Rolls
of
Connecticut Men
in the
FRENCH AND INDIAN WAR
1755-1762

Volume I
1755-1757

Connecticut Historical Society

HERITAGE BOOKS
2013

HERITAGE BOOKS
AN IMPRINT OF HERITAGE BOOKS, INC.

Books, CDs, and more—Worldwide

For our listing of thousands of titles see our website
at
www.HeritageBooks.com

A Facsimile Reprint
Published 2013 by
HERITAGE BOOKS, INC.
Publishing Division
5810 Ruatan Street
Berwyn Heights, Md. 20740

Originally published by the Society
Hartford
1903

This was originally published as the
*Collections of the Connecticut Historical Society
Volume IX*

— Publisher's Notice —

In reprints such as this, it is often not possible to remove blemishes from the original. We feel the contents of this book warrant its reissue despite these blemishes and hope you will agree and read it with pleasure.

International Standard Book Numbers
Paperbound: 978-1-55613-890-4
Clothbound: 978-0-7884-8103-1

COLLECTIONS

OF THE

Connecticut Historical Society.

VOLUME IX.

HARTFORD:
PUBLISHED BY THE SOCIETY.
1903.

[This copy is one of three hundred published by the Connecticut Historical Society for the State of Connecticut under the provisions of a special act of the General Assembly.]

The Case, Lockwood & Brainard Company, Hartford, Conn.

OFFICERS OF THE SOCIETY.

Elected May 20, 1902.

PRESIDENT, SAMUEL HART.

VICE-PRESIDENTS,
- JAMES J. GOODWIN, HARTFORD.
- JAMES TERRY, NEW HAVEN.
- RICHARD A. WHEELER, STONINGTON.
- MORRIS W. SEYMOUR, BRIDGEPORT.
- THEODORE S. GOLD, CORNWALL.
- FRANK FARNSWORTH STARR, MIDDLETOWN.
- ELLEN D. LARNED, THOMPSON.
- E. STEVENS HENRY, ROCKVILLE.

RECORDING SECRETARY, ALBERT C. BATES.
CORRESPONDING SECRETARY, W. DE LOSS LOVE.
TREASURER, JOHN E. MORRIS.
LIBRARIAN, ALBERT C. BATES.
AUDITOR, JOSEPH G. WOODWARD.

MEMBERSHIP COMMITTEE,
- SAMUEL HART, *ex officio*.
- JOSEPH G. WOODWARD.
- JULIUS GAY.
- JOHN E. MORRIS.
- HORACE E. MATHER.
- JANE T. SMITH.
- ALBERT C. BATES.
- JOSEPH L. BLANCHARD.

LIBRARY COMMITTEE,
- SAMUEL HART, *ex officio*.
- FRANCIS H. PARKER.
- THOMAS S. WEAVER.
- FREDERICK W. PRINCE.

PUBLICATION COMMITTEE,
- SAMUEL HART, *ex officio*.
- ALBERT C. BATES.
- LEVERETT BELKNAP.
- GEORGE S. GODARD.

COMMITTEE ON MONTHLY PAPERS,
- P. H. WOODWARD.
- CHARLES B. WHITING.
- ARTHUR L. SHIPMAN.

INTRODUCTION.

This volume of Rolls is published under the provisions of a recent Special Act of the General Assembly making an annual appropriation of one thousand dollars to the Connecticut Historical Society ; one of the purposes specifically named in this act being "to publish its rolls of soldiers in the revolutionary and colonial wars, not heretofore printed." Another provision is that the Society "shall deposit in the State Library three hundred copies of each catalogue, report, or other work published" under this act, to be disposed of by the State Librarian. This is the second important work issued under the provisions of this act.

At a meeting of the Standing Committee of the Society held on the twentieth of last May it was "Voted that a volume of Rolls of Connecticut Men who served in the French and Indian War 1755–1762 be prepared and published," and the librarian as editor of the Society's publications was directed to undertake the work without delay. This volume is the result of that vote. It was anticipated that all of the rolls of the Connecticut men in that war could be published in one volume, but as the printing progressed it was found necessary, in order to make a volume of convenient size and to conform to the size of the previous volumes of the series, to divide the work into two volumes. It is expected that the second volume will be issued without delay.

Some fifteen years ago the old Seymour house on Governor street, Hartford, which had been the home of the Seymour family for many years, passed by sale into other hands. The heirs who had the disposition of the property first removed from the house everything that was considered as of personal interest or as having special value ; the miscellaneous odds and ends remaining were sold to a local second-hand dealer. Among other things secured by this dealer was a large and miscellaneous assortment of ancient manuscripts gathered by him, it is said, partly from old trunks in the garret and partly from an old desk and some boxes stored in an outbuilding. The lot had scarcely reached the dealer's store before it was seen and purchased, without having been examined by either party to the trade, by the late Judge Sherman Wolcott Adams of Hartford, for a sum but little above the paper-stock price at which the dealer had secured it. Judge Adams' antiquarian instinct led him to believe that a collection from such a prominent family would probably contain documents of great historical value, and in this he was not mistaken. It is not the purpose of this introductory sketch to describe this collection of manuscripts except so far as it relates to the work in hand. Among the documents were about two hundred and thirty-five original muster and pay rolls of Connecticut men serving in the French and Indian War 1755–1761. A well-known Hartford book collector, since deceased, became, in some way now unknown, associated with Judge Adams in the examination and perhaps in the ownership of the collection. Through him these rolls were offered for sale to the State at a round price. The late Charles J. Hoadly, the State Librarian, refused to purchase them, claiming that they were a part of the archives and were State property, and more than intimating that, if necessary, steps would be taken to obtain possession of the rolls by due process of law. Some time later Judge Adams and Dr. Hoadly, who were the best of friends, came to an agreement by which, after Dr. Hoadly had examined them, the State paid a nominal sum, said to have been fifty dollars, for the rolls, and Judge Adams relinquished all claim to them, and they were placed with the other archives in the State Library. They have remained together as a distinct collection and are kept separate from the few other rolls of this war which were previously among the archives in the Library. How these rolls came into the possession of the Seymour family is not known. It is probable that at the close of the war they remained in the possession of some official and thus descended in the family from one generation to another, and had never been actually in the State's possession. When received at the Library, these rolls were in a very dilapidated condition. Later, after having been assorted and arranged, they were repaired in a manner which, while not entirely satisfactory, has done much to preserve them from further injury. Since they were copied for this work, the rolls for 1755 and 1756 have been mounted by the Emory process and each year bound in a handsome and convenient

volume. In printing this volume these rolls, out of respect for Judge Adams, have been designated as the "Adams Papers."
The majority of the rolls printed in this volume and of those which will appear in the succeeding volume are from these Adams Papers in the State Library. In addition there are rolls from the series lettered "War," 5, 6, 7, 8, 9, among the bound volumes of archives in the State Library, a number from the archives of the Connecticut Historical Society, a few from private sources, and several from the New York Historical Society's Collections for 1891. Items have also been gleaned from a volume of army accounts 1755-1758 in the Comptroller's Office, from the printed series of the Records of the Colony of Connecticut, and from the file of the *Connecticut Gazette* in the Yale University Library.

The greater part of the copy for this volume was prepared by the editor, and the proof of every roll has been read by him with the original manuscript. The index cards, which were written by Miss Alice M. Gay of Hartford, were also all compared by him with the printed sheets before they were printed.

The names and official positions of general, regimental, and company officers, gathered from scattered sources, have been arranged for convenience at the beginning of each campaign, regiment, and company. So far as could be ascertained, the residence of each officer is given. Where the residence does not appear in the records but has been added by the editor, it is enclosed in brackets. In a number of instances where there were two or more rolls of the same company covering the same period, only one has been printed in full and a reference made to the others.

This work does not profess to be more than a list of men who served as soldiers, with an account of their service and such further records as will aid in identifying them. Consequently much has been omitted in the printing of these rolls which has appeared irrelevant to the object in view. It has seemed outside the scope of the work to give the amount of bounty received, the sum per month or the total amount of pay received, the number of months and days in service when dates of both enlistment and discharge are given, and numerous similar items. As the location of the manuscript of each roll is given, the curious can find such items as occur by reference to the originals.

Headings and indorsements of rolls as well as all names have been spelled exactly as in the original manuscripts, but the abreviations for months have been made uniform, ditto marks have been introduced and a few variations made in arrangement for the sake of uniformity. In indexing the volume names have, in general, been given their recognized spelling instead of following the manifold variations which are found in the rolls. But all important variations of surnames that appear are given in parentheses at the beginning of the index of each name, while occasional cross-references call attention to the occurrence of more than one recognized spelling.

ALBERT C. BATES,
Chairman of the Publication Committee,
and Editor of this Volume.

THE SOCIETY'S LIBRARY, JANUARY 17, 1903.

CAMPAIGN OF 1755.

GENERAL AND STAFF OFFICERS.

William Johnson [of Warrensburgh, near Schenectady, N. Y., appointed by a council of governors and] approved of for Lieutenant-General and Commander-in-Chief, March, 1755. [Was wounded while commanding the troops in the battle of Sep. 8. For the victory won by this battle he was made a baronet of Great Britain Nov. 27. Resigned his commission early in December.]

Phineas Lyman [of Suffield] nominated Major-General and Captain of the first company in the first regiment March, 1755. [At the battle of Sep. 8, after Gen. Johnson was wounded, the chief command devolved upon Gen. Lyman.] Discharged Dec. 6.

Rev. George Beckwith [of Lyme] nominated Chaplain, March, 1755.
Rev. Benjamin Throop of Norwich appointed Chaplain, Aug. 1755.
Rev. John Norton of Middletown appointed Chaplain, Aug. 1755. Was in service until Dec. 1, 1756. [*State Library, War 5, 276.*]

Dr. Timothy Collins of Litchfield appointed Physician and Surgeon, Aug. 1755.
Dr. Jonathan Marsh of Norwich appointed Physician and Surgeon, Aug. 1755.
Dr. Samuel Ely of Durham appointed Physician and Surgeon Aug. 1755. Served in Col. Chauncey's regiment from Sep. 1 to Oct. 31
[*State Library, War 5, 273.*]
Dr. Timothy Warner [of   ] appointed Physician Oct. 1755; his wages to commence from his entering into said service.
Nathaniel Porter, served as Physician from April 5 to Nov. 13.
[*State Library, War 5, 273.*]

Isaac Doolittle [of New Haven], served as Armourer from June 9 to Aug. 6 and from Sep. 10 to Dec. 6. [*State Library, War 5, 274.*]

Col. Thomas Wells [of Glastonbury],
Maj. Jabez Hamlin [of Middletown],
Maj. John Hubbard [of New Haven],
Col. Gurdon Saltonstall [of New London],
Col. Hezekiah Huntington [of Norwich],
Capt. Theophilus Nichols [of Stratford],
} Appointed Commissaries to provide transports, provisions and other necessaries, March, 1755.

Elihu Lyman of New Haven, appointed Commissary of the provisions and muster-rolls, March, 1755.
Lieut.-Col. Nathan Whiting [of New Haven], acted as Commissary at Fort Edward during the winter of 1755–1756.
[*State Library, War 6, 14.*]

Maj. Nathan Payson [of Hartford] appears to have been with the garrison at Fort Edward in the winter of 1755-1756.
[*The above from Colonial Records, except as noted.*]

Note: The General Assembly in March, 1755, ordered the raising of 1,000 men, to be divided into two regiments of six companies each, and impowered the governor to take measures for the raising of 500 additional men should it become necessary. This additional force was raised about the end of August in consequence of letters received from General Johnson. The companies were added to the two regiments already raised, probably three companies to each regiment. At about the same time the Assembly authorized the raising of two additional regiments, each to consist of 750 men, divided into nine companies.

FIRST REGIMENT—MAJ.-GEN. PHINEAS LYMAN.

REGIMENTAL OFFICERS.

Phineas Lyman [of Suffield] nominated Major-General and Captain of the first company, March, 1755. Discharged Dec. 6.

John Pitkin [of Hartford] nominated Lieutenant-Colonel and Captain of the second company, March, 1755. Discharged Oct. 23.

Robert Dennison [of New London] nominated Major and Captain of the third company, March, 1755. Discharged Oct. 30.
[Colonial Records.]

FIRST COMPANY—MAJ.-GEN. LYMAN.

Phineas Lyman [of Suffield], Major-General and Captain. [Colonial Records.]
Aaron Hitchcock [of Suffield], First Lieutenant and Captain.
Medina Fitch of Windsor, Second Lieutenant. [Colonial Records.]
Eliphalet Whittlesey [of Newington], Ensign.

A Muster Roll of the Company in His Majesties Service under the Command of Major Gen'll Lyman Esq'r.

Mens Names	Quality	Time of entrance in the Service		Time of Discharge		Dead or Taken
Phinehas Lyman Esq'r	Ma'r Gen'l	Apr'l	5	Dec'r	6	
Aron Hitchcock	Lieu't	"	"	Sep'r	27	
Aron Hitchcock	Cap't	Sep'r	27	Dec'r	6	
Medinah Fitch	Lieu't	Apr'l	5	"	"	
Eliph't Whittlesey	Ens'n	"	"	Sep't	10	
Elihu Kent	Serj't	"	21	"	"	
"	Ens'n	Sep'r	10	Sep'r	27	
"	Liu't	"	27	Dec'r	6	
Ithamar Binham	Clerk	Apr'l	14	"	"	
John Charter	Serj't	"	"	"	"	
Nehe'a Harmon	"	"	21	Oct'r	29	
Joseph Negus	"	"	28	Dec'r	2	
Phinehas Chapen	Corp'l	"	14	Sep'r	26	
"	Serj't	Sep'r	27			Nov 2
John Stanard	Corp'l	Apr'l	21	Oct'r	10	
Nth'l Osborn	"	"	14			Oct'r 24
Ephr'm Adams	"	"	28	Oct'r	26	
Tho's Griffen	Drum	"	30	Dec'r	6	
John Brown	Cent'l	"	5	Oct'r	27	
John Shield	"	"	7	Dec'r	12	
Moses H. Hutching'n	"	"	"	"	2	
Joshua Reed	"	"	12	Oct'r	3	

CAMPAIGN OF 1755.

Mens Names	Quality	Time of entrance in the Service		Time of Discharge		Dead or Taken
Jon[a] Edgerton	Cent[l]	Apr[l]	14	Oct[r]	18	
Hezē Reed	"	"	"	Dec[r]	6	
Simon Wolcott	"	"	"	"	2	
Thomas Watson	"	"	"	"	6	
Solomon Hall	"	"	"	"	6	
Henry Woodward	"	"	"	Sep	27	
Benja[n] Scott	"	"	"	Oct[r]	10	
John Starns	"	"	"	"	"	
Solomon Wills	"	"	"	Nov[r]	4	
Israel Perkins	"	"	"	"	18	
Benja[n] Davis	"	"	"	Dec[r]	6	
David Parsons	"	"	"	"	"	
Jacob Redington	"	"	17	Oct[r]	3	
Abel Cross	"	"	"	Dec[r]	6	
Oliver Barker (?)	"	"	21	Oct[r]	10	
[ ]	"	"	"	"	27	
[ ] Southwell	"	"	"	"	29	
Phin[s] Lyman	"	"	"	Nov[r]	4	
Joel Adams	"	"	"	Dec[r]	8	
Alex[r] Dunlap	"	"	"	"	6	
Joseph King	"	"	"	Nov[r]	2	
Hen[y] Nickalson	"	"	"	Dec[r]	6	
Josiah Smith	"	"	"			Sep[r] 9
Cor[s] Shaw	"	"	"	Nov[r]	26	
Noah Pumroy	"	"	"	"	15	
George Slaughter	Drum Maj[r]	July	9	Oct[r]	10	
Elihu Kent	Adjutant	Sep[r]	10	Dec[r]	6	
Nath[ll] Warner	Cent[l]	Apr[l]	21	Oct[r]	29	
W[m] Thrall	"	"	"	Nov[r]	2	
Isaac Hall	"	"	"	"	5	
Cain (?) Smith	"	"	"	June	24	
Ely Warner	"	"	"	Oct[r]	21	
Will[m] Youngs	"	"	"	Nov[r]	15	
James Hatlock	"	"	23	Oct[r]	27	
Abner Meacham	"	"	26	Dec[r]	3	
Abner Pease	"	"	"	Nov[r]	19	
Phillip Simons	"	"	"	Dec[r]	2	
Will[m] Knowlton	"	"	28	"	"	
Eph[r] Lyon	"	"	"	"	"	
Tho[s] Parry	"	"	"			Oct 15
Sam[ll] Sacher	"	"	"	Dec[r]	2	
Sam[ll] Cobourn	"	"	"	Nov[r]	25	
Robert Snow	"	"	"	Dec[r]	6	
George C[ ]	"	"	"	"	2	
Sam[ll] Thrall	"	"	"	Oct[r]	10	
John Adams	"	"	"	Nov[r]	3	
Semi[o] Ward	"	"	"	"	"	
Mri[l] Jackson	"	"	"	Oct[r]	18	
Sam[l] Humphry	"	"	"	"	"	
Amasa Mills	"	"	"	Nov[r]	25	
Abraham Ates	"	"	"			Nov[r] 20
Daniel Gains	"	"	"	Dec[r]	6	
John Grayham	"	"	"	May	26	
Stephen Holcomb	"	"	"	Oct[r]	10	
John Rice	"	"	"	"	27	
Eld[d] Holcomb	"	"	"	Dec[r]	6	

FIRST REGIMENT.

Mens Names	Quality	Time of entrance in the Service		Time of Discharge		Dead or Taken
Ezary Holcomb	Cent¹	Apr¹	28	Oct^r	18	
Wm Gaines	"	"	"	Nov^r	2	
Mic¹ Mills	"	"	"	Dec^r	6	
Oth¹¹ Moses	"	"	"			Deserted June 25
Noah Gleson	"	"	21	Dec^r	6	
Icha^d Hatch	"	"	28			Octr 12
David Wilson	"	"	28	Nov^r	2	
Aron Simons	"	May	28	Oct^r	27	
Josi^a Bodget	"	Apr¹	30			Decr 7
Nath¹ Pease	"	June	3	Oct^r	27	
Judah Hayse	"	"	2	Dec^r	2	
Thos Lyons	"	Apr¹	28	Nov^r	26	
Dudly Hayse	"	May	26	Oct^r	10	
Mick¹ Holcomb	"	June	24	Dec^r	6	
Eleaz^r Smith	"	Apr¹	21	"	"	
John White	"	"	"	"	"	
Ephr^m Adams	Serj^t	Oct^r	26	"	"	
Henry Woodward	Corp¹	Sep^r	27	Nov^r	2	
"	Serj^t	Nov^r	3	Dec^r	6	

[Indorsed] Major Gen¹ Lyman 1755   [*State Library, Adams Papers.*]

SECOND COMPANY—LIEUT.-COL. PITKIN.

John Pitkin [of Hartford], Lieutenant-Colonel and Captain.
Lemuel Hull of Killingsworth, First Lieutenant.
James Jones of Colchester, Second Lieutenant.   [*Colonial Records.*]
Eliphalet Whittlesey [of Newington], Second Lieutenant.

A Muster Roll of Lieu^t Colonel John Pitkins Company. Being the Second Company in the first Rigement, rais'd by the Colony of Connecticut for the Reduction of Crown Point in April 1755 With the time of their Inlisting, and of their being Discharged, and how long in Said Service, and the sum of each mans Wages. &c. &c. &c.

		Dates of their Inlistments 1755		Return'd home & Discharged		Dead
John Pitkin	Col.	Apr.	5	Oct^r	23	
Lem¹ Hull	Lieut.	"	"	"	6	
James Jones	"	"	"			Sepr 8
Jno Keeny	Serg.	May	13	Sep.	23	
Isaac Turner	"	Ap¹	12	Dec^r	3	
Dan¹ Cone	"	"	14	"	7	
Chas Buckland	"	"	10	Oct^r	21	
Wm Stanton	Clerk	May	14	Dec^r	8	
Jona^n Avery	Corp.	Ap¹	14	Sep.	27	
Peleg Redfield	"	"	15	Nov^r	24	
Alex^r Keeny	"	May	3	Dec^r	1	
Reu. Chittenden	Drum.	Ap¹	26			Oc^r 28
Jere^h Stevens	"	"	16			" 5
Amos Raiment	Soldier	"	12	Sep.	25	
Aaron Pratt	"	"	21	Oct^r	30	
Benj. Keeny	"	May	13	Dec^r	1	

CAMPAIGN OF 1755.

Name	Rank	Dates of their Inlistments 1755	Return'd home & Discharged	Dead
Samuel Evens	Soldier	May 7	Aug. 30	
Nath[ll] Dewey	"	Ap[l] 10	Dec[r] 5	
Josiah Stanclift	"	" 12	Nov[r] 2	
Abner Elgar	"	" 14	Sep[r] 27	
Will[m] Brown	"	" 10	Nov[r] 7	
Asa Burnham	"	" "	Dec[r] 5	
Benj. Brewer Jun[r]	"	May 6	Oct[r] 25	
Benoni Evens	"	Ap[l] 10	Dec[r] 1	
Benoni Loomiss	"	" "	" "	
Moses Evens	"	" "	Oct[r] 25	
Elisha Parker	"	" 25	Nov[r] 26	
Samuel Evens Jun[r]	"	" 14	Dec[r] 1	
Gideon King	"	" 21	Nov[r] 8	
Joseph Keeny Jun[r]	"	" 19	Oct[r] 31	
Ozias Bissell	"	" 21	Nov[r] 8	
Sam[ll] Chandler	"	" 29	Oct[r] 29	
Simon Gains	"	" 21	Dec[r] 1	
Thom[s] Brewer Jun[r]	"	May 15	Sep[r] 29	
John Benjamin	"	" 14	Nov[r] 2	
Israel Harding	"	" 26	" 26	
Suckhecun	"	Ap[l] 10	" "	
Giles Willcocks	"	" 14	Oct[r] 29	
James Redfield	"	" 14	Sep[r] 30	
Ichabod French	"	" 23	Dec[r] 9	
Thomas Stevens	"	" 19	Sep[r] 23	
Reuben Turner	"	" 12	Dec[r] 3	
Tho[s] Rooty	"	" 16	Sep. 5	
Jona. Shepherd	"	" 19	Dec[r] 9	
Joseph Daton	"	" 20	Oct[r] 29	
Aaron Stevens	"	" 12	" 20	
Moses Wright	"	" 15	" 4	
Eben[r] Belding	"	" 28	Sep[r] 8	
Abrah[m] Brooker	"	" 20	Dec[r] 3	
Ezek[l] Hull	"	" 12	Oct[r] 6	
Abr[m] Stevens	"	" "	Sep[r] 27	
Miles Wright	"	" 15	Nov[r] 3	
Ezra Crain	"	" 21	Oct[r] 20	
Reuben Keley	"	" 14	Dec[r] 9	
Aaron Kelcey	"	" 13	" "	
Joseph Carter	"	" 21	Oct[r] 27	
John Nichols	"	" 11	" 10	
Edw[d] Hutchens	"	" 13	" 27	
Jesse Chatfield	"	" 12	" 20	
Dan[ll] Franklen	"	" 14	Dec[r] 9	
Ezer Ephraims	"	" 16		Sep. 8
Gid[n] Fox	"	" 19	Oct[r] 8	
Sam[ll] Wells	"	" 14	" "	
Simeon Menter	"	" 19	" 26	
Benj. Bragg	"	" 14	Dec[r] 8	
John Ryaut	"	" 19	Oct[r] 20	
Leb. Tubbs	"	" 14	" 16	
Jed. Fox	"	" 14	" 8	
James Webb	"	" 20	Dec[r] 8	
Benj. Tubbs	"	" "	Oct[r] 26	
Israel Rowlee	"	" "	" "	
Amos Jones	"	" 14	Dec[r] 8	

FIRST REGIMENT.

		Dates of their Inlistments 1755		Return'd home & Discharged		Dead
Willm Dodge	Soldier	Ap^l	14	Oct^r	26	
And^w Clark	"	"	20	Nov^r	15	
Elijah Thomas	"	"	14	Oct^r	8	
Judah Spencer	"	"	"	"		26
Abner Scovel	"	"	20	Dec^r	8	
Peter Homan	"	"	14	Oct^r	26	
Daniel Shiels	"	May	27	Dec^r	5	
Thos Keeny Junr	"	"	26	Sep^r	25	
John Abbey Junr	"	Ap^l	14	Oct^r	5	
Willm Ross	"	May	21	Dec^r	5	
Elip. Whittlesey	Lieut.	Sep^r	10	Nov^r	30	
Danl Brewer	Soldier	Apr.	19	Oct^r	8	

[Indorsed]   Coll^o Pitkins Muster Roll 1755
   Jno. Abbee Jr
   Saml Evens &c
   Jos. Keeny
   Simon Gains p

[*State Library, Adams Papers.*]

A Muster Roll of Lieu^t Colonel John Pitkins Company, being the Second Company in the first Rigement, rais'd for the Reduction of Crown Point, April 1755, Time of Inlistments, and Discharge &c &c &c

	Inlistments.		Return'd home & Discharg'd	
Reuben Kelcey	Ap^l	14	Dec.	9
Jno Ryant	"	19	Oct.	20
Lebbeus Tubbs	"	14	"	16
Jedidiah Fox	"	14	"	8
Benajah Tubbs	"	20	"	26

[The other names are as in the roll above.]

[*Connecticut Historical Society.*]

THIRD COMPANY—MAJ. DENNISON.

Robert Dennison [of New London], Major and Captain.
Ebenezer Billing Jr, of Stonington, First Lieutenant.
John Tyler of Preston, Second Lieutenant.

[*Colonial Records.*]

Major Robart Denison Company A Roal

Officers and Soldiers Names	Time of Enlistment		Discharged		Dead and Captivated
Maj^r Robar^t Denison	Apr^l	2	Oct.	30	
Lieu^t Ebenz Billing	"	"	Dec.	10	
Lieu^t John Tyler	"	"	"	"	
Sar Andrew Denison	"	7	Oct.	30	
Sar Jabez Billing	"	10	"	26	
Sar George Crary	"	"	Dec.	10	
Sar Mason Wattles	"	7	Oct.	20	
Clark Wm Billing	"	10	Dec.	10	

CAMPAIGN OF 1755.

Officers and Soldiers Names	Time of Enlistment		Discharged		Dead and Captivated
Drum Jacob Rathbon	Apr¹	10			Sep. 8
Corp Thoms Mynor	"	7	Oct.	18	
Corp James Deen	"	10	"	29	
Corp Edward Mott	"	12	"	26	
Corp Wᵐ Force	"	11	"	"	
Asa Crocker Cent¹¹	"	7	Dec.	6	
Nehemiah Smith	"	"	"	"	
James Puffer	"	"	Nov.	15	
Stephen Taylor	"	"	"	8	
Jonathan Mynord	"	8	Sep.	29	
Joseph Kelogg	"	10	Nov.	8	
Levy Wells	"	"	"	"	
Nathan Parks	"	"	Oct.	16	
John Button	"	"	"	20	
Levy Bompas	"	"	Dec.	10	
Samll Billing	"	"	Oct.	28	
Elisha Blackman	"	"	"	18	
Peter Coeghegan	"	"	Dec.	4	
Jeremiah Downs	"	"	"	"	
Josph Comstock	"	"	"	"	
Wm. Fagans	"	11	"	"	
Samll. Hill	"	10	Oct.	28	
Daniel Back	"	"	Dec.	8	
Ebenez Billing	"	"	Nov.	9	
Nathan Barran	"	"			Oct. 8
Joseph Hewit	"	"	Dec.	10	
Christopher Avery	"	"			Sep. 8
Robison Bomp	"	"	Dec.	1	
John Avery	"	"	"	10	
Jonas Babcock	"	11			Oct. 16
Jerremiah Bennet	"	"	Oct.	14	
Joseph Randol	"	"	Nov.	4	
Nathanel Bowdis	"	"	Sep.	28	
Reubin Jones	"	"	Dec.	8	
John Petty	"	17			June 12
James Dean Serj	Oct.	30	Dec.	1	
Peter Bowdish	Apr.	11	Oct.	16	
Caleb Benjamin	"	"	"	28	
Thomas Cogan	"	12	Nov.	8	
Benjamin Kinne	"	"	Oct.	16	
Lemuel Stewart	"	"	Nov.	9	
Jahleal Billing	"	"			Oct. 15
Joseph Ellot (?)	"	"	Oct.	18	
Rufus Hill	"	"	Nov.	12	
Amos Fox	"	"	"	6	
Samll Avery	"	"	Dec.	1	
Ezekel Yarrington	"	"	"	8	
Benjamin Park	"	"	"	"	
Elijah Brumbly	"	"	Oct.	20	
Thomas Reed	"	"	Nov.	8	
John Fish	"	13	Oct.	15	
Ichabod Dickinson	"	"	Dec.		
James Hagar	"	"	Oct.	30	
Jonathan Luis	"	"			Nov. 12
John Skesuck	"	"	Nov.	15	
Peter Cocghets	"	"	Dec.	8	
Solomon Chebuck	"	"	Oct.	30	

FIRST REGIMENT.   11

Officers and Soldiers Names	Time of Enlistment	Discharged	Dead and Captivated
James Possetouce	Apr. 12	Oct. 12	
Thomas Laraby	" "	Aug. 20	
Medad Benton	" "	Oct. 28	
Caleb Bundy	" "	Nov. 18	
Samll Fitch	" "		Oct. 29
James Butler	" "	Nov. 4	
Isaac Herrings	" "	" 18	Oct. 18
George Ashbow	" "		
John Jurdin	" "	Nov. 8	
James Murfee	" "	" 15	
Samll Mosure	" 16	" "	
Jonathan Weeks	" "	" 8	
Thomas Robison	" "	Sep. 8	
John Mejon	" 28	Nov. 8	
Wm. Grover	" 20	" "	
Joseph Mynor	" "	Oct. 15	
Solomon Tyler	June 3	Dec. 30	
Joseph Mack	June 9	Oct. 30	
Robart Warrin	Apr. 7	May 28	
Willm Billing Serjt	Oct. 21	Dec. 10	
Edwd Mott Serjt	" 27	" "	
Thomas Robinson Drumr	Sep. 9		" 8

[Indorsed] Majr Robert Denison 1755
            Jeremiah Bennet p

[State Library, Adams Papers.]

FOURTH COMPANY—CAPT. PAYSON.

Nathan Payson [of Hartford], Captain and Major.
Andrew Ward [of Guilford], First Lieutenant.
Thaddeus Mead of Norwalk, Second Lieutenant. [*Colonial Records.*]

A Roll of Major Nathan Paysons Company with the time of Their Inlistment and what their Wages amounted to at the time of being Discharg'd, Dead, Deserted, &c &c

		Dates of Inlistment 1755	Discharged	Dead
Nathn Payson	Capt	Apr. 5	Sep. 26	
"	Majr	Sep. 26	Jan. 1	
Andw Ward	Lieut.	Apr. 5	Nov. 24	
Thads Mead	"	" "	Sep. 22	
Abrm Pinney	Serj.	" 16	Nov. 5	
Ithamr Andruss	"	May 21	" 19	
Belias Ward	"	" 7	" 8	
Jno Pearson		Apr. 11	Sep. 15	
Jno Stimson	Corporals	May 18	" 26	
Wm Seymore	Clerk & Drummer	" 14	Oct. 28	
Alexr Sloan	"	" 11	Sep. 15	
Philandr Pinney	"	" 16	Oct. 24	
Jos. Gilbert	"	Apr. 25	Nov. 11	
Lews Giveit	"	" "	" 24	

CAMPAIGN OF 1755.

Name	Rank	Dates of Inlistment 1755	Discharged	Dead
Dan¹ Sanders	Soldur	Apr. 10		Sep. 8
Jonathⁿ Welch	"	" 14	Oct. 13	
Edwᵈ Cadwell	"	" 11	Sep. 15	
Jonathⁿ Sparkes	"	" "	Nov. 11	
John Stanly	"	" 7	Sep. 24	
Elisha Tillison	"	" 12	" 26	
Isaac Drake	"	" 10		Oct. 22
Jnᵒ Barnard	"	" 15	Nov. 19	
Joel Marshall	"	" 11	" "	
Sam¹ Foot	"	" 17	" 26	
Isaac Wisk	"	" 24	Oct. 13	
Wᵐ Willson	"	" 21	" 19	
John Ranney	"	" "	Sep. 26	
Jnᵒ Ranney Junʳ	"	" "	Oct. 13	
Joseph Storer	"	" "		Sep. 12
Benjᵃ Dimick	"	" 24	Oct. 24	
Enos Bartholomew	"	" 18	" "	
Benjᵃ Buckman	"	" 26	Deserted Aug. 1	
Jonᵃ Babcock	"	" 24	Sep. 24	
George Fisher	"	" 22	" 18	
Isaac Johnson	"	" [ ]		[ ]
John Streeter	"	" 30	Oct. 24	
Jonathⁿ Rust	"	" 11	Nov. 19	
Isaac Butholph	"	" 20	" 13	
Robᵗ Beekerstaff	"	May 1	Oct. 6	
Asher Seward	"	" 5	Nov. 10	
Enos Bishop	"	" 7	" 11	
Nath¹ Bishop	"	" 9	" 18	
Joseph Dudley	"	" 20	" "	
Timᵒ Spencer	"	" "	" 10	
Ezek¹ Hosford	"	" 21	Sep. 26	
Timothy Hartt	"	" "	Nov. 18	
Abel Dodge	"	" "	" 24	
John Loree	"	" "	" 18	
Zachᵃ Lane	"	" "		Oct. 4
Beliaz Hill	"	" "	Sep. 26	
Samuel Brown	"	" 22	Nov. 19	
Eliphal¹ Loomis	"	Apr. 22	Oct. 13	
Nath¹ Spining	"	May 5	Nov. 8	
John Cooper	"	" 20	Deserted June 17	
Daniel Hatter	"	" "	" " "	
William Greene	"	Apr. 11	Oct. 19	
Isaac Sherwood	"	" 12	" "	
Eliakim Stephens	"	" "	Deserted May 12	
Josiah Camfield	"	" 14	Nov. 26	
Seth Raymond	"	" "	" 18	
Joel Prindle	"	" 21	" 26	
Jnᵒ Dimoret	"	" "	Oct. 16	
Daniel Weed	"	" "		Sep. 19
Epenetus Prindle	"	" "	Sep. 26	
Nath¹ Weskott	"	" "	Nov. 24	
Jnᵒ Robison	"	" "	" 18	
John Roberts	"	" 22	" 25	
Willᵐ Manro	"	" "	Oct. 13	
Willᵐ Bates	"	" "	" "	
Dan¹ Jackson	"	" "	" 24	

FIRST REGIMENT. 13

		Dates of Inlistment 1755	Discharged	Dead
James Brown	Soldur	Apr. 22	Nov. 25	
Hez. Gilbert	"	" "	" 10	
Jonathⁿ Mills	"	" "	" 12	
Jacob Thorncraft	"	" "	Oct. 13	
Jesse Beers	"	" 24	Aug. 21	
Willᵐ Bloggett	"	" "	Nov. 1	
Samˡ Warden	"	" "	" 23	
James Castilow	"	" 25	" 18	
Nicholas Robins	"	" "	" 25	
Jonᵃ Benedick	"	" 28	Oct. 27	
Theophilˢ Morison	"	" "	Nov. 9	
John Lifeet	"	" 30		Deserted May 28
John Ward	"	" 18		" " "
John Gurney Junʳ	"	May 21	Sep. 18	
Thomˢ Scranton	"	" 7	" 1	

[Indorsed] Capᵗ N. Payson 1755
Andʷ Ward Lᵗ
Jno. Ward pr
Belias Ward Corpl

[*State Library, Adams Papers.*]

FIFTH COMPANY — CAPT. PATTERSON.

John Patterson of Farmington, Captain. [*Colonial Records.*]
Stephen Holmes, First Lieutenant.
Stephen Smith of Litchfield, Second Lieutenant. [*Colonial Records.*]

A Roll of Capᵗ John Patterson's Company with the time of Inlistment and what their Wages Amounted to, at the time of their Being Discharged, Dead Deserted &c. &c.

		Time of Inlistment 1755	Descharged 1755	Dead & Taken
Jnᵒ Patterson	Capt.	Apr. 5	Nov. 24	
Stephⁿ Holmes	Lieut.	" 5	" "	
Stephⁿ Smith	"	" 5	Sep. 19	
Ezekˡ Lewis	Serjt.	" 7	Nov. 24	
David Pike	"	" 9	" "	
Benjᵃ Culver	"	" 14	Oct. 13	
Willᵐ Andrus	"	" 10	" 16	
Nathˡ Churchil	Corpl.	" 14	" 13	
"	Serjt.	Oct. 14	Nov. 11	
Enoch Curtis	Corpl.	Apr. 10	Oct. 15	
"	Serjt.	Oct. 16	Nov. 4	
Samˡ Osborn	Corpl.	Apr. 14	Oct. 1	
Jonᵗʰ Gillit	"	" 10	" 16	
"	Clerk	Oct. 17	Nov. 24	
Titus Harrison	"	Apr. 14	Oct. 13	
Benjᵃ Stevens	Drum.	" 11		Sep. 5
Anthᵒ Hoskins	Soldier	" "	Sep. 26	
Amariah Plumb	"	" 14	Oct. 13	
Andrew Norton	"	" "	Nov. 24	

CAMPAIGN OF 1755.

Name	Rank	Time of Inlistment 1755	Discharged 1755	Dead & Taken
Benjᵃ Heckock	Soldier	Apr. 14	Nov. 24	
Barthol° Jacobs	"	" "	Oct. 13	
"	Corpl.	Oct. 14	Nov. 19	
Bela Lewis	Soldier	Apr. 10	" 24	
Bethel Clark	"	" 14		Oct. 11
Benjᵃ Grimes	"	" 12	Nov. 21	
Caleb Wolcott	"	" 14	Oct. 4	
Cotton Mather	"	" 9		Oct. 17
Caleb Hurlbut	"	" 16	Nov. 24	
Daniel Wright	"	" 10	" "	
Daniel Squire	"	" 9	" "	
Ebenezʳ Burlison	"	" 14	Oct. 15	
"	Corpl	Oct. 16	Nov. 24	
Ebenʳ Curtis	Soldier	Apr. 11	Sep. 24	
Elisha Fox	"	" 10	Nov. 24	
Elnathan North	"	" 11	Oct. 24	
Elizʳ Bartholomew	"	" 15	" "	
Eliphᵗ Tuttle	"	" "		Nov. 10
Ephᵐ Whaples	"	" 10	Sep. 19	
Francis Flemming	"	" "	Nov. 24	
Giles Kilborn	"	" 14	Oct. 20	
Gideon Dunham	"	" "	Nov. 19	
George Miller	"	" "	" 24	
Hezᵉ Brunson	"	" "	Oct. 4	
Henry Kircum	"	" 10	" "	
Henry Cook	"	" 11	" 24	
Jabez Peck	"	" 9		Oct. 17
John Bird	"	" 14	Sep. 16	
Joseph Blanchard	"	" "	Oct. 13	
Job Andrus	"	" 10	Nov. 24	
Job Alford	"	" 11		Sep. 27
John Belding	"	" 7	Oct. 20	
Isaac Chamberlain	"	" 10	Nov. 24	
James Lusk	"	" 7	" "	
John Squire	"	" 9	" "	
John Walling	"	" 12	Oct. 24	
John Collens	"	" 11	Nov. 21	
Israel Hall	"	" 14	Sep. 20	
John Carvener	"	" 9	Nov. 24	
Joel Dibble	"	" 14		Taken Aug. 31
Josiah Dibble	"	" "	Oct. 20	
John Panter	"	" 15	Nov. 21	
Joab Hosington	"	" 9	" 24	
Nathˡ Culver	"	" 14	Oct. 13	
Nehᵉ Smedly	"	" 15	" 4	
Noah Porter	"	" "	Nov. 24	
Oliver Lewis	"	" 12	Oct. 13	
Phenⁱ Curtis	"	" 11	" 4	
Roger Andrus	"	" 10	Nov. 24	
Roswell Hubbard	"	" 9	" "	
Robert Linsea	"	" 11	Sep. 26	
Agur Galard	"	" 10	Nov. 21	
Robert Vine	"	" 14	" "	
Samˡ Bird	"	" 10	" "	
Samˡ Elwell	"	" "	" 24	
Samˡ Weston	"	" 11	Oct. 15	
"	Corpl	Oct. 16	Nov. 24	

FIRST REGIMENT.

		Time of Inlistment 1755	Discharged 1755	Dead & Taken
Stephⁿ Winchel	Soldier	Apr. 10	Oct. 1	
Saml Pike	"	" 14	" 13	
Simeon Stow	"	" 10	Sep. 24	
Steadman Young	"	" 9		Oct. 15
Willm Jacobs	"	" 11	Oct. 4	
Willm Greaves	"	" 15	" 20	
Saml Addams	"	" 10	Nov. 20	
Cummus Indian	"	" "	" "	
Wonks Indian	"	" "	" "	
Peter Sanchuse	"	" 14		Aug. 31
James Woves	"	" 10	Oct. 13	
Hatc Touse	"	" 15	Nov. 24	
David Touse	"	" 16	Oct. 20	
Richard Negro	"	" 9	" 1	

[Indorsed]   Capt Jno Patterson 1755
    Saml Weston p
    Danl Wright p

[*State Library, Adams Papers.*]

The Accompts of Billiting Capt Patersons Company from the Time of their Enlistment to ye 9th of June 1755

	Weeks	Days
Joseph Brancher		
Hatchet Touse		
Richard Torrowa	7	5

[The other names are as in the roll above.]

[*State Library, War 5, 208.*]

SIXTH COMPANY—CAPT. PIERCE.

Ezekiel Pierce of Plainfield, Captain.
James Tracy of Windham, First Lieutenant.
John Cotten of Pomfret, Second Lieutenant.

[*Colonial Records.*]

Capt Ezekiel Perce 1755 Pay roll Saybrook

Officers and Soldiers Names and Qualities	April 1755 ye time of each mans Enlistment	Discharged	Killed in Battle dyed in Sickness
Ezekiel Pierce Capt.	5	Nov. 10	
James Tracy Leut.	"	" 9	
John Cotten Leut.	"	Dec. 9	
Bennedick Saterlee Serg.	14	Nov. 2	
Elijah Simons Serg.	"	Oct. 29	
Charles Lewis Serg.	16		Sep. 8
Elias Stevens Serg.	14		Nov. 8
Samuel Porter Corp.	"		Sep. 30
Thomas Fuller Corp.	16	Nov. 4	
Ebenezer Goold Corp.	14		Jan. 25
Joel How Corp.	16		Dec. 7

CAMPAIGN OF 1755.

Officers and Soldiers Names and Qualities	April 1755 ye time of each mans Enlistment	Discharged	Killed in Battle dyed in Sickness
Andrew Spaulding Clark	14	Sep. 8	
Andrew Spaulding Serg.	Sep. 9	Dec. 9	
Leonard Reed Drumer	14		Oct. 13
John Hall Drummer	Oct. 14	Dec. 9	
Nathaniel Ripley	15	Sep. 9	
Nathaniel Ripley Clark	Sep. 9	Nov. 8	
William Parrish	14	Oct. 1	
William Parrish Corp.	Oct. 2	Jan. 7	
Gillum Phillips	14	Dec. 9	
Calub Astin	16	Oct. 20	
Samuel Adams	15	" "	
William Baulding	"	" 30	
Samuel Bennet	"		Sep. 8
Joseph Brown	12	Nov. 4	
[J]onathan Bingham	14	Dec. 9	
[S]tephen Baker	16	" 3	
Charles Biles	14	Nov. 23	
James Collor	16	Dec. 9	
Isaac Canady	15	" 20	
Seth Cary	16	July 31	
Jonathan Cady	15	Dec. 9	
Jonathan Coye	16	" 5	
Zedekiah Coy	"		Nov. 18
Thomas Cook	15	Dec. 9	
Joseph Commos	"	Oct. 12	
George Dunham	"	" 31	
John Thompson	12	Nov. 4	
Abijah Ward	15	" 27	
Joseph Williams	"	Dec. 9	
Nehemiah Dodge	16	" "	
John Diggins	"	" "	
Amos Fosset	15		Dec. 3
Joseph Farnum	16	Dec. 9	
Solomon Farnum	"	Nov. 26	
Robert Havens	14	Oct. 20	
Ruben Jerould	16	Nov. 10	
Lewis Jones	"	" 8	
Moses Jones	"	" "	
John Heard	14	Oct. 5	
Eleazer Hibbord	15	Nov. 6	
James Hide	"	Dec. 9	
William Harrington	16	Oct. 31	
Benjamin Holding	14	" 19	
John Hall	16	" 14	
John Harris	"	" 3	
Adonijah Kingsley	"	Nov. 9	
John Knight	"	Oct. 12	
John Mulhins	"	" 10	
Lewis Moore	"	Dec. 9	
Daniel Evens	15	" "	
Joseph Trewsdell	"	Oct. 31	
Isaiah Farnum	16	Dec. 9	
Elisha Munsel	15	Oct. 16	
Clement Neff	16	Nov. 4	
Lemuel Peirce	14	Oct. 20	
Eliab Parker	16	" 31	

FIRST REGIMENT.

Officers and Soldiers Names and Qualities	April 1755 ye time of each mans Enlistment	Discharged	Killed in Battle dyed in Sickness
Henry Preston	16	Dec. 9	
Thomas Pool	15	" "	
Solomon Pettingal	16	" "	
Jehiel Robins	"	Nov. 26	
Samuel Root	15	" 30	
Josiah Reed	"	" 2	
Charles Ripley	14	" 23	
Benjamin Robison	16		Oct. 6
Joseph Robison	"	Dec. 9	
Jacob Spaulding	14	Oct. 20	
Israel Sabins	16	Dec. 9	
Asa Stevens	"	" "	Sep. 8
John Searles	"	Oct. 6	
William Shapley	15		Sep. 11
Joseph Sandars	16		
Moses Sparkes	"	Oct. 12	
Ebenezer Smith	"		Sep. 8
Simon Rooney	"	Oct. 17	
Jeremiah Shenteys (?)	"	" 30	
Annanirus Porridge	15	Nov. 4	

[Indorsed] Capt Ezekiel Perce 1755 Pay roll
Saybrook
Eben^r Smith p

[State Library, Adams Papers.]

CAPT. TERRY'S COMPANY.

John Terry [of Lebanon] Captain.
Prince Tracy [of Windham] Lieutenant.
Isaac Williams [of Pomfret] Lieutenant.
A Muster Rol of the Company in the Colonys Service under ye Command of John Terry Capt viz.

Mens Names Both officers and Soldiers	Quality	Time of each mans Enlistment	Dischd	Dead
[ ] Terry	Capt.	Aug. 25	Dec. [ ]	
]acy	Lieut.	" "	"	[ ]
]ams	"	" "	"	
]bbens	Serj.	Sep. 3	"	[ ]
]ldo	"	Aug. 27	"	
]	"	" 25	[	
]	"	" 28		
]ger	Corp.	" 29	]"	[ ]
] Hide	"	" 31	"	
] Roundy	"	" 25	"	]
James Badlack	"	" 27	"	9
Bezeleel Badger	Serj.	Oct. 13	"	"
Patrick Butler	Clerk	Aug. 28	"	"
Jeremiah Hall	Drum.	Sep. 10	"	10
Nathan Fitch	Private	Aug. 25	Oct. 13	
Nathan Fitch	Corp.	Oct. 13		
Abraham Fitch	Private	Aug. 25		
William Scranton		" 27	Dec. 3	
Jeremiah Foster		" 28	Nov. 25	
Gideon Dyke		" 29	Feb. 15	
Stephen Hardenwill^m		. " "	Dec. 9	

CAMPAIGN OF 1755.

Mens Names Both officers and Soldiers	Quality	Time of each mans Enlistment		Dischd		Dead
Richard Cary		Aug.	29	Dec.	9	
Thomas Huntington		"	"	Nov.	25	
Peleg Woodworth		"	"	Dec.	9	
Timothy Lomays		"	30	"	"	
Michael Lahey		"	"	Nov.	5	
Joshua Bill		"	29	Dec.	9	
Jabez Rous		Sep.	1	Jan.	6	
John Watson		"	2	Dec.	9	
[ ] Chrouch		"	"	Oct.	21	
[ ]terman		"	3	Dec.	9	
[ ]ler		"	"	Oct. [ ]		
[ ]n		"	"	Dec. [ ]		
[ ]ay		"	"			
[ ] Junr		Aug.	26			
[ ]ebster		Sep.	8			
[ ]oner		"	5			
[ ] Bacon		"	3			
[ ]Lamb		Aug.	29			
[ ]rd Torrowara		Sep.	11	Dec. [ ]		
[ ]amin Craft		"	"	"		
[ ]imon Cady		"	10	"		
Thomas Lamb		"	"	"	10	
Ichabod Brown		"	"	"	"	
Joshua Ramand		"	"	"	"	
John Trusdel		Aug.	28	"	"	
Ebenezer Doe		"	27	Nov.	25	
Thomas Gooddel		Sep.	4	"	"	
Jeremiah Utley Junr		"	2	Dec.	10	
John Davison		"	1	"	"	
Champion Crocker		"	"	"	"	
Timothy Squier		Aug.	29	"	"	
Amaziah Blancha^d		Sep.	4	Oct.	6	Dead
Jonothan Canany		Aug.	26	Dec.	9	
Theodor Simons		"	"	"	"	
[ ]isha Bingham		"	"	"	"	
[ ]anes Backes		"	"	"	"	
[ ] Fobes		"	"	Oct. [ ]		Dead
[ ]el Ormby		"	31	[ ]		
[ ] Ormby		"	"			
[ ]ens		Sep.	3			
[ ]eacham Junr		Aug.	27			
[ ]art		"	"			
[ ]rnum		"	"			
[ ]lton		"	"			
[ ] Stevens		Sep.	1			
[ ] Johnson		Aug.	28			
Joseph Wilson		"	"	Dec.	9	
John Wright		"	"	Nov.	25	
Jeremiah Everit		"	26	Dec.	9	
Nathaniel Holb^k		"	"	"	11	
Daniel Moulton		Sep.	1	Nov.	20	
Azariah Sang^r		Aug.	28	Dec.	9	
James Shearman		"	29	"	"	
Daniel Squair		"	"	"	"	

[*Connecticut Historical Society.*]

This company marched from Lebanon Sep. 15.

[*Connecticut Historical Society, MS. letter of Jonathan Trumbull.*]

FIRST REGIMENT.

A Pay Rool of The Company under Comand of Cap[t] John Terry. February 27th 1756 Rec[d] of Jonathan Trumble of Lebanon The Several Sums annexed To our Several Names, In full for our Service in Said Company.

Names	Quality	
John Terry		
Prince Tracy		
Isaac Williams		
Josiah Throop	Searg.	
Barzeliel Badger	Corp.	
W[m] Hide	"	
Paterick Butler	Clerk	
Nathan Fitch	Private [and] Corp.	
Abraham Fitch	Private	
W[m] Scranton	"	{ dispute between Isaa (?) Woodwor (?) Master & y[e] Apprentice
Jeremiah Forster	"	
Gideon Dike	"	
Step[n] Harding Williams	"	Simon Newcomb master
Peleg Woodworth	"	
Tim[o] Loomiss	"	
Michael Lahey	"	
Joshua Bill	"	
Jabez Rous	"	
John Watson	"	
David Crouch	"	
Darius Waterman	"	
Josiah Taylor	"	
Zek[l] Lyman	"	[signed] Ezekiel Lyman.
Amos Treadway	"	
Eb[ar] Bill Jr.	"	
Shadrack Webster	"	
Zaccheus Downer	"	
Barnabas Bacon	"	
Eb[n] Lamb	"	
Nath[ll] Holbrook	"	
Daniel Moulton	"	
Tho[s] Huntington	"	
Rich[d] Torowara	"	belongs to Farmington
Patt Butler	"	
Rich[d] Casy	"	
W[m] Southworth	"	{ Inlisted 31st August, returned with the rest
John Fobes		

[Indorsed] Lebanon

[*Connecticut Historical Society.*]

Note: This roll contains the autographs of most of the soldiers named.

A Pay Rool of the Company under Comand of Cap[t] Jn[o] Terry. Feb[ry] 27th 1756 Rec[d] of Jonathan Trumble of Lebanon The several Sums annexed To our Several Names, In full for our Services in Said Company

Names	Quality
Eb[n] Bibbins	Serg.
Sam[ll] Roundy	Corp.
James Badlack	"

CAMPAIGN OF 1755.

Names	Quality	
Theodore Simons	Priv.	
Abisha Bingham	"	
Sylva[s] Backuss	"	
Jn[o] Fobes	"	{ Jon[th] Smith recd it of Mr J Trumble, Smith Married his Sister N B The Brother of John Fobes wants his wages.
Nath[ll] Ormby	"	
Ep[h] Ormby	"	
Amos Bibbens	"	Amos Allen Master to Sd Bibbens
Dan[ll] Meacham Jr.	"	
Josiah Hibbert	"	
Elijah Farnam	"	
Jacob Preston Jr.	"	
Joseph Stevens	"	
Caleb Johnson	"	
Joseph Wilson	"	
Jn[o] Wright	"	
Jere[h] Everit	"	
Jon[th] Canaday	"	
Nath[ll] Holbrook	"	
Aza Sanger	"	[signed] Azariah Sanger
James Sherman	"	Joshua Kendal master of James Sharmon
Dan[ll] Squire	"	
Dan[ll] Moulton	"	

[Indorsed] Windham

[*Connecticut Historical Society.*]

Note : This roll contains the autographs of most of the soldiers named.

A Pay Rool of the Company under Command of Cap[t] Jn[o] Terry.

Feb[ry] 27th 1756 Rec[d] of Jonathan Trumble of Lebanon The Several Sums annex[d] To our Several Names In full for our Service in S[d] Company.

Names	Quality	
Jon[a] Waldo	Serg.	
Sam[ll] Cole	"	
Jere[h] Hall	Drum.	
Benj[a] Craft	Private	
Simon Cady	"	
Th[o] Lamb	"	
Ich[a] Brown	"	Ephraim Ingalls master
Joshua Raymond	"	
Jn[o] Trusdel	"	Sam[ll] Rennells master
Eb[r] Dodge	"	
Th[o] Gooddel	"	{ Paid to Leut. Isaac Williams by order from Goodales Gardian
Jn[o] Davison	"	
Champion Crocker	"	Besa (?) Smith master
Tim[o] Squier	"	
Amaz[h] Blanchard	"	Cap[t] Terry paid for his Coffin boards
Jere Utley Jr	"	
L[t] Isaac Williams	Lieut.	

1756 March 15th Rec[d] of Jonathan Trumble for Amaziah Blanchard's for a Month's pay to be paid his Father W[m] Blanchard he the S[d] Amaziah being Dead

[Indorsed] Pomfret

[*Connecticut Historical Society.*]

Note : This roll contains the autographs of most of the soldiers named.

[   ] Honnered Committy of War I being Inlisted the Seventh Day of September under Capt John Tary of Lebanon in Jenaral Lymons Ridgemet in a Expadetion Against Cronpoynt your Honners Please to Pay onto Joshua Raymond the Premeum for finding myself a Blanket and in So doing you will a Blige me

Benjamin Craft.
[*Connecticut Historical Society.*]

CAPT. PUTNAM'S COMPANY.

Israel Putnam [of Pomfret] Captain.

The company was paid from Sept. It consisted of three commissioned officers and seventy non-commissioned officers and men.

[*State Library, War 5, 239.*]

Note: Humphreys' Life of Putnam is authority for the statement that he "commanded a company in Lyman's regiment."

SECOND REGIMENT—COL. ELIZUR GOODRICH.

REGIMENTAL OFFICERS.

Elizur Goodrich [of Wethersfield] nominated Colonel and Captain of the first Company, March, 1755. Discharged Dec. 8.
Nathan Whiting [of New Haven] nominated Lieutenant-Colonel and Captain of the Second Company, March, 1755. Discharged Dec. 8.
Isaac Foot [of Branford] nominated Major March, 1755. Died [at Greenbush, N. Y.] Oct. 7.

[*Colonial Records.*]

FIRST COMPANY—COL. GOODRICH.

Elizur Goodrich [of Wethersfield], Colonel and Captain. [*Colonial Records.*]
Jehosaphat Starr [of Middletown], Adjutant, First Lieutenant and Captain.
Daniel Rockwell of Norwich, Second Lieutenant. [*Colonial Records.*]
Ebenezer Orvis, Ensign. [of Farmington ?]
Nicols Nicols, Ensign and Lieutenant.

A Muster Role of Colonel Elizor Goodrich Company With the time of there Inlistment &c

Officers & soldiers Names & quality		Time of Inlistment		Discharged		Dead or Captivated	
Elizor Goodrich	Colo.	Apr.	5	Dec.	8		
Jehoshaphat Starr	Lut.	"	"	Oct.	15		
"	Capt.	Oct.	16	Dec.	8		
Daniel Rockwell	Lut.	Apr	5	"	"		
Ebenez Orvis	Ens.	"	"	Aug.	25		
Jehos^t Starr	Adj.	"	"	Dec.	8		
Nicols Nicols	Serj.	"	11	Aug.	25		
"	Ens.	Aug.	25	Sep.	15		
"	Lieut.	Sep.	15	Nov.	27		
Elijah Woodruf	Serj.	Apr.	10	Oct.	16		
John Blin	"	"	9	Nov.	27		
John Kilburn	"	"	10	Dec.	8		
Joseph Preston	Corp.	"	16			Sep.	8
Isaac Goodal	"	"	10	Sep.	17		
Sam^{ll} Crandal	"	"	17	Nov.	27		
Ashbil Webster	"	"	15	Sep.	12		
Timothy Herlihy	Clark	"	26	"	15		
"	Ens.	Sep.	15	Nov.	27		
John Holding	Drum.	Apr.	15	Oct.	8		
Jacob Andrews	Private	"	18	Dec.	8		
Joseph (?) Bartlit		"	12			Sep.	8
Timothy Brooks		"	10	Nov.	27		
Sam^{ll} Bayley		"	15	Sep.	26		
Josiah Bushnal		"	24	"	"		

SECOND REGIMENT.

Officers & soldiers Names & quality	Time of Inlistment	Discharged	Dead or Captivated
Caleb Benton	May 6		Sep. 8
John Merrit	Apr. 15	Nov. 27	
Simeon Bengham	" 23	Dec. 8	
Thomas Clark	" 12	" "	
Uriah Clark	" 19		Sep. 15
Mosis Cleaveland	" 28	Oct. 8	
Benjm Dix	" 12		Sep. 4
Willm Day	" 14	Nov. 27	
Thomas Antony	May 29	Oct. 17	
Wilson Rowlinson	Apr. 16	" 29	
David Rusel	May 6	" 15	
Issaac Robbin	Apr. 28	Dec. 8	
Joseph Renolds	" 17	Sep. 27	
Elish Renolds	" 21	Oct. 1	
Benjm Smith	" 10	" 30	
Benja' Starkwather	" "	" 3	
Garsham Smith	" 11	Dec. 2	
Sam'l Shilling	" 12	Oct. 1	
Enoch Stratton	" 13	" "	
Joseph Slate	" 14	" 29	
Issaac Smith	" 15	" 28	
Ezekil Strong	" 16	Sep. 18	
Willim Ellicott	" 18	Dec. 8	
Joseph Forbs	" 14	Oct. 18	
John Fox	" "	" 30	
Thomas Garrald	" 19	" 16	
Hugh Graham	" 22		Desarted
Joseph Green	May 1	Dec. 8	
Sam'l Guye (?)	Apr. 10	Sep. 26	
Peter Tocomwas	" 24	Sep. 28	
Willim Wilkinson	" 10	Dec. 2	
Joseph Wares	" "	Oct. 16	
Jefrie Welding	" 14	Nov. 27	
Sam'l Wright	" 15	Oct. 16	
Jonathan Ward	" 24	" 17	
David Way	" 28	Dec. 8	
Richard Wallace	May 16	Oct. 1	
Jotham Hall	Apl. 27	" 10	
James Jackson	" 17	Dec. 8	
John Jackson	" 19	Sep. 16	
James Kiman	May 4	Dec. 8	
Joseph Hale	Apr. 12	Oct. 1	
Feman Burnham	" 24	Dec. 8	
Lot Loveland	" 10	Oct. 8	
Elizor Loveland	" 14	Nov. 27	
John Lattemor	" 12	Oct. 28	
John Linsey	" 15	" 18	
Noah Mors	" 18	Nov. 27	
Ebenez Miller	" 29	Oct. 28	
Willim Mason	" 15	Nov. 27	
Seth Mix	" 18	Dec. 6	
Ambros Nicolson	" 14	Nov. 27	
Elisha Porter	" 10	" "	
Lamuel Peas	" 12	" "	
James Powers	" 17	Oct. 17	
Samon Smith	" 19	Nov. 6	
Benjm Stoddard	" 17	Dec. 8	

CAMPAIGN OF 1755.

Officers & soldiers Names & quality	Time of Inlistment	Discharged	Dead or Captivated
David Stoddard	Apr. 16	Dec. 8	
Ezekil Tubbs	" 10	Nov. 27	
Mahue Tuper	" 21	" "	
Nathan Weeb	" 16		Sep. 8
Gideon Woodward	" 21		" 13
John Williams	" 23	Sep. 20	
David Cole	" 24	Dec. 8	
Sam¹¹ Russil	May 1	Oct. 10	
Nicolas Williams	July 1	" "	
John Tylor	Aug. 1	Nov. 1	

[Indorsed] Co¹¹ Elizur Goodrich 1755
Benaj^h Starkweather p

[State Library, Adams Papers.]

SECOND COMPANY — LIEUT.-COL. WHITING.

Nathan Whiting [of New Haven], Lieutenant Colonel and Captain.
Nathaniel Porter of Sharon, First Lieutenant.
John Jefferies of Cornwall, Second Lieutenant.

[Colonial Records.]

A Roll of Col° Nathan Whiting's Company with the Time of Inlistment and what their Wages amounted to, at their Death Desertion being Discharged &c &c

Names & Quality	[ ] of [ ]listg [ ]5	Discharged	Dead
Col° Nath^n Whiting	[ ]r¹ 5	Dec. 8	
Lieu^t Nath¹ Porter	"	Oct. 28	
Lieu^t John Jeffery	"	Dec. 8	
Serj^t Ezek¹ Fitch	10	Sep. 29	
Serj^t Jo^s Sperry	6	Dec. 8	
Serj^t Jo^s Blackman	[ ]	Oct. 18	
Serj^t Asa Richardson	9	" 3	
Corp¹ Thos Pain	14	Aug. 31	
Serj^t Thos Pain	[ ]p^t 1	Oct. 16	
Corp¹ Isaac Bird	[ ]r¹ 17	Sept. 8	
Isaac Bird Clerk	[ ]p^t 9	Nov. 20	
Corp¹ Ed^w Bumps	[ ]r¹ 15	Sep. 30	
Ed^w Bumps Serj^t	[ ]t^r 1	Dec. 3	
Jon^th Chipman Corp¹	[ ]r¹ 17	Oct. 31	
Jon^th Chipman Clerk	[ ]v^r 1	Dec. 5	
Benj^a Wells Clerk	[ ]r¹ 6		Sep. 8
Tim° Talmage Drum^r	5	Oct. 1	
James Arnold	10	Dec. 6	
Abr^a Buell	11	Oct. 8	
Nath¹ Buell	[ ]	Dec. 3	
Charles Cook	11	Oct. 1	
Ezra Cogswell	"	Sep. 29	
Aaron Cogswell	"	" "	
Amos Clark	15		Sep. 25
Tim° Chittendon	11	Dec. 8	

SECOND REGIMENT.

Names & Quality	[ ] of listg [ ]5		Discharged		Dead	
James Doney		15	Oct.	8		
Willm Denslow		5	"	10		
John Denslow		"	"	"		
Willm Duplex		14	Nov.	26		
Jon^th Everit		11	Dec.	8		
James Ellis		14	Oct.	3		
Saml Fales		11	"	18		
Saml Freeman		10	Nov.	26		
Hez^a Ford		17	Oct.	3		
[Twelve or fifteen names missing here.]						
Andrew Lisk	Apr.	10	Oct.	18		
Arunah Lothrop		11				
Willm Lyman		"	Oct.	11		
Dan Mansfield		10	Dec.	2		
David Morgan		12			Sep.	27
John Metchel		"	Sep.	30		
John Mitchel Corp^l	Oct.	1	Dec.	8		
Thomas Marvin	Apr.	11	Sep.	8		
Thomas Marvin Corp^l	Sep.	9	Dec.	8		
Phillip Munger	Apr.	17	Nov.	20		
Lot Norton		"	Sep.	26		
Joel Roberts		11	Nov.	13		
Charles Royce	May	28	Oct.	15		
Isaac Royce	Apr.	17	"	25		
Tim^o Royce		11	"	27		
Steph. Russell		5	"	9		
Robert Roundy		16	Dec.	10		
Ichab^d Stark		8	Oct.	28		
Enos Sperry		13	"	11		
Elij^a Smith		5	Dec.	8		
Joseph Stoddard		11			Sep.	8
Eden Sperry		7	Oct.	18		
Saml Squire		9	"	13		
Simeon Strong		17	Sep.	24		
Elij^a Skinner		"	Oct.	23		
Tim^o Thorp		10	"	18		
Isaac Todd		11	"	16		
Eliph^a Thomson		14	"	10		
Saml Thomas		18	Dec.	6		
Hez^a Tuttle		5	"	8		
John Tuttle		11	"	"		
Danl Tuttle		"	Nov.	10		
David Webb		"	Dec.	8		
Reuben Woodworth		10	"	2		
David Woodworth		"	"	"		
Benj^a Woodworth		11	"	8		
Benj^a Woodworth Jr.		17	Oct.	27		
John Hanmer		10	Nov.	26		
Sampson Amos		"	Dec.	10		
Peras Richards		"	"	2		
Amos Thorp		8			Sep.	8
Eliph^a Thorp		10			"	"
Matthias Smith		"	Sep.	30		
Matthias Smith Serj^t	Oct.	1	Dec.	4		

[Indorsed] Col. Nath^n Whiting 1755
Lot Norton p

[*State Library, Adams Papers.*]

THIRD COMPANY—MAJ. FOOT.

Isaac Foot [of Branford], Major and Captain.
Stephen Powell of Lebanon, First Lieutenant.
Matthew Huntington of Mansfield, Second Lieutenant.
Richard Darrow, Second Lieutenant.

[*Colonial Records.*]

A Muster Roll of the Company in His Majesties Service under the Command of Major Isaac Foot. 1755

Mens Names	Quality	Time of Entrance into Service	Time of Discharge	Dead or Taken
Isaac Foot	Maj^r	Apr. 5		Oct. 7
Steph. Powel	Lieu^t	" "	Oct. 8	
Mtth^w Huntington	"	" "		Sep. 22
John Dunbar	Serj^t	" 17	Sep. 27	
Richd Darrow	"	" 14	" 22	
Richd Darrow	Lieu^t	Sep. 23	Nov. 22	
John Barns	Serj^t	Apr. 14	Dec. [ ]	
Edward Marcy	"	" 30	Oct. 2	
Abr^a Foot	Clerk	" 5	Sep. 26	
Jonah Todd	Drum.	May 14	" 29	
Eleaz^r Done	Corp^l	Apr. 22	Oct. 9	
Joseph Blakslee	"	" 11	Sep. 15	
Joseph Blakslee	Serj^t	Sep. 16	Oct. 14	
Levi Leet	Corp^l	Apr. 17	Sep. 11	
Levi Leet	Serj^t	Sep. 12	Nov. 9	
Nathⁿ Carpenter	Corp^l	Apr. 23	Oct. 4	
Nathⁿ Carpenter	Serj^t	Oct. 5	Dec. 1	
Eldad Mix	Cent^l	Apr. 7	Nov. 30	
James Pierpont	"	" 11	Oct. 2	
Jared H[ ]	"	" "	" [ ]	
[ ]iles	"	" "	Sep. [ ]	
[ ]les	Corp^l	Sep. 16	Nov. 29	
[ ]oyce	Cent^l	Apr. 11		Sep. 8
[ ]es	"	" 7	Aug. 22	
[ ]tkins	"	" 11	Sep. 25	
[ ]ellogg	"	" 11		Nov. 18
[ ]tholomew	"	" 12	Nov. 30	
[ ]lant	"	" "	Sep. 26	
[ ]ith	"	" "		Sep. 8
[ ]is	"	" "	Oct. 8	
[ ]house	"	" "	Nov. 21	
[ ]rtis	"	" "	" 30	
[ ]rtis	"	" 10	Sep. 30	
[ ]islot	"	" 12	Nov. 29	
[ ]lall	"	" 14	" 21	
[ ]lmson	"	" "	" 30	
[ ] Curtis	"	" "	" "	
[ ]arker	"	" "	Oct. [ ]	
[ ]tings	"	" "	" 25	
[ ]arks	"	" "	Nov. 29	
[ ]lakslee	"	" "	Oct. 24	
[ ]ncer	"	" "	Aug. [ ]	
[ ]ilmot	"	" "	Oct. [ ]	
[ ]num	"	" 15		Sep. 8
[ ]ves	"	" "		Nov. 12
[ ] Roys	"	" "	Sep. 18	
[ ]oys	Serj^t	Sep. 19	Nov. [ ]	
Eben. Prindle	Cent^l	Apr. 15	Oct. [ ]	

SECOND REGIMENT.

Mens Names	Quality	Time of Entrance into Service	Time of Discharge	Dead or Taken
John Ball	Cent^l	Apr. 17		Oct. 8
Eben^r Hatch	"	" "	Oct. 5	
Elias Benton	"	" "	" 25	
Ezra Ludington	"	" "	Nov. 29	
Wm Tanterpan	"	" "	" 30	
Solomon Lewis	"	" 23	Oct. 15	
Saml Goodsell	"	" 22	Nov. 8	
James Ludington	"	" 23	Aug. 31	
Jehoida Wheadon	"	" 21	Nov. 30	
Benj^a Alcy	"	" "	Sep. 26	
Joseph Ives	"	" 29	Nov. 29	
Ruben Bachelor	"	May 3	Oct. 8	
Is^c Sherman Kimberley	"	" 30	Nov. 8	
Christ^o Wickwire	"	Apr. 11	Oct. 18	
Jo^s Rowlandson	"	" 17	Nov. 30	
Tim^o Plant	"	" 18	Sep. 17	
Ambrose Tuttle	"	" 14	" 1	
Zach^r Parker	"	" 22	Dec. 1	
Benj^a Hanks	"	" "	Oct. 1	
Experience Davis	"	" 23	Dec. 1	
Jacob Dena	"	" 26	Nov. 8	
Phillip Rice	"	" "	Oct. 27	
Ezek^l Abbie	"	" 21	Dec. 2	
Christ^o Green	"	" 19	Oct. 16	
John Leach	"	May 5		Sep. 8
Peleg Heath	"	" 5	Dec. 1	
Nathl Fenton	"	Apr. 17		Sep. 8
Richard Leach	"	" 17	Oct. 26	
Amos Ames	"	" 23	Dec. 1	
Winter Green (?)	"	" 28	Nov. 5	
Thomas Fowler	"	" 24	Oct. 20	
John Frame	"	May 5	Dec. 1	
Noah Davis	"	Apr. 28		Sep. 8
Eben^r Gary	"	" 21	Nov. 17	
Isaac Dexter	"	May 6	Sep. 27	
Abr^a Redington	"	" "	Sep. 30	
Moses Parker	"	Apr. 14	Oct. 24	
Pi. Pito	"	" 23	Dec. 2	
Jonth Russell	"	" 22	" "	
Tim^o Plant	Corp^l	Sep. 18	" 1	
Parmen^s Bumsil	Cent^l	Apr. 17	wounded and paid	

[*State Library, Adams Papers.*]

FOURTH COMPANY—CAPT. SANFORD.

Samuel Sanford, Jr., of Milford, Captain.
David Waterbury, 3d., of Stamford, First Lieutenant.
Gershom Fulford of Waterbury, Second Lieutenant.   [*Colonial Records.*]

This company consisted of three commissioned officers and eighty-one non commissioned officers and soldiers.   [*State Library, War 5, 206.*]

FIFTH COMPANY—CAPT. WHITING.

Samuel Whiting of Stratford, Captain.
David Lacy of Fairfield, First Lieutenant.
Thomas Barnum, 3d., of Danbury, Second Lieutenant.

[*Colonial Records.*]

This company consisted of three commissioned officers and eighty non-commissioned officers and men.

[*State Library, War 5, 209.*]

SIXTH COMPANY—CAPT. HINMAN.

Benjamin Hinman of Woodbury, Captain.
Benjamin Ruggles of New Milford, First Lieutenant.
Tarball Whitney of Canaan, Second Lieutenant.

[*Colonial Records.*]

A Mustor Role of Capt Benj^m Hinmans Company In Colo^{ll} Elez^r Goodrich's Regiment Novemb^r ye 30th A D 1755

Officers and Soldiers Names & quality		Time of Inlist.		Discharged		Dead or captivated
Benj^m Hinman	Capt	Apr.	5	Nov.	30	
Benj^m Ruggles	Lieu^t	"	"	Sep.	28	
Tarbul Whitney	"	"	"	Nov.	28	
Adam Hinman	Serj^t	"	23	Sep.	28	
David Mun	"	"	17	Oct.	29	
Samuel Hide	"	"	21	Sep.	30	
Hezekiah Baldwin	"	"	22	Oct.	26	
Joseph Ruggles	Cor.	"	18	Sep.	28	
Asel King	"	"	16	Jan.	31	{ Ser^t Jan 31 to 30 Sep.
Rubin Hurlburt	"	"	21	Oct.	12	
John Felows	"	"	25	"	18	
John Parks	Clark	"	19	Nov.	30	{ Ser^t to Nov. 28 to Sep. 28
Elez^r Clark	Drum.	"	29	"	"	
Abijah Hinman		"	16	Oct.	10	
Nathan Baldwin		"	"	Nov.	30	
Nathan Jackson		"	"	"	"	
Benj^m King		"	"	Sep.	27	
Elijah Hinman		"	"	Nov.	10	
Noble Hinman		"	"	"	"	
Samuel Hull		"	"	Sep.	28	
Samuel Hicok		"	"	Oct.	26	
James Radford		"	"	Nov.	30	
Elisha Peck		"	"	Sep.	3	
Daniel Culvor		"	"	Oct.	12	
Joel Smith		"	"	"	30	
Titus Hinman		"	"	Nov.	30	
Gideon Curtis		"	17	"	"	{ Cor. Nov. 30 to Oct. 10
Lemuel Lewis		"	21	Oct.	10	
Tilley Blackslee		"	17	Nov.	30	
John Ranolds		"	19	Oct.	10	
Nathan Lavensworth		"	23	Nov.	30	

SECOND REGIMENT.

Officers and Soldiers Names & quality	Time of Inlist.	Discharged	Dead or captivated
Zaceous Wellor	Apr. 21	Sep. 30	
Uriah Sharp	" 23	Nov. 30	
Caleb Holbrook	" "	" "	
Noah Hurlburt	" 21	Oct. 10	
James Huff	" 23	Nov. 30	
Peruda Isbal	" 21	" "	
Abijah Hurd	" 23	Oct. 8	
Zebulon Norton	" 19	Nov. 30	
Jon[th] Blackslee	" "	Sep. 30	
John Tiff	" 17	Oct. 8	
Solomon Squior	" 21	Nov. 30	
Nathan Hurlburt	" "	Oct. 16	
Amos Hurd	" "	" 2	
Gideon Tuttle	" 23	Nov. 30	{ to Oct. 12 Corp { to Nov. 30
Elias Whitmor	" 21	" 2	
John Drinkwator	" 22		Sep. 8
Benj[m] Summors	" "	Sep. 30	
Larrance Hollond	" 21	Nov. 30	
Abram Taylor	" 23		Sep. 8
Joseph Lines	" 22	Oct. 29	
Henry Burhorns	" 18	" 10	
Tim° Morgan	" 19	" 8	
Edward Culvor	" 18	Sep. 30	
Robbart Summors	" 21	Nov. 30	
Isaac Buck	" 23	" "	
Joseph Beeman	" 22	Sep. 30	
Isaa Bochford	" 19	" "	
Stephen Bristol	" 18	" "	
Isral Canfield	" 22	Oct. 10	
Nathaniel Wallis	" "	Nov. 30	
Issacor Norton	" 19	" 21	
Ebenez[r] Leanord	" 22	" 30	
Joel Hamblin	" 28	Sep. 28	
Abraham Kurby	" 25	Oct. 2	
Samuel Ransom	" 21	Nov. 28	
Samuel Kellogg	" 26	Sep. 26	
Phillep Cool	" 25	Nov. 28	
Asa Lyon	" 28	Oct. 26	
Jedediah Richards	" 24	Nov. 2	
Moses Taylor	" "	Oct. 24	
Nehemiah Brown	" 21		Sep. 8
Edward Foster	" "	Nov. 28	
Robert Bruce	" 30	Dec. 31	
Joshua Adams	" 25	Oct. 14	
Richard Bignald	May 2	Nov. 28	
Iseph Prindle	" 5	Sep. 26	
Lenord Spolding	" "	Nov. 28	
Noah Stephens	" "	Oct. 27	
William Ward	" "	Dec. 20	
Dan Gregory	" "	Nov. 28	
Baley Austen	" "	Oct. 14	
John Collor	Apr. 22	" 24	

[Indorsed] Cap[t] Benj Hinman 1755
Tarball Whitney L[t]
W[m] Ward

[State Library, Adams Papers.]

CAMPAIGN OF 1755.

SEVENTH COMPANY — CAPT. PECK.

James Peck [of New Haven], Captain.
Amos Hitchcock [of New Haven] First Lieutenant.
Asa Royce, Second Lieutenant.

A Muster Role of Capt James Peck^s Company the 7th Company in Co^{ll} Elizur Goodrich^s Regiment (viz)

Officers & Soldiers Names & Quality		Time of Inlistment		Discharged		Dead
Capt James Peck*		Aug.	21	Dec.	9	
Leu^t Amos Hitchcock		"		"	7	
Leu^t Asa Royce		"		"	9	
Sam^{ll} Gilberd	Serg^t		26	"	7	
Wm Cables	"	Sep.	3	"	9	
Charles Alling	"		9	"	"	
Eliakim Robenson	"		16	"	7	
Dan^{ll} Tuttle	Corp.	Aug.	26	"	9	
Elnathan Ives	"	Sep.	4	"	"	
Joel Munson	"		9	"	"	
Eben^r Beech	"		"	Nov.	26	
Dan^{ll} Russel	Clerk		1	Dec.	7	
Joel Potter	Drummer	Aug.	26	Oct.	28	
Daniel Mallery			28			Nov. 14
Amos Potter			"	Dec.	9	
Eben^r Humerston			"	"	"	
James Atwater			29	"	"	
John Thomson		Sep.	1	"	7	
Step^n Thomas			4	Nov.	26	
Charles Royce			2	"	"	
Jno Strickling			4	Oct.	19	
Benj^m Rexford			"	Dec.	2	
James Powers			7	Nov.	26	
Jno Titus			"	"	"	
Asa Goodyear			9	Dec.	9	
Noah Woolcut			"	"	"	
Joel Bradley			"	"	"	
David Tharp			"	"	"	
Eben^r Woolcut			"	"	"	
Benj^m Todd			"			Nov. 6
Jos. Woolcut			"	Dec.	9	
Joel Basset			"	"	"	
David Bishop Jr			"	"	"	
Alvin Bradly			"	"	"	
Jere. Atwater			"	"	7	
Caleb Gilberd			"	"	9	
Jonah Bradly			"	"	"	
Sam^{ll} Austin			"	"	"	
Joel Gilberd			"	Nov.	18	
Jonth Sacket			"	"	15	
David Beers			8	Dec.	9	
Ezra Sperry			9	"	"	
Richardson Minor			"	"	"	
Nathan Ford			"	"	4	
David Hind			"	Nov.	3	
Eph^m (?) Turrel			"	"	"	

* James Peck Jr. [*State Library*, War 5, 238.]

SECOND REGIMENT.

Officers & Soldiers Names & Quality	Time of Inlistment	Discharged	Dead
Sam¹¹ Newton	Sep. 9	Dec. 9	
Joshua Sperry	"	" "	
Tim° Peck	"	" "	Dec. 7
Epinetus Buckingham	"		Deserted Oct. 27
Jack a Negro	Aug. 28		
Jon^th Wood	Sep. 9	Nov. 3	
James Turner	4	" 24	
Ezekiel Tuttle	1	" 3	
John Hill	"	Dec. 9	
Nick Howell	"	Nov. 26	
Step^h Cooper Jr	"	Dec. 9	
John Cornish	"	Nov. 26	
John Rusheck (?)	4	Dec. 9	
Abram Cooper	8	Nov. 12	
Michal Gilberd	9	Dec. 9	
David Bishop	"	" "	
Obed^h Hotchkis	"	" "	
Christ^r Alling	"	" "	
Joseph Food	4		
Obed Bradly	9	Nov. 6	
Jude Blacksley	"	Dec. 9	
Amos Alling	"	Nov. 26	
Abner Hall	"	" 24	
Jay Humerston	"	Dec. 9	
Jon^th Tharp	"		Nov. 14
Amos Ludington	11	Dec. 9	
Step^h Granis Jr	"	" "	
Benj^m Russel	"	" "	
Sam¹¹ Granis	"	" "	
Denison Grainger	"	" "	
Simeon Bradly	"	" "	
Levy Furbs	"	" "	
Isaac Potter		" 3	
Jared Robenson	9	" 26	
Sam¹¹ Osborn	"		
Isaac Brocket	11	Nov. 24	
John Robenson	9	Dec. 9	
John Conner	11		Deserted Sep. 27
Sam¹¹ Woodward	"		" " 17

[Indorsed] Capt James Pecks Muster Rool 1755]
Christopher Allyn
Amos Allyn

[State Library, Adams Papers.]

This company marched from New Haven Sept. 12.

[Connecticut Gazette.]

CAMPAIGN OF 1755.

CAPT. BELLOWS' COMPANY.

Samuel Bellows [of Salisbury], Captain.
Charles Woodrooff [of Litchfield], First Lieutenant.
John Nicholls [of Stratford ?], Second Lieutenant.

Muster Roll of Capt[n] Samuel Bellowes in Col[o] Elizur Goodrich's Regiment of Foot for the Intended Expedition aganst Crown Point is as follows Viz

Mens Names	Office	Time of Entering into Service	When Deserted or Died or Discharged
Sam[ll] Bellowes	Capt.	Aug. 21	Dec. 5
Charles Woodrooff	1 Lieut.	"	" 6
John Nicholls	2 "	"	" 7
Elnathan Ashman	Serj.	Sep. 8	" 5
Abel Barns	"	" 1	" 6
Thadeus Lacy	"	Aug. 26	" 7
Ashbell Goodrich	"	Sep. 1	" 6
Amaz[h] Ashman	Clark	Sep. 3	" 5
Ezra Davis	Corp.	1	Nov. 30 died
Eaton Jones	"	10	Dec. 6
Dan[ll] Hurlbut	"	Aug. 26	" 7
Jesse Stevens	"	Sep. 8	" 5
John Davis	Drum	1	" 6
Jeams Adams	Cent[ll]	8	" 5
Nath[ll] Ashbow		Aug. 31	" "
Woolston Brockway		Sep. 1	" 6
John Barritt		Aug. 25	" 7 (?)
Tho[s] Barker		"	Nov. 22 Alt
Josiah Baldwin		"	Dec. 6
Rich[d] Burton		"	" 7
Amos Brownson		"	" "
Melath[es] Chapman		Sep. 1	" 6
Eli Cattin		"	" "
Phin[s] Castle		Aug. 26	" 7
Abij[h] Cressee		25	Dec. 20 Died
Tho[s] Dikes		Sep. 3	Nov. 22 Alt[d]
W[m] Dennin		9	Nov. 22 Alt[d]
Nath[ll] Davis		"	Dec. 6
Beriah Dudley		1	" "
Dan[l] Dudley		"	" "
Sam[ll] Dean		Aug. 25	" 7
George Edmonds		31	" 5
David Forde		Sep. 1	" 6
Seth Farnam		Aug. 31	" "
Woolston Gifford		Sep. 3	" "
Charls Goodwin		1	" "
Jn[o] Gordon		2	" "
Ephraim Gitto		"	Nov. 22 Alt[d]
Silas Hill		Aug. 25	Nov. 22 Alt[d]
Eben[r] Henman		"	Dec. 7
Benj[a] Henman		"	" "
Jahi[ll] Hurd		"	" "
Peter Johnson		Sep. 5	" 6
Isaac Handford		2	" 7
Zeb[h] Jackson		Aug. 25	" "
W[m] Kilworth		Sep. 8	" 5
Roswell Kilborn		1	" 6
Josiah Lewis		Aug. 25	" "

SECOND REGIMENT.

33

Mens Names	Office	Time of Entering into Service	When Deserted or Died or Discharged
Edwd Lewis		Aug. 2	Nov. 22 Alt^d
Wm Marsh		Sep. 8	Dec. 5
George Marsh		10	" 6
Eben^r Mitchell		Aug. 25	" 7
Zach^h Owen		Sep. 4	" 5
Felix Powel		Aug. 31	Nov. 22 Alt^d
Benj^a Peet		Sep. 1	Dec. 6
Ebed Pettit		Aug. 27	" 7
Alex^r Pettery		Sep. 10	" "
Elisha Roe		" 8	Nov. 15 Died
Caleb Root		" "	Dec. 5
Joseph Root		12	" 7
Nathan Simons		1	" 5
Andrew Squire		Aug. 25	" 7
Eli Sharp		Sep. 2	" "
Thos Tuttle		8	" 5
Amos Turner		3	" 6
Robt Torrence		Aug. 25	" 7
Ichab^d Tulley		26	" "
Enos Titus		27	" "
Jno Vallance		Sep. 8	" 5
Parce Walters		10	Nov. 22 Alt.
George White		3	Dec. 6
Jno Wilcox		1	Nov. 22 Alt.
Simeon Wheeler		"	Dec. 7
Tim^o Walker		Aug. 25	" "
Zach^h Walker		"	" "
Warham Gibbs		30	" 6
Justus Gibbs		"	" "
Uriah Cattin		Sep. 1	" "
Sam^{ll} Akerly		"	Dec. 3 Died
Silvanus Stevens		10	Dec. 20 Died
Edwd Lake		Aug. 25	Dec. 7
Robt Durgey		Sep. 12	" "
Joshua Owen		1	" 5
Men advanc^d			
Amaz^h Asman	Serj.	Nov. 15	
Eaton Jones	Clark	"	
Felix Powel	Corp.	"	
Joseph Root	Serj.	Sep. 20	
Phin^s Castle	Corp.	Oct. 1	
Men Altered			
Lacey	Cent^{ll}	Sep. 20	
Dan^{ll} Hurlbut		Oct. 1	
Joseph Root		Nov. 15	

[Indorsed] Capt Samuel Bellows 1755 Salisbury
Jno. Wilcox p

[*State Library, Adams Papers*]

Note: This company was either the eighth or ninth in this regiment.

CAMPAIGN OF 1755.

THIRD REGIMENT—COL. ELIPHALET DYER.

REGIMENTAL OFFICERS.

Eliphalet Dyer [of Windham], Colonel and Captain of the first company, September 1, 1755. Discharged Sept. 10.
Joseph Worster [of Stratford], Lieutenant-Colonel and Captain of the second company, September 1, 1755.
John Payson [of Hartford], Major and Captain of the third company, September 1, 1755. Discharged Dec. 9.

FIRST COMPANY—COL. DYER.

Eliphalet Dyer [of Windham], Colonel and Captain.
Moses Griswould [of Windsor], First Lieutenant.
Ebenezer Griswold, Second Lieutenant. [*Colonial Records.*]
Christopher Palmer, Ensign. [*Colonial Records.*]

A Roll of Col° Eliphalet Dyer's Company with the time of Inlistment and what their Wages amounted to, and at their Death, Desertion Being Discharged &c. &c.

Names	Quality	Time of Inlistm^t 1755	Descharged	Dead & Taken
Eliphalet Dyer	Col.	Sep. 1	Dec. 10	
Moses Griswould	Lieut.	"	" 8	
Ebenezer Griswould	"	"	" "	
Christopher Palmer	Ens.	"	" 12	
David Seymour	Adj.	18	" 10	
John Spencer	Serj.	12	Nov. 8	
Joshua Ripley	"	"	Dec. 10	
Joseph Holcom	"	"	" 8	
Jonth Smith	"	13	" "	
Eleaz^r Palmer	Clerk	11	" 10	
Richard Crese	Drum.	12	" "	
Joseph Durkee	Corp	"	" "	
Elijah Portor	"	10	" "	
Giles Elsworth	"		" 8	
Jonathan Brooks	"	[ ] 14	" "	
Marverrick Johnson	Centin^l	10	Nov. 26	
Saml Dodge		"	Oct. 29	
Amos Marsh		"	Dec. 10	
Amos Bruster		11	" "	
Willm Gilbert		"		Nov. 22
Willm Smith		"	Dec. 10	
Zacher^h Parker		"	" "	
Jacob Fenton Jr.		"	" "	
Benj^a Cary		"	Jan. 2	

THIRD REGIMENT.

Names	Quality	Time of Inlistmt 1755	Descharged	Dead & Taken
Phenias Manning		Sep. 11	Nov. 3	
Thomas Bingham		"	Oct. 26	
Thomas Bingham	Serj.	Oct. 7	Dec. 10	
Nathan Robinson		Sep. 11	Nov. 26	
John Warren		"	"	"
John Russ		12	Dec. 10	
Abijah Harris		"	"	"
Ezekiel Holt		"	"	"
Cornel^a Coburn		"	Oct. 27	
Zebadiah Holt		"	Dec. 10	
John Bedlack		"	"	"
Francis Bennit		"	"	"
Joshua Hibbard		"	"	"
John Robins		13	"	12
Stephen Curtis		12	"	10
Nathl Bingham		11	"	8
John Fletcher		12	Oct. 30	
Asa Strong		"	Dec. 8	
Saml Parker Jr.		"	Nov. 11	
Ozias Strong		13	Jan. 2	
Benj^a Luce		12	Dec. 10	
Joseph Turner		"	"	"
Thomas Butler Jr.		"	"	"
Nathl Holt		"	"	8
John Thrall		"	"	"
Elijah Alderman		"	"	"
Elijah Addams		"	"	"
John Phelps		"	Nov. 17	
Eldad [ ]		"	Dec. 8	
Joseph Pinney			"	"
John Stiles		11		
Bildad Easton		12	Nov. 30	
Isaac Terry Holcomb		"	"	3
Josiah Tilley		"	"	26
Elijah Alford		"	Dec. 8	
Stephen Griffing		"	"	"
Joseph Hides		"	"	"
Abner Marshall		"	"	"
Martin Winchel		"	"	"
Micha More		"	"	"
Jehiel Winchel		"	"	"
John Ripnear		8	"	"
Eliakim Seymour		10	"	"
Eli Whaples		"	"	"
Hill Hollister		14		
Stephen Dewolf		"	Nov. 22	
David Taylor		15	"	3
John Watrous		"	"	26
Thomas Edy		"	Dec. 8	
Nathl Hail		"	Nov. 26	
Amos Williams		"	Dec. 8	
Jonth Robbins Jr		"	Jan. 9	
Tim^o Andrus		16	Nov. 8	
Ephraim Goodrich		"	"	13
Thomas Brigdon Jr.		13	"	26
Richard Kilborn		12	Dec. 8	

CAMPAIGN OF 1755.

Names	Quality	Time of Inlistm^t 1755	Descharged	Dead & Taken
Jonathan Griswould		Sep. 13	Dec. 8	
Roger Riley		"	" "	
John Hanmer		"	" "	
John Buck		"	" "	

John Rippenson Served as an Armourer In the Camp to the value of three weeks.

[Indorsed]   Co^l Dyers Muster Rool
David Seymour Adj^t
Eliakim Seymour
Jacob Fenton

[*State Library, Adams Papers.*]

SECOND COMPANY — LIEUT.-COL. WOOSTER.

Joseph Wooster [of Stratford], Lieutenant-Colonel and Captain.

[*State Library, War 5, 237.*]

Benjamin Lee [of Plainfield], First Lieutenant.
Asaph Putnam, Second Lieutenant.

[*Colonial Records.*]

The company consisted of three commissioned officers and fifty-six non-commissioned officers and soldiers.

[*State Library, War 5, 237.*]

THIRD COMPANY — MAJ. PAYSON.

John Payson [of Hartford], Major and Captain.
John Corbin [of Killingly], Lieutenant.
Thomas Gallop [of Plainfield], Lieutenant.

A Muster Roll of the Company in his Majesty^s Service, under the Command of John Payson Maj^r viz.

Mens Names	Quality	Time of Entrance in the Service	Until what Time in the Service
John Payson	Major	Sep. 1	Dec. 9
John Corbin	Lieut.	"	" "
Thos Gallop	"	"	" 13
Hez^h Smith	Serj.	13	" 5
Eben^r Frizell	"	9	Nov. 25
Thos Herd	"	11	" 10
Peter Leavens	"	9	" 25
John Throop	Corp.	"	Dec. 5
Edward Spauldin	"	"	" "
Willm Manning	"	"	Nov. 25
Ephr^m Carpenter	"	"	Dec. 5
Sam^{ll} Morris Jr.	Clerk	"	Nov. 22
Nath^{ll} Bacon	Drum	"	" 25
Joseph Wright	"	12	Dec. 5
Ithamar Amidown		9	" "

THIRD REGIMENT. 37

Mens Names	Quality	Time of Entrance in the Service	Until what Time in the Service
Elezar Bateman		Sep. 1	Dec. 5
Thos Bugbee		"	" "
Shubael Child		"	" "
Danl Corbin		"	" "
Eliphalet Carpenter		10	Nov. 25
Benja Dana		9	Dec. 5
Benja Deming		"	" 9
Jabez Corbin Junr		10	" 5
Eliphat Goodale		9	" "
Thos Wilson		"	" "
Eleazer Covell		"	" "
Zebadiah Marsh		"	" "
Levi Hicks		"	" "
Noah Merrit		"	" 9
Darius Wadkins		"	" 5
Nathll Ormsbee		"	" 9
Isaac Stone		"	" "
Isaac Leavens		10	Nov. 25
Jeremh Jackson		11	Dec. 9
Jonath Wallis		9	" 5
Nathll Coller		"	" 1
Willm McClanen		"	" 5
Mathew Hammond		12	Nov. 25
Peter Brown		"	Dec. 5
Elisha Chamberln		"	" "
Thos Fox Junr		"	" "
Saml Bloyce		"	" 9
John Stone Junr		"	" 5
Abrm Scott		"	" 9
James Horsemore		"	" "
Willm Nelson Junr		"	Nov. 22
Willm Powers		"	Dec. 9
Uriah Carpenter		"	" "
Asa Child		"	" 5
Daniel Squire		"	" 9
John Russell		"	Nov. 22
Saml Chandler		"	Dec. 5
Thos Gould		"	Nov. 25
Saml White		"	Dec. 5
Daniel Bugbee		"	" "
Ammi Cooper		"	" "
Jonath Haskell		"	" 9
Leml Lyon		"	" "
Thos Allen		13	" 1
Nathll Walker		"	" 5
Barnabas Cady		"	" 8
Josiah Russell Jr		7	" 1
Lemuel Williams		"	" "
Nathll Sabins		"	" 5
John Ames		8	Nov. 10
Nathl Spauldin		9	Dec. 5
George Abbott		13	Nov. 25
Littlefield Nash		9	Dec. 10
Negro Cesar		7	" "
Negro Catto		9	" 9
Jonathan Knap		13	" "
Edmund Burk		"	

CAMPAIGN OF 1755.

Mens Names	Quality	Time of Entrance in the Service	Until what Time in the Service
Sam[ll] Barrows		Sep. 1	Dec. 5
Uriah Lee		"	" "
James Corbin		"	" "
John Carpenter Jr		"	Oct. 16
Benj[a] Paull Negro		"	Dec. 9
Sam[ll] Cotes		"	" 5
John Williams		14	" 1
James Dixen		"	" 5
John Cadwell		13	" 1

[Indorsed] Major John Paysons Muster Roll for Exped[a] 1755

[*State Library, Adams Papers.*]

FOURTH COMPANY—CAPT. ALLYN.

Benjamin Allen [of Windsor], Captain. [*Colonial Records.*]
Dennis Bement [of Enfield], First Lieutenant.
Henry Chapin [of Hartford ?], Second Lieutenant. [*Colonial Records.*]

A Muster Roll of Cap[t] Benjamin Allyn[s] Company with the time of their Inlistment and what there Wages Amounted to at the time of being Discharged

Names	Quality	Dates of Inlistment	Discharged	Dead
Benjamin Allyn	Capt.	Aug. 30	Dec. 8	
Dennis Bement	Lieuts.	"	"	
Henry Chapin		"	"	
Joseph Winchel	Sergts	"	Nov. 24	
Isaac Tucker		"	"	
Silas Wells		"	Dec. 4	
Phinehas Drake		"	8	
Abner Pryer	Clerk	"	"	
Thomas Osburn	Corp	"	"	
Hezekiah Persons		"		
Jonathan Pinney		"	Nov. 24	
Johathan Buckland		"	Dec. 8	
John Strong	Drum	"	"	
Jonah Gillet		"	"	
Moses Taylor	Soldier	Sep. 2	Nov. 29	Dead
Joseph Moor Jun[r]		3	Dec. 2	
John Japhet		"	Nov. 26	
Jonathan Gillet Jun[r]		"	Dec. 21	Dead
Daniel Filley		"	3	
Robart Westland Jun[r]		"	8	
Roger Crow		"		
Joel Soper		4	Nov. 24	
Ebenezer Loomis		"	Dec. 8	
Gideon Pryer			"	
Zebulon Winslow		5	"	
Hezekiah Wills		"		
John Cotton		"	Nov. 14	
Ozias Grant		"	Oct. 13	
Giles Wolcott		"	Dec. 6	
Elijah Evens		"	1	
Asa Perry		"	6	
Nathaniel Eaton		"	8	
David Bissill Jun[r]		"	"	

THIRD REGIMENT.   39

Names	Quality	Dates of Inlistment	Discharged	Dead
Oliver Day		Sep. 5	Nov. 13	
Ephistian Allyn		"	Dec. 8	
Peter Wolcott		"	Nov. 13	
William Thompson		"	Dec. 6	
Daniel Eaton Jun[r]		"	8	
Ebenezer Belknap		"	29	
Elijah Loomis		"	"	
Zephaniah Snow		"	8	
Gideon Loomis		"	"	
Elisha Williams		"	2	
Asher Isham		7	8	
John (?) M[c]Larran (?)		8	6	
Nathaniel Copely Jun[r]		"	6	
Elisha Denslow (?)		"	1	
Andrew Shelen (?)		"	Nov. 30	Dead
Charles Loomis (?)		"	Oct. 25	
Thomas Hoskins		"	Dec. 8	
Ebenezer Tillotson		9	Nov. 13	
Reubin Cook		10	Dec. [ ]	
Simeon Alcott		Sep. 4	8	
Silas Blodgett		"	"	
Aaron Fuller		"		
James Farrington		"	29	
Samuel Billings		"	Dec. 8	
Abial Pease		"	29	
Ely Parker		8	Dec. 8	
Benjamin [ ]ker		"	"	
Appleton Holister		"	"	
John Coomes		5	"	
Moses Pease		"	"	
Samuel Wright		6		
Stephen Pease		4	Nov. 24	
Ephraim Gleason		6	Dec. 8	
Eldad Pearsons		5	Nov. 24	
Joseph Bement		4	Oct. 8	
Joseph Booth		"	Dec. 8	
Warham Pease		"	Nov. 24	
Noah Pearsons		"	Dec. 8	
Benjamin Hall		"	Nov. 15	
David Bullen		"	Dec. 8	
Asahel Sexton		"	"	
Benjamin F[ ]		"	21	
Nathan Wood		"	8	
Ephram Parker		8	8	
John Horsmer		3	29	
Partrick Ocornally		4	Nov. 26	
Noah Hunt		6	Dec. 2	
John Abbott		9	Dec. 1	
Zacheus Crow		5	Nov. 24	
Reubin Crow		3	"	
John Eggleston		9	Dec. 8	
John Cole Jun[r]		8	Oct. 22	
George Tryon		"	Nov. 27	
Elijah Barret		9	Dec. 8	
Charles Burnham		"	"	

[Indorsed]   Cap[t] Benj Allyn 1755
             Isaac Tucker Serg[t]

[*State Library, Adams Papers.*]

CAMPAIGN OF 1755.

SIXTH COMPANY—CAPT. ABEL.

Joshua Abel [of Norwich] Captain. [*Colonial Records.*]
James Comstock, First Lieutenant.
John Mack, Second Lieutenant. [*Colonial Records.*]

Capt Joshua Abells Muster Roll for the year 1755

Officers and Soldiers Names and Quality	Time of Enlistment	Discharged	Deserted
Joshua Abell Capt	Sep. 1	Dec. 13	
James Comstock Lieu^t	"	" "	
John Mack "	"	" "	
Jabez Post Serg^t	3	" "	
Elihu Hide "	"	" 5	
Andrew Backus Serj^t	5	" 13	
John Griswould "	6	" "	
Elisha Abell Clark	3	" "	
Nathan^{ll} Chipman Corp^l	11	Nov. 11	
Anthony Freyzor "	"		Deserted
Nathan Comstock "	"	Oct. 22	
Sam^{ll} Peck "	9	Dec. 13	
Elisha Calkin Drum	"	" "	
John Swaddle "	11	Nov. 2	
Jedidiah Hide Junr	3	Dec. 4	
Beriah Bill	"	" 13	
John Brown Junr	"	" 5	
Jered Wintworth	"	" 13	
Aaron Cleaveland	"	" "	
David Alger	"	" "	
John Brown	"	" "	
Jabez Jones	"	" "	
John Lee	8	" "	
Sam^{ll} Uncos	5	" "	
James Burnam Junr	9	Nov. 2	
James Strange	4	Dec. 5	
Joshua Aucom	6	Nov. 2	
Sollomon Hewitt	8	Dec. 13	
Levi Hide	"	" "	
George Chebucks	"	" "	
John Nanapum	9	" "	
Henary Shuntup	"	Nov. 2	
Abraham Tecomwas	"	Dec. 13	
Simeon Abell	"	" "	
Nathan^{ll} Ashpo	10	Nov. 25	
Nathan^{ll} Palmer	9	Dec. 13	
Thomas Mix	11	" "	
Isaac Hearington	9		Deserted
William Goff	"	Dec. 13	
Jethro Smith	11	Nov. 25	
Sam^{ll} Avery	"	Dec. 13	
Hezekiah Chapman	"		
Thomas Thomson	"	Nov. 11	
Joshua Baker Junr	"	Jan. 23	
William Allin	"	Nov. 25	
Nathan^{ll} Thomson	"	" 2	
Daniel Griffing	"	Dec. 13	
Robart Fergo	"	Jan. 16	
John Apley	"	Dec. 13	

THIRD REGIMENT.

41

Officers and Soldiers Names and Quality	Time of Enlistment	Discharged	Deserted
Thomas Leach	Sep. 11	Dec. 13	
Peter Button	" "	" "	
William Macken	9	Oct. 7	
Sam¹¹ Keeney	"	Dec. 13	
Gideon Beebe	"	Nov. 11	
Abel Beckwith	"	Dec. 5	
Sam¹¹ Beckwith	"	" 13	
Nathan Caswell	14	" "	
Steaphen Ransom	5	Oct. 22	
George Lewis	"	Dec. 13	
Asa Sawyer	"	" "	
John Trible	"	Nov. 25	
Joseph Emerson	"	Dec. 13	
Steaphen Emerson	"	Nov. 25	
Nathan¹¹ Emerson	"	Dec. 13	
Philip Beckwith	8	" "	
John Bennett	"	Oct. 22	
Daniel Miner	"	Dec. 5	
Ezekiel Rogers	"	" 13	
Ichabod Beckwith	"	Oct. 29	
Joseph Clarke	"	Nov. 25	
Jacob Tillison	"	Dec. 13	
John Huntley	"	" "	
Jonathan Huntley	9	Nov. 4	
Andrew Averey	"	Dec. 30	
Addom Mannering	"	" 13	
Elihu Crocker	10	" "	
William Sobuck	"	Nov. 25	
Simon Dewolf	"	Dec. 13	
William Tillison	"	" "	
Joseph Rogers	"	Nov. 25	
Sollomon Gee	"	Dec. 13	
Jonathan Church	11		Deserted
Joseph Johnson	"	Dec. 13	

[Indorsed] Capᵗ Joshua Abells Muster Role 1755
Jno. Swadle Drumʳ

[*State Library, Adams Papers.*]

Capᵗ Joshua Abells Company   [*State Library, Adams Papers.*]

Note: This roll contains no information not in the previous roll.

SIXTH COMPANY—CAPT. GROSVENOR.

John Grosvenor [of Pomfret], Captain, Aug.
Nehemiah Lyon, First Lieutenant, Aug.
Israel Putnam [of Pomfret], Second Lieutenant, Aug.

[*Colonial Records.*]

Note: The above are the officers as appointed by the General Assembly, whether they served as appointed is not known. It is probable that Putnam did not serve as Second Lieutenant in this company for he was Captain of a company as early as Sept. John Grosvenor was a member of the Assembly when the appointment was made, so it is probable that he accepted it.

CAMPAIGN OF 1755.

SEVENTH COMPANY—CAPT. PHELPS.

Ichabod Phelps of Hebron, Captain. [State Library, War 5, 28c.]
James Gates, First Lieutenant.
Francis Fenton, Jr., Second Lieutenant.

[Colonial Records.]

A Muster Role of Capt Ichabod Phelps Company.

Officers and Soldiers names and quality	Time of Enlisting		Discharged		Dead and Captivated
Cap Ichabod Phelps	Sep.	1	Dec.	8	
Lieut James Gates	"	"	"	10	
Leu^t Francis Fenton	"	"	Nov.	11	
Sarg. Josiah Mack	"	4	Dec.	2	
Sarg. Israel Champen	"	6	"	11	
Sarg. Sam^{ll} Palmer	"	10	"	"	
Serg^t Sam^{ll} Lilly	"	5	Oct.	27	
Clerk Ebenez^r Sumner	"	1	Dec.	8	
Corp. Thomas Post	"	5	"	24	
Corp. Hezekiah Mack	"	6			Nov. 17
Corp. Thomas Abutt	"	"	Dec.	11	
Corp. Samuel Jones	Nov.	19	"	8	
Samuel Feilding	Sep.	11	"	"	
Saml Jones	"	11	Nov.	18	
Elijah Haughton	"	5	Dec.	6	
John Northum	"	"	"	8	
Thomas Dunham	"	6	"	"	
Elijah Smith	"	11	"	11	
Asher Merrill	"	"	"	2	
Ebenez. Willcox	"	"	"	8	
Phinehas Allyn	"	5	"	9	
Amos Phelps	"	11	"	21	
John Carter	"	7	Jan.	19	
James Calkins	"	8	Dec.	15	
David Phelps	"	11	"	21	
Abner Mack	"	5	"	11	
Eliphalet Welles	"	"	"	"	
James Noble	"	7	"	8	
John Ellis	"	4	"	24	
Ebenez Brown	"	"	Nov.	26	
Amos Hall	"	"	"	"	
Isaac Fox	"	"	Oct.	18	
Richard Sparrow	"	6	Dec.	15	
Elihu Minor	"	5	"	11	
Nath^{ll} Ackley	"	"	"	"	
John Hungerfoot	"	4	"	10	
Elisha Brage	"	5	"	11	
John Brown	"	6	"	22	
Thomas Cowdry	"	4	"	11	
Giles Stow of Middletown	"	5	Nov.	26	
Nehemiah Gates	"	"	Jan.	10	
Hez^h Ackley	"	4	Dec.	11	
Nathan Willey	"	"			Dec. 29
Elisha Beckwith	"	5	Dec.	11	
Jesse Gates	"	6	"	"	
William Fox	"	4	Nov.	9	
John Bates	"	"	Dec.	24	
Peleg Chamberlin	"	6	Nov.	25	
Joseph Cone	"	4	"	30	

THIRD REGIMENT.

43

Officers and Soldiers names and quality	Time of Enlisting	Discharged	Dead and Captivated
Robert Chapman	Sep. 4	Dec. 11	
Sylvenus Cone	" "		Dec. 17
Oliver Cone	" "	Nov. 11	
Ephraim Tiffany	" "	" "	
Dan Clark	" "	" 3	
Zaccheus Spencer	" "	Dec. 11	
Moses Cowdery	" 5	" "	
Thomas Graves	" 11	Nov. 11	
Noah Phelps	" 5	" 7	
Jonathan Yeomans	" "	" "	
Peter Rice	" 4	Oct. 27	
Elias Lee	" 5	Nov. 7	
Henry Whitticore	" "	" 22	
Moses Hull	" "	" "	
Solomon Warshborn	" 8	" 7	
Jacob Fuller	" 13	" 11	
John Fenton	" "	" "	
George White	" "	" "	
John Eaton	" "	" "	
Nathaniel Hamblin	" "	" 22	
Elijah Robinson	" "	" 11	
Gershom Richinson	" "	" "	
Nathaniel Patten	" "	" "	
Jonathan Pool	" "	" "	
Joshua Kent	" "	" "	
Nathan Holt	" "	" "	
Benjⁿ Sibly Junr	" "	Oct. 27	
Daniel Coleborn	" "	Nov. 11	
William Green	" "	" 22	
Solomon Alcott	" "	" 11	
Ezra West	" "	" "	
Joseph Rider			

[Indorsed]   Capt Ichabod Phelps 1755
                 Ep^m Tiffany
                 Jno. Fenton p
                 Nathan Patten

[State Library, Adams Papers.]

EIGHTH COMPANY — CAPT. HARRIS.

James Harriss, Captain.
Robert Miller, First Lieutenant.
Daniel Griswold, Second Lieutenant.

[Colonial Records.]

A Muster Role of Cap James Harris Company the Time of Enlistment and Discharge with the Number Weeks and days in service

Officers and Soldiers Names and quality	Time of Enlisting	Dischargd	Dead and Captivated
Cap James Harris	Aug. 30	Dec. 12	
Liu^t Robert Miller	" "	Jan. 26	
Liu^t Daniel Griswold	" "	Dec. 12	
Sarg Josiah Dibble	Sep. 1	Nov. 16	

CAMPAIGN OF 1755.

Officers and Soldiers Names and Quality	Time of Enlisting	Dischargd	Dead and Captivated
Sarg George Nettleton	Sep. 4	Dec. 9	
Sarg James Scovel	" 2	Nov. 16	
Sarg Thomas Peirce	" 10	Dec. 12	
Serj¹ Wᵐ Noyes	Nov. 17	" "	
Clerk George Griswold	Sep. 11	" "	
Corp Samˡˡ Pratt	Nov. 17	" "	
Corp Stephen Adsitt	Sep. 5	Nov. 16	
Serj¹ Stephen Adsitt	Nov. 17	Jan. 1	
Corp Jehiel Dwolf	Sep. 8	Dec. 9	
Corp Nathan Lewis	Nov. 18	" "	Sep. 13
Corp Daniel Sears	Sep. 14		died Nov. 18
Corp Samuel Kelsoy Junʳ	" 8	Dec. 9	
Benjamin Pratt Jun	" 13	" 12	
Daniel Pratt Junʳ	" 12	" "	
James Clark	" 11	" 9	
Thomas Wait Junʳ	" 8	Nov. 26	
Jedediah Leonard	" "	Dec. 10	
Ezekiel White	" "	Nov. 24	
Solomon Mack	" 10	" "	
William Rowland	" 8	Dec. 21	
Ely Lewis	" 11	Nov. 24	
John Phillips	" 4	" 26	
Edward Tryon	" "	" 24	
William Gidding	" 8	Dec. 9	
Caleb Chipman	" "		died Nov. 20
Gideon Webb	" "	Nov. 24	
Josiah Nott	" 9	Oct. 24	
Gideon Kintland	" "	Dec. 5	
Simeon Pratt	" "	" 9	
Samuel Prat Jun	" "	Nov. 16	
John Douglass	" "	Dec. 9	
Joseph Mark	" 13	" 8	
William Hough	" 9	Jan. 1	
Elnathan Hurd	" "	Dec. 11	
Eliud Graves	" "	" "	
Aaron Cone	" 11	Nov. 16	
Abner Bushnull	" 9	Dec. 12	
Martin Kintland	" "	" 9	
David Reeve	" "	" 12	
Pabody Greenell	" 10	" 9	
Thomas Spencer	" "	Nov. 16	
Adonijah Buckingham	" 9	Dec. 9	
John Cunningham	" "		Deserted Sep. 23
Samuel Comstook	" "	Dec. 9	
Joshua Wheeler	" "	" 12	
Stephen Chalker Jun	" 12	Oct. 24	
Simeon Chapman	" "	Dec. 9	
Samuel Stannard	" "	Nov. 16 dead	
Ebenez Glading	" "	Dec. 9	
Sylvenus Dudley	" "	" 12	
Ezekiel Still	" "	Oct. 20	
Samuel Sutlick	" 9	Dec. 12	
Elijah Brainard Junʳ	" 10	" 15	
Samuel Horton	" "	Nov. 26	
Samuel Scovel	" "	Dec. 8	
Samuel Hubbard	" "	" "	
John Cone	" "	" "	

THIRD REGIMENT.

Officers and Soldiers Names and quality	Time of Enlisting		Dischargd		Dead and Captivated
Mason Cogswell	Sep.	10	Nov.	16	
Azanah Dickerson	"	11	Dec.	9	
David Thomas	"	"	"	"	
Nathan Lewis	"	13	"	"	
Timothy Taylor	"	"	"	14	
George Smith	"	"	"	9	
John Morehouse	"	12	"	12	
Wm Bushnall	"	"	"	9	
Andrew Clark	"	11	"	12	
William Bradford	"	13	"	"	
John Farman	"	8	"	9	
Robert Newel	"	"	Nov.	24	
Josiah Balding	"	"	Dec.	9	
James Griffing	"	"	"	"	
Joseph Hillyard	"	"	"	"	
Elias Cadwell	"	"	"	"	
Osborn Stephens	"	"	"	12	
Amos Kelsey	"	"	Nov.	16	
Benjn Willcox	"	"	Dec.	9	
Reuben Chapman	"	"	"	"	
Richard Finny	"	"	"	12	
William Noyce Sr (?)	"	25	Nov.	16	

" Serg^t from Novr 16 to Dec. 12

[Indorsed] Capt James Harris 1755
Wm Hough
Joshua Wheeler

[*State Library, Adams Papers.*]

NINTH COMPANY — CAPT. LEACH.

Ebenezer Leach [of Coventry], Captain.
Jedidiah Fay, First Lieutenant.
Brotherton Martin, Second Lieutenant.

[*Colonial Records.*]

A Muster Role of Capt Ebenez^r Leach^s Company

Officers & Soldiers Names and Qualities	The time of Enlisting		Discharg		Dead and Captivated
Capt Ebenez^r Leach	Sep.	1	Dec.	9	
Leu^t Jedediah Fay	"	"	"	11	
Leu^t Brotherton Merten	"	"	"	"	
Serg^t John Ardua	"	3	Oct.	28	
*Serg^t Ebenez^r Swetland	"	2	Dec.	29	
Serg^t Phillip Squier	"	8	"	9	
Serg^t Samuel Woodward	"	6	Nov.	20	
Clark Benj^a Baldwin	"	3	Dec.	11	
Drum Nathanael Bingham	"	5	Oct.	28	
Corp^l Benjamin Jones	"	3	Dec.	9	
Corp^l Stephen Payn	"	"	"	"	
Corp^l Noah Lion	"	8	Nov.	20	
Corp^l John Avery	"	10	Dec.	9	
Ebenez^r Wright	"	7	"	11	
Simon Clark	"	4	Nov.	20	

*Ebenezer Sweatland of Coventry was left sick at Lake George. [*State Library, War 6.*]

CAMPAIGN OF 1755.

Officers & Soldiers Names and Qualities	The time of Enlisting		Discharg		Dead and Captivated	
Isaac Cushman	Sep.	1	Dec.	29		
James Sims	"	8	"	11		
Eliphalet House	"	4	"	9		
James Pineo	"	"	"	25		
Josiah Long	"	8	"	9		
Jonathan Riley	"	3	"	11		
Thomas Runnels	"	"	"	9		
Ephraham Loomis	"	4	"	"		
Joseph Allen	"	"	"	11		
Joseph Ellis	"	"	"	29		
John Finny	"	3	"	9		
Noah Dewey	"	4	Nov.	24		
James Woodwarth	"	"	Dec.	9		
Zephaniah Thayer	"	"	"	11		
Joshua Bill	"	"	"	9		
William White	"	"	"	11		
Nehemiah Glosson	"	2	"	9		
John Morey	"	"			Nov.	13
Aaron Dewey	"	4	Nov.	24		
John Hutchison	"	2	"	"		
Jonathan Swetland	"	8	Dec.	9		
Joseph Simons	"	4	"	"		
Elijah Scott	"	"	"	11		
Micajah Torey	"	"	Nov.	24		
Ephraham Keys	"	8	Dec.	11		
William Bicknal	"	"	"	"		
Thadeah Watkins	"	"	"	"		
Ebenez^r Cary	"	"	Nov.	24		
Josiah Smith	"	"	Dec.	9		
Bartholomy Porter	"	"	"	11		
Timothy Bicknal	"	"	"	"		
James Dewey	"	"	"	"		
Joseph Holms	"	"	"	"		
Nathan Wadkins	"	"	Nov.	20		
Bernebus Edy	"	"	Dec.	11		
Benjamin Walker	"	"	"	"		
Elaxander Ewings	"	"	"	"		
Thomas Chase	"	"	"	"		
John Turner	"	13	"	"		
Seth Charmbling	"	"	Nov.	20		
Hezekiah Johnson	"	"	Dec.	11		
John Reed	"	"	"	"		
Ameziah Wright	"	"	"	"		
William Johnson	"	"	"	"		
Nathan Jenings	"	"	"	"		
Samuel Hunt	"	3	Nov.	20		
Stephen Bump	"	"	"	"		
Adman Grandey	"	"	Sep.	4		
John Medclaf	"	4	Nov.	24		
Amos Chaple	"	8	Oct.	28		
Nathanael Molton	"	6	Dec.	11		
Ebenezer Hide	"	5			Oct.	30
Israel Webster	"	10			Oct.	21
Samuel Gay	"	"	Dec.	11		
John Thomas	"	"	Oct.	18		
Joseph Hills	"	"	Dec.	11		
Samuel Wise	"	"	Nov.	26		

THIRD REGIMENT.

Officers & Soldiers Names and Qualities	The time of Enlisting	Discharg	Dead and Captivated
Jehiel Woodwarth	Sep. 8	Dec. 9	
Thomas Brooks	" 10	Sep. 17	
Lemuel Harding	" "	Dec. 11	
Edward Carter	" "	" "	
Nathanael Dodge	" "	Sep. 17	
Daniel Ishum	" "	Nov. 24	
Titus Carrier	" "	Dec. 28	
Benj^a Shipman	" "	Nov. 24	
John Bill	" "	Dec. 9	
David Simons	" "		Deserted Sep. 5
Joseph Case	" 12	Oct. 1	

[Indorsed]   Capt Eb^r Leech 1755 Coventry
            Isaac Cushman p
            Eb^r Hide p
            Micajah Torey p

[*State Library, Adams Papers.*]

FOURTH REGIMENT—COL. ELIHU CHAUNCEY.

REGIMENTAL OFFICERS.

Elihu Chauncey [of Durham] appointed Colonel and Captain of the first company, Aug. 1755. Discharged Dec. 9.
Andrew Ward, Jr., [of Guilford] appointed Lieutenant-Colonel and Captain of the second company, Aug. 1755. Discharged Dec. 10.
William Whiting [of Norwich] appointed Major and Captain of the third company, Aug. 1755. Discharged Dec. 13.

[*Colonial Records.*]

FIRST COMPANY—COL. CHAUNCEY.

Elihu Chauncey [of Durham], Colonel and Captain.
John Camp, Jr., [of Durham], First Lieutenant.
Didymus Parker, Second Lieutenant.
Giles Hull [of Guilford], Ensign.

[*Colonial Records.*]

A Muster Roll of the Company under the Command of Col. Elihu Chauncey.

Officers and Soldiers Names	Time of Enlisting	Time of Discharge	Deserted
Col° Elihu Chauncey	Sep. 1	Dec. 9	
Lieu^t Jn° Camp	" "	" 15	
Lieu^t Didemus Parker	" "	Nov. 30	
Ens^n Giles Hull	" "	Dec. 10	
*Nathan Dewolff Commissary	" 22	" 13	
Ser^t Maj^r Nath^{ll} Moss	" 12	" 9	
Ser^t Henry Brooks	" "	Oct. 28	
Ser^t Moses Seaward	" "	Nov. 30	
Ser^t Laban Andrus	" "	Dec. 7	
Ser^t Lemuel Hand	Oct. 18	" 9	
Clerk Jn° Wadsworth	Sep. 4	" 11	
Corp Lemuel Hand	" 9	Oct. 18	
Corp Evan Roice	" 12	Dec. 7	
Corp Sam^{ll} Adams	" "	Oct. 27	
Corp Eliez^r Benham	" "	Dec. 6	
Corp Jo^n Hotchkiss	Oct. 18	" 7	
Corp Mathias Hitchcock	" "	" "	
Drum^r Sam^{ll} Hitchcock	Sep. 12	" 6	
Nathan Seaward	" 9	Nov. 30	
Heth Camp	" "	Dec. 9	
Epaphras Not	" 11	" "	
Jo^a Johnson	" "	" 16	
Dan^{ll} Cone	" "	" 9	

* Of Saybrook. [*Colonial Records.*]

FOURTH REGIMENT.

Officers and Soldiers Names	Time of Enlisting	Time of Discharge	Deserted
Titus Fowler	Sep. 9	Nov. 30	
Eliez[r] Baldwin	" "	Dec. 15	
Enos Fairchild	" 2	" 4	
Morriss Henning (?)	" 3		Oct. 1
Cristopher Vansants (?)	" 8	Dec. 4	
Will[m] Andras	" "	" 9	
David Smith	" 6	" 4	
David Squer	" 2	Nov. 26	
Benjamin Cook	" 4	Dec. 8	
Nathan Curtiss	" 9	" 15	
Noah Robinson	" 6	" 9	
John Seaward	" 4	Nov. 30	
Zebulon Walkley	" 10	Dec. 9	
Nath[ll] Roice	" 12	Nov. 14	
Amos Clark	" "	" 18	
Tim[o] Moss	" "	Dec. 8	
John Badger	" "	" 4	
Eliez[r] Dolittle	" "	" 8	
Phineas Atwater	" "	" "	
Caleb Lewiss	" "	" "	
John Hodgkiss (?)	" "	Nov. 18	
Edward Tuttle	" "	" 17	
Benj[n] Hitchcock	" "	Dec. 8	
Dan[ll] Andras	" "	" "	
Amos Dolittle	" "	" 4	
Will[m] Wheeler	" "	Oct. 27	
John Smith	" "	Dec. 8	
Elam Cook	" "	" "	
John Hodgkiss Ju[r]	" "	" "	
Henry Hodgkiss	" "	" "	
Dan[ll] Culver	" "	Oct. 30	
Enos Tyler	" "	Nov. 26	
Lot Hudson	" "	" "	
Tho[s] Brooks	" "	Dec. 8	
Hez[ah] Lewiss	" "	Nov. 22	
Sam[ll] Rexford	" "	Dec. 8	
Matthias Hitchcock	" "	Oct. 18	
Eph[m] Preston	" "	Dec. 18	
Dan[ll] Tyler	" "	" "	
Sherborn Johnson	" "	" 8	
Eli Smieth	" "	Oct. 30	
James Shepherd	" "	Dec. 8	
Sam[ll] Penfield	" "	" "	
Solomon Yale	" "	" "	
Aaron Yale	" "	Oct. 18	
Tho[s] Yale	" "	Dec. 8	
Abel Curtiss	" "	" 6	
Joseph Waye	" "	" 8	
John Darro	" "	Nov. 12	
Hawkins Hart	" "	Dec. 8	
Benjamin Fenn	" "	Oct. 10	
Jo[a] Moss	" "	Dec. 8	
Tho[s] Merwin	" "	" "	
Jacob Francis	" "	" "	
Abr[m] Hall	" "	Nov. 22	
Titus Hall	" "	Dec. 8	
Dan[ll] Bates	" "	" 9	

CAMPAIGN OF 1755.

Officers and Soldiers Names	Time of Enlisting	Time of Discharge	Deserted
John Sutleif	Sep. 12	Nov. 7	
Elihu Atwater	" "	Dec. 8	
John Hitchcock	" "	Jan. 10	
Elisha Steel	" 20	Dec. 10	
Moses Beach	" 12	" 8	

[Indorsed] Colo. Elihu Chauncey 1755
Sam¹ Penfield p

[*State Library, Adams Papers.*]

SECOND COMPANY—LIEUT.-COL. WARD.

Andrew Ward, Jr. [of Guilford], Lieutenant Colonel and Captain.
Joseph Wilford, First Lieutenant.
Thomas Hill [of Fairfield], Second Lieutenant.

[*Colonial Records.*]

Officers and Soldiers Names and qualities	Time of Enlistment	Discharged	Dead or Captivated
Andrew Ward Lieut. Col.	Sep. 1	Dec. 10	
Ichabod Scranton Lieut.	"	" 8	
Thomas Hill 2 "	"	Nov. 3	
Moses Hatch Serj	9	" "	
James Benton "	4	Dec. 8	
Josiah Watrous "	8	" "	
Sam¹ Bartlett "	"	" "	
Samuel Watrous Corp	6	" "	
Abraham Hubbard "	8	" "	
Nathan Chittenden "	"	" "	
Ebenezer Graves "	"	" "	
Stephen Ranney Clerk	4	" "	
Seth Bishop Drum	"	" "	
Rufus Hardy	"	" "	
Jared Leet	"	" "	
Jehiel Ward	"	" "	
Gilbert Hall	"	" "	
Nathaniel Johnson	"	" "	
Samuel Doud	8	" "	
Amos Bishop	"	" 3	
Samuel Evans	"	" "	
David Dudly	"	" "	
Charles Stone	"	" "	
Jehiel Willcock	"	" "	
Ashbel Norton	"	Nov. 25	
Philemon French	"	" "	
Reuben Hand	"		Nov. 12
John Norton	"	Oct. 30	
Wait Hotchkiss	"	Nov. 12	
Jonathan Cramton	"	Oct. 30	
Jared Chittenden	"	" "	
Reuben Kelley	"	" "	
Levy Monger	"	" "	
Aaron Hill	"	Dec. 8	
Joseph Fowler	"		Oct. 29
Daniel Adkins	"		Nov. 28

FOURTH REGIMENT.

Officers and Soldiers Names and qualities	Time of Enlistment	Discharged	Dead or Captivated
Daniel Frairey	Sep. 8		Nov. 16
Eber Benton	"	Nov. 4	
John Wright	"	" 30	
Beriah Norton	"	" "	
Elias Graves	"	" "	
Selah Lee	"	Dec. 8	
Isaac Hatch	"		Oct. 26
Miles Chittenden	"	Dec. 8	
Edward Howd	"	" "	
Ebenezer Evets	"	" "	
John Cranton	"	" "	
Jonathan Palmer	"	" "	
Ebenezer Field	"	" "	
Abraham Stone	"	" "	
Philemon Hall	"	" "	
Timothy Bishop	"	" "	
Stephen Benton	"	" "	
Nathaniel Bishop	"	" "	
Jehiel Williams	"	" "	
Daniel Thomas	"	" "	
Wm Hull	"	" "	
Timothy Eliot	"	" "	
Zebulon Cretenden	"	" "	
Stephen Sweat	"	" "	
Zenoth Bradley	"	" "	
Timothy Hand	"	" "	
Nathan Graves	"	" "	
Timothy Stephens	"	" "	
James Frances	"	" "	
Robert Isbel	"	" "	
Cornelius Palmerly	"	" "	
John Saunders	"	" "	
Elihu Benton	"	" "	
Roger Rose	"	" "	
Phelex Norton	"	" "	
Timothy Leet	"		
Ephraim Payson	"		
Ahiel Thompson	"	Nov. 24	
Adam Willcox	"	" "	
Gideon Hale	"	" "	

[Indorsed] Col^o Wards Muster Roll Pay Roll 1755
Ichab^d Scranton 1 L^t   Jehiel Ward
Jno Norton   Beriah Norton
Ashbel Norton   Levi Monger p

[*State Library, Adams Papers.*]

THIRD COMPANY—MAJ. WHITING.

William Whiting [of Norwich], Major and Captain. [*Colonial Records.*]
Lankester Gorton, First Lieutenant.
John Shaw, Second Lieutenant. [*Colonial Records.*]

A muster Role of Major William Whitings Company with the Time of Enlistment and discharge and Number of Weeks and days in Service

CAMPAIGN OF 1755.

Officers and Soldiers Names and Quality	Time of Enlistment	Discharg	Dead and Captivated
Maj. Wm Whiting	Sep. 1	Dec. 13	
Lieu^t Lankester Gorton	" "	Nov. 22	
Lieu^t John Shaw	" "	" 13	
Sarg Joshua Welch	" 6	Oct. 20	
Sarg Joseph Fox	" 3	" 22	
Sarg Jeremiah Whipple	" 4	" 21	
Sarg Walter Watrous	" "	Dec. 13	
Corp Elijah Cady	" 6	" 14	{ to Oct 20 { Sarg to Dec. 14
Corp Joseph Rudd	" 8	" "	
Corp Walter Chapel	" "	Nov. 22	{ to Oct. 22 { Sarg. to Nov. 22
Corp John Fillmor	" "	Dec. 13	
Clark Samuel Whiting	" 3	" 16	
Drum^r Thomas Kelking	" 10	" 1	
Drum^r Jabez Stebbens	" 8	" 13	
Joseph Bingham	" 12	" "	{ to 22 Oct. { Sarg. to Dec. 13
Eleazer Tracy	" "	" "	
Ezra Fitch	" 5	" "	
William Henson	" 3	Nov. 22	{ to 20 Oct. { Corp. to 22 Nov.
Henry Fillmore	" 4	" 16	
John Gilbert	" 6	Nov. 14	
Ephraim Wells	" "	Dec. 31	
Ammariah Lyon	" 8	Nov. 10	
Richard Hervy	" 5	Dec. 16	
Peter Hambleton	" 6	" 13	
Isaac Bigelow	" "	" "	
John Roberts	" "	" "	
Peter Murdock	" 10	Oct. 23	
Gideon Burchard	" "	Nov. 18	
Jahlal Peck	" 11	Dec. 13	
Joshua Downer	" "	Oct. 23	
Ephraim Wheeler	" 4	Nov. 23	
Daniel Collens	" "	Dec. 13	
George Austen	" 7	Nov. 12	
James Cobb	" "	" "	
Elisha Pain	" "		died Nov. 27
Samuel Herrick	" 8	Dec. 13	{ to Oct. 22 { Corp. to Dec. 13
Christopher Huntington	" "	" "	
Ebenezar Jackson	" 10	" "	
Dier Spalding	" "	" "	
Elisha Rudd	" "	Nov. 22	
John Burdock	" 7	Dec. 13	
Jonah Chapman	" "	" "	
David Mynard	" 5	" "	
Bartholomew Crossman	" 8	" "	
David Fuller	" "	Nov. 1	
Andrew Minor	" 12	Oct. 18	
Ezekiel Watterman	" "	Dec. 13	
Aruna Lothrop	" 10	" "	
James Smith	" 4	" "	
John Bulkley	" "	Nov. 22	
Israel Roberts	" "	Oct. 19	
James Murfey	" 6	Dec. 13	
Jethro Weeks	" "	" "	

FOURTH REGIMENT. 53

Officers and Soldiers Names and Quality	Time of Enlistment		Discharg		Dead and Captivated
Abraham Chapman	Sep.	8	Nov.	22	
William Bishop	"	"	Dec.	13	
James Hacket	"	5	Nov.	22	
Andrew Chapel	"	"	Dec.	13	
Michael McDaniel	"	"	Nov.	22	
Ebenez Shaw	"	4	Dec.	13	
William Bristow	"	5	Oct.	19	
William Cardall	"	"	Dec.	13	
Zaccheus Wheeler	"	8	"	"	
Stephen Beebe	"	"			
John McClemmon	"	5	Nov.	22	
Thos Crossman	"	8	"	10	
Daniel Loomis	"	12	Dec.	13	
Daniel Huntington	"	"	"	"	
Isaac Davis	"	"	"	"	
Abel Spalden	"	6	Oct.	18	
Francis Story	"	11	"	16	
Joseph Ford	"	14	Dec.	13	
Alexander Farly	"	9	Nov.	22	
Peter Oliver	"	3	Dec.	13	
John Shore	"	6	Nov.	22	
Prince Negro	"	"	Dec.	13	
Jupeter Negro	"	8	"	"	
Solomon Sipio	"	6	"	"	
Rich Skate	"	10	"	20	
John Indian	"	3	Nov.	22	
Thomas Scipio	"	"	"	"	
Naman Moses	"	6	"	13	
John Lomer	"	14	"	"	
Joseph Derrick	"	6	"	"	
Coll Mathews	"	"	Oct.	20	

N B. Stephen Beebe was a soldier taken Sick and had Reced his months pay 26/8 wch was omitted in the within Muster Roll.

[Indorsed] Major Wm Whiting 1755

[*State Library, Adams Papers.*]

FOURTH COMPANY—CAPT. LEWIS.

Eldad Lewis [of Southington], Captain.
Isaac Higby [of Middletown], First Lieutenant.
David Whitney [of Canaan], Second Lieutenant.

[*Colonial Records.*]

A Roll of Capt Eldad Lewis^s Company with the Time of Inlistment and what their Wages Amounted to, at their Death Desertion Being Discharged, &c &c

	Time of Inlistmt 1755		Dischargd		Dead & Deserted
Eldad Lewis Capt	Sep.	1	Nov.	24	
Isaac Higbee Lieut.	"	"	"	"	
David Whiting "	"	"	"	"	
Joel Clark Serj.	"	3	"	"	
Joel Clark Clerk	"	"	"	"	
Saml Root Serj.	"	11			Desert^d Oct. 24

CAMPAIGN OF 1755.

	Time of Inlistmt 1755	Dischargd	Dead & Deserted
Timº Clark Serj.	Sep. 11	Nov. 24	
John Webster Serj.	" "	Oct. 24	
Ashbel Porter ⎤	" "	Nov. 24	
Samˡ Higby ⎪ Corp.	" 3	" "	
Isaac Prichard ⎬ and	" 11	" "	
Ephrᵃ Parker ⎪ Drum.	" "	" "	
Ambrᵃ Sloper ⎦	" "	" "	
Abraham Waters	" "	" "	
Abel Gunn	" "	" "	
Allen Roys	" 12	" "	
Amos Cook	" "	" "	
Asa Barns	" "	" "	
Barnᵃ Hugh[ ]	" "	" "	
Benjᵃ Scott	" 11	" "	
Benjᵃ Wetmore	" "	" "	
Benjᵃ Stillwell	" "	" "	
Benjᵃ Turril	" "	" "	
Caleb Jones	" 12	" "	
David Wetmore	" 11	" "	
David Hungerford	" 7	" "	
Danˡ Upson	" 11	" "	
Danˡ Winstone	" "	" "	
Ebenʳ Hossington	" 14	" "	
Ezekˡ Scott	" 11	" "	
Eliphᵃ Scott	" "	" "	
Ebenʳ Bracket	" 12	" "	
Elias Wetmore	" 11	" "	
John Scott	" "	" "	
Joseph Twiss	" "	" "	
Joseph Barrot	" "	" "	
John Barrot	" "	" "	
Jesse Alcock	" "	" "	
Joseph Rogers	" 14	" 1	
Elihu Morse	" 11	" 24	
Abrᵃ Woster	" "	" "	
Jesse Parker	" "	" "	
James Doolittle	" "	" "	
Josiah Stow	" "	" "	
Joseph Luding[ ]	" "	Sep. 29	
Jonᵗʰ Preston	" "	Nov. 24	
Love Thomas	" [ ]	" "	
Linos Hopson	" 12	" "	
Medad Munson	" "	" "	
Moses Foot	" 11	" "	
Moses Hall	" 12		Oct. 25
Moses Brunson	" 11	Nov. 24	
Nathˡ Hitchcock	" "	Oct. 24	
Nathˡ Messenger	" "	Nov. 24	
Peter Tem	" 7	" "	
Joseph Merion	" 12	" "	
James Scarrit	" "	" "	
Job Bracket	" "	" "	
Hait Hall	" "	" "	
Samˡ Upson	" 11	" "	
Solº Barrit	" "	" "	
Stephⁿ Winston	" "	" "	
Stephⁿ Blaklee	" "	" "	

FOURTH REGIMENT.

	Time of Inlistmt 1755		Dischargd		Dead & Deserted
Samuel Baken	Sep.	12			Nov. 26
Weight Woster	"	11	Nov.	24	
Sam¹ Wheden	"	"	"	"	
Jabez Tuttle	"	"	"	"	
Thomas Way	"	"	"	"	
John Collens	"	12	"	"	
Willida Williams	"	"	"	"	
William Pike	"	11	"	"	
Zealous Adkins	"	"	"	"	
Zebulun Peck	"	"	"	"	
Rememᵇ Baker	"	"	"	"	
Sam¹ Warner	"	3	"	"	
Abijah Barns	"	11	"	,	
Enos Ford	"	"	"		
Thomas Fenn	"	"	"	"	
Peter Judson	"	"	"	"	
Elnathan Tharp	"	12			
Sam¹ How	"	11	Sep.	23	
Ebenʳ Saxstone	"	"	Nov.	24	
Matthʷ Johnson	"	12	"	"	
Nath¹ Lewis	"	11			
Moses Austin	"	12	Sep.	25	
Barthol° Pond	"	"			

[Indorsed] Capᵗ Eldad Lewis 1755
Ebenezer Hossington

[State Library, Adams Papers.]

FIFTH COMPANY — CAPT. HANFORD.

Samuel Hanford [of Norwalk], Captain.
Joseph Hoit [of Stamford], First Lieutenant.
Josiah Starr, Jr., [of Danbury], Second Lieutenant.

[Colonial Records.]

Colony of Connecticut. A Muster Roll of Capᵗ Samuel Hanfords Company

Officers & Soldiers Names & Qualitys	Inlisted		Discharged	
Capᵗ Samˡˡ Hanford	Sep.	1	Jau	1
Lᵗ Josiah Starr	"	"	Dec.	7
Lᵗ Isaac Isaacs	"	"	"	14
Serjᵗ Joseph Bendict	"	4	"	9
" Jabez Cable	"	8	"	5
" Ebenʳ Weed	"	5	"	7
" Foster Lewis	"	4	"	14
Clerk Matthew Smith	"	11	"	7
Corpˡ Samˡˡ Selleck	"	5		
" John Trowbridg	"	12	Nov.	8
" Nathan Gregory	"	"	Dec.	7
" Deodate Davenpot	"	4	"	3
Drum. Elisha Bendict	"	5	"	9
Nathˡˡ Weed	"	4	"	20

CAMPAIGN OF 1755.

Officers & Soldiers Names & Qualitys	Inlisted		Discharged	
Jonathan Green	Sep.	4	Dec.	20
Charles Weed	"	"	"	7
Fairchild Bouton	"	"	"	14
Stephen De wolf	"	"	Oct.	23
Wᵐ Raymond	"	"	Sep.	30
Joseph Lockwood	"	"	Oct.	20
John Sloson	"	"	Dec.	7
Abraham Dann	"	"	"	"
Timᵒ Lawrence	"	"	Nov.	8
John Sewake	"	"	Dec.	14
Epinetus Bishop	"	6	"	7
Esrael Sloson	"	8	"	"
Ebenʳ Crizzy	"	"	"	"
Thadeus Bates	"	5	Nov.	7
Ebenʳ Sloson	"	"	Dec.	7
John Suard	"	"	"	"
Stephen Seamore	"	"	"	14
John Greenslit	"	"	Oct.	24
Joseph Goldsberry	"	"	Nov.	27
Jabez Dibble	"	"	Oct.	30
Austin Smith	"	"	"	20
Mathew Mead	"	8	Jan.	1
Joseph Jennens	"	"	Nov.	27
Jonathan Dean	"	"	Jan.	22
Elijah Gregory	"	"	Dec.	7
Moses Hoyt	"	"	"	14
Eleazor Williams	"	9	"	1
Nathaniel Darrow	"	"	"	"
Nathaniel Westcoat	"	"	"	7
John Stone	"	"	Oct.	23
Jabez Brown	"	10	Dec.	7
Jabez Canfield	"	11	"	"
Timᵒ Sᵗ John	"	"	"	14
Ichabod Olmsted	"	"	"	7
John Platt	"	"	"	"
Abijah Abbott	"	"	"	14
Eliakim Nickols	"	12	"	7
Samuel Brown	"	"	"	"
Edmund Brown	"	13	Oct.	24
John Bill	"	9	Dec.	7
Levi Taylor	"	12	"	1
Freegift Hays	"	"	Oct.	18
John Lockwood	"	"	Dec.	7
Obadiah Siscult (?)	"	"	"	"
Stephen Hoyt	"	9	"	"
John Numan	"	"	"	1
Israel Bendict	"	12	"	9
Joseph Brodbrooks	"	8	"	7
Mathew Barnum	"	6	"	1
Abraham Benett	"	"	"	7
Daniel Berlow	"	12	Nov.	27
Nehemiah Bearllee	"	8	Dec.	7
Benjamin Bass	"	"	"	"
Josiah Crofoot	"	12	"	1
Eleazor Dibble	"	11	"	7
Samˡˡ Duning	"	12	"	"
Ebenʳ Gregory	"	6	"	"

FOURTH REGIMENT.

Officers & Soldiers Names & Qualitys	Inlisted	Discharged
Aaron Garrison	Sep. 8	Dec. 1
Andrew Fairchild	" 11	Oct. 7
Benjamin Fairchild	" 8	Dec. 7
Jedediah Frost	" 12	" "
Elnathan Knap	" 8	" "
James Knap	" 12	" "
David Pickett	" "	" 1
Luke Roberds	" 11	" 7
John Stevens	" 12	" "
James Sturdevant	" 8	" "
Isaac Smith	" 12	Oct. 20
John Wilks		

add Paid to Nehemiah Gregory who Enlisted but was wounded and so left behind

add Mr Isaac Isaacs who Servd as Adjutant In Collo Chaunceys Regim{t} from 1 Sepr to 14 Decemr

[Indorsed] Capt Samuel Hanford 1755 Fairfield County

[State Library, Adams Papers.]

SIXTH COMPANY—CAPT. PETTIBONE.

Samuel Pettibone [of Goshen], Captain.
Abraham Daton [of New Milford (?)], First Lieutenant.
Jehiel Barnum [of Kent], Second Lieutenant.

[Colonial Records.]

The Muster Roll of Capt Saml Pettibone's Company in Coll. Chauncey's Regiment

Mens Names	Quality	Time of Inlisting in ye Service	Time of Dismission	Dead Deserted or Taken
Saml Pettibone	Cap.	Sep. 1	Dec. 2	
Abraham Daton	1 Lt.	" "	Oct. 28	
Jehiel Barnum	2 "	" "	Dec. 3	
Zacheus Griswold	Serj.	" 8	" 2	
Isaac Moses	"	" 5	" 3	
John Dibol	"	" 15	Oct. 29	
David Barnam	"	" 8	Dec. 3	
Arkelus Buell	Clerk	" 16	Nov. 29	
John Cohoon	Drum.	" 8	Dec. 3	
Jonathan Berry	Corp.	" "	Nov. 3	
Stephen Thompson	"	" "	Dec. 5	
Lemuel Warner	"	" 5	Nov. 12	
John House	"	" 9	Dec. 2	
Daniel Bebe		" 8	Nov. 11	
John Slauson		" "	Dec. 3	
Saml Hurlbutt		" "	Nov. 9	
Eliezer Barrett		" "	Dec. 13	
James Agard		" "	" 3	
Daniel Clarke		" "	" "	
Jeremiah How		" 8	" 2	
Asaph Wright		" [ ]	" "	
Moses Miller		" 8	" "	

CAMPAIGN OF 1755.

Mens Names	Quality	Time of Inlisting in ye Service		Time of Dismission		Dead Deserted or Taken
Isaac Humphrey		Sep.	8	Dec.	2	
Timothy Gaylord		"	12	"	"	
Caleb Swetland		"	6	"	3	
Elisha Harris		"	13	"	2	
Sylas Butler		"	8	"	1	
Samuel Farrand		"	5	Oct.	12	
Eli Roberts		"	"	Dec.	4	
Joseph Bostwick		"	"	"	"	
Israel Baldwin		"	"	"	"	
Abraham Smith		"	"	"	5	
John Buck		"	"	"	4	
Benjamin Weller		"	"	"	"	
Coolee Weller		"	9	Nov.	11	
Daniel Buck		"	5	Dec.	4	
Abel Buck		"	"	"	1	
Jesse Barzlee		"	"	"	4	
Elisha Murry		"	"	"	"	
Samuel Buck		"	"	"	"	
Joseph Washborn		"	"	"	"	
James Lake		"	"	"	"	
Israel Noble		"	"	"	"	
Jacob Gallucia		"	6	Oct.	28	
Matthew Bostwick		"	"	Dec.	1	
Joseph Miles		"	5	"	4	
Samuel Hotchkiss		"	3	Oct.	28	
Ezra Duning		"	8	Dec.	4	
Stephen Borsworth		"	6	Nov.	22	
Benj[a] Hurlbutt		"	14	Dec.	3	
Abraham Fuller		"	8	"	4	
Heman Swift		"	"	"	"	
Jonathan Morgan		"	"	"	"	
Park Bement		"	"	"	"	
Joseph Pratt		"	"	Nov.	26	
James Stuart		"	"	Dec.	4	
Asa Church		"	9	"	2	
Elisha Slauson		"	"	"	10	
Benj[a] Dibol		"	"	"	9	
Ezra Chapman		"	"			Nov. 28
Elisha Hollister		"	"	Dec.	2	
Samuel Corbe		"	"	"	"	
Sam[l] Miller		"	"	"	"	
Benedick Woodward		"	"	Nov.	27	
Timothy Rowley		"	"	Dec.	2	
John Millard		"	"	"	"	
Thomas Griffith		"	8	"	"	
Ezra Squire		"	16	"	"	
Abel Abbott		"	"	Nov.	23	
Jonah Todd		"	13	Oct.	25	
Samuel Seeal		"	25	Nov.	27	

[Indorsed] Cap[t] Sam[l] Pettybone Goshen 1755
Asaph Wright p

[*State Library, Adams Papers.*]

FOURTH REGIMENT. 59

SEVENTH COMPANY — CAPT. BUCKINGHAM.

Josiah Buckingham [of Milford], Captain.
Jabez Thompson, First Lieutenant. [*Colonial Records.*]
Nehemiah Dickinson, Second Lieutenant.

A Muster Role off Cap⁺ Josiah Buckingham's Company 7ᵗʰ Company in Colonel Elihu Chancey's Esqʳ his Regiment

Officers & Soldiers Names & Quality		Times of Enlistment		Discharged		Dead	
Josiah Buckinham	Capt.	Sept.	1	Dec.	9		
Jabez Thompson	Lieut.	"		"	21		
Moses Dickerson	"	"		"	9		
Benjⁿ Hind	Serj.		8	Jan.	5		
Eliazer Hawkins	"		4	Dec.	9		
Jonⁿ Boardman	"		8	Oct.	28		
Samˡˡ Hoadley	"		11	Dec.	7		
Samˡˡ Smith	Corp.		6	Dec.	9		
Joseph Prudden	"		12	"	"		
Peter Wooster	"			Oct.	19		
Peter Wooster	Serj.	Oct.	19	Jan.	5		
Moses Mallery	Corp.	Sep.	8	Dec.	9		
John Griffin	Clark		6	"	"		
Parpeton Barker	Drum.		11	"	"		
Joseph Woodrugh	Priv.		8	Oct.	19		
Joseph Woodrough	Corp.		19	Dec.	9		
William Gibson			8	"	"		
Elihu Sandford			"	Jan.	5		
Peter Perrit			"	Dec.	9		
John Duran			"	"	"		
David Collings			"	"	16		
Nathan Burril			"			Dec.	18
Epinetus Platt			"	Dec.	9		
Richard Bristol			"	"	"		
Willᵐ Fowler			"	"	16		
Joel Hind			"	"	9		
Nathan Clark			"	"	"		
Isaac Treat			"	"	"		
John Arnold			"	"	"		
Amos Baldwin							
David Gillet			11	Nov.	17		
Joel Parrish			8	Jan.	5		
John Woodrough			11	Dec.	9		
Henry Summers			8	"	"		
Jonathⁿ Northrop			"	"	"		
Andrew Northrop			"	"	"		
Ephraim Northrop			"	"	7		
Elihu Jonson			"	"	9		
Richard Bonfouy			"	"	"		
Gideon Baley			"	"	"		
Benjⁿ Towner			"	Oct.	21		
Tim° Spencer			11	Dec.	7		
Moses Goodrich			"	"	9		
Ebenʳ Jonson			"	"	7		
David Wheden			"	"	"		
Stepⁿ Rogers			"	"	9		
Jos° Bartholomew			"	"	7		
David Goodrich							

CAMPAIGN OF 1755.

Officers & Soldiers Names & Quality	Times of Enlistment	Discharged	Dead
John Kincade	Sep. 11	Oct. 21	
Phyneas Foot	"	Dec. 9	
Richard Lucas	"	"	7
Willm Harrison	"	"	"
Jacob Barker	"	"	"
Dan^ll Palmer	"	"	"
Jorden Smith	"	"	"
Eben^r Buttler	"	Oct. 21	
Moses Harrison	"	Dec. 7	
Phyneas Baldwin	"	"	9
Step^n Todd	"	"	7
Titus Munson	"	"	"
Jacob Foot	"	"	"
Ruben Wheden	"	"	"
Eben^r Trusdell	"	"	"
Abram Tylor	8	"	9
Abram Towner	"	"	"
Dan^ll Beats	"	"	"
Sam^ll Webb	"	"	"
Elkana Higgins	"	"	"
Jon^n Beats	"	"	"
Abijah Buckingham	"	Nov. 3	
Joseph Morris	12	Dec. 9	
Nath^ll Perry	"	"	"
Elisha Wooster	"	"	"
Silas Lee	"	"	"
Benjn Bristol	"	"	"
Joseph Russel	"	"	7
Andrew Weed	"	"	"
Zack^h Fairchild	4	"	20
Charles Burrell	12	"	7
John Smith	5	"	9
Dan^ll Chatfield	"	Jan. 5	
David Holtbrook	6	Dec. 9	
Sam^ll Hale	8	"	5
Pharoh Necko	4	"	9
Sam^ll Botchford	5	"	"

[Indorsed]   Capt Josiah Buckinham 1755

[*State Library, Adams Papers.*]

EIGHTH COMPANY — CAPT. HOBBY.

Thomas Hobby, Captain.
Nathan Holly, First Lieutenant.
John Barnes, Second Lieutenant.

[*Colonial Records.*]

A Muster Roole of Capt Thomas Hobby's Company In Collonal Elihu Chaunceys Regiment

Officers & Souldiers Names & Quallitys	The time of Enlistment	Discharge	Deserted
Capt Thomas Hobby	Sep. 1	Dec. 6	
Lieu^t Nathan Holly	"	"	"
Lieu^t John Barnes	"	"	"
Serj^t Ruben Ferris	5	"	"

FOURTH REGIMENT.

Officers & Souldiers Names & Quallitys	The time of Enlistment		Discharge		Deserted
Serj¹ Peter Ferris	Sep.	6	Dec.	6	
Serj¹ Josiah Stebbins		3	"	4	
Serj¹ David Sill		10	"	6	
Clerk Nathan Betts		16	Oct.	26	
Drummer Jon^th Brooks		11	Dec.	5	
Corp¹ Matthew Benedict		"	Oct.	26	
Corp¹ Daniel Whelply		5	Dec.	7	
Corp¹ William Scott		3	"	6	
Corp¹ Joseph Mead		11	"	4	
Jeremiah Lockwood		5	"	6	
Peter Beay		"	"	8	
Nathaniel (?) Mead (?)		"	"	6	
Andrew Worden		"	"	8	
John Johnson Junr		"	"	6	
Sackett Reynolds		"	"	"	
Jeseph Peters		"	"	"	
Samuel Ferris		6	"	12	
James Martin		"	"	6	
Joseph Peck		"	"	"	
Eliphalet Peck		"	"	7	
James Welch		"	"	6	
Gedion Hait		"	"	"	
Edward Tharps		"	"	"	
Vallentine Burch		"	"	"	
Gershom Mead		8	"	24	
Zopher Willmoth		"	"	"	
Richard Mandor		"	"	8	
Michael Mesenger		"	"	7	
Morris Kelley		11	Oct.	18	
David White		"	Dec.	7	
John Jarman		12	"	6	
John Moor		"	"	"	
Joseph Hutchenson		"	"	8	
Jabez Nortrup		3	"	6	
Aaron Osburn		"	"	5	
William Nortrup		"	Oct.	9	
Simon Molatto		"	Dec.	6	
James S¹ John		4	"	"	
James Whitney		"			Nov. 20
Preserved Tayler		5	Dec.	5	
[ ]h Riggs		"	"	"	
[ ] Lobdell		11	"	"	
[ ] Smith		"	"	"	
James Jones		"	"	"	
Daniel Goodrich		"	"	"	
Jonathan Gates		"	"	"	
Ebenezer Lobdell		"	"	"	
Daniel Tharps		"	"	"	
John Deen		6	"	6	
Jacob Rundell		15	"	5	
Jonathan Sillsberry		"	"	6	
Samuel Chapel		13			Nov. 5
David Walls		10	Dec.	6	
Nathan Walter		"	"	"	
Stephen Tumbling		"	"	"	
Barnaby Graham		14	"	"	
Enos Mojer		"	"	"	
Elisha Tumbling		16			

CAMPAIGN OF 1755.

Officers & Souldiers Names & Quallitys	The time of Enlistment	Discharge	Deserted
John Nicklos	Sep. 18	Dec. 6	
Jabez Brunson	22	" "	
Edward Cogswell	"	" "	
Joseph Rundell	23	" "	
Jabez Hall	"	" "	
Jacob Kenney Ju^r *	24	" "	
Elisha Chapman	"	" "	
Andrew (?) Buckly	"	" "	
[ ] Nuel J^r	"	" "	
[ ] Tryton	26	" "	
David Elmer	27	" "	
Ebenezer Pardey	10	" "	
Thomas White	15	" "	
Thomas Barnes	24	" "	
William Danells	11	" "	
Daniel Rockwell	"	" "	

Deduct 14 Days alowd the people to come home on 10 of the Soldiers in this Muster Roll who stay^d at ye Fort wth Capt Hobby, Capt ½ month Lieu^t ½ month

[Indorsed]   Cap T[ ]o H[   ]y 1755
             And^w Worden p

[State Library, Adams Papers.]

NINTH COMPANY—CAPT. PETTIBONE.

Jonathan Pettibone [of Simsbury], Captain.   [*Colonial Records.*]
John Leavitt [of Suffield], First Lieutenant.
Hezekiah Humphreys [of Simsbury], Second Lieutenant.   [*Colonial Records.*]

A Muster Roll of the Company in His Majesties Service under the Command of Captain Jonathan Pettibone In Co^{ll} Elihu Chancys Regment

Mens Names	Quality	Time of Entrance in the Service	Time of Discharg	Dead or Taken
Jonathan Pettibone	Cap.	Aug. 30	Dec. 5	
John Leavitt	Lieut.	" "	" "	
Hezekiah Humphy	"	Sep. 1	" 2	
Noah Humphy	Serj.	" "	Nov. 5	
Simeon Adams	"	" 5	Dec. 6	
Jonathan Case	"	" 8	" 2	
John Edgcom	"	" 5	" 5	
Emanuel Nearing	Corp.	" 6	" "	
Joseph Smith	"	" 8	Nov. 27	
Abra^m Dibel	"	" 11	Dec. 3	
Thomas Winchel	"	" 4	" "	
John Phelps	Clerk	" 1	Nov. 2	
Seth King	Drum.	" 9	" 11	
Israel Curtis	Cent^{ll}	" 1	" 29	
John Slawter	"	" "	Dec. 2	

* Continued in service, in garrison at Fort Edward, until April 1756 when as he was on his way home to New Milford he was captured by the Indians and held in captivity until Aug. 1760. [*Colonial Records.*]

FOURTH REGIMENT. 63

Mens Names	Quality	Time of Entrance in the Service		Time of Discharg		Dead or Taken	
George Bunce	Cent[ll]	Sep.	1	Dec.	2		
Jedediah Case	"	"	"	Oct.	28		
Martin Case	"	"	"	Dec.	2		
Abel Moses	"	"	"	Oct.	28		
Joseph North	"	"	"			Nov.	28
Jacob Tuller	"	"	"	Nov.	19		
Elijah Holcomb	"	"	4	"	6		
Azriah Phelps	"	"	"	Oct.	26		
Tim° Alderman	"	"	"	Dec.	2		
Dan[ll] Trapue	"	"	"	"	"		
Sam[ll] Cane	"	"	"	"	"		
Tim° Hogkis	"	"	5	Nov.	26		
Sam[ll] Woodford	"	"	"	Dec.	2		
Apelton Woodroff	"	"	"	"	12		
Dan[ll] Owin	"	"	"	Nov.	26		
Elihu Andress	"	"	"	Dec.	2		
Phinehas Bunce	"	"	7	"	"		
Sollomon Bewil	"	"	8	"	"		
Jacob Read	"	"	"	"	"		
Noah Humphry	"	"	"	Oct.	29		
Stephen Person	"	"	"	Dec.	3		
Noah Bull	"	"	"	"	"		
Noah Merrills	"	"	"	Nov.	30		
Moses Marsh	"	"	9	"	"		
Sam[ll] Lewis	"	"	"	"	29		
Sam[ll] Merrils	"	"	"	"	"		
John Miller	"	"	"	"	28		
Salvenes Willcoks	"	"	11	Dec.	2		
John Mills	"	"	5	"	3		
Joseph Dyar	"	"	"	Oct.	2		
Sam[ll] Higley	"	"	8	"	25		
Moses Dibel	"	"	"	Dec.	3		
Return Holcomb	"	"	"	"	2		
Isaac Barber	"	"	"	Nov.	27		
Josiah Graves	"	"	"	Dec.	14		
Hezekiah Phelps	"	"	"	Nov.	28		
Joseph Segar	"	"	"	Dec.	3		
John Lilley	"	"	11	"	"		
Benj[a] Addams	"	"	10	"	2		
Aaron Moses	"	"	"	"	"		
Isaac Enos	"	"	"	"	"		
Salvenas Humphry	"	"	"	Oct.	28		
Sandras More	"	"	11	Dec.	2		
Isaiah Rice	"	"	"	"	3		
Tho[s] Portor	"	"	8	"	"		
Dan[ll] Robarts	"	"	10	"	2		
Joseph Brownson	"	"	1	Nov.	26		
Moses Ball	"	"	2	Dec.	8		
Jonathan Olds	"	"	5	"	3		
Aaron Phelps	"	"	"	Jan.	10		
John Stanard	"	"	"	Oct.	30		
David Miller	"	"	6	Nov.	3		
Henery Bloggit	"	"	7	Oct.	30		
Paul Kent	"	"	8	Jan.	24		
John Conlin	"	"	10			Oct.	26
James Halladay	"	"	"	Dec.	1		
Eusebeas Marther	"	"	"			Oct.	30

CAMPAIGN OF 1755.

Mens Names	Quality	Time of Entrance in the Service	Time of Discharg	Dead or Taken
David Bement	Cent[ll]	Sep. 10	Nov. 23	
Phin⁸ Pumroy	"	" "	" 22	
Charles Kent	"	" "	Oct. 30	
Elijah Easton	"	" "	Dec. 23	
Tho Roe	"	" "	Nov. 28	
Joseph Old	"	" "	" 2	
John Hathway	"	" "	Dec. 5	
John Fowler	"	" "	Nov. 11	
Joel Kent	"	" 11	Jan. 24	

[Indorsed] Cap[t] Jon[a] Pettybone 1755

[State Library, Adams Papers.]

NEW YORK REGIMENT.

REGIMENTAL OFFICER.

Eliezer Fitch [of Windham] nominated Major, May 1755
[*Colonial Records.*]

Note: Upon request from the Colony of New York the General Assembly of Connecticut gave liberty for the enlisting of three companies from Connecticut "on the pay and encouragements" of New York, to be commanded by their own company officers and in a regiment having a Connecticut Major.

CAPT. HALL'S COMPANY.

Street Hall of Wallingford nominated Captain, May 1755.
David Baldwin of Milford nominated First Lieutenant, May 1755.
[*Colonial Records.*]
Ebenezer Dyar [of New Haven], Second Lieutenant.

A List of the Company under the Command of Capt. Street Hall Esq[r] of Wallingford Enlisted in his Majesty's Service in the pay of the province of New York.

Street Hall, Esq[r]., Capt.
David Baldin, 1st Lieut.
Ebenezer Dyar, 2 Lieut.
Josiah Stanly
Justus Holt
John Rowlison
James Osburn
Isaac Cook
John Andrus
David Spencer
Anthony Miller
Jonathan Wright
Frederick Chappel
James Hartford
Nath[ll] Yale
Waitstill Cook
Stephen Ives
Elisha Brackett
John Dudley
Daniel Tharp
Barnabas Merwin
Jonathan Bull
Ethan Curtiss
John Rose
Sylvanus Bishop

Nathan Osborn
Phinehas Beech
Nathan Andrews
Benjamin Huff
Israel Daton
Nath[ll] Cook
Timothy Carrington
Nath[ll] Hitchcock
Sam[ll] Whedone
Sam[ll] Bayley
Jason Cooper
Peter Davis
Will[m] Brown
Eldad Curtiss
Josiah Dudley
Hezekiah Brackett
Sam[ll] Towner
Benjamin Griswold
Benjamin Chittingden
Thomas Watson
Nicholas Elsworth
Amaziah Busk
David Page
Ephraim Camp
John Tom

CAMPAIGN OF 1755.

Will. Tom
Enos Potter
James Henman
Benjⁿ Cooke, J^r
John Atwood
Bate Hall
Israel Frisbe
John Kimbol
Willm Right
Peter Sip
Adam Saintgood
Peter President
Permenas Bunnel
Francis Blague
John Low
Moses Earl
Denis Covert
James Parker
Moses Wooster
Israel Smith
Samuel Lyon
Edward Wooster
Timothy Dirgey
David Colkoon
Samuel Halbart

Daniel Kenney
Samuel Waller
Abiraham Stoddard
Elijah Hamblin
Jedediah Jewet
Paul Atwell
John Thomas
Nathaniel Dike
Larance Parkle
John Howde
Joseph Ball
Arch^d Blare
Timothy Turner
Eben Warner
Sam^{ll} Smith
Jedediah Morehouse
Thadeus Carter
David Cooke
Charles Dutton
Joseph Miles
Elnathan Street
Eben^r Bracket
Mordica Cuff
James Corbit
Joseph Bishop

June 21st 1755 Then mustered aforenamed Ninety Seven private soldiers as able Bodied Effective Men &c.

Test Elihu Chauncey, Commiss^r of ye Musters.

Norwalk 23d June 1755.

[*New York Historical Society, Collections 1891.*]

A Muster Roll of Captain Street Hall's Company Time of their Enlistment also Acc^t of their Wages from ye date their Enlistment until ye first July.

Street Hall, Captain
David Baldwen, Lev^t
Eben^r Dyar, Lev^t

1755			Number Days
May 22	Josiah Stanly,	} Sergants	40
30	Stepⁿ Marwin,		32
24	Jno Roalingson,		38
June 13	Arch^d Blare,		18
May 30	Isaac Cooke,	} Corporal	32
23	David Spencer,		39
26	Ethan Curtis,		36
26	Silvanus Bishop,	Drummer	36
24	David Hall,	Clark	38
	Antony Miller		38
	Israel Daton		38
	Stephen Ives		38
	Samuel Totson		38
	Phineas Beach		38
26	Bale Hall		36
	Sam^{ll} Baley		36
	Jonth Wright		36

NEW YORK REGIMENT.

1755		Number Days
May 26	Benjⁿ Griswell	36
	Nathaniel Yale	36
	Elisha Bracket	36
	John Dudly	36
	Peter Davis	36
	James Coben	36
	Thadeus Carter	36
	Michael Doolittle	36
	James Hertford	36
27	Nathan Osbon	35
	Israel Smith	35
	John Thomas	35
	John Lowe	35
	James Parker	34
	Francis Blake	34
	David Page	34
	Daniel Thorp	34
	Jason Cooper	34
	James Henman	34
	Fred^k Chappel	34
	Benj. Chidderton	34
	Nicholas Elsworth	34
28	Asa Page	34
	Josiah Dudly	34
	Benjⁿ Hough	34
	Ephraim Camp	34
	Hez^h Bracket	34
	Abram Jacobs	34
	Enos Hitchcock	34
	Wm Brown	34
30	Ephraim Andrus	32
	Stephen Pirkens	32
	Jonth Bull	32
	Elded Curtis	32
	Weitstal Cooke	32
	John Andrus	32
	Israel Frisbe	32
	Permemas Bunnel	32
	Nathl Dike	32
31	Denis Covert	31
June 1	John Atwell	30
	Enos Potter	29
	Nathan Andrus	29
	Reuben Hitchcock	29
	Thomas Gill	29
3	Lawrance Parklee	28
5	Jedediah Jewel	26
	Sam^{ll} Lyons	26
	John Hoade	26
	Elijah Hamlin	26
6	Stephen Mix	25
	Paul Atwell	25
10	Eben^r Warner	21
	Saml Harlbut	21
	Saml Waller	21
	David Calhoun	21
	Timo. Dirkee	21

CAMPAIGN OF 1755.

1755		Number Days
June 11	Aberam Stodard	20
	Daniel Kenny	20
	Moses Erle	20
13	Tim° Turner	18
	Jeded^h Morehouse	18
	Edward Wooster	18
	Moses Wooster	18
16	Sam¹ Smith	15
17	Joseph Ball	14
23	Josiah Nettleton	8
	Daniel Worden	8
	Joshua Perry	8
26	Wm Hopkins	5
July 3	Sam^ll Baley Jr.	0
7	Gideon Parrish	0
May 17	1 Captain	45
	1 Levtenant 1st	45
	1 Levtenant 2d	45
June 3	Timo. Carrington detained by Attachment	28
	Nath^ll Cook, ⎫ sick	28
	Nath^ll Hitchcock, ⎭	28
May 28	Thomas Walston, ⎫	34
June 2	Willm Tom, ⎬ Deserters	29
	John Tom, ⎭	29
May 24	Amaz^h Bush, Deserter	38
	Will Tom since appeared	29
	3 Days over charged for Lorence Parklee	

Street Hall

[New York Historical Society, Collections 1891.]

A Muster Roll of Capt. Street Hall's Company from ye 1th Novemb^r to 2th December both days Included vizt.

Josiah Stanlay,
Jn° Roulingson,
Stephen Merwin, } Serj^ts.
Isaac Cook,

Ethen Curtis,
John Thomas, } Corporals.
Stephen Mix,

Enos Potter,   Drummer.

Moses Earl	Jason Cooper
Benjamin Griswell	Peter Davis
Sam¹ Bayle	Eldad Curtis
Michale Dowlittle	Bate Hall
Jonathan Wright	Israel Frisbe
Frederick Chappel	Francis Blake
James Hartford	Enos Hitchcock
Nathanale Gale	Sam¹ Lyon
Waitstell Cook	Ed Wooster
John Dudly	David Calhoun
Daniel Tharp	Sam^ll Waller

NEW YORK REGIMENT.

Paul Atwell
Larance Parkle
John Howde
Sam¹ Smith
Joshua Perrey
William Hopkins
Sam¹¹ Tietson
Ruben Hitchcock
Sam¹¹ Bayles J^r
Dennis Covert
Ebenezer Warner
Asa Page
Phinehas Beach
Nathanall Dike
Benjamin Chitterton
    Street Hall.

William Brown
Daniel Worden
William Tom
Stephen Perkins
Sam¹¹ Hurlbert
Gideon Parish
Permineas Bunnel
Nathan Andrews
Hezekiah Bracket
James Parker
Moses Wooster
James Coben
Stephen Joes
Antony Miller
Ephraim Andrews

        Albany ye 4 Decr 1755
                [*New York Historical Society, Collections 1891.*]

CAPT. SLAPP'S COMPANY.

John Slapp of Mansfield nominated Captain, May 1755.
Samuel Stanton of Stonington nominated First Lieutenant, May 1755.
Samuel Gaylord of Middletown nominated Second Lieutenant, May 1755.
                                                  [*Colonial Records.*]

    A Muster Roll of ye Soldiers Enlisted in Capt. John Slap's Company raised in this Colony in ye Pay of New York to be Imployed in Conjunction with ye Forces of the other Governments in Building Forts & removeing Encroachments on his Majesties Lands to ye Northward of Albany.
                John Slap, Capt
                Sam¹¹ Stanton, 1st Lieut.
                Sam¹¹ Gaylord, 2 Lieut.

Willm Billings
Dan¹ Bellows
Benjamin Brooks
Willm Dewy
Jabez Green
Eleazer Robinson
Thos Atwood
Joseph Preston
John Gennings
Ebenezer Crocker
Uriah Carpenter
Joseph Shaddock
Richard Webber
Joseph Russ
John Abbe J^r
Clement Neff
Dan¹ Rust J^r
Benajah Edwards
Anson Whitney
Ebenezer Dunham

John Rice
Joseph Pumham
Job Amos
Ephraim Dean
Nath¹ Curtiss
Nath¹ Chappel
Ruben Atwood
Benjamin Larkin
Thos Walbridge
Aaron Eaton
Dan¹ Rust
Benjamin Buel
Zepurah Cooper
Joseph Rust
Willm Hodgkins
Wm Pollard
Wm Loyd
Asa Bowdish
John Brown
John Rayn

CAMPAIGN OF 1755.

Elias Avery
Peter Dye
Simon Sparhauk
Richard Thomas
Benjamin Coyes
Josia Hawkins
Jonathan Paheag
Tho⁸ Kinis
Joseph Garret
Bristo Park
Woodbury Starkweather
Dan¹¹ Ford
Nath¹¹ Wells
Ebenezer Davis
Ruben Hutchinson
Nathan Lillie
Elijah Fitch
Dan¹¹ Rose
Josiah Whitney
Isaac Sawer
Ebenezer Lyman
Resolved Wheeler
Mercy Throop
King Palmer
Tho⁸ Martin
Sam¹¹ Metcalf
Tho⁸ Goodrich
Sam¹ Foster
Dan¹ Killum

Justus Dayley
John Lord
Ephraim Goodrich
Dan¹ Bliss
Charles Bartlet
Tho⁸ Loveland
Tho⁸ Powel
Tho⁸ Selkreg
Joseph Lewiss
Edmund Reding
Tim° Raney
Isaac Hail
Abel Friel
Tho⁸ Blake
Charles Squire
Sam¹¹ Cotton
Jabez Barns
Josiah Ferrill
Eleazer Gaylord
Rufus Yarrington
Tho⁸ Sweete
Nath¹ Miller
Robart Stevens
Sam¹¹ Judd
Josiah Savage
Sam¹¹ Spelman
Robert Stevenson
Aaron Stevens

Certified pʳ Elihu Chauncey Commissary of yᵉ Musters Durham 4th July 1755.

Joseph Butts
Zechariah Bicknel
Ebenezer Steel
John Silkregg
Nath¹¹ Tyler
Moses Whitney
Joseph Garret
Sam¹¹ Gilbert
Josiah Hawkins

Josiah Savage
Josiah Torrill Jʳ
Eleazer Gaylord Jʳ

Daniel Bellows ⎫
Willm Billing   ⎬ Sergeants
Benjn Brook   ⎪
Thomas Goodrich ⎭

Richard Nicholson
Robert Cook
Benjamine Tidd
Nathaniel Lane

Ezekiel Whitney
James Roberts
Joseph Lewis
Ebenezer Larrabe
Robert Durkee
Sam¹¹ Cotton
Ezekiel Crocker
Daniel Ford

Nathaniel Tyler
Thomas Kindress
Samuel Tracey

Ebenezer Davis   ⎫
Ruben Hutchinson ⎬ Corp¹ˢ
Nathan Lilly   ⎭
Elijah Fitch, Clark.
Charles Squire, Drumʳ

Daniel Danison
John Smith
Silas Bobbet

[*New York Historical Society, Collections 1891.*]

NEW YORK REGIMENT.

A Muster Role of Capt. John Slapps Company With ye Admounts of Their Wages from ye last Day of October to ye first of Second of December which is 32 Days. Albany December ye 4th 1755.

John Slapp, Esqr, Capt.   32^d
Sam^{ll} Stanton, 1st Liev^t 32^d
Sam^{ll} Gaylord, 2 Lev^t 33^d

Danl Bellows,
Willm Billings, } Serj^t
Benjn Brooks,
Thomas Goodrich,
Ebenez^r Davis,
Nathan Lylley, } Corp^{ls}
Josiah Savage,
Charls Squire,   Drummer

Timothy Ranny
Eben^r Lymon
Thomas Lovland
Joseph Buts
Benjn Coys
Zaikriah Briknal
Joseph Rust
Daniel Killum
Epharim Goodrich
Richard Webber
Eben^r Croker
Josiah Terril
Joseph Lewis
Aron Stevens
Willm Duey
Willm Hopkins
Willm Pollard
Nathl Miller
Edmun Redding
Willm Loyd
Moses Whitney
John Silkrig
Elezar Robbertson
Josiah Preston
Wath: Curtis
Danl Rust, J^r
Nath^{ll} Will, 2 days
Charls Bartlett
Climon Neff
Sam^{ll} Guilburt
Sam^{ll} Cotton

John Brown
Benajah Edwards
Sam^{ll} Judd
Ezekil Whitney
Jonathan Pawkaigh
Syrus Hawkins
James Robbords, 2 days
John Ryon
Brister Park
John Gennius
Asa Bowdish
Joseph Pomham
Peter Dye, 2 days
Robart Stevenson
Jabez Barns
John Lord
Joseph Garrot
Thomas Kines
John Rice
Roburt Stevens
Elezar Gaylord
Thomas Sweete
Justes Dale
Roburt Durke
Simon Sparhawk
Epharian Dean
Thomas Blake
Woodbury Starkwether
Daniel Ford, 5 Days
Josiah Whitney
Aron Whitney

John Slapp

[*New York Historical Society, Collections 1891.*]

CAPT. DIMOCK'S COMPANY.

Samuel Dimock of Saybrook nominated Captain, May 1755.
[*Colonial Records.*]
Christopher Helms, First Lieutenant.
Benjamin King of Woodbury nominated Second Lieutenant, May 1755.
[*Colonial Records.*]

CAMPAIGN OF 1755.

A Muster Roll of the Private Soldiers Enlisted in Capt. Dimocks Company in ye Pay of New York.

Sam^ll Dimock, Capt.
Christopher Helms, 1st Lieut.
Benjamin King, 2^d Lieut.

John Griswold
Saml Tooly
David Franklin
Hez^ah Atwell
George Dibble
John Tacker
Sam^ll Reve
Stephen Spencer
Thos Webb
Zepheniah Mitchel
Gershom Rowley
Tim^o Persivel
Eliakim Spencer
Edward Fuller
Israel Rowley
Jedadiah Brockway
John Toroomp
Dan^ll Sireas
Simon Baguet
Sam^ll Mack
Richard Doves
John Shaw
Zebulon Dudley
John Loveland
Benjamin Hubbard
Sam^ll Hudson
Thomas Graves
Elisha Kirtland
Jabez Howland
Sam^ll Baldwin
Ebenez^r Pelton
Increase Billings
Willm Button
Elihu Palmer
Elisha Guard
Francis Simmons
Eliab Farman
Benjn Woodworth
Archibald Johnson
Henery Chip
Joseph Toby
Thos Drinkwater
Andrew Baldwin
Calvin Leavenworth
Roger Clark
Sam^ll Cummins
John Eglestone

John Indian
Robert Pow
Nathl Divine
Moses Fisher
Saml Raments
Andrew Coly
Joshua Roggers
John Chapts
Ruben Rusk J^r
Adrew Corre Compt
Thos Sherman
Sam^ll Teall
Benjn Ackley
Jack Mulatt
John Yeant
John Wetmore
Cornelius Cone
Stephen Downer
Nath^ll Hall
Thos Lamb
Lemuel Touey
Charles Pawheag
Caleb Shaw
Danl Comstock
James Warner
Willm Brown
Allin Leet
Saml Reynolds
David Crouch
Joseph Maxley
Peter Buck
Ruben Toney
Benjn Waggs
Sam^ll Todd
Christopher Tooley
B. Williams
Nathan Fisher
Cornelius Hannabel
Sam^ll Bennet
Willm Perige
Thos Sherman
Benjn Harry
Christopher Crouch
Japhet Pompey
Charles Sharpes
Zacheus Hill

Certifyed p^r Elihu Chauncey Commiss^y of ye Muster.
Durham July 16th Day Anno Domini 1755

[*New York Historical Society, Collections 1891.*]

NEW YORK REGIMENT. 73

A Muster Roll of Capt. Sam¹ Dimock's Company Time of there Enlistment, Wages & Billiting due until Aug¹ 1st Included 1755.

		Days
May 17	Samuel Dimock Capt.	75
	Christ^r Helme Lieut	75
	Benjamin Kingland Lieu^t	75
May 9	Allen Leet Serg^t	54
25	Benjn Woodworth Serg^t	38
May 27	Elisha Kartland Serg^t	36
June 10	Thomas Drinkwater Serj^t	53
June 25	Elliab Farnam Corp^l	38
June 9	Timothy Pacifull Corp.	54
June 4	Jabez Howland Corp^l	59
July 7	N^{ll} Hall Drum^r	25
June 2	John Griswould Clerk	60
June 30	Stephen Downer	32
18	Samuel Bolden	43
19	Increase Billings	42
22	William Button	39
2	Andrew Baldwin	60
16	Edward Bostrick	45
July 7	William Brown	24
2	Samuel Bennet	30
June 4	Samuel Cabel	58
19	Roger Clark	42
9	Samuel Cummins	54
July 11	Andrew Coley	21
4	Cornelius Coen	28
1	Christop^r Crouck	31
June 30	Danil Comstock	32
July 10	Ebenezar Crosby	22
14	Samuel Camfield	18
June 5	George Dibel	58
June 18	Zebulon Dudley	43
12	N^{ll} Divine	49
29	John Ergetstone	33
2	David Franklin	60
10	Edward Fuller	53
July 9	Moses Fisher	23
7	Nathan Fisher	25
June 18	Thomas Graves	43
20	Ellisha Gard	41
18	Samuel Hudson	43
July 10	Cornelius Hannaball	22
June 19	Archabel Johnson	42
23	John Loveland	38
2	Calvin Leavenworth	60
27	William Lord	36
July 12	Thomas Lamb	20
June 9	Zephaniah Michel	54
16	Samuel Mack	45
July 10	William Markham	22
12	Joseph Mosely	20
June 20	Elihu Palmer	41
July 19	William Perigoo	23
June 19	Ebenezer Pelton	42
5	Samuel Reves	57
12	Israel Rowley	49
9	Gershom Rowley	54

CAMPAIGN OF 1755.

		Days
June 30	Samuel Renols	32
30	Thomas Shearman	32
3	Stephen Spencer	59
18	John Shaw	43
July 20	Jabez Spencer	12
June 20	Francis Summers	41
9	Elliakim Spencer	54
2	Samuel Teall	60
June 5	John Tacker	57
July 7	Christ[r] Tooly	25
June 2	Samuel Tooley	60
3	Thomas Webb	59
July 14	James Warner	18
7	Boaz Williams	25
June 7	Jonathan Washbone	56
July 1	John Wetmore	31
July 5	Samuel Rament	27
July 3	Joshua Rogers	29
June 8	Richard Dorus	43
12	Simon Bagonet	49
20	Peter Buck	41
25	Henry Chip	36
July 8	John Chopts	24
June 14	Andrew Currecompt	47
10	Reuben Rousk	51
26	John Indian	37
12	Dan[l] Sejrus	49
30	Benjamin Harrak	32
July 10	Charles Pawheagg	22
June 10	Robert Powe	51
June 19	Jacob Pompey	42
20	Tafett Pompey	41
July 5	Reben Rusk 2[d]	27
June 1	Thomas Shearman	61
22	Charles Sharper	39
July 8	Zacheus Still	24
June 12	John Towump	49
23	Joseph Toley	38
20	Chareuel Toucy	41
17	Robben Toucy	44
July 10	Samuel Toodd	22
July 10	Benjamin Flagg	22
June 5	John Ycout	58
12	Isack Molatt	49

These names were dropped in the Roll for Aug[t] 1755: Thomas Graves, Thomas Lamb and Ebenezer Pelton.

Sam[ll] Dimock.

[*New York Historical Society, Collections 1891.*]

A Muster Roll of Capt. Sam[l] Dimocks men, Nov[r] 30th, 1755.

Capt. Sam[l] Dimock
Left. Christopher Helms
Le[t] Benj[n] King
Serj[t] Allin Leat
Serj[t] Benj[n] Woodworth

Serj[t] Elisha Kirtland
Serj[t] Jabez Howland
Corp[l] Eliab Farnam
Corp[l] Tim[o] Persival
Corp[l] Zebulon Dudly

NEW YORK REGIMENT.

Drm^r Nath^{ll} Hall
John Grisewould
Stephen Downer
Saml Baldwin
W^{ll} Butten
Andrew Baldwin
W^{ll} Brown
Sam^{ll} Benet
Sam^{ll} Cable
Roger Clarke
Saml Canfield
Andrew Cooley
Cornelus Cone
Christopher Crouch
Danil Comstock
Ebenezer Croseby
George Dibble
John Egleston
David Franklin
Moses Fisher
Thomas Graves
Elisha Garb
Sam^{ll} Hutson
Cornelus Hanabal
Archabald Johnson
John Loveland
W^{ll} Lord
Zephoniah Mitchle
Saml Mack
W^{ll} Markham
Joseph Moxly
Elisha Palmer
W^{ll} Pereggo
Sam^{ll} Rynols
Thomas Sherman
Stephen Spencer

John Shaw
Jabez Spencor
Francis Sumers
Saml Teal
John Tacker
Christopher Tooly
Sam^{ll} Tooly
Thos Webb
James Warner
Boaz Williams
Jonathan Washbon
Joun Wetmore
Sam^{ll} Rayment
Joshua Rogers
Richard Dorus
Peter Buck
John Chops
Andrew Curri Comp
Ruben Rusk
John Indian
Daniel Sirus
Benjⁿ Harry
Charles Powheage
Robert Pone
Jacob Pompey
Japhet Pompey
Ruben Rusk 2^d
Tom Sherman
Charles Charper
Zackeus Stell
John Tromp
Joseph Toby
Lem^{ll} Zone
John Yeout
Sam^{ll} Todd
Benjⁿ Waggs

Albany ye 5 Decr 1755.

I doe declare on ye holy Evangelist of Almighty God that the men whose names are mentioned in the within rool or List where in actual service in my Comp^y from the 1 Day of Novr to ye 2 of Decr both days Included Except those marked otherwise.

Sam^{ll} Dimock.

Sworn before me
Day & year above
   Jno De Peyster.

[*New York Historical Society, Collections 1891.*]

CAMPAIGN OF 1755.

COL. BAGLEY'S REGIMENT.

REGIMENTAL OFFICERS.

Jonathan Bagley [of Massachusetts] appointed Colonel, Nov. 25, 1755.
Nathan Whiting [of New Haven] appointed Lieutenant-Colonel, Nov. 25.
Edmun Mathews [of New York] appointed Major, Nov. 25, 1755. [He probably did not accept the appointment.]
[*Capt. Nathaniel Dwight's Journal.*]

Note : These appointments were made by commissioners from the several colonies assembled at Albany.   [*Maj. Robert Rogers' Journals.*]

Nathan Payson [of Hartford], Major as early as Nov. 29, 1755.
[*State Library, War 5, 280.*]

Ebenezer Dyer of New Haven, Fort Major and Commissary at Fort Edward, Nov. 1755 to April 1756, when he was captured.
[*Colonial Records.*]

Hear followeth the orders of the Day
Head Quarters Camp Lake George
Twesday 25th Novr 1755

That 232 men officers included out of the Massachusetts Troops 193 men officers included out of the Connecticut Troops 154 men officers included out of the New York Troops 95 men officers included out of the New Hampshire Troops and 76 men officers included out of the Rhode Island troops be given to Garrison Fort William Henry and Fort Edward which body of men are to be Considered as a Regiment of which Jon^a Bagley Esqr to be Co^{ll} Nathan Whiting Esqr to be Lieut Co^{ll} and Edmun Mathews Esqr to be Maj^r. 430 of the s^d Reg^t under the Command of Lt Co^{ll} Whiting to Garrison Fort Edward.

[*Capt. Nathaniel Dwight's Journal.*]

LIEUT.-COL. WHITING'S COMPANY.

Nathan Whiting [of New Haven], Lieutenant-Colonel and Captain.
Nicholas Nichols [of Stratford], Lieutenant.
Timothy Hierlihy, Lieutenant and Adjutant.

A Muster Roll of Lieu^t Colonel Nathan Whitings Company with the Time of Inlistment, Dead Captivated, Discharged, Weeks and Days in Service, Wages Due &c.

Officers & Soldiers Names & Quality		Time of Inlistmt		Dischargd		Dead
Nathan Whiting	Col.	Dec.	8	May	30	
Nathan Whiting	Capt.	"	"	"	"	
Nicholas Nichols	Lieut.	Nov.	27	"	"	
Timothy Hierlihy	"	"	"	"	"	
Timothy Hierlihy	Adj.	"	"	"	"	
Noah Chapel	Serj. Maj.	"	26	"	"	
John Blin	Serj.	"	27	Mar.	10	
Thomas Pain	"	"	23	May	30	
William Day	"	"	27	"	"	
Stephen Emason	"	"	23	"	"	

COL. BAGLEY'S REGIMENT.

Officers & Soldiers Names & Quality		Time of Inlistmt		Discharg'd		Dead
Samuel Freeman	Corp.	Nov.	26	Apr.	22	
Samuel Freeman	Serj.	Apr.	22	May	30	
Ezekiel Tubs	Corp.	Nov.	27	"	30	
Phelix Powel	"	"	22	"	27	
Ebenezer Beech	"	"	26	"	30	
Elijah Smith	Clerk	"	23	"	29	
Elizur Clark	Drum.	"	30			Jan. 19
Enos Sperry	Soldier	"	23	Jan.	28	
Enos Sperry	Corp.	Jan.	28	May	29	
John Merritt		Nov.	27	"	30	
Jesse Welding		"	"	"	"	
Elizur Loveland		"	"	"	[ ]	
Noah Morss		"	"	"	30	
William Mason		"	"	"	"	
Ambrose Nicholson		"	"	"	"	
Elisha Portor		"	"	"	"	
Lemuel Peas		"	"	"	"	
William Duplex		"	26	"	29	
John Hammer		"	23	"	"	
Stephen Thomas		"	26	"	"	
James Powers		"	"	"	"	
John Titus		"	"	"	30	
Nicholas Howel		"	"	"	29	
John Cornish		"	"	"	30	
Amos Allin						Captivated Apr. 21
John Weed		Dec.	7			May 23
Elisha Pierce		"	"			Dec. 13
Pierce Walter		Nov.	23	May	30	
Thomas Barker		"	22	"	"	
Wilston Gifford		"	"	"	29	
John Gording		"	"	Mar.	18	
Ephraim Gittow		"	"	May	29	
Silas Hill		"	"	"	30	
David Wheeler		"	24	"	29	
John Rice		"	"	"	30	
Owen Fluskey		"	23			Captivated Apr. 21
David Austin		Jan.	26	May	30	
John Brown		"	"	"	"	
Daniel Owen		Nov.	23	"	29	
Charles Rice		"	26	"	"	
Joseph Brunson		"	23	"	30	
John Japhet		"	"	"	"	

[Indorsed] Col¹¹ Nathan Whitings Garrison Pay Roll

[*State Library, War 5, 298.*]

MAJ. PAYSON'S COMPANY.

Nathan Payson [of Hartford], Major and commander of the company until the week ending Dec. 20. He returned to Connecticut about that time and probably resigned his command before leaving Fort Edward.

Noah Grant [of Windsor], probably First Lieutenant until the week ending Dec. 20. After that time he was Captain.

E. Waterman, Lieutenant.

Joseph Winchell [of Suffield], Ensign.

[*State Library, War 5, 276-283; Colonial Records 10, 11.*]

CAMPAIGN OF 1755.

Capt Noah Grants Garrison Pay Roll

Mens Names		Time of Enlisting		Discharged		Captivated
Noah Grant	Capt.	Nov.	23	Mar.	26	
E. Waterman	Lieut.	"	26			Apr. 21
Jos. Winchel	Ens.	"	"	May	21	
Israel Harden	Serj.	"	"	"	"	
Maverick Johnson	"	"	"	"	"	
Caleb Johnson	"	"	25	"	"	
Saml Stoddard	"	"	"	"	"	
Charles Ripley	Corp.	"	"	"	"	
John Church	"	"	"	"	"	
John Wright	"	"	"	"	"	
John Trible	"	"	"	"	"	
Jer^h Foster	Drum.	"	"	"	"	
John Warren	Cen^l	"	26	"	"	
Saml Wordin		"	23	"	"	
Jos. Clark		"	25	"	"	
Nathan Robinson		"	26	"	"	
Jos. Stevens		"	25	"	"	
Eben^r Dodge		"	"	"	"	Apr. 21
Reuben Crow		"	24	"	"	
Danl Filley		Dec.	3	"	"	
Josiah Filley		Nov.	25	"	"	
Abiel Leonard		"	23	"	"	
Israel Warner		"	25	"	"	
Giles Stow		"	"	"	"	
Jethro Smith		"	"	"	"	
Jos. Rogers		"	"	"	"	
Jno Kneeland		"	22	"	"	
Benj^m Fields		Dec.	7	Mar.	2	
Thom^s Goodale		Nov.	25	May	21	
Thos Huntington		"	"	"	4	
Thos Graves		"	"	"	21	
Andrew Chappel		Dec.	7	"	[ ]	
Amos Hall		Nov.	25	"	21	
Eben^r Brown		"	"	"	"	
Elisha Parker		"	26	"	"	
Saml Cravat		Dec.	6	"	"	
Willm Allin		Nov.	25	"	"	
Jno Hills		Dec.	6	"	"	
Levi Webster		Nov.	23	"	"	
Peleg Chamberlin		"	25	"	"	
Willm Carter		"	"	"	"	
Henry Rose		"	"	"	"	
Willm Sobuck		"	"	"	"	
Nathl Ashbo		"	"	"	"	

[Indorsed] Capt Noah Grants Garrison Pay Roll with the Gratuity Months Pay Included in it
Noted 12 July 1764 J L

[State Library, War 5, 299.]

[Another roll having the same names and dates bears an indorsement signed] Noah Grant Windsor June ye 21 : 1756

[State Library, War 5, 300.]

COL. BAGLEY'S REGIMENT. 79

CAPT. PUTNAM'S COMPANY.

Israel Putnam [of Pomfret], Captain.
Nathaniel Porter, Lieutenant.
Henry Chapam, Lieutenant.

A Roole of Cap[t] Israel Putnames Company in Garrison att Fort Edward December y[e] 5th 1755

Mens Names and Qualities	Time of Inlisting 1755	Discharged	Dead and Captivated
Cap[t] Isral Putnam	Nov. 25	May 30	
Lieu. Nat[ll] Porter		Apr. 26	
Lieu. Henry Chapam		" 29	
Ser[t] Hez[h] Persons	Nov. 24	May 24	
Ser[t] Peter Leavens	" 25	" "	
Ser[t] Peleg Sundurling	Dec. 10	Apr. 26	
Ser[t] Will[m] Manning	Nov. 25	May 30	
Cor[ll] David Cleaveland	" "	" "	
Cor[ll] Nath[a] Hale	" 26	" "	
Cor[ll] David Whitmore	" 24	" "	
Cor[ll] Thomas Lyon	" 25	Apr. 6	
Drum Nat[a] Bacon	" "	May 30	
Clerk Isaac Deana	" "	" "	
Robert Auston	" "	Apr. 4	
Matthew Davis	" "	May 30	
Daniel Isham	" 24	" "	
Michajah Torrey	" "	Apr. 4	Dyed Apr. 8
Eliphelett Carpenter	" 25	May 30	
Samuel White	" "	" "	
Littlefield Nash	" "	" "	
Jeremiah Jackson	" "	" "	
Peter Bowen	" "	" "	
Timothy Harrinton	" "	" "	
Giles Harris	" "	" "	
Ebenezer Cary	" 24		
John Auston	" 25	Apr. 9	
Aaron Dewey	" 24	May 30	
John Waters	" 25	" 29	
Eli Lewes	" 24	" 23	
Samuel Horton	" 26	" 30	
Ezekiel White	" 24	Apr. 21	Cap[td] Apr. 21
Robert Newell	" "	May 29	
Samuel Webb	" 25	Mar. 20	
Gideon Webb	" 24	May 29	
Solomon Mack	" "	" "	
Zeccheus Crow	" "	" "	
Roger Crow	" "	" 28	
Charles Biles	" 23	" 30	
Edward Tryon	" 24	" 29	
Eldad Parson	" 25	" "	
Stephen Peeas	" 24	Mar. 20	
Whearhom Peeas	" "	" "	
Thomas Brigdon	" 26	May 29	
James Hartford	" 25	" "	
Thomas Eddy	" "	Mar. 20	
George Gregory	" "	" 29	

Mens Names and Qualities	Time of Inlisting 1755	Discharged	Dead and Captivated
John Medkif	Nov. 24	Jan. 23	
John Phillips	" 25	Dec. 25	
John Hutchinson	" 24	Jan. 22	
Benj^a Shipman	" "	Feb. 7	

the three Last Died at the time Set Down

[Indorsed] Capt Israel Putnams Garrison Pay Roll with ye Gratuity Months Pay Included in it.
Noted 12 July 1764 J L

[*State Library, War 5, 241.*]

CAPT. GAYLORD'S COMPANY.

The following men are noted as being in this company, the earliest and latest dates they are mentioned being here given.

Jabez Howland	Nov. 29, 1755	Jan. 13, 1756
Joseph Huxley or Muxley	Nov. 29, 1755	Jan. 13, 1756
Cornelis Cone	Nov. 29, 1755	Jan. 12, 1756
Jabez Spencer	Nov. 29, 1755	Dec. 29, 1755
Nathaniel Curtie or Curtice	Nov. 29, 1755	Dec. 13, 1755
Ebenezer Lyman	Nov. 29, 1755	Nov. 29, 1755

[*State Library, War 5, 276-284.*]

William Billings appears to have been a member of this regiment. He is mentioned from Nov. 29, 1755, to Jan. 13, 1756.

[*State Library, War 5, 276-284.*]

MISCELLANEOUS.

CAPT. SAVAGE'S COMPANY.

Joseph Savage [of Middletown ?], Captain.
Noah Grant [of Windsor], First Lieutenant.
Isaac Sawyer [of Hebron], Second Lieutenant.

A muster Role of Capt Joseph Savages Company with the Time of Enlisting and discharge with the Time of Service and Entire Wages

Officers and Soldiers Names & qualitys	Time of Enlisting		Dischargd		Dead and Captivated	
Cap. Joseph Savage	Aug.	25	Dec.	6		
Lieut. Noah Grant	"	"	Nov.	23		
Lieut. Isaac Sawyer	"	"	Oct.	3		
Sarg. Hez. Summer	"	30	Dec.	6		
" Solomon Grant	"	28	"	"		
" Ebenez Loomis	Sep.	1	"	1		
" Stephen Scovel	Aug.	29	"	13		
Corp. Fenner Ward	"	30	Nov.	20		
" Benjamin Buel	Sep.	2	Dec.	1		
" Abraham Palmer	Aug.	28	"	6		
" Polycarpus Smith	Sep.	3	"	"		
Clerk Joshua Booth	Aug.	25	Nov.	18		
Jonathan Clark	Sep.	2	"	6		
Joseph Goff	"	"			Oct.	12
David West	"	1	Nov.	6		
Sylvanus Higgins	"	2	"	"		
John Reaves	"	1	Dec.	1		
Solomon Sage	Aug.	29	"	14		
Elijah Stocking	Sep.	1	"	6		
Thomas Sheapard	"	"	Oct.	6		
Amos Dewey	"	"	Dec.	6		
Waitstill Wilcox	"	"	"	20		
Thomas White	"	"	"	6		
John Sumner	"	"	Nov.	20		
John Barker	"	"	Dec.	6		
Simeon Barnes	Aug.	29	"	"		
John Fox	Sep.	1	"	"		
James Master	"	"	"	"		
Owin Flusko	"	"	Nov.	23		
Samuel Clark	Aug.	29	Dec.	6		
Justus Taylor	Sep.	1	"	"		
Peter Rich	"	2	"	"		
Samuel Goff	"	"	"	"		
Hezekiah Cook	"	1	"	"		
Marcus Cole	"	"	"	"		
John Bevins	"	2	"	"		
Stephen Bacon	"	"	"	"		
Giles Dowd	Aug.	30	"	"		
Recompence Roberts	"	"	"	"		
Ebenez Doolittle	"	"	"	"		
Barakiah Fairbank	"	"	"	"		

CAMPAIGN OF 1755.

Officers and Soldiers Names & qualitys	Time of Enlisting		Dischargd		Dead and Captivated	
Samuel Cravatt	Aug.	30	Dec.	6		
Peter Butler	"	"	"	"		
Benjn Cornwell	"	"	Oct.	6		
Abijah Lee	"	"	Dec.	6		
Abiel Leonard	"	29	Nov.	23		
Nathaniel Ranny	"	28	Dec.	13		
Amos Savage	"	29	"	6		
John Gipson	"	"	"	"		
Jethro Dellino	Sep.	1	"	7		
Solomon Loomis	"	"	"	"		
Andrew Chapel	"	"	"	"		
Joshua Morgan	"	"	"	"		
Thomas Bawden	Aug.	28	"	"		
Jeames Bundy	Sep.	1	"	"		
Josiah Cook	"	"	"	"		
Aaron Woodward	"	"	"	"		
Elakim Root	"	3	"	"		
Jonathan Bill	"	"	"	"		
Josiah Read	"	"	"	"		
Solomon Dean	"	"	"	"		
Stephen Richardson	Aug.	28	"	"		
Benjamin Field	"	"	"	"		
Nathan Flint	Sep.	1	"	"		
John Hills	"	3	"	6		
Azariah Wells	"	"	Nov.	12		
Dan Barnard	"	"	Dec.	7		
Ebenezar Skinner	Aug.	28	"	6		
John Gott	Sep.	2	"	"		
Samuel Hodge	"	5	"	11		
Abraham Fox	"	"	"	6		
David Dickerson	"	"	"	"		
John Waddams	"	"	"	"		
Levi Webster	"	2	Nov.	23		
Abel Mattoon	"	"	Feb.	1		
Timothy Bush	"	1	Dec.	6		
John Kneeland Junr	"	2	Nov.	23		
Simeon Darby	"	"			Nov.	5
Eleazar Chambirlen	"	"	Dec.	6		
Abner Brown	"	3	"	"		
William Waters	"	"	"	"		
Matthias Gates	"	"	"	"		
Ezra Gates	"	"	"	"		
Daniel Shipman	"	"	"	"		
Timothy Waters	"	"	"	"		
Joshua Baily	"	"	"	"		
Nathaniel Mott	"	"	"	"		
John Holmes Junr	"	"	"	"		
Simeon Owen	"	2			Dec.	3
William Daniels	"	3	Dec.	6		
Ephraim Wright	"	4	"	"		
Henry Waters	"	5	"	"		
Beriah Wright	"	"	"	"		

[Indorsed] Capt Joseph Savage Muster Roll 1755
Elijah Stocking p
Thos Shepard   [*State Library, Adams Papers.*]

Note: This roll bears the memorandum "No 9." It was probably the ninth company in either the first or second regiment.

MISCELLANEOUS. 83

CAPT. BILLINGS' COMPANY.

Roger Billings [of Preston], Captain.
Charles Whiting [of Norwich], First Lieutenant.
John Lay [of Lyme?], Second Lieutenant.

Officers and Soldiers Names & Quality		Time of Enlisting 1755		Dischargd		Dead and Captivated
Cap. Roger Billings		Aug.	21	Dec.	18	
Lieut. Charls Whiting		"		"	"	
Lieut. John Lay		"		"	"	
Sar. Heart Leffingwell			26	"	8	
Sar. Elisha Waterman		"		Nov.	26	
Able Coye	Serj.	"		Dec.	6	
Jona^n Davison	"	"		"	16	
Jedediah Waterman	Clerk	"		"	"	
Lemuel Bingham	Drum		27	"	6	
Saben Durge	Corp.	"		"	12	
John Chappel	"		25	"	4	
Saml Stoddard	"		29	Nov.	25	
John Smith	"	Sep.	9	Dec.	16	
Joseph Benjamin		Aug.	26	"	"	
Joseph Hall			27			dead Dec. 12
Joseph Stannard			29			dead Jan. 1
Ichabod Fergo			27	Nov.	25	
Elijah Williams		"		Dec.	16	
Benjamin Mackris		"		"	"	
Azariah Jones		"		"	"	
Thomas Jewet		"		"	"	
Josiah Benjamin		Sep.	10	"	"	
Jacob Bennet		"		"	"	
Ebenezer Prentice		"		"	"	
John Putnam			1	"	29	
George Perker		"		"	12	
Gershom Hail		"		"	"	
James Greenlif		"		"	"	
Jacob Read		"		"	"	
Henry Rose			2	Nov.	25	
Timo^y Herrington		"		"	"	
Rufus Hatch		"		Dec.	29	
John Mardock		Aug.	24	"	16	
Robert Cragg		Sep.	9	Nov.	25	
Robert Dunlop		"		Dec.	28	
James Kinney			2	"	12	
David Kinney		"		"	29	
Isaac Walker		Aug.	26	"	12	
Joseph Coye		"		"	"	
Aron Dow		Sep.	2			Dead Nov. 25
Sam^{ll} Thornton			3	Dec.	16	
Samuel Williams		"		"	20	
Peleg Billings		Aug.	26	Nov.	28	
Thomas Wilkee		Sep.	1	Dec.	16	
Jena Waldow		"		"	4	
John French		"		"	"	
Elijah Taylor		"		"	"	
Wm Wintworth		Aug.	29	"	12	
Charles Hills		Sep.	1	"	"	
Ezekiel Cook		"		"	"	
Peter Deful		Aug.	29	"	"	

CAMPAIGN OF 1755.

Officers and Soldiers Names & Quality	Time of Enlisting 1755	Dischargd	Dead and Captivated
John Church	Aug. 28	Nov. 25	
Jos^h Welch	"	" "	
David McLane	29	" 12	
Willm Gaylord	Sep. [ ]	" "	
Aron Fergo	[ ]	" 25	
Ambros Post	Aug. 28		dead Nov. 4
Alpheus Chapman	Sep. 1	Dec. 8	
Joseph Lloyd	10	" 4	
Benja^n Post	Aug. 28		dead Dec. 4
Zack Johnson	Sep. 28	Dec. 4	
Daniel Jompo	Aug. 28	" "	
Eben^r Tanner	Sep. 3	" "	
Ambros Lewis	Aug. 26	" "	
Maugunet Indian	"	" "	
Sam^ll Weisle	Sep. 3	" "	
Jonat^n Alcom	"	" 12	
Thomas Alcom	"	" "	
Sampson Shawcot	Aug. 28	" "	
Ellick Church	26	" "	
Jos^h Chequipes	Sep. 3	" "	
Isaac Tawdecommewas	1	" "	
Hez^h Wright	"	" "	
Caleb Geer	8	Oct. 17	
John Geer	"	" "	
Job Wood	6	" 20	
Elias Jones	Aug. 29	Sep. 30	
Sam^ll Stoddard	Sep. 8	" 10	
Ezra Tracy	"	Oct. 17	
Ely Gay	1	Dec. 12	
George Peter	Aug. 29	" "	
James Freeman	"	Sep. 9	
Sam^ll Doud	26	" 3	

[Indorsed]   Capt Roger Billing 1755

[*State Library, Adams Papers.*]

INDEPENDENT COMPANY.

Dr Independants

	Lead lbs	flints		Lead lbs	flints
Caleb Benjamin	21	6	Elijah Curkem (?)	1	3
John Cadwell	3	6	Augustus Fitch	2	
Leu^t Smith	3		Benjamin Carver	4	4
Oliver Hills	1		Joseph Dickens	4	4
Benjamin Gilbert	2		William Lewis	4	6
Nathaniel Goodwine	0	4	Augustus Fitch	2	6
Daniel Marsh	3	4	Richard Edwards	4	
Hezekiah Porter	4	6	Daniel Bull	3	
Joseph Rogers	3	4	William Nichols	3	
George Steel	3		Jonathan Burnham	3	4
Samuel Barnard	2	4	Eleazer Abby	3	6
John Nash	3	4	David Roberts	3	6
Joseph Moor	3	4	Samuel Porter	4	6

MISCELLANEOUS.

	Lead lbs	flints		Lead lbs	flints
Edward Forbs	3	6	David Case	1	6
Francis Wilson	2		John Kilburn	1	
Samuel Chapman	1	4	Samuel Evans	3	4
Charles Elsworth	3	4	Phinehas Nash	3	4
Noah Barbur		3	Elezer Holister	3	4
Jonah Allyn	4	6	Josiah Benton	1	
Ely Dewey	2	6	Samuel Benton	2	4
Jed. Spencer	3	6	Benj^a Slater	2	4

[*State Library, War 5, 236.*]

Note: This document appears to be a list of names of soldiers in several companies raised in 1755 to whom lead and flints were delivered. It contains, besides the following, the names of soldiers in the companies of Captains Allyn, Leach, and Phelps.

CAPT. DAVID BANKS' COMPANY.

Captain David Banks [of Fairfield ?] entered the service in September in command of a company of eighty three persons, three of whom were commissioned officers.

[*State Library, War 5, 234.*]

DR. HUBBARD'S COMPANY.

Dr. Leverit Hubbard with an independent company of above eighty men set out from New Haven on horseback Sept. 14 to join Gen. Johnson's army. The company was raised within six hours upon receipt of news the previous day that the English army was surrounded. The company probably returned in a few days.

[*Connecticut Gazette, Nos. 24, 26.*]

CAPT. HINMAN'S COMPANY.

Timothy Hinman of Woodbury, Captain.
Wait Hinman, First Lieutenant and Ensign.
Matthew Mitchel, Second Lieutenant.

This company of 44 volunteers set out from Woodbury on or about Sept. 11, 1755, and went eight or ten miles beyond Sheffield when they were ordered to return. They were in service four days.

[*State Library, War 6, 114.*]

CAPT. HOSMER'S COMPANY.

Captain Stephen Hosmer and a number of soldiers under his command served as a garrison at Pantusick, 30 miles north from Canaan, until Sept. 8, 1755.

[*State Library, War 6, 30.*]

COLCHESTER SOLDIERS.

Listed into his Majesties Service in the Present Expedition

Out of the first or North Company in Colchester

Eliphalet Wills
Israel Rowley
Benjamin Brooks
James Robarts Junr
William Daniels
Daniel Shipmon

Eliezer Chamberlin
John Northam
Joshua Booth
John Brown
John Sunkaway
Joshua Nonsuch under Boston Pay

Out of Westchester Company

Timothy Hamblin ⎫
Mathew Lewes   ⎬ under Boston
Timothy Bartlet ⎭
Timothy Waters
William Waters Junr
Henry Waters
Ezra Gates

Mathew Gates
Nathaniel Mott
Policarpus Smith
Elijah Thomas
John Holmes
Abner Brown
Zephaniah Mitchel

Out of the South Company

Ensign James Jones
Samuel Wells
Levi Wells
Stephen Taylor
Elijah Taylor
John Jorden
Benaiah Tubs
Gideon Fox
Simeon Mentor
Nehemiah Smith
Peleg Chamberlin
Peter Hambleton
John Robart

Isaac Bigelow Junr
Ephraim Wells
Prince Servt to Capt Lomis
Peter Servt to the Widdow Lomis
Timothy Start
Ruben Wells   ⎫
David Brown   ⎪
James Boag   ⎪
David Daniel   ⎬ under
Ezra Downer   ⎪ Boston
Jack Bond   ⎪
Jabez Brooks   ⎪
Stephen Start   ⎭

Out of New Salem Company

John Gilbert
Joshua Welch
William Dodge
Israel Harden
James Webb
——— Martin
Jonah Chapmon
John Burdick
Rabard Stanton

Lewis Tattington
John Quon
Amos Jones
Jedadiah Renolds
David Fuller
John Grant   ⎫ under
James Wickwire ⎭ Boston
William Jones ⎫ Gone to List
Daniel Lomis ⎭

[Indorsed] Acc^o of Soldiers Gone from Colchester 1755

[*Connecticut Historical Society.*]

Colchester September the Eleventh 1755

An Account of Sunderies Impressed for the use of the Soldiers Going to Reinforce the armey Gone against Crownpoint p^r order of Co^{ll} Jonathan Trumble and apprised by Men under Oath

Delivered to Neel Carter
" " Peleg Chamberlin
" " Eliphalet Wells
" " John Northam
" " Abner Brown
" " Denis Delane

Delivered to David Simons: they say is run away
" " John Northam
" " Daniel Isham
" " Titus Carrier
" " Benjamin Shipman
" " Nathan Dodge

[Indorsed] Colchester Acc° of Horses &c for the soldiers Decr 22, 1755
[*Connecticut Historical Society.*]

John Gold, probably of Lebanon, was a soldier in Capt. Porter's company.
Pyras Indian, in Lieut.-Col. Nathan Whiting's company.
Joseph Allen, page 46, was of Lebanon.
Joseph Blackman, page 24, was of Lebanon. He enlisted May 8.
Josiah Long, James Sims and Jonathan Swetland, page 46, were of Andover parish in Lebanon; Joseph Simons, Ephraham Loomis and James Woodworth were of the North parish in Lebanon; and Jonathan Riley was of Coventry.
[*Connecticut Historical Society.*]

Matthias Smith of Lebanon and Edward Foster of Canaan in Col. Goodrich's regiment were wounded at Lake George.
[*State Library, War 6, 119.*]

Abijah Ives Jr. of Wallingford in Major Isaac Foots company lost his right arm.
[*State Library, War 6, 118.*]

Lieut. Benjamin Ruggles, Hezekiah Baldwin and Joseph Lines, all of New Milford, in Capt Benjamin Hinman's company were wounded Sept. 8.
[*State Library, War 6, 108, 109.*]

Charles Cook of New Haven was wounded Sept. 8.
[*State Library, War 6, 105.*]

Lieut. Henry Chapin of Hartford served since some time in Aug. When returning home from Fort Edward he was surprised and captured by the enemy April 21, 1756.
[*State Library, War 6, 110.*]

Ebenezer Dodge of Woodstock a soldier in Capt. John Terry's company, re-enlisted under Col. Nathan Payson and was with the garrison at Fort Edward until April 1756 when he was captured and carried to Canada, remaining in captivity until Oct. 15, 1759. [*Colonial Records.*]

Lieut. Benjamin Ruggles, page 28, was wounded in the engagement of Sept. 8. [*Colonial Records.*]

Ebenezer Dyer of New Haven entered into the service at Fort Edward as Fort-Major and Commissary; was captured in April 1756.
[*Colonial Records.*]

New Haven Oct° 1755

We have near   men now Employed ag^t The Enemy
about 300 gone to Nova Scotia
300 were Encouraged to inlist in Gov Shirley & Sr Wm Pepperell's Regiments, & it was Supposed one or both Them (?) would have Gone in the service Genl Johnson's Army are Engaged in.
3000 are gone into the Service under Genl Johnson On the Pay & subsistence of this Colony
300 are gone into the Same Service on the Pay of New York
75 Stationed at The Forts in The County of Hampshire, in the Massachusetts Bay
———
3975

3075 of W^ch are in the Actual pay of This Government

[Jonathan Trumbull.]
[*Connecticut Historical Society, Trumbull MSS.*]

CAMPAIGN OF 1756.

GENERAL AND STAFF OFFICERS.

John Winslow [of Plymouth, Mass.,] appointed by Gen. William Shirley and approved of to be Commander-in-Chief of the forces raised for the expedition against Crown Point, March, 1756.

Phineas Lyman [of Suffield] appointed Major-General and second officer over all the forces ordered to be raised to go on the expedition against Crown Point &c., March, 1756. Discharged Dec. 1.

Rev. David Jewet of New London,
Rev. John Norton of Middletown,
Rev. Jonathan Lee of Salisbury,
Rev. John Grayham of Woodbury, } appointed chaplains, March, 1756.

Timothy Collins of Litchfield,
Leveret Hubbard of New Haven, served 6 months 16 days. [*State Library, War 6, 359.*]
Jonathan Marsh of Norwich, served from March 26 to Oct. 22. [*Comptroller's Office, Treasurer's Book.*] } appointed Physicians and Surgeons, March, 1756.

Pelatiah Bliss of Suffield,
Elisha Lord of Farmington,
John Redfield of Durham,
Joseph Clark of Wallingford,
Jabez Fitch, Jr., of Canterbury, } appointed Physician's and Surgeon's Mates, March, 1756.

Elihu Lyman [of New Haven] appointed Commissary of Stores, March, 1756.

Ithamar Bingham of Windsor appointed Commissary of the Hospital, March, 1756.

Benjamin Bancroft of Suffield appointed Commissary in the first regiment, March, 1756.

Ebenezer Sage of Middletown appointed Commissary in the second regiment, March, 1756.

Thaddeus Mead of Norwalk appointed Commissary in the third regiment, March, 1756.

Phineas Stanton of Stonington appointed Commissary in the fourth regiment, March, 1756.

Thomas Wells [of Glastonbury],
Hezekiah Huntington [of Norwich],
Gurdon Saltonstall [of New London],
Jabez Hamlin [of Middletown],
John Hubbard [of New Haven],
Theophilus Nichols [of Stratford], } appointed Commissaries of purchase and transportation, March, 1756.

[*The above from Colonial Records, except as noted.*]

William Stanton, Commissary. [*Comptroller's Office, Treasurer's Book.*]
John Ketchum, Commissary. [*Comptroller's Office, Treasurer's Book.*]
John Ripnear, Armourer from April 16 to Nov. 29, 1756.
[*State Library, War 6, 364.*]
Eleazer Dean, Armourer. [*Comptroller's Office, Treasurer's Book.*]

Note: The General Assembly in February, 1756, resolved to raise 2500 men, officers included, for the coming campaign; this force to be divided into four regiments of eight companies each. In October following, in consequence of a letter from the Earl of Loudon, the Assembly resolved to raise eight additional companies, to be added to the four regiments already raised as the ninth and tenth companies. No evidence has been found to show that these additional companies were in service and it is probable that they were not raised on account of the lateness of the season. Half-pay from December 17, 1755, to the date of reënlistment was allowed to officers and soldiers who had served in the previous campaign and a gratuity of one months pay was granted to officers and soldiers who had served in garrison during the winter.

FIRST REGIMENT—MAJ.-GEN. PHINEAS LYMAN.

REGIMENTAL OFFICERS.

Phineas Lyman [of Suffield] appointed Major-General and Captain of the first company, March, 1756. Discharged Dec. 1. [*Colonial Records.*]

John Payson [of Hartford], Lieutenant-Colonel and Captain of the second company, March 26, 1756. Discharged Oct. 20.
[*State Library, War 6, 312.*]

Joseph Storrs [of Mansfield], Major and Captain of the third company.
[*State Library, War 6, 60.*]

Benjamin Bancroft of Suffield appointed Commissary, March, 1756.

Rev. Jonathan Lee of Salisbury, Chaplain. [*Colonial Records.*]

Timothy Collins of Litchfield, Surgeon, disabled by illness Oct. 2.
[*State Library, War 6, 171.*]

Elisha Lord of Farmington, Surgeon's Mate, served from April 5 to Dec. 3, 1756, with one month's absence during that time.
[*State Library, War 6, 371.*]

William Abernarther, Surgeon's apprentice. [*State Library, War 6, 171.*]

—— Stoughton, Adjutant. [*Comptroller's Office, Treasurer's Book.*]

Aaron Beach, Armourer, from "latter end of May" to "latter end of Aug.," 1756. [*State Library, War. 6, 348.*]

FIRST COMPANY—MAJ.-GEN. LYMAN.

Phineas Lyman [of Suffield], Major-General and Captain. [*Colonial Records.*]
Samuel Chandler [of Woodstock], Captain Lieutenant.

Elihu Kent [of Suffield], Second Lieutenant.
John Charter, Ensign and Lieutenant. [*Colonial Records.*]

Officers and Soldiers Names	Time of Inlisting	[ ]	Dead
Gen. Phinehas Lyman	Mar. 26	Dec. 1	
Cap. Samuel Chandler	" "	" "	
Lieut. Elihu Kent	" "	Nov. 1	
Ens. John Charter	" "	Sep. 20	
Leiut. John Charter	Sep. 20	Dec. 1	
Serg. Nehemiah Ferman	Mar. 29	Sep. 20	
Ens. Nehemiah Farman	Sep. 20	Dec. 1	
Clerk David Parsons	Mar. 29	Jan. 13	
Serg. Nehemiah Chandler	Apr. 5		Aug. 9
" Joel Adams	Mar. 29	Dec. 16	
" John Atchinson	Apr. [ ]	Oct. 15	

CAMPAIGN OF 1756.

Officers and Soldiers Names	Time of Inlisting	[ ]	Dead
Corp. Abner Meacham	Apr. 5	Sep. 10	
Serg. Abner Meacham	Sep. 10	Dec. 1	
Corp. Zerah Kibbe	Apr. 9	Nov. 12	
" Oliver Barker	Mar. 29		deserted Sep. 30
Philip Simons	Apr. 5	Sep. 10	
Corp. Philip Simons	Sep. 10	Dec. 1	
" Seth King	Apr. 1	" 14	
Peter Bishop	" 15	" 1	
John White	Mar. 29	Oct. 12	
Alex^d Dunlap	" "	Dec. 1	
Stephen Holcomb	" "		deserted Mar. 29
David Bennet	[ ]	Dec. 1	
Phinehas Lyman Junr	[ ]	Nov. 1	
George Slaughter	[ ]	Dec. 6	
[ ]	[ ]	" 1	
Noah [ ]roy Junr	[ ]	Nov. 12	
John Carvaneer	Apr. [ ]		deserted Sep. 2
James Halladay	" "	Oct. 12	
Joseph Rogers	" 3	Dec. 1	
Ezekiel Hale	Mar. 29	" "	
Zebulun Norton	Apr. 14		deserted Oct. 11
Oliver Keny	Mar. 29		
Shadrach Norton	Apr. 14		deserted Oct. 11
Joseph Chandler	" 2	Oct. 12	
Frances Baxter	" 3	" "	
Noah Pearsons	" 5	Dec. 1	
John Rumeril	" "	Oct. 12	
Daniel Hale	" "	Dec. 1	
Moses Pease	" "	" "	
Joel Pease	" "	" "	
Paul Kibbe	" "		Nov. 5
Israel Markham	" "	Oct. 12	
Benj. Booth	" "		Nov. 6
Stephen Markham	" "	Oct. 12	
William Collins	" 8	Dec. 14	
Daniel Pratt	" "	Oct. 12	
Ebenezar Wood	" "	Dec. 1	
Joseph Phelt	" 9		Nov. 30
Joshua Gary	" "		" 28
Michael Holcomb	" 14		deserted Apr. 14
Jacob Terry Junr	May 3	Dec. 1	
Isaac Orsborn	" "	Oct. 2	
Nathan Whipple	Apr. 9	Dec. 1	
Oliver Evens	" 10	Oct. 2	
Edmund Evens	" 9	" "	
Elijah Mainard	May 19		Aug. 18
Edmund Grover	Apr. 8	Oct. 12	
John Shertleef	" 18		Sep. 18
Benj. Scott	" 8	Nov. 12	
James Haddlock	" "	" "	
William White	" "	Dec. 1	
Nathaniel Brace	" "	Nov. 12	
Isaac Smith	" 4		Nov. 11
Josiah Granger	May 3		Sep. 1
Joel Granger	Apr. 18		" 20
John Hixley	" 9	Dec. 1	
Stephen Winchel	Mar. 29	" "	
Joshua Adams	" "		deserted July 25

FIRST REGIMENT.

Officers and Soldiers Names	Time of Inlisting	[ ]	Dead
John Read (?)	May 3		deserted July 17
Elphalet Spencer	Apr. 4		deserted Sep. 27
Corp. Joel Granger	Sep. 20		Nov. 1
Dan¹ Sheldon	May 11	Dec. 1	
Charles Gillet	" "	" "	
Jone Bone	Apr. 4	Oct. 12	
Samuel Granger	Mar. 29	" "	
Joseph Buel	May 13	Dec. 1	
John Law	" 10	Nov. 10	
Adj^t John Stoughton	Mar. 26	Dec. 1	
Edward Foster	30 Apr.	1 Dec.	
Jonathan Parsons	29 Mar.	12 Nov.	
Jesse Austion	5 Apr.	1 "	
Bildad Granger	3 May	13 Oct.	
John Winchel	4 Apr.	1 Dec.	
Jon^a Allen	29 Mar.	12 Nov.	
Michael Wilson	2 Apr.		
George Slaughter			deserted

[Indorsed] Maj^r General Lymans Muster Roll 1756

[*State Library, Adams Papers.*]

Phinehas Lyman Mag^r Genl Colonal and Captain
Samuel Chandler Capt Lieu^t
Elihu Kent 2^d Lieu^t
John Charter Ens^n
Red^d Jonathan Lee Chaplain
John Laws A d Camp
Timothy Collins Surgeon
Elisha Lord Surgeons mate
Benjamin Bancroft Comissary
John Stoughton Adjutant
Nathaniel Ripley Quartermaster
Eliazar Done Armourer
Nehemiah Harmon Serj^t Maj^r Confined
John Atchinson ⎫
Joel Adams   ⎬ Serj^t
Nehemiah Chandler ⎪   Dead
Abner Meacham ⎭
David Parsons Clerk
Zerah Kibbe ⎫
Philip Simons ⎬ Corp^l
Joel Granger ⎪
Oliver Barker ⎭   gone home without leave
George Slaughter Drum Maj^r
Oliver Evens Drumer

[The above officers' names are followed by the names of the privates as on previous roll.]

[Indorsed] General Lymans C^o 1756
    Camp at Fort William Henry Oct. 13, 1756
        Henry Leddel Muster Mast^r Genl

[*State Library, Adams Papers.*]

CAMPAIGN OF 1756.

Names & Rank of Such as Served Last year now in Maj[r] Gen[ll] Lymans Com[y]

Phin[s] Lyman Maj[r] Gen[l]
Cap[t] Sam[ll] Chandler
Lieu[t] Elihu Kent
Serj. Jn[o] Charler
Benj[a] Bancroft
Serj Neh. Farman
David Parsons
Oliver Barker
John White
Alexander Dunlap
Joel Adams
David Bement
Phinehas Lyman
George Slaughter
Henry Riedson
Noah Pumroy
Philip Simons
Micael Holcomb
Abner Meacham
Benj[a] Scot
James Hadlock
Stephen Winchel Drum.
Seth King Drum.
James Halladay
Joseph Rogers
Noah Parsons
Moses Pease
Oliver Evans
Ezekiel Hale
Edmund Evans
Zeb. Norton
Frances Baxter
Joshua Geary
Edward Foster

[Indorsed] Maj[r] Gen[ll] Lymans Half Pay Roll

[*State Library, War 5, 312.*]

SECOND COMPANY—LIEUT.-COL. PAYSON.

John Payson [of Hartford], Lieutenant-Colonel and Captain.
James Tracy [of Windham], First Lieutenant.
Ezekiel Fitch, Second Lieutenant.   [*Colonial Records.*]

A Muster Roll of Lieu[t] Col[o] Jn[o] Paysons Company with the Time of Their Inlistment Dead Deserted Discharged weeks and Days in Service at what p[r] week Intire wages &c 1756

Mens Names and Quality		Time of Inlistmt	Discharg'd	Dead
Lieut. Col. Jn[o] Payson		Mar. 26	Oct. 20	
James Tracy	1st Lieut.	" "		Sep. 21
Ezek[l] Fitch	2[d] "	" "	Dec. 2	
Elijah Simons	Serj.	Apr. 2	Oct. 20	
Asa Richardson	"	" 1	Dec. 2	
Nathan Lilly	"	" 6	Oct. 16	
Darias Waterman	"	" 2		deserted Oct. 10
Sam[ll] Morris	Clerk	May 8	Oct. 1	
Joseph Wattles	Cor.	Apr. 5	Dec. 2	
Sam[ll] Adams	"	" 22	" "	
Joseph Farnam	"	" 13	" "	
Nath[ll] Ormsbee	"	May 8	" "	
Henry Moriss		" 12	Nov. 17	
Asa Stephens		Apr. 12	Oct. 16	
Nath[ll] Ripley		" 2	Dec. 7	
Joseph Reynolds		May 12		Sep. 1
Joshua Bill		Apr. 3		" "
Roger Carary		May 8	Oct. 16	
Eanos Bartholomew		" "	" 20	
John Streetor		" 10	" "	
Will[m] Gourden		" "	Dec. 2	
Isaac Canada		Apr. 2	" "	

FIRST REGIMENT.

Mens Names and Quality	Time of Inlistmt		Discharg'd		Dead
Rheuben Bingham	Apr.	6	Dec.	2	
Aaron Eaton	"	"	Nov.	1	
Henry Preston	"	"	Dec.	2	
Isaac Robinson	"	5	"	"	
John Knight	"	3	"	"	
John Lilly	"	6	Oct.	16	
Isaac Dodge	"	"	Dec.	2	
Benj[n] Holding	"	3	"	"	
Will[m] Ripley	"	8	Oct.	20	
Josiah Fuller	"	3	Dec.	2	
Nath[ll] Spencer	"	2	"	"	
Simon Cady	"	9	Nov.	4	
Stephen Baker	"	13	Oct.	17	
Joseph Russ	"	8	Dec.	2	
Barthol[w] Durkee	"	"	Oct.	17	
Hez. May	"	"	Dec.	2	
Caleb Austin	"	"	"	"	
Joshua Lyon	"	13			Sep. 29
Abiel Lyon	"	"	Oct.	17	
George Parker	"	2	Dec.	2	
Elijah Woodworth	"	5	"	"	
Elihu Bascum	"	9	Nov.	14	
Ezek[l] Huntington	"	7	Dec.	2	
Peter Bowdish	"	12	"	"	
Will[m] Parrish	"	6	Oct.	20	
John Watson	"	2	Dec.	2	
Mich[l] Layhah	"	5	"	"	
David Woodworth	"	2			Never joyned
Dan[ll] Molton	"	3	Dec.	2	
Joseph Hammond	"	6	"	"	
Oliph[r] Thorp	"	2	Oct.	10	
Benj[n] Butler	"	5	Dec.	2	
Aaron Buck	"	8			deserted Sep. 26
Benj[n] Cary	"	"	Sep.	16	
James Dodge	"	14			Sep. 26
Nathan Caull	"	13	Dec.	2	
James Hide	"	12			Sep. 13
George Dunham	"	5	Dec.	2	
Joseph Trusdell	"	15	Nov.	4	
Jon[th] Canada	"	8	Oct.	16	
Dan[ll] Squire	"	"	Dec.	2	
Moses Sparks	"	"	Oct.	16	
John Wise	"	6	Dec.	2	
Phenihas Maning	"	9	Oct.	16	
Will[m] Blanchard	"	27	Dec.	2	
Zaccheus Downer	"	15	"	"	
Ebenez[r] Bibbins	"	6	Oct.	15	
Elisha Bowman	"	15			Oct. 2
Sam[ll] Bass	"	12	Dec.	2	
Piras Richards	"	"			Never Joyned
Anani[a] Porrage	"	3	Dec.	2	
Simon Pooney	"	12			Sep. 15
Jn[th] Peagon	May	19	Oct.	20	
Hez. Wobbon	"	20	"	"	
Jn[o] Sunsamon	"	21	"	"	
Benj[n] Paul	"	8	Dec.	2	

[Indorsed] L[t] Col[o] John Payson Muster Roll January 1757
John Knight   [*State Library, Adams Papers.*]

A muster roll of this company, signed by Henry Leddel Muster Mast. General, is dated Camp at Fort Wm Henry, Oct. 13, 1756.

[*State Library, War 6, 312.*]

Names & Rank of Such of Lieu^t Co^{ll} Eleazer Fitch's Company as were in last years Service & are to Have Half Pay

Lieut. James Tracy	John Watson
" Ezekiel Fitch	Michael La
Serj. Elijah Simons	David Woodworth
" Asa Richardson	Dan^{ll} Molton
Corp. Nathen Lilley	James Hide
" Peter Bowdish	George Dunhem
" Wm Parrish	Jos. Trusdel
Serj. Eben^r Bibbens	Jonath. Canada
Clerk Nath^{ll} Ripley	Dan^{ll} Squire
Darius Waterman	Moses Sparks
Joseph Farnum	Phinehes Maning
Asa Stevens	Benj^a Cary
Isaac Canada	Pyrus Richard
Aaron Eaton	John Frame
Henry Preston	Joshua Hebard
John Knight	Clerk Saml Morriss
Ananias Porrage	Wm Gordon
Benj^a Holden	Benj^a Paul
Jonah Fuller	John Streeter
Simon Cady	Roger Crary
Stephen Baker	Enos Bartholomew
Simon Poon	Henry Morris
Caleb Austen	Maj^r Jon^o Payson
George Parker	

[Indorsed] Lt Col^o Eliezer Fitch's half pay Roll

[*State Library, War 5, 330.*]

This company consisted of 48 men from Middletown, 20 men from Woodstock and two men from Hartford. [*State Library, War 6, 296.*]

Note: The General Assembly had appointed Eliezer Fitch as Lieutenant-Colonel of the regiment and Captain of this company, but he appears not to have accepted the appointment. [*Colonial Records.*]

THIRD COMPANY—MAJ. STORRS.

Joseph Storrs [of Mansfield], Major and Captain. [*State Library, War 6, 60.*]
John Levinze, First Lieutenant. [*Colonial Records.*]
Thomas Baldwin, Second Lieutenant. [*State Library, War 6, 53.*]

Names of Sundry now in Maj^r Stores Company who were in last years Service & have right to Half Pay

Benj^a Rider	April 14	Jonathan Knap	April 15
Thomas Sumner	13	Eleazer Covel	15
Nathl Walker	15	Timothy Squire	9
Thomas Willson	9	Jonathan Cady	9

FIRST REGIMENT. 99

Peleg Heath	April 6	Jaacob Fenton	May 10
Pite Peito	6	John Fletcher	April 28
David Stodderd	May 8	John Brown	3
Levi Wells	10	John Cross	13
Thomas Jewel	June 4	Abell Cross	13
Gershom Hale	4	Nath[ll] Bingham	June 4
Richard Leech	April 6	Henry Whitaker	April 15
Ephraim Dewey	27	Zach[h] Parker	June 4

[Indorsed] Maj[r] Joseph Stores for half pay

[*State Library, War 5, 317.*]

To the Hon[ble] The Com[tte] of The Pay Table of The Colony of Connecticut
    Gentlemen
        Upon The Desire of Maj[r] Joseph Storrs Esq[r] I Have on The Day of The Date hereof Taken The Muster of The following Able Body'd Effective Men by him enlisted into his Majesty's Service for the Present Intended Expedition against Crown point &c being forty Eight in Number as follows

Jonathan Cady	William Stephens
Stephen Russel	Jonathan Knapp
Thomas Willson	Abishai Hollon
Timothy Knight	John Williams
Thomas Sumner	Robert Paddock
Greenfield Randal	Timothy Squire
David Barret	John Fletcher Jun[r]
John Joslen	John Royse
Joseph Winter	Richard Leach
Benjamin Ellis	Edmund Freeman y[e] 3rd
Simeon Wakefield	Asa Humphrey
Jacob Barrett	Peleg Heath
Samson Barrett	Mickel Lunsford
John Day	Abel Cross
Jesse Addams	Benjamin Rider
Eleazer Covel	Joseph Kent
Michel Hulet	John Cross
Eleazer Childs	Henry Whittaker
Nathaniel Walker	Robert Croford
Joshua Powel	William Dewey
Benoni Cuttler	Josiah Reed
Jehiel Brooks	Huckens Storrs Jun[r]
Simeon Bloss	Pyte Pyto
Jacob Daly	Ephraim Baldwin

        Mansfield 5th May Anno Domini 1756
            Test Shubael Conant Colonel

[Indorsed] Col[o] Conants Muster of 3[d] Compa 1st Regiment retund June 10th 1756 p Maj[r] Storrs

[*State Library, War 6, 126.*]

To the Honb[le] Com[tee] of The Pay Table of the Colony of Connecticut
    Gentlemen
        Upon the Desire of Maj[r] Joseph Storrs Esq[r] I have on The Day of The Date hereof Taken the Muster of The following able

CAMPAIGN OF 1756.

Bodyed Effective men by him enlisted in to his Majestys Service in the present Intended Expedition against Crown point &c being 24 in number

Jacob Fenton
John Brown
John More
Elijah Blodget
Jacob Green
David Stoddard
John Bettee
Elexander Lille
Levy Wells
Zeckeriah Parker
Daniel Cook
John Austin

Azariah Hall
Nathaniel Bingham
Ebenezer Bingham
Aaron Geer
John Ames
William Wedge
William Burnham
Lemewel Buzel
Gershom Hale
Thomas Jewet
John Beckwith
Prince Hopkins

Mansfield June y[e] 8th A D 1756
p Shubael Conant Colonel
[*State Library*, War 6, 127.]

This company contained 73 men; 42 of them marched from Mansfield and 31 from Killingly. [*State Library*, War 6, 297.]

FOURTH COMPANY—CAPT. PUTNAM.

Israel Putnam [of Pomfret], Captain.
Thomas Gallop, First Lieutenant. [*Colonial Records.*]
George Crary [of Voluntown], Second Lieutenant.
[*State Library*, War 6, 56.]

A Roll of Sundry Men of y[e] Company under command of Cap[t] Israel Putnam in y[e] Expedition against Crown point A Dom 1756 Who at y[e] Time of making up y[e] Muster roll of S[d] Company being Enterd as Deserters were not allowd Pay but are Since on further evidence of y[e] circumstances of their leaving y[e] army are now allowd y[e] Same by y[e] Pay Table

Mens Names and Rank	Time of Enlisting	When Discharged or Dead
Serj[t] Moses Bronch	Apr. 8	Oct. 14
Corp[l] Reuben Jones	" 12	5
Corp[l] David S[ ]pard	May 8	16
John Heard	Apr. 2	15
Stephen Downer	" 13	16
Ezekiel Apley	" 12	"
Malachy Cady	" 15	"
Cull Matthews	" 2	"
Jabez Holms	" 13	15
Cato Negro	" 13	14
Benj[a] Bragg	" 8	15
Benj[a] Sherman	" "	20
Ebenezer Benjamin	" 9	16
Thomas Gallup	May 10	"
Jeremiah Shontup	Apr. 2	"
Nathan Dow	" 20	14
Stephen Harris	" 1	Dec. 2

FIRST REGIMENT.

Mens Names and Rank	Time of Enlisting	When Discharged or Dead
Joseph Clark	June 14	Oct. 15
John Hide	July 14	"
Joseph Squuntup	Apr. 13	14
Jacob Williams	" "	9
Benj Keeny	" 23	16
George Dorrance	" 9	6
Stephen Downer Jr	" 8	5

[*State Library, War 6, 299.*]

This company contained 74 officers and men; 51 of them marched from Plainfield and 23 from Pomfret. [*State Library, War 6, 299.*]

Capt Putnam Half Pay Roll

Men Enlisted by ye Lieu^{ts} Gallup & Crery

Thomas Gallup Leut.	Mar. 26	Benjamin Kinne	Apr.	23
George Crary Sarg.	" "	Thomas Reed	"	8
Benedick Saterly Sarg.	Apr. 2	Elijah Brumby	"	"
Elijah Cady Sarg.	" "	Benjamin Bragg	"	"
Ezekel Whitney	" 1	Robart Dixon	"	9
John Heard	" 2	Ruphas Parks	"	"
Jeams Aply	" "	Ruben Jons	"	12
Nathan^l Fabens	" "	Benjamin Park	"	13
Coll Matthew	" "	William Bordman	"	14
Jeremiah Sheentup	" "	Ebenezer Davis Corp	"	23
Benjamin Sharman	" 8	Stevan Downer	"	13
Robart Heavens	" 9	Ebenezer Williams Drum Maj.	May	8
William Herronton	" 8	David Sheapard Corp.	"	"
Elexander Kee	" 9	Negro Ceser	"	10
Isaac Stone	" 12	Thomas Gallup	"	"
Negro Cato	" 13			

Men Enlisted by Capt Putnam himself after others were gone

Capt Israel Putnam		Jonathan Coye	
John Hide		Jeremiah Jackson	May 31
Corp^l Joseph Ross		Nathl Coller	
Corp^l Thomas Lyon		James Hartford	May 31
Andrew Spaulding Serj^t		John Truesdell	
Isaac Hide		Littlefield Nash	May 31
Joseph Clark		Roger Crow	May 31
Charles Biles	May 31		

N. B. all above in this Column they not Enlisting into ye Service til very late viz about ye Middle of July it was Supposd reasonable their Half pay Should not run on So farr but end about ye time the last of ye army went up and their Half pay was accordingly Computed to end on ye 16th of June all except ye five above who in fact listed ye 31st of May whose half pay was computed according to their Enlistment.

[Indorsed] Capt Putnams Comp^a Half Pay Roll

[*State Library, War 5, 306.*]

CAMPAIGN OF 1756.

FIFTH COMPANY—CAPT. WHITING.

Samuel Whiting [of Stratford], Captain.
Samuel Hubbel [of Kent], First Lieutenant.
Nathan Godfrey, Second Lieutenant. [*Colonial Records.*]

Names and quality of the men in last Comp^a Now in Capt Samuel Whitings Compeney

	Month and Day of inlistment			Month and Day of inlistment	
Samuel Whiting Capt.	Apr.	1	Thomas Sturgis	Apr.	20
Samuel Hubbel Lieut.	"	"	David Henrix	"	29
William Thorpe	"	5	Preserved Tayler	"	8
John Fanning	"	19	Josia Bears	"	5
Benjamin Davis	"	9	Jesper Baley	"	3
Thomas Rowland	"	20	Thomas Nichols	"	6
Andreow Cable	"	19	Benjamin Squier	"	9
Ezekill Leathers	"	21			

[*State Library, War 5, 325.*]

This company contained seventy four officers and men and marched from Stratford. [*State Library, War 6, 311.*]

SIXTH COMPANY—CAPT. HITCHCOCK.

Aaron Hitchcock [of Suffield], Captain. [*Colonial Records.*]
Jonathan Humphrey [of Simsbury], First Lieutenant.
[*State Library, War 6, 60.*]
Benjamin Royce, Second Lieutenant. [*Colonial Records.*]

A Muster Roll of Capt Aaron Hitchcock's Company

Mens Names	Quality	Time of Enlisting		Discharged		Dead
Aaron Hitchcock	Capt.	Mar.	26	Dec.	1	
Jonathan Humphrey	Lieut.	"	"	"	"	
Benjamin Rice	"	"	"	Nov.	12	
John Chick	Serj.	Apr.	14	Dec.	1	
Joseph Smith	"	"	19	"	"	
Even Rice	"	"	8			deserted Sep. 5
Austin Mygate	"	"	10	Dec.	10	
Noah Humphrey	"	Sep.	6	"	1	
Paul Kent	Clerk	Apr.	10	"	"	
John Slaughter	Corp.	"	19	"	"	
Oliver Kent	"	Mar.	29	Oct.	23	
Enos Doolittle	"	Apr.	10			Oct. 28
Mical Jacson	"	May	20	Dec.	1	
Stephen Winchell	Drum.	Apr.	26	"	"	
Benjamin Adams	Private	"	14	"	"	
Samuel Alyn	"	May	3	"	"	
Josiah Alyn	"	Apr.	5	"	"	
Elihu Alderman	"	May	6	"	"	
Amos Andros	"	Apr.	8	Oct.	25	
Asael Andros	"	"	23	Dec.	1	

FIRST REGIMENT.

Mens Names	Quality	Time of Enlisting	Discharged	Dead
Abner Barnes	Private	May 28		Nov. 7
Elihu Beach	"	Apr. 24	Dec. 1	
Timothy Blackmoor	"	Aug. 26	Nov. 11	
Henry Blodgett	"	May 24	Oct. 20	
George Bunce	"	" 26	Dec. 1	
Daniel Canadice	"	Apr. 11	Oct. 29	
Andrew Corycomb	"	May 13		
Jason Cooper	"	June 3	Dec. 1	
John Dayly	"	Apr. 14	Nov. 12	
Benjamin Demick	"	" "	Dec. 1	
Ebeneazer Doolittle	"	" 18	" "	
Moses Gains	"	" 16	" "	
Jacob Hensdill	"	June 8	" "	
John Harmon	"	May 26	" "	
Elijah Hodgkiss	"	Apr. 9	Oct. 18	
Amos Horseford	"	" 14	Nov. 17	
Benjamin Judd	"	May 22	Dec. 1	
Noah Kent	"	Mar. 31	" "	
Joseph King	"	May 26	" "	
Hezekiah Lewis	"	Apr. 13	Oct. 7	
Joseph Lewis	"	May 18	Dec. 6	
Samuel Lewis	"	Mar. 31	" 1	
Oliver Lewis	"	May 10	Sep. 22	
Ambroise London	"	Apr. 16	Dec. 6	
Lemuel Mooffitt	"	June 1	" 1	
Roger Mygate	"	Apr. 13	" "	
London Negro	"	" 20	" "	
Jedediah Alcott	"	" 16	Jan. 10	
Abner Phelps	"	" 20	Aug. 20	
Jonathan Piney	"	" 14	Dec. 1	
Joseph Piney	"	" 22	" "	
Nathaniel Piney	"	June 10	" "	
John Quick	"	May 25		deserted June 29
Johnn Return	"	Apr. 14	Dec. 1	
William Roberts	"	" "	" "	
Phinehas Southwell	"	" 10	Nov. 14	
Elisha Spencer	"	May 3	Dec. 1	
John Spencer	"	" 4	Oct. 9	
William Thrall	"	Apr. 17	Aug. 20	
Jacob Taylor	"	June 6	Oct. 16	
Sangola	"	Apr. 15	Nov. 8	
Moses Webster	"	June 4	Oct. 15	
Jonathan Westover	"	May 6		Sep. 21
Joseph Woolcott	"	Apr. 26	Nov. 5	
John Wallyn	"	May 10	Dec. 1	
Martin Winchell	"	Apr. 16	Aug. 20	
Noah Humphrey	"	May 1	Sep. 6	
Joseph Blanchar	"	" 6	Aug. 26	

Asa Francis
Titus Hall
Clemen Hopson
Barnabas Merwin } These Never Joyned ye Reg^t
Henry Merwin
Oliver Whitmoor
Andrew Corycomb

[Indorsed] Capt Aaron Hitchcock Muster Roll Jan^{ry} 1757

[*State Library, Adams Papers.*]

A muster roll of this company, signed by Henry Leddel Must. Mast. General, is dated Camp at Fort William Henry Oct. 13, 1656.

[*State Library, Adams Papers.*]

Names & Rank of Such & were in last years Campaign & now in ye Company of Capt Aaron Hitchcock

Aaron Hitchcock Capt	Mar.	26	Joseph Smith Corp.	Apr.	19
Sam^ll Lewis	"	31	John Slaughter	"	"
Paul Kent Clark	Apr.	10	Thomas Winchal Corp.	"	20
Phinehas Southwel	"	"	Joseph Piney	"	22
Sangore Warre	"	15	Noah Humphrey Serj.	May	1
Henry Blodgit	Mar	24	Joseph Blanchar	"	6
John Chick Serj	Apr.	14	Oliver Lewis	"	10
Benj^m Demick	"	"	John Walen	"	"
Benj^m Addams 2^d	"	"	Mickel Jackson	"	20
Marten Winchal	"	16	George Bunce	"	26
Wm Thrall	"	17			

listed by ye Capt
Joseph King   May 26

[Indorsed] Half Pay Roll of Such in Cp^t Hitchcocks as were enlisted by Lieu^t Humphrey

[*State Library, War 5, 323.*]

The Names & Rank of Such of ye Men now in Capt Aaron Hitchcocks Company as are Enlisted by Lieu^t Rice & were in last years Service

Serj. Benj^a Royce	Mar.	26	Andrew Curricomb	May	13
Corp. Evan Royce	Apr.	8	John Spencer	"	4
Hezekiah Lewis	"	13	Joseph Lewis	"	18
Joseph Woolcot	"	26	Jason Cooper	June	3
Ebenezer Doolittles	"	8	Nat Pinny	"	10

[Indorsed] Half Pay Roll for Some of Capt Hitchcocks Men
[*State Library, War 5, 318.*]

SEVENTH COMPANY—CAPT. BALDWIN.

David Baldwin [of Milford], Captain.   [*Colonial Records.*]
Samuel Lawrence [of Simsbury], First Lieutenant.
[*State Library, War 6, 60.*]
Samuel Clarke, Second Lieutenant.

David Baldwin Capt		
Samuell Lawrence Lieu^t	at Albany Sick	
Samuel Clarke 2 Lieu^t		
Peter Wooster Serjants		
John Edgcomb "	Sick	
Elihu Sanford "	Confined	
Nathan Davis "	Sick at Fort Edward	
Silas Baldwin Clark	Sick at Saratoga	
Elisha Wooster Corporals		
Noah Gleason "		
John Thomas "		
Solomon Thomas "	Confined	

FIRST REGIMENT.

Samuell Peck Drumer   gone home without Leave
Atwell Paul
Andrus Ephraim   Dead
Alderman Thomas   Confined
Albert Nathanale   Deserted Sep. 20
Alderman Timothy   Dead July 26
Adams Daniel   Deserted Sep. 23
Adams Timothy   with the sick at Alb^y
Bunnel Luke   Sick at Fort Edward
Barberer Isaac   Dead Sep 21
Brocket Hezekiah   Sick
Bonner Partrick   never Joyned
Blague Jeremiah   Sick at Fort Edward
Canfield Jeremiah   gone to Alb^y wth Leave
Case Jacob
Collens Jacob   Sick at Albany
Case Richard   Confined
Cush Roben
Craft Peter   Deserted half moon July 20
Cowell Joshua   Dead Sep. 8
Chepunck John   Dead Sep. 26
Clinton Shuball   Dead Oct. 5
Cam George   Dead   "   "
Curtis Eliphalet   Sick at Fort Edwd
Dayton Israel   Dead
Fulford John
Gains William   gone to Alb^y sick
Graham Benjamin   on Com^d at half moon
Horskin Shuball   Confined
Hodge Thomas
Hatchet Tousey John   Sick at fort Edwd
Humphry Jonathan   Deserted Sep. 20
Humphry John   never Joyned
Holcomb Stephen   never Joy^d
Hatch John
James Tom
Killam Moses   Sick at fort Edward
Lylle Phillip   Sick
Lattemore Jonathan   Sick
Macdaniel John   Dead
Mills Amsey
Mitchel George   Sick
Miles Daniel   Deserted in Connecticut
Mansfield James   never Joyned
Pond Peter
Plumb Charles
Peas Benjamin   Sick at Fort Edwd
Pettebone Jacob   Sick
Priest Phillip   Deserted Fort Edwd
Ross William
Roben Samuel
Rice Isaiah   Deserted Fort Edwd
Robards Daniel
Russell William   Discharged half moon
Smith Samuell
Stanly Josiah   at Fort Edward
Sullivan Thomas   Sick
Tharp Daniell
Tolles Samuell   Dead

CAMPAIGN OF 1756.

Tutsson Samuell   absent
Whitney Henry   on Command Alb^y
Worden Daniel   Deserted half moon
Woodcock Barnabas   Sick at fort Edward
Will Tom   "   "   "   "
Wade Stephen
Whitticus Jo   Sick

[Indorsed]   Camp at Fort William Henry Oct. 13, 1756 Henry Leddel
             Muster Mast. General
             Capt Baldwin's Co Muster Roll 1756.

[*State Library, Adams Papers.*]

A Roll and Manifest of Such Men as serv'd last Year in the Expedition against Crown Point &c and are now enlisted to serve in Capt David Baldwins Company, their half Pay stated &c

Mens Names & Ranks in last Years Service	Day of their new inlisting	Mens Names & Ranks in last Years Service	Day of their new inlisting
David Baldwin 1 Lieut	Mar. 26	Robin Cush	Apr. 2
Peter Wooster Serj.	Apr. 12	Samuel Tatson	" 17
Josiah Stanly "	" 16	Daniel Tharp	" 16
John Fulford Corp.	" 27	William Russell	" 17
Elihu Sanford	" 9	John Chegpunck	" 14
Henry Whitney	" "	Hezekiah Bracket	" 17
Samuel Smith	" "	Jason Cooper	" "
George Mitchel	" 2	Elisha Wooster	" 22
Benjamin Graham	" "	Daniel Warden	" "
Israel Daton	" 13	John Hatch	" 29
Paul Atwell	" 10	John Thomas Corp.	" 20
Thomas Hodg	" 8	Jeremiah Blade	May 13
John Hatchetousey	" 2	Thomas Sullivan	Apr. 20
Thomas James	" 9	James Mansfield	May 6
Thomas Will	" "		

[Indorsed]   Capt David Baldwin's Rolls of half pay 1756

[*State Library, War 5, 309.*]

This company marched from Milford.   [*State Library, War 6, 291.*]

Half Pay Roll Containing ye Names Rank & Number of Weeks and Days and Each ones perticuler half pay according to ye Act of Assembly allowing half pay to Such as were in ye last years Service

Names and Ranks	Times of Enlistment	Names and Ranks	Times of Enlistment
Serj. Jno Edgcomb	April 14	Isaiah Rice	April 13
Corp. Emond Nearing	19	Amasa Mills	14
Corp. Wm Ross	16	William Gains	13
Danl Robards	14	Timothy Alderm^n	20
Isaac Barber	12	Noah Gleasen	16
Jacob Tuller	19		

[*State Library, War 5, 310.*]

FIRST REGIMENT. 107

EIGHTH COMPANY—CAPT. BILLINGS.

Ebenezer Billings [of Stonington], Captain. [*Colonial Records.*]
Nathan Leonard [of Preston], Lieutenant.
William Billings [of Preston], Lieutenant. [*State Library, War 6, 52.*]

A Muster Role of Capt Ebenezer Billings Company & the Time of Enlisting & Discharged & Number of Weeks & Days in Service

Officers & Soldiers Names & quality	Time of Enlisting	Discharged	Dead & Captivated
Capt. Ebenez^r Billings	Mar. 26	Oct. 25	
Lieut. Nathan Leonard	"	Nov. 6	
Lieut. Wm Billings	"	Dec. 5	
Sarj. Jabez Billing	Apr. 1	" "	
Sarj. Jonas Frink	"	Oct. 25	
Sarj. John Smith	"	" "	
Sarj. John Avery	"	Dec. 5	
Corp. John Prentice	"	" 10	
Corp. Luis Jones	9	Nov. 2	
Corp. Jehu Fish	2	Dec. 5	
Corp. Increas Billing	12	" 20	
Clark Ichabod Dickinson	1	Oct. 30	
Drum. Elisha Prentice	8	Nov. 2	
Jesse Billing	2	Dec. 5	
Theophilus Fitch	3	Oct. 14	
Joseph Ellot	8	Nov. 18	
Ebenezer Billing	1		Dd Oct. 13
Ebenezer Hill	"		Dead July 24
Charles Avery	2	Oct. 28	
Daniel Back	1	" 13	
Nathan Jones	4	Nov. 3	
Samuel Tracy	"		Dyd Dec. 1
John Whipple	"	Oct. 12	
Jonas Hewit	"	Dec. 5	
Jesse Williams	8	" "	
Barzilla Burrus	6		
Elijah Jones	7	Nov. 4	
John Babcock	8	" "	
Thomas Laraby	9	" 1	
Robison Bomp	6		Dyd Oct. 22
Ebenez^r Yarrington	"		Dyd " 23
Theophilus Stanton	7	Sep. 20	
Nathanael Wells	9	Oct. 28	
Benjamin Avery	"	Dec. 10	
Samuel Huntington	6		July 25
Joseph Williams	5	Oct. 30	
James Brown	9	Dec. 5	
John Geer	8	" 20	
Jeremiah Jackson	12	" "	
Moses Jones	9	Oct. 25	
Joseph Randol	8	Dec. 12	
Jonathan Calking	6	May 19	
Samll Thornton	"	Dec. 5	
John Robarts	"		Oct. 28
Andrew Herrick	"	Oct. 18	
Thomas Green	"	Dec. 20	
Cypprian Davison	"	Nov. 1	
Bethuel Brumbly	"	Dec. 5	

CAMPAIGN OF 1756.

Officers & Soldiers Names & quality	Time of Enlisting	Discharged	Dead & Captivated
Elezer Herrick	Apr. 6	Dec. 30	
Ezra Williams	"	" 20	
Daniel Ray	8	Oct. 20	
Benjamin Coye	6	Dec. 5	
Thomas Brayman	12	" 20	
Solomon Ritch	"	Oct. 10	
Benj^m Braymon	"	Dec. 5	
Wm Walbridg	"	" "	
Ephraim Coye	6	Nov. 30	
Asa Davison	9	Oct. 20	
Simeon Rouse	6	Dec. 5	
Isaac Herrington	1	Oct. 12	
Nathan^{ll} Tyler	9	" 13	
James Hagar	1	Dec. 5	
Joseph Commewas	6	Oct. 10	
John Skesucks	8	Dec. 4	
Jams Possetous	9	" "	
John Cousin	10	" 5	
George James	"	" 19	
Williams Charls	11		July 25
Daniel Charls	"	Dec. 5	
Solomon Chebuck	"	" "	
Peter Quotcheats	10	" "	
Pompy March	12	Nov. 8	
John Mezen	13	Dec. 5	
Sam^{ll} Apes	"	" "	
Charles Sharpor	14	" 4	
Joseph Cheets	8		Dyd Nov. 1
Sam^{ll} Tode	1	Dec. 4	

[Indorsed] Capt Eben^r Billing Muster Roll 12 January 1757

[*State Library, Adams Papers.*]

A muster roll of this company, signed by Henry Leddel Must. Mast. General, is dated Camp at Fort Willm Henry, Oct. 13, 1756.

[*State Library, Adams Papers.*]

NINTH COMPANY—CAPT. SEYMOUR.

Jonathan Seymour of Hartford, Captain.
Moses Griswold of Windsor, First Lieutenant.
John Case of Simsbury, Second Lieutenant. [*Colonial Records.*]

Note: These officers were appointed by the Assembly, but no evidence has been found that they were commissioned or that the company was raised.

TENTH COMPANY—CAPT. LEE.

Benjamin Lee of Plainfield, Captain.
Isaac Williams of Pomfret, First Lieutenant.
Benjamin Follett of Windham, Second Lieutenant. [*Colonial Records.*]

Note: These officers were appointed by the Assembly, but no evidence has been found that they were commissioned or that the company was raised.

SECOND REGIMENT—COL. DAVID WOOSTER.

REGIMENTAL OFFICERS.

David Wooster [of New Haven] appointed Colonel and Captain of the first company, March, 1756.
William Whiting [of Norwich] appointed Lieutenant-Colonel and Captain of the Second Company, March, 1756. Discharged Dec. 3.
Jehosaphat Starr [of Middletown] appointed Major and Captain of the third company, March, 1756. Discharged Nov. 2.
Ebenezer Sage of Middletown appointed Commissary, March, 1756.
[*Colonial Records.*]
Charles Whiting, Adjutant, May 2 to Dec. 3, 1756.
[*State Library, War 6, 313.*]
Christopher Palmer, Adjutant, 5 weeks and 2 days.
[*Comptroller's Office, Treasurer's Book.*]
Thaddeus Noble, Armourer, April 23 to Oct. 26, 1756.
[*State Library, War 6, 354.*]

FIRST COMPANY—COL. WOOSTER.

David Wooster [of New Haven], Colonel and Captain.
Isaac Isaacs, Captain-Lieutenant.
[*Colonial Records.*]
———— Hotchkis, Second Lieutenant.
Christopher Palmer [of Stonington], Ensign.
[*Colonial Records.*]

A Victualing Role of Col David Woosters Company from the Time of Entring into the Service to the 12th of May A D 1756 Enclusive

Mens Names	Weeks	Days	Mens Names	Weeks	Days
Col Wooster	6		Obediah Siscatt	5	
Capt Lieu^t Isaacs	6		Jabez Brown	5	2
Lieu^t Hotchkis	5	2	John Lockwood	4	1
Wm Seymour	4	6	Moses Hoyt	4	6
James Castelo	4	6	John Hekock	4	5
John Dimerat	4		Wm Barronet	4	
John Roberts	4	5	Jos Riggs	4	5
Alexand^r Sloan	4	5	Jon^a Brooks	2	2
Wm Monrow	2	3	Ebenez^r Bates	4	6
Josiah Canfield	5	1	Seeley Gregory	4	2
John Greenslitt	4	6	Josiah Lockwood	4	2
Neh^m Gregory	1	5	Jo^s Dulittle	5	1
Saml Selleck	4	6	Philip Tauquin	5	
Mathew Mead	4	6	Albert Williams	5	1
Nathl Westcoat	4	5	James Hekock	3	6
Jos Lockwood	4	2	Jo^s Stebbins	4	1
Ebenez^r Weed	4	5	Wm Cable	4	1
Samuel Brown	5		Elijah Smith	4	1

CAMPAIGN OF 1756.

Mens Names	Weeks	Days	Mens Names	Weeks	Days
John Warren	4	6	David Sluicer	5	
Barak Taylor	4	5	Nathan Washburn	5	
Zebulon Bass	3	2	Jabez Crain	5	2
George Patchen	3	5	Tho⁸ Taney	3	4
Jon⁴ Whelply Jun⁺	4		Jo⁸ Marven	4	6
Daniel Smith	3	1	Henry Wooster	4	3
David Growmon	1	2	Zadok Hawkins	1	5
Tim⁰ Fountain	3	5	Nath¹¹ Dike	4	5
Job Bartram	4	2	James Anoquin	3	
Jo⁸ Peck	3	2	David Bears	1	2
Tho⁸ Stevins	5	5	Sam¹¹ Hull	5	2
Edward Wooster	4	5	Elias Wetmore	2	1
Anthony Carpenter	5		Caleb Suckenup	5	5
Zeph⁴ Tucker	4		Jon⁴ Mansfield	1	
Jon⁴ Gillet	4		John Mills	4	
Daniel Munse	3	6			

[Indorsed] A Victualing Role of Part of Col⁰ Woosters Company May 12ᵗʰ A D 1756

[*State Library, War 5, 339.*]

May A D 1756 A List of men Their Ranks and Half Pay that Were in the Service Last Year and the time of their Entrance into the preasant Service in Colo. David Woosters Company

Mens names	Time of Entrance	Ranks
Isaac Isaacs	April 5	Lieut. & Adj.
Edward Wooster	" 9	Serj.
Wᵐ Seymour	" 8	Corp.
Ebenez⁺ Sloan	" 9	"
Samuel Sellick	" 8	"
Ebenez⁺ Weed	" 9	Serj.
Job Barteram	" 12	"
Elias Wetmore	" 27	Corp.
Caleb Suckenux	" 2	Private
Samuel Hull	" 5	"
Nath¹ Dike	" 9	"
Anthony Carpenter	" 7	"
James Anoguin	" 22	"
James Castelo	" 8	"
John Demerat	" 14	"
John Roberts	" 9	"
Wᵐ Monrow	" 25	"
Josiah Canfield	" 6	"
John Greenslitt	" 8	"
Nehᵐ Gregory	" 30	"
Matthew Mead	" 8	"
Nath¹¹ Westcoat	" 9	"
Joseph Lockwood	" 12	"
Obediah Siscatt	" 7	"
Jabez Brown	" 5	"
John Lockwood	" 13	"
Sam¹¹ Brown	" 7	"
Moses Hoyt	" 8	"
John Hekock	" 9	"
Wᵐ Barronet	" 14	"

SECOND REGIMENT.

Mens names		Time of Entrance		Ranks
Joᵃ Riggs	. . . . . .	April	9	Private
Jonathⁿ Brooks	. . . . . .	"	26	Drum.
David Bears	. . . . . .	May	3	Private
Christopher Palmer	. . . . .			Ensign

N. B Christoph Palmers own half pay & Marching Money was ordered May 22ᵈ 1756

[Indorsed] A Return Role of the Half Pay Officers and Souldiers in Col Wooster's Compʸ May 7ᵗʰ A D 1756

[*State Library, War 5, 319.*]

The company contained 75 men and marched from New Haven.

[*State Library, War 6, 290.*]

SECOND COMPANY—LIEUT.-COL. WHITING.

William Whiting [of Norwich], Lieutenant-Colonel and Captain.
Charles Whiting [of Norwich], First Lieutenant.   [*Colonial Records.*]
Ichabod Fitch, Second Lieutenant.

A Muster Roll of Lieuᵗ Colonel William Whiting's Company with the Time of their Inlistment Dead and Captivated, Discharged, Weeks and Days in Service, Entire Wages &c &c

Officers and Soldiers names and Quallity		Time of Inlistiment		Discharged		Dead & Captivated
William Whiting	Lt. Col.			Dec.	3	
William Whiting	Capt.			"	"	
Charles Whiting	1 Lt.			Oct.	28	
Ichabod Fitch	2 Lt.			Dec.	20	
Joseph Bingham	Serj.	Apl.	5	"	3	
William Billings	"	"	"	"	"	
James Deans	"	"	6	"	"	
Jahleel Peck	"	"	12	"	"	
Joseph Rudd	Corp.	"	"	"	"	
Eliphalet Kimball	"	"	8	"	"	
Solomon Andrews	"	"	"	"	"	
Jeremiah Bingham	"	"	12			Oct. 10
Jabez Fitch	Clerk	"	5	Dec.	3	
Thomas Colking	Drum	"	6	"	"	
Thomas Aslen		"	12	Sep.	14	
John Ashpo		"	3	Dec.	3	
Jacob Andres		"	8	"	"	
John Burdick		"	"	"	"	
John Buckley		"	5			
Lemuel Binghom		"	8	Oct.	25	
Jacob Burnom		"	"	"	1	
Caleb Bishop		"	29	"	13	
Samuel Crandel		"	6	Dec.	3	
James Chappel		"	28	"	"	
Nathan Chappel		"	8	Sep.	26	
James Cyman		"	"	Dec.	3	
Solomon Cooper		"	10	"	"	
Denis Delany		"	5	Nov. 17		

CAMPAIGN OF 1756.

Officers and Soldiers names and Quallity	Time of Inlistiment	Discharged	Dead & Captivated
Jeremiah Downs	Apl. 6	Dec. 3	
John Downs	" 12		Nov. 11
Samuel Drummer	" 21	Nov. 2	
Joseph Edgerton	" 12	Dec. 9	
Jacob Epheram	" 6		Deserted
Samuel Fales	" 20		Sep. 1
Rezen Gear	" 7	Dec. 3	

[Sixteen names missing here.]

Nathaniel Preston	Apr. 8	Sep. 28	
Eliphalet Peehe	" 21	Dec. 3	
Isaiah Rothbon	" 12	" "	
John Robens	May 11	" "	
Benjamin Shaw	" 10	Oct. 1	
Henry Shuntup	Apr. 23	Dec. 3	
Samson Shawcut	" 10	" "	
Zebalon Tubbs	" 12	Sep. 26	
Amos Tannor	May 3	Dec. 3	
Ebenezer Tannor	Apr. 5	" "	
Isaac Tecomwass	" 8	" "	
Abraham Tecomwass	" 10	" "	
Pompy Uncas	" 5	" "	
Samuel Uncas	" 11	" "	
Benjamin Uncas	" 6	" "	
Thomas Walbridg	" "	" 9	
John Wood	" 28	" 3	
Ebenezer Walbridg	" "	" "	
Ebenezer Wood	" 20	Sep. 30	
Jonathan Walden	" 8	Nov. 18	
John Welch	" "		Dec. 15
Ebenezer Welch	" "	Oct. 14	
William Wintworth	" 9	Dec. 3	
Jonathan Wade	" 30	Oct. 13	
John Wamponey	" 7	Dec. 3	
Hezekiah Wright	" 8	" "	
John Lee	" 17		

[Indorsed] Colº Wm Whiting Campain 1756
Ebenr Walbridge
Thos Walbridge

[State Library, Adams Papers.]

William Whiting Lieut. Col. and Capt.
Charles Whiting first Lieutenant
Ichabod Fitch second Lieutenant   at Fort Edward
William Billings Serj.   Sick at Albany
James Deains   "   Sick
Jahleel Peck   "
Joseph Rudd   "
Jabez Fitch   Clerk
Jeremiah Bingham Corp.   At Albany Sick
Eliphelet Kimball   "
Solomon Andrews   "
Jacob Andrews   "

SECOND REGIMENT.

Thomas Colkin Drum
Austin Thomas   Sick at Albany
Ashbow John
Burdie John
Bulkley John
Bingham Lemuel   Sick at fort Edward
Burnham Jacob   Sick at Alb^y
Bishop Caleb   "
Bingham Joseph   Sick at fort Edward
Crandell Samuel
Chappel James   At Fort Edward
Chappel Nathan   Sick at Alb^y
Cyman James
Cooper Solomon
Delany Dennis
Downs Jeremiah
Downs John   Sick
Drummer Samuel   "
Edgerton Joseph
Ephraim Jacob   never Joyned
Fails Samuel   Dead
Geer Reason
Huntington Christopher
Harvy Richard   Sick at Alb^y
Hodgkin Ebenezer   Sick at fort Edwd
Huntly Elisha   Sick at Alb^y
Harris Jonathan
Jackson Joseph   Sick at Alb^y
Teequips Joseph
Jones Jabez   Sick
Jonathan Zachariah   Sick at Albany
Johnson Joseph
Kellogg Joseph
Mynard David   Sick
Mattason David
Minor Andrew
Nanapum John
Preston Nathaniel   Sick at Albany
Peecke Eliphelet
Rathbone Isaiah
Robbins John
Shaw Benjamin   Sick at Alb^y
Shuntup Henry
Shanket Sampson
Tubs Zebulon   Sick at Alb^y
Tanner Amos
Tanner Ebenezer
Tocomwas Isaac
Tocomwas Abraham
Uncus Pompey
Uncus Samuel
Uncus Benjamin
Walbridge Thomas
Wood John
Walbridge Ebenezer
Wood Ebenezer   Sick at fort Edward
Walden Jonathan
Welsh John

Welsh Ebenezer Sick Alby
Wintworth William
Wade Jonathan Sick fort Edwd
Wompanage John
Wright Hezekiah
Pork (?) Nathan

Signed by Henry Leddel Must. Mast. General from the Camp at Fort William Henry Oct. 13, 1756, as a correct muster.

[Indorsed] Lieut Colo Compy Muster Roll 1756

[*State Library, Adams Papers.*]

THIRD COMPANY — MAJ. STARR.

Jehosaphat Starr [of Middletown], Major and Captain.
Nathaniel Porter of Mansfield, First Lieutenant.
Timothy Heirlehy [of Middletown], Second Lieutenant.

[*Colonial Records.*]

Joseph Green, Lieutenant.

A Muster Roll of Major Jehosaphat Starr's Company with the Time of Their Inlistment Dead Captivated Discharged and Deserted Weeks and Days in Service with the Intire Wages 1756

Mens Names and Quality	Time of Inlistment		Discharged		Dead or Captivated
Jehosaphat Starr Maj.	Mar.	26	Nov.	2	
Nathaniel Porter 1st Lieut	"	"	"	12	
Timothy Hierlihy 2d "	"	"	Oct.	28	
Joseph Green "	Oct.	29	Jan.	3	
Cornelius Cornwell Serj	Apr.	19	Dec.	3	
Joseph Green Serj. Maj.	"	3	Oct.	29	
John Sumner Serj.	Mar.	29	Dec.	3	
Samuel Hare "	"	30	"	"	
Samuel Winship Clerk	"	"	"	"	
Aaron Stevens Corp.	Apr.	9	"	"	
Cornelius Cone "	"	12	"	"	
Phenner Ward "	Mar.	30	"	"	
Daniel Sozer (?) "	Apr.	6	"	"	
Joseph Harris Drum	"	"	"	"	
Thomas Anthony [ ]	"	4	[ ]		
Ezekiel Abby	June	8	Oct.	3	
Abner Abby	"	"			Sep. 19
Elijah Barns	Apr.	28	Dec.	3	
Charles Barns	"	10	"	"	
Solomon Barns	"	19	Sep.	27	
John Blake	Mar.	30	Dec.	3	
Marcheus Cole	Apr.	5	Oct.	2	
Ebenezer Crosby	"	27	Dec.	3	
Elihu Cotton	Mar.	30	Oct.	2	
Daniel Cone	"	"	Dec.	3	
John Combs	Apr.	26	Aug.	26	
Ebenezer Cole	"	14	Oct.	7	
John Connor	"	8	Nov.	11	
John Couch	June	7			Nov. 30
Giles Doud	Mar.	30	Nov.	4	
Justice Dailey	Apr.	14	Dec.	3	

SECOND REGIMENT.

Mens Names and Quality	Time of Inlistment	Discharged	Dead or Captivated
Ebenezer Doolittle	Mar. 30	Dec. 3	
Lot Demick	Apr. 8	Nov. 12	
Amos Dormond	June 8		Sep. 4
Jeremiah Everet	" 7	Dec. 3	
Caleb Fairchild	Apr. 1	Jan. 5	
Jeremiah Foster	" 8		Dec. 1
Elisha Fairchild	" 27	Nov. 12	
Robert Fairchild	" 8	Dec. 3	
Phillip Goff	" 13	Oct. 5	
John Green	Mar. 30	Dec. 3	
David Gilbert	Apr. 8	" 1	
Richard Hubbard	Mar. 30	" 3	
Jonathan Hubbard	Apr. 12	" 3	
Samuel Harris	June 8		Aug. 30
Zacheus Higbee	Apr. 19	Dec. 3	
John Keeney	" 10		Deserted May 8
Ezekiel Leete	" 5	Oct. 28	
William Markham	May 3	Dec 3	
James Mattocks	Apr. 2	Nov. 4	
Lewis Mears	Mar. 29	Oct. 15	
Elias Marsh	June 8		Nov. 22
Michael Nathan	" 6	Dec. 3	
Harris Prout	" 2	" "	
Ebenezer Prout	" 9	Sep. 28	
Timothy Patterson	" 1	Nov. 4	
Ephraim Powell	Mar. 30	Dec. 3	
Ezra Robberds	" 29	" "	
Recompence Robberds	" 30	" "	
Moses Rowley	Apr. 27		Deserted May 8
Constant Rogers	" 1	Dec. 3	
David Rice	June 7	" "	
Simeon Robeson	" 8	Sep. 13	
David Starr	Apr. 5	Nov. 4	
Benjamin Strong	" "		Deserted May 8
John Stemson	" 10	Dec. 2	
James Sprage	June 8	" 3	
Thomas Shephard	Mar. 30	Oct. 11	
George Starr	" "	Aug. 24	
Samuel Spelman	Apr. 2	Nov. 15	
Israel Standish	June 7	Jan. 7	
Elias Wetmore	Apr. 12	Nov. 15	
Jonathan Ward	" 6	Dec. 3	
Isaac Woodward	" 2	Sep. 25	
Samuel Wise	" 6	Oct. 5	

[Indorsed] Capt Jehosop^{tt} Starrs Pay roll 1756 Justus Dayly pr^{te}

[*State Library, Adams Papers.*]

A muster roll of this company, signed by Henry Leddel Muster Mast General, is dated Camp at Fort William Henry Oct. 13, 1756.

[*State Library, Adams Papers.*]

CAMPAIGN OF 1756.

A Roll & Manifest of such Men as Serv'd Last Year in the Expedition Against Crown Point &c. and Now Inlisted to Serve in Major Jehosaphet Starrs Company, their half Pay.

Mens Names & Rank in Last Years Service			Mens Names & Ranks in Last Years Service		
Jehosaphat Starr	Capt.	Mar. 26	Recompence Roberts	Private	Mar. 30
John Keeny	Serj.	Apr. 10	Eben' Doolittle	"	" "
Joseph Green	"	" 3	Justice Dayly	"	Apr. 14
Luis Mears	"	Mar. 29	Giles Dowd	"	Mar. 30
Phener Ward	Corp.	" 30	Elias Wetmore	"	Apr. 12
Cornelias Cone	"	Apr. 12	James Murfey	"	" 10
Ezra Roberts	"	" 2	Aaron Stephens	"	" 9
John Conner	Private	" 8	Sam¹ Spellman	"	" 3
Thoˢ Shepard	"	Mar. 30	Dan¹ Cone	"	Mar. 30
Jonᵃ Ward	"	Apr. 6	Lieut. Nath¹¹ Porter		Apr. 26
Ebenʳ Crosby	"	" 27	Ezekiel Abbe		June 8
John Sumner	"	Mar. 29	Jeremiah Averit		" "
Marcus Cole	"	Apr. 5	Timothy Hierlihy		May 31
Thoˢ Anthony	"	" 4	Willm Markham		" 3
John Combs	"	" 26			

[Indorsed] Majʳ Jehosᵗ Starr half pay Roll

[*State Library, War 5, 329.*]

Jehosaphat Star, Major and Captain
Nathaniel Porter, First Lieuᵗ
Timothy Hierliky, Second Lieuᵗ
Cornelius Cornwell ⎫
Joseph Green ⎬ Serjantᵗ
John Sumner ⎪
Aaron Stevens ⎭
Cornelius Cone ⎫
Phineas Ward ⎬ Corporals
Daniel Sizer ⎪
Makens Cole ⎭
Sam¹ Minship, Clerk
Joseph Harris, Drumer
Thomas Anthony
Ezikel Abby
Abner Abby
Elijah Barnes
Charles Barnes
Solomon Barnes
John Blake
Ebenezer Crosbey
Eliheu Cotton
Daniel Cone
John Courby
Ebezer Cole
John Conner
John Couel
Giles Doud
Justine Daily
Ebenezer Doolittle
Lot Dimick
Amos Dermand
Jeremiah Everett
Philip Goff
John Green
Daniel Gilbert
Samuel Hare
Richard Hubbard
Jonathan Hubbard
Samuel Harris
Zacheeus Higbee
Ezikel Lide
William Markham
James Mattock
Lewis Mears
Elias Marsh
Nicholas Nathan
Haris Prout
Ebenezer Prout
Timothy Patterson
Ephraim Powell
Ezra Robarts
Recompense Roberts
Constant Rogers
Daniel Rew
Simeon Robinson
David Starr
John Stinson
James Sprague
Thomas Shepard
Samuel Spelman
Israel Standish

[Indorsed] Col. Thatchers Regt. Contains Ten Companies 1756

[Joseph Thatcher was a Colonel in the Massachusetts service and this roll is found among the archives of that State.]

[*Massachusetts Archives, 94, 296.*]

SECOND REGIMENT. 117

FOURTH COMPANY—CAPT. PORTER.

Nathaniel Porter [of Lebanon], Captain.
Lancaster Gorton, First Lieutenant.
John Durke, Second Lieutenant. [*State Library, War 6, 51, 56, 58.*]

May ye 12th 1756 A List of Men their Rank and Pay and half pay that were In the Service Last year, and are now going Into the Service in Capt. Nath^{ll} Porter^s Company

Mens Names	Rank	Time of entrance	Mens Names	Rank	Time of entrance
Nathl Porter	Lieut. & Doct^r	March 26	Andrew Lisk		April 4
			John McClannin		" 8
Lancaster Gorton	Lieut.	" "	Michael McDonald		" "
Wm Pollard	Serj.	April 8	Makum Mcfarding		" 13
Thos Marvel	Corp.	" 4	James Powers		" 9
John Swaddle	Drum.	" 9	Brister Park		" 8
Wm Lyman	Private	" 4	Benjⁿ Pettis		" 13
Wm Southworth		" "	James Strange		" 9
Benjⁿ Woodworth		" "	Richard Seate		" "
John Bill		" "	Stephen Williams		" 7
John Gould		" 6	Jehiel Woodworth		" "
Eben^r Bill		" "	John Carter		" 29
Bariah Bill		" 8	Jon^{tm} Ryley		" 4
John Brown		" 7	Aaron Cogswell		" "
Moses Cleveland		" 9	Jon^{tn} Everit		" "
Thos Cocheequis		" 15	Benaj^h Larkins		" 26
Alexander Fairly		" 8			

Names of three Men More of ye last year army not Conteind in ye Roll on ye other Side

Nehemiah Clossen	April 8	James Woodworth	April 6
Francis Storer	" 5		

[*State Library, War 5, 311.*]

Corp. John Bill was Serj. from October 1 to December 2.
Andrew Lisk was Corp. from October 1 to December 2.

[*State Library, War 6, 301.*]

The Company contained 74 men.

[*Comptroller's Office, Treasurer's Book.*]

FIFTH COMPANY—CAPT. HARRIS.

James Harris, Jr., Captain.
Isaac Turner, First Lieutenant.
Cornelius Higgens, Second Lieutenant. [*Colonial Records.*]

Capt James Harriss Billiting Bills and Half Pay Roll for Anno 1756

Names		Inlistments	Names		Inlistments
James Harris	Capt.	March 26	Willm Stanton	Clerk	April 1
Isaac Turner	Lieut.	"	Zebulon Dudley	Corp.	7
Cornelius Higgens	Lieut.	"	Joseph Dayton	"	3
Geo. Nettleton	Serj.	April 19	Peter Homan	"	19
Thomas Pierce	"	8	Dan^{ll} Franklen	"	7
Justus Buck	"	9	Barzilla Willey	Drum.	23
John Griswould	"	8	Abraham Bishop		5

CAMPAIGN OF 1756.

Names	Inlistments		Names	Inlistments	
John Tooker	April	5	Joseph Hillard	April	8
George Dibble		7	John Hurd		11
Jabez Bates		8	Aaron Bailey		12
Aaron Cone		9	Timothy Stevens		"
Eliud Graves		"	Joel Thompson		15
Samuel Cone		"	Levy Monger		"
Willm Harrisson		13	Elihu Johnson		5
Sam^{ll} Webster		"	Daniel Bates		8
Willm Giddings		"	Richard Bonfoy		9
Samuel Willey		14	William Hough		7
John Dibble		15	John Doglass Junr		6
Joshua Gladding		"	John Watts	May	7
Silas Gladding		19	Benj. Bunday		10
Peter Murdock		17	Sam^{ll} Whittelsey		3
Richard Beebe		23	Charles Riley		10
David Beebe		"	John Leathercote		11
Martin Beckwith		24	John Rowland		3
Elnathan Smith		7	Benj. Arnolds		16
Caleb Baldwin		"	Joseph Dudley		"
Reuben Kelcey		"	Edward Merrels		15
Peter Hull		"	Dan^{ll} Bagneak	April	17
Nath^{ll} Parker		"	James Simons	May	13
Samuel Tuley		8	Benanivel (?) Bonfoy	April	21
Abraham Stevens		"	David Thomas	May	17
Aaron Stevens		"	Ezekiel Bailey	April	26
Reuben Turner		"	James Stevens		8
Ezra Crain		"	Obediah Oliver	May	21
Thomas Stevens		11	Sam^{ll} Jackson		1
Moses Wright		13	Abner Bushnal		24
Miles Wright		14	Thomas Miller		"
William Hull		8	Samuel Higgins		23

The Whole Company Marched May 25th

[Indorsed] Capt Harris's Billiting and Half Roll

[*State Library, War 5, 322.*]

A List of the men Belonging to Capt James Harris's Company That were in service last Campaign, & in w^t Comp^y they Served.

Mens Names	Dates of Inlistment		Company last in	Rank in Last Year
James Harris Capt.	March	26	his own	Capt.
Isaac Turner Lieut.		"	Pitkin	Serj.
Geor. Nettleton Serj.	April	19	Harris	"
Thos Peirce "		8	"	"
John Griswell "		"	Demick	Clark
Wm Stanton Clark		1	Pitkin	"
Zebelun Dudley Corp.		7	Demick	Corp.
Joseph Dayton "		3	Pitkin	Soldier
John Toocker		5	Demick	"
George Dibble		7	"	"
Aaron Cone		9	Harris	"
Eliud Graves		"	"	"
Wm Gidding		13	"	"
Samuel Willey		14	Lamson	"
Peter Murdock		17	Maj. Whiting	"

SECOND REGIMENT.

Mens Names	Dates of Inlistment	Company last in	Rank in Last Year
Peter Homan	April 19	Pitkin	Soldier
Reuben Kelcey	7	"	"
Daniel Franklen	"	"	"
Samuel Toolly	8	Demick	"
Abraham Stevens	"	Pitkin	"
Aaron Stevens	"	"	"
Reuben Turner	"	"	"
Ezra Crain	"	"	"
Thomas Stevens	11	"	"
Moses Wright	13	"	"
Miles Wright	14	"	"
William Hull	8	Ward	"
Joseph Hillard	"	Harris	"
Timothy Stevens	12	Ward	"
Joel Tompson	15	"	"
Levy Mongar	"	"	"
Elihu Johnson	5	Buckingham	"
Daniel Bates	3	"	" *
Benj. Towner	"	"	"
Richd Bonfoy	9	"	"
William Hough	7	Harris	"
John Leathercoat	May 11	Lampson	"

*This man was either in Capt Buckingham, or Collo Chauncys Company.

Saybrook May 8, 1756

[Indorsed] Capt James Harris half pay Roll.

[*State Library, War 5, 316.*]

A Roll of Such Soldiers as Servd in the Campain of 1755 and now Enlisted into ye Company under Command of Capt James Harris & thereby entitled to half pay from 17 Decemr 1755 to their Enlisting

David Thomas   May 17
Abner Bushnel   24

[The other names are as in the roll above.] [*State Library, War 5, 301.*]

This company contained 76 officers and men and marched from Saybrook. [*State Library, War 6, 234.*]

SIXTH COMPANY — CAPT. WOODWARD.

Israel Woodward, Captain.
Asa Royce, First Lieutenant.
Joel Clark, Second Lieutenant.   [*Colonial Records.*]

A Muster Roll of Capt Israel Woodwards Company in the Expedition against Crown Point Anno 1756.

Names	Quality	Time of Enlistment	Discharged	Deserted
Capt Israel Woodward	Capt.	Mar. 26	Dec. 5	
Asa Royce	Lieut.	" "	" "	
Joel Clark	"	" "	" "	
Oliver Welton	Serj.	Apr. 9	" "	

CAMPAIGN OF 1756.

Names	Quality	Time of Enlistment		Discharged		Deserted
Enoch Curtis	Serj.	Apr.	6	Dec.	5	
David Clark	"	Mar.	30	Sep.	28	
David Woodward	"	Apr.	7	"	"	
Ethan Curtis	Corp.	"	4	Oct.	4	
James Doolittle	"	"	9	"	18	
Joab Hoesington (?)	"	"	4	Dec.	5	
adv^d to Serj. 28 Sep.						
Abiel Robarts	"	"	2	Nov.	2	
adv^d to Serj. 28 Sep.						
Moses Frost	Drum.	"	9	Dec.	5	
Joseph Blake	Centin^l	"	"	Sep.	24	
Israel Calkins	"	"	"	Oct.	18	
Charles Warner	"	"	"	Nov.	2	
Elnathan Prichard	"	"	"	Oct.	20	
Ezekiel Scott	"	"	"	"	24	
adv^d to Corp. 28 Sep.						
Moses Brownson	"	"	"	Dec.	5	
Samuel Lounsbury	"	"	"	Oct.	18	
John Parker	"	"	"	Sep.	6	
John Fenn	"	"	"	Oct.	2	
Samuel Frost	"	"	"	Dec.	5	
Isaac Terril	"	"	"	Oct.	28	
Nathl Weed	"	"	"	"	2	
Wm Munson	"	"	7	Dec.	5	
Jacob Guild	"	"	"	Sep.	28	
Jeremi Gillett	"	"	"	Dec.	5	
Peleg Woodworth	"	"	"	Sep.	26	
Benj^a Ellis	"	"	"	Dec.	5	
John Gibbs	"	"	"	Sep.	28	
Samuel Woodward	"	"	"	"	"	
Willm White	"	"	"	Oct.	28	
Hezek^h Davenport	"	"	"	Nov.	20	
Benj^a Woodworth	"	"	"	"	"	
Reuben Woodworth	"	"	"	Oct.	16	
Stephen Dullf	"	"	4	Sep.	6	
Samuel Adams	"	"	2	Nov.	28	
Ephraim Allyn	"	"	3	Sep.	22	
Simeon Stow	"	Mar.	30	Nov.	30	
John Barrett	"	"	"	"	22	
William Horton	"	"	"	Dec.	14	
Samuel Pike	"	Apr.	2	Nov.	10	
adv^d to Corp. Sep. 28						
Judah Palmer	"	Mar.	29	Sep.	28	
Asa Brownson	"	"	"	Nov.	15	
John Brownson	"	"	"	Dec.	5	
Parmineus Bunne	"	Apr.	2	"	"	
Jonath^n Wright	"	"	"	Nov.	5	
Elijah Clark	"	"	"	Dec.	10	
Nathan Benham	"	"	3	"	5	
Voluntine Hitchcock	"	"	4	"	"	
Joel Roberts	"	"	"	Nov.	5	
Israel Squire	"	"	"	July	20	
Ezekiel Curtis	"	"	2	Dec.	5	
John Thomas	"	"	"	Nov.	2	
Remēber Baker	"	"	5	"	5	
Nathl Hitchcock	"	"	4	Dec.	5	
Joseph Bunnel	"	"	3	Nov.	12	

SECOND REGIMENT.

Names	Quality	Time of Enlistment	Discharged	Deserted
Jehiel Dayton	Centin[l]	Apr. 3	Oct. 26	
Benj[a] Williams	"	" 6	Nov. 5	
Tho[s] Bray	"	" 4	" 2	
Nath[l] Messenger	"	" 5	Dec. 5	
Henman Worster	"	" 6	Sep. 30	
Nath[l] Pardy	"	" 7	" 28	
Eliab Parker	"	" 9	Dec. 5	
Joseph Foot	"	" 2	Nov. 5	
Luke Fox	"	" 5	Oct. 28	
John Haystens	"	" "		Oct. 2
Nathan Wright	"	" "	Dec. 5	
John Strickland	"	" 7	Oct. 2	
Jotham Hall	"	" "	Aug. 25	
John Butler	"	" "	Sep. 29	
Peleg Spencer	"	" 10	" 27	
Benj[a] Aly	"	" 8	Nov. 28	
Stephen Bagley	"	" 9		May 9
Nathan Woodw[d]	Clerk	Mar. 26	Oct. 18	
Seth Thayer	Cent[l]	Aug. 25	Dec. 5	
Oliver Terril	"	Apr. 9	" "	

[*State Library, Adams Papers.*]

A Roll & Manifest of Such Men as Servd last Year in y[e] Expedition against Crown Point &c and now Enlisted to Serve in Cap[t] Woodward's Company their half pay Stated &c

Mens Names & Rank in last Years Service			Mens Names & Rank in last Years Service		
Asa Roys Lieut.	Apr.	8	William Hough	Apr.	10
Enoch Curtis Serj.	Mar.	30	John Hasting	"	6
Ethan Curtis "	Apr.	5	Benjamin Eley	"	8
Joel Clark "	Mar.	29	Jothan Hall	"	"
Simeon Stow Cent[l]	"	30	Ezek[ll] Scott	"	9
John Barrett	"	"	James Doolittle	"	"
Samuel Pike	Apr.	2	Moses Brunson	"	"
Parmen[s] Bunnel	"	4	Peleg Woodworth	"	"
Jonath[n] Wright	"	"	Ruben Woodworth	"	"
Israel Squire	"	5	Benjamin Woodworth	"	"
Remember Baker	"	"	William White	"	"
Nath[l] Hitchcoock	"	4	Jesse Perken (?)	"	2
Henman Wooster	"	11	Moses Frost Drum.	"	9
Jacob Hosington	"	2	Samuel Frost Centinel	"	"
Sam[ll] Adams	"	"	John Fenn Jun[r]	"	"
Nath[ll] Messenger	"	12	John Calkin	"	"
Joseph Foot	"	3	John Parker	"	5
John Strickland	"	8	Elieb Parker	"	9

SEVENTH COMPANY — CAPT. GRANT.

Noah Grant [of Windsor], Captain.
Medina Fitch [of Windsor], First Lieutenant.

[*Colonial Records.*]

Josiah Gates, Second Lieutenant.

A Muster Role of Cap[t] Noah Grants Company and y[e] Time of Enlisting & Discharged & Num[r] of Weeks in Servis

CAMPAIGN OF 1756.

Names and Quality	Time Enlisted	Discharged	Dead and Captivated
Capt. Noah Grant	Mar. 26		Sep. 20
Lieut. Med[h] Fitch	" "	Dec. 1	
Lieut. Josiah Gates	" "	" "	
Serj. Hez[h] Parsons	June 8	" 20	
Serj. Solomon Wells	Apr. 8	Sep. 30	
Serj. Benajah Tubs	" 9		Oct. 20
Serj. Ozias Bissell	June 9	Oct. 11	
Clark Nathan Webb	May 7	" 10	
Serj. John Shields	Sep. 30	Nov. 14	
Corp. John Shields	Apr. 1	Sep. 30	
Corp. Eli Parker	" 9	Dec. 1	
Corp. Will[m] Dodge	" 1	Nov. 9	
Corp. Benj[n] Davis	" 8	Dec. 3	
Drum. Nath[l] Pirce	May 28	" "	
Jonathan Birge	June 9	" 1	
Nath[ll] Bordman	" "	" "	
Jese Belknap	Apr. 9	" 9	
John Bingham	" 12	Nov. 17	
Aaron Beach alias Jn[o] Trible	June 9	Dec. 3	
John Chambers	Apr. 2	" 30	
Jonah Chapman	" 4	" 1	
Solo[n] Cooper	June 9	" 30	
Nath[ll] Dart	" "	" 1	
Jedediah Darling	" "	" "	
David Dunham	Apr. 1	" 6	
Richard Downer	" 20		Deserted Sep. 16
Alixander Dodge	" 6	Dec. 1	
John Dodge	" "	" "	
Will[m] Eaton	" 8	" 24	
Thomas Ellsworth	May 28	Sep. 28	
Lott Fuller	June 9	Dec. 1	
Daniel Filley	" 8	Nov. 9	
Solomon Hall	Apr. 8	Dec. 1	
Ichabod Hinkly	" "	" 25	
David Hatch	" "	" 1	
Elisha Hubard	" 1	Nov. 25	
Benj[n] Hubard	" 27	Dec. 1	
Petter Hambleton	" 1	" "	
David Johnson	" "	" "	
Hez[h] Kilborn	" 8	Nov. 20	
Elijah Kilborn	" 4	Dec. 1	
Noah Lyon	" 8		Oct. 20
Joseph Luce	" "	Nov. 9	
W[m] Josiah Lewes	" 11	Dec. 1	
Prince Negro	" 4	Oct. 30	
Jupeter Negro	" "	Dec. 13	
Josiah Owen	" 8		Oct. 18
Josiah Pinny	" 9	Dec. 1	
Eanos Parker	" 3	" "	
Daniel Pirce	" 9	" "	
Daniel Rust	June 9	Nov. 9	
Joseph Rogers	" "	Dec. 20	
Rufus Root	Apr. 8		Dec. [ ]
Joshua Read	" [ ]	Dec. 1	
James Simons	" 9	" 5	
George Smith	" 3	" 1	

SECOND REGIMENT.

Names and Quality	Time Enlisted	Discharged	Dead and Captivated
Abner Scovell	Apr. 9	Dec. 1	
Soloⁿ Sipio	" 7	" "	
Isaac Tucker	June 21		
George Tryon	" "	Dec. 30	
Caleb Talcutt	" 9	Oct. 30	
Zephaniah Thayr	" "	Dec. 1	
James Tattington	Apr. 4		Oct. 10
Jacob White	" 8	Dec. 3	
Israel Warner	May 29	" 1	
Salvanus Willebe	Apr. 8	" 20	
Timothy Wheeler	" "	" 24	
Samuel Wells	" 21	Oct. 11	
Eph^m Wells	" 1	" 19	
Ichabod Wells	June 9		Sep. 15
James Webb	Apr. 8	Jan. 1	
Zebulon Warterman	" 29	Dec. 1	
Willm Young	" 12		Oct. 23
Joseph Sparks	May 1		Never Joyned
James Hunt	June 22		" "

[Indorsed] Captain Noah Grants Muster Roll Jan^{ry} 1757
Isaac Tucke^r
Nathl Dart

[State Library, Adams Papers.]

A muster roll of the same company, signed by Henry Leddel Muster Mast General, is dated Camp at Fort William Henry Oct. 13, 1756.

[State Library, Adams Papers.]

May A D 1756   A List of Men, their Ranks, & Half Pay that were in the Service last Year, & the Time of their Entrance into the preasant Service in Capt Grants Company. Inlisted by Lieu^t Gates

Mens Names	Time of Entn.	Ranks
Benajah Tubbs	April 4	Corp^l
Abner Scovel	9	Private
Willm Dodge Junr	6	"
James Webb	8	"
Ephraim Wells Junr	1	"
Jonah Chapman	2	"
Saml Wells	20	"
Prince Negro	4	"
Jupitur Negro	4	"
Solomon Scipio	7	"
Peter Ambleton	1	"

The eight beneath Enlisted by Capt Grant himself

Serj. Hez Parsons	June 8	
Corp. Ozias Bissell	9	
Corp. Jno Trebble	9	
Daniel Rust	9	
Joseph Rogers	9	
Israel Warner	May 30	
Zeph^h Thayre	June 9	
Daniel Filley	8	

CAMPAIGN OF 1756.

Mens Names	Time of Entn.	Ranks
Lieut Noah Grant	Mar 26	
Isaac Tucker	June 21	
George Tryon	21	

[Indorsed] Lieut Joseph Gates Half Pay Roll for Men Enlisted by him & allso Capt Noah Grant & 8 men listed by him Half Pay

[*State Library, War 5, 323.*]

Names & quality of Men In Capt Grants Company who were in last Campain & now listed by Lieut Fitch

Lieut Medina Fitch	March 26	Joshua Reed	April	8
Serjt John Schield	April 1	Solomon Hall		8
Corporal Noah Lyon	8	Eli Parker		9
Benja Daviss	8	William Young		12
Solomon Wells	8			

[*State Library, War 5, 315.*]

EIGHTH COMPANY—CAPT. RUGGLES.

Benjamin Ruggles [of New Milford], Captain.
Samuel Elmor, First Lieutenant.
Jehiel Barnum [of Kent], Second Lieutenant. [*Colonial Records.*]

May 7th 1756 Capt Benj Ruggles Half Pay Roll for Such as were in last years Service & are now in his Compa for ye Service of the Current Year

Names and Rank of those who were in ye last years Service & are to have Half Pay	Enlisted April	Names and Rank of those who were in ye last years Service & are to have Half Pay	Enlisted April
Serjt Hez Baldwin	6	Henry Burhorn	12
" Isaac Morse	"	Israel Canfield	11
" David Barnum	8	Elijah Slossen	6
Centls Isaac Buck	6	Dan. Barns	"
Robert Summers	"	Benedick Woodward	19
Timo Durkee	"	George White	7
Moses Fisher	"	Israel Rowlee	8
Joseph Lines	"	Caleb Swelling	13
Isaac Botchford	8	Nathll Devine	14
Orrisimus Titus	14	Jonatha Morgan	8
Benja Weller	12	Reuben Prime	"
Eli Robards	8	Lieut Benja Ruggles	7
Edward Colver	12	Lieut Jehiel Barnum	"

[Indorsed] Capt Benj Ruggles half pay Role

[*State Library, War 5, 303.*]

The company contained 75 officers and men and marched from New Milford. [*State Library, War 6, 314.*]

NINTH COMPANY—CAPT. PRESTON.

Ephraim Preston of Wallingford, Captain.
Benjamin Hyne of Milford, First Lieutenant.
Asa Morris of New Haven, Second Lieutenant.

[*Colonial Records.*]

Note: These officers were appointed by the Assembly, but no evidence has been found that they were commissioned or that the company was raised.

SECOND REGIMENT.

TENTH COMPANY — CAPT. LEE.

Josiah Lee of Farmington, Captain.
Jonathan Jones of Saybrook, First Lieutenant.
Peleg Redfield of Killingworth, Second Lieutenant.

[*Colonial Records.*]

Note: These officers were appointed by the Assembly, but no evidence has been found that they were commissioned or that the company was raised.

THIRD REGIMENT—COL. NATHAN WHITING.

REGIMENTAL OFFICERS.

Nathan Whiting [of New Haven] appointed Colonel and Captain of the first company, March, 1756. Discharged Dec. 2.
Nathan Payson [of Hartford] appointed Lieutenant-Colonel and Captain of the second company, March, 1756.
John Patterson [of Farmington] appointed Major and Captain of the third company, March, 1756. Discharged Dec. 5.
Thaddeus Mead of Norwalk appointed Commissary, March, 1756.
[*Colonial Records.*]
John Lee, Surgeon's Mate, from April 5 to Dec. 9, 1756.
[*State Library, War 6, 357.*]
Samuel Gaylord, Adjutant, served 8 months and 25 days.
[*State Library, War 6, 353.*]

FIRST COMPANY—COL. WHITING.

Nathan Whiting [of New Haven], Colonel and Captain.
Amos Hitchcock [of New Haven], Captain-Lieutenant.
[*Colonial Records.*]
Samuel Gaylord [of Middletown], Captain-Lieutenant.
Richard Darrow, Second Lieutenant
Ezekiel Lewis, Ensign. [*Colonial Records.*]
Samuel Hawkins, Ensign.

A Muster Roll of Col° Nathan Whiting's Company with the Time of their Inlistment, Dead, Deserted, Descharg'd Weeks and Days in Service, at what p^r week, Entire Wages &c 1756

Mens names & quality	Time of Inlistm^t	Discharged	Dead
Nathan Whiting Col°	Mar. 26	Dec. 2	
Amos Hitchcock Capt L^t	" "	Oct. 28	
Richard Darrow 2^d L^t	" "	Sep. 20	
Samuel Gaylord Capt L^t	Oct. 29	Nov. 30	
Ezekiel Lewis Ens.	Mar. 26	June 6	
Samuel Hawkins Ens.	June 6	Dec. 1	
Jos. Sperry Serj^t Maj^r	Mar. 31	" "	
Thomas Pain Serj^t	May 21	" 2	
Daniel Tuttle "	Apr. 5	Oct. 12	
Jonathan Palmer "	" 17		Sep. 27
John Mitchel "	" 14	Dec. 18	
Samuel Hawkins Clerk	" 8	June 6	
Tim° Talmage Drum Maj^r	Mar. 31	Oct. 12	
Joel Potter Drum^r	Apr. 10	" "	
Ebenezer Beech Corp^l	" 5	Nov. 9	
Jabez Hotskiss "	" 6	Oct. 13	
Jesse Johnson "	" 12	Sep. 30	

THIRD REGIMENT. 127

Mens names & quality	Time of Inlistm^t		Discharged		Dead	
Jesse Johnson Serj^t	Sep.	3	Dec.	18		
Isaac Johnson Corp^l	Apr.	20	Nov.	10		
Abraham Cooper priv^t	"	24	Dec.	1		
Amasa Hitchcock	"	5	"	"		
Amos Tuttle	"	8			Deserted Aug. 1	
Bilious Hill	"	15	Oct.	2		
Caleb Gilbert	"	6	Dec.	18		
Cornelius Johnson	"	9	Oct.	11		
David Wheadal	"	24	Dec.	1		
Dan Mansfield	"	26	"	12		
Dan Carrington	"	"	Oct.	15		
Daniel Fox	"	5	"	11		
David Thompson	"	22	May	23		
David Ludington	"	23			Sep.	13
Elijah Hoskins	"	12	Dec.	1		
Eliphalet Thompson	"	6	"	"		
Ebenezer Walder	"	12	"	18.		
Enos Sperry	"	17			Nov.	10
Frederick Chapple	May	10	Dec.	1		
George Miller	Apr.	15	"	"		
Hezekiah Tuttle	"	5	"	"		
Jacob Curtis	"	"	"	"		
Joseph Warner	"	19	Oct.	13		
John Hill	"	21	Nov.	10		
James Tuttle	"	10	"	29		
James Thomas	"	12	Oct.	11		
Jonathan Wade	"	6			Sep.	17
Isaac Pain	"	"	Dec.	1		
John Rollins	Mar.	31			Deserted Apr. 15	
John Tucker	Apr.	16	Dec.	6		
James Plant	"	17			Deserted Aug. 1	
James Powers	"	20			" " 27	
Joseph Chaucus	"	7	Dec.	1		
James Adkin Bralton	"	8	Oct.	11		
James Ludington	"	23			Sep.	3
John Russuck	"	21			Deserted July 1	
John Seebury	"	19	Dec.	2		
Isaac Todd	"	20	"	1		
Joseph Ball	"	5	"	"		
Joseph Tilison	"	29	"	"		
Matthias Smith	"	30	"	"		
Nathaniel Harris	"	6	Oct.	11		
Noah Merrill	"	9	"	2		
Nathl Andrus	"	5	Dec.	1		
Philemon Potter	"	"	"	"		
Phelix Powel	May	10				
Phenias Tyler	Apr.	24	Oct.	15		
Richard Lucas	May	4	Dec.	1		
Roger Bissell	Apr.	15			Deserted July 1	
Samuel Hugens	"	5	Oct.	11		
Stephen Thomas	"	20	Nov.	29		
Stephen Cooper	"	12	Dec.	1		
Silvanus Bachus	"	21	Oct.	10		
Thomas Trickey	"	6	Dec.	1		
Thomas Dikes	"	5				
Timothy Bristol	"	"	Dec.	1		
Timothy Turner	"	3	"	"		

128   CAMPAIGN OF 1756.

Mens names & quality	Time of Inlistm[t]		Discharged	Dead
William Lewis	Apr.	6	Oct. 13	
William Mansor	"	5	Nov. 10	
William Denslow	"	"	Dec. 1	
William Bassett	"	8		Deserted Aug. 1
William Jacobs	"	5	Oct. 11	
William Duplex	Mar.	26	Dec. 10	
Zepheniah Webster	Apr.	29		

[Indorsed] Col° Nathan Whiting Pay Roll January 1757

[*State Library, Adams Papers.*]

Noah Merrls	April	9
Billious Hill	"	"
Gorge Miller	"	14
Roger Bisel	"	"
Ezekiel Lewis (?) Sarg.	March	26
Matthias Smith "	April	30
Nathan Whiting Esq[r] Lieu[t] Co[ll]	March	26
Amos Hitchcock 1 Lieu[t].	"	"
Richard Darrow 2 "	"	"
Corp. Enos Sperry	May	15
James Powers	"	"
Stephen Thomas	"	"
Thomas Dike	April	19

[Indorsed] Col° Nathan Whitings half pay Roll

[*State Library, War 5, 326.*]

SECOND COMPANY—LIEUT.-COL. PAYSON.

Nathan Payson [of Hartford], Lieutenant-Colonel and Captain.
Samuel Gaylord [of Middletown], First Lieutenant.
Timothy Seymour [of Hartford], Second Lieutenant.

[*Colonial Records.*]

A List of the Half pay Men in My Company
Cap[t] Sam[ll] Gaylord

Serj. Josiah Savage	April 1	Savage Triscott	June 25
Corp. Daniel Kellom	5	Corp. Charles Ripley	1
Elezar Gaylord	1	Serj. Israel Harding	1
Wait Wilcocks	1	Serj. William Manning	1
Robert Stevenson	1	Eleazor Smith	1
Joseph Slate	2	Clerk John Barnard	1
John Reeve	2	Serj. Marvrick Johnson	1
John Fox	1	Serj. Noah Chappel	1
John Gypson	6	Eliphelit Carpenter	15
Thomas Loveland	5	Littlefield Nash	14
William Brown	6	Thomas Goodale	April 27
Rufus Yarrington	14	Jonathan Sparks	June 13
Jabez Tuttle	May 31	Roger Clerk	May 23
Timothy Peck	31	Daniel Corbin	June 15
Timothy Ranney	24	Thomas Bugbee	1

THIRD REGIMENT.

The Names of those Three y^t are in Albany Gould Upon Suspecion of Burning a house on the house on ye East side of half Moon
Timothy Peck of Col Payson Comp
Elijah Thomas Cap Hide Compay
    Bushop Co^l Lee's Compay

[Indorsed]   Capt Saml Gaylord half pay Roll

[*State Library, War 5, 303.*]

A Muster Roll of half Pay in Nathan Payson Coll's Company.

Mens Names	Quality	Time of Enlisting	Mens Names	Quality	Time of Enlisting
Saml Gaylord	Capt	March 26	Rufus Yarington	Soldier	April 14
Wm Manning	Serj.	June 1	Tim^o Peck	"	May 31
Israel Harding	"	" "	Jabez Tutler	"	" "
Josiah Savage	"	April 1	Timothy Ranny	"	" 24
Charles Ripley	Corp.	June 1	Thos Goodell	"	April 27
Danl Kelom	"	April 5	Noah Chappell	"	June 1
Wait Willcox	Soldier	" 1	Samuel Wardin	"	" "
Robt Stevenson	"	" "	Thos Bugbee	"	" "
John Fox	"	" "	Eliph^t Carpenter	"	" 15
John Reive	"	" 2	Danl Corbin	"	" "
Joseph Slate	"	" "	Marvick Johnson	Serj.	" 1
Wm Brown	"	" 6	Eleazer Gaylard	Corp.	April 1
John Gipson Junr	"	" "	John Barnard	Serj.	June 18
Joshua Rogers	"	" "	Eleazer Smith	Corp.	" 1
Thos Loveland	"	" 5	Jonathan Sparks	"	" 18

[Indorsed]   Co^l Nathan Paysons Half Pay Roll

[*State Library, War 5, 307.*]

Aaron Beach served in this company for about seven weeks beginning April 8; later was Armourer in Gen. Lyman's regiment.

[*State Library, War 6, 348.*]

This company contained 76 officers and men, and marched from Woodstock and Windham.

[*State Library, War 6, 304.*]

THIRD COMPANY—MAJ. PATTERSON.

John Patterson [of Farmington], Major and Captain.
Nicholas Nichols [of Stratford], First Lieutenant.
Samuel Brooks, Second Lieutenant.
                          [*Colonial Records.*]
Ezekiel Lewis, Second Lieutenant.

Officers and Soldiers Names and Quality		Time of Inlistment	Discharg^d	Dead
John Paterson	Major	Mar. 26	Dec. 5	
Nicholas Nichols	Lieut.	" "	" 6	
Samuel Brooks	"	" "		May 28
Ezekiel Lewis	"	May 29	Dec. 6	
David Pike	Serj.	Mar. 30	Nov. 17	
David Andrus	"	" "	" 12	

CAMPAIGN OF 1756.

Officers & Soldiers Names and Quality		Time of Inlistment		Discharg'd		Dead	
Timothy Brooks	Serj.	Mar.	30	Oct.	24		
Samuel Gridly	"	"	"	"	30		
Nathaniel Churchill	Clark	Apr.	2	"	"		
Gideon Goodrich	Corp.	Mar.	30	"	24		
Bille Leuis	"	Apr.	2	Dec.	2		
Benony Lomis	"	Mar.	31	Oct.	24		
Samuel Bidwell	"	"	30	"	"		
Noah Gridly	Drum	Apr.	3	"	30		
Elihu Andrus		Mar.	30	Dec.	2		
Elisha Andrus		Apr.	3			Dec.	7
Joseph Brewer		Mar.	31			Sep.	30
Daniel Brown		Apr.	3			"	22
Daniel Robison		"	5			Nov.	10
Joseph Bobin		"	2	Dec.	2		
John Collins		Mar.	30	Oct.	19		
Isaac Chamberlin		"	29			Oct.	20
John Cole		Apr.	5			Sep.	21
Nathaniel Dewey		"	1	Oct.	24		
Moses Dickerson		Mar.	31	"	30		
Stephen Dwolf		"	27	Dec.	1		
William Ebenathy		"	30	"	5		
Francis Fleming		Apr.	1	"	2		
Elisha Fox		"	6	"	5		
Ephraim Goodrich		"	3	"	2		
Jonathan Gains		"	5	Oct.	15		
Jeremiah Gillitt		"	2			July	26
Jonathan Griswold		"	5			"	17
Timothy Goodrich		Mar.	30			Aug.	30
Jonathan Hough		"	"	Dec.	1		
Abraham Hills		Apr.	2	Oct.	20		
John Holms		"	5	Dec.	1		
Salah Hubbard		"	3	"	2		
Benjamin Hecoks		Mar.	30	"	"		
Phineis Rowlison		Apr.	5	May	31		
John Jacobs		"	"	Dec.	1		
John Lord		"	"	"	15		
David Lensey		"	2	Nov.	18		
Thomas Lusk		Mar.	27	"	30		
John Lensey		"	"	"	12		
Theopleas Morison		"	30	"	"		
Elnathan North		"	27	Oct.	24		
Joseph Norton		Apr.	8	Dec.	1		
Joseph Peters		"	3	"	"		
Amariah Plumb		"	"	"	"		
Stephen Person		Mar.	30	"	"		
Charls Rylee		"	"	Nov.	16		
Samuel Squier		"	29	"	12		
Moses Squier		"	"	"	"		
Nathan Sparks		Apr.	3			Dec.	2
Enoch Stratton		Mar.	31	Oct.	25		
Joseph Segers		Apr.	10	Dec.	1		
Jonathan Treet		"	5	"	"		
Elisha Titerson		"	3	Nov.	10		
Stephen Tayler		"	"	Aug.	15		
Ezekiel Wright		"	6	Oct.	24		
Amos Williams		"	3	Dec.	1		
Joseph Ware		Mar.	31	"	"		

THIRD REGIMENT.

Officers and Soldiers Names and Quality	Time of Inlistment	Discharg^d	Dead
Samuel Wright	Apr. 3	Dec. 2	
John Williams	Mar. 30	" "	
Nicholas Williams	Apr. 6	" "	
James Wonor (?)	Mar. 30	Oct. 30	
John Japhit	Apr. 4	Dec. 2	
David Tousey	" 5	Nov. 16	
Wonks Nobigin	" 2	Dec. 2	
Samuel Poley	" "	June 28	
Ambo Negro	Mar. 30	Nov. 1	
Bristol Negro	Apr. 5	Dec. 1	
Thomas Tossitt	" "		Sep. 28
Samuel Burd	Mar. 30	Dec. 1	
Charls Bartlitt	" "	" 2	
Jonathan Bidwill	Apr. 6	" 15	
Samuel Adam	" 8	Nov. 15	
John Caucucor (?)	" 5		{ Deserted ye Later End of Aprell
James Welkeson	Mar. 30		{ In Ap^r D^rm of Co^ll Wost[ ] Regiment

[Indorsed] Major John Patterson's
Muster Roll Jan^ry 1757
Jno. Holmes

[State Library, Adams Papers.]

A muster roll of the same company, signed by Henry Leddel Muster Mast General, is dated Camp at Fort William Henry Oct. 13 1756

[State Library, Adams Papers.]

An accompt of Maj^r John Paterson's Company when they Enlisted, & their Respective Billetings 1756

Bela Lewis	April 2	James Wover	March 20
Rossell Hubbert	" 3	John Carvenear	April 5
Elisha Tilletson	" "		

[The other names are as in the previous roll.]

[State Library, War 5, 340.]

List of those y^t ware in ye service Last yere and ye Capesaty thay ware in w^h ye time of Enlistment in ye presnt Expedison w^t Majer Paterson and how many Days thay ware under half paye with ye sume Due:

Capt. John Paterson	March 26	Ameriah Plum	April 3
Sarg. David Pike	March 30	Elishua Tillerson	" "
" Temithy Brooks	" "	Jonath^n Hough	March 30
" Nath^ll Churchell	April 3	Sam^ll Bird	" "
Corp^l Belle Lewis	" 2	Stephen Person	March 30
John Lord	" 5	Epaham Goodrith	April 3
Nath^ll Devey	" 1	Amos Willems	" "
Joseph Peters	" 5	Charles Bartlet	March 30
Elihu Andrus	March 30	Enoch Straton	" 31
John Collens	" "	Benone Lomis	" "
John Lensey	" 27	Joseph Ware	" "
Francs Flaming	April 1	Theophlus Moreson	" 30
Stephen Dewolf	March 27	Benj^a Hecok	" "
Elnathan North	" "	John Willems	" "
Isaac Chamberlan	" 29	Elishua Foox	April 6

CAMPAIGN OF 1756.

Rosell Hubard	April	3	James Woes	March	30
David Tousey	"	5	Sam[ll] Adem	April	8
Wonks	"	2	Sam[ll] Wright	"	3
Neckels Willams	"	6			
added June 26th 1756					
Lieu[t] Nicholas Nickols	June	1	John Japhet	June	1

[Indorsed] Maj[r] Jn[o] Patersons Half Pay Roll

[State Library, War 5, 320.]

FOURTH COMPANY — CAPT. SLAPP.

John Slapp [of Mansfield], Captain. [Colonial Records.]
Ephraim Keyes [of Ashford], First Lieutenant. [State Library, War 6, 60.]
Solomon Grant, Second Lieutenant. [Colonial Records.]
Israel Harding, Lieutenant.
Robert Durkee, Lieutenant.

A muster Role of Cap[t] John Slapps Compeny With The acount of the mens Enlistments to the Day of thair Dis Charge

Mens Names and Rank	Time of Enlistment		Time when Discharged		Dead or Captivated
Capt. John Slapp	Mar.	26	Oct.	26	
Lieut. Ephareham Keys	"	"	"	11	
Lieut. Sal[a] Graint	"	"			June 25
Sarj. Hana[r] Woodward	Apr.	2			" "
Sarj. Robart Durke	"	8	Oct.	29	
Sarj. Isack Daxter	Mar.	30	Dec.	2	
Nathan Rise	May	3	"	"	
Corp. Edward Hutcher[ ]	Mar.	30			June 25
Corp. John Tomson	Apr.	2			Deserted Aug. 8
Corp. Ebenes[r] Bicknol	"	"	Nov.	17	
Corp. Josiah Roote	"	25	Oct.	14	
Clark John Wodkins	"	6			Oct. 8
Drum Charets Hunt	May	11			Deserted May '24
Ephram Kiys	Apr.	1	Dec.	2	
William Beckiat	"	2	"	"	
Humphary Richardson	"	"			June 25
Josiah Reede	"	"	Sep.	21	
Joseph Brown	"	"	Dec.	1	
Azariah Wales	"	"			June 25
Nichols Worters	"	"	Oct.	18	
Sipe Wood	"	"	Oct.	27	
Jeames Chaghorn (?)	"	"	"	26	
Jeames Chambers	"	24	June	26	
Joseph Willson	"	3	Oct.	11	
Jonathan Bill	"	4	Nov.	12	
Banj. Cagshall	"	"	Oct.	8	
Josiah Duning	"	"			
Jeames Palmer	"	"	Oct.	8	
Aron Strong	"	"	"	15	
Clamant Neff	"	5	Dec.	2	
Timethy Ladd	"	"	"	1	
Ruben Alwood	"	"	Oct.	8	
Gurdn Fowler	"	"	Sep.	18	

THIRD REGIMENT.

Mens Names and Rank	Time of Enlistment		Time when Discharged		Dead or Captivated
John Ginings	Apr.	6	Aug.	12	
Silas Flinte	"	"	Dec.	2	
Nathan Write	"	"	"	"	
Abraham Rust	"	"	Oct.	8	
John Praston	"	"	Dec.	2	
George Cateny	"	"	"	"	
Jeans Sheermon	"	"	Oct.	15	
David Cross	"	"	Nov.	11	
Jonathan Eastmon	"	"			June 25
Salvanis Snowe	"	7	Dec.	2	
Joseph Carpander	"	"	Jan.	26	
Amas Praston	"	8			Oct. 15
Fradrack Cortis	"	"	Dec.	2	
Daniel Canade	"	"	Oct.	17	
Zabediah Caborn	"	"			June 25
George Caborn	"	"	Dec.	2	
John Badlock	"	"	Oct.	8	
Samuell Carpand'	"	"	Sep.	10	
Robart Backer	"	"	Oct.	4	
Epharahm Deeain	"	"	Nov.	1	
Tors Cooper	"	"	Oct.	8	
Abraham Downer	"	9	"	"	
Arune Snowe	"	"	"	"	
Timethy Glushar	"	"			Oct. 11
Ezare Sibely	"	"	Oct.	8	
Joseph Rider	"	"	Dec.	2	
Staven Johnson	"	10	Oct.	8	
Elesar Robartson	"	"	Dec.	2	
Joseph Hopkins	"	12			Deserted Apr. 19
Richard Wabber	"	"	Jan.	9	
Zachariah Deeain	"	"	Oct.	7	
Jonathan Sanger	"	14	Aug.	12	
Barnabus Eddy	"	"	Dec.	2	
Hasaciah Carpendr	"	"	"	"	
Thomas Roote Jur	"	19	Oct.	8	
Neale Eastmon	"	"	Aug.	16	
Joseph Pumham	"	4	Oct.	8	
John Farnam	"	20	"	4	
Daniel Knolten	"	19	Dec.	2	
John Amedown	"	21			Oct. 19
Daniel Squiar	May	6	Nov.	11	
Peter Whitne	"	"	Oct.	15	
John Harrick	"	20			Deserted
Edman Rading	"	10	Dec.	2	
Benjmon Davis Ju'	Apr.	12	Oct.	8	
Israel Harding Leut.	July	12	Dec.	3	
Robert Durkee Lieut.	Oct.	29	"	"	
James Chamberlin Sarj.	June	26	Oct.	8	
Joseph Carpenter Corp.	"	"	Dec.	2	
Neal Eastman Drum	Aug.	16	Oct.	17	

[Indorsed]   Cap^{tn} John Slapps Muster Roll 1756
[*State Library, Adams Papers.*]

Zebadiah Coburn of Windham, was captured June 15 by the Indians about 12 miles north of Osuck Fort, was carried to Canada and kept captive 13 months.

Jonathan Eastman of Woodstock was captured.
Thomas Willson of Killingly (apparently of this company) was captured.
[*State Library, War 6, 271, 279.*]

FIFTH COMPANY — CAPT. ALLEN.

Benjamin Allen [of Windsor], Captain.
Henry Chapin [of Hartford ?], First Lieutenant.
Ebenezer Orvis, Second Lieutenant. [*Colonial Records.*]

A Muster Roll of Capt Benjamin Allyns Company 1757

Mens Names	Quality	What Time Inlisted	When Returned Home	
Henry Chapin	Lieut.	Apr. 30	Oct. 18	
Ebenezer Orvis	2^d "	Mar. 26	"	
Benjamin Allyn	Capt.	Mar. 26	Dec. 1	
Charles Buckland	Serg.	Apr. 1	Dec. 1	
Ebenezer Belknap	"	"	"	
Phinehas Drake	"	5	Nov. 21	
Jonathon Pinney	"	2	Dec. 1	
Abner Prier	Clerk	1	"	
Timothy Marsh	Soldier	June 19	Nov. 28	
John Strong	Drum.	Apr. 5	Dec. 1	
Benjamin Keney	Corp.	Mar. 30	"	
David Bissill	"	Apr. 1	"	
Jonathon Gillet	"	8	20	
Hozeah Clark	"	"	Oct. 7	
Charles Burnham	Soldier	Mar. 30	Dec. 1	
Eliphilet Loomis	"	31	Oct. 7	
Zebulon Winslow	"	Apr. 2	Dec. 1	Servt to Saml Skinner
Ozias Grant	"	"	"	
Jonathon Booth	"	"	9	
Jonathon Bemont	"	"	1	
Aaron Williams	"	"	Sep. 29	Died
Ebenezer Loomis	"	"	Nov. 13	
Gideon Prier	"	5	Dec. 1	
John Hosmer	"	"	Nov. 13	
Thomas Jarrals	"	"	Dec. 1	
John Egleston	"	"	"	
Josiah Standliff	"	"	"	
Joseph Moore	"	"	"	
Elijah Holcomb	"	"	Nov. 1	
Samuel Shilling	"	"	Oct. 14	
Keump Penegue	"	"	"	
Jonathon Egleston	"	"	7	
Elijah Owen	"	"	Dec. 1	
Ezekiel Scott	"	"	Oct. 18	
John Holcomb	"	6		Never Join^d
Stephen Holcomb	"	"		Never Join^d
Christopher Crow	"	"	Oct. 1	
Henry Wolcutt	"	"	Dec. 1	
Ebenezer Drake	"	8	Oct. 25	
Hezekiah King	"	"		Never Join^d
Joseph Keney	"	"	Dec. 1	
Elijah Martan	"	"	Oct. 25	Died
Gideon Drake	"	"	17	
Zebulon Isham	"	"	18	Died
Job Drake	"	"	30	Died
Job Marshel	"	"		Never Join^d
Asa Phelps	"	"		Never Join^d
William Barnes	"	12	Oct. 6	Died

THIRD REGIMENT.   135

Mens Names	Quality	What Time Inlisted		When Returned Home		
Eli Simons	Soldier	Apr.	14	Dec.	1	
Charles Gaylord	"	"	"	Oct.	14	
Ralf Fargo	"		12	Sep.	15	Died
Jonah Fargo	"		19	Dec.	20	Died
Micah Avery	"		"			Never Join^d
John Mullen	"		20	Nov.	22	
Norman Greene	"		"	Oct.	18	
Saml Belcher	"		"		10	Died
John Soper	"	May	13	Nov.	18	
Joshua Geery	"		17			Never Join^d
William Smith	"		"	June	12	Deserted
Reubin Coal	"		18	Dec.	1	
Eli Holcom	"		28	"	"	
Joel Palmers	"		"	Oct.	12	
Noah Barber	"		"		4	
Moses Barber	"		"		16	
Jonathan Gillet	"		29		14	
Benjamin Gilbort	"		"		"	
Josiah Clark	"		"		"	
Christopher Minor	"		"		"	
Elijah Cooke	"		"		"	
Jonah Allyn	"		"	Dec.	1	
Alexander Farly	"		"		"	
William Stevens	"		"		"	
Amos Westland	"		"	Oct.	7	
Zaccheus Crow	"		"	Dec.	1	
Samuel White	"		"	Oct.	18	
Saml Gilbort	"		24	June	20	Deserted
John Warters	"	June	5	Dec.	1	
Ebenezer Smith	"		15		"	
Daniel Read	"		18	Nov.	18	
Abrah^m Filley	"		19	Oct.	14	
Nathan^l Loomis	"		"	"	8	
Martin North	"		"	Dec.	1	
Elnathan Gilbort	"		25	Oct.	14	
Mathew Grant	"	May	29			Never Join^d

Hartford January 1st 1757
Errors Excepted pr

[Indorsed] Capt Benj Allyns Muster Roll Jany 1757
            Chas Buckland Serjt
            Benj^a Keeny Corp^l
            Eben^r Smith p.

[*State Library, Adams Papers.*]

Muster Roll of Capt Benjamin Allens Company who [   ] half Pay and the time.

Names	Quality	time when the whole pay begun		Names	Quality	time when the whole pay begun	
[ ]n Allyn	Capt	March	26	John Strong	Drum.	April	5
[ ] Chapin	Lieut.	April	29	Jonathan Pinney	Corp.	"	2
[ ] Orvis	2^d "	March	26	Benj^a Kinney	"	March	30
[ ]s Drake	Serj.	April	5	Charles Burnham	"	"	"
[ ] Buckland	"	"	1	Eliphilet Loomis	"	"	31
Abner Pryer	Clerk	"	"	David Bissell		April	1

Names	Quality	time when the whole pay begun		Names	Quality	time when the whole pay begun	
Ebenezer Belknap		April	1	Stephen Halkom		April	6
Zebulon Winslow		"	2	Semuel Gilburd		May	24
Ozias Grant		"	"	Alexander Farlie		"	29
Ebenez^r Loomis		"	3	Robart Westland		"	"
Josiah Standliff		"	5	William Smith		"	17
Gideon Pryer		"	"	Joshua Gery		"	"
John Hosmer		"	"	Elijah Holcomb		April	5
Thomas Jarrall		"	"	Jonathan Gillet	Clerk	"	8
John Eggleston Junr		"	"	Samuel Shiling		"	5
Joseph Moore Junr		"	"	Keup Penigue		"	"

[On the back is]

April 5 Ezekel Scott
" 8 Jonathan Gillet Clark in [ ]
" 12 William Barnes
" 14 Charles Gayler
" 5 Samuel Shiling Cor^l Gutre[ ]
" 5 Keup Pinigue Capt Sanferd (?) [ ]
" 20 John Miller
May 18 Ruben Cole

[Indorsed] Capt Benj^a Allyn Half Pay Roll

[*State Library, War 5, 327.*]

This company marched from Hartford. [*State Library, War 6, 202.*]

SIXTH COMPANY—CAPT. HIDE.

Caleb Hide [of Lebanon], Captain. [*Colonial Records.*]
Amos Hitchcock [of New Haven], Captain.

Jedidiah Waterman, First Lieutenant.
Joseph Blackman, Second Lieutenant. [*State Library, War 6, 50, 57.*]

A Muster Role of the Sixth Company in the Third Rigement in the Sarvace of the Collony of Connecticut Under Command of Amos Hitchcock Capt Viz

Naims boath of Oficers & Soalders	Quality	Time of Inlist or Emprest		When Discharg^d		Dead
Caleb Hide	Capt.	Mar.	26	Nov.	10	
Amos Hitchcock	"	Oct.	29	Dec.	5	
Jedediah Waterman	Lieut.	Mar.	26	Oct.	26	
Joseph Blackman	"	"	"	"	20	
James Read	Serg.	Apr.	15	Dec.	3	
Benj^a Brooks	"	"	8	Oct.	13	
Timothy Thorp	"	"	7	Sep.	20	Dead
Jonathan Edgerton	"	"	8	Dec.	2	
Zabdial Rogers	Clark	"	13	Oct.	20	
John Jackson	Corp.	"	8	Dec.	2	
Elijah Thomas	"	"	"	"	14	
Zepheniah Hart	"	"	5	Sep.	27	
James Roberts	"	"	15	Dec.	14	
Ezekel Strong	Drum.	"	10	Nov.	2	Dead

THIRD REGIMENT.

Naims boath of Oficers & Soalders	Quality	Time of Inlis^t or Emprest	When Discharg^d	Dead
Timothy Bush	Privet	Apr. 16	Oct. 10	
Isaiah Dible		June 17	" 19	
Nathan Osburn		Apr. 8	" 5	Dead
Samuel Devenport		June 10	" 17	Dead
Giles Harris		" 1	Nov. 30	
Cleomant Stoderd		" 6	Dec. 14	Dead
Joseph Atkin		" 14	Nov. 23	
Csreal Beckweth		" 10	Aug. 13	Dead
John Gott		" 12	Nov. 30	
Asa Robinson		Apr. 8	" "	
Zebede Howerd		" 1	" "	
Simon Baxter		June 23	July 21	
James Sparrer		" 3	Oct. 11	
James Booge		" "	Nov. 20	
John Nothum		" 14	Dec. 14	
Daniel Shipman		Apr. 16	" "	
Benj^a Willey		June 10	Nov. 10	Dead
Joshua Fox		" 3	Dec. 4	
Jonathan Coy		Apr. 5	Aug. 7	Dead
David Bosworth		May 10	Oct. 16	
Joseph Sweet		June 9	Sep. 24	
Hezekiah Holdredg		Apr. 10	Dec. 3	
William Lam		" 5	" 2	
Zepheniah Spiar		June 18	Nov. 20	
John Wright		" 8	" 10	
Abner Gay		Apr. 12	Oct. 7	Dead
Abner Hills		" 9	Dec. 2	
Aaron Bunce		June 24	Nov. 10	
James Bill		" 3	" 30	
Abell Webster		" 9	Dec. 2	
William Bentley		Apr. 5	Oct. 22	Dead
Isaac Fox		May 3	" 6	
Samuel Wright		June 3	" 11	
Sampson Amous		Apr. 6	Nov. 20	
Ruben Strongue		" 5	Oct. 13	
John House		June 10	" 7	
Daniel Armstrong		Apr. 23	Nov. 10	
Thomas Cocks		" 9	Dec. 2	
Simon Chalcom		" 4	Sep. 20	Dead
Joshua Sherrin		June 8	Dec. 2	
Edward Howard		Apr. 7	" "	
Eliakem Hitchcock		" 15	Oct. 13	
John Crocker		June 8	" 10	
Amos Larken		Apr. 9	" 22	
Thomus Weeb		June 12	" 17	
Seath Beech		" 3	Sep. 15	Dead
Joseph Bayle		May 29	Oct. 28	
Joseph Foot		June 21	" 8	Dead
Sam^ll Blackmon		" 8	" 10	
Daniel Gillit		" 21	Sep. 23	Dead
Thomus Wilke		Apr. 13	Dec. 2	
James Jacobs		" 16	Sep. 17	Dead
Michel Ewen		" 19	Dec. 2	
Josiah Wedg		" 21	Nov. 20	Dead
John Gurley		May 20	Oct. 30	
George Lewis		" 3	" 16	
Selus Tefany		" "	Dec. 12	

138   CAMPAIGN OF 1756.

Naims boath of Oficers & Soalders	Quality	Time of Inlis^t or Emprest	When Discharg^d	Dead
Sam^{ll} Baldwin		May 5	Oct. 16	
Ceaser Allin		" 6	Dec. 10	Dead
Isaac Tatton		" 3	Oct. 13	
Nathaniel Curtis		" 5	Dec. 9	Dead
Sam^{ll} Colwell		" "	May 5	Deserted
Denis Calcheese (?)		" "	" "	"

    [Indorsed] Capt Hide & Capt Amos Hitchcox for ye Company Raised by Capt Caleb Hide Muster Roll Jany 1757
                  1756
                  Silas Tiffany
                  Jno. Wright p
                  Seth Bush

                                          [*State Library, Adams Papers.*]

SEVENTH COMPANY—CAPT. HAWLEY.

Nathan Hawley [of Stratford], Captain. [*Colonial Records.*]

Jabez Hall, First Lieutenant.

Joseph Benedict, Second Lieutenant. [*Colonial Records.*]

        Nathan Hauley Captain
        Jabez Hall first Lieut at Albany sick
        Joseph Benedict 2nd Lieut " "
        Jon^a Silsby Sarj^t at Fort Edwd sick
        Saml Comstock Sarj^t
        John Trowbridge "
        Geo. Follet   " at Fort Edwd sick
        Ebenezer Hanford Clark "   "   "
        Ambros Nicholson Corp
        Elisha Murray   "
        Abijah Abbot   "   left at Fort Edwd sick
        John McClennen
        Ebenezer Osborn Drumer at Albany wthout leave
        Adams Abraham at Albany wthout leave
        Arnold Isaac at Fort Edwd sick
        Barse Joseph "   "   "   "
        Bishop Epenetus
        Bolt John at Albany sick
        Betts Timothy at Albany without Leave
        Boughton John "   "   "   "
        Boughton Saml at Fort Edwd sick
        Bartrum John at Albany wthout leave
        Button Peter at Fort Edwd sick
        Chapman Abraham
        Carley Jedediah at Albany wthout leave
        Dan Abraham
        Fairchild Andrew at Fort Edwd sick
        Finch Nathl "   "   "   "
        Farress Josiah in Camp sick
        Goldsberry Jos.
        Hodge Tim^o Albany wthout leave
        Hodge Ezekiel   "   "   "
        House John   "   "   "

THIRD REGIMENT.

Higgins Benj[a] at Fort Edw[d] sick
Hanford Stephen sick at Albany
Hanford Gershom
Kellog Jon[a] at Albany w[th] leave
Ketchum Benj[a]
Lacy Seth at Albany sick
Levake John at Fort Edw[d] sick
Lawrence Sam[l] at Albany sick
Lovelace James at Albany w[th]out leave
M[c]Daniel Michael
Moltrop Benj[a] at Fort Edw[d] sick
Mills David
Raymond W[m]
Resco Thomas at Albany w[th]out leave
Richardson Tho[s] sick at Albany
Smith Jedediah at Albany w[th]out leave
Smith Richard at Fort Edw[d] sick
Smith Eben[r]
Sealey Nehemiah at Albany sick
Sherod Abell without leave at Albany
S[t] John Isaac
Scipio sick at Albany
Tomlin Elisha at Albany without leave
Truesdell Sam[l]
Utter John at Albany w[th]out leave
Wildman John
Wilks John at Albany sick
Wolleps Benj[a]
Peters Jos Never Join[d]
Jesse Clinton Dead

[Indorsed] This muster roll, signed by Henry Leddel Muster Master General, is dated Camp at Fort William Henry Oct. 13, 1756.

[*State Library, Adams Papers.*]

The following Name are Solders that Was in y[e] Servis Last Summer Sertified per
Nathan Hauley Cap[tn]

Serj. Joseph Bennerdeck	April	6	Elisha Murry	April 23
" Jonathan Silsbe	May	28	Abraham Aadams	May 10
Corp. John Trowbridge	April	15	Jediah Sweet	" 23
" John House	"	25	John Welks	" 14
" Ambrous Nickalson	May	28	David Austin	" 28
Ebennetous Bishup	April	9	Neamiah Barsley	April 25
Jonathan Kelog	"	14	Joseph Goolsbery	May 28
Jonathan Green	"	19	Epheram Wheler	" "
John Lewak	"	"	Abraham Chapman	" "
Will[m] Raymond	"	"	Micael MacDoneld	" "
Abraham Dan	May	2	Joseph Peters	" "
Jabez Hall	April	15	John Mack Clenen	" 30
Elish Tomblin	"	23	Benj[m] Higens	June 6
Eben[r] Pardy	"	25	John Bartram	May 12
Benj Bacss (?)	"	"	Benjamin Wallaps	June 4
Andrew Farechild	May	10	Abijah Abbott	April 19

Cap[t] Nathan Hawley half pay as Leiut

[Indorsed] Cap[t] Na[n] Hawleys half pay Roll

[*State Library, War 5, 308.*]

CAMPAIGN OF 1756.

EIGHTH COMPANY—CAPT. JEFFRY.

John Jeffry [of Cornwall], Captain.
Charles Woodruff [of Litchfield], First Lieutenant.
Nathaniel Everts, Second Lieutenant.

[*Colonial Records.*]

    A Muster Roll of ye Company y^t Served under the Command of as their Captain against Crown Point &c in the Pay of the Colony of Connecticut Anno 1756

Names & Qualities of Officers and Soldiers		Time of Enlistment	Discharged	Dead
John Jeffery	Capt.	Mar. 26	Nov. 30	
Charles Woodruff	Lieut.	"	26	
Nath^{ll} Everts	"	"	29	
Elnaⁿ Ashman	Serj.	Apr. 9	"	
Moses Chamberlin	"	"	Dec. 1	
Isaac Bird	"	"		Oct. 29
More Bird	"	19		Sep. 4
Sam^{ll} Dean	Clerk	5	Nov. 30	
James Bentley	Corp.	7	Sep. 4	
James Bentley	Serj.	Sep. 5	Oct. 16	
Joseph Prindle	Corp.	Apr. 9	9	
Joseph Prindle	Serj.	Oct. 10	Nov. 29	
Ruben Dean	Corp.	Apr. 9	17	
George Richman	"	6	29	
Jonathⁿ Caswall	Drum.	"		Sep. 10
Asa Landon		"	Sep. 19	
Asa Landon	Drum.	Sep. 20	Nov. 29	
Nath^{ll} Buel		Apr. 6	Sep. 4	
Nath. Buel	Corp.	Sep. 5	Nov. 29	
Coonrod Kline		Apr. 6	Oct. 9	
Coonrod Kline	Corp.	Oct. 10	Nov. 29	
Ashbel Patterson		Apr. 5		June 30
Abraham Race		8		
Andrew Barton		6	Oct. 4	
Benj^a Griswould		9	Nov. 29	
Bartho^w Barrat		"	16	
Calob Root		5	"	
David Handy		Aug. 9	Dec. 1	
David Austin		May 21	" 5	
Daniel Skiner		Apr. 6	Nov. 29	
Daniel Barns		June 7	Dec. 1	
Eliphlet Owen		Apr. 6	Nov. 29	
Ebenez^r Flicher		9	16	
Ebenez^r Jewel		6	29	
Ebenez^r Allin		15	Sep. 10	
Ebenez^r Allin Ju^r		9	Nov. 29	
Gad Farnum		18	26	
Hez^h Foord		9	30	
John Mackmaners		June 5	Taken at Albany by a Regular officer	
Isaac Bates		Apr. 9	Nov. 30	
Isaac Green		"		June 30
Israel Barns		6		May 30
John Evarts		"	Nov. 29	
John Brinsmad		"	21	
Justis Gebbs		16	Dec. 1 { never joynd till 11 Nov^r	

THIRD REGIMENT. 141

Names & Qualities of Officers and Soldiers	Time of Enlistment	Discharged	Dead
Josiah Dibble	Apr. 9	Nov. 30	
John Tannar	"	Oct. 1	
Joseph Dean	"	Nov. 30	
John Dean	"	Sep. 28	
Jonath\n Hurlbort	5	Nov 17	
John Winter	9	29	
Joseph Lindly	18	Dec. 1	
Joseph Waugh	"	Aug. 9	
Jona Moore	15	Nov. 29	
John Rose	9	"	
John Scott	"		deserted May 18
James Fuller	"	Nov. 29	
Josiah Rice	June 7	30	
John Nickols	May 17	29	
Moses Dean	Apr. 5	16	
Philop Mongar	9	Aug. [ ]	
Rich\d Bignal	20	Nov. 29	
Rob\t Tomes	9	"	
Samuel Owen	"	"	
Solom\n Johnson	5	30	
Samuel Skiner	6	29	
Simeon Stockwell	9	"	
Seth Casey	"	Sep. 28	
Tho\s Tuttel	"	Nov. 24	
Tho\s Chandler	21	29	
Tho\s Davis	15	"	
Tim\y Chittendon	19	Oct. 5	
Uriah Dean	9	Nov. 29	
Waitw\l Willeby	June 7	30	
Will\m Patterson	Apr. 6	29	
Will\m Kilworth	9	"	
Will\m Tew	"	"	
Will\m Woodworth	"	"	
Zeckeus Owen	17	"	
Nath\ll Ashbow	6	"	
Sam\ll Pougoneet	20	Dec. 11	
Fuller Negro	16	1	
Newport Negro	"	"	

    Add Andrew Barton 26 Weeks
        Justus Gibbs 1 mo pay &
        Philip Munger 1 "

[Indorsed] Cap\t John Jeffrey Jan\y 1757 Muster Roll
                                                            [*State Library, Adams Papers.*]

A muster roll of this company is endorsed

    This Comp\y not Musterd being at an Out post
    The above representation is Fact   John Winslow
    Cap\t John Jeffrey\s Must\r Roll
    Asa Landon p

                                                                           [*State Library, Adams Papers.*]

This company marched from Cornwall.   [*State Library, War 6, 307.*]

NINTH COMPANY — CAPT. TYLER.

John Tyler of Preston, Captain.
Elisha Miller of Lyme, First Lieutenant.
Eleazer Tracy of Norwich, Second Lieutenant.

[*Colonial Records.*]

Note: These officers were appointed by the Assembly, but no evidence has been found to show that they were commissioned or that the company was raised.

TENTH COMPANY — CAPT. PHELPS.

Ichabod Phelps of Hebron, Captain.
Gideon Hurlburt of Goshen, First Lieutenant.
Timothy Northum of Colchester, Second Lieutenant.

[*Colonial Records.*]

Note: These officers were appointed by the Assembly, but no evidence has been found to show that they were commissioned or that the company was raised.

FOURTH REGIMENT. 143

FOURTH REGIMENT—COL. ANDREW WARD, JR.

REGIMENTAL OFFICERS.

Andrew Ward, Jr. [of Guilford] appointed Colonel and Captain of the first company, March, 1756. Discharged Aug. 5.
Stephen Lee [of New London] appointed Lieutenant-Colonel and Captain of the second company, March, 1756.
Benjamin Hinman [of Woodbury] appointed Major and Captain of the third company, March, 1756. Discharged Oct. 1.
Phineas Stanton of Stonington appointed Commissary, March, 1756.
[*Colonial Records.*]
Giles Hall, Adjutant, from March 26 to Nov. 23, 1756.
[*State Library, War 6, 362.*]
Rev. David Jewet of New London, Chaplin, for 3 months 3 weeks and 1 day from April 5, 1756.
[*State Library, War, 6, 347.*]

FIRST COMPANY—COL. WARD.

Andrew Ward, Jr. [of Guilford], Colonel and Captain.
[*Colonial Records.*]
Samuel Stanton [of Stonington], Captain-Lieutenant.
John Lay [of Lyme], Second Lieutenant.
Giles Hull, Ensign. [*Colonial Records.*]

A Muster Roll of ye Company that Serv^d under ye Command of Colon^{ll} Andrew Ward as their Captain against Crown Point &c in the Pay of the Colony of Connecticut Anno 1756

Names & Quality of Officers & Soldiers	Time of Enlistment		Discharged		Dead		Deserted	
Andrew Ward	Mar.	26	Aug.	5				
Samuel Stanton					Aug.	29		
John Lay					"	27		
Giles Hull			Nov.	23				
Thom^s Morehouse	Apr.	13	Oct.	15				
Assa Eliot		11	Nov.	25				
Levi Leet		21	"	23				
Urias Avery		20	Oct.	16				
Elihu Palmer		"					Sep.	26
Abraham Kimberly		9	Nov.	23				
Ezra Bishop		1			Oct.	1		
Clamont Minor		10	Nov.	25				
Abraham Foot		9	Aug.	26				
Nath^{ll} Hall	May	3	Nov.	25				
Ebenz^r Beldon	Apr.	13	Sep.	18				

CAMPAIGN OF 1756.

Names & Quality of Officers & Soldiers	Time of Enlistment	Discharged	Dead	Deserted
Wm Brown	Apr. 5	Sep. 26		
Simon Pasahauk (?)	"	Oct. 16		
Isaac Whittel	"	Nov. 25		
David Job	"	Oct. 16		
Thom^s Dibble	6	" 15		
Lemuel Doud	8		Aug. 28	
James Benton	"	Oct. 27		
Elisha Blackman	"	Nov. 23		
Joshua Wright	"	" 9		
Jehiel Ward	9	" 23		
Obidiah Tiller	"	" "		
Henry Ludenton	10	" 13		
Phinous Pond	"		Oct. 16	
Jeremiah Hall	"	Oct. 25		
Stephen Johnson	"	" 13		
Arune Darin	"		Sep. 22	
Sam^{ll} Turner	"	Nov. 25		
Stephen Poheage	"	Oct. 16		
Thom^s Scranton	12		Sep. 16	
Nath^{ll} Bishop	"	Nov. 23		
Aaron Hinman	"	" "		
Nath^{ll} Eldrige	"	" 25		
Charles Acoat	13			Apr. 14
James Done	"	Oct. 2		
Ira Whitmore	"	" 14		
Phineas Bradly	"	Nov. 23		
Phineas Palmer	"	" "		
Daniel Stone	"	" "		
Reuben Kelly	14	Sep. 24		
Peter Davis	"	Nov. 23		
Ozial Cook	"	Oct. 11		
John Bacon	"	Nov. 23		
Christopher Stevens	"	" 24		
Elias Benton	"	Oct. 14		
Timothy Hand	15	Nov. 23		
Benj^m Chittendon	"	Oct. 14		
Nath^{ll} Fellers	16	" 16		
Jonathⁿ Poheage	"	Nov. 1		
Jabez Peters	"	" 11		
Johogada Wheton	18	" 22		
Thom^s Norton	"	Oct. 2		
Stephen Farnum	"	Nov. 23		
Joseph Garrett	19	" 25		
David Hillard	"	" "		
Elisha Gart	"			
John Fish	"	Sept. 19		
Joseph Thomson	20		Aug. 17	
Robert Jackwise	"	Nov. 11		
Isaac Pompy	"	" 24		
Sam^{ll} Freeman	"	" "		
Waitstill Cook	21	Oct. 12		
Sam^{ll} Trusdall	"		Sep. 26	
Abel Badcock	"	Nov. 25		
Reuben Brown	"	" "		
John Graves	24	" 23		
Richd Kenny	27	" 24		
Nemiah Lester	"	" 25		

FOURTH REGIMENT. 145

Names & Quality of Officers & Soldiers	Time of Enlistment	Discharged	Dead	Deserted
John Low	Apr. 27			
Silvanus Dudly	"	Nov. 24		
Francis Summers	May 6	Sep. 28		
Timothy Bradly	7	" 17		
Ichabod Higgens	17	Nov. 24		
Zebulon Bishop	26	" "		

[Indorsed]   1756 Colº Andw Ward Pay Roll & Muster Roll January 1757

    Asa Elliot within allowd Serjts Wages made Ensign Sept 6
    Allso Abraham Kimberly made Serjt October 15
    Jere Hall made Serjt Sept 6
    Stephen Farnum made Corporal Sept 16
    Jehiel Ward   Do   Octobr 16
    and Peter Davis made Clark   Augt 26th
      Jno. Bacon
      Nathl Hall Drm

                    [*State Library, Adams Papers.*]

SECOND COMPANY—LIEUT.-COL. LEE.

Stephen Lee [of New London], Lieutenant-Colonel and Captain.
John Raymond, First Lieutenant.
Nicholas Bishop, Second Lieutenant.

                              [*Colonial Records.*]

Half Pay Roll for ye Men who were in ye last years Service & now in Capt Steph Lees Company

	Month & Day of their Inlistment		Month & Day of their Inlistment
Left John Shaw	Mar. 29	Simon Coy Choy	Apr. 5
Sarg. Jeremiah Whipple	Apr. 2	John Stimson	Mar. 27
Corp. Thomas Miner	5	Joseph Emroson	30
Corp John Chappell	"	Anthany Frasur	29
Jonathan Weeks	Mar. 29	Asa Sawyer	30
Samll Billings	30	Beter Button	Apr. 5
Samll Mager	"	Samll Keeny	"
Joseph Comstock	Apr. 5	Isirl Rowlee	Mar. 30
James Murfey	Mar. 30	Lemeul Toney	Apr. 5
Peter Ollever	"	Charls Pockhage	"
Naman Moger	"	Richard Dorors	2
Jethro Weeks	"	Tom Oacom	Mar. 30
Isril Richards	"	Jonathan Oacom	29
Andrew Chappell	"	Elisha Beckwith	Apr. 5
Joseph Derik	"	Jeames Collour	Mar. 30
Zeccharius Wheeler	Apr. 5	Jeames Right	"
William Bishop	"		

                              [*State Library, War 5, 331.*]

This company consisted of seventy-seven officers and men, and marched from New London.

                              [*State Library, War 6, 308.*]

THIRD COMPANY—MAJ. HINMAN.

Benjamin Hinman [of Woodbury], Major and Captain.
Stephen Smith, First Lieutenant.
Adam Hinman, Second Lieutenant.

[*Colonial Records.*]

A Muster Role of Maj^r Benjamin Hinmans Company in Colo^{ll} Andrew Wards Regim^t

Officers and Sold^r Names & Quallity		Time of Inlistm^t		Discharged		Dead or Captivated
Benj^m Hinman	Maj.	Mar.	26	Oct.	1	
Stephen Smith	Lieut.	"	"	Aug.	12	
Adam Hinman	"	"	"	Nov.	20	
David Mun	Serj.	Apr.	8	Sep.	10	
Samuel Osborn	"	"	2	Nov.	20	
Phenehas Castle	"	"	19	"	"	
Adam Hurd	"	"	15			Nov. 26
Alex Thompson	Clerk	"	1	Nov.	10	
Tely Blackslee	Corp.	"	15	"	20	
John Tiff	"	"	8	Oct.	2	
John Coller	"	"	"	Nov.	20	
Wiliam Greives	"	"	5	"	"	
Peruda Isbal	Dru n	"	8	Dec.	16	
Robert Bruce		"	"	"	"	
Gideon Brownson		"	"	Nov.	20	
Solomon Squior		"	9			deserted Sep. 26
Nathan Jackson		"	"	Nov.	20	
Ebenezor Wornor Junr		"	"	Sep.	23	
Samuel Jenors		"	"	Nov.	20	
Philip Cool		"	8	"	"	
Israel Sumnor		"	10			deserted Sep. 26
Samuel Ransom		"	8	Nov.	18	
Elifalet Raynols		"	16	"	20	
John Raynolds		"	"	"	"	
Jonathan Blackslee		"	15	Sep.	20	
Robart Torrance		"	9	Nov.	20	
Rubin Hinman		"	8	Oct.	1	
Noah Hurlburt		"	15	Sep.	26	
James Huff		"	19	Nov.	20	
Adam Hurlburt		"	20	"	"	
Reubin Allin		"	22	"	"	
John Barrall		"	26	Dec.	10	
Beriah Dudley		"	10	Sep.	20	
Simeon Wheeler		"	20	Oct.	29	
Obadiah Robason		"	19	Nov.	19	
Joel Smith		"	"	"	6	
Asa Lyon		"	"			deserted June 10
William Parks		"	26	Dec.	6	
Ephraim Berry		"	"			Oct. 2
David Holbrook		"	29			Aug. 26
James Fancher		"	"	Nov.	10	
Noble Hinman		"	30	Oct.	2	
Joshua Hurlburt		"	22	Nov.	20	
Jacob Wagner		"	"	Sep.	20	
Aaron Hurlburt		"	15	Nov.	20	
Samuel Hurlburt		"	22	"	"	
Judah Boldwin		"	"	Oct.	22	
Samuel Baker		"	"	Sep.	20	

FOURTH REGIMENT. 147

Officers and Soldʳ Names & Quallity	Time of Inlistmᵗ	Discharged	Dead or Captivated
Reubin Squior	Apr. 19	Nov. 20	
Nathan Boldwin	" 22	Oct. 22	
William Miles	" 13	Nov. 20	
Elezʳ Bartholomew	" 5	" "	
Nathanˡ Daviss	" 7	" "	
Thomas Griffus	" 1	Dec. 8	
Elisha Harris	" 8	Aug. 12	
Elijah Grant	" 5	Dec. 12	
Samuel Chapel	" 9	Nov. 20	
John Groues	" "		deserted June 6
Ebenezer Culvor	" 14	July 29	
Jobe Gibs	" 9		deserted June 6
Hezekiah Agard	" 19		Dec. 10
John Collins	" "	Oct. 4	
Samuel Catling	" "	Nov. 20	
Zephaniah Wicks	" 18	Oct. 10	
Daniel Barnes	" 20	Nov. 20	
Amos Barnes	" 2	" "	
Thomas Hotchkiss	May 20		Sep. 7
Elijah Hinman	" "	Oct. 1	
Justice Pearce	June 3	Nov. 20	
Jedediah Durkee	" "	Sep. 22	
Israel Minor	" 5	Oct. 16	
Paul Peeck	May 3	" 5	
Ebenezʳ Worner	June 30	Sep. 21	
⎧ Francis Gitto			
⎪ Luke Hill Junʳ			
⎨ Petor Garnse			
⎩ John Waddams			

[Indorsed] Major Ben. Hinman's Muster Roll January 1757.
[*State Library, Adams Papers.*]

A billiting roll of the same date gives the same names.
[*State Library, Adams Papers.*]

A muster roll of this company, signed by Henry Leddel Muster Master General, is dated Camp at Fort William Henry 13 Oct. 1756.
[*State Library, Adams Papers.*]

FOURTH COMPANY—CAPT. WELLS.

Edmund Wells [of Hebron], Captain.
John Kilborn, First Lieutenant.
Daniel Cone, Second Lieutenant.
[*State Library, War 6, 60.*]

A Roll of Capᵗ Edmund Wells's Company with yᵉ time of Inlistment and what their wages amounted to at there Death Desertion Being Discharged &c &c

Mens Names	Quaˡʸ	Time of Inlistment 1756	Discharᵈ	Dead 1756
Edmund Wells	Capt.	Mar. 26	Dec. 6	
John Kilborn	1 Lieut.	" "	Oct. 7	
Daniel Cone	2 "	" "		Sep. 17
Ebenezʳ Sumner	Serj.	Apr. 1	Nov. 26	
Pollicarpos Smith	"	" 26	Oct. 5	

CAMPAIGN OF 1756.

Mens Names	Quaty	Time of Inlistment 1756	Dischard	Dead 1756
Orlandor Mack	Serj.	Apr. 1	Nov. 26	
Timothy Percifull	"	May 30	Oct. 16	
Thos Sumner	Clerk	Apr. 1	" 20	
Ebezr Sumner	"	Oct. 20	Nov. 26	
Isaac Smith	Serj.	" 5	" "	
Jabue (?) Strong	"	" 16	" "	
Isaac Gooddell	Corp.	Apr. 12	Oct. 4	
Jabue Strong	"	" 14	" 16	
Zeph Mitchell	"	" 23	Nov. 26	
John Harris	"	" 28	" "	
Samll Feilding	"	Oct. 4	" "	
Isaac Bigelow	Drum.	May 19	Oct. 20	
Ancel Annable	Privit	" 30	" 16	
John Brown		Apr. 2	" 7	
Thos Brewer		" 12	Sep. 26	
Joshua Baly		" 28	Nov. 26	
Nathll Brown		" 1	Sep. 15	
Barll Brainard		" 28	Oct. 16	
Thos Carrier		" 8	Aug. 25	
John Curtice		May 30	" "	
Silvanas Cone		" "	Nov. 26	
Hosea Curtice		Apr. 1	Oct. 13	
Calab Cook		May 29	Nov. 26	
Wm Cox		Apr. 12	Oct. 16	
Isaac Dunham		June 2		Oct. 3
Jeremy Dinney		Apr. 12	Dec. 1	
Joseph Davis		May 30	Nov. 27	
David Dean		Apr. 16	Never Joynd Company	
Labeas Eddy		" 7		Nov. 16
Nathn Fisher		May 4	Sep. 25	
Samll Fox		" 17	Oct. 16	
Willm Fox		June 1	" "	
Garsham Fox		Apr. 23	Sep. 25	
Samll Fox Jr		May 4	Deserted Sep.	
Lemuel Fox		" "	" Sep. 21	
Samll Feilding		Apr. 1	Oct. 4	
John Foord		" 12	" 16	
Henry Gray		May 29	Nov. 26	
Eli Gay		Apr. 1	Dec. 1	
John Gilbord		May 30	Oct. 16	
Moses Hutchinson		Apr. 1	Nov. 26	
John Holdrig		" 30	Sep. 27	
Jarad Knowlton		May 30	Oct. 2	
Roswell Knowlton		Apr. 28	" 12	
Nethll Moot		" 25	Nov. 13	
Abner Mack		" 1	" 21	
Samll Mack		" 24	Oct. 16	
Joseph Mitchell		" 25		Sep. 26
John Mitchell		" 23	Sep. 25	
James Noble		" 1	Oct. 20	
Benja Ollcot		May 30	Nov. 27	
Timothy Osborn		Apr. 1	Dec. 1	
Uzziel Owen		" "	Sep. 27	
Gersham Rowlee		May 30	Nov. 27	
Isaac Robin		Apr. 11	Oct. 16	
Isaac Robin Jr		June 2	Nov. 26	

FOURTH REGIMENT.

Mens Names	Qua'y	Time of Inlistment 1756	Dischar'd	Dead 1756
Eliekem Spencer		May 30	Nov. 27	
Henry Smith		" 29		Nov. 25
Isaac Smith		Apr. 20	Oct. 5	
Benj^a Tucker		" 12	Nov. 26	
Joseph Taylor		" 23	Sep. 23	
Joseph Taylor Jr		May 10	Nov. 27	
Nath^{ll} Taylor		" 14	" "	
Joseph Tuttill		Apr. 12	Oct. 16	
Levis Tattinton		May 19	Nov. 27	
Solomⁿ Wickwier		" 29	Deserted Sep. [ ]	
Nathⁿ Wickwier		" "	Sep. 10	
Tim^y Waters		" 30	Oct. 12	
Willm Warters		Apr. 28	Deserted Sep. 21	
Benj^a West		May 29	Nov. 6	
John West		" 24	Dec. 12	
Sam^{ll} Warters		Apr. 1	Nov. 26	
Levi Webstor		May 3	" "	

[*State Library, Adams Papers.*]

A muster roll of this company, signed by Henry Leddel Muster Master General, is dated Camp at Fort William Henry Oct. 13, 1756.

[*State Library, Adams Papers.*]

A Role & Manifest of Such Men as Serv'd last year in ye Expedition against Crown point &c and are now Enlisted to Serve in Capt Wells's Company their half pay Stated &c

Mens Names & Rank in last years Service	Mens Names & Rank in last years Service
John Kilborn Serj.	Josuah Baley
Daniel Cone "	John Hares
Ebenez^r Sumner Clerk	Willm Warters
Moses Hutchinson	Thos Brewer
Ely Gay	Nath^{ll} Mott
John Brown	Isaac Bigelow
Isaac Gooddall Corp.	John West
Levi Webster	Wm Fox
Sam^{ll} Feilding	Benj Tinker
Orlandor Mack	James Noble
Isaac Smith	Silvanos Cone
Abner Mack	Eliakem Spencer
Policarpos Smith Corp	Timothy Warters
Nathan Fisher	Isaac Robbin Jr.
Zepheniah Michall	Gershom Rowlee Corp.
Sam^{ll} Mack	Timothy Parsifell "

[*State Library, War 5, 314.*]

FIFTH COMPANY—CAPT. WATERBURY.

David Waterbury, 3d, [of Stamford,] Captain.
Reuben Ferris, First Lieutenant.
Timothy Lockwood, Second Lieutenant.

[*Colonial Records.*]
[*State Library, War 6, 63.*]

A Role of Capt David Warterburry's Company in Col^o Ward's Reg^t

Names	Quality	Time of Inlistment 1756	Discharged 1756	Dead
David Warterbury	Capt.	Mar. 26	Nov. 26	
Reuben Ferris	Lieut.	" "	" "	
Timothy Lockwood	"	" "	" 12	
Israel Smith	Serj.	Apr. 3	" 26	
Caleb Knap	"	" "	" 8	
James Wardel	"	" "		Captivated July 17
John Newman	"	" 8	Nov. 26	
Jeremiah Finch	"	July 17	" 12	
Ebenezer Slauson	"	Nov. 8	" 26	
Daniel Welply	"	" 12	" "	
Peter Warterbury	Clerk	Apr. 3	" 2	
Israel Smith	"	Nov. 2	" 26	
Jeremiah Finch	Corp.	Apr. 7	July 17	
Ebenezer Slauson	"	" 8	Nov. 8	
Ehenezer Crissey	"	" 8	" 10	
Daniel Welply	"	" 10	" 12	
David Newman	"	July 17	Oct. 6	
Francis Wilmouth	Drum.	Apr. 24	June 29	
Timothy Reynolds	Centinel	" 20		Captivated July 17
Charles Williams		" 5	Nov. 26	
Michael Messenger		" "		Captivated May 29
Ezekiel Salar		" "	Nov. 26	
Jeremiah Jagger		" "	" "	
David Barley		" "		Oct. 13
Isac Slauson		" 7	Nov. 8	
John Holly		" "	" 26	
Stephen Ambler		" "		Oct. 18
Youngs Weed		" 8	Nov. 12	
John Denslow		" "		July 19
Joseph Ferris		" "		Dec. [ ]
Abraham Bates		" "	Nov. 26	
Moses Smith		" "	" "	
Ebenezer Knap		" 9		Sep. 7
William Gales		" "	Nov. 26	
Silvanus Slauson		" "	" "	
Nathan Ferris		" "	Dec. 23	
John Delevand		" 4	Nov. 26	
Jonathan Weeb		" 10	" "	
Jonathan Weed		" "		July 17
James Steward		" "	Nov. 30	
Jeremiah Lockwood		" 12	" 8	
Richard Mangrel		" 13	" 26	
Charles Denslow		" 17	" 8	
Jonas Knap		" 19		Oct. 11
James Wright		" "	Nov. 8	
Ely Reynolds		" 8	" 26	
Lockwood Astin		" "	" "	
Daniel Hubbard		" "		July 17

FOURTH REGIMENT.

Names	Quality	Time of Inlistment 1756	Discharged 1756	Dead
John Mow		Apr. 24	Nov. 26	
John German		" 9	Oct. 6	
Thomas George		" "	" 31	
Edward Tharps		" "	Nov. 26	
James Parmer		" 10	" 8	
Samuel Parmer		" "	" 26	
Thomas Ask		" "	" "	
Jonas Winchel		" "		
Jonathan Sellick		" "		
Isack Bea		" 11	Oct. 6	
Titus Reynolds		" "	Nov. 26	
Peter Avery		" 13	" "	
Peter Mashel		" "		Aug. 20
Nehemiah Knap		" 10	Nov. 26	
James Moger		" 13	" 12	
Pack Ferris		" "	" 26	
Joseph Morgin		" "	Oct. 6	
William Johnson		" 16	Nov. 12	
David Newman		" 19	July 17	
Israel Slossman		" "		Aug. 12
James Mead		" 21	Nov. 24	
John Rickey		" 23		Sep. 13
Daniel Chapman		" 7	Nov. 26	
Moses Lockwood		" 6	" "	
John Adams		" "	" "	
Silas Mashel		" "	" 8	
Samuel Lockwood		" "	" 26	
Nathaniel Jesup		" "	" "	
Abraham Lockwod		" 8	" "	
Ebenezer Reynolds		" 7	" 8	
Hezekiah Cosher		" 6		Oct. 14
David Perday		" 10	Nov. 26	
Hezekiah Davis		" "	" "	
John Peck		" 8	Oct. 28	

[*State Library, Adams Papers.*]

A muster roll of this company, signed by Henry Leddel Muster Mast General, is dated Camp at Fort William Henry Oct. 13, 1756.

[*State Library, Adams Papers.*]

Names & Rank of Such as were in last years service & are now in Cap[t] Waterburys Comp[y] & have right to Half Pay

David Waterbury	Lieut.	Charles Williams
Reuben Feriss	Serj.	Michael Messenger
Timothy Lockwood	Drum.	Ezekiel Sealy
Israel Smith	Serj.	Jeremiah Jagger
Caleb Knap	"	David Barly
James Wardwel[r]	Corp.	Youngs Weed
John Newman Jr.		John Denslow
Ebenezor Slauson		Abraham Bates
Ebenezer Cresey		Silvanus Slauson
Timothy Reynolds	Corp.	Nathan Ferris

CAMPAIGN OF 1756.

John Delavan
Jonathan Webb
Jonathan Weed
Jeremiah Lockwood
Richard Mandell
Lockwood Austin
John Moe
John Jerman
Thomas George
Thomas Ask

Edward Thanks

Peter Avery
James Mogier
Pack Terris
Israel Slauson
Moses Lockwood
John Adams
Nathan Jessup
Hezekiah Casher
Hezekiah Davis
Daniel Whelply Corp.

[*State Library, War 5, 313.*]

[*State Library, War 5, 333.*]

SIXTH COMPANY — CAPT. WHITTLESEY.

Eliphalet Whittlesey [of Newington], Captain. [*Colonial Records.*]
Edward Marcy [of Ashford], First Lieutenant. [*State Library, War 6, 54.*]
Thomas Foster, Second Lieutenant. [*Colonial Records.*]
John Shaw, Second Lieutenant.

A Muster Role of Capⁿ E Whitteleys Company 1756

Mens Names	Quality	Time of Inlistment	When Discharged	Dead and Captivated
E. Whitteley	Capt.	Mar. 26	Nov. 25	
Edward Marcy	Lieut.	" "	Sep. 16	
Thomas Foaster	"	" "		Sep. 30
John Shaw	"	Sep. 6	Nov. 1	
Jonathan Brooks	Serj.	Apr. 1	" 16	
Moses Erles	"	" 8	" 27	
Abner Curtis	"	" 9	" 25	
Gemalial Deming	"	" 2	Sep. 28	
Josiah Wright	Clark	Mar. 31	" "	
Henry Kurcom	Corp.	" "	Nov. 25	
Uryah Carpenter	"	Apr. 8	Sep. 30	
Timothy Royce	"	" 2	" 28	
Moses M[ ]	"	" 10	" 7	
Benj^a Winchil	Drum	" 1	Oct.(?)20	
Amos Lawrance		" 6	Nov. 25	
Joshua Ramont		" 8	" 27	
Bille Blin		Mar. 31		
Martin Brunson		Apr. 1	Oct. 20	
Asa Barnes		" 15	" 18	
Gideon Barnes		May 24	Nov. 25	
John Brown		Apr. 8		Oct. 20
John Bugbe		" 20	Sep. 30	
David Barnes		" 8	Nov. 13	
John Bell		May 1	" 25	
Thomas Boner (?)		" 22	" 3	
Thomas Bulkly		" 27	" 25	
Backos Negroe		April 11	Nov. 25	
Lenard Cady		" 5	Oct. 20	

FOURTH REGIMENT. 153

Mens Names	Quality	Time of Inlistment	When Discharged	Dead and Captivated
John Collins		April 25	Oct. 20	
Abner Curtis Jr.		" 1	" 31	
James Coburn		" 30	" 18	
William Clark		May 22	" 31	
Samel Cotten		" 23	Nov. 25	
James Curtis		Mar. 30		
Abrom Dayley		Apr. 8	Oct. 10	
Daniel Gaines		" 3		
[ ]		May 17		
[ ]		Mar. 30	Oct. 18	
John Hide		Apr. 10		Deserted June 30
William Johnson		" 8		Sep. 30
Richerd Killorn		" 5	Nov. 13	
Eben Killo		May 27	" 25	
Ephram Loyon		Apr. 8	" 27	
Nathan Loyon		May 5	" "	
John Lattemore		Mar. 30	Oct. 27	
Amos Murey (?)		Apr. [ ]	[ ] 30	
John Mechall		" 12		Oct. 4
Robrt Martin		May 11	Oct. 18	
James Martin		Apr. 5	" 20	
Robert Martin Ju{r}		" "	Nov. 25	
William Nott		May 27	" "	
Ebenez. Prindel		Apr. 11	Oct. 20	
John Poolen		" 13	" "	
Isaac Parsons		May 3		Sep. 11
Ezrah Prindel		Apr. 3	Nov. 25	
Elisha Parker		" 10	" "	
James Parker		May 10	" 27	
Stephen [?]		Apr. 6	" 12	
Willson Roolleson		May 27	" "	
Benja Raxford		Mar. 29	Oct. 10	
Benja Smith		" 31	Nov. 16	
John Squire		Apr. 8	Oct. 20	
Mosis Smith		" 1		Oct. 19
Gershom Smith		May 27	Oct. 18	
David Spensor		" 22	" "	
Ebenr Sanford		Apr. 8	" 20	
Suckhegun		Mar. 30	Nov. 25	
Josiah Tharpe		Apr. 8	Sep. 30	
John Teese		" "	Nov. 27	
Pick Fripe		" "	" "	
Abrom Foster		" "	Oct. 18	
Richard Foroway		" 2		July 22
Jonathan Wright		Mar. 30	Nov. 25	
Fransis Whittmore		Apr. 28	" "	
Jonathan Webb		Mar. 29	" 3	
Ely Whaples		Apr. 3	" 25	
Cabil Woolcot		Mar. 31	Sep. 28	
Mosis Whitney		Apr. 8		May 8
Isaac Suncemon		May 19	Nov. 27	

[Indorsed] Capt Eliph{t} Whittleseys Muster Roll Jany 1757
Jno Lattimer
Eli Whaples

[State Library, Adams Papers.]

CAMPAIGN OF 1756.

Names & Rank of Such as were in ye last years Service & are now of ye Compa of Capt Elipht Whitlesey

Lieut. Elipht Whittlesey
Corp Jonathn Brooks
Ely Whaples
Richard Kilborn
Richard Torroway
Asa Barns
Elisha Parker
John Collins
Timothy Rice
Moses Matthews
James Coborn
Ebenezer Prindle
Henry Kircum
Caleb Woolcot
John Lattimer
Suekheagon Indian
Benja Smith
Benjamin Roseford (?)

James Curtice
Hill Hollister
Serj. Edward Mercy
Serj. Moses Earles
Joshua Raymond
Ichabod Brown
John Bugbye
Wm Nolton
Epm Lyon
Moses Whitney
Abraham Dayley
Wm Huff
David Spencer
Saml Cotten
John Bell
Isaac Suncemon
Willson Rowleson
Gershom Smith

[Indorsed] Capt Elipt Whittlesey's Roll of half pay
[State Library, War 5, 324.]

Of this company, 56 men marched from Wethersfield and 20 from Pomfret.
[State Library, War 6, 289.]

SEVENTH COMPANY—CAPT. LACEY.

David Lacey [of Fairfield], Captain.   [Colonial Records.]
Gideon Tomlinson, First Lieutenant and Captain.
[Colonial Records. State Library, War 6, 237.]
Gershom Huble, Second Lieutenant.

David Lacy Captain gone to Albany sick
Gideon Tomlinson 1st Lieut.
Gershom Huble 2nd "   Sick at Albany
Daniel Tunell Serj. at Alby Sick
James Morehouse "   wth the Captn
Elisha Risdon "   at Alby Sick
Elizer Hall "   wth the Captain
David Wheeler Clerk Confined
John Tredwell Corp. Sick at fort Edward
Ebener Foot "   Sick at Albany
Gilbert McKinsey "   "   "   "
Daniel Beardsle "   with the Captain
Joseph Phippene Drumer Sick at Alby
Andros Joseph
Adams Daniel at Alby Sick
Anguvine Lewis wth the sick at Alby
Allexander William sick fort Edwd
Blackman John at Alby Sick
Bennet Charles sick at fort Edwd
Bennet Gershom
Bennet Lewis with the Lieut
Bennet Daniel sick at Alby

FOURTH REGIMENT.

Beach Nathan   Sick Albany
Beach Daniel   Sick fort Edwd
Beach Richard
Burton Robert   Sick at fort Edwd
Burton William   on Comm^d Alb^y
Burton George
Cooley Benj^a never Joyned
Cooley Joseph   at Alb^y Sick
Castle John   "   "   "
Chapman Hope   wth the sick Alb^y
Chops John
Dascomb Thomas   at Alb^y Sick
Dascomb Thos Junr "   "
Defratus Lewis   Confined
Daniel Henry   Sick at fort Edwd
Downs John   sick at Alb^y
Evis Benj^a
Flora John
Frost Benj^a
Gregory Gilead   at Alb^y Sick
Hollowell Willm "   "   "
Hall Icabud
Hinman Elihu   at Alb^y Sick
Judson Henry
Jones James   Sick at fort Edwd
Knap John   wth the sick at Alb^y
Lord Samuel   Sick at Alb^y
Lion Samuel   at Fort Edwd Sick
Lion Abell   at Albany Sick
Lacy Isaac   "   "   "
Man John
Man Samuel   at Albany Sick
Man Mathew   with the Sick at Alb^y
Morehouse Jehu   Dead
Meker Daniel   Left with the sick at fort Edwd
Mills Ebenezer   Sick at Alb^y
Metauk Taukus
Moynot Peter   Dead
Morehouse Jethro
Nodine Lewis   Sick at Alb^y
Nicholas Elnathan   wth the sick F. Edwd
Peet Daniel   Sick at Albany
Sealey Ephraim
Shelley Timothy   on Command at Alb^y
Stratton David   at Albany Sick
Shirmon Thos
Turrell Nathan   at Alb^y Sick
Tredwell Jacob   at fort Edwd with the Sick
Treadwell Ephraim   at Fort Edward sick
Webb Distrow
Ward Samuel   at Alb^y Sick
Wakelee Abell   with the Captain
Whaley Jon^a with the Sick at Alb^y
Brooknis Cyrus   never Joyned
Beadlee Enos   Dead.

This muster roll, signed by Henry Leddel Muster Master General, is dated Camp at Fort William Henry Oct. 13, 1756.

[*State Library, Adams Papers.*]

CAMPAIGN OF 1756.

Names & Rank of Men who were in last years Service & now have right to Half Pay in Capt Lieu^t Lacys Company

	Month & Day of Inlistment			Month & Day of Inlistment	
Lieut. David Lacy	April	1	Jonathan Waley	April	23
Serj. James Morehouse		5	Henry Judson		6
Drum. Ebenezer Foot		6	Denius Coleman		8
Benjⁿ Evis		3	Lewis Angevine		20
Gershom Bennet		5	Samuel Lord		21
Robert Burton		19	Samuel Man		14
Disborow Webb		5	Daniel Addams		17
Nathan Beech		5	Talker Metauk, Indian		17
William Burton		5	Lewis Bennet		14
John Knap		6	John Chops, Indian		17
John Castle		5	Tom Shermon, Indian		15
John Man		3	Nathan Turrell		20
Eliezer Hall		13	John Treedwell	May	3
Hope Chapman		21	John Meanwell		7
Benj^a Frost		21	David Wheeler		8
Jehu Morehouse		21	Matthew Man		8

[*State Library, War 5, 305.*]

Capt. David Lacey died and First Lieutenant Gideon Tomlinson succeeded him as Captain.

[*State Library, War 6, 237.*]

This company marched from Stratfield.

[*State Library, War 6, 237.*]

EIGHTH COMPANY — CAPT. WOOD.

John Wood [of Danbury], Captain. [*Colonial Records.*]
Jonah Daten, First Lieutenant.
John Benedict, 3d, Second Lieutenant. [*Colonial Records.*]

```
John Wood      Captain      at Alby Sick
Jonah Daten    First Lieut.  "   "    "
John Benedict 2nd    "       at Fort Edwd Sick
Ezra Stevens   Sarj.         at Alby Sick
Ebenezer Leonard "
Saml Canfield         "      on Commd Alby
John Stevens          "      Sick at Alby
Abell Prindle  Clerk
Jona Birched   Corp.         Sick at fort Edwd
James Morehouse "
Daniel Wildman        "      wh the Teams
Joseph Hubbard
Abraham Towner Drumer        Sick at Alby
Anguvine Zacha
Ambler John    fort Ed Sick
Arnold James   never Joyned
Benedict Lemuel  fort Ewd Sick
Beardslee James  Sick at Alby
Burret Eleazer   with the Liefts
Barnum Ebenezer  Sick at fort Edwd
Barns Joseph   Sick at Albany
```

FOURTH REGIMENT.

Barns Benj[a]   Dead
Barnum David
Canfield Daniel   Sick at Alb[y]
Curtiss Samuel
Chapell Nathan[1]
Debill Nathan   Sick at Alb[y]
Dickinson Nathan   "   "   "
Daten Josiah   never Joyned
Douglass Domini   Sick at fort Edw[d]
Davis Thadeus   on Command Alb[y]
Dodge Joseph   never Joyned
Ferry Charles
Fairchild William   Sick at fort Edw[d]
Green David   Sick at Alb[y]
Gregory David   Deserted Fort Edw[d]
Hendrick Benoni   on Com[d] at Alb[y]
Hollister Nathan[1]   Deserted at Fort Ed.
Hubard John   Sick at Albany
Hill Silas
Hays Jonathan
Harris David   Sick at Alb[y]
Hamlin Elijah   Deserted at fort Edw[d]
Huble Jepthah   at Alb[y] with the sick
Jarvis Thomas   Sick at Albany
Kimburly Fitch   Sick at Alb[y]
Ketchum Ezra   Dead
Lobdell Jacob   sick at Alb[y]
Lyon Samuel
Lyon John   Confined
Murray William   Sick at fort Edw[d]
Moger Jehiel   Sick at Albany
Northrop Abraham
Nichols Joseph   Sick at Alb[y]
Nuttleton Amos
Nicholson Eliphaz   Sick at Alb[y]
Omstead Nathan   Dead
Osborn Moses   with the Captain
Osborn John   Sick at Albany
Peek Charles   Deserted
Perry Elisha
Perry John
Prindle John
Prindle Isaac   sick at fort Edw[d]
Peirce Francis   sick at Alb[y]
Peirce Jonathan   sick at fort Edw[d]
Rockwell Daniel
St. John James   sick at fort Edw[d]
Stephens Abraham   "   "   "   "
Shepherd John   Deserted half moon
Sealey Zadock   Sick fort Edward
Spees John   "   "   "
Sumers Ebenezer   "   "   "
Vedito John   Sick at Alb[y]
Whitney James   "   "   "
Waterbury Gideon   "   "   "
Wildman Richard   "   "   "

This muster roll, signed by Henry Leddel Muster Master General, is dated Camp at Fort William Henry Oct. 13, 1756.

[*State Library, Adams Papers.*]

CAMPAIGN OF 1756.

Capt Jno Woods Half Pay Roll for Such in his Comp^a as were in last years Campain.

	Month & Day of Enlistment			Month & Day of Enlistment	
Corp. Joseph Hubberd	April	9	Charles Ferry	April	8
Ebenezer Leonard		9	Joseph Barns		14
Benoney Hendrix		13	Jonathan Hays		16
Jeptha Hubbel		12	James Morehouse	May	3
Nathan Dickenson		9	Samuel Curtice	Apr.	7
Josiah Daten		11	John Stevens		9
Samuel Lyon		9	Ebenezer Barnum		13
Elijah Hamblin		12	John Perry		8
Abraham Stevens		12	Nath^{ll} Worden		10
Francis Pierce		12	John Spees		8
Moses Osburn		7	James Whitney	May	4
Richard Wildman		10	James St John		5
Charles Peek		8	Daniel Rockwell		5
Joseph Dodge		15	Silas Hill	April	9
Samuel Canfield		7			

[Indorsed] Capt John Woods half pay Roll

[*State Library, War 5, 321.*]

Abraham Stephens in this company was of Danbury.

[*State Library, War 6, 269.*]

NINTH COMPANY—CAPT. HOIT.

Joseph Hoit of Stanford, Captain.
Samuel Adams, Jr., of Stratford, First Lieutenant.
Jedidiah Hull of Fairfield, Second Lieutenant.

[*Colonial Records.*]

Note: These officers were appointed by the Assembly, but no evidence has been found to show that they were commissioned or the company raised.

TENTH COMPANY—CAPT. STODDARD.

Moses Stoddard of Litchfield, Captain.
Adam Gallop of Groton, First Lieutenant.
Daniel Fitch of Norwalk, Second Lieutenant.

[*Colonial Records.*]

Note: These officers were appointed by the Assembly, but no evidence has been found to show that they were commissioned or the company raised.

MISCELLANEOUS.

LIEUT. SMITH'S COMPANY.

Samuel Smith, Lieutenant, and the company under his command were paid Dec. 22, 1756, for garrisoning the Massachusetts frontier.

[*Comptroller's Office, Treasurer's Book.*]

SERJ. GOODRICH'S COMPANY.

Charles Goodrich, Serjeant, and nine privates under his command were paid Nov. 11, 1756, for garrisoning the Massachusetts frontier.

[*Comptroller's Office, Treasurer's Book.*]

SOLDIERS DECEASED.

A List of the Connecticut Troops who have Dyed in Albany.

Names	Quality	Date		of what Company
Israel Barns	P. Soldier	May	27	Capt. Jefferys
John Weed	"	"	23	{ Col. Whitings at F. Edward
William Lansford	"	June	8	Maj. Stores
Enos Bearsley	"	July	19	Capt. Leacy
Thomas Sherwood	"	Aug.	5	Capt. Whiting
Benjamin Wells	Serj.	"	18	" "
Nathan Wickwire	Pr. S^r	"	28	Col. Lee
Ichabod Wells	"	Sep.	12	Capt. Grant
John Brown	"	"	16	Maj. Stores
Daniel Cone	Lieut.	"	17	
Elisha Tomling	P. Sol.	"	"	
John Ryley	"	"	18	Capt. Porter
John Carter	"	"	"	" "
James Bearsley	"	"	20	Capt. Wood
John Westover	"	"	21	Capt. Hitchcock
William Buck	"	"	20	Capt. Porter
George Cam	"	"	16	Capt. Whitting
Samuel Trusdel	"	"	24	Col. Ward
Thomas Foster	Lieut.	"	28	Capt. Whittelsey
Isaac Buel	P. Sold.	"	29	Capt. Porter
Luke Fulford	"	"	"	Col. Payson
Aaron Williams	"	"	"	Capt. Allyn
Jonathan Palmer	Serj.	"	"	Col. Whiting
Joshua Lyon	P. Sol.	"	"	Col. John Payson
Gershom Clenton	"	"	"	Capt. Hawley
Elisha Bowman	"	Oct.	2	Col. J. Payson

CAMPAIGN OF 1756.

Names	Quality	Date		of what Company
Willm Johnson	P. Sol.	Oct.	2	Capt. Whittelsey
Ezekiel Baley	"	"	4	Capt. Harris
Isaac Dunham	"	"	"	Capt. Wells
Joseph Foot	"	"	8	Capt. Hides
Isaac Chamberlin	"	"	9	Maj. Patterson
Nathan Osburn	"	"	"	Capt. Hides
Cyprian Rood	"	"	10	Capt. Putnam
Jonas Knap	"	"	11	Capt. Watterbury
Timothy Grasier	"	"	"	Capt. Slapp
Jeremiah Bingham	"	"	9	Col. Whiting
Joseph Cheat	"	"	11	Capt. Billings
Sipio Negro	"	"	14	Capt. Hawleys
Phineas Pond	"	"	16	
Daniel Smith	"	"	19	Capt. Whittelsey
Willm Fairchild	"	"	22	Capt. Wood
James Talington	"	"	20	Capt. Allyn
Elijah Martain	"	"	21	" "
John Bowman	"	"	24	Capt. Whittelsey
Enos Doolittle	"	"	28	Capt. Hitchcock
Willm Murry	"	"	30	Capt. Wood
Josiar Hanley	"	"	"	Capt. Boldwin
Ezekiel Strong	"	Nov.	3	Capt. Hides
Peter Moredock	"	"	6	Capt. Harriss
Samuel Cone	"	"	"	" "
Abner Barns	"	"	7	Capt. Hitchcock
Wm Young	"	"	9	Capt. Grant
Gala Peters	"	"	10	Col. Ward
Peter McFelling	"	"	11	Capt. Porters
Josiah Weedge	"	"	15	Maj. Stores
Elezar Solwell	"	"	16	
Nathaniel Brace	"	"	25	Gen. Lyman
Henry Smith	"	"	26	Capt. Wells

E. Lyman's letter accompanying this list is dated Albany, Dec. 6, 1756.

[*State Library, War 6, 367, 368.*]

Ezekel Fitch
Asa Richardson
Timothy Thorp
Oliver Thorp
Jonathan Evirt
Benajah Strongue
Zacceas Downer
Stephen Hardin Williams
David Woodwoth
Samuel Freeman

Abraham Fitch
Derias Waterman
William Southworth
John Watson
Benjamin Butter
Ezekiel Huntington
Elihue Baskim
Nathan Fitch
Jos Blackman
Pyras

The above persons are those that are in the Expediton against Crown pinte

            Josiah Rockwell Clark

[Indorsed] Capt Jos Fitch's Return 1756
            [*Connecticut Historical Society.*]

MISCELLANEOUS.

Lebanon June ye 4 1756 The Acount of the Men that are Inlisted Within the Limits of Capt Caleb Hides Company

John Goold	John Vaghan
Benj Woodworth	Elijah Dewey J{r}
Lemuel Woodworth	Joshua Bill
Thomas Marvel	David Lomis
Wm Lyman	Ebenr Bill J{r}
Frances Story	Jonathan Coye
Andrew Lisk	John Hamer
Wm Dewey	

[*Connecticut Historical Society.*]

Soldiers named in commissary's account, 1756.

Thomas Bingham	in Capt. Putnam's	company
Thomas Bingdon	" " "	"
Charles Bills	" " "	"
Thomas Hutten	" Noah Grant's	"
Nathan Parks	" Maj. Paterson's	"
Wm Harison, died,	" Capt. James Harris'	"
Samuel Brooks	" Col. Lee's	"
William Theley	" " "	"
Jesse alias John Minord	" " "	"
Thomas Brigdon	" Capt. Putnam's	"
George Boyles	" " "	"
Thomas Huntington	" Capt. Noah Grant's	"
Ebenezer Garey	" Capt. Joseph Hodges	"
Saml Morier	" Col. Lee's	"

[*State Library, War 6, 330.*]

The following soldiers were raised from the 12th regiment of militia, Jonathan Trumbull, Colonel.

Impressed June 9 from the company in Colchester

Ephraim Rowley   Joel Chamberlin

Inlisted May 27 from the company in the society in Andover; "the number that have inlisted are seven."

Thomas Rennals, a Battow man
John Bill
Nehemiah Closson
Eleazer Closson } these in Goverments service
Jonathan Dewey
Solomon Bill
Moses Hutchinson

[These names follow, in the handwriting of Col. Trumbull.]

Jon{th} Bill	Jno Gibbs Junr
Jno Bingham	James Smalley
Arunah Snow	Simeon Chappel
David Woodward	Jno Wise
Jacob Guile	Haz Davenport
Benja Ellis	Willm White Junr
Saml Woodward Junr	Jere Gillet
Benja Woodworth	Nathl Curtis
Reuben Woodworth	David Dodge Batto man
James Woodworth	Thos Washbun went to{ds} Boston

[Indorsed] Capt Leach & Capt Cushman's Return

[Cushman commanded the company in the second society in Lebanon.]

CAMPAIGN OF 1756.

The following soldiers from the 12th regiment of militia, Jonathan Trumbull, Colonel, were a part of the quota ordered raised in October

From the company in the south part of Millington Robert Harvey enlisted, Hez. Usher enlisted, James Steward, Jr., detached.

Impressed from the company of the parish of Goshen in Lebanon.
John Wise
Ephraim Carpenter
Gideon Gay
Benoni Clark

Impressed from the company in the first society in Hebron.
Daniel Cogswell
Abijah Man
David Dean
Nathan Fuller
Gideon Jones
Tim° Sewart

Impressed from the troop under the command of Dan Throope
James White
Ebenezer White
Joseph Waters

Impressed from the south company in the first society in East Haddam.
John Warner
John Wetmore
Joseph Church, a gunsmith

From the north company in the parish of Hadlyme in East Haddam Abel Willey Junr detached, Richard Booge inlisted

Impressed from the north company in the first society in Lebanon,
John Hadlock Junr
Samuel Hatch
Wm Lisk

Detached from Colchester
Asa Treadway
Shubel Smith
Nathan Chapman

Inlisted from Glastenbury
Amos Strong
David Smith
Richard Dicknson
John Neland

[*Connecticut Historical Society.*]

Reuben Jones of Capt. Putnam's company was wounded.
[*State Library, War 6, 214.*]

John Law served as Aid-de-Camp and Secretary to Gen. Lyman.
[*State Library, War 6, 206.*]

Col. Nathan Whiting served as Quartermaster-General.
[*State Library, War 6, 243.*]

Owen Fluskey of Middletown captured April 21, 1756, and carried a prisoner to Canada, escaped Aug. 7, 1757.
[*Colonial Records.*]

John Broadstreet deserted from Col. Wooster's Company.
[*Connecticut Gazette, No. 61.*]

Letter from Albany dated June 7 states that Lieut. Brooks a Connecticut gentleman has been massacred.
[*Connecticut Gazette, No. 62.*]

Capt. Stevens of Danbury with about 40 men is mentioned, apparently as being in Pennsylvania.

[*Connecticut Gazette, No. 66.*]

Peleg Woodworth and Jn° Wanepoom, soldiers.

[*Comptroller's Office, Treasurer's Book.*]

Pelatiah Bliss, Surgeon's Mate died in the service before Feb. 9, 1757.

[*State Library, War 7, 96.*]

Isaac Tucker, Armourer from July 1 to Oct. 15, 1756.

[*State Library, War 7, 92.*]

Note: A great part of the eight companies designated as the ninth and tenth companies of each regiment had been raised when, in consequence of a letter received late in October from the Earl of Loudon, they were dismissed.

[*Colonial Records.*]

CAMPAIGN OF 1757.

Note: The General Assembly in February, 1757, resolved to raise 1400 men for the next campaign, to be formed into one regiment of fourteen companies, to act in conjunction with the regular troops under the command of the Earl of Loudon. In October the Assembly ordered the enlisting of three companies of ninety-four men each, officers included, out of the troops already in service, to remain in service through the winter. A vessel of war was purchased and put in service by order of the Assembly. An alarm in August, at the time of the capture of Fort William Henry, called out many of the militia.

COL. LYMAN'S REGIMENT.

REGIMENTAL OFFICERS.

Phineas Lyman [of Suffield] appointed Colonel and Captain of the first company, Feb. 1757. Discharged Dec. 2.

Nathan Whiting [of New Haven] appointed Lieutenant-Colonel and Captain of the second company, Feb. 1757. Discharged Nov. 24.

Nathan Payson [of Hartford] appointed Major and Captain of the third company, Feb. 1757. Discharged Dec. 2.
[*Colonial Records.*]

Timothy Hierlihy [of Middletown], Adjutant from March 8 to Dec. 1, 1757.
[*State Library, War 7, 98.*]

Rev. Benjamin Pomeroy [of Hebron], Chaplain from Aug. 2 to Oct. 2, 1757.
[*State Library, War 7, 109.*]

Rev. Asa Spaulding of Fairfield entered the service as Chaplain May 19, 1757, and received pay for seven month's service.
[*State Library, War 7, 93.*]

Elisha Lord [of Farmington], Surgeon March 3 to Oct. 16, 1757.
[*State Library, War 7, 105.*]

Silas Baldwin [of Derby], Surgeon's Mate from May 30 to Oct. 30, 1757
[*State Library, War 7, 119.*]

Silas Baldwin [of Derby], Surgeon from Oct. 30, 1757, to May 24, 1758.
[*State Library, War 7, 91.*]

David Adams [of Canterbury], Surgeon's Mate from March 3, 1757, to April 30, 1758.
[*State Library, War 7, 118.*]

Jabez Hamlin [of Middletown],
Hezekiah Huntington [of Norwich], } appointed Commissaries of purchase, Feb. 1757.
Theophilus Nichols [of Stratford],
[*Colonial Records.*]

Josiah Wright, Commissary at Fort Edward, Nov. 1757.
[*State Library, War 7, 133.*]

FIRST COMPANY—COL. LYMAN.

Phineas Lyman [of Suffield], Colonel and Captain.
Aaron Hitchcock [of Suffield], Captain-Lieutenant.
John Stoughton [of Windsor], Lieutenant.
Ezekiel Lewis, Ensign.
[*Colonial Records.*]
Partrick Welsh, Ensign.

A pay Roll of Colonel Lymans Company in the Conecticut Regiment 1757

CAMPAIGN OF 1757.

Mens Names & Quality	Time of Inlisting	Discharged	Dead
Phinehas Lyman Col.	Feb. 21	Dec. 2	
Aaron Hitchcock Capt. Lieut.	" "	" "	
John Stoughton Lieut.	" "	" 6	
Ezekiel Lewis Ens.	" "	July 20	
*Partrick Welsh "	July 21	Dec. 2	
Nathaniel Riply Q M		Sep. 21	
John Stoughton "	Sep. 22	Dec. 6	
John Chick Serg. Maj.	Mar. 29	Sep. 19	
†David Pique Serg.	" 7	Nov. 29	
Joel Adams "	" 17	" 11	
Seth King "	" 16	Sep. 21	
Giles Wolcott "	" 31	June 30	
Ebenezer Belknop "	May 31	Dec. 2	
Aseph Kent "	Nov. 2	Nov. 11	
John Elsworth Clark	Apr. 4	Dec. 2	
Elijah Alderman Corp.	Mar. 27	Nov. 14	
William Rows "	June 5	Dec. 2	
William Thomson "	" "	Nov. 11	
Nathan Rice "	Apr. 1	June 4	
Ebenezer Belknop "	" 7	May 30	
Hoseah Wilcoks "	Nov. 2	Dec. 2	
Ashel Kent "	Mar. 28	Nov. 1	
Stephen Winchel Dm Maj.	Apr. 2	" 11	
Roger Crow Drum	Mar. 27	Dec. 1	
Jonathan Ashly Privat	" "	" 2	
William Andrus	Apr. 11	" "	
Elihu Andrus	" 8	June 4	
Samuel Adams	Mar. 26	Dec. 2	
Asel Bissel	" 27	" 3	
Hezekiah Bissel	" 7	Nov. 11	
Samuel Bird	" 9	Dec. 7	
Benjamin Baker	" 14	Nov. 11	
Jonathan Booth	" 15	" "	
Jese Belknop	" "	Dec. 2	
George Briant	Apr. 13		July 4
Elisha Burnom	Mar. 21	Dec. 7	
Eldad Barbar	Apr. 2	Nov. 20	
John Bodwill	July 1	Dec. 11	
Silas Coy	Apr. 2	Sep. 15	
Hoseah Curtis	Feb. 21	Dec. 2	
Silvanos Curtis	Mar. 21	" "	
Rubin Cole (?)	" 28	" "	
John Conner	Apr. 10	" "	
Abel Collins	Mar. 15		Never Joynd
Stephen Deming	Apr. 11		Nov. 1
Jeremiah Daly	Mar. 27	Dec. 1	
Abraham Dibble	July 12	" 2	
Joel Eno	Mar. 28	Nov. 10	
John Egleston	Apr. 8	" 2	
Bildad Eston	" "	Oct. 15	
Josiah Philley	" 7		Sep. 13
Israel Freman	" 5	Nov. 14	
Francis Fleming	Feb. 24		Deserted

* Lately of ye 35th Reg^t   [*General Orders of 1757.*]
† David Pike reduced to the ranks Sept. 17 ; restored to Serg. Oct. 8.
                                                        [*General Orders of 1757.*]

COL. LYMAN'S REGIMENT. 169

Mens Names & Quality	Time of Inlisting	Discharged	Dead
Obediah Gleson	Mar. 7	Dec. 2	
William Gayns	" 28		Sep. 1
Stephen Griffin	" "	Sep. 29	
Normon Green	" 12	Nov. 14	
Gideon Gyllit	Apr. 11		Sep. 9
Return Holcomb	Mar. 15	Nov. 14	
Silas Holcomb	" 28	" 11	
Elijah Holcomb	Apr. 4	" 30	
James Huston	Mar. 23		Never Joynd
Richard Hudleston	" 28	Dec. 2	
Ruben Holiberd	Apr. 5	Nov. 24	
Oliver Hanchet	Mar. 4	Dec. 2	
Apleton Holister	Aug. 19	" "	
David Johnson	Mar. 15	Nov. 11	
John Japhet	" 29	Dec. 2	
Nathan Kelsey	Apr. 7	" 1	
Ebeneser King	Mar. 17	" 2	
Jese Mathews	" 15	" "	
John Mills	Apr. 3	" "	
Jobe Marshal	" 7	Aug. 10	
Amasa Marshal	" 11	" 19	
Othniel Moses	Mar. 27	Nov. 1	
Bethuel Norton	" 21	Dec. 2	
Walpole Negro	" 26	" "	
William Negro	Apr. 20	" 11	
John Need	Mar. 17	Nov. 11	
Wonks Nobikin	" 14	" 26	
Uziah Owin	Feb. 21	Dec. 2	
Gersham Orvis	Mar. 28		Deserted Aug. 9
Simeon Plumb	" 15	Nov. 14	
Joseph Piney	Apr. 5	Dec. 2	
Dan Pumroy	Mar. 11	Nov. 24	
Enos Parker	Apr. 6	" 11	
Jonathan Pascho	" 7	Dec. 2	
Noah Peas	Feb. 25	" "	
Nathan Rice	June 5	" 3	
Jonathan Remington	Mar. 28		July 11
John Rice	" "	Oct. 15	
John Ross	Apr. 5	Dec. 2	
Joseph Row	" 12	Nov. 2	
Joseph Roger	Mar. 12	Dec. 2	
Samuel Robins	" 9	Nov. 11	
Elisha Stodard	Apr. 10	" 25	
David Soper	Mar. 30	" 30	
James Tuller	" 28		July 26
Elisha Tylletson	" 2		Oct. 12
[ ]	July 1	Nov. [ ]	
David Towsey	Mar. 17	" 11	
Benjamin Tucker	" 27		Deserted Apr. 18
Benjamin Twing	" "		Never Joynd
Hoseah Wilcoxson	" 28	Nov. 1	
John Winchel	Apr. 2	" 11	
Samuel Worner	Mar. 26		Aug. 9
John Wolling	Apr. 7	Dec. 1	
Elihu Wylson	" 8		Never Joynd
Zebulon Winslow	Mar. 7		Sep. 17
Daniel Wolling	Apr. 7	Nov. 11	

Mens Names & Quality	Time of Inlisting	Discharged	Dead
John Waters	Apr. 11	July 17	
George Webster	Feb. 21	Aug. 18	
William Ross	" 26	June 4	
William Thomson	Mar. 22	" "	
Joseph Negro	Sep. 30		Oct. 25
Elthura Lambson	Mar. 8	July 11	
George Steel	" 27	Aug. 18	
Nathaniel Riply	Sep. 21	Dec. 3	

N B. The Soldiers whose Names are underwritten 'tis Supposed March'd in their Return from Canaan to their Respective homes on the Colony's Cost therefor to their Names is Annexd the Number of Days each Soldier probably lived at ye Governments Cost and the charge is made at 14^d p Day and stopt out of the pay now if hereafter any of said Soldiers give proper Evidence y^t they had not So much at the Colonys Cost they are to be considered accordingly

	Days		Days
Ebenezer Belknap	3	Appleton Holister	4
Elijah Alderman	"	Azoah Owen	"
Jon^a Ashly	"	Hosea Wilcox	2
Hez. Bissil	"	Roger Crow	"
Jesse Belknap	"	Wm Andrus	"
Elisha Burnam	"	Sam. Adams	"
Eldad Barbar	"	Sam. Bird	"
John Bodell	"	Sylv. Curtis	"
John Conner	"	Ruben Cole	"
Obadeah Gleson	"	Jere. Daley	"
Elij^h Holcomb	"	Abra. Dibble	"
John Japhet	"	Jesse Matthews	"
Jos. Pinny	"	John Mills	"
Jon^a Pasco	"	Bethuel Norton	"
Jos. Rogers	"	Woux Nobicen	"
Nathan Royce	4	David Soper	"
Hoseal Curtiss	4		

[Indorsed]   Capt Amos Hitchcock of Genl Lyman's Comp^y Muster Roll Feb^r 15 1758
Bildad Easton

[State Library, Adams Papers.]

A Muster Role of Co^l Phinehas Lymans Company 1757

[Indorsed]   Jno. Ellsworth

[State Library, Adams Papers.]

Christian Taylor appears on
A Muster Roll of Major Genl Lyman's Company Fort Edward Octr 3^d 1757

[Indorsed]   Benj^a Pomeroy Chaplin
Jonth Ashley p

[State Library, Adams Papers.]

COL. LYMAN'S REGIMENT.   171

SECOND COMPANY—LIEUT.-COL. WHITING.

Nathan Whiting [of New Haven], Lieutenant-Colonel and Captain.
[*Colonial Records.*]
Jabez Thompson, First Lieutenant.
Benjamin Hine [of Milford], Second Lieutenant.
Abraham Foot [of Branford], Ensign.   [*Colonial Records.*]

A pay Roll of Lieut Colo Nathan Whitings Company in General Lyman Regiment for the year 1757

Mens names & quality		Time of Inlistment		Discharged		Dead	
Nathan Whiting	Lieut. Col.	Feb.	21	Nov.	24		
Jabez Thompson	1st Lieut.	Mar.	8	"	"		
Benjn Hine	2rd "	"	"	"	"		
Abram Foot	Ens.	Feb.	23	"	"		
Joseph Sperry	Sergt.	Mar.	4	"	"		
Eli Hawkins	"	"	11	"	"		
John Barns	"	"	28	"	"		
David Collins	"	"	"	"	"		
Jesse Johnson	Corp.	"	25	"	"		
Hezh Tuttle	"	"	"	"	"		
John Fox	"	"	24	"	"		
John Smith	"	"	12	"	"		
Benjn Humphrey	Viel Clerk	"	10	"	"		
Nicholas Howel	Drum	"	1	"	"		
David Austin	Privt	Feb.	23	"	"		
Anthony Angivine		Mar.	23	"	"		
James Atwater		"	29	"	"		
Henry Bates		"	"	"	"		
Jonathan Butler		"	17	"	13		
Samuel Botchford		"	14	"	24		
David Bishop		"	27	"	"		
Justice Baldwin		"	23	"	"		
Benjn Brackett		"	26	"	"		
Jotham Bulckley (?)		"	"	"	"		
James A. Brolton		"	31	"	8		
John Conner		"	4			Aug.	6
Daniel Chatfield		"	10	Nov.	24		
Isaac Cook		"	29	"	"		
Abrahm Cooper		Feb.	28	"	"		
Wade Cooke		Mar.	23	"	"		
John Clark		"	27	"	"		
William Duplex		Feb.	24	"	"		
Ezra Dodge		Mar.	29	"	"		
Joseph Downs		"	25	"	"		
William Duncan		Apr.	2	"	13		
Zachah Fairchield		Mar.	12	"	24		
Thomas Fling		Apr.	1	"	"		
Daniel Fox		Mar.	29	"	13		
Jesse Ford		Apr.	3	"	24		
Benjn Graham		Mar.	21	"	"		
Caleb Gilbert		"	26	"	"		
Michael Gilbert		Apr.	4	"	"		
John Gibbins		"	1	"	"		
Samuel Hale		Mar.	11	"	8		
Thomas Hodge		"	28	"	24		
Aaron Hine		"	27	"	"		
Abraham Jacobs		"	26	"	8		
John Kencade		"	28	"	24		

CAMPAIGN OF 1757.

Mens names & quality	Time of Inlistment		Discharged		Dead	
Moses Killum	Mar.	28	Nov.	30		
Tim° Ludington	"	31	"	24		
James Lemons	"	28	"	"		
Isaac Mallery	Apr.	2	"	"		
George Mitchel	Mar.	25	"	28		
Joseph Osbourn	"	"	"	13		
Abra^m Osbourn	"	26	"	24		
Benjn Peas	"	18	"	"		
Charles Plumb	"	14	"	13		
Nathan Palmer	Apr.	4	"	24		
Caleb Palmer	"	7	"	"		
Seth Plumb	"	5	"	"		
Benjn Pairpoint	Mar.	26	"	"		
Azuriah Pratt	"	28	"	"		
Timothy Plant	"	"	"	"		
Benjn Parmilee	"	"	"	13		
Philemon Potter	Apr.	5	"	24		
Aaron Page	Mar.	31	"	"		
Ebenez^r Roberts	"	21	"	"		
Benjn Russell	"	15	"	"		
David Rogers	Apr.	7	"	"		
Edward Rogers	Mar.	28	"	"		
David Royce	"	23	"	"		
Israel Smith	Apr.	4	"	"		
Eden Spery	Mar.	9	"	"		
Abel Summers	"	22	"	"		
William Stevens	"	25	"	"		
Nathl Silhrig	"	26	"	13		
Thomas Trickey	Feb.	26	"	24		
Stephen Thomas	"	28	"	13		
Daniel Tharp	Mar.	18	"	"		
Benjn Trim	"	23	"	24		
Ezekiel Tuttle	"	26	"	"		
Aaron Tuttle	"	"	"	"		
James Thomas	"	28	"	"		
Andrew Tuttle	"	"	"	"		
Ambrose Tuttle	"	29			Sept.	1
Josiah Whitney	"	19	Nov.	24		
Daniel Winston	"	6	"	13		
Moses Wooster	"	11	"	24		
Henry Wooster	Apr.	8	"	8		
Suckhegan Indian	Mar.	2	"	13		
James Rockwell	"	6	"	8		
Jn° Hatchet Towsey	"	8	"	24		
John Charles	"	9	"	13		
Thomas James	"	8	"	24		
Benjn Alley	"	9	"	13		
Jeffery Negro	"	28	"	24		
John Seabury	Apr.	14	"	"		
James Denison	"	12	"	"		
John Hatch	"	1	"	13		
Abra^m Brunson	"	26	"	24		
Jeohoida Wheadon	"	4	'	"		
Aaron Osmore	"	29	Aug.	30		

[Indorsed] Col° Nathan Whiting's Muster Roll December 1757
    Edwd Rogers p   [*State Library, Adams Papers.*]

Col° Nathan Whiting's Billeting Roll Decem^r 1757
                                    [*State Library, Adams Papers.*]

COL. LYMAN'S REGIMENT.

THIRD COMPANY — MAJ. PAYSON.

Nathan Payson [of Hartford], Major and Captain.
Samuel Wells, Jr. [of Hartford], First Lieutenant.
Noah Humphrey [of Simsbury], Second Lieutenant.

[*Colonial Records.*]

David Parsons, Ensign.
John Chick, Ensign.

Mens names & quality		Time of Inlistment		Discharged		Dead	
Nathan Payson	Maj.	Feby.	21	Dec.	2		
Samuel Wells	1st Lieut.	"	23	Nov.	30		
Noah Humphry	2nd "	"	23	Oct.	23		
David Parsons	Ensign	Mar.	5	Sept.	20		
John Chick	"	Sept.	20	Nov.	29		
Mavark Johnson	Qu. Mr Serj	Mar.	31	"	11		
Charles Buckland	Serg.	"	1	"	30		
Abner Meacham	"	"	24			Oct.	29
Philip Rice	"	"	18	Dec.	1		
William Grant	"	"	29	Sept.	12		
Jonathan Gillett	"	Oct.	29	Nov.	30		
Eliphaz Stell	Clerk	Mar.	29			Aug.	11
Elisha Done	"	Aug.	12	Nov.	30		
Benjn Keeney	Corp.	Mar.	1	"	"		
Daniel Sexton	"	"	29	"	6		
Benjn Grimes	"	"	30	Oct.	18		
Jonathan Robberds	"	"	1	Sept.	19		
William Stevens	"	Sept.	20	Nov.	30		
John Abott	Private	Mar.	31	Oct.	21		
Asahel Andrews	"	Apr.	8	Nov.	27		
Caleb Benjamin	"	Mar.	1	"	30		
Jonathan Bemant	"	"	29	"	11		
Joseph Blanchard	"	"	17	"	30		
Joseph Booth	"	"	18	"	11		
Stephen Cone	"	"	29	"	"		
Nathaniel Chapin	"	"	9	"	"		
Andrew Clerk	"	"	29	"	"		
Ashbel Charter	"	"	1	"	"		
David Case	"	Apr.	4	"	10		
Ebenezer Comes	"	Mar.	9	Oct.	26		
Lemuel Deming	"	"	1	Nov.	5		
Hezekiah Deming	"	"	29			July	29
Daniel Eaton	"	"	"	Nov.	30		
John Forgoson	"	"	10	"	5		
Edward Forbs	"	"	1	"	10		
Ephraim Flint	"	"	29			Aug.	31
Samuel Felt	"	"	10	Nov.	30		
Solomon Griswold	"	"	9	"	11		
Alexander Grant	"	"	29	"	"		
Luke Gridley	"	"	30	"	5		
Jonathan Gillett	"	"	29	Oct.	28		
Charles Gaylord	'	Apr.	8	Nov.	11		
Samuel Goudy	"	Mar.	9	Dec.	1		
Roger Griswold	"	"	14	Sept.	5		
Benjn Hulbert	"	July	30			Nov 1st	
Benjn Hale	"	Mar.	1	Nov.	5		
Elisha Humphrey	"	Aug.	9	"	11		
Solomon Hall	"	Apr.	5	"	30		
Silvenus Humphrey	"	Mar.	28	"	29		
David Hayden	"	"	30	"	"		

CAMPAIGN OF 1757.

Mens names & quality		Time of Inlistment		Discharged		Dead
Thomas Jerrald	Private	Mar.	8	Aug.	23	
Harding Jerrald	"	"	1	Nov.	5	
Jnº Kenp Perigo	"	Apr.	5			July 26
Eben^r Bloggett	"	"	27	July	30	
Benoni Loomis	"	Mar.	1	Nov.	30	
John Matson	"	"	30	Sept.	19	
Isaac Mix	"	"	29	Nov.	30	
Thomas Middleton	"	"	"	"	"	
Patrick McColoney	"	"	23	"	"	
John McClelen	"	"	29	"	"	
Ashbel Moses	"	"	28			Oct. 12
Theophilus Morrison	"	"	1	Nov.	30	
Aaron Noble	"	Apr.	21	"	"	
John Ormsbury	"	Mar.	29	Oct.	22	
Samuel Porter	"	"	8	Nov.	30	
Clother Pryor	"	"	14	"	"	
Warham Parsons	"	"	29	Dec.	1	
Eldad Parsons	"	"	"	Nov.	11	
Joshua Pomroy	"	"	"	"	"	
Daniel Pratt	"	"	19	"	"	
Noah Parsons	"	"	9	"	"	
William Pryor	"	"	29	"	"	
Shubal Reed	"	"	"	"	30	
John Rogers	"	"	14	"	5	
Hezekiah Reed	"	"	29	"	30	
Ezra Rodden	"	"	"			Aug. 31
Daniel Riordan	"	Aug.	4	Nov.	30	
Nathaniel Rogers	"	Mar.	29			Aug. 10
Amos Shepard	"	"	"	Nov.	30	
Jonathan Skinner	"	"	"	Sept.	13	
Zepheniah Snow	"	"	"	Nov.	30	
William Stevens	"	"	"	Sept.	19	
Ebenezer Sperry	"	Apr.	14	"	3	
Joseph Spencer	"	Mar.	31	Nov.	5	
Levi Strong	"	"	29			July 25
William Smith	"	Apr.	18	Deserted Apr. 20		
Jacob Tuller	"	Mar.	11	Nov.	5	
David Taylor	"	"	29	Aug.	27	
Jonathan Tyler	"	"	30	Nov.	29	
Jonathan Webster	"	"	29	"	30	
Jonathan Wood	"	"	"	"	"	
Zepheniah Webster	"	"	"	"	"	
Stephen Wood	"	"	"	"	11	
James Wallice	"	"	9	"	30	
Zipron Watson	"	"	30	Sept.	3	
John Wilson	"	"	"	"	"	
David Wilson	"	"	29	Nov.	30	
Isaac Whisk	"	"	7	"	29	
Jonathan Ward	"	"	31			Aug. 9
Abner Webb	"	"	19	Aug.	23	
Alexander Wilcott	"	"	29			Sept. 7
Samuel Waters	"	Apr.	8	Nov.	4	
Asahel Simons	"	Mar.	9	Aug.	4	
John Ripnier	"	"	29	Nov.	5	
Owen Fluskey	"	Aug.	27	"	30	
Nathan De Woolf	"	Sept.	13	"	5	
Elizer Robberds	"	"	19	"	30	
Roger Humphrey	"	Mar.	28	Aug.	9	

COL. LYMAN'S REGIMENT.

N. B. The Soldiers whose Names are underwritten 'tis Supposed Marched on their Return from Canaan to their Respective homes on the Colony's Cost therefor to there Names Annexed ye Number of Days each Soldier probably lived in said manner and the charge is made at 14^d per Day and Stopt out of the pay now if hereafter any of said Soldiers give proper evidence that thay had not so much at the Colony's Expense thay are to be considered accordingly

	Days		Days
Charles Bucklin	3	Luke Gridly	2
Jon^a Gillett	3	Joseph Spencer	2
Benj Keeny	3	Jon^a Tyler	2
Wm Stevens	3	David Hayden	2
Jno Abbott	3	Eben^r Sperry	2
Caleb Benjamin	3	David Taylor	2
Joseph Blanchard	3	Benj Grimes	2
Lamuel Deming	3	Asael Andrus	2
Jno Furgeson	3	Sylv^a Humphry	2
Edward Forbes	3	John Mattson	2
Benjamin Hale	3	Cyprian Watson	2
Harding Jarrold	3	Saml Felt	4
Benoni Loomis	3	Solomon Hall	4
Isaac Macks	3	Clothier Prior	4
Tho. Middleton	3	John Rogers	4
Patrick McCullog	3	Zeph^h Snow	4
Jno McLarin	3	Jon^a Webster	4
Amos Shepherd	3	John Wilson	4
Zeph^h Webster	3	David Wilson	4
James Wallace	3	Abner Webb	4
Saml Waters	3	Matt^w Dewolf	4
Jno Rippaneor	3	John Amsbury	4
Owen Flusky	3	Shubal Reed	4
Elijah Roberts	3	Hez. Reed	4
David Case	3	Saml Gowdy	4
William Grant	3	Warhan Parsons	4
Daniel Eaton	3	Daniel Sexton	4
Tho. Jarrold	3	Ebenezer Comes	4
Jon^a Wood	3	Roger Griswold	4
Jacob Tuller	3	Danl Rierdon	4
Theoph Morrison	3	Elisha Doan	4
Isaac Whesk	3	Philip Royce	5

John Wilson Dyed the 27th Day of Sept.

[Indorsed] Col^o Nathan Payson Muster Roll Decem^r 1757
 Chas Buckland Serj^t
 Zepheniah Webster
 David Taylor

[State Library, Adams Papers.]

A Muster Role of N. Paysons Company 1757

[Indorsed] Jon^a Roberts
 Chas Buckland Serj^t
 Bej^a Keeny

[State Library, Adams Papers.]

CAMPAIGN OF 1757.

A Muster Roll of Colonel Nathan Payson's Company Fort Edward Oct. 17, 1757, is signed By General Lymans orders Timothy Hierlihy Adjutant

[Indorsed] Sam¹ Wells Lt
Ep^m Flint
Zephaniah Snow p
Sam¹ Porter

[State Library, Adams Papers.]

FOURTH COMPANY — CAPT. PUTNAM.

Israel Putnam [of Pomfret], Captain.
George Creary [of Voluntown], First Lieutenant.
Samuel Porter, Second Lieutenant.
Benjamin Hayward, Ensign.

[Colonial Records.]

Jonathan Tuttle appointed Corporal June 27.

[General Orders of 1757.]

Israel Putnam and Benjamin Hayward are mentioned as being in the service.

[General Orders of 1757.]

The company contained ninety eight men, of whom fifty four had been in service before.

[State Library, War 7, 83.]

FIFTH COMPANY — CAPT. HUBBEL.

Samuel Hubbel [of Fairfield], Captain.   *[State Library, War 7, 81.]*
Josiah Walker, First Lieutenant.   *[State Library, War 7, 87.]*
Nathan Stephens, Second Lieutenant.
Abel Prindle, Ensign.

[Colonial Records.]

[The headings of this roll have been torn off.]

Mens Names and Quality		Time of Inlistment		[Discharged]	[Deserted]
Sam¹¹ Hubbel	Capt.	Mar.	2	Nov. 26	
Josi^a Walker	Lieut.	"	"	"	
Nath^n Stephens	"	"	"	Oct. 10	
Abel Prindle	Ens.	Feb.	23	Nov. 13	
Jo^s Sturgis	Serj.	Mar.	3	26	
Joel Parish	"	"	2	"	
Dan¹ Herrington	"	"	14	"	
Robt Summers	"	"	8	13	
Isaac Sterling	Corp.	"	2	26	
Arch^d Blair	"	"	7	"	
Disbrow Webb	"	"	8	13	

COL. LYMAN'S REGIMENT.

Mens Names and Quality		Time of Inlistment		[Discharged]		[Deserted]	
Nathⁿ Beach	Corp.	Mar.	2	Nov.	13		
Jn° Smedly	Clerk		9		26		
Andr^w Cable	Drum		17		13		
Ezek^l Leathers	Centn^l		2		"		
Saml Morhouse			"		10		
Jo^s Budington			"		26		
Lewis Angevine			"		13		
Jn° Arnold			"		26		
Victor Baker			"		"		
Jn° Bassett			"		"		
David Wheeler			7		"		
Stephⁿ Thorp			"		"		
Willm Thorp			"		"		
Willm Hallowel			"		"		
Squire Wakeman			"		"		
Jn° Griffin			8		10		
Saml Jacock			"		26		
Saml Truesdel			"		"		
Thad^s Davis			"		"		
Jn° Lyon			"		"		
Eli Sharp			"	Dec.	8		
Nathⁿ Dickenson			"	Nov.	26		
Danl Adams			"		"		
Willm Chartee			9		"		
Is^a Sherwood			"		"		
James Redfield			11		"		
Anth° Carpenter			"		"		
Tim° Shelley			12		"		
Danl Nichols			"		"		
Charles Ferry			14		"		
Luke Roberts			"		"		
Simon Caulkens			"		10		
Jn° Spees			"	Dec.	8		
Saml Gorham			15	Nov.	26		
Tim° Hogden			19		"		
David Barnam			22		13		
[Some names gone here]							
Elisha Benidict		Mar.	28	Nov.	26		
Moses Osburn			"		"		
Isach^r Nicholson			"		"		
Tim° Picket			"		"		
Ben° Hendrick			"		"		
Danl Jackson			"		13		
Thos Butler			"			Apr.	9
Silamon Hubbel			"		26		
Jasper Baily			"		13		
Nehe^m Sealy			"		26		
Isaac Hill			"		"		
Jo^s Hubbard			"		"		
Noble Benedict			"		"		
Amos Nettleton			"		"		
Hez^e Lyon			29		"		
Nathl Johnson			"		"		
Danl Rumsey			"		"		
Seth Buckley			30		"		
Jabez Sherwood			"		10		

CAMPAIGN OF 1757.

Mens Names and Quality	Time of Inlistment	[Discharged]	[Deserted]
Thoˢ Stirges	Mar. 31	Nov. 26	
Isaac Cable	"	"	
Jacob Cadwell	Apr. 1	"	
Samˡ Lyon	2		Deserted
Ned Odel	"	13	
Jehiˡ Moger	"	26	
Francis Pierce	5	"	
Samˡ Patchen	"	"	
Abrᵐ Addams	6	"	
Jnº Nott	7	13	
Nathˡ Cady Blackman	"	26	
Benjᵃ Frost	"	"	
David Stratton	"	"	
Samˡ Hendrix	"	10	
Benjᵃ Davis	8	26	
Thadˢ Bennit	"	13	
Aron Wheeler	"	26	
Danˡ Wakeman	9	"	
Danˡ Peet	"	13	
Zadᵏ Blackman	10	10	
Jehu Morehouse	11	26	
Toby Boston	"	13	
Joˢ Woods	May 13	"	

[Indorsed] Capᵗ Samˡ Hubbel Pay Roll 1757
  Fairfield
  Francis Pierce

[*State Library, Adams Papers.*]

A Muster Roll of the Company Raised in the fourth Regiment in this Colony, under the Command of Capᵗ Samˡˡ Hubbell of Fairfield and Mustered by me the subscriber on the days & months set in the Margin

1757		Capᵗ Samˡˡ Hubbell
		1 Lt. Josiah Walker
		2 Lᵗ Stevens
		Ensⁿ Prindle
March	7	Joel Parrish
		John Arnold
		Victor Baker
		John Basset
	8	Ezekiel Leathers
		Lewis Angevine
		Nathan Beach
		Willᵐ Thorp
		Willᵐ Hallowell
		David Wheeler
		Joseph Sturgis
	9	Willᵐ Carte
	11	Carpenter
		James Redfield
	12	Squier Wakeman
		John Griffin
	15	Samˡˡ Trusdell
		Samˡˡ Jacobs
		Nathan Dickson
		John Lyon
March	15	Eli Sharp
		Thaddeus Davis
		Robert Summers
		Danˡˡ Adams
	16	John Smedley
		Samˡˡ Morehouse 3ᵈ
		Stephen Thorp
		Isaac Sterling
		Disbrow Webb
		Timothy Shelly
		Danˡˡ Nickols
	17	Andrew Cable
		Archibald Blair
		Danˡˡ Herrington
		Charles Ferry
		Luke Roberts
		Simon Calkins
		John Spees
	19	Samˡˡ Gorham
	21	Timothy Hodgdon
	25	Hugh Brooks
		David Barnum
		Hezekiah Brownson
		Samˡˡ Curtis

COL. LYMAN'S REGIMENT.

March 25	Willm Roberts		April 1	Thomas Butler
26	Joseph Budington			Silliman Hubbell
	Tom Sherman Indian			Nath^{ll} Blakman
	John Chops Indian			Jasper Baly
	John Sherwood			Thomas Sturgis
	Isaac Sherwood			Sam^{ll} Henrys
31	Jacob Cadwell			Nehemiah Seely
April 1	Thomas Sherwood			Zadock Dickinson *
	John Knap			Lewis Nodine *
	Elisha Bendict			Isaac Hill
	Moses Osborn		March 31	Joseph Hubbard
	Isaker Nickerson			Noble Benedict
	John Olmstead			Amos Nettleton
	Timothy Picket		April 5	Francis Perce
	Isaac Cable		6	Abraham Adams
	Dan^{ll} Rumsey		4	Ned Odell Negro
	Nath^{ll} Johnson		8	Aaron Wheeler
	Jabez Sherwood			Benjⁿ Davis
	Hezekiah Lyon			Sam^{ll} Patchen
	John Nott			Benjⁿ Frost
	Lem^{ll} Lyon			Toby Boston negro
	Nehemiah Bennett *			Dan^{ll} Peat
	John Coggeshall *			Zadock Blackman
	Benony Henrys			David Stratton
	Jehiel Mosier			Nathan Price
	Dan^{ll} Jackson			Sam^{ll} Beach

The two Last hired men in their rooms as the Capt Informed me but I have forgot their names

* Imprest Supposed never went

And^w Burr Muster Master

[*State Library, War 7, 81.*]

SIXTH COMPANY—CAPT. WATERBURY.

David Waterbury, 3d [of Stamford], Captain.
Reuben Ferris [of Greenwich], First Lieutenant.

[*Colonial Records.*]

John Taylor, Second Lieutenant.
Josiah Stebbins, Ensign.

April the 14 Day Ad 1757

A List of Men Belonging to Cap^{tn} David Waterberry Raised for the Present Expedition in the Regiment Commanded by Col^o Phinehas Lyman, Under The Command of His Excellency the Earl of Loudoun

	Inlisted			Inlisted
David Waterbury Capt. *	1757	Peter Verdin Corp. *	Mar.	4
Reuben Ferris 1st Lieut. *		Joseph Moris " *		24
John Taylor 2d "		Jeremiah Jagger Corp. *		10
Josiah Stebbins Ens *		Moses Lockwood " *		6
Nathan Ferris Serg. *	Mar. 1	Abraham Bates Clark *		25
William Gale " *		Daniel Elmer Drum		7
Isaac Whelply "	25	Ebenezer Bates *		16
Reuben Taylor	14	John Loder		28

	Inlisted			Inlisted	
William Josiah Lewis *	Mar.	22	Isaac Saint John *	Mar.	16
Sands Raymond		24	Sephen Moris		15
Samuel Wordin *		2	Daniel Tharps		22
David Dan		1	Jedediah Nash *		"
Peter Slason		27	Barak Taylor *		"
Zopher Wilmoth *		28	Samuel Sherwood*		"
Philip Canedy		29	David Olmsted		24
William Barnite *		10	Nathan Yeras		"
Josiah Smith		8	Thomas Hays		25
Charles Denslow *		3	Phinehas Taylor		"
Moses Smith *		25	Amos Knaap		28
Silvanus Slason *		29	Nehemiah Nickes		29
Abijah Seely		"	John Rockwel *		"
Andrew Reboe *		31	Adkison Hilton		30
Foster Lewis *		4	Nathaniel Squier		31
Nathan Dickson		8	Nathan Gray		4
Samuel Provorce *		20	John Deen *		5
Alexander Sloem *		3	Ebenezer Lobdell *		7
Thomas Ask *		11	Nahaniel Wescot *		8
James Castalow *		3	Stephen Daton		"
Caleb Reynolds *		21	Abraham Camp		"
Samuel Palmer *		28	Ezra Green		"
Jacob Palmer		21	Athaniel Silleck		9
James Ferris		25	Daniel Jackson *		13
Nathaniel Close		17	John Demorat *		"
Nathaniel Jesup *		6	Seely Gregory *		14
Ebenezer Reynolds *		17	John House *		23
Silas Palmer		15	Robert Forquar		5
Thomas George *		29	James Mead *	Feb.	28
William Leeke *		28	Jonthan Weeb *		"
John Jerman *		28	Reuben Jager		"
Ephraim Lockwood		6	Ebenezer Waterberry		"
Daniel Reynolds		"	Charles Williams *		26
David White *		7	Yoangs Weed *		28
Stephen Eget		"	Thomas Nickals *	Apr.	1
Pack Ferris *		17	Robert Lockwood		2
John Mow *		21	Benjamin Peters *		5
Morris Kelley *		29	Daniel Steward		7
John Lockwood		14	James Dauchy		2
Joseph Baterson		"	John Stone *		8
John Tomson		15	Stephen Jackson		6
Jesse Beears *		"	Eliakim Sickels *		11
Robert Downs		16			

Those that Are thus Mark^d * have been in the Service before

[*State Library, Adams Papers.*]

SEVENTH COMPANY—CAPT. FITCH.

Adonijah Fitch [of New London], Captain.
John Durkee [of Norwich], First Lieutenant.

[*Colonial Records.*]

Jabez Huntly, Second Lieutenant.
Eleazer Tracy [of Norwich], Ensign.

[*Colonial Records.*]

COL. LYMAN'S REGIMENT. 181

Muster Rool For the Seventh Company in General Lymans Regiment in the Colony of Connecticut under the Command of Cap^{tn} Adonijah Fitch 1757 Viz

Names both of Officers & Soldiers	Quality	Time of Inlistment	Discharge	Dead
Adonijah Fitch	Capt.	Feby. 23	Dec. 5	
John Durkee	1st Lieut.	" 23	Nov. 3	
Jabez Huntly	2nd "	Mar. 15	" 30	
Eleazer Tracy	Ens.	Feby. 23	" 3	
* Joseph Comstock	Serg.	Mar. 1	" 30	
Jabez Fitch	"	Feby. 24	" 3	
Joseph Mack	"	Apr. 2	Oct. 20	
Ebenezer Jackson	"	Mar. 8	" 12	Dead
Silas Waterman	Clerk	Feby. 24	Nov. 3	
† Jacob Andros	Corp.	Mar. 29	" 30	
Thomas Walbrig	"	" 14	" "	
Thomas Andros	"	" 1	Sept. 27	Dead
Joseph Keleg (?)	"	Feby. 28	Nov. 30	
John Chapell	Drum.	Mar. 1	" "	
John Partin	Private	" "	" "	
Sans Raymond	"	" "	" "	
Alpheus Chapman	"	" "	" "	
Benjamin Hopkins	"	" "	Oct. 15	
John Gurley	"	" "	Nov. 3	
Moses Hutchison	"	" "	" 30	
John Shaw	"	" 3	" "	
Samuel Billings	"	" "	" "	
John Hatch	"	" 7	Oct. 15	
Charlott Hill	"	" "	Nov. 30	
John Wells	"	" "	" 3	
Nathan Sabin	"	" 9	" 30	
Samuel Bebe	"	" 10	" "	
Jonathan Weeks	"	" 11	" "	
Amos Tanner	"	" 16	Aug. 11	
John Button	"	" 15	Nov. 30	
Simon Choychoi	"	" 18	" "	
Samuel Wackwett	"	" "	" 3	
Peter Button	"	" 11	Sep. 29	
Ebenezer Hoghkin	"	" 24	Nov. 30	
Joseph Willobey	"	Apr. 11	Oct. 29	
Ichabod Lay	"	" 16	Sept. 29	
Levi Bumpus	"	Feby. 24	Nov. 3	
Joseph Doubleday	"	" "	" "	
Joseph Welch	"	" "	" 30	
John Robin	"	" 25	" 3	
Jabez Jones	"	" "	July 4	Captivated
James Powars	"	" "	Nov. 30	
Ezekiel Cook	"	" 28	" "	
Joseph Johnson	"	" "	" "	
Pompey Unkus	"	" "	" 3	
David Bosworth	"	" "	" 30	
Joseph Cooper	"	Mar. 11	Aug. 26	Dead
Nezer. Tanner	"	" "	Nov. 3	
Joseph Chowhorn	"	" 1	" "	
Josiah Fuller	"	" 2	Oct. 15	

* Reduced to the ranks July 21. [*General Orders of 1757.*]
† Promoted to Serj. Sept. 24. [*General Orders of 1757.*]

CAMPAIGN OF 1757.

Names both of Officers & Soldiers	Quality	Time of Inlistment		Discharge		Dead
Benjamin Unkus	Private	Mar.	2	Oct.	29	
Peter Tecommowas	"	"	"	Nov.	30	
Isaac Tecommowas	"	"	"	June	10	Captivated
Samson Shawcott	"	"	"	Nov.	30	
Joseph Sina	"	"	4	"	3	
Richard Scate	"	"	"	July	26	Dead
Jacob Epharim	"	"	5	Nov.	8	
Samuel Unkus	"	"	6	"	30	
Amasa Mix	"	"	"	Oct.	5	Dead
Phinias Burchard	"	"	9	Nov.	30	
John Wampanegg	"	"	11	"	3	
Jacob Reed	"	"	"	June	10	Dead
David McLane	"	"	12	Nov.	30	
John Ashbo	"	"	"	"	"	
Samuel Hoscott	"	"	14	July	24	Dead
Moses Cleaveland	"	"	2	Sept.	9	Dead
John Brown	"	"	19	Nov.	30	
Peter Mossett	"	"	15	"	3	
Joseph Lewis	"	"	18	"	30	
Thomas Henry	"	"	29	"	3	
Matthias Norton	"	"	"	"	"	
Thomas Chogegins	"	"	"	"	"	
Henry Jones	"	Apr.	11	"	30	
Edward Murphey	"	"	1	Oct.	15	
* Gideon Dike	"	Feby.	26	Nov.	30	
Joseph Chequipos	"	Mar.	5	"	"	
Christopher Huntington	"	"	7	"	3	
Levi Hide	"	"	3	"	"	
James Balding	"	"	8	"	30	
John Williams	"	"	12	"	3	
† James Cobb	"	"	11	"	"	
Solomon Chebucks	"	"	17	Sept.	29	
John Couzens	"	"	12	Aug.	13	Dead
Samson Amos	"	Feby.	26	Nov.	3	
Benjamin Wentworth	"	Mar.	4	June	10	Captivated
Stephen Otis	"	"	17	Nov.	3	
Moses Huntly	"	"	"	"	30	
Thomas Graves	"	"	21	"	"	
Nathan Bennet	"	"	"	Sept.	29	
Stephen Chapman	"	"	22	Nov.	30	
Josiah Bennitt	"	"	23	Sept.	29	
Rubin Tatson	"	"	24	Aug.	12	
Tobey Negro	"	Apr.	12	Oct.	13	Dead
Rowland Rogers	"	Mar.	21	"	29	
Jonathan Fox	"	"	23	Nov.	30	
Hezekiah Atwell	"	"	17	Oct.	29	
Paul Pride	"	Apr.	18	Nov.	30	

[*State Library, Adams Papers.*]

---

* Promoted to Corp. Sept. 24. [*General Orders of 1757.*]
† Promoted to Corp. Sept. 24. [*General Orders of 1757.*]

COL. LYMAN'S REGIMENT.

EIGHTH COMPANY—CAPT. SLAPP.

John Slapp [of Mansfield], Captain.
                                                                [*Colonial Records.*]
Elijah Simons, First Lieutenant.
Robert Durkee [of Windham], Second Lieutenant.
Elijah Porter [of Coventry], Ensign.
                                                                [*Colonial Records.*]

    1757 A Role of the Company under the Command of Capt John Slapp Lieu^{ts} Elijah Simons & Robert Durke & Ens^n Elijah Porter Mustered by me the Subscriber Containing ye Time of Each Particular Soldiers inlistment & time of their Muster

	Inlisted		Discharged	Dead by Sickness	Killd by Eny
* Serj^t Josiah Smith	Mar.	7			
† " Charles Ripley		8			
" Caleb Austin		9			
" Jedidiah Geer		14			
James Shearman		1			
John Stimpson		9	Aug. 1		
Edmund Redding		7			
Thomas Knoulten		1			
Daniel Rust Clerk	Feb.	26			
Simon Grover	Mar.	7		Oct. 10	
Josiah Cook	Feb.	26			
Joseph Rust	Mar.	7			
Nathaniel Preston		14			
Ephraim Dean Corp.		"			
Jehiel Robins		10			
John Canada		9			Captivated July 1
George Coburn		10			
Daniel Utley		"		Aug. 5	
John Fees		"			
Asa Cheedle		"			
Amos Bruister Corp.		8			
Thomas Heath		"			
William Neff		14			
Clement Neff Junr, Drum		7			
Moses Coye		15			
Cypio Wood	Feb.	26			
James Claghorn	Mar.	15			
Nathaniel Spencer		10			
Ebenezer Hebard		9			
Elijah Hebard		10			
Jonathan Canada		9			
Amos Bibben		8			July 23
Ephraim Ormsbey		"			
Annanias Porrage		1			
Moses Cleaveland		14			
Robert Roundey Junr		8			

  * Reduced to the ranks Oct. 17. Restored to Serj. Oct. 25.
                                                                [*General Orders of 1757.*]
  † Reduced to the ranks, but restored to Serj. Oct. 8.
                                                                [*General Orders of 1757.*]

CAMPAIGN OF 1757.

Name	Inlisted	Discharged	Dead by Sickness	Killd by Eny
Solomon Farnum Corp.	Mar. 10			
Daniel Knoulten	15			
Wilson Whiton	"			
Rice Edwards	"			June 10
Pite Pito	18			Deserted Apr. 4
Michael Lahey	7			
Jedidiah Lee	19			
Joseph Fenton	20			
Hezekiah King	24			
Thomas Kingsbury Corp.	7			
Jeremiah Reed	25			
David Royse or Rice	"			Deserted Sep. 5
Jacob Fuller	"			
Jeremiah Abbe	"			
Joseph Preston	26			N. Joynd
Ebenezer Brown y[e] 3[d]	28			
Joseph Cummus	12		Sep. 12	
Benjamin Stark	Apr. 1			
Matthew Waller	Mar. 31			
Josiah Reed	30			
John Gray	Apr. 3			
Nathaniel Rust	2			
Joseph Russ	Mar. 9			
Elijah Blochet	Apr. 1			
Jabez Green	Mar. 9			
James Torrey	Apr. 1			
Ezra West	"			
Aaron Fuller	"			
Joshua Convers				
Moses Cook	Mar. 20			
Peter Royse or Rice	Apr. 4		Oct. 10	
John Woolcutt	5			Captivated June 10
Joseph Green	"			
Jasper Baley	"			Deserted April 16
Jonathan Pidge	6			
Joseph Rider	7			
William Parrish Jun[r]	"			
Daniel Fowler	"			
Samuel Coats	"			
Richard Lues	"			
Willi[m] Montowomuck	8			June 10
Andrew Moredock	"			
Foxon Dean	"			
John Trescott	"		Aug. 15	
Obediah Walker	"			
Throope Chapman	9			
Seth Deming	11		Sep. 1	
Isaiah Bugbee	"			
William Blanchard	Mar. 7			
John Finney	Apr. 11			
Enoch Johnson	"			
Daniel Squier	13			
David Canada	14			
James Brayman	"			N. Joynd

Shubael Conant Muster Master of S[d] Company

N. B. no more than two of the Seven Soldiers by act of Assembly Granted to be raised in ye first Regiment for the filling up ye above Company, have appeared by me to be Mustered, by means Whereof in The above Roll there is 5 Wanting to Compleet S^d Company

Shubael Conant as above

[Indorsed] Capt John Slapp &c Muster Roll 1757
Joseph Rider p

[*State Library, Adams Papers.*]

The information of Officers, Discharged, Dead, Killed and Captived given above, together with the name John Timus, Deserted May 13, are added from A Muster Roll of Capt John Slapp's Company Fort Edward Oct. 17, 1757 ; By General Lyman's orders

Timothy Hierlihy Adj^t

[Indorsed] Elij^h Porter Ens
Jos. Rider p
James Torrey p

[*State Library, Adams Papers.*]

NINTH COMPANY — CAPT. JEFFRIES.

John Jeffries [of Cornwall], Captain.
Samuel Elmor, First Lieutenant.
Adam Hinman [of Woodbury], Second Lieutenant.
Hezekiah Baldwin [of New Milford], Ensign.

[*Colonial Records.*]

Searj^t Dickinson reduced to the ranks Sept. 19 and Corp. David Handee promoted Searj^t in his room.

[*General Orders of 1757.*]

John Jeffries and Hezekiah Baldwin are mentioned as being in the service.

[*General Orders of 1757.*]

This company marched with its full quota of one hundred men.

[*State Library, War 7, 75.*]

TENTH COMPANY — CAPT. WHITTLESEY.

Eliphalet Whittlesey [of Newington], Captain. [*Colonial Records.*]
Timothy Hierlihy [of Middletown], First Lieutenant.
Nicholas Nichols [of Glastenbury], Second Lieutenant.
John Sumner, Ensign.

[*Colonial Records.*]

A pay Roll of Capt Eliphalet Whittelsey's Company in General Lyman's Regiment for the year 1757

Mens Names & quality	Time of Inlistmt	Discharged	Dead
Eliphalet Whittelsey Capt.	Feb 23	Dec. 1	
Timothy Hierlihy 1 Lieut.	Mar. 8	"	
Nicholas Nichols 2 "	Feb. 23		5
John Sumner Ens.			10
Jonathan Brooks Serj.	Mar 4		1

CAMPAIGN OF 1757.

Mens Names & quality	Time of Inlistmt	Discharged	Dead
*Epaphras Nott Serj.	Mar. 12	Dec. 1	
Francis Hollister "	10	"	
Jonathan Johnson "	25	Nov. 20	
Josiah Wright Clerk	1	Dec. 1	
Hill Hollister Corp.	14	"	
Moses Bordman "	26	Nov. 15	
Timothy Brooks "	8	10	
Peter Butler "	Apr. 2	Dec. 10	
Noadiah Heart Drum.	"	Aug. 30	
Obediah Allen priv.	Mar. 27		Sep. 11
Thomas Anthony	5	Dec. 2	
Charles Bartlett	15	Nov. 11	
John Beckley	28	24	
Silas Beckley	"		Nov. 11
Elisha Belding	20	Nov. 11	
Samuel Bowers	29		Oct. 2
Nathan Brooks	30	Nov. 10	
Thomas Buckley	8		June 10
John (?) Buckley	9	Dec. 1	
Thomas Bunn	1	Nov. 25	
William Clark	1	11	
Daniel Cone	5	Dec. 1	
Noah Coles	14	Sep. 16	
Moses Dickinson	31	Nov. 11	
Bennoni De Woolf	29	Dec. 2	
Stephen DeWoolf	28	Nov. 16	
Ambrose Egelstone	7	Dec. 1	
John Foster	5	Nov. 10	
Joseph Fox	31	Dec. 2	
Benjamin Galpen	28	"	
John Goff	26	1	
Caleb Goodrick	Apr. 8	"	
John Hadlock	Mar. 28	Nov. 11	
Jotham Hall	16	deserted May 22	
Joseph Harris	9	Dec. 1	
John Hart	28	"	
Daniel Hill Junr	30	Nov. 11	
Aaron Hinman	14	Dec. 2	
John Holmbs	8	Nov. 11	
Martin Hooker	14		June 10
Thomas Horner	24		Nov. 13
Samuel Hubbard	28	Nov. 24	
Roswell Hubbard	"	Dec. 1	
Jonathan Hubbard	7	2	
John Jacobs	9	Nov. 11	
Davis Johnson	Apr. 7	15	
John Keenland	Mar. 9	Oct. 18	
Timothy Lankton	14	Nov. 20	
Peter Latch	28	Nov. 20	
John Lattimer	4	Dec. 1	
Daniel Lewis	Apr. 5	2	
Robert Lindsey	1	1	
John Lindsey	Feb. 28	Nov. 11	
David Lindsey	Mar. 26	Dec. 1	

* Appointed Serj.-Maj. Nov. 2. [*General Orders of 1757.*]

COL. LYMAN'S REGIMENT. 187

Mens Names & quality	Time of Inlistmt	Discharged	Dead
Lot Loveland	Feb. 28	Sep. 1	
Andrew Lusk	"	Dec. 1	
Thomas McCleave	Mar. 28	Oct. 18	
Timothy McKeough	"	Dec. 1	
James Mattocks	Apr. 7	10	
John Meeker	Mar. 9	Nov. 11	
Lewis Mears	23		Sep. [ ]
Charles B. Miller	20		Aug. [ ]
Noah Moss	Apr. 7		deserted Apr. 18
James Murphey	Mar. 8	Dec. 2	
William Nott	"	Nov. 24	
John Rany	Apr. 4	10	
Stephen Ranney	Mar. 28	Dec. 1	
Jonathan Robbins	9	Nov. 24	
[ ]	[ ]	11	
Wilson Rowlandson	1		deserted Apr. 27
Moses Scott	26	Dec. 2	
Ephraim Shayler	15	5	
Samuel Shilling	8	Nov. 11	
James Simons	Apr. 4	Dec. 3	
Timothy Stedman	9	Aug. 14	
Giles Stow	Mar. 7		deserted Aug. 17
Simeon Stow	8	Dec. 1	
Isaac Stratton	Feb. 28	"	
John Treat	Mar. 26	8	
Thomas Turner	23	Aug. 9	
Andrew Warner	"	Nov. 10	
Joseph Wares	Feb. 25	Dec. 2	
John Washbon	Mar. 28	1	
David Way	"	Nov. 11	
Samuel Wells	1		Nov. 12
James Welsh	9	Nov. 10	Nov. 10
David West	Apr. 2	Dec. 1	
Aaron West	Mar. 30		Nov. 10
Wait Whaples	15		Sep. 17
Nathan Whittelsy	Apr. 11	Dec. 3	
Samuel Williams	Mar. 26	1	
Jonathan Wright	1	"	
Daniel Wright	17	Sep. 1	
Henry Halling	Aug. 31	Nov. 11	

[Indorsed] Capt Elipht Whittlesey Muster Roll Decr 1757 pay Roll
  Jno. Holmes
  Wait Whaples

[*State Library, Adams Papers.*]

ELEVENTH COMPANY — CAPT. WELLES.

Edmund Welles [of Hebron], Captain.
Ezekiel Fitch, First Lieutenant.
John Cone, Second Lieutenant.
Timothy Northam, Ensign.

CAMPAIGN OF 1757.

Names	Places whence they came	Time of Inlisting or Impressing	When Mustered	
Andrews Oliver	Easthaddam	Mar. 23	Apr. 4	
Ames John	Colechester	Apr. 3	" 15	
Ackley Nicholas	"	" 12	" 18	
Ackley Attar	"	" "	" "	
Abbot Price	Lebanon	" "	" 12	
Bush Timothy	Hebron	" 9	" 13	
Bonfory Purmort	Lebanon	" 12	" 12	
Bragg Benj^a	"	" "	" "	
Beach John	Hebron	" 6	" 16	
Beckwith Jonath	Colechester	" 12	" 18	
Brown William	"	" 6		
Clark Dan	Easthaddam	Mch. 15	" 4	
Chapman Daniel	"	" 26	" 8	
Chapman Samuel	Lebanon	" 15	Mar. 15	
Cox William	Hebron	" 7	" 17	Drum.
Chappel Andrew	"	" 21	" 31	
Culver James	"	Feb. 24	" 17	
Coates Amos	Lebanon	Apr. 8	Apr. 19	
Coledwell Jedediah	Norwich	" 14		
Culver David	Hebron	Feb. 24	Mar. 17	
Dibble Isaiah	Easthaddam	Mar. 15	Apr. 4	
Dunbar James	Hadlime	Apr. 13	" 13	
Dewey Jonathan	Hebron	Mar. 31	" 4	
Dudley Zebulon	Saybrook	Apr. 8	" 18	
Daniels Asa	Easthaddam	" 10	" "	
Dodge Thos	Colechester	" "	" "	
Dickinson Nathan	Hebron	" 8	" 21	
Dunham Obadiah	"	" 18	" 25	
4th Serg. Forster Jeremiah	Lebanon	" 10	" 12	
Fox Joel	Colechester	Mar. 30	" 2	
Fuller Jonathan	Easthaddam	Apr. 8	" 14	
Freeman Zacheus	"	" 13		
Ford John	Hebron	" 12	" 18	
Fox Asa	E. haddam	Mar. 30	" 2	
Fox Joshua	"	Apr. 9		
Fergo Ich^a	Norwich	" 12	" 12	
*Gillit Jeremiah	Lebanon	" 7	" 7	Putnam
Goward William	Hebron	" 11	" 11	
Graves Mark	E. haddam	" 13	" 13	
*Gillet Israel	Lebanon	" 12	" 12	
Hutchinson Asa	Hebron	Mar. 15	Mar. 31	
Hill Elijah	Lebanon	Apr. 12	Apr. 12	
Hatch Sam^{ll}	"	" "	" "	
Hitchcock Eliakim	Colechester	" 18	" 23	
Harden Thos	"	" 12	" 14	
Holdridge Hezekiah	Hebron	" 6	" 13	
Jones Sam^{ll}	"	" 16	" 16	1 Corp.
Ingham Alexander	"	" 6		
Kenny James	Glassenbury	" 21	" 21	
John Ephraim				
Joel Negro	Colechester	May 31	May 31	
Loveridge John	"	Mar. 26	Apr. 2	
Larkin Amos	Lebanon	Apr. 12	" 15	

---

* Crossed out in the original manuscript.

COL. LYMAN'S REGIMENT. 189

Names	Places whence they came	Time of Inlisting or Impressing	When Mustered	
Loomiss Ephraim Jun	Lebanon	Apr. 8	Apr. 18	
Lisk And	"	" 12	" 12	
*Morse Noah	Hebron	" 8	" 8	
†1st Searg. Mack Orlando	"	Mar. 17	Mar. 22	
*Marsh Silas	Lebanon	Apr. 12		
2nd Searg. Moulton Daniel	"	" 13	" 13	
Mattoon Abel	Hebra	" 6	Apr. 13	
Minor Jon	Colechester	" 9	" 25	
‡Mack Abner	Hebron	" 12	" 12	
Osborn Tim	"	" 6	" 6	
Oxford Negro	E. haddam	Mar. 31	" 2	
Pumroy Elijah	Lebanon	Apr. 7	" 7	
Parker George	"	Mar. 9	Mar. 9	
Root Caleb	Hebron	Apr. 6	Apr. 14	
Ransom Mathew	Lyme	" 12	" 15	
Richardson Ebenezer	Lebanon	" 8	" "	
Stedman Tho	"	" 10	" 12	
Stevens George	Colechester	" 15	" 17	
Squibb Christ	Lebanon	Mar. 13	Mar. 30	
Skinner Ebenezer	Hebron	Apr. 6	Apr. 14	Clerk
Sweetland Elijah	"	" 12	" 13	
Scipio Solomon	Colechester	" 7	" 14	
Snow Arunah	Lebanon	" 8	" 15	
§Skinner Tho	Hebon	" 16	" 16	
Strong Amos	Glassenbury	" 6	" 18	
Stark Zeph	Lebanon	" 9	" "	
Shipman Dan	Colechester	Mar. 15	" 20	Corp.
*Tuttle Jonathan	Lebanon	Apr. 9	" 9	
Tinker Ellis	Hebron	" 10	" 14	
Thatcher Jared	Lebanon	" 12	" 12	
Vorse Henry	"	" 8	" 14	
Webster Levi	Colechester	" 10	" 12	
Willey Sam	Easthaddam	Mar. 17	" 7	
Webster Oliver	Lebanon	Apr. 7	" "	
Woodworth David	"	" 9	" 9	
Wright Ephraim Jun	Hebron	" "	" "	
Whipple Zebulun	Stonington	" 12	" 12	
Wadsworth Sam	Hebron	Mar. 7	Mar. 17	
Wright Beriah	"	Apr. 6	Apr. 6	
Walbridge W	Coventry	" 12	" 13	
Webster Asel	Lebanon	" 8		
Williams Har. Stephen	"	" 7	" 7	
Ephraim John	"	" 12	" 12	
Wetmore Jn	Easthaddam	" 8	" 14	
3d Serg. Welles Ephraim	Colechester	" 12	" "	
Webster Abram	Lebanon	" "	" 15	
Woodworth Benj	"	" 8	" "	
Welles Samuel Indian	Colechester	" 5	" 20	

[*Connecticut Historica Society.*]

---

* Crossed out in the original manuscript.
† Called Jr. on another roll.
‡ In room of Israel Gillet of Leb
§ Jones Sam Cor. In his stead

A Muster Roll of the Company under the Comand of Capt Edmund Welles.

[*Connecticut Historical Society.*]

A Billeting Bill for ye Company under Command of Capt Edmond Wells in pay of this Colony Anno 1757 Manifesting the time when each person was Mustered when Marchd, ye time each person was Billeted & amount thereof

[*State Library, Adams Papers.*]

TWELFTH COMPANY—CAPT. GALLOP.

Ben Adam Gallop [of Groton], Captain. [*State Library, War 7, 79.*]
William Billing [of Preston], Lieutenant.
Jedediah Waterman, Lieutenant.
William Roe Minor, Ensign. [*Colonial Records.*]

Muster Role of Capt Benadam Gallups Company the time of Enlisting & Number of Weeks & days in the Service.

Officers & Soldiers Names & Quality	Time of Enlisting		Discharged		Dead & Captivated	
Capt. Benadam Gallup	Feb.	23	Dec.	2		
Lieut. Wm Billing	"	28	"			
Lieut Jed^d Waterman	Mar.	26	"			
Ens. Wm Roe Minor	Feb.	23	"			
Serj. Thos Giles	Mar.	12	"			
*Serj. Elias Avery	"	1	"			
Serj. Oliver Coit	"	4	"			
*Serj. Charles Avery	"	20	"			
Clark Robert Niles	Feb.	24	"			
Corp. Jon^a Simons	Apr.	6	"			
*Corp. Jeptha or Joseph Hewett	Mar.	22	Nov.	10		
*Corp. Simeon Rouse	"	1	Dec.	2		
Corp. David Amos	"	5	Oct.	1		
Drum. Wm Holdridge	Apr.	7	Nov.	15		
*Saml Thorington or Thornton	Mar.	4		10		
Saml Jones	"	8	Aug.	29		
*Benjamin Cay or Coy	"	1	Nov.	10		
*James Brown	"	8	Dec.	2		
Jonathan Safford	Feb.	27	Nov.	20		
Christo^r Billing	"	26		15		
Ruben Randol	"	24			Sep.	9
Joseph Palmer	"	"	Dec.	2		
*Sam^ll Wheeler	Mar.	1	"			
John Guile	"	30	Nov.	15		
Levi Hill	"	22		10		
Ambrose Fish	"	"	Dec.	2		
Peter Ellis	"	18			Aug.	3
Stephen Bennit	"	29	Dec.	2		
*Daniel Bogue	"	24	"			
Thomas Andrus	"	28	Oct.	29		
*John Church	Feb.	26	Dec.	2		
*Nathl Etherige	"	"	Oct.	29		
*Willm Brown	"	25			Never Joyned	

COL. LYMAN'S REGIMENT. 191

Officers & Soldiers Names & Quality	Time of Enlisting	Discharged	Dead & Captivated
Matthew Melony	Mar. 1	Dec. 2	
*Robert Jaquish	Feb. 22	"	
*Peter Davis	" 23	"	
*Isaac Whittle	" 22	"	
*Francis Summers	" 26	"	
*Joseph Randol	Apr. 4	"	
John Johnson	" 1		July 9
Joseph Yeomans	" 7	Nov. 10	
*Hezekiah Right	" 8	"	
*Ambrose Lewis	Mar. 1	Dec. 2	
Benj^a Dunlap	Apr. 9	"	
*Isaac Herington	Mar. 1	"	
John Armstrong	Apr. 4	Nov. 10	
*Jeremiah Jackson	" 12	Dec. 2	
Thos Quocheets	" "		July 26
*Elkanah Meech	" 13	Sep. 1	
*Willm Apes	Feb. 26	Dec. 2	
*Joseph Eliot	Mar. 28		Apr. 27
Asa Edy	" "	Dec. 2	
Cyprian Downer	" "	"	
*George Whitney	" 2	Nov. 10	
*George James	" 6	26	
*Peter Quocheets	" 1	Dec. 2	
*Daniel Charles	" "	"	
*James Possetouse	Feb. 26		Aug. 12
*Alick Church	Mar. 1	Dec. 2	
*Sampson Derrick	" "	Nov. 10	
*Amos Babcock	Apr. 1	"	
Zack Butler	" 2	Oct. 29	
*Rufus Hatch	Mar. 1	Dec. 2	
Chris^o Denison	" 4	Oct. 28	
*Jeremiah Utley	" 8	29	
*Lem^{ll} or Samuel Stewart	" 22	Dec. 2	
*Willm Perrigo	Feb. 23	"	
Stephen Williams	" 24	Oct. 29	
Jerem^h Haley	Mar. 3	Nov. 15	
John Latham	" "	Dec. 2	
*Sam^{ll} Stoddard	" 25		Never Joined
Matthew Martin	" 15		July 20
James Babcock	" 3		Oct. 11
Amos Holdridge	" 15	Nov. 20	
David Yeomans	" 18	Dec. 2	
*James Colyer	Feb. 22		Deserted Aug. 14
Thomas Ennes	" 25	Nov. 10	
*Joseph Garrit	Mar. 9	"	
*James Hagar	Feb. 24	"	
*James Megg	" 22	Dec. 2	
*Lem^{ll} Toney	Mar. 18	"	
John Quiomps	" 2		May 16
*John Plato	Feb. 28	Nov. 10	
*Sam^{ll} Crandol	Apr. 4	"	
John Vargison	" 6	Dec. 8	
John Duffey	" 1	Oct. 29	
Willm Denison	Mar. 4	Nov. 15	
*Sam^{ll} Corning	Apr. 4	Dec. 2	
*Willm Fagins	Feb. 26	"	
Jonathan Hasting	Mar. 5	Nov. 15	

CAMPAIGN OF 1757.

Officers & Soldiers Names & Quality	Time of Enlisting	Discharged	Dead & Captivated
John Stedman	Mar. 20	Dec. 2	
*Daniel Cozumps	Feb. 22		Oct. 3
*Jabez Jethro	" 25	Dec. 2	
*Joseph Cozumps	" 22	"	
James Nead	Mar. 2	"	
Jack Punise	" 12	Oct. 29	
Charles Scudob	Apr. 1	2	
John Toney	Feb. 24	Nov. 10	
*Joshua Toby	" 25	"	
George Toney	Mar. 3	Dec. 2	

[Indorsed] Capt Ben Adam Gallops Muster Roll 1757
Stephen Benett p.

[State Library, Adams Papers.]

Another roll has the following heading: Acompt of the Billiting Due to the 12 Company Comanded by Capt Benadame Gallop

[State Library, Adams Papers.]

A Role of the Men Enlisted under Capt Benadam Gallup Lieu^t William Billing 2^d Lieu^t Jedediah Waterman and Ensign William Roe Miner being the Company Raised in the Third and 8th Regiments in this Colony for the Ensuing Campaign with the Time of their Enlistment

N. B. those with * this marke were in the Army Last Summer or the Summer before.

From this list the marks have been added on the above roll.

[State Library, Adams Papers.]

THIRTEENTH COMPANY—CAPT. PRESTON.

Ephraim Preston [of Wallingford], Captain.

[Colonial Records.]

Archibald McNeil [of New Haven], First Lieutenant.
Jonathan Beebe, Second Lieutenant.

[Colonial Records.]

Moses Matthews, Ensign.
Archibald McNeil [of New Haven], Ensign.

A muster Roll of Capt. Preston's Company Dec. 15th 1757

		Time of Inlisting	Time of return	
Ephraim Preston	Capt.			
Archibald M^{c}neil	1st Liet.			
Jonathan Beebe	2nd "			
Moses Matthews	Ens.			
Israel Calkins *	Serg.	Mar. 1	Aug. 6	Killed
Phinehas Beech	"	Feb. 28	Nov. 14	
Wm Greave	"	Mar. 10	" 23	
David Hamilton	"	" 13	" 13	
Ephr^m Preston	Clerk	Feb. 25	" 23	
Lemuel Hand	Corp.	Mar. 26	" "	
Anthony Horskin	"	" 10	" 9	

* Taken prisoner and carried to France, whence he returned in 1758.

[Colonial Records.]

COL. LYMAN'S REGIMENT. 193

Name	Rank	Time of Inlisting		Time of return	
Nath^{ll} Weed	Corp.	Mar.	22	Nov.	13
John Barrett	"	"	10	"	23
Israel Terrel	Drum^r	"	"	"	"
Ebenezer Prindle		Feb.	25	"	23
Hezek^h Brockit		"	26	"	"
Timothy Bristol		"	28	"	13
Reuben Hitchcock		"	"	"	23
Nath^{ll} Andrews		"	"	"	13
Aner Ives		"	"	"	"
Nathan Benham		"	"	"	"
Ambrose London		"	"	"	23
John Daily		"	"	"	13
James Martin		"	"	"	23
Enos Hitchcock		"	"	"	13
Benj^a Cook		"	"	"	"
Volentine Hitchcock		Mar.	2	"	"
Dan^{ll} Kenady		"	3	Dec.	5
Permen^s Buñel		"	4	Nov.	23
Israel Squire		"	"	Dec.	5
Nathan Wright		"	5	Nov.	13
Gideon Parker		Feb.	25	"	23
Job Haden		Mar.	10	"	13
Gideon Allen		"	12	"	"
Stephen D'Wolf		"	"	"	"
Barna^s Hough		"	"	"	23
Sam^{ll} Bailey		"	"	"	"
Moses Wright		"	11	"	13
Jesse Hotchkiss		"	16	"	23
Wait Wooster		"	17	"	"
Mose Bidwell		"	26	"	"
Wm Andrews		"	"	"	"
Aaron Luddinton		"	9	"	"
Paul Chipman		"	5	"	9
Zera Beebe		"	1	"	23
Andrew Currecum		"	5	"	9
Justus Daly		"	15	"	13
Wm Horton		"	10	"	"
James Barret		"	12	"	23
James Baldwin		"	5	"	"
Saml Wheadon		"	26	"	"
Silas Merriman		"	"	"	"
David Newel		"	"	"	"
Saml Upson		"	"	"	"
Andrew Colver		"	"	"	13
Andrew Beardslee		"	"	"	23
Barnabas Merwin		"	"	"	"
Ezra Prindle		"	"	Dec.	5
Levi Munson		"	"	Nov.	13
Ichabod Stark		"	"	"	25
Wm Maltby		"	"	"	9
Henry Cook		"	9	"	23
Saml Merwin		"	26	"	"
Barna^s Dunham		"	25	"	"
Jesse Cook		"	26	"	"
Jonth Mansfield		"	28	"	13
Uzal Barker		"	"	"	23
Josiah Stow		"	"	"	"
Stephen Scott		"	"	"	"

CAMPAIGN OF 1757.

Name		Time of Inlisting	Time of return	
Samˡ Fenn		Mar. 28	Nov. 23	
" Lownsbury		" "	" "	
Charles Squire		" 26	" "	
Bartholemew Pond		" 28	" "	
Joseph Benham		" 25	" 13	
Samˡ Seaward		" 26	" 23	
Danˡ Meaker		" "	" "	
John Roe		" "	" 13	
Wᵐ Miles		" 10	" 23	
Nathˡˡ Davis		" "	" 13	
Danˡˡ Barns		" "	" 23	
Josiah Lewis		" "	" "	
James Blancherd		" 13		Deserted
Eliezer Bartholʷ		" "	Nov. 13	
Samˡˡ Dutton		" 26	" 23	
Onesimas Titus		" "	" "	
John Welton		" "	" 9	
Edward Johnson		" "	" 13	
Jedidiah Smedley		" "	" 23	
Abel Harrison		" "	" "	
Henry Ingraham		" "	" "	
Eliphalᵗ Reynold		" "	" "	
James Fancher		Apr. 2	" "	
Amos Palmerly		" "	" "	
John Lewis		" "	" "	
Zepheʰ Wix		Mar. 10	" "	
Caleb Hurlibut		" "	" "	
Danˡˡ Speek		Apr. 8	" 13	
John Smith		" 11	" 23	
Simeon Ross		" "	" 9	
Ephraim Preston	Capt.	Feb. 23	" 23	
Archibald McNeil	Lieut.	Mar. 8	" "	
Jonathan Beebee	Lieut.	Feb. 23	" "	
Moses Mathews	Ens.	Mar. 8	" "	
Archibald McNeil as Ens.		Feb. 23	Mar. 7	

Litchfield Regiment

[*State Library, Adams Papers.*]

The foregoing is A Roll of yᵉ Company under yᵉ Command of Ephraim Preston Capt Being yᵉ 13 Company in Colᵒ Lyman's Regiment

[*State Library, Adams Papers.*]

FOURTEENTH COMPANY—CAPT. WARD.

Andrew Ward [of Guilford], Captain. [*Colonial Records.*]

Peleg Redfield [of Killingworth], First Lieutenant.

Thomas Pierce [of Plainfield], Second Lieutenant. [*Colonial Records.*]

Zebulon Butler [of Lyme], Ensign.

A Muster Roll of Capt. Andrew Ward's Company that Servᵈ under the command of Lieut Coloⁿ Nathan Whitting att No 4
In the Pay of the Coloney of Connecticut anno 1757

COL. LYMAN'S REGIMENT. 195

Name		Time of Inlistment		Time viz weeks & days	
Andrew Ward Capt.		Feb.	23	39	2
Peleg Redfield Lieut		"	"	"	"
Thomas Peirce "		"	"	37	5
Zebulun Butler Ens.		"	"	"	"
Ichobod French Segt		Mar.	28	33	0
Benjamain Wellman "		"	"	34	4
Benjamain Wellman "		"	"	"	"
David Rosseter "		"	"	"	"
Isaac Sherman Kimborly Corp^ol		"	"	"	"
Gedion Webb "		"	7	35	5
William Jacobs "		"	28	33	0
Samuel Hutson "		"	"	34	4
Moses Whitte Clerk		"	"	33	0
Lumen Ward Drumer		"	"	34	4
Noah Bishop		"	"	33	0
Semieon Sexton		"	"	34	4
Edward Benten		"	"	"	"
Samuel Foot		"	"	"	"
Samuel Hand		"	"	"	"
Thomas [ ]		"	"	"	"
Jesse Cramton		"	"	"	"
Timothy Hand		"	"	"	"
Jannah Miges		"	"	"	"
Rebuen Kelley		"	"	"	"
Joiel Thompson		"	"	"	"
Samuel Johnson		"	"	33	0
Josiah Benten		"	"	32	3
Melezer Fowler		"	"	34	4
Lucas Carter		"	"	"	"
Abraham Turner		"	"	32	3
Dan Dickerson		"	"	33	0
Noah Norton		"	"	34	4
Stephen Hall		"	"	"	"
Irah Whitmore		"	29	"	"
Christopher Stevens		"	"	35	5
Elezor Isbell		"	"	"	"
Samuel Griffing		"	"	37	1
Elihua Wellock		"	28	34	4
James Stevens		"	"	"	"
Michael Merite		"	"	"	"
Gershom Tollees		"	"	"	"
Miles Wright		"	"	"	"
David Franklin		"	"	33	0
Samuel Tooley		"	"	"	"
Joseph Tooley		"	"	34	4
Robert Newell		"	5	37	4
Elihuia Wellman		"	28	34	4
George Chatfield		"	"	"	"
Christopher Tooley		"	"	"	"
James Bellemey		"	"	"	"
Roger Rose		"	"	33	0
Jonathan Shepeard		"	"	34	4
Aaron Smith		"	"	"	"
William Crook		"	"	33	0
Samuel Beailey		"	"	34	4
William Beailey		"	"	33	0
David Buller		"	"	"	"
John Bone		"	"	"	"

CAMPAIGN OF 1757.

	Time of Inlistment		Time viz weeks & days	
Thomas Deibell	Mar.	28	34	4
Edmund Shipmon	"	"	"	"
Nathan Pelton	"	"	"	"
Samuel Grenall	"	"	"	"
John Tucker	"	5	36	0
Jabez Beats	"	10	37	1
Elishia Chapman	"	28	34	4
Joseph Grimes	"	"	"	"
James Done	"	"	"	"
Samuel Comstock	"	"	"	"
Ebner Bushnall	"	"	33	0
John Wats	"	17	36	1
Daniel Comstock	"	28	32	3
Jonathan Ingham	"	"	34	4
Semeion Hough	"	"	33	0
Samuel Webb	"	"	"	"
James Colley	"	"	32	3
Abner Beckwith	"	29	34	4
Elihia Lee	"	"	35	2
Joshua Minor	"	"	"	"
Richard Hutson	"	"	35	1
John Daniels	"	"	"	"
Thomas Munsell	"	"	34	5
Cyrus Leiwes	"	"	"	"
John Keef	"	"	34	4
Richard Tinney	"	"	36	0
Richard Dorais	"	"	33	5
William Dollover	"	"	35	1
John Miller Tubs	"	"	34	5
Joseph Simons	"	"	36	6
Reuben Clearck	"	28	34	4
Elishia Robins	June	4	24	6
Joseph Coley	Apr.	2	32	2
Samuel Blackman	"	8	33	1
Simon Hurd	"	2	32	2
Jonas Moses	"	8	31	3
Hope Chapmond	"	11	32	5
Abraham Northrop	"	9	33	0
Edmund Pulphard	"	4	"	5

[Indorsed] Capt Andrew Wards Muster Roll Decem^r 16, 1757

[*State Library, Adams Papers.*]

MILITIA COMPANIES.

CAPT. MORGAN'S COMPANY.

Joseph Morgan [of Groton], Captain.
John Stanton [of Groton], Lieutenant.
Thomas Fitch, Ensign.

"Colony" of Connecticut to Cap[t] Joseph Morgan & Comp[a] for Service Marching to relief of Fort W[m] Henry at y[e] Alarm August last

Joseph Morgan Capt.
John Stanton Lieut.
Thomas Fitch Ens.
William Morgan Serj.
Benj. Woodworth "
James Walworth Clerk
Nat. Hall Drummer
Benajah Williams
Lethon (?) Avery
Sim Chester
Amos Lester
Nathan Foresey (?)
Abel Bayly
James Mills
James Wyllys
Joshua Morgan
John Wood Jun[r]
Elijah Adams
Thos Cunningham
Elisha Baker
David Dill
Gideon Leeds
Thom. Story
Ozias Buddington
Jed Williams
John Munsell
Sam. Allyn Jun[r]
Jon[a] Russ
Mortimore Stodard
Rob[t] Williams
Josh. Chapman
John Widger Jun[r]
W[m] Allyn
Joseph Williams
Eben[r] Williams
Dan[ll] Whipple Jun[r]
Jn[o] Swaddle
Tho[s] Spencer
Eben[r] Stoddard
John Lenien
Rich[d] Smith
Andrew M[c]Farthing
James Avery 3[d]
Caleb Haly
Tim[o] Lamb
Christopher Ellis
Oliver Wells
Andrew Lamb
Dan[ll] Lamb Jun[r]
Joseph Wells
James Barrows
Amos Barrows Jun[r]
Dan[ll] Mark 3[d]
Philip Covell
Tho[s] Parke Jun[r]
David Crouch
Simeon Smith
Lem[l] Barrows Jun[r]
Aaron Starke
Jerem[h] Collver
Will. Floyd
John Morgan Jun[r]
Dan[l] Williams
David Fanning
W[m] Fanning
Naum Maynard
Elkenah Morgan
Solo. Story
Solomon Geer
Jos. Malleson Jun[r]
Abel Spicer
Eben[r] Starke
Jn[o] Dickenson
Benajah Williams
Caleb Haynes Jun[r]
Horse drivers
Simeon Avery
Peter Brown

Each of the above named served 15 days.

[*State Library, War 7, 2.*]

CAMPAIGN OF 1757.

CAPT. BARKER'S COMPANY.

Abner Barker, Captain.
Simeon Hunt, First Lieutenant.
Samuel Davis, Second Lieutenant.
John Holmes, Ensign.

To The Coloney of Conecticut to Abner Barker Cap[t] of the Company under his Command In Co[ll] Shubel Connant Regement for their Service at the time of the Alarem for ye Relief of fort William Henery and Parts ajacent.

Abner Barker Capt.	Samuel Hendrick
Simeon Hunt 1 Lieut.	Hezekiah Smith
Samuel Davis 2 Lieut.	Nathan Watkins
John Holmes Ens.	Joseph Mason
Ebenezer Root Serj.	John Sumner
Epraham Clough "	Ebenezer Bosworth
Joseph Crocker "	James Parker
Joshua Barges "	Calven Eaton
John Works "	Jacob Kendal
Abner Hatch Clerk	Ebenezer Cheney
Ameriah Rockwell Corp.	Benjamin Hutcherson
Daniel Chandler "	Thomas Abbot
Soloman Walls "	Thomas Lyon
Joseph White "	Henery Lyon
John Root	William Laird
Asa Strong	Samuel Green
Bildad Curtice	Elijah Robardson
Dudley Dorman	Solomon Cushman
Stephen Palmer	John Reed
Levy Dow	Ezra Alden
Elijah Clark	Joseph Colburn
Eliphalet Edwards	William Washburn
Henery Dyer	Moses Snow
Medad Root	Jonathan Lille
Joseph Edwards	Benjamin Renolds
Ozias Halkens(?)	Benjamin Rider
Amos Dorman	Israel Standish
Samuel Root Jun[r]	Moses Carey
Lamuel Long	Lenard Pike
Israel Bruster	Danil Marcom
Elijah Carpenter	Timothy Butler
Thomas Fowler	Josiah Fuller
Ebenezer Brown Jun[r]	Moses Johnson
Gurden Fowler	Timothy Torrey
Ezekel Herrick	Elijah Scot
Elisha Adams	Elijah Fenton
Benjamin Luce	Peleg Heath
William Willson	Samuel Commans
Nathan Porter	William Cushman
Thomas Porter	Timothy Holt
Stephen Richardson	Peter Whitney
Timothy Lad	Moses Orcut
Pheneas Crosman	George Sawens
John Thompson	Elisha Parker
Benjamin Enos	Jered Thompson
Daniel Bagger	William Johnson
Jeremiah Bishop	Benjamin Stodard
Moses Ward	Jonathan Pool
Caleb Abbot	Joseph Mirick
William Fuller	Isaac Stoel

Each of the above named served two weeks from Aug. 10 to Aug. 24, 1757, except Serj. John Works and Timothy Torrey who each served six days.

David Orcut, Samuel Roberson, Amos Richardson, and Joseph Turnner were occupied seven days going to Canaan and bringing back horses from there.

Seven of the above named rode horses from Willington, three from Stafford, fifteen from Ashford, twenty seven from Coventry, and six from Union.

[*State Library, War 7, 3.*]

CAPT. MARSH'S COMPANY.

John Marsh [of Litchfield], Captain.
Ruben Averid or Averiel, Lieutenant.

Colony of Connecticut to Capt John Marsh and the Company under his Command in Colon^l Ebenez^r Marsh^s Regim^t at the time of Alarm for Relief of Fort Wm Henry and Places Adjacent

	Days in Service		Days in Service
Jn° Marsh Capt Aug. 7 to Aug. 23, 1757	16	Alex^a Miller	"
		Thos Porter	"
Ruben Averid or Averiel Aug. 8 to Aug. 23, 1757	15	Ahirah Hill	"
		Jese Horsford	"
		Eliph^a Easton	"
Ephr^m Smedly Serj.	16	George Marsh	"
Benj^a Woodruff "	16	Steph^n Webster	"
Moses Chamberlin "	16	Joshua Mason	"
Hendrik Venduzer "	16	Jn° Ferry	"
Nathl Goodwin Clerk	16	Ruben Sacket	"
Gideon Harrison Corp.	16	Simeon Phinny	"
Titus Harrison "	"	Eben^r Curtiss	"
Cladus Briton "	14	Oliver Phinny	"
Asael Bruns [ ] "	"	Dan [ ]swell	"
Peruda Isbell	16	Isaac Tickner	"
Gad Farnum	"	Isaac Swain	"
Elex Waugh	"	Danl Lee	"
Jo^s Linsly	"	Eben^e Loomis	"
Hez^e Orton	"	Ahi^l Bronson	"
Jere^m Kilburn	15	Cornel^s Dutcher	14
Isaac Johnson	"	Tunas Surdam	"
Abr^m Bewel	"	Ruluff Ducher	"
Zeb^n Walkley	"	Eliph^a Jewel	"
Thos Doolittle	"	Jn° Rose	"
Amos Barns	"	Edward Histing	
Noah Stone	"	Caleb Gibbs	7
Jn° Osburn	"	Zebulun Gibbs	"
Tim° Peck	"	Jo^s Veal	"
Saml Beach	"	Abij^a Clammens	"
Barnius Beach	"	Went to bring back horses	
Asher Culver	"	Jacob Woodruff	7
Oliver Dickerson	"	Abel Barns	"
Mark Prindle	"	Simeon Lyman	5
Jn° Stoder	"	Danl Comstock	"

Thirty eight of the above named rode horses from Litchfield, twelve from Kent, four from Woodbury and four from Salisbury.

[*State Library, War 7, 4.*]

CAMPAIGN OF 1757.

CAPT. BROWN'S COMPANY.

Isaiah Brown [of Stratford], Captain.
Israel Curtiss [of Stratford], Lieutenant.
Enoch Daviss [of Ripton in Stratford], Lieutenant.
Joseph Burton [of Stratford], Ensign.

    Colony of Connecticutt To Capt. Isaiah Brown and the Company under his Command In Col^l Andrew Burrs Regiment for their Service at the Time of the Alarm For Relief of Fort Willm Henry and parts Adjacent August 1757

Isaiah Brown Capt.
Israel Curtiss Lieut.
Enoch Daviss "
Joseph Burton Ens.
John Hubbel   Serj.
Abner Curtiss   "
Hudson Blackleach "
Josiah Brinsmaid   "
Nathan Curtiss Clerk
Saml Curtiss   Corp.
Howkins Nichols "
Danl Judson   "
Eben^r Foot   "
Samuel Curtiss
Saml Wells
Eben^r Coe
David Baldwin
Danl McCune
Isaac DeForrest
Elnathan Benjamin
Stephen Porter
Ephraim Warner
Michael Cosbee
Brewster Curtiss
Benjamin Bennit
George Lewiss
Stephen Beers
John Booth
Abraham Tomlinson
Phinehas Sherman
Silas Nichols
Saml Judson
Ephraim Curtiss
Joseph Birdsey

Phinehas Hill
David Silby
Eben^r Beardsley
James Fairchild
Peter Blackman
Edmund Pendleton
Nehem^h Loring French
Elias Baldwin
Benj^m Nichols
Lemuel Judson
Joshua Beardslee
John Gill
David Lake
James Fairchild Junr
Joseph Beardslee
Elnathan Peet
Phinehas Lake
Thomas Curtiss
Saml Hauley
Jacob Wakeley
Archibald Phipeney
Wm Wainright
Ephraim Furnee
Jesiel French
John Jones
Nathan Clark
Israel Beardslee
Michael Seley
Joseph Moss
Abiel Berrs
Saml French
Hesekiah Wheeler
Gideon Sherwood
Eliakim Walker

Each of the above named served sixteen days, from Aug. 7 to 23, 1757
Reuben Dean served fourteen days
Each of the above named rode a horse from Stratford.

                                                         [*State Library, War 7, 5.*]

CAPT. BRADLEY'S COMPANY.

Daniel Bradley [of New Haven], Captain.
James Morgan [of Redding in Fairfield], Lieutenant.
Phineas Chapman [of Fairfield], Lieutenant.
John Reed [of Redding in Fairfield], Ensign.

MILITIA COMPANIES.

Colony of Connecticut to Capt Daniel Bradley and the Company under his Command in Col^o Andrew Burr^s Regiment, for their Service at the time of Alarm for Relief of Fort Willm Henry and Parts Adjacent

Danil Bradley Capt.
James Morgan Lieut.
Phin^s Chapman "
John Reed Ens.
Ebenez^r Banks   Serj.
Gershom Coley   "
Solomon Morehouse   "
Ebenez^r Couch   "
John Hull Clerk
Peter Hull Corp.
Joshua Desbrow Corp
Seth Hull J^r "
Seth Hull   "
Jedediah Hull
John Hubbel
Luther Gould
Ebenez^r Ogden
Elnath^n Bradley
John Staples
Ebenez^r Wakeman
Willm Lord
Ebenez^r Bennitt
Cornel^s Stratton
Tim^o Burr
Joseph Smith
Joseph Burr
John Mills
Aaron Genings
Jonth Robenson
Oliver Whitlock
Seth Sandford
James Bartram
Thadeus Dikeman
Tim^o Sandford
John Gray
James Hull
Willm Truesdell
Elihu Deforrist
Hezeki^a Smith
Ebenez^r Williams
Jese Northe

Josiah C[   ]field
John Griffing
Thom^s Fairchilde
Giershom Fairchild
Lazarus Beach
John Malery
Jonth Meeker
Joshua Hall
Joseph Lyon
John Phinney
Willm Holley (?)
Paul Bartram
Isaac Hall
Ebenez^r Mills
Thomas Cable
Abr^m Andrus
Ebenez^r Godfry
Abel Nichols
Saml Hendrick
Hez^e Gray
John Hurlbut
John Higgens
Hez^e Elwood
Nathl Shaw
John Godfry
Dan Dunkens
Isaac Gorham
Thomas Allen
Danl Sturges
Danl Beers
Ichabod Denmores
Ebenez^r Baker
Jason Disbrow
Gershom Fanton
David Addams
Danl Godfry
Jese Ogden
Thadeus Squire
Jebez Canfield
David Platt
David Couch

Each of the above named served sixteen days, from Aug. 7 to 23, 1757. Each of the above named rode a horse from Fairfield.
Eben^r Green, James Gray, Dan^{ll} Dean, Eph^m Jackson and Eleazar Smith attending ye Return of the Horses 16 Days each.

[*State Library, War 7, 6.*]

MAJ. ELIOT'S COMPANY.

Aaron Eliot [of Killingworth], Major and Captain.
Ichabod Scranton, Lieutenant.
Joseph Bradly [of Guilford], Second Lieutenant.

CAMPAIGN OF 1757.

The Muster Roll of the First Company of a Detachment from yᵉ Seventh Ridgment of yᵉ Coloney of Conecticut for yᵉ Relief of Fort Wᵐ Henry

Name	Days in Service	Name	Days in Service
Aaron Eliot Maj. & Capt.	17	Phenius Steevens	16
Ichabod Scranton Lieut.	15	Roger Steevens	"
Joseph Bradly 2 "	"	Josiah Kelcey	"
John Eliot Clerk	"	Benjⁿ Merrels	"
Joseph Waterous Serj.	"	Nathˡˡ Steevens	"
Ebenezer Chettenton "	"	David Buel	"
David Dible "	"	Abner Farnam	"
Stephen Farnam "	"	Benjⁿ Baning	"
Stephen Whittelcy Corp.	16	Asa Jones	"
Wise Wright "	"	Noah Lane	"
Wellcum Giddings "	"	Joseph Hull	"
Edward Tryon "	"	Elias Graves	15
Ziba Loveland	"	Nathan Hill	"
Isaac Bates	"	Benjⁿ Bradly	"
Levi Bartholomu	"	James Bishop	"
Ambrose Restand	"	Ebenezer Feild	"
John Buckingham	"	Daniel Hand	"
William Ingraham	"	Ezra Wellcoks	"
Thomas Jones	"	Giles Hamblen	"
Jeremiah Chalker	"	Ebenezer Munger	"
Eliakim Jones	"	Gilbert Dudly	"
Ebenezer Ingham	'	Ambrose Everts	"
Joseph Kertlend	"	Jehiel Willcoks	"
John Deneson	"	Isi Norton	"
Edward Shipman	"	Stephen House (?)	12
Elias Meges	"	Stephen Buckingham	8
Orsbon Steevens	"	Edward Shipman	16
Josiah Carter	"	John Denison	"
Cornelius Chatfield	"	Joy Ward	8
Aaron Steevens	"	Ely Graves	11
Hiel Kelcey	"	Samˡˡ Parmele	"

Various members of the company rode horses from Killingworth, Guilford, and East Guilford.

[*State Library, War 7, 8.*]

CAPT. CONE'S COMPANY.

Daniel Cone [of East Haddam], Captain.
John Chamberlin [of Colchester], Lieutenant.
John MᶜCall [of Millington in East Haddam], Lieutenant.
Ephraim Fuller, Ensign.

Colony of Connecticut to Capᵗ Daniel Cone and the Company under his Command in Col. Jonathan Trumbleˢ Regimᵗ for there Service at the time of Alarm for Relief of Fort Wᵐ Henry and Places Adjacent

Danˡ Cone Capt.
Jnº Chamberlin Lieut.
Jnº MᶜCall "
Ephrᵐ Fuller Ens.
Eleazʳ Braynard Serj.
Willᵐ Welch "
Jnº Church "

Timº Parsivel Serj.
Stephⁿ Gardner Clerk
Danˡ Warner Corp.
Benjᵃ Fuller "
Elijᵃ Ackly "
Willᵐ Doge "
Elijᵃ Kilborn Drum.

MILITIA COMPANIES.

David Willey
Tim° Cone
Tim° Northam
Steph Spencer
Fredrick Spencer
Ezek Crocker
John Hungerford
Jn° Shaw
Edmund Marsh
Elishil Booge
Jo^s Beckwith
Christ° Holmes
Lem^l Willey
Danl Williams
Thos Knowlton
Willm Akins
Silv^a Youngs
Jared Braynard
Benj^a Olcott
Nathan^l Ackley
James Cook
Tim° Gates
Jn° Chamberlin
Deliverence Waters
Asahel Taylor
Jo^s Borden
Sterling Graves
James Bogue
Steph. Chapman
Lem^l Hungerford
Thos Webb

Mich^l Scovel
Hez^e Usher
James Sparrow
Isaac Tatton
Alex: Stewart
Saml Dodge
Jn° Tenant
Jonth Harris
James Forsyth
Jonah Chapman
James Ransome
Elisha Chapman
Jonth Gilbert
Rufus Randel
Asa Jones
Thos Brooks
James Rogers
Christ^r Minor
Jn° Hambleton
Danl Fuller
Abr^m Ackley
Nathan Beebe
Arter Scovel
Danl Emmons
Jn° Sheperson
Eben^r Smith
Ruben Cone
Levi Gates
Willm Markum
Elisha Beckwith
Nathl Taylor

Each of the above named served fifteen days, from Aug. 9 to Aug. 24, 1757.

Joseph Parker served nine days.

Eli Warner served eight days.

Amos Rothburn, Thos Cowdry and Roswell Knowlton each served seven days.

Sixty-two of the above named rode horses from East Haddam.

Elisha Johnson, James Forsyth, Thom^s Jones, Caleb Beebe, Nathl Sparrow, Eb^r Cook, and Eliak^m Spencer each seven days; Robert Hungerford and Christ° Holmes each three days to bring back horses.

[*State Library, War 7, 9.*]

A Role of the Company Under the Command of Capt Daniel Cone Belonging to the Twelfth Rigement Under the Command of Col° Jonathan Trumbull Esqr

[*Connecticut Historical Society.*]

CAPT. DOWNS' COMPANY.

Ebenezer Downs [of Southbury in Woodbury], Captain.
Gideon Stoddard [of Woodbury], Lieutenant.
Matthew Mitchel [of Southbury in Woodbury], Lieutenant.

CAMPAIGN OF 1757.

Dr the Colony of Connecticut To Capt Ebenezer Downs and Company under his Command for his Servis in the Alarm for the Releif of fort Wm Henry And plases Adjasent In the month of August 1757

	Served Weeks	Days		Served Weeks	Days
Ebenezer Downs Capt.	4	1	Enos Hawly	2	3
Aug. 7 to Aug. 18			Josiah Baset	"	"
Gideon Stoddard Lieut.	2	3	Gideon Curtis	"	"
Aug. 7 to Aug. 23			David Cresy	"	"
Matthew Mitchel Lieut.	2	3	Roburt Edmond	"	"
Aug. 7 to Aug. 23			Benjamin Wornor	"	"
Joseph Hecok Serj.	2	3	Gideon Bronson	"	"
Return Strong "	"	"	William Hopson	"	"
Thadeus Lasy "	"	"	Gideon Hecok	"	"
Gideon Holester "	"	"	Peter Castel	"	"
Joseph Perce Clerk	"	"	Joshuah (?) Judson	"	"
Eldad King Corp.	"	"	Roburt Potter	"	"
Obediah Wheeler "	"	"	John Runels	"	"
Abner Mallery "	"	"	Matthew Duten	"	"
Ruben Hulbut "	"	"	Carpenter Sanford	"	"
Benjah King	"	"	Edward Smith	"	"
Nathan Hurd	"	"	Peleg Stone	"	"
Tille Blakly	"	"	Benjamin Sanford	"	"
Jedediah Hurd	"	"	Ebenezer Hulbut	"	"
Timothy Allen	"	"	John Barit	"	"
Nathan Minor	"	"	John Calhone	"	"
Thomas Knowls	"	"	Joseph Burch	"	"
Benajah Hawly	"	"	Daniel Hurd		14
Bushnal Benidik	"	"	Sam^{ll} Hurd		"
Joseph Washbon	"	"	Amos Bronson		11
John Stoddard	"	"	Thomas Roots		8
Timothy Terrill	"	"	Ruben Castel		"
Daniel Keny	"	"	Daniel Judson		"
Seth Minor	"	"	Sam^{ll} Galpin		"
David Jonson	"	"	Selah Strong		6
Timothy Walker	"	"	Noah Frisbe		"
Gideon Brister	"	"	Gideon Squir		"
Jesse Roots	"	"	Samuel Knowls		"
Daniel Shirman	"	"	David Hecok		"
Daniel Hecok	"	"	Benjahmin Prince		"
John Hunt	"	"	Ruben Hinman		"
Gideon Tuttel	"	"	Jams Durky		"
Jams Mory	"	"	Daniel Hulbut		"
Elisha Stoddard	"	"	To bring back horses		
Nathan Hine	"	"	Sam^{ll} Minor		8
Phenes Potter	"	"	Ezekil Baker		"
Sam^{ll} Hinman	"	"	David Squir		3
Thadeus Curtis	"	"			

[*State Library, War 7, 10.*]

CAPT. DAY'S COMPANY.

Benjamin Day [of Colchester], Captain.
Jonathan Kilburn [of Colchester], Lieutenant.
Solomon Phelps [of Marlborough in Colchester], Lieutenant.
John Peters [of Gilead in Hebron], Ensign.

MILITIA COMPANIES. 205

Dr Colony of Connecticut to Capt Benjamin Day and the Company under his Command in Col^o Jonathan Trumbles Regim^t for there Service in the Late Alarm for Relief of Fort Wm Henry and Places Adjacent Augst 1757

	Days in Service		Days in Service
Benj^a Day Capt. from Aug. 8 to Aug. 23	15	Jno Carter	15
Jonth Kilburn Lieut.	"	Gid^n Post	"
Solom^n Phelps "	"	Jo^s Tuttle	"
John Peters Ens.	"	Jno Hazard	"
Eben^r Willcocks Serj.	"	Israel Dodge	"
Jno Johnson "	"	Elij^a Thomas	"
Henry Champion "	"	Joel Chamberlin	"
Dav^d Miller "	"	Ebe^n Cole	"
Thos Sumner Clerk	"	Jo^s Taylor	"
Thos Perrin Corp.	"	Elij^a Northam	"
Abr^m Palmer "	"	Aron Gillet	"
Saml Kellogg "	5	Miles Wright	"
Robt Loveland Drum	15	Jno Roberts	"
Willm Root	"	Phillip Judd	"
Gideon Jones	"	Nathl Kellogg	"
Willm Chamberlin	"	Jos^l Archer	"
Dav^d Dean	"	Roger Phelps	"
Silven^s Phelps	"	Girshom Fox	"
Saml Wright	"	Saml Beebe	"
Elisha Beach	"	Amos Wells	"
Edwd Howard	"	Robt McCleave	"
Danl Gott	"	Jo^s Spencer	"
Thos Frink Crouch	"	Bildad Waterman	"
Asa Robenson	"	Jacob Worthington	"
George Blanchard	"	Parker Jones	"
Tim^o Stewart	"	Amos Dodge	"
Ezra Cogswell	"	Caleb Loomis	"
Jab^z Dunham	"	James Crocker	"
Jno Chamberlin	"	Ezra Gates	"
Jno Jones	"	Jo^s Watrous	"
Jonth Root	"	Allen Willey	"
Jonth Tillotson	"	Stephen Ackley	"
David Blish	"	Jno Bigalow	"
Stal Worthy Waters	"	Noah Weston	"
Job Stiles	"	Elij^a Smith	"
Jno Whitcomb	"	Silas Fox	"
Abij^a Briant	"	Benj^a Day	"
Jo^s Carrier	"	Jo^s Kellogg	14
Saml Raymond	"	John Kilburn	10
Abr^m Fox	"	Jno Rowley	8
Jno Talcott	"	Thos Dunham	7
Obe^d Culver	"	Jonth Brown	10
Nathl Phelps	"	Benj^a Archer	7
Jo^s Blish	"	Jno Blish	6
Josh^a Smith	"	To bring back horses	
Asher Merrils	"	Barret Phelps	9
Nich^o Bond	"	Jo^s Williams	"
Henry Curtiss	"	David Smith	8
Jno Ellis	"	Jonth Dunham	2
James Cocks	"	Danl Tillotson	"

Seventy-six of the above named rode horses from Colchester.

[*State Library, War* 7, *11.*]

CAMPAIGN OF 1757.

CAPT. DUNHAM'S COMPANY.

Samuel Dunham [of Sharon], Captain.
Samuel Hubbell [of Kent], Lieutenant.
Caleb Jewet [of Sharon], Lieutenant.

A Muster Roll of a Comp^a of Militia under Command of Capt Saml Dunham on ye Alarum to relieve Fort Wm Henry &c August 1757

Capt Sam^{ll} Dunham
Lieu^t Sam^{ll} Hubbell
" Caleb Jewet
Serj^t John Davise
" John Gray
" Ebenez^r Beaman
" Ashbell Goodrich
Clerk Jonath Hawley
Corp^l Solomon Johnson
" Dan^{ll} Beebe
" James Pardy
" Heamon Swift
Dan^{ll} Raymond
Phinehes Fountain
Joseph Landers
Elijah Strong
David Griswould
Benjamin Hunter
Jonath Hunter
Solon n Dunham
John Marvin ye 3^d
George White
David Ford
Penuel Bacon
Eleazer Curtice
Daniel Mack
James Phelps
Bela Brownson
Elijah Smaley
Luke Swetland
Nathen Tibbals
Isaiah Curtice
Azeriah Pratt
Peleg Chamberlin Ju^r
Sam^{ll} Cocksure
Benj^a Dibble
Israel Rowley
Jedidiah Hubbel
William Pollet
James Stewart
Isaiah Gibson
John Ransom
Abraham Fuller
Ebenezer Peck
Nehemi^h Gregory
Sela Abbet
Ichabod Squire
Stephen Lee
John Clothier
Isaac Cushman
Matthias Chapman
Garret Vineger
John White
Ambrose Clothier
Talmadge Bishop
Timoth. Spaulding
Hezekiah Foord
William Pierce
Benj^a Bisbye
John Allen
Stephen Pangmon (?)
Dan^{ll} Rowland
Thomas Harriss
Dan^{ll} Gifford
Moses Dean
Zach^h Dibble
Jno Millard Junr
Elias Chapman
Christoph^r Cartwright
John Pardy
Sam^{ll} Corby
Dudley Hamilton
Sam^{ll} Hambleton
Dan^{ll} Champion
Jesse Marvine
Isaac Doty
Silas Hamblin
Thomas Tracy
David Millard
Alex^r Spencer
Stephen Jackson
John Simons
Solomon Hutchinson
Moses Read Junr
John Pettit
David Cole
Nath^{ll} Curtice
Elijah Calkins
Benedick Woodward
Benj^a Frisby
Jonath^n Swain
James Betts Junr
Wm Tickner Junr
Dan^{ll} Thurston
Abraham Mudge
Eben^r Mudge ye 3^d
Zenas Goodrich
Ebenezer Pettit
Joseph Carter

MILITIA COMPANIES. 207

Each of the above named served fifteen days, except Elijah Smaley served eighteen, Nathan Tibbals and Joseph Carter each sixteen, and for Isaiah Curtice no time is given.

[*State Library, War 7, 12.*]

LIEUT. PHELPS' COMPANY.

David Phelps [of Simsbury], Lieutenant.

D[r] Colony of Connecticut to Lieu[t] David Phelps and the Company under his Command in Colon[ll] Joseph Pitkins Regiment at the Time of the Alarm for the Relief of Fort William Henry and places adjacent, who went out under the command of Cap[t] Ammi Trumble, and Continued in the Service under the Command of Lieu[t] David Phelps. August 1757

	Days in Service		Days in Service
David Phelps Lieut.	13	Samuel Rockwell	14
Aug. 8 to Aug. 21		Samuel Palmer	"
Israel Jones Serj.	14	Benjamin King	"
Aug. 8 to Aug. 22		James Fareman	"
Parmenus King Serj.	"	Ebenezer Meacham	"
David Bissell "	"	Timothy Pease	"
William Bissell Clerk	"	Daniel Perkins	"
John M[c]Knight	13	John Slater Corp.	13
Joseph Young	"	Mathew Grant	14
John Vineing	14	to bring back horses	
Simon Wolcott	"	Ephraim Willcockss	10
Oliver Stoughton	"		
Nath[ll] Drake Jun[r]	"	John Slaughter horse journey	
Ebenezer Loomis	"	95 miles	

[*State Library, War 7, 13.*]

CAPT. GROSVENOR'S COMPANY.

John Grosvenor [of Pomfret], Captain.
Ebenezer Holbrook [of Pomfret], First Lieutenant.
John Cotton, Second Lieutenant.

A Muster Role of the Company under the Command of Cap[t] John Grosvenor In the Late Allarm who Marched In y[e] Month of Aug[st] 1757

John Grosvenor Capt.
Ebenez[r] Holbrook 1 Lieut.
Jn[o] Cotton 2 "
John Robins Sarj.
Moses Earl "
Jn[o] Johnson "
Josiah Sabin "
Josiah Brown Corp.
Jn[o] Fisk "
Beno. Cuttler "
Jn[th] Coye "

Nath[el] Stowell Clerk
Elij[h] Sharp Drum.
Jn[o] Sumner
Elij[h] Chandler
James Williams
W[m] Coye
Veren Danniells
Semeion Lee
Jn[o] Jefferds
Jn[o] Sanders
Nahum Hall

CAMPAIGN OF 1757.

Thoˢ Liscomb
James Holmes
Nathˡˡ Goodale
Wᵐ Blackmore
Cyperⁿ Stephens
Nathˡˡ Barns
Abᵐ Statter
Jnᵗʰ Collar
Jnᵗʰ Patton
Jn° Anderson
Jn° Smith
Thomˢ Gould
Jn° Grover
Jn° Sprauge
Jehoial Brook
Elijʰ Cady
Stepⁿ Brown
Joshua Powell
David Peregoe
Jn° Batinan
Samˡˡ Harinton
Benjᵃ Tucker
Benjᵃ Webben
Benjᵃ Craft
James Ramond
Joshᵃ Chaze
Nathˡˡ Wolcott
Dan Davison
Wᵐ Stephens
Jehᵈ Brown
Jn° Bilbowa
Wᵐ Shearman

Seth Hide
Jesse Darbee
Abijʰ Goodale
Zachᵃ Hubbard
Abner Adams
James Daruse
N[   ] Pike
Jn° Trusdell
Abjʰ Tucker
Barthoʷ Durkey
Jn° Hibbard
Jnᵗʰ Aldrige
Lenoard Cady
Wᵐ Cooper
Aden Durkey
Asa Pike
George Allen
Jn° Glazar
Samˡˡ Glazer
Parks Moffit
Jn° Felshaw
Jacob Whitmore
Jn° Cuttler
Jn° Stephens
Ebenzʳ Covell
Asa Church
Elihu Larrance
Jn° Henrick
Benjᵃ Grover
James Caplin (?)
Danˡˡ Robinson
Robᵗ Coats

Each of the above named served fifteen days, except Danˡˡ Robinson who served thirteen, and Robᵗ Coats who deserted

Ebenezer Grosvenor attended to the return of the horses six days.

Horses were ridden by various members of the company from Pomfret and Killingly.

[*State Library*, War 7, 14.]

LIEUT.-COL. WHITNEY'S COMPANY.

David Whitney [of Canaan], Lieutenant-Colonel.
Daniel Lawrence Jr. [of Canaan], Lieutenant.
Joshua Whitney [of Canaan], Lieutenant.
Benjamin Stevens [of Canaan], Ensign.

A Muster Roll of Lieut. Colˡ David Whitneys Company of Militia for Relief of Fort William Henry &c August A D 1757

Mens Names & Rank Canaan Men	In Service Weeks & Days		Mens Names & Rank Canaan Men	In Service Weeks & Days	
David Whitney Lieut. Col.	2		Lemuel Roberts Serj.	2	
Danˡ Lawrance Junʳ Lieut.	1	4	Ezra Knapp "	2	
Joshua Whitney "	2		Amazʰ Ashman "	2	
Benjᵐ Stevens Ens.	2		James Addams "	2	
Samˡ Gaylord Adj. Gʳ	2		Ephraim Hewitt Corp.	2	

MILITIA COMPANIES.

Mens Names & Rank Canaan Men	In Service Weeks & Days		Mens Names & Rank Canaan Men	In Service Weeks & Days	
John Collen Corp.	2		Nath¹ Hamlin	1	5
James Hodgkiss "	2		Jacob Kingsbury	2	
Noah Allin "	2		Herman Kenickerbaker		6
Sam¹ Briant	1		Hezekiah Loomiss	2	
John Brinsmaid	2		Dan¹ Lawrance	1	1
Elijah Cleavland	1	1	Gideon Lawrance	2	
Abiel Camp	2		Rufus Lawrance	2	
Joseph Clark	2		Jona. Moor Junr	1	
Charles Duppee	2		Simon Newcomb	2	
James Dunham	2		Jona. Owen	1	
Elizur Dickinson	2		Amos Peirce Comss^y	2	
Gabriel Dutcher	2		Thos Peirce	2	
Josiah Dean	1	1	Nath¹ Porter	1	6
James Evans	2		Thos Patterson	1	4
David Fellows	2		Job Rothbone	2	
Amos Fuller	1		Sam¹ Roberts	2	
Samuel Forbs	2		Elias Reed	1	6
Jonathan Fellows	1	1	Thos Reed	2	
Andrew Stevens		3	Eben^r Stevens	2	
Thomas Williams	2		Noah Strong	1	6
Willm Fitch	2		Hartman Vanduser	1	
Jos. Trumble Fitch	2		Jesse Stevens	2	
Justus Gaylord	2		Phineas Walker	2	
John Higbee	2				

[*State Library, War 7, 15.*]

CAPT. LEE'S COMPANY.

Josiah Lee [of Farmington], Captain.
Isaac Hurlbut, Lieutenant.
Joseph Deming, Lieutenant.

Dr The Colony of Connecticutt to Capt Josiah Lee and the Company under his Command Raised in the 6th Regiment in said Colony for their Service in the Alarm for the Relief of Fort William Henry and parts adjacent.

	In Service Weeks & Days			In Service Weeks & Days	
Josiah Lee Capt.	2	4	John Belding	2	5
Aug. 7 to Aug. 24			Deliverance Blin	"	"
Isaac Hurlbut Lieut.	"	"	John Crane	"	"
Joseph Deming "	"	"	Ebenez^r Dickinson	"	"
Timothy Hubbard Serj.	"	"	Ozias Griswold	"	"
Josiah Goodrich "	"	"	Elias Hurlbutt	"	"
David Hills "	"	"	William Loveland	"	"
Seth Bird Clerk	"	"	Thos Newson	"	"
Nath¹ Goodrich Serj.		10	Roger Robbins	"	"
Alexander Chalker "		9	Thos Mygatt	"	"
Jo. Crowfoot Corp.	2	4	Jonah Fox	"	"
Eben^r Goodrich "	"	"	Samuel Peas	"	"
John Kelsey "	"	"	Peleg Weldon	"	"
Noah Gridley Drum.	"	"	Gideon Hollister	"	"
Daniel Wilcox Corp.		8	James Butler	"	"

14

CAMPAIGN OF 1757.

Name	In Service Weeks & Days		Name	In Service Weeks & Days	
Lemuel Deming	2	5	Matthew Dunham	2	4
Samuel Wolcott	"	"	Benj[a] Beckly	"	"
Tim[o] Francis	"	"	Richard Riley	"	"
Chester Welles	"	"	Ebenezer Sanford	"	"
Tim[o] Griswold	"	"	Alexander Chalker	1	3
Francis Hanmer	"	"	Benjamin Andrus	"	"
Samuel Buck	"	"	Benjamin Winchell	1	
Solomon Deming	"	"	David Collins		3
Menas (?) Smith	"	"	Stephen Andrus		7
Robert Collins	"	"	Elihu Wright		8
John Riley	"	"	Samuel Brownson		7
John Church	"	"	Hez[h] Francis		"
Nath[ll] Bordman	"	"	Billee Blin		"
Hez[h] Goodrich	"	"	David Blin		"
Josiah Goffe	"	"	Elisha Stoddard		"
Jacob Goffe	"	"	Appleton Hollister enlisted		
Timothy Taylor	"	"	at Fort Edward y[e] 9th		
Abraham Goodrich	"	"	day		
David Mather	2	4	Phineas Rowlandson deserted at Half Moon the 8th day		
Elnathan North	"	"			
Benj[a] Smith	"	"			
Ebenezer Dickinson	"	"	Ambrose Nicholson Serj.	2	2
David Kilborn	"	"	Sam[ll] Bidwell Corp	"	"
Tho[s] Lusk	"	"	Jon[a] Webster	"	"
Amos Wright	"	"	Stephen Taylor	"	"
Abel Andrus	"	"	Tho[s] Loveland	"	"
Hez[h] Attwood	"	"	John Stevens	"	"
Elisha Whaples	"	"	Jon[a] Miller	"	"
Francis Deming	"	"	Peter Goodrich	"	"
Eli Whaples	"	"	Elisha Goodrich	"	"
Epaphras Andrus	"	"	Amos Matson	"	"
John Bordman	"	"	Jon[a] Wickham	"	"
Jonathan Stoddard	"	"	Gideon Sage	"	"
Theodore Seymour	"	"	Henry Nicholson	"	"
Silas Brownson	"	"	Adonijah Scott		10
Job Root	"	"	the 14 Men next above named were Sent by Cap[t] Sam[ll] Talcott [of Glastenbury] out of his Company after Cap[t] Lee March[d] with y[e] rest of his Comp[a]		
Matthew Hart	"	"			
Solomon Rugg	"	"			
Samuel Squire	"	"			
Jesse Cole	"	"			
Archer Willson	"	"			
William Hills	"	"			
Titus Brownson	"	"	Elias Wright		7
Joseph Hopkins	"	"	Cha Hurlbut		"
Zechariah Hart	"	"	Caleb Galpen		"
James Steel	"	"	Uriah Wickham		"
David Hart	"	"	Amos Porter		"
Josiah Gilbert	"	"	Dan[ll] Wilcox Jun[r]		"
Roger Mygot	"	"	Job Norton		"
John Gurney	"	"	These went with pack horses and brought back the other horses.		
Zacheus Bacon	"	"			
John Tooley	"	"			

Nine of the above named rode horses from Middletown, fifteen from Farmington, and thirteen from Wethersfield.

Jeduthan Smith and Tho[s] Matson, not of y[e] Company, rode horses from Glastenbury.

[*State Library*, War 7, *16*.]

CAPT. TRUMBLE'S COMPANY.

Ammy Trumble [of Windsor], Captain.
John Hanchett [of Simsbury], Ensign.

A pay Role for the men under the Command of Cap[t] Ammy Trumble in the Alarm in the year 1757 in their march to the releif of Fort Edward and parts Adjacent that have not been Paid

John Hanchett Ens.
Sam[ll] Smith   Serj.
Joseph Negurs   "
David Addams   "
Robert Grainger   "
Israel Dibble   Corp.
Timothy Mather   "
Hugh Thomson
Ben Adams   delinquent
John Bissell
Noah Stiles
Joel Prior
Zebedee Osburn
Joseph Allin Jr.
Job Ellsworth
Israel Ossburn
Benony Stiles
Shadrach Barber
Silas Simons
Josiah Blotchett
Ezra Grant
Ephestus Allin
Timothy Bissell
Joel Hawkins
Jeremiah Ballard
Nath[l] Peirce
Elijah Evans
Silas Stepheson
Jonathan Mason
James Ollcott
Charles Wait
David Peirce
Caleb Jones Jr
Shobal Parsons
Judah Bemont
Joseph Peirce Jr. Deserted 9 Aug.
James Simons
John Allin
Stephen Markim
Nath[ll] Markim
Judah Haise
Benjamin Bruer
Serajah Stratten Jr.
Ichabod Grimes
George Bunts (?)
Jonathan Lattemore
Thomas Winchel Jr.
Thomas Spencer
John Rising Jr.
Jonathan Rising Jr.

Joseph Rimmington
Aaron Granger
Nathan Higly
Elijah Alvord
Zekera Negro
Petro Negro
Thomas Hail
Richard French
Silas Kibbe
Benjamin Hall
Thomas Dyer
Elijah Graham
Nath[ll] Alvord Jr.
Michael Mills
Michael Jackson
Jacob Davis Jr.
Joel Higly
Elijah Herington
Elihu Olderman
Sam[ll] Thrall
Joseph Moore
Roger Moore
Abner Marshel
Ezra Brown
Roger Phelps
John Alvord
John Adams 2[d]
Sam[ll] Palmer
Jonathan Allin
Sam[ll] Adams
Edmund Bemont
Ebenezar Loomise
Jacob Winchel
Rubin Woolworth
Simon Kindall
Abner Granger
Ruben Spencer
Phinehas Southwell
John Harmon
Nath[ll] Warner
Joseph Hastins
Joseph Phelan
Seth Sheldin
Joel Smith
Benjamin Gillit
Jonathan Dewey
Epraim Leason
John Norton Jr.
Abel Roce
James Smith Jr.

[*State Library, War 7, 17.*]

CAMPAIGN OF 1756.

CAPT. JOHNSON'S COMPANY.

Nathaniel Johnson [of Guilford], Captain.
Timothy Hill, Lieutenant.
Samuel Bartlet, Lieutenant.

    Colony of Connecticut to Capt Nathaniel Johnson and the Company under his Command in Col^o Samuel Williard^s Regiment for their Service at the time of Alarm for Relief of fort Willm Henery and Parts adjacent August 1757

Name	Days in Service	Name	Days in Service
Nathaniel Johnson Capt. Aug. 8 to Aug. 22	15	John Forsdick	15
Timothy Hill Lieut.	"	Stephen Savage	"
Sam^{ll} Bartlet "	"	Thelus Ward	"
Benjamain Fowler Serj.	"	Jered Leet	"
Joiel Canfield "	"	Josep Chittenden	"
William Collins "	"	Thomas Caldron	"
Jonathan Evarts "	"	Amos Hodgkis	"
Reuben Leet Clerk	"	Mark Hodgkis	"
John Evarts Corp.	"	Samuel Ludenton	"
Philemon French "	"	Aaron Jones	"
Aaron Parmlee "	"	Stephen Chittenden	"
Felex Norton "	"	Samuel Bishop	"
Abrham Bartlet Drum.	"	Samuel Field	"
Jered Benten	"	Stephen Miges	"
Joshua Bishop	"	Samuel Field 2^d	"
Peter Falmon	"	Shuball Shelley	"
Ebnezer Hatch	"	Joseph Dudley	"
Samuel Hart	"	Caleb Chapmon	16
Jacob Coann	"	Joseph Bushnell	"
Daniel Chittenden	"	Jesse Bushnell	"
Samuel Fitch	"	Mathew Post	"
David Fowler	"	Daniel Lay	"
Samuel Loper	"	Joseph Carter	"
John Bartlet	"	Jeremiah Kelcey	"
Joseph Chitsey	"	Daniel Devall	"
Charles Falkner	"	Reuben Post	"
Daniel Hill	"	Ephraim Kelcey	"
Joseph Stone	"	John Shipmon	"
Zebulon Norton	"	Nathan Surthworth	"
Thomas Griswold	"	Moses Baldwin	"
Mark Spencer	"	John Duglis	"
Phineas Johnson	"	Ebnezer Warner	"
Luther Chittenden	"	Zerackiah Church	"
Ashnar (?) Stone	"	William Hough	"
Jered Sheperd	"	Samuel Watrous	22
Timothy Cudweley (?)	"	Zebuloun Cruttenden	"
Timothy Spencor	"	Four horse men	
William Star	"	Reuben Norton	12
David Norton	"	David Bishop	"
Isaac Pendfield	"	John Hubbard	"
		Thomas French	"

    Sixty-one of the above named rode horses from Guilford.

                                                          [State Library, War 7, 18.]

MILITIA COMPANIES. 213

LIEUT. HALL'S COMPANY.

Abijah Hall [of East Hampton in Middletown], Lieutenant.
Jacob Hall, Ensign.

Dr Colony of Connecticut, To Lt Abijah Hall & the Company under his Command In Co^l John Chester Rigiment for there Service at the Time of Alarm for the Releaf of Fort Wm Henry and parts Adjasent Augt 1757

	Days in Service		Days in Service
Abijah Hall Lieut.	19	Sam^{ll} Akin	16
Aug. 8 to Aug. 26		Aron Roberts	"
Jacob Hall Ens.	15	Elisha Hale	"
Aug. 8 to Aug. 22		John Ufford	"
Stephen Gates Serj.	16	Sam^{ll} Brown	"
Aug. 8 to Aug. 23		Thos White	"
Job Bates Serj.	19	Eben^r Harding	"
Aug. 8 to Aug. 26		James Bill	"
Fenner Ward Serj.	15	Eben^r Cole	"
Aug. 8 to Aug. 22		Justis Taylor	"
Silan Dunham Clerk	19	Simion Youngs	"
Aug. 8 to Aug. 26		Daniel Hubbard	"
Charls Goodrich Corp.	8	Joshua Griffin	"
Aug. 8 to Aug. 17		Joshua Branord	"
John Hinkley Corp.	11	Joseph Dart	"
Aug. 8 to Aug. 20		Jonathan Branord	"
Recompence Robrts Corp.	16	John Vansant Deserted	12
Aug. 8 to Aug. 25		Richard Goodale "	"
Stephen Jenkins	16	Sith Knowls	"
Aug. 8 to Aug. 23		Danel Brewer'	5
Benjⁿ Adley (?)	"	John Miller	19
Daniel Shepard	"	Nehamiah Gales	10
John Penfield (?)	"	David Baley	"
Lackins (?) Good[ ]	"	Isaac Baley	"
Nath^{ll} Savage	"	Heman Swift	"
Joseph Stote	"	John Cook	"
Marshel Stocking	"	James Knowls	"
Colins Yeomans	"	To Cary Back horses	
Gideon Hall	"	Joseph Chapman	8
Amos Stocking	"		

[*State Library, War* 7, *19.*]

CAMPAIGN OF 1757.

CAPT. BALDWIN'S COMPANY.

John Baldwin [of Stonington], Captain.
Joseph Palmer [of Voluntown], Lieutenant.
Amos Danilson [of Stonington], Ensign.

The Colony of Conecticut D^r to Capt John Baldwin Capt of ye Company under his Command in Cor^l Christopher Avery Rigment for thier Servise at ye time of ye Alarm for ye Releef of Fort Wm Henry and Parts adjacent 1757

	Days in Service		Days in Service
John Baldwin Capt.	16	Sam^{ll} Fellows	16
Aug. 9 to Aug. 24		Thomas Baxter	"
Joseph Palmer Lieut.	"	John Babcock	"
Amos Danilson Ens.	"	John Prentice	"
Joseph Denison Serj.	"	Joseph Smith	"
Ichabod Palmer "	"	Gideon Dikenson	"
Jehu Fish	"	Christopher Brown	"
Jesse Billings "	"	Abr^m Birdict	"
Seth Smith Clerk	"	John Brumbly	"
Nathan Cobb Drum.	"	Nehemiah Palmer	"
Saml Prentice Corp.	"	Wait Winkley	"
Thomas Pabodie "	"	Pell Collins	"
Silvester Cheasbrough "	"	Joseph Noyes	"
Saml Billings "	"	John Beebee	"
Rufus Hill	"	Daniel Yeomans	"
Moses Clark	"	John Stanton	"
Joshua Swan	"	Uriah Willbour	"
Lemuel Lamb	"	Jeremiah Ingraham	"
Hezekiah Muck	"	David Utley	"
Jones Hewit	"	Christopher Palmer Jr.	"
Joshua Prentice	"	Jeremiah Brown	"
Willm Swan	"	Reuben Brown	"
Benjamin Hewit Jr.	"	James Cornish	"
Amaziah Yarington	"	Caleb Niles	"
Henery Dauning	"	Amos Rathbun	"
Saml Hallet	"	Joseph Frink	"
Jonth Brewster	"	Stephen Main	"
John Gambel Jr.	"	Peter Pawheague	"
Daniel Brown	"	Charles Pawheague	"
Walter Clark	"	Stephen Symonds	"
David Balie	"	Reuben Toney	"
Daniel Bennit Jr.	"	Daniel Hamer	"
John Deruse	"	Jeffery Codgjoh	"
Sam^{ll} Stockwell	"	Stephen Brown	18
Nathl Swan	"	Theopholas Fitch	10
Sam^{ll} Minor ye 3^d	"	Seth Wright	7
Sam^{ll} Hewit	"	James Chapman	"
Isaac Willcox	"	Willm Willcocks	"
Elias Raynolds	"	Amos Brown	"
Reubin Hewit	"	Silvester Baldwin	10
Arnold Neph	"	Epheram Brewster	"
George Jaquease	"	Thomas Williams	"
Jonth Wiatt Palmer	"	Willm Swift	1
Joseph Tift	"	Asell Clark	"
Willm Brown	"	Thomas Lyman	"

[*State Library, War 7, 20.*]

CAPT. STOUGHTON'S COMPANY.

Samuel Stoughton [of Windsor], Captain.
Moses Thrall [of Bolton], Lieutenant.
George Cooly [of Somers], Ensign.
Samuel Chapman [of Tolland], Ensign.

Dr Coloney of Connecticutt to Capt Sam^{ll} Stougton and the Company under his Command in Col. Joseph Pitkins Regiment for their Service at the Time of the Alarm for Relief of Fort William Henry and parts Adjacent August Anno 1757

	Days in Service		Days in Service
Sam^{ll} Stoughton Capt.	14	Jo^s Whitcomb	15
Aug. 8 to Aug. 21		John Stricklin	"
Moses Thrall Lieut.	15	Jesse Craw	"
Aug. 8 to Aug. 22		Tim^o Scott Jr.	"
George Cooly Ens.	14	John Abbott Jr.	14
Aug. 9 to Aug. 22		Abner West	"
Saml Chapman Ens.	"	Thatcher Lothrop	"
John Fullor Serj.	"	Jacob Fellows	"
Aug. 9 to Aug. 22		Nathan Harvey	"
Solomon Wells Serj.	"	David Hatch	"
Ozios Bissell "	15	John Eaton	"
Aug. 8 to Aug. 22		Ichabod Hinkly	"
Abel Foster Serj.	"	George Nye	"
John Allyn Clerk	"	Timothy Delano	"
Aug. 8 to Aug. 21		William Benton	"
Nathan Messenger Corp.	15	Solomon Loomis	"
Aug. 8 to Aug. 22		Sam^{ll} Huntington	"
Jonathan Buckland Corp.	"	Jabez Bradly	"
Jos Cogswell "	"	Sam^{ll}·Benton Jr.	"
Thomas Chapman "	5	Sam^{ll} Aborns	"
Aug. 8 to Aug. 12		Jonathan Ladd Jr.	"
Job Strong	15	Simon Chapman	"
Jonth Smith	"	Francis West	"
Ralph Cox	"	Rufus West	"
Bariah Loomis	"	Joseph Davis	"
Jared Knowlton	"	John Starns Jr.	"
Hezekiah Wells	"	Amos Ward	"
Gershom Bartlett	"	Sam^{ll} Ellis	"
Charles Kellogg	"	Oliver Chapin	"
Crafts Goodrich	"	Asa Wood	"
Wm Thayer	"	Benjamin Jones	"
Joshua Fuller	"	Daniel Sexton Jr.	"
Jo^s Spencer	"	Mathew Bewil	"
John Colman Jr.	"	Josiah Field Jr	"
Sam^{ll} Bartlett	"	Aaron Horton	"
Wm Jones	"	Benjamin Allin Jr.	"
Isaac Hills	"	Isaac Brunson Jr.	7
Brenton Paine	"	Sam^{ll} Barnard	4
Daniel Baker	"	Persons Negro	2
Elihu Johnson	"	Saml Stoughton riding from Farm-	
Benjamin Grant Jr	"	inton to Windsor 1 day	
John McKenny	"	Moses Trall Jr. and a horse from	
Uriah Coy	"	Boston to Sheffield	
Richard McCartey	"	Thomas Hall 4 days	

Twenty-four of the above named rode horses from Tolland, twenty-one from Bolton, twenty-one from Litchfield, and three from Windsor.

The Soldiers whose Names are underwritten were ordered by ye Captain to continue wth the Company but deserted returnd & never again joynd s^d Company

Elijah Owen	Sam^ll Whipples
Elijah Strong	Noah Pease
Nath^ll Heyden Jr.	James Farrington
Aaron Strong Jr.	Obadiah Spencer
Elisha Hubbard	James Pease 4th
Josiah Stantleff	Noadiah Kibbe
William Booth	Josiah Wood Jr.
Lem^ll Hatch	John Osborn
Daniel Squire	Thaddeaus Billings
Israel Warner	Nathl Tiffany Jr.
Eleazar West	Sam^ll Rockwood Jr.
David Eaton	Charles Wood
Benjamin Jones Jr.	Barzeliel Atchinson
Oliver Evans	Gideon Smith
Charles Kibbe	

Abner Burroughs, Joseph Sparks, Joshua Reed Detached but never appeared.

[State Library, War 7, 21.]

CAPT. WHITE'S COMPANY.

Stephen White [of Stanwich in Greenwich], Captain.
Caleb Mead [of Greenwich], Lieutenant.
Ezekiel Lockwood [of Greenwich], Ensign.

A Roll of the Company under the Command of Captain Stephen White Captn in the 9th Regiment in the Colony of Connecticut under the Command of Colonel Jonathan Hait who in the Late alarm Marched for the Succour & Relief of fort William Henry & the parts Adjacent, the time they were in Service &c. in August A Dom 1757

	Days in Service		Days in Service
Stephen White Capt.	16	Joshua Smith	17
Caleb Mead Lieut.	17	Deliverance Mead	"
Ezekiel Lockwood Ens.	"	Amos Partelo	"
Samuel Johnson Serj.	"	Denham Palmer	"
Reuben Holms "	"	James Waring	"
Nathaniel Lockwood Serj.	18	Nath^ll Cross	"
Daniel Whelply "	20	Abraham Randall	"
John Perot Clerk	22	Reuben Reynolds	"
Bezaleel Brown Corp.	17	Joseph Newman	"
Job Austin "	"	Joseph Knap	"
Samuel Ferris "	"	David Pardee	"
John Jurden "	"	Silvanus Jesup	"
Simon Ingersol	"	Ezra Newman	"
Nathan Lockwood	"	Benjamin Webb	"
James Knap	"	Whitman Smith	"
Eben^r Whiting	"	Willm June (?)	"
Silvanus Ferris	"	Abr^m Holly	"
Christ^r Hartman	"	Robert Bard	"
Thos Penoyr	"	David Smith	"

MILITIA COMPANIES.

	Days in Service		Days in Service
William Lyon	17	Mead Marshal	17
Halsted Wood	"	Jabez Ferris	"
Nathaniel Mead	"	Abr^m Todd Junr	12
Thad^s Selleck	"	Isaac Newman	"
Jeremiah Green	"	Joseph Mead	"
Abr^m Hait	"	Horton Reynolds	"
Nath^{ll} Mead Junr	"	Henry Mead	"
David Knap	"	Joseph Coe	"
James Green	"	Peter Ferris	"
William Wilson	"	James Peck	20
John Hobby	"	Sam^{ll} Smith	"
Jesse Mead	"	Elijah Mead	9
Felix Acherly	"	Benjamin Hobby	"
Benjⁿ Mead	"	John Knap	7
John Marshal	"	Joseph Peck	4
Nath^{ll} Holly	"	James Scoit Deserted	7
John Holms	"		

Thirty-seven of the above named rode horses from Horseneck, seventeen from Stanwich parish, and eleven from Greenwich.

Isaac Newmen Horton Rennals
Joseph Meed Henry Meed

These four were employed to return the horses.

[*State Library, War 7, 22.*]

CAPT. NOBLES' COMPANY.

Daniel Nobles [of New Fairfield], Captain.
Daniel Parks [of Sharon], Lieutenant.
Joseph Canfield [of New Milford], Lieutenant.

Dr Colony of Connecticut to Capt Daniel Nobles and the Company under his Command in Col. Ebenezer Marsh's Regiment for their Service at the Time of Alarm for Releif of Fort William Henry and parts Adjacent August Anno 1757.

	Days in Service		Days in Service
Danl Nobles Capt.	16	Samuel Dunham Corp.	15
Aug. 8 to Aug. 24		Aug. 8 to Aug. 23	
Danl Parks Lieut.	15	Joshua Dickingson Corp.	"
Aug. 8 to Aug. 23		Solomon Goodrich "	"
Joseph Canfield Lieut.	17	Peletiah Chapman Drum.	"
Aug. 7 to Aug. 24		Aug. 8 to Aug. 23	
Benjamin Gaylord Serj.	16	Benj^a Ruggles	17
Aug. 8 to Aug. 24		Amos Collens	"
Jethro Hatch Serj.	"	Arthur Bostwick	"
Jonathan Gillett "	17	Saml Warner	"
Aug. 8 to Aug. 25		Heath Garlick	"
John Penoyer Serj.	"	Ebenez^r Leonard	"
Isaac Bostwick Clerk	16	Zadock Bostwick	"
Aug. 8 to Aug. 24		Paul Welch	"
Ebenezer Bostwick Corp.	15	David Farriss	"
Aug. 8 to Aug. 24		Elizur Warner	"

	Days in Service		Days in Service
John Henry Nearing	17	Elijah Thompson	15
Jehiel Hawley	16	John Bentley	"
Benj^a Ovet	"	Thos Rowley	"
Isaac Hitchkock	"	Saml Dooty	"
John McEven	"	William Goodrich	"
Aaron Benedict	"	James Betts	"
James Osborne	"	Timothy Treat	"
Shadrak Hubbel	"	Oliver Burton	"
Robert Hawkins	"	Cornelius Hamlin	"
Ep^m Buck	"	Amos Boardman	"
Josiah Daton	"	Danl Curtice	"
Emerson Cogswel	"	Nathl Warner	"
Abel Curtiss	"	David Maning	"
Jacob Galusha	"	Bartholomew Heath	"
Joseph Lamb	"	Saml Hurlbutt	"
John Cobb	"	David Elmer	"
Saml Peet	"	Elijah Wood	"
Ichabod Palmer	'	Reuben Munroe	"
Ebenezer Sealy	15	Joseph Gould	"
Jeremiah Fuller	"	Amos Weller	"
Josiah Raymond	"	Joshua Chaffee	"
Joseph Pratt	"	Jonth Huff	"
Eley Rowley	"	Amos Tyler	"
Isaac Fuller	"	Jesse Ford	"
Edward Wilcox	"	Josiah Strong	"
Peleg Sturdevant	"	Tim^o Brockway	"
John Slauson	"	Tim^o Carrier	"
Aaron Rowley	"	Stephen Marvin	"
John Lake	"	Azariah Griswould	"
Jonth Berry	"	Joseph Marvin	"
Elias Church	"	Josiah Strong Jr	"
Luke Fisher	"	Jarvis Munge (?)	7
Luke Steward	"	Benj^a Summers	6
Lewis Mills	"		

Thirty-three of the above named rode horses from Sharon, twenty-one from Milford, nineteen from Kent, and eleven from New Milford.

[*State Library, War 7, 23.*]

CAPT. HENMAN'S COMPANY.

Wait Henman [of Woodbury], Captain.
John Nichols [of Stratfield in Stratford], Lieutenant.
Ephram Bakor [of Woodbury], Lieutenant.

The Coloney of Connectut to Wait Henman Capt of the Company under his Command in Col Ebenzer Marshs Ridgment for their Servis at the time of the alarram for the Relefe of fouet william Henery and pleacs ajasent 1757

	Days in Service		Days in Service
Wait Henman Capt.	17	Ahijah Mitchel Serj.	
Aug. 7 to Aug. 25		Hezkiar Thomson	"
John Nichols Lieut.		Elezor Mitchel	"
Ephram Bakor "		Joseph Pery Clerk	
David Barnums Serj.		Joseph Gilbert Corp.	

MILITIA COMPANIES.

	Days in Service		Days in Service
Sam[ll] Judson Corp.		Joseph Hurlburt	17
Abraham Brownson "		Jos Gunthy	"
Jeddiah Dorkey "		Jonathan Royce	"
Amos Mortin	17	Justice Gibbs	"
Anthony Stoddord	"	Michel Honn	"
Amos Hicok	"	Nathaniel Sanford	"
Abijah Thomirlin	"	Noah Tuttle	"
Benj[a] Henman	"	Noah Hurlburt	"
Benj. Galpin	"	Remember Backor	"
Charls Strong	"	Ruben Thomas	"
Charls Smith	"	Richard Burton	"
David Clohon	"	Sam[ll] Logan	"
David Foot	"	Sam[ll] Cantis	"
David Drkey	"	Lem[ll] Castle	"
David Wheler	"	Salomon Squier	"
David Henman	"	Stephen Squire	"
David Porter (?)	"	Sam[ll] Castle	"
David Stiles	"	Titus Beach	"
David Martin	"	Tim[o] Judson	"
Daniel Cresey	"	Thomas Minor	"
David Levensworth	"	Thadus Judson	"
David Minor	"	Tim[o] Cale	"
Daniel Reed	"	Thomas Dank	"
Edward Lake	"	Tim[o] Fuller	"
Ebenzor Wheler	"	Willam Yongs	"
Sam[ll] Walen	"	William Balden	"
Elijah Brownson	"	William Edmun	"
Elijah Hurlburt	"	Zorakiah Walker	"
Elihu Smith	"	Zacheas Weller	"
Elish Clark	"	Phylemon Way	"
Edward Tirsby (?)	"	Abisha Mosely	"
Gideon Holly	"	James Nichols	"
Gideon Mun	"	Ephraim Baldwen	"
Groshum Lake	"	Sam[ll] Squire	"
Gideon Walker	"	Delevrensce (?) Kinne (?)	"
Jehiel Peet	"	Ichabod Tutle	"
John Walker	"	Benj[a] Estmon	"
Ebenezar Hurlburt	"	Hezakiah Noble	"
Justice Blachly	"	Israil Canfield	"
John Hurlbut	"	Isaac Buck (?)	"
John Jackson	"	Cele (?) Waller (?)	"
Israel Sumner	"	Nathan Mortin	10
John Atwell	"	William Black	"
John Creday (?)	"	Asa Preston	4

The men that Brought Back the horses

Andrew Nichols	10	Jese Bockar (?)	5
Nash Tuttle	9	Abijah Stoddard	7
Tim[o] Browson	"	Richard Smith	"
Hezekiah Prulee	"	Isah Gilbort	"
John Levensworth	7	John Marchant (?)	"
David Foot	5	John Kinne (?)	
Robert Durkey	"		

[*State Library, War 7, 24.*]

CAPT. WOODRUFF'S COMPANY.

Joseph Woodruff [of Milford], Captain.
Joseph Riggs [of Derby], Lieutenant.
Benjamin Ferm [of Milford], Lieutenant.

A Muster roll of ye Comp^a of Militia under Command of Capt Joseph Woodruff on ye Alarum Augt 1757 for Relief of Fort Wm Henry &c.

	Days in Service		Days in Service
Joseph Woodruff Capt.	19	Henry Whitney	19
Joseph Riggs Lieut.	18	David Woodruff	"
Benj^a Fenn "	19	Joseph Buckingham	"
John Sandford Serj.	"	Eliph^t Humervile	"
Abner Gunn "	"	Harriss Jones	"
Edward Worster "	18	David Lambert	16
Elisha Worster "	"	Sam^{ll} Worster	"
Wm Gillet Clerk	19	Zephaniah Tucker	18
Ezekiel Newton Corp.	"	Henry Clinton	"
Danl Worster "	18	Henry Worster	"
Joseph Sandford "	19	Amos Basset	"
Nathl Perry "	18	Sam^{ll} Durand	"
Samuel Oviat	19	John Washburn	"
Samuel Smith	"	Eliada Pettit	"
Fitch Welch	"	Sam^{ll} Pierson	"
Jonath Fowler	"	Sam^{ll} Belchier	"
James Davidson	"	Eli Tomlinson	"
Fletcher Prudden	"	Lemuel Chatfield	"
Solomon Baldwin	"	John Honde	"
Joseph Clark	"	Nathan Pierson	"
Sam^{ll} Durond	"	Nathan Washburn	"
Nehemiah Nothrop	"	John Griffin	"
Epinelus Platt	"	James Perry	"
James Fenn	"	Daniel Warden	"
David Down	"	Nathan Buckingham	"
Robert Arnold	"	Jabez Harger	"
David Miles	"	Noah Cande	"
Reuben Bristoll	"	David Smith	"
Barnabus Woodcock	"	Phinehas Johnson	"
Elijah Hine	"	Phinehas Lee	"
Phinehas Camp	"	Jonathan Lumb	"
Isaac Camp	"	Stephen Hull	"
John Perrit	"	John Crowfoot	"
Lazarus Northrop	"	Jehiel Smith	10
Andrew Baldwin	"	Timothy Botchford	"
Benj^a Buckingham	"	James McRay	"
Moses Northrop	"	Hezekiah Hine	"
Elihu Baldwin	"	Charles Johnson	"
Abraham Baldwin	"	John Whitmore	"
Lamberton Smith	"	Benj^a Clark	20
Charles Prindle	"	Michael Peck	"
Oliver Smith	"	Abel Northrop	6

[*State Library, War 7, 25.*]

MILITIA COMPANIES. 221

CAPT. SMEDLEY'S COMPANY.

James Smedley [of Fairfield], Captain.
William Bennet [of Stratfield in Stratford], Lieutenant.
Isaac Bennet [of Stratfield in Stratford], Lieutenant.
Joseph Squire [of Fairfield], Ensign.
John Cable [of Fairfield], Ensign.

Dr Colony of Connecticut to Capt James Smedley and the Company under his Command in Col° Andrew Burr^s Regiment for their Service at the time of Alarm for Relief of Fort Willm Henry and Parts adjacent August 1757

	Days in Service		Days in Service
James Smedley Capt.	16	Danl Cable	16
Aug. 7 to Aug. 23		Benj^a Hubbel	"
Willm Bennet Lieut.	"	Nehemⁱ Smith Odell	"
Isaac Bennet "	"	John Fairweather	"
Joseph Squire Ens.	"	Frances Jackson	"
John Cable "	"	Joseph Hall	"
Ebenez^r Wakman Serj.	"	Wolcott Hawley	"
Abrah^m Gould "	"	Selvenus Sterling	"
James Morehouse "	"	Fredr^k Hawley	"
John Burr "	"	Ebenez^r Perry	"
Saml Penfield Clerk	"	Tim° Fairchild	"
Abel Seely Corp.	"	George Graves	"
Abel Genings "	"	Willm Jackson	"
Seth Bradly "	"	Danl Bennit	"
Georg Burr "	"	Saml Seely	"
Hezek^a Bennit Drum.	"	Tim° Tredwell	"
Seth Burr	"	Thomas Beach	"
Moses Nichols	"	Adin Jackson	"
David Smith	"	Benj^a Coley	"
Eleaz^r Sherwood	"	Lewis Bennet	"
Thos Dymon	"	Epra^m Tredwill	"
Ephr^a Burr Jr.	"	Saml Murwin	"
John Whitehead	"	John Olmsted	"
Joseph Stirges	"	Justus Olmsted	"
Jeremⁱ Osborn	"	Nathan Burr	"
Seth Sturges	"	Ruben Lake	"
Peter Hendrick	"	Elnathⁿ Wheeler	"
Benj^a Meaker	"	Saml Bostwick	"
Willm Grant	"	Timothy Lyon	"
David Pachen	"	John Cable	"
Ezra Burr	"	Willm Orborn	19
Willm Butington	"	Deliverence Wakely	"
Wolcot Chancy	"	Elisha Risden	"
Josep Davis Jr.	"	Onesimus Bradley	6
Danl Morehouse Jr.	"		

Sixty-four of the above-named rode horses from Fairfield.

[*State Library, War 7, 26.*]

TORRINGTON COMPANY.

Colony of Connecticut for Service at y⁰ Alarm in August 1757 for Defence of Fort Wm Henry

	Days in Service		Days in Service
Noah Wilson	15	John Whetner	15
Gad Marshel	"	Epaphras Loomis	"
Israel Averett	"	Isechar (?) Loomis	"
Saml Cowles	"	Martin North	"
Jonathen Coe	"	Abra^m Tilley	"
Aaron Loomis	"	Matt^w Grant	"
Beriah Hills	"		

Each of the above named rode a horse from Torrington.
Deduct 6 Days overchargd to Israel Abott & Beriah Hill

[*State Library, War* 7, 27.]

CAPT. LEWIS' COMPANY.

Eldad Lewis [of Southington], Captain.
John Norton [of Durham], Lieutenant.
John Sutliff [of Waterbury], Lieutenant.
Gideon Hodgkiss [of Waterbury], Ensign.

D^r the Colony of Conecticut to Eld Lewis Capt of ye Company under his Command in Colo^l Benja^n Halls Redgement for their Servis at ye time of the alarm for Relief of Fort William Henry and places ajasant 1757

	Days in Service		Days in Service
Eldad Lewis Capt. Aug. 7 to Aug. 26	19	Elisha Rust	18
John Norton Lieut.		Ebn^r Hubard	"
John Sutliff "	18	Rufus Clark	"
Gideon Hodgkiss Ens.		Abraham Wallers	"
Danl Killum Serj.	"	Simeon Hart	"
Stephen Welton "	"	Nath^ll Hitchcock	"
Joab Horsington "	"	Merven Beckwith	"
Stephen Bates "	"	Petter Powers	"
Dan^ll Potter Clerk	"	Eliakim Welton	"
Noadiah Graves Corp.	"	Nath^ll Hubard	"
Elihu Moss "	"	John Whaling	"
Tho Richards "	"	Robert Scott	"
Stephen Mathews "	"	Hez^h Brown	"
Ambrus Slooper	"	David Merrils	"
Nath^ll Mesanger	"	Abner Munson	"
Sam^ll Woodruff	"	Shadrak Benham	"
Lem^l Lewis	"	Dan^ll Barns	"
John Stoten	"	Saml Spary	"
Eben^r Pike	"	Eldad Mix	"
Jason Hazard	"	William Hordly	"
Solomon Barrit	"	Joseph Wornar	"
John Bell	"	Charles Wornar	"
Seth Woodruff	"	Oliver Turrel	"
William Parsons	"	Jesse Allcok	"
		Abrah^m Prichard	"

MILITIA COMPANIES.

	Days in Service		Days in Service
Sam¹ Judd	18	John How	18
John Silkrag	"	Asher Blaklee	"
Joel Roburds	"	William Clark	"
Dan¹¹ Williams	"	Jehial Hull	"
Joel Frost	"	James Henmon	"
David Hungerford	"	Benjⁿ Gittum	"
Tho Cole	"	Oliver Bates	"
Tho Hammon	"	Jonathⁿ Waklee	"
Tho Williams	"	Henry Suard	"
Weith Scot	"	Ambrus Field	"
Williams Judd	"	Benjⁿ Cook	"
Jonathⁿ Garnsey	"	John Camp	"
Simeon Beebe	"	Sam¹¹ Loveland	"
Tho Hecock	"	David Squier	"
Sam¹ Richards	"	William Wheeler	"
Nath¹ Edwards	"	John Fowler	"
Abner Wettmore	"	Benjⁿ Barns	"
Nathⁿ Foot	"	Ambrus Egleston	"
Isaac Merimon	"	Went to take back horses	
Reuben Blaklee	"	Samuel Root	9
Phenehas Curtis	"	Medad Lewis	"
Ephr Allin	"	Isaac Brownson	"
Jonathⁿ Cook	"	Roger Prichard	"
John Fancher	"	Richard Seymour	"
Ezra Sanford	"	Silas Hodgkiss	"
Abisha Castel	"	Zachary Sanford	"

Forty-eight of the above named rode horses from Waterbury, two from Wallingford, and ten from Southington.

[*State Library, War 7, 28.*]

CAPT. BUEL'S COMPANY.

Solomon Buel [of Litchfield], Captain.
Benjamin Gibbs [of Litchfield], Lieutenant.
Gideon Hulbut [of Goshen], Lieutenant.

A Muster Roll of a Company of Militia under command of Capᵗ Solomon Buel on yᵉ Alarum for Relief of Fort Wᵐ Henry Aug 1757

Names & Rank	Days in Service	Names & Rank	Days in Service
Capᵗ Solomon Buel	17	David Case	17
Lieuᵗ Benjᵃ Gibbs	"	Uriah Catlin	"
Serjᵗ Benjᵃ Colver	12	Eli Catlen	"
" David Landon	17	Sam¹¹ Catlen	"
Clerk Timo Stanly	"	Theodore Catlen	8
Corp¹ Benjᵃ Kilborn	"	Barnabas Doolittle	17
" Seth Farnum	"	Silvanus Bishop	"
Zebⁿ Taylor	"	Aaron Stodder	"
Beriah Stone	"	Moses Barns	"
Rosewell Killborn	"	Archalus Buell	"
Zebⁿ Bissell	"	Benjᵃ Webster	"
Justus Sealey	"	Elijah Grant	"
David Welch	23	George Baldwin	"

CAMPAIGN OF 1757.

Names & Rank	Days in Service	Names & Rank	Days in Service
Lemuel Orton	17	Joel Strong	17
Jonath Mason	"	Gooff Negro	"
Jacob Smith Jr.	"	John Fulford	n m
Paul Peck	"	Joshua Meed	n m
Benj[a] Frisbye	"	Isaiah Williams	n j
Joshua Rosseter	"	Eldad Curtice	n j
Solomon Linley	"	of Woodbury	
Jacob Harrison	"		
Thomas Peck	"	Lieu[t] Gideon Hulbut	17
Brian Stadder	"	Serj[t] Joseph Lee	"
W[m] Hall	"	Corp[l] Benj[a] Ives	"
Sam[ll] Barnard	"	Benj[a] Reaves	"
Eli Emmans	"	Jonath Waddams	"
Joseph Waugh	"	Jeremiah How Jr.	"
Nath[ll] Benton	"	Giles Griswould	"
John Walkins	8	Pierce Walter	"
Joseph Picket	D	Elisha Blin	"
Eben[r] Colver	D	Asaph Wright	"
Elijah Marsh	n m	David Ives	"
Fuller Negro	11	Samuel Smith	"
Zeb[n] Gibbs Jr	8	Wertil Willoughbye	"
[ ] Sandford	17	Joseph Hinman	"
[ ]hfield		Joseph Haskins	"
		Stephen Tuttle	"
Serj[t] Simeon Wheeler	"	Chiliab Smith	"
Corp[l] Solomon Steel	"	Jn[o] Beech	"
Joseph Wheeler	"	Jonath Pettibone	D
John Gorden	"	James Pinnock	n m
Ephraim Gitteau	"	Moses Wright	17
David Phelps	"	Elisha Thompson	n m
Benj[a] Chapmon	"	Tim[o] Gaylard	n m
John Hamilton	"	Elias Deming	n m
Abirom Peet	"	Jn[o] Kilborn	n m
Dan[l] Dudley Jr.	"	Jn[o] Thompson	n m
Tho Doolittle	"	Aaron Miller	n m
Joel Munger	"	Israel Dibble	n m
Ezekiel Steel	"	Titus Hill	11
Asahel Hooker	"	of Goshan	

Names of those who returnd the Horses in this Company

Jehiel Grant	8	W[m] Hooker	8
Josiah Smith	"	Timo Stanley	7
Benj[a] Birge	"	John North	"

N. B. y[e] meaning of y[e] letter D in y[e] 2[d] Column Signifys Deserted The letters n m Signifys never moved and n j never Joynd

[*State Library*, War 7, *29.*]

LIEUT. MALTBIE'S COMPANY.

Daniel Maltbie [of Northford in Branford], Lieutenant.

The Colony of Connecticut to Lieut. Daniel Maltbie Lieut of the Company under his Command In y[e] 2[d] Regiment under Col[l] Newton for their Service att y[e] time of the Alarm for the Relief of Fort W[m] Henry and parts Adjacent August 1757

MILITIA COMPANIES.

		Days in Service			Days in Service
Daniel Maltbie Lieut.	8 to 23	15	Sam¹ Linsley Jr.	8 to 23	15
Solomon Seaward Serj.	"	"	Jacob Linsley	"	"
Benj^m Baldwin Corp.	"	"	Thomas Stanly	"	"
Daniel Harrison	"	"	Simeon Harrison	"	"
Uzel Wardel	8 to 24	16	Joseph Foot	"	"
Nath¹ Harrison Jr.	"	"	James Howd	"	"
Dan¹ Rose	"	"	Joseph Talmage	"	"
James Smith	"	"	John Munson	"	"
Dan¹ Goodrich	"	"	Eli Bradly	"	"
Gideon Rogers	"	"	Ephraim Foot	"	"
Jonathan Johnson	"	"	Reuben Wheadon	8 to 22	14
Sam¹ Stant	"	"	Edward Brockway	"	"
Elisha Frisbee	"	"	John Elwell	"	"
Demetrius Cook	"	"	Jared Barker	8 to 18	10
Jacob Frisbee	"	"	Eben^r Barker	8 to 17	9
Phinehas Baldwin	"	"	Stephen Darin	"	"
Jonathan Russel	8 to 23	15	Stephen Palmer	"	"
Sam¹ Baldwin	"	"	Went to bring back horses		
Dan¹ Baldwin Jr.	"	"	Joseph Barker	8 to 16	8
Jude Ludinton	"	"	Abraham Page	"	"
Joseph Butler	"	"	Josiah Bartholomy	"	"

Twenty-six of the above named rode horses from Branford.
Obadiah Winters, Henry Ludington, Solomon Rose Deserters
Isaac Linsley, Jurden Smith, Jonathan Foot, Thomas Keson Delinquents
[*State Library, War 7, 30.*]

CAPT. HITCHCOCK'S COMPANY.

John Hitchcock [of New Milford], Captain.
Abel Wright [of New Fairfield], Lieutenant.

Dr Coloney of Connecticut to Capt John Hitchcock and the Company under his Command in Colonel Ebenezer Mash^s Regiment for their Service at ye time of Alarm for Relief of Fort Willm Henry and Places adja^t August 1757

		Days in Service			Days in Service
John Hitchcock Capt.	6 to 23	18	David Harriss	6 to 22	17
Abel Wright Lieut.	7 to 23	17	Eli Robards	"	"
Janathan Benedick Serj. 6 to 23		18	Jesse Beardsley	"	"
			Isaac Deforreest	"	"
Israel Baldwin Serj.	6 to 23	"	Nath^ll Beacher	"	"
John Benedick	7 to 23	17	Abel Mott	"	"
Ephraim Seeley	"	"	Justus Miles	"	'
Abel Hine Clerk	6 to 24	19	David Hitchcock	6 to 23	18
Epenetus Platt Corp.	6 to 22	17	Wm Hambling	"	"
Joseph Lines	6 to 24	19	Abraham Gillit	"	"
John Peet	7 to 22	16	Nath^ll Smith	"	"
Ebenez^r Seeley	"	"	Benjn Brownson	"	"
Ezra Benedick	6 to 22	17	Thomas Oviatt	"	"
Jude Ferris	"	"	Job Goold	"	"
Benjn Hurlbutt	"	"	John Hull	"	"
Mertin Warner	"	"	Nathan Canfield	"	"

CAMPAIGN OF 1757.

	Days in Service			Days in Service	
Asahel Bostwick	6 to 23	18	Ezekiel Curtis	7 to 14	8
Reuben Booth	"	"	Zacheus Brush	"	"
Edward Collins	"	"	Allien Ball	"	"
Joseph Canfield	"	"	Ebenez^r Lacy	"	"
Ephraim Beardsley	"	"	Nathan Barnum	7 to 23	17
James Prime	"	"	Alexander Fairchild	"	"
Joshua Wallis	"	"	Charls Knap	"	"
John Brownson	6 to 26	21	Hezek^h Stevens	"	"
Abraham Warner	7 to 24	18	Jonathan Wiks	"	"
Josiah Chuchwell	7 to 22	13	Ebenezer Pardy	"	"
Joseph Gray	"	"	Ebenez^r Umstead	"	"
Aaron Gaylord	"	"	Serajah Beardsley	"	"
Elisha Wood	"	"	Joseph Stevens	"	"
Willm Cogswell	"	"	Josiah Barse	"	"
John Handerson	"	"	Jedediah Wheeler	"	"
Morgin Noble	"	"	Gideon Beardsly	"	"
Ephraim Guttree	"	"	Ralph Trobridge	"	"
Simeon Stockwell	"	"	Seth Trobridge	"	"
Sam^{ll} Raymond	"	"	Elijah Waller	"	"
James Lake	"	"	David Green	7 to 12	6
Elijah Palmer	"	"	Zibe Brownson	"	"
Mertin Negro	"	"	Elnathan Botchford	6 to 19	14
Joseph Giddings	"	"	Chesher Wanzer		Deserted
Benjn Seeley	"	"	Men went to bring back horses		
Nath^{ll} Hollister	"	"	Stephen Noble		6
Fithen Sill	"	"	James Terrill		"
Silus Hill	"	"	Sam^{ll} Prindle		"
Willm Barns	"	"	Nathaniel Brown		"
Asahel Tryon	"	"	Samuel Comstock		"
Daniel Stuard	"	"	Justin Miles		"
Stephen Tombling	"	"	Isaac Bisco		"
Enoch Hubbel	"	"	Willm Goold		"
Edmond Hawse	"	"	Daniel Prindle		"
John Pepper	"	"	Elnathan Hall		"
Caleb Hitchcock	6 to 14	9			

Sixty-five of the above named rode horses from New Milford, and eighteen from New Fairfield.

[*State Library*, War 7, 31.]

CAPT. HULL'S COMPANY.

Lemuel Hull [of Killingworth], Captain.
Isaac Turner, Lieutenant.
Stephen Lane, Lieutenant.

The Colony of Connecticut to Capt Lemuel Hull & Company of Soldiers under his Command for Service Marching to relief of Fort Wm Henry &c in the Alarm August 1757

	Days in Service		Days in Service
Lemuel Hull Capt.	16	Abra Towner Serj.	16
Isaac Turner Lieut.	"	Jedi Kirtland "	"
Stephen Lane "	"	Silvanus Graves "	"
Jedediah Griswold Clerk	"	Dan^{ll} Bates Corp.	"
Dan^{ll} Franklin Serj.	"	John Marbel "	"

MILITIA COMPANIES.

Name	Days in Service	Name	Days in Service
Sam¹ Scofield Corp.	16	Hez. Lane	16
Josiah Redfield	"	Philip Laget	"
Joseph Ardnel	"	Jere. Nettleton	"
Abra Bishop	"	Dan¹¹ Parnell	"
Prosper Brainard	"	Dan Parnel	"
Nathan Baley	"	Simⁿ Pratt	"
Increase Brainard	"	Hez Pratt	"
Hez Baly	"	Timᵒ Ray	"
James Brooks	"	Eliphᵗ Stevens	"
Jona Bates	"	Ruben Stevens	"
Phinˢ Comstock	"	Eliakim Stevens	"
Joshua Cone	"	Rubⁿ Shaylor	"
Jacob Clark	"	John Smith	"
Tho. Clark	"	Elijah Scovel	"
James Cumstock	"	Edmond Snow	"
Christopher Clark	"	Sam¹¹ Squire	"
Ebenʳ Gleeding	"	Zach. Still	"
Nathan Hull	"	Dan¹¹ Smith	"
Sam Hull	"	Isaac Thomas	"
Ebenʳ Horton	"	Thomas Tyly	"
Dan¹ Hubbard	"	Josh. Wheeler	"
Timᵒ Hubbard	"	Returning horses	
Oliver Kelsey	"	Dan¹ Buel	16
Jonᵃ Kelsey	"	Stephen Nott	12
William Nobles	"	Charles Williams	"
Dan¹ Lane	"		

Six of the above named rode horses from Haddem, nine from Killingworth, and six from Saybrook.

[*State Library*, *War* 7, *32*.]

CAPT. STEVENS' COMPANY.

Uriah Stevens [of Canaan], Captain.
Jonathan More [of Salisbury], Lieutenant.
Joseph Lee, Lieutenant.

Dʳ Colony of Connecticut to Capᵗ Uriah Stevens and yᵉ Company under his Command in Colᵒ Ebenezer Marshes Regimᵗ for their Service at the time of Alarm for Relief of Fort Wᵐ Henry & parts adjacent August 1757

Name	Days in Service	Name	Days in Service
Uriah Stevens Capt. 7 to 20	14	Baley Austin	14
Jonᵃ More Lieut.	"	Benj. Everts	"
Joseph Lee "	"	Joseph Benton	"
John Frankland Serj.	"	David Benton	"
Isaac Peck "	"	Richard Bignal	"
Joshua Jewel "	"	Elipht Buel	"
Sylvanus Everts "	"	Bartᵒ Barrett	"
John Stevens Clerk	"	Sam¹ Brinsmade	"
Gamaliel Whiting Corp.	"	Elkanah Brigs	"
Dan¹ Bingham "	"	Simⁿ Cleveland	"
Jabᶻ Bingham "	"	James Claghorn	"
David Bidwell "	"	Luke Camp(?)	"

CAMPAIGN OF 1757.

	Days in Service		Days in Service
Jn° Everetts	14	Nat¹¹ How	14
James Fuller	"	Elisha Hurlbut	"
Dan¹ Furgason	"	Walter Hewit	"
Ebenezer Fletcher	"	Isaac Johnson	"
Alpheus Holmes	"	Seth Kent	"
Ebenezer Jewel	"	Elijah Kelogg	"
Lawrence Knickorbecker	"	Joseph Kellogg	"
Ezekiel Landon	"	Peter Knap	"
Nat¹ Loomis	"	Is° Lawrence	"
David Lord	"	Nehemiah Lawrence	"
Sam¹ Norton	"	Moses Nash	"
John Nicholls	"	Josʰ Prindle	"
Jerᵉ Reed	"	Joseph Pangman	"
Nat. Roberts	"	Dan¹ Rathbone	"
Ebenezer Reed	"	Nat¹ Root	"
John Strong	"	Solomon Wright	"
Sam¹ Skinner	"	Elisha Richards	"
Matt. Tousley (?)	"	Sam¹¹ Strickland	"
Dan¹ Warren	"	Ruben Stevens	"
Sylvanus Woodworth	"	Moses Spalding	"
Jn° Welding	"	Jn° Sprague	"
Nat. Winslow	"	Jacob Spalding	"
Jonʰ Allyn	"	Robᵗ Tomrus (?)	"
Augusʰ Bryan	"	David Tusner (?)	"
Gideon Ball	"	Sam. Whitcker	"
Seth Bardin	"	Wᵐ Whitney	"
Caleb Church	"	Thoˢ Knap	"
James Clark	"	Abram Bardin	10
Tho. Chandler	"	Jonᵃ Hancock	"
Stephen Comstock	"	Uriah Stevens Jr.	"
Elisha Forbes	"	Asael Beebe	8
Thomas Goodwyn	"	David Lawrence	12
John Gillit	"	Asa Root	"
James Hinshaw	"	Thoˢ North	9
Russel Hart	"		

Ninety-two of the above named rode horses from Canaan

[*State Library, War 7, 33.*]

MAJ. TALCOTT'S COMPANY.

Elizur Talcott [of Glastenbury], Major and Captain.
Elisha Griswold, Lieutenant.
Samuel Smith [of Hartford], Cornet.
Comfort Sage [of Middletown], Quartermaster.

Dʳ The Colony of Connecticot to Majar Elizur Talcott Majʳ of the Sixth Regᵗ in the Colony of Connecticott and Captain of the Troop of Horse in Said Regᵗ for Servics in the Alarm for the Relief of Fort Willᵐ Henry &c and Troop Under his Command. August

	Days in Service		Days in Service
Elizur Tallcott Maj. 8 to 22	15	Adonijah Lewes Corp.	17
Elisha Griswold Lieut. " "	"	Nathˡˡ Tallcott "	15
Sam¹ Smith Cornet 8 to 24	17	Sam¹ May "	11
Comfort Sage Qt-Mast. 8 to 22	15	Joseph Bacon "	17

MILITIA COMPANIES.   229

	Days in Service		Days in Service
Nath[ll] Colman Corp.	15	Gidian Hale	15
Jonathan Stow Trumpeter	"	Elisha Woolcot	"
John Lancton "	"	Sam[l] Dix	"
Jonathan Hubbard	16	David Mitchel	"
William Renells	"	Josha Welles	"
Moses Hale	"	Dan[ll] Woodhoues	"
John Holden	"	Elisha Stillman	"
John Robbins	"	Jonathan Steel	"
Willit Ranney	15	Janna Churchill	"
Fort[s] Taler	"	John Willcox	"
Jonathan Stocking	"	Seth Smith	17
Timo. Shattuct	"	Josiah Boardman	"
Eben[r] Johnson	"	Dan[ll] Araut	14
Stephen Treet	"	Stephen Hollester	"
Jos. Grave	"	Gedian Dunham	"
Edward Hamlin	"	Solomon Dunham	"
Elizur Boardman	"	Asel Porter	"
John M[c]Ky	"	Edward Perterson	"
Elihu Cotton	"	Sam[ll] Hooker	"
Tho[s] Gelberd	"	Jos. Stillman	"
John Welles	"	David Williams	"
Jonathan Holden	"	Gasham Blin	18
Timo. Morley	"	Peter Pees	"
Isaac Smith	"	Sam[ll] Perce	12
Thoder Hale	"	Cephas Smith	"
Tho[s] Perterson	"	John May	7
Dan[l] Hale	"	Nathan Jones	24

Twelve of the above named rode horses from Glastenbury, twenty-two from Middletown, nine from Farmington, and nineteen from Wethersfield.

[*State Library, War 7, 34.*]

CAPT. PITKIN'S COMPANY.

William Pitkin, Jr. [of Hartford], Captain.
Gideon Wolcott [of Windsor], Lieutenant.
Samuel Smith, Lieutenant.

D[r] Colony of Connecticut to Cap[t] William Pitkin Jun[r] and the Company under his Command in Col[o] Joseph Pitkins Regement for their Service at the time of Alarm for Relief of Fort Will[m] Henry and parts Adjacent August 1757

	Days in Service		Days in Service
William Pitkin Capt. 7 to 24	17	John Benton	17
Gideon Wolcott Lieut.	"	John Crow	"
Samuel Smith "	14	Abel Easton	"
Caleb Sheldon Serj.	17	Andrew Cook	"
Jonth Pinney "	"	Titus Bigelow	"
John Keney "	14	Moses Smith	"
Rich[d] Cook "	9	Samuel Easton Jr.	"
Sam[ll] Eavens Jr. Corp.	17	William Warren Jr.	"
John Newel Jr. "	"	Joel Marshel	"
Hosea Clark "	13	William Andruss Jr.	"
Jonth Birge "	18	Benjamin Waters	"

CAMPAIGN OF 1757.

Name	Days in Service	Name	Days in Service
John White Jr.	17	Jonathan Eglistone	17
Gershom Nott	"	Joel Griswold	"
Phineas Foster	"	Thomas Hoskins	"
Joseph Colyer	"	Noah Brown	"
Joseph McKey	"	Benoni Thomson	"
Elisha Buckland	"	Noah Porter	"
John Cook	"	Gad Stanly	"
Simon Gains	"	Johna Pitkin	16
Justus Smith	"	Samuel Olmsted	"
Ezekiel Ensign	"	Israel Smith	"
Joseph Waters	"	Solomon Williams	"
Uriah Goodwin	"	Mosses Forbs	"
Timothy Olmsted	"	Roswel Judson	"
George Horsmer	"	Benjamin Risley	"
Henry Walbridge	"	William Stanly	"
Robert Sloan	"	Caleb Olmsted	"
Ezra Pratt	"	Griffen Sweet	"
Charles Camel	"	Aaron Pratt	"
Dosethus Humphry Jr.	"	Allyn Merril	"
James Curry	"	Ichabod Norton	"
Silas Andrus	"	William Lewis	"
Elisha Andrus	"	Charles Seymour	"
Jon^th Gilbert	"	Mathew Norton	"
Samuel Hooker	"	Benj^a Andrus	"
Richard Wallis	"	Titus Bunnel	"
Gurden Munsell	"	Reuben Smith	"
Thomas Bancroft	"	Joseph Baker	"
Hezekiah Wills	"	John Porter	"
Jeremiah Bissell	"	Zebulon Warner	"
Thomas Elsworth Jr.	"	John Apanatha	"
Peter Wolcott	"	Elisha Scott	"
Oliver Skinner	"	Isaac Gleason	"
Mathew Bissell	"	James Pitkin	18
Oliver Chamberlen	"	Abel Allyn	"
Daniel Bower	"	Aaron Booth	"
Jon^th Drake	"	Thomas Foster	"
Timothy Strong	"	James White Jr.	"
Elijah Loomis	"	John Chambers	"
Gideon Loomis	"	Nath^ll Boardman	"
Nathaniel Copley	"	Joseph Tucker	"
David Austin	"	Elias Skinner	"
Frances Drake	"	Ezekiel Olcotts	"
Jedidiah Eglestone	"	Jon^th Wright	"
John Grant	"	James White Jr.	"
Joel Barber	"	Jonth. Barber	9
Elijah Cook	"	Jon^th Filley Jr.	13
Joseph Marvin	"	Isaac Phelps	8
Daniel Filly	"	Wm Rockwell	5
Abel Barber	"	Nath^ll Dart	14
Jedediah Scott	"	Jon^th Stanly Jr.	10

Twenty of the above named rode horses from Hartford, thirteen from Farmington, three from Windsor, and four from Bolton.

Allyn Seymour, Eleazer Root and Samuel Moody each served seven days attending return of the horses, Stephen Belding and Titus Olcott each one day.

[*State Library, War 7, 35.*]

CAPT. PECK'S COMPANY.

James Peck [of New Haven], Captain.
Abraham Thompson [of New Haven], Lieutenant.

A Muster Role of Capt James Peck's Company the First Company that went out of the Second Regement in this Colony Commanded by the Honourable Roger Newton Esqr Cor^l under the Command of John Hubbard Esqr Major of Said Regement in ye Late Alarmn for ye Defence of Fort Wm Henry and Parts Adjacent Augt 1757

		Days in Service			Days in Service
James Peck Capt.	7 to 24	18	Asa Ludington	8 to 24	17
Abraham Thompson Lieut.		17	Robert McCleve	"	"
	8 to 24		Joseph Mansfield	"	"
Samuel Gilberd Serj.	8 to 24	"	John How	"	"
Tim° Mix Jr.	" "	"	Amos Potter	"	"
Dan Carrington	" "	"	Stephen Potter	"	"
Adonijah Sherman Clerk		18	Tim° Potter	"	"
	8 to 25		Joel Potter	"	"
Joel Basset Corp.	8 to 24	17	Israel Potter	"	"
Jeremiah Atwater Corp.		"	Icabod Russel	"	"
	8 to 24		Abel Russel	"	"
Sylvanus Bishop Drum.		"	Isaac Stiles	"	"
	8 to 24		Israel Sperry	"	"
John Austin	8 to 24	"	Stephen Sheapard	"	"
Jonah Bradly	"	"	Eben^r Tuttle	"	"
Eleazer Brown	"	"	Gershom Tod	"	"
Isaac Bishop	"	"	Isaac Tod	"	"
Stephen Basset	"	"	Abner Tod	"	"
Lemuel Bradly	"	"	James Turner	"	"
David Basset	"	"	James Thompson	"	"
Amos Bishop	"	"	Samuel Thompson	"	"
Azariah Bradly	"	"	Samuel Tuttle	"	"
Jacob Bradly	"	"	Moses Tharp	"	"
John Cornish	"	"	Eliphalet Thompson	"	"
Eben^r Chidsey	"	"	Gaskin Woodward	"	"
Charles Bishop	"	"	Joseph Hotchkis	"	"
Samuel Davenport	"	"	Eben^r Lines	"	"
Wm Densly	"	"	John Spencer	"	"
John Denison	"	"	Peter Caveler	"	"
William Everton	"	"	Ithermer Tod	"	"
Mathew Forde	"	"	Abel Beecher	8 to 27	20
Joel Gilberd	"	"	Horse drivers		
Jn° Gordon Jr.	"	"	Samuel Chatterton		10
Eben^r Humerston	"	"	Isaac Holt		"
James Hille	"	"			

[*State Library, War 7, 36.*]

CAPT. LEONARD'S COMPANY.

Nathan Leonard [of Preston], Captain.
John Tyler [of Preston], Lieutenant.
Thaddos Cock (?), Ensign.

Dr the Coloney of Conecticut to Nathan Leonard Capt of ye Compney under his Command in Colol Christopher Avry Ridgment for their Sarvis at ye time of the Alarm for ye Reliefe of fort william Henery and places ajesent &c August 1757

	Days in Service		Days in Service
Nathan Leonard Capt. 9 to 24	16	Ebenezr Benjamin	16
John Tyler Lieut.	"	Thomas Braman	"
Thaddos Cock(?) Ens.	"	James Avrill	"
Asa Kenne Serj.	"	Amasa Cook	"
Benjamon Kimbal "	"	Joseph Hatch	"
Jonas Frink "	"	Nemiah Gats	"
Joseph Rose Clerk	"	Joseph Jonson	"
John Kay Corp.	"	Benjamin Braman	"
Stephen Tucker "	"	Ebenezr Clark	"
Tho Rix "	"	Joshua Meach	"
Danil Freeman "	"	Rozel Morgain	"
Robert Herick	"	David Kimbel	"
Israil Burton	"	Benjaman Bruster	"
Elezer Prentice	"	Jonas Woodward	"
William Thorn	"	Samll McFarlen	"
Danel Stanton	"	William Buten	"
Elezer Herrick	"	John Kimbal	"
Henerey Herrick	"	Stephen Starkwether	"
Iachabod Potter	"	Nathan Fobs	"
Rufus Branch	"	Simon Tracy	"
Danil Clark	"	Ezra Tracy	"
Elias Geer	"	Zepheniah Rude	"
Charls Button	"	Joseph Story	"
Christepher Green	"	John Tifft	"
Josiah Rose	"	Jacob Kimbel	"
Elijah Herrick	"	Stephen Downer	"
Jeremiah Parke	"	Samll Renails	"
Abel Geer	"	Caleb Bundy	"
John Geer	"	Elias Jones	"
Josiah Rusel	"	Amos Avry	"
David Green	"	Asisted in the Return of the horses	
Abia Coye	"	James Geer	10
Joseph Kimbal	"	James Clark	"
John Mordock	"	Elias Lord	8
Medad Benton	"	Nathanil Morss	8
Seth Sabens	"	Ruben Jones	"

Twenty-four of the above named rode horses from Preston.

[*State Library, War 7, 37.*]

CAPT. LATTIMORE'S COMPANY.

Jonathan Lattimore Jr., Captain.
John Rogers [of New London], Lieutenant.
Thomas Rogers [of New London], Lieutenant.
Edward Lewiss, Ensign.

Dr Colony of Connecticut To Captain Jonathan Lattimore Junr and the Company under his Command In the 3d Regiment under Coll Gurdon Saltonstal for their Service att the Time of Alarm for the Releif of Fort Wm Henry and parts Adjacent August 1757

MILITIA COMPANIES.

Name	Days in Service	Name	Days in Service
Jonathan Lattimore Jr. Capt. 9 to 23	14	Bedgood Woolfinch	14
		Elihu Austin	"
John Rogers Lieut. 9 to 13	4	Thomas Attwel	"
Tho⁸ Rogers " 9 to 23	14	Ichabod Powers	"
Edward Lewiss 9 to 13	4	Edward Hawkins	"
Edward Lewiss Ens. 13 to 23	10	Christopher Green	"
Jeremiah Whipple Serj.	14	Dan¹ Bowls	"
Wm Bishop	"	John Gardner Goldsmith	"
Joseph Prentice "	"	Jason Comstock	"
Isaac Lester "	"	Sylvester Clifford	"
Amos Lattimore Clerk	"	Green Plumb	"
Nath¹ Waterhouse Corp.	"	Morriss Fowler	"
Benjm Kelly "	"	Peter Crocker	"
James Chapman "	"	James Beebe	"
Benjm Atwel Jr.	"	Dan¹ Harriss	"
Isaac Thompson Jr.	"	Sam¹ Caulkins	"
Zadox Bosworth	"	Jubez Mannering	"
Peleg Church	"	Noah Mosier	"
Rainford Comstock	"	Sam¹ Udal	"
Willm Camp	"	Wm Daton	"
Wm Goff	"	Bonijus Beebee	"
John Gardner	"	Walter Beebee	"
Samuel Minor	"	Ruford Comstock	"
Benjm Scrivener	"	Jethro Wicks	"
Asa Williams	"	Jeremiah Minard	"
Sam¹ Wickwire	"	Timothy Dannills	"
Joub Beebe	"	George Dowglas	"
John Otis	"	Sam¹ Thompson	"
Moses Fargo	"	James Tooley	"
Wm Minard	"	Benjm Brown	"
Silas Whipple	"	Nero Raimond	"
Abraham Chapman	"	Thomas Minard 9 to 16	7
Nath¹ Chappel	"	William Wheeler "	"
James Danills	"	Nathan Parks "	"
Jesse Minard	"	Nehemiah Rogers "	"
Sam¹ Bishop	"	Laford Daton "	"
John Cobb	"	Uriah Rogers 9 to 17	8
Jos. Butten	"	Jonathan Morgan "	"
John Way	"	Timo. Beckwith "	"
Wm Chapel Jr.	"	James Rina "	"
Amariah Lyons	"	Corp. Elijah Hammond	Deserter
Jos. Chapel	"	Comfort Chapman	"
Alexander Merrels	"	Ephm Beach	"

Twenty-four of the above named rode horses from New London.

[*State Library, War 7, 38.*]

CAPT. WHITMORE'S COMPANY.

Jacob Whitmore [of Middletown (?)], Captain.
Samuel Stow [of Middletown (?)], Lieutenant.
Caleb Hubbard [of Middletown (?)], Lieutenant.

CAMPAIGN OF 1757.

Names & Rank	Days in Service	Names & Rank	Days in Service
Capt. Jacob Whitmore	15	Joel Robards	
Lieut. Sam'll Stow	"	Sam'll Wise	19
" Caleb Hubbard	16	Thomas Pierpont	17
Serj. Christ'r Hamblin	15	Giles Miller	"
" Eben Savage	16	William Hall	16
" Stephen Johnson	"	George Stow	"
" Cornelius Cornwell	"	David Starr	"
" Zebediah Mix	14	Constant Bosworth	"
Corp. Sam'll Higbye	16	William Riley	"
" Dan'll Cornwell	15	William Ward	"
" W'm Banks	18	W'm Rockwell	"
" Eleazer Gaylard	16	Thomas Brigden	"
Clerk Amos Johnson	"	Caleb Brintnell	"
Drum. Sam'll Forster	"	Robert Fairchild	"
Sam'll Lewis Sage	15	Dan'll Southmead	"
Nath'll Miller	18	Nathan Robenson	"
Gershom Butler	15	Edward Collins Whitmore	17
Joshua Plumb	"	W'm Marks	16
Joseph Savage	17	Ebenezer Cook	"
Jedidiah Sage	15	Stephen Ward	"
Abijah Cornwell	"	Amos Barns	"
Ebenezer Doude	17	Benj'a Smith	"
Josiah Scovel	15	Josiah Prior	"
Aaron White	"	Amos Tryon	"
Joseph White	"	Dan'll Brooks	"
Ebenezer Prout	16	Thomas Blague	"
John Guernsey		Elisha Sears	"
Jedidiah Hubbard	16	Darius Weston	"
Solomon Barns	"	Jeremiah Hubbard	"
Jedidiah Johnson	"	Elisha Fairchild	"
Eben'r Robbards Jr.	"	Abijah Lee	"
Daniel Barns	17	Lemuel Sizer	"
Benj'a Birdseye	18	Reuben Clark	"
Ichabod Miller	"	Giles Doude	"
David Gilbert	17	Ebenezer Elton	"
Oliver Wetmore	"	Jn'o Boardman	"
Ebenezer Robards	15	Uziel Clark	"
Zacheus Higbye	17	Simon Dewolf	11
Joseph Higbye	"	George Hubbard	17
Ebenezer Doolittle	"	Assisting about y'e Return of Horses &c	
George M'cKey	18		
Charles Hamblin	16	Hez'h Hubberd	6
Ezra Robards	17		

[*State Library, War 7, 40.*]

CAPT. HULL'S COMPANY.

Samuel Hull [of Wallingford], Captain.
Enos Brooks [of Wallingford], Lieutenant.
Ebenezer Bunnell [of New Cheshire in Wallingford], Lieutenant.
Joel Holcomb [of Wallingford], Ensign.

D'r The Colony of Connecticut to Sam'll Hull Cap't & Company under his Command in Col'o Benj Halls Regim't for their Service at y'e time of the Alarm for Relief of Fort William Henry and parts adjacent August 1757

MILITIA COMPANIES.

	Days in Service		Days in Service
Sam[ll] Hull Capt. 7 to 25	18	Caleb Everts	18
Enos Brooks Lieut.	"	Titus Allyn	"
Eben[r] Bunnel "	"	Hermon Munson	"
Joel Holcomb Ens.	"	Joseph Miles	"
Enos Attwater Serj.	"	Dan[l] Doolittle	"
Benj. Culver "	"	Giles Doolittle	"
Step[n] Culver "	"	Sam[l] Tyler	"
Gamaliel Parker "	"	Bartho[w] Andrus	"
Elnathan Ives Corp	"	Thad[s] Carter	"
Isaac Roys "	"	Street Yale	"
Step[n] Yale "	"	Amos Horsford	"
Matthias Hitchcox "	"	Charles Peck	"
Elias Bates Clerk	"	Sam[l] Doolittles	"
Eli Doolittle	"	Abra. Stanly	"
Bela Lewis	"	Asall Beach	"
Tim[o] Moss	"	Jn[o] Dairaw	"
Peter Munson	"	Linus Hopson	"
Ebenezer Moss	"	Edward Fenn	"
Phil. Doolittle	"	Hawkins Hart	"
Noah Griggs	"	Asa Francis	"
Eben[r] Tuthill	"	Charles Yale	"
Thomas Newton	"	Eben[r] Judd	"
Zac[h] Ives	"	Allen Roys	"
Elihu Attwater	"	Asa Barns	"
John Ward	"	Noah Andrus	"
Ruben Doolittles	"	Jer[a] Edwards	"
Henry Hotchkiss	"	Moses Andrus	"
Andrew Durand	"	Diamond Berry	"
David Barns	"	Samuel Austin	"
Abra. Tyler	"	Joseph Merriams	"
Benj. Doolittle	"	Sam[ll] Cavat (?)	"
Dan[l] Andrus	"	Tim[o] Roys	"
Elam Cook	"	John Ives	"
Elijah Hotchkiss	"	Joshua Ives	"
Lem[l] Kelogg	"	Elisha Goodrich	"
Titus Hitchcock	"	Lem[l] Colins	"
David Brooks	"	Joseph Mathews	10
W[m] Wheeler	"	Ebenezer Mattoon	5
Wait. Hotchkis	"	Miles Marks	7
Clem[t] Hopson	"	Elijah Scovel	10
Edmond Austin	"	Giles Curtiss	Deserted
Dan[l] Wrexford	"	Nath[l] Cook	"
Elnathan Thorp	"	Attending the return of horses	
Asa Page	"	Thomas Brooks	10
Miles Hall	"	Samuel Adams	"
Colier Peck	"		

Thirty-one of the above named rode horses from Wallingford
[*State Library*, *War 7, 41.*]

CAPT. PERKIN'S COMPANY.

John Perkins [of Newent in Norwich], Captain.
John Safford, Lieutenant.
Elisha Edgerton [of Norwich], Ensign.

CAMPAIGN OF 1757.

The Colony of Conecticut D^r to Capt John Perkins and Company that marched from Norwich in ye Alarm in August A D 1757 for ye Releaf of forts Wm Henry and places Adjacents is as followeth

	Days in Service		Days in Service
John Perkins Capt. 8 to 23	16	William Frasher	15
John Safford Lieut.	17	Ezra Freman	"
Elisha Edgerton Ens.	16	Jason Fergo	"
John Hughs Serj.	14	Ebenezer Falles	"
Jahleah Peck "	"	Nathaniel Fillmore	"
Thomas Crocker "	"	Samuel Griswould	"
Daniel Hide Serj.	15	John Gager	"
Joseph Rudd "	"	John Hide	"
John Kingsley "	"	Ezekiel Hide	"
Nathan Durke "	"	Abnor Hide	"
Stephen Gifford "	"	Eliab Hide	"
Nathan Brewster Serj.	29	William Huntington	"
Thomas Leffingwell Clerk	14	Cypron Herrick	"
Jacob Perkins Corp.	15	Enoch Horskins	"
Elisha Huntington "	"	Benjamin Jones	"
Solomon Huath (?) "	"	Ephraim Ingraham	"
Solomon Petingal "	"	Ichabod Jewett	"
Thomas Calkins Drum.	13	Isaac Johnson	"
Jonathan Lawrance "	16	Jabez Kingsley	"
Nathan Ames	"	Daniel Kimbal	"
Samuel Anderson	"	Joseph King	"
Caleb Bishop	"	Daniel Ladd	"
Ruben Bishop	"	John Ladd	"
Ebenezer Baldwin	"	Jonathan Lathrup	"
Thomas Jewett	"	Simeon Lester	"
Joseph Jackson	"	Jeremiah Leffingwell	"
David Lappim	"	Joseph White	"
Silas Liley	"	Jacob Pember	"
Simon Perkins	"	Lemuel Petingal	"
Joseph Rust	"	Jabez Rouse	"
Thomas Adams	15	Increse Rudd	"
Benjamin Avery	"	John Smith	"
Joshua Arnold	"	Abijah Smith	"
Jonathan Avery	"	Joshua Smith	"
Labeus Armstrong	"	Elijah Tenney	"
Ezekiel Armstrong	"	Samuel Tracy (?)	"
John Ames	"	Hezekiah Tracy	"
Nathaniel Brag	"	Joseph White	"
James Bramble	"	Daniel Wills	"
Asa Backus	"	Jonathan Walden	"
Ozias Backus	"	John Waterman	"
Joseph Biggalow	"	Thomas Waterman	"
John Burnam	"	Joseph Walbridge	"
Nathaniel Crandal	"	Ezekiel Waterman	"
Daniel Cornel	"	Ebenezer Welch	"
Ezra Corning	"	Joshua Wills	"
Aron Cleveland	"	Benidick Arnold	14
Constant Crocker	"	Robert Ames	"
James Downer	"	Simeon Abel	"
Edward Doge	"	John Birchard	"
Joshua Edgerton	"	John Birchard Jr.	"
Daniel Edgerton	"	Beriah Bill	"
Jonathan French	"	Eleazer Burnam	"
Ebenezer Fillmore	"	Abel Benjamins	"

MILITIA COMPANIES.

	Days in Service		Days in Service
Nathaniel Collens	14	Elihu Morgan	14
Nathan Caswell	"	Joseph Park	"
John Deming	"	Peter Pride	"
Jacob Fuller	"	Nathaniel Peabody	"
Samuel French	"	John Prentice	"
Joseph Ford	"	David Rogers	"
Joseph Giddens	"	Elisha Rudd	"
Benjamin Gorten	"	Ebenezer Rude	"
Reason Gear	"	Phenias Smith	"
George Grist	"	Benjamin Spicer	"
John Hartshorn	"	Samuel Tubs	"
Elijah Huntington	"	Moses Tracy	"
John Hamilton	"	Ezra Williams	"
Ebenezer Harris	"	Ezra Waterman	"
Gersham Hale	"	Thomas Wilke	"
Gideon Haskil	"	Rufus Welch	"
Rufus Jones	"	Job Wood	"
Jeremiah Kingsley	"	Lemuel Vorce	"
Labeus Lothrup	"	Joseph Williams	"
John Loomer	"	John Kennedy	"
Asa Lord	"	Christophors Downing	13
Benajah Leffingwell	"	Nathan Bushnell	9
James Lankester	"	Henry Munsel	11

The men that attended y⁰ Return of y⁰ Horses

Cap. Matthew Hide	7	Samuel Bishop	7
Elihu Hide	"	Matthew Perkins	"
John Hide Jr.	"	Joseph Perkins	"
Joseph Loomer	"	Benjamin Fitch	"
Samuel Spiler	"	Stephen Fitch	"
Benjamin Huntington	"	Daniel Story	2
Stephen Tatman	"		

[*State Library, War 7, 42.*]

CAPT. BARNUM'S COMPANY.

John Barnum [of Danbury], Captain.
Josiah Starr [of Danbury], Lieutenant.
Abel Judson [of Newtown], Lieutenant.
Benjamin Benedick [of Danbury], Ensign.

Dᵣ Coloney of Connecticut to Capᵗ John Barnum and the Company under his Command in Colonel Andrew Burrˢ Regiment for their Service at the time of alarm for Releif of Fort Willᵐ Henry and Places adjacienet

	Days in Service		Days in Service
John Barnum Capt. from Aug. 6 to Aug. 23	18	Ebenzʳ Bristor Serj.	18
		Amos Terrill	"
Josiah Starr Lieut.	"	Nathan Gregory Clerk	"
Abel Judson "	"	Joseph Bristor Corp.	"
Benjamin Benedick Ens.	"	Nathaⁿ Benedick "	"
John Trobridge Serj.	"	David Picket "	"
Jonathⁿ Fairchild "	"	Isaac Botchford "	"

CAMPAIGN OF 1757.

	Days in Service		Days in Service
Joseph Atherton	18	Noah Pamerly	18
Francis Barnum	"	Ezra Peck	"
Francis Benedick	"	Amiel Peck	"
Lemuel Benedick	"	Aron Peck	"
Zadok Benedick	"	Jonathan Prindle	"
Theophilus Benedick	"	John Prindle	"
Jonathan Beebe	"	James Prindle	"
Sam'l Baylee	"	Ashbel Ruggles	"
Sam'l Barnum	"	Oliver Rugg	"
Ebenez'r Boughton	"	Joseph Starr	"
Daniel Barly	"	Jonathan Starr	"
Silus Benedick	"	Abra'm Stevens	"
Theophilus Botchford	"	Isaac Sherwood	"
Thaddeus Baldwin	"	Amos Smith	"
Elijah Botchford	"	Simeon Shepard	"
Joseph Bunnel	"	Thomas Stilson	"
Sam'l Burrell	"	Stephen Trowbridge	"
Joel Botchford	"	Abner Taylor	"
Caleb Church	"	Thomas Tousey	"
Daniel Canfield	"	Timothy Wileman	"
Moses Corbin	"	David Whitlock	"
James Cagwin	"	Nehemiah Whitlock	"
Joel Camp	"	Benj'n Williams	"
Ezra Dibble	"	Sam'l Wileman	"
Ezra Duning	"	Jedediah Wheeler	"
Daniel Dibble	"	Daniel Winton	"
John Egleston	"	Elijah Whitney	"
Peter Foot	"	Robard Winchel	"
Benj'n Griffen	"	Matthew Barnum	17
Obediah Gray	"	Lemuel Bangs	"
James Glover	"	Ebnezer Gregory	"
Henery Glover	"	Gershom Summers	"
Sam'l Griffeth	"	Gideon Church	8
Will'm Holley	"	Sam'l Deming	13
Elijah Hull	"	Will'm Nickeson	"
Sam'l Hoyt	"	Jonathan Keeler	5
James Hayes	"	John Wilks	19
Nathan Hoyt	"	An account of horse Drivers	
James Knap	"	Abraham Wileman	8
David Knap	"	Jonathan Hoyt	"
Brasy Knap	"	James Benedick	"
Ezra Kellog	"	Daniel Starr	"
Ebenez'r Munson	"	Comfort Hoyt	"
Will'm Northrup	"	Eliezer Dibble	"
Amos Northrup	"	Jonathan Booth	"
Abiel Philips	"	Will'm Burch	"
Jesse Peck	"	Jotham Sherman	"
Ebenez'r Picket	"		

[*State Library, War 7, 44.*]

CAPT. WADSWORTH'S COMPANY.

William Wadsworth [of Farmington], Captain.
Jonathan Gillet, Lieutenant.
John Hungerford [of Farmington], Lieutenant.

MILITIA COMPANIES.

Mens Names & Rank	Days in Service	Mens Names & Rank	Days in Service
Capt. W[m] Wadsworth	16	W[m] Burnham	16
Lieut. Jonath Gillet	"	Jonath Burnham	"
" Jn[o] Hungerford	"	Joseph Keeney	"
Serj. Judah Woodruff	"	Malachy Corning	6
" Peter Judson	"	Asahell Cheeney	16
" John Seymour	"	W[m] Cook	9
" Edmund Beaman	17	Amos Bull	14
Clerk James Wadsworth	16	Barnabas Benton	4
Corp. Joel Catlen	14	Cyprian Webster	14
" Abijah Collon	16	Jesse Goodwine	"
" Hez Wadsworth	"	Stephen Rosseter	"
" Reuben Cook	"	Benj[a] Robenson	"
Rezin Gridley	"	Job Alford	"
John Porter Jr.	"	Jonath Hopkins	4
David Hart	"	John Collins	16
Daniel Warner	9	Joel Spencer	8
Gideon Hart	16	Jacob Roys	17
Daniel Owen	"	Matth[w] Hungerford	16
Elnathan Hart	7	Gershom Tuttle	16
Elisha Prat	16	Josiah Barns	"
Elihu Newell	11	Matthew Smith	"
Amos Cowles	"	Abell Collins	"
Timothy Woodruff	16	Elijah Ensign	"
John Judd	"	Elisha Steel	"
Phinehas Cowles	"	Ashbell Wells	"
Nodiah Hooker	"	Eleaz[r] Ensign	"
Joseph Root	"	George Kellogg	"
Serajah Horseford	"	Joel Soper	13
Hezekiah Beech	"	Stephen Olmstead	16
Semeon Strong	"	Josiah Clark	"
Elisha Hart	"	Zenos Brace	"
Elijah Wempy	"	Daniel Butler	"
Zimri Moody	"	Joel Marshell	"
Solomon Woodruff	"	Uriah Sheppard	"
Salmon Burr	"	W[m] Pratt	"
John Fowler	"	Asahel Burnham	"
Daniel Brewer	"	Caleb Church	"
Eleazer Cowles	"	Thomas Waters	"
Eleazer Burnham	"	Richard Shew	"
Azariah Williams	"	Ebenezer Catlin	11
Nath[ll] Crow	17	Matthew Webster	16
William Brown	"	Nehemiah Cadwell	8
Abraham Forbs	16	Asahel Smith	16
Caleb Olmstead	13	Amos Lawrence	8
Aaron Pratt	"	Barzeleel Gurney	16
Jonathan Porter	16	John Soper	"
Roger Porter	"	Horse Drivers	
Eldad Smith	"	Daniel Curtice	7
John Smith	"	Ezek[l] Lewis	"
Matthew Cadwell	"	Stephen Smith	"
John Brewer	"	John Steell	10
Semeon Keeney	"	Isaac Bunce	8
George Risleey	"	Jacob Hinsdell	9
Nehemiah Abby	"	Gideon Burr	"

[*State Library, War 7, 45.*]

CAPT. COIT'S COMPANY.

Isaac Coit, Captain.
Aron Cleavland, Lieutenant.
Corneales Waldor, Lieutenant.

D^r the Coleney of Conecticut to Isaac Coit Capt of ye Compney under his Command in Co^{ll} John Dyar Ridgment for their Sarvis at ye time of ye alaram for Release of fort William Henery and plases ajasant &c August 1757

	Days in Service		Days in Service
Isaac Coit Capt. 9 to 23	15	William Park	15
Aron Cleavland Lieut.	"	Phinihas Tyler	"
Corneales Waldor "	"	David Gats	"
John Dawglis Serj.	"	Thomas Aston	"
David Pain "	"	Thomas Demick	"
Joseph Williams "	"	James Pelcit	"
Sam^{ll} Adams "	"	Elezer Brown	"
Andrew Spalding Clerk	"	Berzila Handey	"
Elemuail Williams Corp.	"	Asa Cleveland	"
Ebenez^r Parish "	"	Ruben Park	"
Eliflet Kimbail "	"	Nathan Howard	"
David Ames "	"	Olivar Lovicey	"
Nehemiah Stephens	"	Elkeney Homos	"
Abel Peirce	"	Joseph Baldon	"
Jonas Shepord	"	Joshua Nowling	"
Benjamin Hutching	"	Jacob Geer	"
Jeremiah Bennet	"	Jonathan Wheeler	"
Tilley Parkhurst	"	Benjamin Morss	"
John Wheeler	"	Jonuthan Miner	"
Jonas Wheeler	"	Patrick Ray	"
Joseph Underwood	"	Sam^{ll} Edmon	"
David Spolding	"	William Megonniail	"
Nathenil Kingsbury	"	Sam^{ll} Wells	"
Adam Clark	"	Elijah Hamblin	"
Benjamin Clark	"	John Skinnar (?)	"
Danil Harris	"	John Safford	"
Jonathan Parkhust	"	Joseph Morey	"
William Bingham	"	Danil Kenady	"
Josiah How	"	Jonathan Willkson	"
Jacob Smith	"	Elias Rouse	"
Joseph Butt	"	Zepheniah Brigs	"
Shubel Cleveland	"	Philip Alsworth	"
Obadiah Jonson	"	Peter Garey	"
Sam^{ll} Answorth	"	John Seaton	"
Epheraim Gibson	"	Danil Smith	"
Stephen Bond	"	Stephen Harrais	"
William Munrow	"	Samson How	"
James Woodward	"	Ebenez^r Williams	8
Henery Frost	"	Ebenez^r Kingsbuary	"
Stephen Downing	"	Joseph Borg	4
John Simes	"	John Carter	7
Joseph Jones	"	Gorg Aston	"
Zecheriah Waldor	"	Joseph Safford	"
Benjamon Shepord	"	Nathan^{ll} Lotrap	8
Increas Cartor	"	Isaac Hide	"
Peter Stephens	"	Joseph Park	3
Thomos Bettes	"	Zackriah Frink	"
Williman Bond	"		

MILITIA COMPANIES. 241

Twenty-six of the above named rode horses from Plainfield, forty-six from Canterbury, and eleven from Voluntown.

[*State Library, War 7, 46.*]

CAPT. FITCH'S COMPANY.

Perez Fitch [of Stamford], Captain.
Thaddeus Mead [of Norwalk], Lieutenant.
Noah Chappel, Lieutenant.

Dr Colony of Connecticut to Capt Perez Fitch and the Company under his Command in Col^o Jonth Hoyts Regim^t for their Service at the time of alarm for Relief of Fort Wm Henry and parts Adjacent August 1757.

	Days in Service		Days in Service
Perez Fitch Capt. 7 to 23	16	Ezek^l Osburn	16
Thadd^s Mead Lieut.	"	Nathan Smith	"
Noah Chappel "	"	Silas Scofield	"
Carey Leads Serj.	"	John Smith Jr.	"
Jno Greensleete "	"	Peter Scott	"
George Follet "	"	Saml Seely	"
Charles Stewart "	"	Abr^m Scofield	"
Joseph Naggs Foster Clerk	"	James Shelding	"
Saml Seward Corp.	"	Edward Tharp	"
Willm Bostwick "	"	Ruben Weede Jr.	"
Jonth Scofield "	"	Epenet^s Weede Jr.	"
Joseph Mead "	"	David Webb Jr.	"
Jno Andruss	"	Josiah Waterbury	"
Hez^e Arnold	"	Saml Bishop Jr.	"
Jonth Brown	"	Jacob Clark	"
Silas Bishop	"	Jabez Dibble	"
Abij^a Bishop	"	Silas Garnsey	"
Silvenus Brown	"	Josi^a Hoyt	"
Peter Clark	"	Asa Jones	"
David Clawson	"	James Little	"
Jonth Clawson	"	Dan^{ll} Richards	"
Peter Dunill (?)	"	Abij^a Reede	"
Josiah Dean	"	Peter Reed	"
Hez^e Davis	"	James Reed	"
Gabrel Flemming	"	Thad^s Scofield	"
James Finch	"	Stephen Tuttle	"
Sam^{ll} Garnsey	"	Jonas Weede Jr.	"
Roger Gail	"	David Brown	"
Isaac Hoyt	"	Ebenez^r Hawley	"
Deodaty Hoyt	"	Thomas Waterbury Jr.	"
Jo^s Heusted Jr.	"	Thos Reed	"
David Hoyt 3^d	"	Sam^{ll} Richards Jr.	"
Eben^r Hoyt Jr.	"	Jno Willson	15
Silvenus Hoyt	"	Jere^m Osburn	"
Nathan Hoyt	"	Gabrel Bennit	"
Jo^s Hoyt 3^d	"	Ezekiel Bradly	"
Jno Holms Jr.	"	Sam^{ll} Brooks	"
Jno Hawley Jr.	"	Joseph Cable	"
Joshua Jum (?)	"	Benj^a Higgens	"
James Knap	"	Jno Jones	"
Israel Knap	"	Hez^e Osburn	"
David Knap	"	James Smith	"

16

	Days in Service		Days in Service
Jere^m Willson	15	Benj^a Ketch	15
Ebenez^r Wood	"	Elisha Amsden	18
Jno Morehouse	"	Nathan Hawley Jr.	10
Willm Northam	"	Saml Waterbury	6
Joseph Stebbens	"	Hez^a Gilbert	5
Danl Mills	"	James Tonge	"
Eben^r Osburn	"		

Fifty-five of the above named rode horses from Stamford, seventeen from Middlesex, and twenty-two from Ridgefield.

Mem^o Jacob Weed Jr. Nath^ll Waterbury Jr. James Scofield Seymour Sellick & John Bill of Stanford Nathan Tuttle Peter Betts of Norwalk being detach^d for ye within Refuse to Join said Comp^a &c

[*State Library, War 7, 47.*]

CAPT. CARPENTER'S COMPANY.

John Carpenter [of Woodstock], Captain.
Josiah Child, Lieutenant.
Diah Johnson, Lieutenant.

A Muster Role of the Company under the Command of Capt John Carpenter In ye Late Recruits who Marched Aug^st A D 1757

Mens Names	Days in Service	Mens Names	Days in Service
Capt. Jno Carpenter	16	Ab^m Daily	16
Lieut. Josiah Child	"	Henry Merrett	"
" Diah Johnson	"	Abij^h Nichols	"
Serj. Wm Maning	"	Nath^ll Ormsbee	"
" Stephen Marcy	"	Jn^th Perry	"
" Isaac Stone	"	Luke Upam	"
" Benj^a Johslen	"	Noah Sanders	"
Clerk Zeb^h Sabin	"	Wm Whitemore	"
Drum. Elis^h Marcy	"	Elnathan Walker	"
Corp. Tim^o Perrin	"	Eliph^t Goodale	"
" Jn^th Knap	"	Sam^ll Dodge	"
" Dan^ll Corbin	"	Ezekiel Abbe	"
" Jese Carpenter	"	Benj^a Marcy	"
Benj^a Bacon	"	Zeb^n Marcy	"
Jno Bishop	"	Jn^th Allerton	"
Thos Fox Jr.	"	Elisha Goodale	"
Amasa Frisell	"	Darias Watkins	"
Abij^h Griggs	"	Dan^ll Allard	"
Abel Hammond	"	Increase Child	"
Jer^h Jackson	"	Benj^a Dana	"
George Lyon	"	Lemuel Lyon	"
Jno Nelson	"	Stephen Lyon	"
Eph^m Peake	"	David Lyon	"
Joseph Bugbee	"	Wm Powers	8
Benj^a Deming	"	Stephen Squire	16
Jno Barrett	"	Joseph Town	"
Elis^h Child	"	Joseph Newell	"
Ezra Corbin	"	Nathan Bixby	"
Nath^ll Elithorp	"	Peter Levens	"

MILITIA COMPANIES. 243

Mens Names	Days in Service	Mens Names	Days in Service
Wm Marsh	16	Noah Barrows	Deserted
Neh^h Clark	"	John Burrows	16
Stephen Tucker	"	Jnth Bacon	Deserted
Thos Shapley	Deserted	Ebenez^r Foster	"
Calvin Torry	"		

Mens names who were Imploy'd to Bring back the Horses

Joseph Peake	11	Henry Lyon	2
Joseph Frisell	"	Dan^{ll} Bacon	"
David Barrett	"	Uriah Marcy	"

[*State Library, War 7, 48.*]

CAPT. STEVENS' COMPANY.

Uriah Stevens [of Canaan], Captain.
Jonathan Moore [of Salisbury], Lieutenant.
Joseph Lee [of Goshen], Lieutenant.

A Muster Rool of Capt Uriah Stephens's Comp^a in Col. Ebenezer Marsh's Regiment for Relief of Fort William Henry &c August Anno Dom. 1757.

Mens Names & Rank	Weeks & Days in Service		Mens Names & Rank	Weeks & Days in Service	
Uriah Stevens Capt	2	0	Lawrence Kirnickerb^r	2	0
Jonth Moore Lieut.	"	"	Ezekiel Landon	"	"
Joseph Lee "	"	"	Nathl Loomis	"	"
Jno Franland Serj.	"	"	David Lord	"	"
Isaac Peck "	"	"	Saml Norton	"	"
Joshua Jewel "	"	"	Jno Nickols	"	"
Silvanus Everets "	"	"	Jonth Reed	"	"
John Stevens Clerk	"	"	Nath^{ll} Roberts	"	"
Gam^l Whiting Corp.	"	"	Eb^{zr} Reed	"	"
Danl Bingham "	"	"	John Strong	"	"
Jabez Bingham "	"	"	Saml Skinner	"	"
David Bidwel "	"	"	Mathew Towsley	"	"
Bayley Austin	"	"	Danl Warren	"	"
Benj^a Everets	"	"	Syrenus Woodworth	"	"
David Everets	"	"	John Welden	"	"
Joseph Benton	"	"	Nathl Winslow	"	"
David Benton	"	"	Jonth Allen	"	"
Richard Bignal	"	"	Abram Bardin	1	3
Eliphalet Bewel	"	"	Gustin Bryant	2	0
Bartholomew Barrett	"	"	Asahel Bebee	1	1
Saml Brimsmade	"	"	Gideon Barns	deserted	4
Elkanah Briggs	"	"	Gideon Ball	2	0
Simon Cleaveland	"	"	Seth Barden	"	"
James Claghorn	"	"	Caleb Church	"	"
Luke Camp	"	"	James Clark	"	"
John Everets	"	"	Thos Chandler	"	"
James Fuller	"	"	Stephen Cumstock	"	"
Danl Furgison	"	"	John Dean	deserted	6
Eb^z Fletcher	"	"	Elisha Forbs	2	0
Alfeus Holmes	"	"	Thos Goodwin	"	"
Eb^z Jewel	"	"	John Gillett	"	"

CAMPAIGN OF 1757.

Mens Names & Rank	Weeks & Days In Service		Mens Names & Rank	Weeks & Days In Service	
James Henshaw	2	0	Joseph Pangman (?)	2	0
Russel Hunt	"	"	Dan¹ Wrathbone	"	"
Nath¹ Stow	"	"	Nath¹ Root	"	"
Elisha Hurlbutt	"	"	Solomon Wright	"	"
Jonth Hancock	1	3	Asa Root	1	5
Walter Hewitt	2	0	Elisha Richards	2	0
Isaac Johnson	"	"	Samuel Strickland	"	"
Seth Kent	"	"	Uriah Stevens Jr.	1	3
Elijah Kellogg	"	"	Reuben Stevens	2	0
Joseph Kellogg	"	"	Moses Spaulding	"	"
Peter Knapp	"	"	John Sprague	"	"
Isaac Lawrence	"	"	Jacob Spaulding	"	"
Nehem^h Lawrence	"	"	Robert Thoms	"	"
David Lawrence	1	5	David Turner	"	"
Moses Nash	2	0	Sam¹ Whitaker	"	"
Phillip Monger	deserted	3	William Whitney	"	"
Thos North	1	2	Thos Knapp	"	"
Joseph Prindle	2	0			

[*State Library, War 7, 50.*]

CAPT. GOYT'S COMPANY.

Isaac Goyt or Got, Captain.
———— Cleaveland, Lieutenant.

Account of Ammonition &c Delivered to the Several Captains & Companys Raised in Augst A : D : 1757 of the Colony Stores Viz^t

Capt Goyts Company

Joseph Jones
Samuel Adams
Elkanah Holmes
Stephen Harriss
Benjamin Shephard
Joseph Underwood
Phinehas Taillor
Thos Battiss
Elijah Hamlin
Moses Ward
Thos Austin
Ebenezer Parrish
Capt Isaac Got
Nathan Howard
Dan¹ Harriss
Lt Cleaveland
Abell Peirce
Cornelious Waldo
Barzillai Hende
Stephen Downing
Ephram Gipson
Shubell Cleaveland
James Pellet
Jonas Wheeler
Benj Hutching
Sam¹ Ainsworth
Wm Bingham
Dan¹ Gates
James Woodward
Elias Rouse
John Sims
Lemuel William
Josiah Hobbord
Jacob Geers
Josh. Paulding (?)
Adam Clark
Jonas Shephard
David Spaulding
Wm Monro
Josiah How
W^m McGunnego
Increse Carty (?)
Wm Parke
Phinehas Tailor
Dan¹ Gale
Skilijen (?)
David Emeas
Joseph Baldwin

MILITIA COMPANIES. 245

Jonath. Wheeler
Asa Cleaveland
John Douglass
Eleazer Brown
Jonath. Minor

Dan¹ Smith
John Seeton
Peter Gery (?)
Zachariah Waldo
John Wheeler

[*State Library, War 7, 54.*]

CAPT. PETTIBONE'S COMPANY.

Jonathan Pettibone [of Simsbury], Captain.
Juddah Holcomb [of Simsbury], Lieutenant.
Jonathan Terry [of Enfield], Lieutenant.

    the musterrole Role of the Ofesers and Solgers that went with Capt Jonathan Pettibone in his Companey to fourt Edword in the allarram in August last 1757 and allso the time that they was gon in Said Survis

	Days		Days
Capt Jonathan Pettibone	17	the midel Companey in Simsbury	
Lif^t Juddah Holcomb	"	Richard Addoms	17
Surgent Nethaniel Spring	"	Isaac Grimes	"
Surgent John Foot	"	Moses Gains	"
Corporall Elijah Case	"	Jesse Holcomb	"
Ezekiel Willcocks	"	Barnabus Meacham	"
Jeremiah Willcocks	"	Josiah Alfird	"
Job Case	"	Asael Owen	"
Silas Read	"	Michel More	
Ebenezer Smith	16		
Jedidiah Case	17	Samon brook Companey	
Solomon Case	"	William Stronge	17
Jesse Case	"	Isaias Rice	"
Noah Phelps	16	Joseph Bowker	"
Joseph Tiff	"	Simeon Holcomb	"
Elihu Larrance	"	Obed Holcomb	"
Dudely Humphry	17	Silas Hays	"
Rogur Case	16	Zenos Hays	"
Elisha Moses	"	Timothey Case	"
Michal Segor	17	John Read Jr.	"
John Larrance	"	Joseph Willcocks Jr.	"
Timothey Phelps	"	Richard Case Jr.	"
		Samuel Barber Jr.	"
		Ezekiel Case	
		Moses Lily	18

So far Coms Simsbury Solgers

    the number of the Oficiers and Solger that doth belong to the town Suffield are as followeth to wit

Clark Daniel Austin	17	Aaron Phelps	17
Surgent Benjeman Harman	"	James Holladay	"
Jonathan Norton	"	Corporall Joseph Old	"
Jonathan Shelding	"	Daniel Spencer Jr.	"
Stephen Old	"	Calib Allin	"
Samuel Harman	"	Zacheas Hanchitt Jr.	"
John White	"	Jobe Fowler	"
Joseph Brunnson	"	Abel Rising	"
Isaac Hall	"	Jeremiah Nelson	"

    these foregoing are the names of Suffield men besids sum that Came Home without leave

CAMPAIGN OF 1757.

these folowing names are the names of the Solgers that do belonge to the town of windsor

	Days		Days
Edward Griswold Jr.	17	Alvin Owen	17
Abraham Phelps	"	Elisha Phelps	"

the folowing names are those that belonge Enfield

Lift Jonathan Terry	17	Abiel Bush	17
Corporall Isaac Kibbe	"	Elias Purkins	"
Ezekel Pryor	"	Jonathan Parsons	"
Henery Chandler	"	Nehemiah Rumrell	"
Nathaniel Parsons	"	David Kibbe	"
Eldad Phelps	"	Benjam Simons	"
Obediah Hulburd	"	Joel Pease	"
Abel Pease	"	Ruben Pirkins	"

So fur Coms Enfield Solgers

New hartford november the 8th 1757 we the Subscribors being Detached In the last alarram for their Releaf at Lake george went under the Command of Capt Jonathan Pettibone of Simsbury

Surgant John Edgecomb	14	Roger Olmsted	16
Israel Loomis	"	Ashbel Andrus	15
Thomas Ollett	17	Samuel Merralls	16
Justios Lewis	14	Samuel Benham	15
Elifihelet Ensign	"	John Miller	14
Jonathan Goodwine	16	Corparall Eber Andrus	"
Ashbel Kellogg	"	Uriah Seymar	15
Samuel Duwglass	15	Isaac Cadwill	16
Moses Marsh	16	John Rise	"

So far Coms new Hartford men

the following Solgers names belong to farmington

Ager Gailord	17	Joseph Gailord	17
Aaron Wiard	"	Thomas Cupper	8
Jacob Bartholemu	"	Josiah Ives	17
Justus Peck	"	James Hasdell	"

So far Coms farmington Solgers

the following Solgers names beloning to Torranton

Charles Mather	13	Ephraim Durrum	14
Elijah Gaylord	"		

So far Coms torranton Solgers

the following names are the Solgers that Doth belonge to Harwinton

Abraham Sperry	17	Abijah Webster	17
Eli Dewey	"	James Hopkins	"
Stephen Willcox	"	Daniel Messinger	"

So far Coms Harrinton men

Accot of Such as Attended ye Return of ye Horses here Follows

Timo Moses	16	Jonath Case	1
Joseph Case Jr.	2	Samll Stone Butler	4
Samll Derwin	6	Oliver Lewis	3
Wm Saymore	"	John Granger	2

[*State Library, War 7, 55.*]

MILITIA COMPANIES. 247

CAPT. LYMAN'S COMPANY.

Moses Lyman [of Goshen], Captain.
Stephen Smith [of Litchfield], Lieutenant.
Ebenezer Norton [of Goshen], Lieutenant.

Colony of Connectcut to Capt Moses Lyman and the Compeney under his Command In Colonel Eben Marsh Regment for ye Service at ye Time of alaram for ye Relief of fort Wm Henry and Places a

	Days in Service		Days in Service
Moses Lyman Capt.		Samuel Horsford	14
from Aug. 7 to 21	15	Benoni Peck	"
Stephen Smith Lieut.	"	Levi Croker	"
Ebenezer Norton "	"	Wodrof Emons	"
John Wright Ser.	"	Benjamin Daley	"
Benone Hills "	"	Phinas Spalding	"
Wait Deming Cla.	"	John Peas	"
John Evets Serj.	"	Jonathan Chandler	"
Nathanel Evets "	13	Eathen Allen	"
Stephen Thonson (?) Cor.	15	Barzilla Dudley	"
Charles Brustar "	"	William Duglas	"
Jeremiah Woolcut	"	John Dibel	"
Abel Phelps	"	John Dibel ye 2	"
Samuel Frainces	"	Asa Landon	2
Sephen Godwin	"	Asa Hill	8
Martain Wilcocks	"	Jonah Case	"
Billias Hill	"	Edmund Beech	"
Nathanell Standley	"	Eben Hill	"
Asaph Hall	"	John Dibel	"
Daniel Horsford	14	Samuel Henman	7
Jonathan Baldwen	"	Medad Hills	"
Jesse Toba	"	Samuel Baldwen	"
Ichabad Rogars	"	Samuel Wright	6
William Tromble	"	Lent Ells (?)	2
Ebenezer Stevens	"	William Warner	11
Moses Read	"	Samuel Lewes	15
Elijah Owen	"	William Tromble	12
Samuel Chipman	"	Billi Morgan	12
Philep Spencer	"	George Bissel	10
Samuel Benton	"	Samuel Tousley	6
Jonathan Hull	"	Philop Chatfield	"
Joseph Meriels	"	James Bird	"
Amos Hanchet	"	Josiah Stodard	6
Thomas Tutel	"	Joshua Harris	"
Isaac Benton	"	Thomas Russel	"
Joseph Bird	"	Nemiah Pers	"
Elijah Skinner	"	Noah Foard	"
Simeon Strong	"		

Twenty-four of the above named rode horses from Goshen, one from Litchfield, four from Canaan, three from Sharon, twenty-five from Salisbury, and seventeen from Cornwall.

[*State Library, War* 7, *56*.]

CAMPAIGN OF 1757.

CAPT. RUDD'S COMPANY.

Jonathan Rudd [of Windham], Captain.
Eli Stutson, Lieutenant.
Jonathan Kingsbury, Lieutenant.
Zacheriah Bicknell, Ensign.

The Colony of Conecticut Dr To Cap Jonathan Rudd and Company under his Command Being ye first Company of militia detached or drafted out of ye 5 Rigement of s^d Colony on ye 9 and 10th Days of August A D 1757 to march for ye Releaf of fort Wm. Henry and Places Adjacent.

	Days in Service		Days in Service
Jonathan Rudd Capt. 9 to 23	15	Samuel Huntington	15
Eli Stutson Lieut.	16	Michal Cary	"
Jonathan Kingsbury "	15	Jonathan Luce	"
Zacheriah Bicknell Ens.	"	Eliphelit Palmer	"
Benjamin Talcot (?) Serj.	"	Nathan Hebberd	"
William Holt "	"	Phinehas Manning	"
Oliver Hincher "	9	Jonathan Waldo	"
Abram Spafford "	14	David Lilley	"
Josiah Eaton Cleark	15	Amasa Palmer	"
Amos Moss Corp.	"	Barnabas Anabel	"
Samuel Roundy "	"	Pelatiah Kimbal	"
James Stedman "	"	Eliazer Butler	"
Josiah Chandler "	"	Daniel Hebberd	"
Isaac Crane Drum.	"	Jonah Smith	"
Samuel Adams	17	William Yerington	"
Isaiah Wood	4	Ruben Bingham	"
Christopher Hide	"	Eliphaz Kingsley	"
Elisha Wright	"	Nathan Robenson	"
Silvanus Backus	15	Henry Preston	"
Eleazer Robinson	"	Joseph Marten	"
Moses Spafford	"	Jonathan Hovey	"
Joshua Ginings	"	John Gould	"
Stephen Brown Jr.	"	Caleb Fortnor	"
Daniel Redington	"	Joshua Burnam	"
Moses Coltson	"	Nathaniel Ford	"
Stephen Johnson	"	Samuel Ashley	"
Benajah Bingham	"	Nehemiah Holt	"
Elijah Bibbins	"	James Perl	"
William Mordock	"	John Curtis	"
Abisha Bingham	"	Daniel Denison	"
Eleazer Cary	"	John Hammon	"
John Frame	"	John Greanslit	"
Elijah Bingham Jr.	"	Jeremiah Durke	"
Oliver Parish	"	Malatiah Bingham	"
Daniel Allen	"	Gideon Marten	"
Elijah Frik	"	David Fisk	"
Verrin Balch	"	Thomas Chaffe	"
John Balcom Jr.	"	John Preston Jr.	"
Benjamin Hanks	"	William Daney	"
Richard Wabber	"	Christopher Webber	"
Richerd Cary	"	Lamuel Holms	"
Samuel Case	"	Abijah Kendal	"
Jonathan Crosby Jr.	"	William Kyes	"
Ebenezer Hinkly	"	Daved Chaffe Jr.	"
Daniel Hovey Jr.	"	Thomas Hill	"

MILITIA COMPANIES.

	Days in Service		Days in Service
Solomon Welch	15	Uriah Hanks	14
Joseph Snow	"	Amos Clerk	"
Josiah Bugbe Jr.	"	Elisha Eldrich	"
James Commins	"	Benjamin Hayward	"
Peter Estman	"	Amos Lawson	"
Thomas Atwood	14	John Waldo	"
James Bundy	"	James Haston	"
Asa Baldwin	"	Andrew Burnam	"
John Turner	"	Daniel Ross	"
Shubel Dimeck ye 3d	"	Joseph Skiff	16
John Dunham	"	was a Serjant 11 days	
Jaduthan Dimmoak	"	Moses Walcut	15
Nathaniel Kidder (?)	"	Joshua Holt	11
Joseph Hovey	"	Josiah Hebberd	8
Daniel Waterman	"	Daniel Baldwin	9
Joshua Palmer	"	Joseph Jacobs	11
Ebenezer Clerk	"	Elisha Barrows	"
Thomas Brown	"	Jonathan Daney	9
Jabez Fitch	"	Oliver Smith	11
John Worner	"	Jacob Waters	"
William Riply	"		

The men that attended to ye Return of ye Pack Horses

Noah Gilbord	10	Elnathan Maynord	9
John Baker	"	Asa Spafford	2
John Manning	"	Timothy Laraby	"
Elijah Bingham	"	Nathaniel Ford	"
Benjamin Bingham	"	Jedadiah Dana	"

Thirty-eight of the above named rode horses from Windham.

[*State Library, War 7, 59.*]

CAPT. FITCH'S COMPANY.

Joseph Fitch [of Lebanon], Captain.
Abel Buwel [of Lebanon], First Lieutenant.
Thomas Loomis [of Goshen in Lebanon], Second Lieutenant.
Joseph Marsh, Ensign.

The Colony of Connecticut Dr to Capt Joseph Fitch Capt of the Company under his Command in Coll Jonth Trumble's Regiment for their Service at the time of the Alarm for the Relief of Fort Wm Henry and Parts Adjacent Augt 1757

	Days in Service		Days in Service
Joseph Fitch Capt. from Aug. 9 to 24	17	Asa Richerson Corp. Wm Lyman "	16 "
Abel Buwel 1 Lieut.	16	Joshua Fuller "	"
Thomas Loomis 2 Lieut.	"	Benjm Ellis "	"
Joseph Marsh Ens.	"	John Vauhn Drum.	"
Samuel Seybury Serj.	"	Wm Huntington	"
Elijah Sprague "	"	John Huntington Jr.	"
John Eggington "	"	Thos Marvin	"
Benjm Woodworth "	"	Danll Indian	"

CAMPAIGN OF 1757.

Name	Days in Service	Name	Days in Service
Zac. Downer	16	John Polly	16
Hugh Wylley	"	Amos Chappel	"
Amos Treadaway	"	Benoni Clark	"
Walter Aldon	"	Daniel Clark Jr.	"
Wm Bayley	"	John Wise Jr.	"
Abraham Fitch	"	Pennygreen Whealer	"
Benjⁿ Buttler	"	Nathan Lee	"
Zebulon Case	"	Caleb Gifford	"
Banajah Strong	"	Epharain Carpenter	"
Edmond Grandee	"	Aron Tharp	"
Nehemiah Palmer	"	Tim^o Loomis	"
Wm Aldon	"	Elijah Webster	"
Sam^{ll} Hunt	"	James Hill	"
Dan Hide	"	Gideon Gay	"
Josiah Taylor	"	John Baskum	"
Sam^{ll} Mitcalf	"	Amos Clark	"
Dan^{ll} Skinner	"	James Symes	"
Nath^{ll} Halbrook Jr.	"	Banajah House	"
Sam^{ll} Alling	"	Jabez Dike	"
Benjⁿ Wright	"	Eben^r Baldwin	"
Nath^{ll} Bliss	"	Silas Long Jr.	"
John Tiffiny	"	Nehemiah Claston	"
Josiah Wickwire	"	Elijah Bill	"
Walter Woodworth	"	Abraham Blackman Jr.	"
Elisha Toby	"	Ezekiel Haughton	"
Isaac Bayly	"	Zebulon Tubbs	"
Ezekiel Calkin	"	Joshua Bill	"
Perez Swift	"	Elijah Dewey	"
Caleb Lyman	"	Samuel Bristal Jr.	"
Jonth Finny	"	Zibah Gifford	"
Lemuel Devey	"	Nath^{ll} Porter	11
Sam^{ll} Pemfield	"	Robert Thompson	"
Wm Alling	"	James Gifford	12
Elisha Porter	"	Walter Hide	"
John Enlish	"	Simeon Gray	"
Zephaniah Post	"	John Sherwin	4
Christopher Pees	"	Benjⁿ Owen	"
John Damming	"	Ezra Loomis	9
Eliphalet Woodworth	"	John Bliss	"
Wadworth Bruster	"	Benj^m Sweatland	6
Solomon Curtis Jr.	"	Samuel Wells	12
Stephen Hunt Jr.	"	John Avery	"
Jeremiah Proad (?)	"	Samuel Williams	5
Thos Alling	"	Elijah Hide	"
John Wise	"	Eleazar Wells	"
John Gold	"	Joseph Wadsworth	"
Jonth Russel	"	Wm Tory	"
Thos Clark	"	Hink Bennet	5
Aaron Dewey	"	David Strong	"
Jahiel Williams	"	Samuel Fuller	"
Benjⁿ Brewster Jr.	"	John Dewey	2
Simeon Metcalf	"	Wm Lusk	"
Joshua Chappel Jr.	"	Benjⁿ Baldwin	"
Elias Bliss	"	Eliphalet House	"
Elijah Strong	"	John Bill	"

Reuben Metcalf 2 days to bring back horses

[*State Library, War* 7, *60.*]

MILITIA COMPANIES.

CAPT. HANDFORD'S COMPANY.

Samuel Handford, Captain.
Samuel Marven [of Norwalk], First Lieutenant.
David Westcoat, Second Lieutenant.

Colony of Connecticut to Capt Sam^{ll} Handford and the Company under his Command in Col^o Jonathan Hoits Regiment, for there Service at the time of Alarm for Relief of Fort Wm Henry and Places adjacent Augst 1757

	Days in Service		Days in Service
Sam^{ll} Handford Capt. from Aug. 7 to 23	16	John Abbot	18
		James Stewart	"
Sam^{ll} Marven Lieut	"	Ephr^a Kimberly	"
David Westcoat "	"	Abij^a Hubbel	"
Jonth Hewsted Serj.	"	Thadd^s Betts	"
Elias Scribner "	"	Ebenez^r Hendrick	"
Matthew Mead "	"	Ephr^a Ketchum	"
Danl Benedick "	"	David Sloan	"
Gould Hoit Clerk	"	Saml Comstock	"
Silas Olmsted Corp.	18	George Pachen	"
Dan^{ll} Betts "	"	Eben^r Cressey	"
Gardiner Olmsted "	16	David Morehouse	"
Saml Benedick "	"	Nathl Weede	"
Danl Hyat Drum	"	Charles Weed	16
Stephen Waren	18	Saml Lawrence	"
Jo^s Stevens	"	Benajah Hoit	"
Enos Tuttle	"	Matthew Seymour	"
Jonas Seeley	"	Eli Reed	"
Deliverence Bennit	"	Ebenetus Bishop	"
Danl Hoyt	"	Matthew Fitch	"
Nathan Jagger	"	John Levake	"
Jo^s Lockwood	"	David Slawson	"
Stephⁿ St John	"	Eliphal^t Kellogg	"
Danl St John	"	Eeb^r Smith	"
Saml Pharoah	"	Matthias St John	"
Abra^m Grigory	"	John Acorn	"
Gemal^l Taylor	"	Jonathⁿ Benidick	"
Seth Taylor	"	Elij^a Grigory	"
Thad^s Taylor	"	Willm Hoyt	"
Ichab^d Olmsted	"	Thomas Lawrence	"
Abra^m Gray	"	John Lockwood	"
Elij^a Benidick	"	John Picket	"
Nathan Jarvis	"	Noah Smith	"
Benjamin Keeler	"	Eben^r Smith	"
James Filleow	"	Elnathⁿ Bears	"
Zebulⁿ Bass	"	Charles Pope	"
Asael Raymond	"	Seth Abbot	"
David Tuttle	"	Solomon Tyler	"
David Betts	"	Silas Hecock	"
Benj^a Betts	"	Seth Griffith	"
James Keeler	"	Willm Belden	"
Jno St John	"	Willm Raymond	"
Andrew Patchen	"	John Harmon	"
Danl Cole	"	Isaⁱ Keeler	"
Joseph Rockwell	"	Ebenez^r Handford	11
Isaac Darrow	"	Ezra Hoyt	"
Saml Gates	"	Nathan Williams	"

252   CAMPAIGN OF 1757.

	Days in Service		Days in Service
John Truesdel	11	John Rockwell	7
Seth Bennidick	7	Humphry Denend	"
Tim⁰ Hoyt	"	John Betts	5
Silas Devenport	"		
To bring the horses back			
Peter Lockwood	9	Nathan Mallory	14
Stephen St John	"		

One hundred of the above named rode horses from Norwalk.

[*State Library, War 7, 64, 65.*]

CAPT. HITCHCOCK'S COMPANY.

Amos Hitchcock, Captain.
Amos Sherman [of Amity in Milford and New Haven], Lieutenant.

A Muster Role of Capt Amos Hitchcock Company the third Company that went out of the 2^d Regement Commanded by ye Honourable Roger Newton Esqr Col^l under ye Special Command of Major John Hubard of S^d Regement in the Late Alarm for ye Defence of Fort Wm Henry and parts adjacent Augt 1757

	Days in Service		Days in Service
Amos Hitchcock Capt. 7 to 24	18	Jos. Collings	17
Amos Sherman Lieut. 8 to 24	17	John Grannis	"
Obediah Hotchkis Serj. 7 to 24	18	Charls Hotchkis	"
Nath^ll Sperry 2^d " 8 to 24	17	Dan^ll Heaton	"
Jude Blachly 3^d " "	"	Jay Humerston	"
Jabez Hotchkis Clerk	26	Jared Hill	"
Aug. 8 to Sept. 2		Isaac Hind	"
Elijah Hotchkis Corp. 7 to 24	18	Jeremiah Toles	"
Tim⁰ Peck 2^d "	17	Steph^n Lounsbury	"
Benajah Peck Drum.	"	Wm Mansor	"
Stephen Hotchkis	18	Nicholas Russel	"
Christopher Alling	"	Hez. Rogers	"
Tim⁰ Ruggles	"	Isaac Sperry	"
William Cuttler	19	Amos Sperry	"
Henry Toles	"	Reubin Sperry	"
Josiah Alling	17	Reubin Sacket	"
The⁰ Baldwin	"	Nehemiah Toles	"
Sam^ll Beech	"	Daniel Tucker	"
Alex^r Bradly	"	Uri Tuttle	"
Jesse Bradley	"	Oliver Tod	"
Seth Barns	"	Hez. Tuttle	"
Ruben Bacheler	"	Eben^r Walner	"
Thaddius Barns	"	Noah Woolcut	"
Benj^m Curtice	"	Abel Ward	"
John Cooper	"	Tim⁰ Payn	"
Caleb Cooper	"	Epharaim Andrews	19
Tim⁰ Cooper	"	Gidion Andrew	"
Stephen Cooper	"	Isaac Brackett	18
John Cornwell	"	Denis Scovet	"

MILITIA COMPANIES.

	Days in Service		Days in Service
John Horton	18	Lemuel Humphrevile	Deserter
Henry Howell	"	John Benham	"
Eben^r Johnson	"	Horse Drivers	
Tim^o Leeke	"	Aaron Day	10
Jos. Peck	"	Yale Bishop	"
Wm Payn	"	James Thompson	"
Elisha Painter	"	James Sherman	"
Caleb Tuttle	"	Gershom Barns	"
John Thompson	"	Wm Bradly	"
Ambros Ward	"	Jesse Blakly	9
Samuel Brooks sick	58	Wm Johnson	"
Wm King Dead	22	Abraham Thompson	"
Jos. Heaton	10	Mathew Gilberd went to Fort	
Jos. Warner	"	Edward with Major Hubbard	17
Danl Pardee	"	John Gordon	3
Stephen Bristol	Deserter		

[*State Library, Adams Papers, in War 7.*]

CAPT. WHITMORE'S COMPANY.

Jacob Whitmore, Captain.

The Colony of Connecticut to Capt Jacob Whitmore & Company by him Commanded March 9 for the Releif of Fort Wm Henry In ye Alarm

The company contained seventy-one men.

[*State Library, War 7, 1.*]

COL. CONANT'S RETURN.

1757 August ye 10th the following is a Muster Roll of ye first Company of militia Detached or Drafted out of ye Militia of ye 5th regiment in the Colony of Connecticut on ye ninth & tenth days of Instant August in order to march for ye Succour Releese & assistance of ye forces under the Command of Maj^r General Webb at Fort Edward Fort William Henry and parts adjacent Which S^d Company is by me the Subscriber (for S^d March & Service) put under the Command of Capt Jonathan Rudd as their Capt & Lieu^t Eli Stetson as their first Lieu^t & Lieu^t Jonathan Kingsbery as their 2nd Lieu^t and Ensⁿ Zechariah Bicknel as their Ensⁿ, With orders forthwith to proceed on S^d March (viz) &c

(mens names)

The Second Company has the Same preface as above Except ye Date Which 1757 August ye 11; and Detached or Drafted out ye 10th of Instant August, and their Capt is Abner Barker, first Lieu^t Simeon Hunt, 2 Lieu^t Samuel Davis their Ensⁿ John Holms

Both Signed at ye End of the Roll

Shubael Conant, Colonel of the 5th Regiment
in the Colony of Connecticut

CAMPAIGN OF 1757.

6 Comp. Capt Kendals Men
Ser^t Oliver Henchet
Thomas Chaffe
John Preston Junr
William Daney
Christopher Webber
Lemewell Homes
Abijah Kendal
William Kyes
Corp^l Josiah Chandler
David Chaffe Junr
Thomas Hill
Solomon Welch
Joseph Snow
Elisha Dexter
Josiah Bugbee Junr
James Cummins
Josiah Eaton
Peter Eastman

1 Comp. Capt John Fitch's Men
Ser^t Benjamin Follett
Drumer Isaac Crane
Joseph Skiff
Selvanus Backus
Eleazer Robinson
Moses Spofford
Joshua Gennings
Stephen Brown Junr
Daniel Redington
Moses Coltson
Stephen Johnson
Benajah Bingham
Elijah Bibben
William Murdock
Abisha Bingham
Eleazer Casey
John Frame
Josiah Hebord
Elijah Bingham Junr
Oliver Parrish
Sam^{ll} Addams
Daniel Allen Junr
Christopher Hide
Elijah Frink
Moses Wallcut

Capt Storrs's Men
Serj^t Abraham Spafford
Thomas Atwood Junr
Elisha Wright
James Bundy ye 3^d
Asa Baldwin
John Turner
Shubael Dimmock ye 3^d
John Dunham Junr
Jeduthan Dimmock
Nath^{ll} Kidder
Joseph Hovey Junr

Daniel Waterman
Joshua Palmer
Ebenezer Clerk

5th Comp. Capt Durkes Men
Lieu^t Jonathan Kingsbury
Ser^t William Holt
Corp^l James Stedman
Joseph Martin
Jonathan Hovey
John Gould
Caleb Falkner
Joshua Holt Junr
Joshua Burnham
Nath^{ll} Ford Junr
Samuel Ashley Junr
Nehemiah Holt
James Perle
John Curtice
Daniel Dennison
John Hammon
John Greenslit
Corp^l Jeremiah Durkee
Malatiah Bingham
Isaac Bennet
James Utley
David Fisk

3 Comp. Capt Rudds Men
Capt Jonathan Rudd
Jonathan Luce
Eliphalet Palmer
Samuel Roundey
Isaiah Wood
Nathan Hebard Junr
Phinihas Manning
Jonathan Waldon
David Lillie
Amasa Palmer
Barnabas Annabel
Palatiah Kimbal
Eleazer Butler
Daniel Hebard
Jonah Smith
William Yarrington
Ruben Bingham
Eliphaz Kingsley
Nathan Robinson
Henry Preston

2nd Comp. Capt Halls Men
Verren Balch
Joseph Jacobs ye 3^d
John Balcom
Benjamin Hanks Junr
Richard Webber
Oliver Smith
Daniel Baldwin Junr
Elisha Barrows Junr

Richard Carey
Samuel Case
Jonathan Crosby Junr
Amos Marsh
Ebenezer Hinkley
Jonathan Daney
Daniel Hovey Junr
Samuel Huntington
Michael Casey

Troop Capt John Howards men
Thomas Brown
Jabez Fitch

John Warner
William Ripley
Henry Brown
Amos Clark
Jacob Waters
Isaac Barrows
Benjamin Hayward
James Halkins
Amos Lawsen
John Waldow
James Haston
Andrew Burnham
Joshua Lasell

[*F. Clarence Bissell, Willimantic.*]

CAPT. LEACH'S RETURN.

August 9, 1759   Andover Souldiers Detached in Lebanon are Viz
James Sims   Jabez Like
Benajah House

And in Coventry are Viz
Eben^r Baldwin   Nehemiah Closson
Silas Long Junr
Elijah Smioth in the room of Zachariah Loomiss
Elijah Bill in the room of Corp^l Sam^{ll} Dagget

And also in Hebron
Jno Sherwine   Zebulon Tubbs
Abraham Blackman Junr   Joshua Bill
Ezekiel Houghton   William Jones
William Sweetland the Father in ye room of y Son Azariah
   [Indorsed] Leah's Return

[*Connecticut Historical Society.*]

CAPT. WORTHINGTON'S RETURN.

Colchester August 9   1757
Pursuant to the within Orders I have Detach^d Twelve able Bodied Men which are one fourth part of ye Company Under my Command
                                        Elijah Worthingⁿ Capt
The Names of which are as Follows Viz

Gershom Fox   Jacob Worthingⁿ
Sam^{ll} Bebee   Amos Ransom
Amos Wells   Parker Jones
Robert Mcleve   John Tozer
Joseph Spencer   Amos Dodge
Bildad Waterman   David Dodge 3^d

   [Indorsed] Capt Elijah Worthington

[*Connecticut Historical Society.*]

CAPT. BULKLY'S RETURN.

To Jon^n Trumble Col^l of ye 12th Regiment in ye Colony of Con^t

Honrd S^r, Pursuant to your order I have Detach^d ye following Persons to march for ye Relief of our friends at Fort Edward &c : & have brought them to ye house of m^r Obadiah Horsfoot Inn keeper in hebron as Directed Viz

Stephen Start	Elijah Northum
Israel Dodge	Aaron Gillett
Asahel Strong	Miles Wright
Joel Chamberlin	John Roberts Ju^r
Eben^r Cole Ju^r	Philip Judd
Jo^s Taylor Ju^r	Nath^{ll} Kellogg Junr

Hebron August 10th 1757

Gershom Bulkly Capt
[*Connecticut Historical Society.*]

CAPT. GATES' RETURN.

At a muster of the north military Company in East Haddam august ye 9th 1757 the acount of the Soldiers Detached for his majestys servis is as folloeth Viz

Serj Timothy Parsival	Joseph Parker
Daniel Williams	Benjamin Olcutt
Thomas Knolton	Nathaniel Acly ye 4th
William Aacanes	James Cook
Silvenos Youngs	Timothy Gates
Jared Brainerd	

Test Caleb Chapman Lieu^t

[Indorsed] Capt Daniel Gates

[*Connecticut Historical Society.*]

CAPT. WEST'S RETURN.

To Coll. Jonathan Trumble Coll. of the 12th regiment In the Coloney of Connecticutt Sir in obediance to your orders of the 8th and 9th instant on the ninth instant I Called together the Company under my Command and have Detached twenty five men out of S^d Company for the service expressed in s^d orders which is the fourth part of my s^d Company and have them here present armd and acquiped according to S^d orders at the house of M^r obediah Horsford in Hebron. the under officers in my S^d Com are also here present the fourth part of them armd and acquiped in readiness to march with the Soldiers if thereto required

from your Humble servant at Command

Joshua West Capt. of ye military Company in Goshen in Lebanon

Dated August ye 10 : 1757

MILITIA COMPANIES. 257

The men Detachd as above s^d are

Jehial Williams
James Start
Benj^m Bruster Junr
Simeon Metcalf
John Bliss Junr
Joshua Chappel Junr
Elias Bliss
Elijah Strong
John Polley
Amos Chappel
Benoni Clark
Daniel Clark Junr
John Wise

Purgran (?) Wheeler
Benjn Owen
Nathan Lee
Caleb Gifford
Eph^m Carpenter
Aaron Thorpe
Timothy Loomis
Elijah Webster
James Hills
Gideon Gay
John Bascom
Amos Clark

Joshua West
[*Connecticut Historical Society.*]

CAPT. DEWEY'S RETURN.

The Reve^nd Benjn Pomroy
Lieu^t Amos Hills
Lieu^t Samuel Jones
Doc^r Benjn Pomroy
Sar. Epharam Taylor
Sar Epheram Wright
Corp Beriah Wright
Drum^r Elijah Dewey
Hezekiah Holdridg
Lasarus Puffer
John Gott
Daniel Gott
Jonathan Root
Edward Howard

John Ford
Aron Baxtor
Ezekil Parish
Timothy Stuard
Thomas Skinner
John Holdridg
Josiah Rockwell
Samuel Felding
Thomas Napping
George Blanchard
Thomas Cox
Samuel Mot
Ezra Cogswel   Dont Go

[Indorsed] Capt Charles Dewey^s Men Inlisted

[*Connecticut Historical Society.*]

CAPT. GILBERT'S RETURN.

to ye Hon^bl Jon^th Trumbel Esqr Col of the 12th Rigement of the Coleney of Connecticut prsuant to your orders to me of the 8th Instant I have Detacht one 4th part of the Company under my Comand & Well Equipt them as the Law Derects & Have orderd them to apper Compleat in thare Arms at the house of mr obadiah horsford by Nine of the Clock in the morning this 9th Day of Agust Instant

Sam^el Gilbert Jr Capt of the first or
second Company in the town of hebron

A List of the Nams of those Detacht

Sr Ebnezer Willcox
Cor Thos Perine
Cor Thos Wells
mr John Tompson
John Talcote

Obadiah Culver
Nathanel Phelps
Asher Merels
John Eles
Nichalas Bond

17

Henery Curtice
Beng Sumner
Jams Cox
Thos Brown

John Carter
Gidon Post
Jos Lulel (?)
John Hazzod

[*Connecticut Historical Society.*]

CAPT. DICKINSON'S RETURN.

To the Honr^d Col° this is to leet your Honer Know that this is the acounte and Nomber of man that Blongue to Capt David Dickeson in the 12 Regement that he hath presd

Sa^r David Miller
Co^r Samuel Kelogg
Jonathan Tillson
David Blish
Staulwortha Woutors Jr. (?)
Job Stils
John Whitcom Jr.
Banjmon Cirtice

Abijah Bryant
Joseph Kelogg Jr.
Joseph Conyer (?)
Jaben Strongue
Samuel Raymont
Ebenezer Coleman
Abraham Fox
Robord Lovemon Jr is Drumer

[*Connecticut Historical Society.*]

CAPT. HOLMES' RETURN.

Colchester 9 August 1757

Pursuant to the within Written Orders, have Assembled the Company under my Command, & have attachd one Quarter part of the Men being twenty in Number, for his Majesties Service & Relief of the fort Now Beseiged

George Holmes Capt.

Serg. William Welch
Drum. Elijah Kilburn
Sam^{ll} Dodge
Stephen Gardner Jun.
John Tennant
Jonathan Harris
James Forsyth Jr.
Jonah Chapman
James Ranson
Elisha Chapman

Joshua Perkins
Jonathan Gilbert
* James Morgan
Rufus Randal
Asa Jones
Tho. Brooks
James Rogers
Christopher Miner
Amos Rothbone
John Hamelton

* Crossed out in the original manuscript.

[*Connecticut Historical Society.*]

CAPT. OLMSTED'S RETURN.

[The following appears to be a list of the men detached from the company of Capt. William Olmsted of East Haddam, Aug. 10, 1757.]

Joshua Smith
Deliverance Waters
Asahel Taylor
Nathanel Taylor

Uriah Clarke
John Chamberlin Jr.
Aaron Griswold impressed
* Ebenezer Cone "

* Also called Ebenezer Cone Jr.

[*Connecticut Historical Society.*]

CAPT. DAY'S RETURN.

Colchestor August ye 9th 1757

In persuance of an order from Colonal Trumble to detach one quarter of my Soldiers to go forthwith in Defence of his Majestis forts (ie to Say) fort Edward and Fort William Henry & places Adjasent thereabouts & according to Sd order I have Taken ye men whose Names are here Inserted P^r me your Humble Servant

Benjamin Day Captain

Benjamin Day Jr.
Calob Lomis Jr.
John Rowly Jr.
Adonijah Foot
James Crocker Jr.
Ezra Gates
John Blish

Joseph Walters
Allin Willee
David Niles
Stephen Ackly
John Bigalow Jr.
Oliver Dean

[*Connecticut Historical Society.*]

CAPT. SPENCER'S RETURN.

August 10th 1757

To Coll^o Jonathan Trumble Hon^d Sir

Pursuant to your Honours orders Detach'd from ye South Comp in millington

Joseph Borden
Hains Graves Delinquent
Sterling Graves
James Booge 2^d
Stephen Chapman
Lemuel Hungerford
Thomas Webb

Micah Scovel
Hez. Usher
James Sparrow
Isaac Tatton
Alex. Steward
Ser. Jacob Burnham Delinquent

Pr Jared Spencer Capt

[*Connecticut Historical Society.*]

LIEUT.-COL. HAVILAND'S COMMAND.

COMMANDING OFFICER.

William Haviland, Lieutenant-Colonel of the 27th regiment of regulars, was in command of the troops at Fort Edward during the winter of 1757–1758.

[*Journals of Maj. Robert Rogers.*]

CAPT. FERRIS' COMPANY.

Reuben Ferris, Captain.
Thomas Pearce, Lieutenant.
Abel Prindel, Lieutenant.
Zebulon Butler, Ensign.

A Pay Role of Capt Reuben Ferris's Company of Rangers at N° 4 1757 : 8

Mens Names and Quality	Time of Inlistment	Discharged	Left the Service
Capt. Reuben Farris	Nov. 18	May 14	
Lieut. Thom^s Pearce	14	"	
Lieut. Abel Prindel	"	"	
Ens. Zebulon Butler	"	"	
Serj. Ichabod French	"	"	
Serj. Isaac Whelply	18	"	
Serj. David Hamilton	14	"	
Serj. Robert Sumers	"	"	
Clerk Moses White	"	"	
Drum. Andrew Cabel	"	"	
Corp. Nathl Weed	"	"	
Corp. Disbrao Webb	"	"	
Corp. Wm Jacobs	"		Apr. 28
Corp. Roger Rose	"	May 14	
Lewis Angavine	"		May 1
Gideon Alin	"	May 14	
Nathl Andrews	"	"	
Benj^a Ally	"	"	
David Butler	"	"	
Wm Bayly	"	"	
Tobe Boston	"	"	
John Bone	"	"	
Noah Bishop	"	"	
Jonathan Butler	"	"	
Nathan Beech	"	"	
Abner Beckwith	"	"	
Abner Bushnell	"	"	
Joseph Benham	"	"	

LIEUT.-COL. HAVILAND'S COMMAND.

Mens Names and Quality	Time of Inlistment	Discharged	Left the Service
Nathan Benham	Nov. 14	May 14	
Eleaz^r Bartholemew	"	"	
Jasper Bayly	"		Apr. 11
Timothy Brister	"	May 14	
Jesse Beers	18		Mar. 2
Thaddeus Benit	14	May 14	
David Bernham	"	"	
John Charles	"	"	
Andrew Culver	"	"	
Philip Canada	18		Mar. 17
Benj^a Cook	14	May 14	
Joseph Coly	"	"	
Wm Crook	"	"	
Wm Dunken	"		Mar. 17
David Dan	18	May 14	
Dan Dickerson	14	"	
Stephen Dulf	"	"	
Stephen Daton	18	"	
John Dayly	14	"	
Justice Dayly	"	"	
Nathl Davis	"	"	
Richard Davas	"		Died Dec. 28
Stephen Edget	18	May 14	
James Ferris	"	"	
Daniel Fox	14	"	
David Franklin	"	"	
Job Hadon	"	"	
Wm Horton	"	"	
Volingtine Hichcock	"	"	
Enos Hichcock	"	"	
Sam^{ll} Hand	"	"	
John Hatch	"	"	
Simeon Hough	"	"	
Simon Hurd	"	"	
Suck Hegon	"		Apr. 7
Eleazor Jisbell	"	May 14	
Sam^{ll} Johnson	"	"	
Aner Ives	"	"	
Edward Johnson	"	"	
Daniel Jackson	"	"	
John Keef	"		Mar. 2
Amos Knap	18	May 14	
Ezekiel Leathers	14		Apr. 11
John Loder	18	May 14	
Epharim Lockwood	"	"	
Jonathan Mansfield	14	"	
Levi Munson	"	"	
Thomas Munsel	"		Apr. 24
Jonas Moses	"	May 14	
John Not	"	"	
Joseph Orsborn	"	"	
Edward Oddle	"	"	
Benj^a Peters	18	"	
Jacob Palmer	"	"	
Benj^a Parmile	14	"	
Sam^{ll} Provoce (?)	18	"	
David Peet	14	"	

Mens Names and Quality	Time of Inlistment	Discharged	Left the Service
Charles Plum	Nov. 14	May 14	
Ebenezer Reynolds	18	"	
Daniel Raynolds	"	"	
John Roe	14	"	
Christopher Stephens	"	"	
Nath¹ Selkrig	"	"	
Daniel Speek	"	"	
Salvanis Sloson	18	"	
Stephen Thomas	14	"	
John Tooker	"	"	
Sam¹¹ Tooly	"	"	
Daniel Tharp	"	"	
Gideon Webb	"	"	
Sam¹¹ Webb	"	"	
Daniel Winstone	"	"	
Moses Wright	"	"	
Nathan Wright	"	"	
Joseph Wood	"	"	
Sam¹¹ Worden	18	"	
Zopher Wilmouth	"	"	
Jn° Webb	"	"	
Nathan Garns	"	"	

[*State Library, Adams Papers.*]

A Muster Role of Capt Reuben Ferriss's Company of Rangers and the Sum of there Bounty N° 4 Novr 30th 1757

[*State Library, Adams Papers.*]

CAPT. PUTNAM'S COMPANY.

Israel Putnam [of Pomfret], Captain.

He was in command of a company of rangers at Fort Edward in Oct. 1757, and was at the fort Nov. 10, 1757.

[*State Library, War 7, 132, 135.*]

He was in service at Fort Edward during the winter of 1757–1758.

[*Humphreys' Life of Putnam.*]

CAPT. DURKE'S COMPANY.

John Durke [of Norwich], Captain.

He was in command of a company of rangers at Fort Edward in Oct. 1757, and was at the fort Nov. 10, 1757.

[*State Library, War 7, 133-135.*]

MISCELLANEOUS.

CAPT. PUTNAM'S COMPANY.

[Israel] Putnam [of Pomfret] appointed Captain of a company of rangers, July 5, 1757.
[*Rufus Putnam's Journal.*]

He appears to have been in command of a company of rangers as early as May 31.
[*General Orders of 1757.*]

CAPT. SEFFORD'S COMPANY.

—— Sefford appointed Captain of a company of rangers, July 5, 1757.
[*Rufus Putnam's Journal.*]

CAPT. BURNHAM'S COMPANY.

Michael Burnham [of Middletown] appointed Captain, May, 1757.
Giles Hall [of Middletown] appointed Lieutenant, May, 1757.

The Assembly directed the purchase and equiping of a vessel to be manned by one hundred men, including officers. The vessel thus put in service was the brigantine Tartar. Permission was given that after Nov. 10 the vessel "may be improved to distress his Majesty's enemies and to protect our trade in the West Indies." During the winter cruise no wages were to be allowed the officers or men.
[*Colonial Records.*]

CAPT. HURLBURT'S COMPANY.

Titus Hurlburt of New London was directed by the Assembly in February, 1757, to enlist twenty men for service in the battery at New London. The men to be commanded by Capt. Hurlburt "or such other captain as may be appointed." The men were dismissed in October.
[*Colonial Records.*]

CAPT. BURNHAM'S COMPANY.

Micheal Burnham, mentioned as Captain of a company in August.

CAPT. WARD'S COMPANY.

Samuel Ward, mentioned as a Captain of a company in August.
[*State Library, War 7, 104.*]

CAPT. WHITMORE'S COMPANY.

Caleb Whitmore, mentioned as Captain of a company in August.
[*State Library, War 7, 104.*]

CAPT. WARNER'S COMPANY.

John Warner, mentioned as Captain of a company in August.
[*State Library, War 7, 104.*]

CAPT. STOCKING'S COMPANY.

George Stocking, mentioned as Captain of a company in August.
[*State Library, War 7, 104.*]

CAPT. ALVORD'S COMPANY.

Jonathan Alvord, mentioned as Captain of a company in August.
[*State Library, War 7, 104.*]

CAPT. GOODRICH'S COMPANY.

Jeremiah Goodrich, mentioned as Captain of a company in August.
[*State Library, War 7, 104.*]

CAPT. MERVIN'S COMPANY.

Matthew Mervin of Lyme, mentioned as Captain of a company in August.
[*State Library, War 7, 54.*]

Eleazar Doane Served from March 26 to October 15.
[*State Library, War 7, 127.*]

Lieut. James Nichols and Quartermaster Richard Seymour, both of Hartford, went into service in August.
[*State Library, War 7, 261.*]

Timothy Peck Jr. of New Haven was in service.
[*State Library, War 6, 281.*]

Charles Burnham was in service.
[*State Library, War 7, 121.*]

Lot Lockwood was in service.
[*State Library, War 7, 122.*]

Paul Kent, Oliver Kent, Martin Breunson, John Lensey and Noah Cole were in service.
[*State Library, War 7, 120.*]

John Brown a soldier died of the small pox.
[*State Library, War 7, 244.*]

John Williams of Norwich was appointed Commissary to received stores at Albany.
[*State Library, War 7, 214.*]

Benjn Humphrevile of New Haven was in service under command of Col. Whiting and was by him appointed Quartermaster at No. 4.
[*State Library, War 7, 256.*]

For the autographs of a number of members of the companies of Capt. Abner Barker, Capt. Benjamin Day, Capt. Isaac Coit and Capt. John Carpenter see War vol. 7, nos. 123–126.
[*State Library.*]

Charles Wright, David Pease and Stephen Markham were in Capt. Ammie Trumble's company. The two last named were of Enfield.
[*State Library, War 7, 252, 254.*]

Moses Seymour and Ebenezer Benton Jr. drew bullets preparatory to going into service.
[*State Library, War 7, 54.*]

ADDENDA AND ERRATA.

A Muster Role of men Mustered and Excepted By the Muster Master Belonging To Capt Andrew Ward. And the Date of there Inlistment And Sum of there Bounty &c.

[The names following appear on this roll in addition to the names printed on pages 195, 196.]

	Time of Inlisting	Time of Being Mustred
Zachariah Marvin Serg^t	March 26	March 29
Tho^m Francis	18	"
Tho^m Francis	28	"
Zipron Dudley	"	"
James Duglas	11	"

[Indorsed] Capt Andrew Ward Copy
Luman Ward Drum
Noah Norton
1755
James Cooley
Jos. Cooley

[*State Library, Adams Papers.*]

[The date, 1755, indorsd on this roll is undoubtedly an error for 1757.]

Thomas Gallop, First Lieutenant in Capt. Putnam's company, 1756, was of Plainfield.

[*Colonial Records.*]

Serj. Story Gott was in service in 1756.

[*State Library, War 7, 121.*]

Nathaniel Porter, page 3, was of Lebanon. See page 117.

David Holmes of Woodstock served as doctor for 7 weeks beginning Nov. 1, 1755.

[*War 6, 232.*]

Doctors Bliss and Warner were the only doctors at Lake George from Conn. Nov. 1, 1755.

[*War 6, 234.*]

Matthias Smith of Wethersfield, late of Lebanon, in Nathan Whiting's company, was wounded at Lake George in 1755.

[*War 6, 241.*]

Adam Hinman of Woodbury in Capt. Benjamin Hinman's company was wounded Sep. 8, 1755.

[*War 6, 253.*]

ADDENDA AND ERRATA.

George Crary, p. 100, was of Preston.
[*War 7, 269.*]

John Wheatley was Lieut. in Joseph Storrs company in July, 1756.
[*War 7, 270.*]

John Raymond, serving in 1756, probably the First Lieut. in Stephen Lee's company, was of New London.
[*War 7, 274.*]

Elisha Waterman of Norwich, a Lieutenant at Fort Edward in the winter of 1755–56, was captured and carried to Canada.
[*War 7, 259.*]

Asa Richardson, p. 96, was of Lebanon.
[*War 7, 268.*]

Ebenezer Dyar, Lieut. in Street Hall's company in 1756 and Fort Major in Jonathan Bagley's regiment, is described as of Canterbury. He was captured April 21, 1756, was carried across the ocean and died in England in 1757.
[*War 7, 246.*]

Page 50. Lieut.-Col. Ward's Company, second line, for Joseph Wilford, First Lieutenand, read Ichabod Scranton, First Lieutenant.

Page 55. Capt. Hanford's Company, second line, for Joseph Hoit [of Stamford], First Lieutenant, read Josiah Starr, First Lieutenant.

Page 59. Capt. Buckingham's Company, third line, for Nehemiah Dickinson, Second Lieutenant, read Moses Dickerson, Second Lieutenant.

Page 92. "The great part" of the men ordered raised in October 1756 had been raised when letters received by the Governor from the Earl of Loudon ordered the companies not to march, whereupon the men were dismissed by order of the General Assembly.
[*Colonial Records.*]

Page 150. Capt. Waterbury's Company, twenty-third line, for Ebenezer Crissey read Ebenezer Crissey.

Page 220. Capt. Woodruff's Company, third line, for Benjamin Ferm [of Milford], Lieutenant, read Benjamin Fenn [of Milford], Lieutenant.

INDEX.

Aacanes, William, 256.
Abbe (Abbee, Abbey, Abbie, Abby).
Abbe, Abner, 114, 116.
Abbe, Eleazer, 84.
Abbe, Ezekiel, 27, 114, 116, 242.
Abbe, Jeremiah, 184.
Abbe, John, Jr., 9, 69.
Abbe, Nehemiah, 239.
Abbot (Abbet, Abbott, Abott, Abutt).
Abbot, Abel, 58.
Abbot, Abijah, 56, 138, 139.
Abbot, Caleb, 198.
Abbot, George, 37.
Abot, Israel, 222.
Abbot, John, 39, 173, 175, 251.
Abbot, John, Jr., 215.
Abbot, Price, 138.
Abbot, Sela, 206.
Abbot, Seth, 251.
Abbot, Thomas, 42, 198.
Abell, Elisha, 40.
Abell, Joshua, 40, 41.
Abell, Simeon, 40, 236.
Abernathy, William, 93, 130.
Aborns, Samuel, 215.
Ackley (Acherly, Ackly, Acly).
Ackley, Abraham, 203.
Ackley, Attar, 188.
Ackley, Benjamin, 72.
Ackley, Elijah, 202.
Ackley, Felix, 217.
Ackley, Hezekiah, 42.
Ackley, Nathaniel, 42, 203.
Ackley, Nathaniel, 4th, 256.
Ackley, Nicholas, 188.
Ackley, Stephen, 205, 259.
Acoat, Charles, 144.
Acorn, John, 251.
Adams (Adam, Addams, Adem, Adoms).
Adams, Abraham, 138, 139, 178.
Adams, Abraham, 179.

Adams, Abner, 208.
Adams, Ben, 211.
Adams, Benjamin, 63, 102.
Adams, Benjamin, 2d, 104.
Adams, Daniel, 105, 154, 156, 177, 178.
Adams, David, 167, 201, 211.
Adams, Elijah, 35, 197.
Adams, Elisha, 198.
Adams, Ephraim, 5, 7.
Adams, James, 32, 208.
Adams, Jesse, 99.
Adams, Joel, 6, 93, 95, 96, 168.
Adams, John, 6, 151, 152.
Adams, John, 2d, 211.
Adams, Joshua, 29, 94.
Adams, Richard, 245.
Adams, Samuel, 15, 16, 48, 96, 120, 121, 131, 132, 168, 170, 211, 235, 240, 244, 248, 254.
Adams, Samuel, Jr., 158.
Adams, Simeon, 62.
Adams, Thomas, 236.
Adams, Timothy, 105.
Adkins, Daniel, 50.
Adkins, Zealous, 55.
Adkins, see Atkin.
Adley, Benjamin, 213.
Adsitt, Stephen, 44.
Agard, Hezekiah, 147.
Agard, James, 57.
Ainsworth (Answorth).
Ainsworth, Samuel, 240, 244.
Akerly, Samuel, 33.
Akin, Samuel, 213.
Akins, William, 203.
Albany, 69, 71, 75, 76, 104, 105, 106, 112, 113, 114, 129, 138, 139, 140, 154, 155, 156, 157, 159, 160, 162, 265.
Albert, Nathanale, 105.
Alcock (Allcok), Jesse, 54, 222.
Alcorn, Jonathan, 84.

Alcorn, Thomas, 84.
Alcott, Jedediah, 103.
Alcott, Simeon, 39.
Alcott, Solomon, 43.
Alcy, Benjamin, 27.
Alden (Aldon), Ezra, 198.
Alden, Walter, 250.
Alden, William, 250.
Alderman (Olderman).
Alderman, Elihu, 102, 211.
Alderman, Elijah, 35, 168, 170.
Alderman, Thomas, 105.
Alderman, Timothy, 63, 105, 106.
Aldrige, Jonathan, 208.
Alexander, William, 154.
Alford (Alfird, Alvord).
Alford, Elijah, 35, 211.
Alford, Job, 14, 239.
Alford, John, 211.
Alford, Jonathan, 264.
Alford, Josiah, 245.
Alford, Nathaniel, Jr., 211.
Alger, David, 40.
Allard, Daniel, 242.
Allerton, Jonathan, 242.
Allen (Alin, Allens, Allin).
Allen, Amos, 20, 77.
Allen, Benjamin, 38, 134, 135, 159, 160.
Allen, Benjamin, Jr., 215.
Allen, Cæsar, 138.
Allen, Caleb, 245.
Allen, Daniel, 248.
Allen, Daniel, Jr., 254.
Allen, Ebenezer, 140.
Allen, Ebenezer, Jr., 140.
Allen, Ephestus, 211.
Allen, Ephraim, 223.
Allen, Ethan, 247.
Allen, George, 208.
Allen, Gideon, 193, 260.
Allen, John, 206, 211.
Allen, Jonathan, 95, 211, 243.
Allen, Joseph, 46, 87.
Allen, Joseph, Jr., 211
Allen, Noah, 209.
Allen, Obediah, 186.
Allen, Reuben, 146.
Allen, Thomas, 37, 201.
Allen, Timothy, 204.
Allen, William, 40, 78.
Allen, see Allyn.
Alley (Ally, Aly).
Alley, Benjamin, 121, 172, 260.
Alling, Amos, 31.
Alling, Charles, 30.
Alling, Christopher, 31, 252.
Alling, Josiah, 252.

Alling, Samuel, 250.
Alling, Thomas, 250.
Alling, William, 250.
Allyn (Alyn), 135.
Allyn, Abel, 230.
Allyn, Amos, 31.
Allyn, Benjamin, 38, 39, 85, 134, 135, 136.
Allyn, Christopher, 31.
Allyn, Ephistian, 39.
Allyn, Ephraim, 120.
Allyn, John, 215.
Allyn, Jonah, 85, 135.
Allyn, Jonh, 228.
Allyn, Josiah, 102.
Allyn, Phinehas, 42.
Allyn, Samuel, 102.
Allyn, Samuel, Jr., 197.
Allyn, Titus, 235.
Allyn, William, 197.
Allyn, see Allen.
Alsworth, Philip, 240.
Alwood, Ruben, 132.
Ambler, John, 156.
Ambler, Stephen, 150.
Ambleton, Peter, 123.
Ames, Amos, 27.
Ames, David, 240.
Ames, John, 37, 100, 188, 236.
Ames, Nathan, 236.
Ames, Robert, 236.
Amity, 252.
Ammidown (Amedown, Amidown).
Ammidown, Ithamar, 36.
Ammidown, John, 133.
Amos (Amous), David, 190.
Amos, Job, 69.
Amos, Sampson, 25, 137, 182.
Amsbury, John, 175.
Amsden, Elisha, 242.
Anable (Anabel, Annabel, Annable).
Anable, Ancel, 148.
Anable, Barnabas, 248, 254.
Anderson, John, 208.
Anderson, Samuel, 236.
Andover, 87, 161, 255.
Andrews, Asahel, 173.
Andrews, Ephraim, 69, 252.
Andrews, Gideon, 252.
Andrews, Jacob, 22, 112.
Andrews, Nathan, 65, 69.
Andrews, Nathaniel, 193, 260.
Andrews, Oliver, 188.
Andrews, Solomon, 111, 112.
Andrews, William, 193.
Andrus (Andres, Andros).

INDEX. 271

Andrus, Abel, 210.
Andrus, Abraham, 201.
Andrus, Amos, 102.
Andrus, Asael, 102, 175.
Andrus, Ashbel, 246.
Andrus, Bartholomew, 235.
Andrus, Benjamin, 210, 230.
Andrus, Daniel, 49, 235.
Andrus, David, 129.
Andrus, Eber, 246.
Andrus, Elihu, 63, 130, 131, 168.
Andrus, Elisha, 130, 230.
Andrus, Epaphras, 210.
Andrus, Ephraim, 67, 105.
Andrus, Ithamar, 11.
Andrus, Jacob, 111, 181.
Andrus, Job, 14.
Andrus, John, 65, 67, 241.
Andrus, Joseph, 154.
Andrus, Laban, 48.
Andrus, Moses, 235.
Andrus, Nathan, 67.
Andrus, Nathaniel, 127.
Andrus, Noah, 235.
Andrus, Roger, 14.
Andrus, Silas, 230.
Andrus, Stephen, 210.
Andrus, Thomas, 181, 190.
Andrus, Timothy, 35.
Andrus, William, 13, 49, 168, 170.
Andrus, William, Jr., 229.
Angevine (Angavine, Angivine, Anguvine).
Angevine, Anthony, 171.
Angevine, Lewis, 154, 156, 177, 178, 260.
Angevine, Zachariah, 156.
Anoguin, James, 110.
Anthony, Thomas, 23, 114, 116, 186.
Apanatha, John, 230.
Apes, Samuel, 108.
Apes, William, 191.
Apley, Ezekiel, 100.
Apley, James, 101.
Apley, John, 40.
Arant, Daniel, 229.
Archer, Benjamin, 205.
Archer, Josi, 205.
Ardnel, Joseph, 227.
Ardua, John, 45.
Armstrong, Daniel, 137.
Armstrong, Ezekiel, 236.
Armstrong, John, 191.
Armstrong, Labeus, 236.
Arnold, Benedict, 236.
Arnold, Benjamin, 118.
Arnold, Hezekiah, 241.

Arnold, Isaac, 138.
Arnold, James, 24, 156.
Arnold, John, 59, 177, 178.
Arnold, Joshua, 236.
Arnold, Robert, 220.
Ashbow (Ashpo), George, 11.
Ashbow, John, 111, 113, 182.
Ashbow, Nathaniel, 32, 40, 78, 141.
Ashford, 132, 152, 199.
Ashley, Jonathan, 168, 170.
Ashley, Samuel, 248.
Ashley, Samuel, Jr., 254.
Ashman, Amaziah, 32, 33, 208.
Ashman, Elnathan, 32, 140.
Ask, Thomas, 151, 152, 180.
Aslen, Thomas, 111.
Atchinson, Barzeliel, 216.
Atchinson, John, 93, 95.
Ates, Abraham, 6.
Atherton, Joseph, 238.
Atkin, Joseph, 137.
Atkin, see Adkins.
Atwater, Elihu, 50, 235.
Atwater, Enos, 235.
Atwater, James, 30, 171.
Atwater, Jeremiah, 30, 231.
Atwater, Phineas, 49.
Atwell, Benjamin, Jr., 233.
Atwell, Hezekiah, 72, 182.
Atwell, John, 67, 219.
Atwell, Paul, 66, 67, 69, 105, 106.
Atwell, Thomas, 233.
Atwood, Hezekiah, 210.
Atwood, John, 66.
Atwood, Ruben, 69.
Atwood, Thomas, 69, 249.
Atwood, Thomas, Jr., 254.
Aucom, see Occom.
Austin (Astin, Aston, Austen, Austion, Auston).
Austin, Bailey, 29, 227, 243.
Austin, Caleb, 16, 97, 98, 183.
Austin, David, 77, 139, 140, 171, 230.
Austin, Daniel, 245.
Austin, Edmond, 235.
Austin, Elihu, 233.
Austin, George, 52, 240.
Austin, Jesse, 95.
Austin, Job, 216.
Austin, John, 79, 100, 231.
Austin, Lockwood, 150, 152.
Austin, Moses, 55.
Austin, Robert, 79.
Austin, Samuel, 30, 235.
Austin, Thomas, 240, 244.
Averett (Averit), Israel, 222.

Averett, Jeremiah, 116.
Averid, Ruben, 199.
Averill (Avrill), James, 232.
Averill, Ruben, 199.
Avery (Avry), Amos, 232.
Avery, Andrew, 41.
Avery, Benjamin, 107, 236.
Avery, Charles, 107, 190.
Avery, Christopher, 10, 214, 232.
Avery, Elias, 70, 190.
Avery, James, 3d, 197.
Avery, John, 10, 45, 107, 250.
Avery, Jonathan, 7, 236.
Avery, Lethon, 197.
Avery, Micah, 135.
Avery, Peter, 151, 152.
Avery, Samuel, 10, 40.
Avery, Simeon, 197.
Avery, Urias, 143.

Babcock, Amos, 191.
Babcock, James, 191.
Babcock, John, 107, 214.
Babcock, Jonas, 10.
Babcock, Jonathan, 12.
Bacheller, Reuben, 27, 252.
Back, Daniel, 10, 107.
Backus (Bachus, Backes), 18.
Backus, Andrew, 40.
Backus, Asa, 236.
Backus, Ozias, 236.
Backus, Sylvanus, 20, 127, 248, 254.
Bacon (Baken), 18.
Bacon, Barnabas, 19.
Bacon, Benjamin, 242.
Bacon, Daniel, 243.
Bacon, John, 144, 145.
Bacon, Jonathan, 243.
Bacon, Joseph, 228.
Bacon, Nata, 79.
Bacon, Nathaniel, 36.
Bacon, Penuel, 206.
Bacon, Samuel, 55.
Bacon, Stephen, 81.
Bacon, Zacheus, 210.
Bacss, Benj., 139.
Badcock, Abel, 144.
Badger, Barzaliel, 17, 19.
Badger, John, 49.
Badlack (Badlock), James, 17, 19.
Badlack, John, 133.
Bagger, Daniel, 198.
Bagley, Jonathan, 76, 267.
Bagley, Stephen, 121.
Bagneak, Daniel, 118.
Bagonet, Simon, 74.
Baguet, Simon, 72.

Bailey, (Baily, Baley, Balie, Bayle, Bayles, Bayley, Bayly, Beailey).
Bailey, Aaron, 118.
Bailey, Abel, 197.
Bailey, David, 213, 214.
Bailey, Ezekiel, 118, 160.
Bailey, Gideon, 59.
Bailey, Hezekiah, 227.
Bailey, Isaac, 213, 250.
Bailey, Jasper, 102, 177, 179, 184, 261.
Bailey, Joseph, 137.
Bailey, Joshua, 82, 148, 149.
Bailey, Nathan, 227.
Bailey, Samuel, 22, 65, 66, 68, 193, 195, 238.
Bailey, Samuel, Jr., 68, 69.
Bailey, William, 195, 250, 260.
Baker (Backer, Backor, Bakor).
Baker, Benjamin, 168.
Baker, Daniel, 215.
Baker, Ebenezer, 201.
Baker, Elisha, 197.
Baker, Ephraim, 218.
Baker, Ezekiel, 204.
Baker, John, 249.
Baker, Joseph, 230.
Baker, Joshua, Jr., 40.
Baker, Remember, 55, 120, 121, 219.
Baker, Robart, 133.
Baker, Samuel, 146.
Baker, Stephen, 16, 97, 98.
Baker, Victor, 177, 178.
Balch, Verrin, 248, 254.
Balcom, John, 254.
Balcom, John, Jr., 248.
Balden, William, 219.
Baldin, David, 65.
Balding, James, 182.
Balding, Josiah, 45.
Baldon, Joseph, 240.
Baldwin (Baldwen).
Baldwin, Abraham, 220.
Baldwin, Amos, 59.
Baldwin, Andrew, 72, 73, 75, 220.
Baldwin, Asa, 249, 254.
Baldwin, Benjamin, 45, 225, 250.
Baldwin, Caleb, 118.
Baldwin, Daniel, 249.
Baldwin, Daniel, Jr., 225, 254.
Baldwin, David, 65, 66, 104, 106, 160, 200.
Baldwin, Ebenezer, 236, 250, 255.
Baldwin, Elias, 200.
Baldwin, Eliezer, 49.
Baldwin, Elihu, 220.
Baldwin, Ephraim, 99, 219.

INDEX.

Baldwin, George, 223.
Baldwin, Hezekiah, 28, 87, 124, 185.
Baldwin, Israel, 58, 225.
Baldwin, James, 193.
Baldwin, John, 214.
Baldwin, Jonathan, 247.
Baldwin, Joseph, 244.
Baldwin, Josiah, 32.
Baldwin, Justice, 171.
Baldwin, Moses, 212.
Baldwin, Nathan, 28.
Baldwin, Phinehas, 60, 225.
Baldwin, Samuel, 72, 75, 138, 225, 247.
Baldwin, Silas, 104, 167.
Baldwin, Silvester, 214.
Baldwin, Solomon, 220.
Baldwin, Thaddeus, 238.
Baldwin, Theo, 252.
Baldwin, Thomas, 98.
Baldwin, see Balden, Baldin, Balding, Baldon, Baulding, Bolden, Boldwin.
Ball, Allien, 226.
Ball, Gideon, 228, 243.
Ball, John, 27.
Ball, Joseph, 66, 68, 127.
Ball, Moses, 63.
Ballard, Jeremiah, 211.
Bancroft, Benjamin, 91, 93, 95, 96.
Bancroft, Thomas, 230.
Bangs, Lemuel, 238.
Baning, Benjamin, 202.
Banks, David, 85.
Banks, Ebenezer, 201.
Banks, William, 234.
Barber (Barbar, Barberer, Barbur).
Barber, Abel, 230.
Barber, Eldad, 168, 170.
Barber, Isaac, 63, 105, 106.
Barber, Joel, 230.
Barber, Jonathan, 230.
Barber, Moses, 135.
Barber, Noah, 85, 135.
Barber, Samuel, Jr., 245.
Barber, Shadrach, 211.
Bard, Robert, 216.
Bardin (Barden) Abram, 228, 243.
Bardin, Seth, 228, 243.
Barges, Joshua, 198.
Barker, Abner, 198, 253, 265.
Barker, Ebenezer, 225.
Barker, Jacob, 60.
Barker, Jared, 225.
Barker, John, 81.
Barker, Joseph, 225.

Barker, Oliver, 6, 94, 95, 96.
Barker, Parpeton, 59.
Barker, Thomas, 32, 77.
Barker, Uzal, 193.
Barlow (Berlow), Daniel, 56.
Barly (Barley), Daniel, 238.
Barly, David, 150, 151.
Barnard, Dan, 82.
Barnard, Jonathan, 12, 128, 129.
Barnard, Samuel, 84, 215, 224.
Barnes (Barns), Abel, 32, 199.
Barnes, Abijah, 55.
Barnes, Abner, 103, 160.
Barnes, Amos, 147, 199, 234.
Barnes Asa, 54, 152, 154, 235.
Barnes, Benjamin, 157, 223.
Barnes, Charles, 114, 116.
Barnes, Daniel, 124, 140, 147, 194, 222, 234.
Barnes, David, 152, 235.
Barnes, Elijah, 114, 116.
Barnes, Gershom, 253.
Barnes, Gideon, 152, 243.
Barnes, Israel, 140, 159.
Barnes, Jabez, 70, 71.
Barnes, John, 26, 60, 171.
Barnes, Joseph, 156, 158.
Barnes, Josiah, 239.
Barnes, Moses, 223.
Barnes, Nathaniel, 208.
Barnes, Seth, 252.
Barnes, Simeon, 81.
Barnes, Solomon, 114, 116, 234.
Barnes, Thaddius, 252.
Barnes, Thomas, 62.
Barnes, William, 134, 136, 226.
Barnite, William, 180.
Barnum (Barnam).
Barnum, David, 57, 124, 157, 177, 178, 218.
Barnum, Ebenezer, 156, 158.
Barnum, Francis, 238.
Barnum, Jehiel, 57, 124.
Barnum, John, 237.
Barnum, Matthew, 56, 238.
Barnum, Nathan, 226.
Barnum, Samuel, 238.
Barnum, Thomas, 3d, 28.
Barrall, John, 146.
Barrett (Barit, Barrat, Barritt, Barrot).
Barrett, Bartholomew, 140, 227, 243.
Barrett, David, 99, 243.
Barrett, Eliezer, 57.
Barrett, Elijah, 39.
Barrett, Jacob, 99.
Barrett, James, 193.

Barrett, John, 32, 54, 120, 121, 193, 204, 242.
Barrett, Joseph, 54.
Barrett, Samson, 99.
Barrett, Solomon, 54, 222.
Barron (Barran), Nathan, 10.
Barronet, William, 109, 110.
Barrows, Amos, Jr., 197.
Barrows, Elisha, 249.
Barrows, Elisha, Jr., 254.
Barrows, Isaac, 255.
Barrows, James, 197.
Barrows, Lemuel, Jr., 197.
Barrows, Noah, 243.
Barrows, Samuel, 38.
Barse, Joseph, 138.
Barse, Josiah, 226.
Barsley, Neamiah, 139.
Bartholomew (Bartholomu, Bartholomy).
Bartholomew, Eleazer, 261.
Bartholomew, Eliezer, 194.
Bartholomew, Elezer, 147.
Bartholomew, Elizur, 14.
Bartholomew, Enos, 12, 96, 98.
Bartholomew, Jacob, 246.
Bartholomew, Josiah, 225.
Bartholomew, Joso, 59.
Bartholomew, Levi, 202.
Bartlett (Bartlitt), Abrham, 212.
Bartlett, Charles, 70, 71, 131, 186.
Bartlett, Gershom, 215.
Bartlett, John, 212.
Bartlett, Joseph, 22.
Bartlett, Samuel, 50, 212, 215.
Bartlett, Timothy, 86.
Barton, Andrew, 140, 141.
Bartram (Barteram, Bartrum).
Bartram, James, 201.
Bartram, Job, 110.
Bartram, John, 138, 139.
Bartram, Paul, 201.
Barzlee, Jesse, 58.
Bascom (Bascum, Baskum).
Bascom, Elihu, 97, 160.
Bascom, John, 250, 257.
Bass, Benjamin, 56.
Bass, Samuel, 97.
Bass, Zebulon, 110, 251.
Bassett (Baset), Amos, 220.
Bassett, David, 231.
Bassett, Joel, 30, 231.
Bassett, John, 177, 178.
Bassett, Josiah, 204.
Bassett, Stephen, 231.
Bassett, William, 128.
Bateman, Elezar, 37.
Baterson, Joseph, 180.

Bates, Abraham, 150, 151, 179.
Bates, Daniel, 49, 118, 119, 226.
Bates, Ebenezer, 109, 179.
Bates, Elias, 235.
Bates, Henry, 171.
Bates, Isaac, 140, 202.
Bates, Jabez, 118.
Bates, Job, 213.
Bates, John, 42.
Bates, Jona, 227.
Bates, Oliver, 223.
Bates, Stephen, 222.
Bates, Thadeus, 56.
Bates, William, 12.
Bates, see Beats.
Batinan, John, 208.
Battiss, Thomas, 244.
Baulding, William, 16.
Bawden, Thomas, 82.
Baxter, Aaron, 257.
Baxter, Frances, 94, 96.
Baxter, Simon, 137.
Baxter, Thomas, 214.
Bea, Isack, 151.
Beach (Beech).
Beach, Aaron, 93, 122, 129.
Beach, Asall, 235.
Beach, Barnius, 199.
Beach, Daniel, 155.
Beach, Ebenezer, 30, 77, 126.
Beach, Edmund, 247.
Beach, Elihu, 103.
Beach, Elisha, 205.
Beach, Ephraim, 233.
Beach, Hezekiah, 239.
Beach, John, 188, 224.
Beach, Lazarus, 201.
Beach, Moses, 50.
Beach, Nathan, 155, 156, 177, 178, 260.
Beach, Phinehas, 65, 66, 69, 192.
Beach, Richard, 155.
Beach, Samuel, 179, 199, 252.
Beach, Seth, 137.
Beach, Thomas, 221.
Beach, Titus, 219.
Beadlee, Enos, 155.
Beardsley (Beardslee, Bearsley).
Beardsley, Andrew, 193.
Beardsley, Daniel, 154.
Beardsley, Ebenezer, 200.
Beardsley, Enos, 159.
Beardsley, Ephraim, 226.
Beardsley, Gideon, 226.
Beardsley, Israel, 200.
Beardsley, James, 156, 159.
Beardsley, Jesse, 225.
Beardsley, Joseph, 200.

INDEX. 275

Beardsley, Joshua, 200.
Beardsley, Serajah, 226.
Bearllee, Nehemiah, 56.
Bears, David, 110, 111.
Bears, Elnathan, 251.
Bears, Josia, 102.
Bears, see Beers.
Beats, Daniel, 60.
Beats, Jabez, 196.
Beats, Jonathan, 60.
Beay, Peter, 61.
Bebee, Asahel, 243.
Bebee, Daniel, 57.
Bebee, Samuel, 181, 255.
Bebee, see Beebe.
Beckiat, William, 132.
Beckley (Beckly), Benjamin, 210.
Beckley, John, 186.
Beckley, Silas, 186.
Beckwith, Abel, 41.
Beckwith, Abner, 196, 260.
Beckwith, Csreal, 137.
Beckwith, Elisha, 42, 145, 203.
Beckwith, George, 3.
Beckwith, Ichabod, 41.
Beckwith, John, 100.
Beckwith, Jonathan, 188.
Beckwith, Joseph, 203.
Beckwith, Martin, 118.
Beckwith, Merven, 222.
Beckwith, Philip, 41.
Beckwith, Timothy, 233.
Beckwith, Samuel, 41.
Bedlack, John, 35.
Beebe, Asael, 228.
Beebe, Bonijus, 233.
Beebe, Caleb, 203.
Beebe, Daniel, 206.
Beebe, David, 118.
Beebe, Gideon, 41.
Beebe, James, 233.
Beebe, John, 214.
Beebe, Jonathan, 192, 194, 238.
Beebe, Joub, 233.
Beebe, Nathan, 203.
Beebe, Richard, 118.
Beebe, Samuel, 205.
Beebe, Simeon, 223.
Beebe, Stephen, 53.
Beebe, Walter, 233.
Beebe, Zera, 193.
Beebe, see Bebee.
Beecher (Beacher), Abel, 231.
Beecher, Nathaniel, 225.
Beers (Beears, Berrs).
Beers, Abiel, 200.
Beers, Daniel, 201.
Beers, David, 30.

Beers, Jesse, 13, 180, 261.
Beers, Stephen, 200.
Beers, see Bears.
Belcher, Samuel, 135, 220.
Belden (Belding, Beldon).
Belden, Ebenezer, 8, 143.
Belden, Elisha, 186.
Belden, John, 14, 209.
Belden, Stephen, 230.
Belden, William, 251.
Belknap, Ebenezer, 39, 134, 136, 168, 170.
Belknap, Jesse, 122, 168, 170.
Bell, John, 152, 154, 222.
Bellemey, James, 195.
Bellows, Daniel, 69, 70, 71.
Bellows, Samuel, 32, 33.
Bement (Beaman, Beeman, Bemant, Bemont).
Bement, Ebenezer, 206.
Bement, Edmund, 211, 239.
Bement, David, 64, 96.
Bement, Dennis, 38.
Bement, Jonathan, 134, 173.
Bement, Joseph, 29, 39.
Bement, Judah, 211.
Bement, Park, 58.
Benedict (Benedick, Bendict, Benidick, Benidict, Benidik).
Benedict, Aaron, 218.
Benedict, Benjamin, 237.
Benedict, Bushnal, 204.
Benedict, Daniel, 251.
Benedict, Elijah, 251.
Benedict, Elisha, 55, 177, 179.
Benedict, Ezra, 225.
Benedict, Francis, 238.
Benedict, Israel, 56.
Benedict, James, 238.
Benedict, John, 156, 225.
Benedict, John, 3d, 156.
Benedict, Jonathan, 13, 225, 251.
Benedict, Joseph, 55, 138, 139.
Benedict, Lemuel, 156, 238.
Benedict, Matthew, 61.
Benedict, Nathaniel, 237.
Benedict, Noble, 177, 179.
Benedict, Samuel, 251.
Benedict, Seth, 252.
Benedick, Silus, 238.
Benedick, Theophilus, 238.
Benedict, Zadok, 238.
Benham, Eliezer, 48.
Benham, John, 253.
Benham, Joseph, 194, 260.
Benham, Nathan, 120, 193, 261.
Benham, Samuel, 246.
Benham, Shadrak, 222.

Benjamin, Abel, 236.
Benjamin, Caleb, 10, 84, 173, 175.
Benjamin, Ebenezer, 100, 232.
Benjamin, Elnathan, 200.
Benjamin, John, 8.
Benjamin, Joseph, 83.
Benjamin, Josiah, 83.
Bennett (Benett, Bennet, Bennit).
Bennett, Abraham, 56.
Bennett, Benjamin, 200.
Bennett, Charles, 154.
Bennett, Daniel, 154, 221.
Bennett, Daniel, Jr., 214.
Bennett, David, 94.
Bennett, Deliverance, 251.
Bennett, Ebenezer, 201.
Bennett, Francis, 35.
Bennett, Gabrel, 241.
Bennett, Gershom, 154, 156.
Bennett, Hezekiah, 221.
Bennett, Hink, 250.
Bennett, Isaac, 221, 254.
Bennett, Jacob, 83.
Bennett, Jeremiah, 10, 11, 240.
Bennett, John, 41.
Bennett, Josiah, 182.
Bennett, Lewis, 154, 156, 221.
Bennett, Nathan, 182.
Bennett, Nehemiah, 179.
Bennett, Samuel, 16, 72, 73, 75.
Bennett, Stephen, 190, 192.
Bennett, Thaddeus, 178, 261.
Bennett, William, 221.
Bentley, James, 140.
Bentley, John, 218.
Bentley, William, 137.
Benton, Barnabas, 239.
Benton, Caleb, 23.
Benton, David, 227, 243.
Benton, Eber, 51.
Benton, Ebenezer, Jr., 265.
Benton, Edward, 195.
Benton, Elias, 27, 144.
Benton, Elihu, 51.
Benton, Isaac, 247.
Benton, James, 50, 144.
Benton, Jered, 212.
Benton, John, 229.
Benton, Joseph, 227, 243.
Benton, Josiah, 85, 195.
Benton, Medad, 11, 232.
Benton, Nathaniel, 224.
Benton, Samuel, 85, 247.
Benton, Samuel, Jr., 215.
Benton, Stephen, 51.
Benton, William, 215.
Berry, Diamond, 235.
Berry, Ephraim, 146.

Berry, Jonathan, 57, 218.
Bettee, John, 100.
Betts, Benjamin, 251.
Betts, Daniel, 251.
Betts, David, 251.
Betts, James, 218.
Betts, James, Jr., 206.
Betts, John, 252.
Betts, Nathan, 61.
Betts, Peter, 242.
Betts, Thaddeus, 251.
Betts, Thomas, 240.
Betts, Timothy, 138.
Bevins, John, 81.
Bewel, see Buell.
Bibbins, Amos, 20, 183.
Bibbins, Ebenezer, 19, 97, 98.
Bibbins, Elijah, 248, 254.
Bickerstaff (Beekerstaff).
Bickerstaff, Robert, 12.
Bicknell (Briknal), Ebeneser, 132.
Bicknell, Timothy, 46.
Bicknell, William, 46.
Bicknell, Zechariah, 70, 71, 248, 253.
Bicknell, see Bignal.
Bidwell, David, 227, 243.
Bidwell, Jonathan, 131.
Bidwell, Mose, 193.
Bidwell, Samuel, 130, 210.
Bigelow (Bigalow, Biggelow).
Bigelow, Isaac, 52, 148, 149.
Bigelow, Isaac, Jr., 86.
Bigelow, John, 205.
Bigelow, John, Jr., 259.
Bigelow, Joseph, 236.
Bigelow, Titus, 229.
Bignal, Richard, 29, 141, 227, 243.
Bignal, see Bicknell.
Bilbowa, John, 208.
Biles, Charles, 16, 79, 101.
Bill (Bills), Beriah, 40, 117, 236.
Bill, Charles, 161.
Bill, Ebenezer, 117.
Bill, Ebenezer, Jr., 19, 161.
Bill, Elijah, 250, 255.
Bill, James, 137, 213.
Bill, John, 47, 56, 117, 161, 242, 250.
Bill, Jonathan, 82, 132, 161.
Bill, Joshua, 18, 19, 46, 96, 161, 250, 255.
Bill, Solomon, 161.
Billings, Christopher, 190.
Billings, Ebenezer, 9, 10, 107, 108, 160.
Billings, Ebenezer, Jr., 9.
Billings, Increase, 72, 73, 107.

INDEX.

Billings, Jabez, 9, 107.
Billings, Jahleal, 10.
Billings, Jesse, 107, 214.
Billings, Peleg, 83.
Billings, Roger, 83, 84.
Billings, Samuel, 10, 39, 145, 181, 214.
Billings, Thaddeaus, 216.
Billings, William, 9, 11, 69, 70, 71, 80, 107, 111, 112, 190, 192.
Bingdon, Thomas, 161.
Bingham (Bengham, Binham), 18.
Bingham, Abisha, 20, 248, 254.
Bingham, Benajah, 248, 254.
Bingham, Benjamin, 249.
Bingham, Daniel, 227, 243.
Bingham, Ebenezer, 100.
Bingham, Elijah, 249.
Bingham, Elijah, Jr., 248, 254.
Bingham, Ithamar, 5, 91.
Bingham, Jabez, 227, 243.
Bingham, Jeremiah, 111, 112, 160.
Bingham, John, 122, 161.
Bingham, Jonathan, 16.
Bingham, Joseph, 52, 111, 113.
Bingham, Lemuel, 83, 111, 113.
Bingham, Malatiah, 248, 254.
Bingham, Nathaniel, 35, 45, 99, 100.
Bingham, Ruben, 97, 248, 254.
Bingham, Simeon, 23.
Bingham, Thomas, 35, 161.
Bingham, William, 240, 244.
Birchard, John, 236.
Birchard, John, Jr., 236.
Birchard, Jonathan, 156.
Birchard, see Burchard.
Bird, Isaac, 24, 140.
Bird, James, 247.
Bird, John, 14.
Bird, Joseph, 247.
Bird, More, 140.
Bird, Samuel, 14, 131, 168, 170.
Bird, Seth, 209.
Birdict, see Burdick.
Birdsey, Benjamin, 234.
Birdsey, Joseph, 200.
Birge, Benjamin, 224.
Birge, Jonathan, 122, 229.
Bisbye, Benjamin, 206.
Bisco, Isaac, 226.
Bishop (Bushop), 129.
Bishop, Abijah, 241.
Bishop, Abra, 227.
Bishop, Abraham, 117.
Bishop, Amos, 50, 231.
Bishop, Caleb, 111, 113, 236.
Bishop, Charles, 231.

Bishop, David, 31, 171, 212.
Bishop, David, Jr., 30.
Bishop, Ebenetus, 139, 251.
Bishop, Enos, 12.
Bishop, Epenetus, 56, 138.
Bishop, Ezra, 143.
Bishop, Isaac, 231.
Bishop, James, 202.
Bishop, Jeremiah, 198.
Bishop, John, 242.
Bishop, Joseph, 66.
Bishop, Joshua, 212.
Bishop, Nathaniel, 12, 51, 144.
Bishop, Nicholas, 145.
Bishop, Noah, 195, 260.
Bishop, Peter, 94.
Bishop, Ruben, 236.
Bishop, Samuel, 212, 233, 237.
Bishop, Samuel, Jr., 241.
Bishop, Seth, 50.
Bishop, Silas, 241.
Bishop, Silvanus, 65, 66, 223, 231.
Bishop, Talmadge, 206.
Bishop, Timothy, 51.
Bishop, William, 53, 145, 233.
Bishop, Yale, 253.
Bishop, Zebulon, 145.
Bissell (Bisel), Asel, 168.
Bissell, David, 134, 135, 207.
Bissell, David, Jr., 38.
Bissell, George, 247.
Bissell, Hezekiah, 168, 170.
Bissell, Jeremiah, 230.
Bissell, John, 211.
Bissell, Mathew, 230.
Bissell, Ozias, 8, 122, 123, 215.
Bissell, Roger, 127, 128.
Bissell, Timothy, 211.
Bissell, William, 207.
Bissell, Zebulon, 223.
Bixby, Nathan, 242.
Blachly, Jude, 252.
Blachly, Justice, 219.
Black, William, 219.
Blackleach, Hudson, 200.
Blackman (Blakman).
Blackman, Abraham, Jr., 250, 255.
Blackman, Elisha, 10, 144.
Blackman, John, 154.
Blackman, Joseph, 24, 87, 136, 160.
Blackman, Nathaniel, 179.
Blackman, Nathaniel Cady, 178.
Blackman, Peter, 200.
Blackman, Samuel, 137, 196.
Blackman, Zadock, 178, 179.
Blackmoor, Timothy, 103.
Blackmore, William, 208.
Blade, Jeremiah, 106.

Blague, Francis, 66.
Blague, Jeremiah, 105.
Blague, Thomas, 234.
Blair (Blare).
Blair, Archibald, 66, 176, 178.
Blake, Francis, 67, 68.
Blake, John, 114, 116.
Blake, Joseph, 120.
Blake, Thomas, 70, 71.
Blakeslee (Blackslee, Blacksley, Blaklee, Blakly, Blackslee).
Blakeslee, Asher, 223.
Blakeslee, Jesse, 253.
Blakeslee, Jonathan, 29, 146.
Blakeslee, Joseph, 26.
Blakeslee, Jude, 31.
Blakeslee, Reuben, 223.
Blakeslee, Stephen, 54.
Blakeslee, Tilley, 28, 146, 204.
Blanchard, Amaziah, 18, 20.
Blanchard, George, 205, 257.
Blanchard, James, 194.
Blanchard, Joseph, 14, 103, 104, 173, 175.
Blanchard, William, 20, 97, 184.
Blin, Bille, 152, 210.
Blin, David, 210.
Blin, Deliverance, 209.
Blin, Elisha, 224.
Blin, Gasham, 229.
Blin, John, 22, 76.
Blish, David, 205, 258.
Blish, John, 205, 259.
Blish, Joseph, 205.
Bliss, 266.
Bliss, Daniel, 70.
Bliss, Elias, 250, 257.
Bliss, John, 250.
Bliss, John, Jr., 257.
Bliss, Nathaniel, 250.
Bliss, Pelatiah, 91, 163.
Blodgett (Blochet, Bloggit, Blotchett, Bodget).
Blodgett, Ebenezer, 174.
Blodgett, Elijah, 100, 184.
Blodgett, Henry, 63, 103, 104.
Blodgett, Josiah, 7, 211.
Blodgett, Silas, 39.
Blodgett, William, 13.
Bloss, Simeon, 99.
Bloyce, Samuel, 37.
Boardman (Bordman), Amos, 218.
Boardman, Elizur, 229.
Boardman, John, 210, 234.
Boardman, Jonathan, 59.
Boardman, Josiah, 229.
Boardman, Moses, 186.

Boardman, Nathaniel, 122, 210, 230.
Boardman, William, 101.
Bobbet, Silas, 70.
Bobin, Joseph, 130.
Bochford, Isaa, 29.
Bockar, Jese, 219.
Bodell, John, 170.
Bodwill, John, 168.
Bolden, Samuel, 73.
Boldwin, Judah, 146.
Boldwin, Nathan, 147.
Bolt, John, 138.
Bolton, 215, 230.
Bomp, Robison, 10, 107.
Bond, Jack, 86.
Bond, Nicholas, 205, 257.
Bond, Stephen, 240.
Bond, Williman, 240.
Bone, John, 195, 260.
Bone, Jone, 95.
Bonfoy, Benanivel, 118.
Bonfoy, Purmort, 188.
Bonfoy, Richard, 59, 118, 119.
Bonner (Boner), Patrick, 105.
Bonner, Thomas, 152.
Booge (Boag, Bogue, Borg).
Booge, Daniel, 190.
Booge, Elishil, 203.
Booge, James, 86, 137, 203.
Booge, James, 2d, 259.
Booge, Joseph, 240.
Booge, Richard, 162.
Booth, Aaron, 230.
Booth, Benjamin, 94.
Booth, John, 200.
Booth, Jonathan, 134, 168, 238.
Booth, Joseph, 39, 173.
Booth, Joshua, 81, 86.
Booth, Reuben, 226.
Booth, William, 216.
Borden, Joseph, 203, 259, 260.
Boston, Toby, 178, 179.
Boston, 86, 161, 215.
Bostwick (Bostrick), Arthur, 217.
Bostwick, Asahel, 225.
Bostwick, Ebenezer, 217.
Bostwick, Edward, 73.
Bostwick, Isaac, 217.
Bostwick, Joseph, 58.
Bostwick, Matthew, 58.
Bostwick, Samuel, 221.
Bostwick, William, 241.
Bostwick, Zadock, 217.
Bosworth (Borsworth).
Bosworth, Constant, 234.
Bosworth, David, 137, 181.

INDEX. 279

Bosworth, Ebenezer, 198.
Bosworth, Stephen, 58.
Bosworth, Zadox, 233.
Botchford, Elijah, 238.
Botchford, Elnathan, 226.
Botchford, Isaac, 124, 237.
Botchford, Joel, 238.
Botchford, Samuel, 60, 171.
Botchford, Theophilus, 238.
Botchford, Timothy, 220.
Boughton, Ebenezer, 238.
Boughton, John, 138.
Boughton, Samuel, 138.
Bouton, Fairchild, 56.
Bowdish, Asa, 69, 71.
Bowdish, Nathaniel, 10.
Bowdish, Peter, 10, 97, 98.
Bowen, Peter, 79.
Bower, Daniel, 230.
Bowers, Samuel, 186.
Bowker, Joseph, 245.
Bowls, Daniel, 233.
Bowman, Elisha, 97, 159.
Bowman, John, 160.
Boyles, George, 161.
Brace, Nathaniel, 94, 160.
Brace, Zenos, 239.
Brackett, Benjamin, 171.
Brackett, Ebenezer, 54, 66.
Brackett, Elisha, 65, 67.
Brackett, Hezekiah, 65, 67, 69, 106.
Brackett, Isaac, 252.
Brackett, Job, 54.
Brackett, see Brockett.
Bradford, William, 45.
Bradley, Alexander, 252.
Bradley, Alvin, 30.
Bradley, Azariah, 231.
Bradley, Benjamin, 202.
Bradley, Daniel, 200, 201.
Bradley, Eli, 225.
Bradley, Elnathan, 201.
Bradley, Ezekiel, 241.
Bradley, Jabez, 215.
Bradley, Jacob, 231.
Bradley, Jesse, 252.
Bradley, Joel, 30.
Bradley, Jonah, 30, 231.
Bradley, Joseph, 201, 202.
Bradley, Lemuel, 231.
Bradley, Obed, 31.
Bradley, Onesimus, 221.
Bradley, Phineas, 144.
Bradley, Seth, 221.
Bradley, Simeon, 31.
Bradley, Timothy, 145.
Bradley, William, 253.
Bradley, Zenoth, 51.

Bragg, Benjamin, 8, 100, 101, 188.
Bragg, Elisha, 42.
Bragg, Nathaniel, 236.
Brainard (Brainerd, Branord, Braynard).
Brainard, Barll, 148.
Brainard, Eleazer, 202.
Brainard, Elijah, Jr., 44.
Brainard, Increase, 227.
Brainard, Jared, 203, 256.
Brainard, Jonathan, 213.
Brainard, Joshua, 213.
Brainard, Prosper, 227.
Bralton, James Adkin, 127.
Bramble, James, 236.
Braman, Thomas, 232.
Branch, Rufus, 232.
Brancher, Joseph, 15.
Branford, 22, 26, 171, 224, 225.
Bray, Thomas, 121.
Brayman (Braman).
Brayman, Benjamin, 108, 232.
Brayman, James, 184.
Brayman, Thomas, 108.
Breunson, Martin, 265.
Brewer (Bruer), Benjamin, 211.
Brewer, Benjamin, Jr., 8.
Brewer, Daniel, 9, 213, 239.
Brewer, John, 239.
Brewer, Joseph, 130.
Brewer, Thomas, 148, 149.
Brewer, Thomas, Jr., 8.
Brewster (Bruister, Bruster).
Brewster, Amos, 34, 183.
Brewster, Benjamin, 232.
Brewster, Benjamin, Jr., 250, **257.**
Brewster, Charles, 247.
Brewster, Epheram, 214.
Brewster, Israel, 198.
Brewster, Jonathan, 214.
Brewster, Nathan, 236.
Brewster, Wadworth, 250.
Briant, Abijah, 205.
Briant, George, 168.
Briant, Samuel, 209.
Briant, see Bryant.
Brigdon, Thomas, 79, 161, 234.
Brigdon, Thomas, Jr., 35.
Briggs, Elkanah, 227, 243.
Briggs, Zepheniah, 240.
Brinsmade (Brimsmade).
Brinsmade, John, 140, 209.
Brinsmade, Josiah, 200.
Brinsmade, Samuel, 243.
Brintnell, Caleb, 234.
Bristol, Benjamin, 60.
Bristol, Reuben, 220.
Bristol, Richard, 59.

Bristol, Samuel, Jr., 250.
Bristol, Stephen, 29, 253.
Bristol, Timothy, 127, 193.
Bristow (Bristor), Ebenezer, 237.
Bristow, Gideon, 204.
Bristow, Joseph, 237.
Bristow, Timothy, 261.
Bristow, William, 53.
Briton, Cladus, 199.
Broadstreet, John, 162.
Brocket, Hezekiah, 105, 193.
Brocket, Isaac, 31.
Brocket, see Brackett.
Brockway, Edward, 225.
Brockway, Jedadiah, 72.
Brockway, Timothy, 218.
Brockway, Woolston, 32.
Brodbrooks, Joseph, 56.
Brolton, James A., 171.
Bronch, Moses, 100.
Bronson, Ahil, 199.
Bronson, Amos, 204.
Bronson, see Breunson, Brownson, Brunson.
Brooker, Abraham, 8.
Brooknis, Cyrus, 155.
Brooks, 162.
Brooks, Benjamin, 69, 70, 71, 86, 136.
Brooks, Daniel, 234.
Brooks, David, 235.
Brooks, Enos, 234, 235.
Brooks, Henry, 48.
Brooks, Hugh, 178.
Brooks, Jabez, 86.
Brooks, James, 227.
Brooks, Jehiel, 99, 208.
Brooks, Jonathan, 34, 61, 109, 111, 152, 154, 185.
Brooks, Nathan, 186.
Brooks, Samuel, 129, 161, 241, 253.
Brooks, Thomas, 47, 49, 203, 235, 258.
Brooks, Timothy, 22, 130, 131, 186.
Brown, Abner, 82, 86, 87.
Brown, Amos, 214.
Brown, Benjamin, 233.
Brown, Bezaleel, 216.
Brown, Christopher, 214.
Brown, Daniel, 130, 214.
Brown, David, 86, 241.
Brown, Ebenezer, 42, 78.
Brown, Ebenezer, Jr., 198.
Brown, Ebenezer, 3d, 184.
Brown, Edmund, 56.
Brown, Eleazer, 231, 240, 245.
Brown, Ezra, 211.
Brown, Henry, 255.

Brown, Hezekiah, 222.
Brown, Ichabod, 18, 20, 154.
Brown, Isaiah, 200.
Brown, Jabez, 56, 109, 110.
Brown, James, 13, 107, 190.
Brown, Jedediah, 208.
Brown, Jeremiah, 214.
Brown, John, 5, 40, 42, 69, 71, 77, 86, 99, 100, 117, 148, 149, 152, 159, 182, 265.
Brown, John, Jr., 40.
Brown, Jonathan, 205, 241.
Brown, Joseph, 16, 132.
Brown, Josiah, 207.
Brown, Nathaniel, 148, 226.
Brown, Nehemiah, 29.
Brown, Noah, 230.
Brown, Peter, 37, 197.
Brown, Reuben, 144, 214.
Brown, Samuel, 12, 56, 109, 110, 213.
Brown, Silvenus, 241.
Brown, Stephen, 208, 214.
Brown, Stephen, Jr., 248, 254.
Brown, Thomas, 249, 255, 258.
Brown, William, 8, 65, 67, 69, 72, 73, 75, 128, 129, 144, 188, 190, 214, 239.
Brownson (Browson).
Brownson, Abraham, 219.
Brownson, Amos, 32.
Brownson, Asa, 120.
Brownson, Bela, 206.
Brownson, Benjamin, 225.
Brownson, Elijah, 219.
Brownson, Gideon, 146, 204.
Brownson, Hezekiah, 178.
Brownson, Isaac, 223.
Brownson, John, 120, 226.
Brownson, Joseph, 63.
Brownson, Moses, 120.
Brownson, Samuel, 210.
Brownson, Silas, 210.
Brownson, Timothy, 219.
Brownson, Titus, 210.
Brownson, Zibe, 226.
Brownson, see Breunson, Bronson, Brunson.
Bruce, Robert, 29, 146.
Brumley, Bethuel, 107.
Brumley, Elijah, 10.
Brumbly, John, 214.
Brumby, Elijah, 101.
Bruns [ ], Asael, 199.
Brunson, Abraham, 172.
Brunson, Hezekiah, 14.
Brunson, Isaac, Jr., 215.
Brunson, Jabez, 62.

INDEX.

Brunson, Joseph, 77, 245.
Brunson, Martin, 152.
Brunson, Moses, 54, 121.
Brunson, see Breunson, Bronson, Brownson.
Brush, Zacheus, 226.
Bryan, Augush, 228.
Bryant, Abijah, 258.
Bryant, Gustin, 243.
Bryant, see Briant.
Buck, Aaron, 97.
Buck, Abel, 58.
Buck, Daniel, 58.
Buck, Ephraim, 218.
Buck, Isaac, 29, 124, 219.
Buck, John, 36, 58.
Buck, Justus, 117.
Buck, Peter, 72, 74, 75.
Buck, Samuel, 58, 210.
Buck, William, 159.
Buckingham, Abijah, 60.
Buckingham, Adonijah, 44.
Buckingham, Benjamin, 220.
Buckingham, Epinetus, 31.
Buckingham, John, 202.
Buckingham, Joseph, 220.
Buckingham, Josiah, 59, 60, 119, 267.
Buckingham, Nathan, 220.
Buckingham, Stephen, 202.
Buckland, 135.
Buckland, Charles, 7, 134, 135, 173, 175.
Buckland, Elisha, 230.
Buckland, Jonathan, 38, 215.
Buckley, Andrew, 62.
Buckley, John, 111, 186.
Buckley, Seth, 177.
Buckley, Thomas, 186.
Buckley, see Bulkley.
Bucklin, Charles, 175.
Buckman, Benjamin, 12.
Buddington, Ozias, 197.
Budington, Joseph, 177, 179.
Buell (Bewell, Buwel).
Buell, Abel, 249.
Buell, Abraham, 24, 199.
Buell, Archalus, 57, 223.
Buell, Benjamin, 69, 81.
Buell, Daniel, 227.
Buell, David, 202.
Buell, Eliphalet, 227, 243.
Buell, Isaac, 159.
Buell, Joseph, 95.
Buell, Mathew, 215.
Buell, Nathaniel, 24, 140.
Buell, Solomon, 63, 223.
Bugbee (Bugbye), Daniel, 37.

Bugbee, Isaiah, 184.
Bugbee, John, 152, 154.
Bugbee, Joseph, 242.
Bugbee, Josiah, Jr., 249, 254.
Bugbee, Thomas, 37, 128, 129.
Bulkley (Bulckley), John, 52, 113.
Bulkley, Jotham, 171.
Bulkley, Gersham, 256.
Bulkley, Thomas, 152.
Bulkley, see Buckley.
Bull, Amos, 239.
Bull, Daniel, 84.
Bull, Jonathan, 65, 67.
Bull, Noah, 63.
Bullen, David, 39.
Buller, David, 195.
Bump, Stephen, 46.
Bumps, Edward, 24.
Bumpus (Bompas), Levi, 10, 181.
Bumsil, Parmens, 27.
Bunce (Bunts), Aaron, 137.
Bunce, George, 63, 103, 104, 211.
Bunce, Isaac, 239.
Bunce, Phinehas, 63.
Bunday, Benjamin, 118.
Bundy, Caleb, 11, 232.
Bundy, James, 82, 249.
Bundy, James, 3d, 254.
Bunn, Thomas, 186.
Bunne, Parmineus, 120.
Bunnel (Bunel).
Bunnel, Ebenezer, 234, 235.
Bunnel, Joseph, 120, 238.
Bunnel, Luke, 105.
Bunnel, Parmenius, 66, 67, 69, 121, 193.
Bunnel, Titus, 230.
Burch, Joseph, 204.
Burch, Vallentine, 61.
Burch, William, 238.
Burchard, Gideon, 52.
Burchard, see Birchard.
Burchard, Phinias, 182.
Burd, Samuel, 131.
Burdick (Birdict), Abraham, 214.
Burdick, John, 86, 111.
Burdie, John, 113.
Burdock, John, 52.
Burhorns, Henry, 29, 124.
Burk, Edmund, 37.
Burlison, Ebenezer, 14.
Burnham (Bernham).
Burnham, Andrew, 249, 255.
Burnham, Asa, 8.
Burnham, Asahel, 239.
Burnham, Charles, 39, 134, 135, 265.
Burnham, David, 261.

Burnham, Eleazer, 236, 239.
Burnam, Elisha, 168, 170.
Burnham, Feman, 23.
Burnam, Jacob, 111, 113, 259.
Burnham, James, Jr., 40.
Burnham, John, 236.
Burnham, Jonathan, 84, 239.
Burnham, Joshua, 248, 254.
Burnham, Michael, 263.
Burnham, William, 100, 239.
Burr, Andrew, 179, 200, 201, 221, 237.
Burr, Ephraim, Jr., 221.
Burr, Ezra, 221.
Burr, Georg, 221.
Burr, Gideon, 239.
Burr, John, 221.
Burr, Joseph, 201.
Burr, Nathan, 221.
Burr, Salmon, 239.
Burr, Seth, 221.
Burr, Timothy, 201.
Burrell, Charles, 60.
Burrell, Samuel, 238.
Burret, Eleazer, 156.
Burril, Nathan, 59.
Burroughs, Abner, 216.
Burrows, John, 243.
Burrus, Barzilla, 107.
Burton, George, 155.
Burton, Israil, 232.
Burton, Joseph, 200.
Burton, Oliver, 218.
Burton, Richard, 32, 219.
Burton, Robert, 155, 156.
Burton, William, 155, 156.
Bush, Abiel, 246.
Bush, Amaziah, 68.
Bush, Seth, 138.
Bush, Timothy, 82, 137, 188.
Bushnell, Abner, 44, 118, 119, 260.
Bushnell, Ebner, 196.
Bushnell, Jesse, 212.
Bushnell, Joseph, 212.
Bushnell, Josiah, 22.
Bushnell, Nathan, 237.
Bushnell, William, 45.
Busk, Amaziah, 65.
Butholph, Isaac, 12.
Butington, William, 221.
Butler, Benjamin, 97, 250.
Butler, Daniel, 239.
Butler, David, 260.
Butler, Ebenezer, 60.
Butler, Eleazer, 248, 254.
Butler, Gershom, 234.
Butler, James, 11, 209.
Butler, John, 121.

Butler, Jonathan, 171, 260.
Butler, Joseph, 225.
Butler, Patrick, 17, 19.
Butler, Peter, 82, 186.
Butler, Samuel Stone, 246.
Butler, Sylas, 58.
Butler, Thomas, 177, 179.
Butler, Thomas, Jr., 35.
Butler, Timothy, 198.
Butler, Zack, 191.
Butler, Zebulon, 194, 195, 260.
Butter, Benjamin, 160.
Button (Buten), Beter, 145.
Button, Charls, 232.
Button, John, 10, 181.
Button, Joseph, 233.
Button, Peter, 41, 138, 181.
Button, William, 72, 73, 75, 232.
Butts (Buts, Butt).
Butts, Joseph, 70, 71, 240.
Buzel, Lemewel, 100.

C[ ] George, 6.
C[ ]field, Josiah, 201.
Cable (Cabel).
Cable, Andrew, 102, 177, 178, 260.
Cable, Daniel, 221.
Cable, Isaac, 178, 179.
Cable, Jabez, 55.
Cable, John, 221.
Cable, Joseph, 241.
Cable, Samuel, 73, 75.
Cable, Thomas, 201.
Cable, William, 30, 109.
Caborn, George, 133.
Caborn, Zabediah, 133.
Cadwell, Edward, 12.
Cadwell, Elias, 45.
Cadwell, Isaac, 246.
Cadwell, Jacob, 178, 179.
Cadwell, John, 38, 84.
Cadwell, Matthew, 239.
Cadwell, Nehemiah, 239.
Cady, 18.
Cady, Barnabas, 37.
Cady, Elijah, 52, 101, 208.
Cady, Jonathan, 16, 98, 99.
Cady, Leonard, 152, 208.
Cady, Malachy, 100.
Cady, Simon, 20, 97, 98.
Cæsar, Negro, 37, 101.
Cagwin, James, 238.
Calcheese, Denis, 138.
Caldron, Thomas, 212.
Cale, Timothy, 219.
Calhone, John, 204.
Calhoun, David, 67, 68.
Calkins (Kelking), Elijah, 206.

INDEX.

Calkins, Elisha, 40.
Calkins, Ezekiel, 250.
Calkins, Israel, 120, 192.
Calkins, James, 42.
Calkins, John, 121.
Calkins, Jonathan, 107.
Calkins, Simon, 178.
Calkins, Thomas, 52, 236.
Calkins, see Caulkins, Colking.
Cam, George, 105, 159.
Camel, Charles, 230.
Camp, Abiel, 209.
Camp, Abraham, 180.
Camp, Ephraim, 65, 67.
Camp, Heth, 48.
Camp, Isaac, 220.
Camp, Joel, 238.
Camp, John, 48, 223.
Camp, John, Jr., 48.
Camp, Luke, 227, 243.
Camp, Phinehas, 220.
Camp, William, 233.
Canaan, 28, 53, 86, 87, 170, 175, 199, 208, 227, 228, 243, 247.
Canada (Canedy), Daniel, 133.
Canada, David, 184.
Canada, Isaac, 16, 96, 98.
Canada, John, 183.
Canada, Jonathan, 20, 97, 98, 183.
Canada, Philip, 261.
Canada, 87, 133, 162, 267.
Canadice, Daniel, 103.
Canany, Jonathan, 18.
Cande, Noah, 220.
Cane, Samuel, 63.
Canedy, Philip, 180.
Canfield (Camfield).
Canfield, Daniel, 157, 238.
Canfield, Israel, 29, 124, 219.
Canfield, Jabez, 56, 201.
Canfield, Jeremiah, 105.
Canfield, Joiel, 212.
Canfield, Joseph, 217, 226.
Canfield, Josiah, 12, 109, 110.
Canfield, Nathan, 225.
Canfield, Samuel, 73, 75, 156, 158.
Canterbury, 91, 167, 241, 267.
Cantis, Samuel, 219.
Caplin, James, 208.
Carary, Roger, 96.
Cardall, William, 53.
Carley, Jedediah, 138.
Carpenter (Carpander), 178.
Carpenter, Anthony, 110, 177.
Carpenter, Elijah, 198.
Carpenter, Eliphalet, 37, 79, 128, 129.
Carpenter, Ephraim, 36, 162, 250, 257.

Case, Zebulon, 250.
Casey (Casy), Eleazer, 254.
Carpenter, Hasaciah, 133.
Carpenter, Jese, 242.
Carpenter, John, 242, 265.
Carpenter, John, Jr., 38.
Carpenter, Joseph, 133.
Carpenter, Nathan, 26.
Carpenter, Samuell, 133.
Carpenter, Uriah, 37, 69, 152.
Carrier, Joseph, 205.
Carrier, Thomas, 148.
Carrier, Timothy, 218.
Carrier, Titus, 47, 87.
Carrington, Dan, 127, 231.
Carrington, Timothy, 65, 68.
Carte, William, 178.
Carter (Cartor), Edward, 47.
Carter, John, 42, 117, 159, 205, 240, 258.
Carter, Increas, 240.
Carter, Joseph, 8, 206, 207, 212.
Carter, Josiah, 202.
Carter, Lucas, 195.
Carter, Neel, 87.
Carter, Thadeus, 66, 67, 235.
Carter, William, 78.
Cartwright, Christopher, 206.
Carty, Incres, 244.
Carvenear, John, 14, 94, 131.
Carver, Benjamin, 84.
Cary (Carey).
Cary, Benjamin, 34, 97, 98.
Cary, Ebenezer, 46, 79.
Cary, Eleazer, 248.
Cary, Michal, 248.
Cary, Moses, 198.
Cary, Richard, 18, 248, 255.
Cary, Seth, 16.
Case, David, 85, 173, 175, 223.
Case, Elijah, 245.
Case, Ezekiel, 245.
Case, Jacob, 105.
Case, Jedediah, 63, 245.
Case, Jesse, 245.
Case, Job, 245.
Case, John, 108.
Case, Jonah, 247.
Case, Jonathan, 62, 246.
Case, Joseph, 47.
Case, Joseph, Jr., 246.
Case, Martin, 63.
Case, Richard, 105.
Case, Richard, Jr., 245.
Case, Rogur, 245.
Case, Samuel, 248, 255.
Case, Solomon, 245.
Case, Timothy, 245.

Casey, Michael, 255.
Casey, Richard, 19.
Casey, Seth, 141.
Casher, Hezekiah, 152.
Castelo, James, 13, 109, 110, 180.
Castle, Abisha, 223.
Castle, John, 155, 156.
Castle, Lemuel, 219.
Castle, Peter, 204.
Castle, Phineas, 32, 33, 146.
Castle, Ruben, 204.
Castle, Samuel, 219.
Caswell, Jonathan, 140.
Caswell, Nathan, 41, 237.
Cateny, George, 133.
Catlin, Eebenezer, 239.
Catlin, Eli, 223.
Catlin, Joel, 239.
Catlin, Samuel, 147, 223.
Catlin, Theodore, 223.
Catlin, Uriah, 223.
Cato, Negro, 37, 101.
Cattin, Eli, 32.
Cattin, Uriah, 33.
Caucucor, John, 131.
Caulkins, Samuel, 233.
Caulkins, Simon, 177.
Caulkins, see Calkins, Colking.
Caull, Nathan, 97.
Cavat, Samuel, 235.
Caveler, Peter, 231.
Cay, Benjamin, 190.
Chaffe, Joshua, 218.
Chaffe, Thomas, 248, 254.
Chaffee, Daved, Jr., 248, 254.
Chalcom, Simon, 137.
Chalker, Alexander, 209, 210.
Chalker, Jeremiah, 202.
Chalker, Stephen, Jr., 44.
Chamberlin, Eleazar, 82.
Chamberlin, Eliezer, 86.
Chamberlin, Elisha, 37.
Chamberlin, Isaac, 14, 130, 131, 160.
Chamberlin, James, 133.
Chamberlin, Joel, 161, 205, 256.
Chamberlin, John, 202, 203, 205.
Chamberlin, John, Jr., 259.
Chamberlin, Moses, 140, 199.
Chamberlin, Oliver, 230.
Chamberlin, Peleg, 42, 78, 86, 87.
Chamberlin, Peleg, Jr., 206.
Chamberlin, William, 205.
Chambers, Jeames, 132.
Chambers, John, 122, 230.
Champen, Isreal, 42.
Champion, Daniel, 206.
Champion, Henry, 205.

Chandler, Daniel, 198.
Chandler, Elijah, 207.
Chandler, Henery, 246.
Chandler, Jonathan, 247.
Chandler, Joseph, 94.
Chandler, Josiah, 248, 254.
Chandler, Nehemiah, 93, 95.
Chandler, Samuel, 8, 37, 93, 95, 96.
Chandler, Thomas, 141, 228, 243.
Chapam, Henry, 79.
Chapin, 135.
Chapin, Henry, 38, 87, 134.
Chapin, Nathaniel, 173.
Chapin, Oliver, 215.
Chapin, Phinehas, 5.
Chapman, Abraham, 53, 138, 139, 233.
Chapman, Alpheus, 84, 181.
Chapman, Benjamin, 224.
Chapman, Caleb, 212, 256.
Chapman, Comfort, 233.
Chapman, Daniel, 151, 188.
Chapman, Elias, 206.
Chapman, Elisha, 62, 196, 203, 258.
Chapman, Ezra, 58.
Chapman, Hezekiah, 40.
Chapman, Hope, 155, 156, 196.
Chapman, James, 214, 233.
Chapman, Jonah, 52, 86, 122, 123, 203, 258.
Chapman, Joseph, 213.
Chapman, Joshua, 197.
Chapman, Melathes, 32.
Chapman, Matthias, 206.
Chapman, Nathan, 162.
Chapman, Peletiah, 217.
Chapman, Phineas, 200, 201.
Chapman, Reuben, 45.
Chapman, Robert, 43.
Chapman, Samuel, 85, 188, 215.
Chapman, Simeon, 44.
Chapman, Simon, 215.
Chapman, Stephen, 182, 203, 259.
Chapman, Throope, 184.
Chapman, Thomas, 215.
Chappel (Chapel, Chaple).
Chappel, Amos, 46, 250, 257.
Chappel, Andrew, 53, 78, 82, 145, 188.
Chappel, Frederick, 65, 67, 68, 127.
Chappel, James, 111, 113.
Chappel, John, 83, 145, 181.
Chappel, Joseph, 233.
Chappel, Joshua, Jr., 250, 257.
Chappel, Nathan, 111, 113.
Chappel, Nathaniel, 69, 157, 233.
Chappel, Noah, 76, 128, 129, 241.
Chappel, Samuel, 61, 147.

INDEX. 285

Chappel, Simeon, 161.
Chappel, Walter, 52.
Chappel, William, Jr., 233.
Chapts, John, 72.
Charler, John, 96.
Charles, Daniel, 108, 191.
Charles, John, 172, 261.
Charles, Williams, 108.
Charmbling, Seth, 46.
Charper, Charles, 75.
Chartee, William, 177.
Charter, Ashbel, 173.
Charter, John, 5, 93, 95.
Chase, Thomas, 46.
Chatfield, Cornelus, 202.
Chatfield, Daniel, 60, 171.
Chatfield, George, 195.
Chatfield, Jesse, 8.
Chatfield, Lemuel, 220.
Chatfield, Philop, 247.
Chatterton, Samuel, 231.
Chaucus, Joseph, 127.
Chauncey (Chancey).
Chauncey, Elihu, 3, 48, 50, 57, 59, 60, 62, 66, 70, 72, 119.
Chauncey, Wolcot, 221.
Chaze, Joshua, 208.
Cheasbrough, Silvester, 214.
Chebuck, George, 40.
Chebuck, Solomon, 10, 108, 182.
Cheedle, Asa, 183.
Cheets (Cheat), Joseph, 108, 160.
Chects, see Quocheets.
Cheney, Asahell, 239.
Cheney, Ebenezer, 198.
Chepunck, John, 105, 106.
Chequipes, Joseph, 182.
Chequipes, Joshua, 84.
Chester, John, 213.
Chester, Sim, 197.
Chettenton, Ebenezer, 202.
Chick, John, 102, 104, 168, 173.
Chidderton, Benjamin, 67.
Chidsey (Chitsey), Ebenezer, 231.
Chidsey, Joseph, 212.
Child, Asa, 37.
Child, Eleazer, 99.
Child, Elisha, 242.
Child, Increase, 242.
Child, Josiah, 242.
Child, Shubael, 37.
Chip, Henry, 72, 74.
Chipman, Caleb, 44.
Chipman, Jonathan, 24.
Chipman, Nathaniel, 40.
Chipman, Paul, 193.
Chipman, Samuel, 247.
Chittenden, Benjamin, 65, 144.

Chittenden, Daniel, 212.
Chittenden, Jared, 50.
Chittenden, Josep, 212.
Chittenden, Luther, 212.
Chittenden, Miles, 51.
Chittenden, Nathan, 50.
Chittenden, Reuben, 7.
Chittenden, Stephen, 212.
Chittenden, Timothy, 24, 141.
Chitterton, Benjamin, 69.
Chogegins, Thomas, 182.
Chops, John, 74, 75, 155, 156, 179.
Chowhorn, Joseph, 181.
Choychoi (Coy Choy).
Choychoi, Simon, 145, 181.
Church, Alick, 191.
Church, Asa, 58, 208.
Church, Caleb, 228, 238, 239, 243.
Church, Elias, 218.
Church, Ellick, 84.
Church, Gideon, 238.
Church, John, 78, 84, 190, 202, 210.
Church, Jonathan, 41.
Church, Joseph, 162.
Church, Peleg, 233.
Church, Zerackiah, 212.
Churchill, Janna, 229.
Churchill, Nathaniel, 13, 130, 131.
Chuchwell, Josiah, 226.
Claghorn (Chaghorn).
Claghorn, James, 132, 183, 227, 243.
Clammens, Abijah, 199.
Clark, Adam, 240, 244.
Clark, Amos, 24, 49, 250, 255, 257.
Clark, Andrew, 9, 45.
Clark, Asell, 214.
Clark, Benjamin, 220, 240.
Clark, Benoni, 162, 250, 257.
Clark, Bethel, 14.
Clark, Christopher, 227.
Clark, Dan, 43, 188.
Clark, Daniel, 57, 232.
Clark, Daniel, Jr., 250, 257.
Clark, David, 120.
Clark, Ebenezer, 232.
Clark, Elijah, 120, 198.
Clark, Elezr, 28.
Clark, Elish, 219.
Clark, Elizur, 77.
Clark, Hosea, 134, 229.
Clark, Jacob, 227, 241.
Clark, James, 44, 228, 232, 243.
Clark, Joel, 53, 119, 121.
Clark, John, 171.
Clark, Jonathan, 81.
Clark, Joseph, 41, 78, 91, 101, 209, 220.

Clark, Josiah, 135, 239.
Clark, Moses, 214.
Clark, Nathan, 59, 200.
Clark, Nehemiah, 243.
Clark, Peter, 241.
Clark, Reuben, 234.
Clark, Roger, 72, 73, 75, 128.
Clark, Rufus, 222.
Clark, Samuel, 81, 104.
Clark, Simon, 45.
Clark, Thomas, 23, 227, 250.
Clark, Timothy, 54.
Clark, Uriah, 23, 259.
Clark, Uziel, 234.
Clark, Walter, 214.
Clark, William, 153, 186, 223.
Claston, Nehemiah, 250.
Clawson, David, 241.
Clawson, Jonathan, 241.
Cleaveland, 244.
Cleaveland, Aaron, 40, 240.
Cleaveland, Asa, 245.
Cleaveland, David, 79.
Cleaveland, Elijah, 209.
Cleaveland, Moses, 23, 182, 183.
Cleaveland, Shubell, 244.
Cleaveland, Simon, 243.
Cleaveland, see Cleveland.
Clenton, Gershom, 159.
Clerk (Clearck), Amos, 249.
Clerk, Andrew, 173.
Clerk, Ebenezer, 249, 254.
Clerk, Reuben, 196.
Cleveland, Aron, 236.
Cleveland, Asa, 240.
Cleveland, Moses, 117.
Cleveland, Shubel, 240.
Cleveland, Simn, 227.
Cleveland, see Cleaveland.
Clifford, Sylvester, 233.
Clinton, Henry, 220.
Clinton, Jesse, 139.
Clinton, Shuball, 105.
Clohon, David, 219.
Close, Nathaniel, 180.
Closson, Eleazer, 161.
Closson, Nehemiah, 117, 161, 255.
Clothier, Ambrose, 206.
Clothier, John, 206.
Clough, Epraham, 198.
Coal, Reubin, 135.
Coats, Amos, 188.
Coats, Robert, 208.
Coats, Samuel, 184.
Cobb, James, 52, 182.
Cobb, John, 218, 233.
Cobb, Nathan, 214.
Coben, James, 67, 69.

Coburn (Cobourn, Coborn).
Coburn, Cornelius, 35.
Coburn, George, 183.
Coburn, James, 153, 154.
Coburn, Samuel, 6.
Coburn, Zebadiah, 133.
Cochecquis, Thomas, 117.
Cock, Thaddos, 231, 232.
Cocks, James, 205.
Cocks, Thomas, 137.
Cocksure, Samuel, 206.
Codgjoh, Jeffrey, 214.
Coe, Ebenezer, 200.
Coe, Jonathan, 222.
Coe, Joseph, 217.
Coeghegan, Peter, 10.
Cogan, Thomas, 10.
Cogshall, Banj., 132.
Coggeshall, John, 179.
Cogswell, Aaron, 24, 117.
Cogswell, Daniel, 162.
Cogswell, Edward, 62.
Cogswell, Emerson, 218.
Cogswell, Ezra, 24, 205, 257.
Cogswell, Jos., 215.
Cogswell, Mason, 45.
Cogswell, William, 226.
Cohoon, John, 57.
Coit, Isaac, 240, 265.
Coit, Oliver, 190.
Colburn (Coleborn), Daniel, 43.
Colburn, Joseph, 198.
Colchester, 7, 86, 87, 142, 161, 162, 188, 189, 202, 204, 205, 255, 258, 259.
Cole, Daniel, 251.
Cole, David, 24, 206.
Cole, Ebenezer, 114, 116, 205, 213.
Cole, Ebenezer, Jr., 256.
Cole, Jesse, 210.
Cole, John, 130.
Cole, John, Jr., 39.
Cole, Marcus, 81, 114.
Cole, Makens, 116.
Cole, Mareus, 116.
Cole, Noah, 265.
Cole, Ruben, 136, 168, 170.
Cole, Samuel, 20.
Cole, Tho., 223.
Coledwell, Jedediah, 188.
Coleman (Colman), Dennis, 156.
Coleman, Ebenezer, 258.
Coleman, John, Jr., 215.
Coleman, Nathaniel, 229.
Coles, Noah, 186.
Coles, see Cowles.
Colking, Thomas, 111, 113.
Colking, see Calkins, Caulkins.

INDEX.   287

Colkoon, David, 66.
Collar, Jonathan, 208.
Coller, John, 146.
Coller, Nathaniel, 37, 101.
Coller, see Collor.
Colley, James, 196.
Collins (Colins, Collens, Collings).
Collins, Abel, 168, 239.
Collins, Amos, 217.
Collins, Daniel, 52.
Collins, David, 59, 171, 210.
Collins, Edward, 226.
Collins, Jacob, 105.
Collins, John, 14, 55, 130, 131, 147, 153, 154, 209, 239.
Collins, Joseph, 252.
Collins, Lemuel, 235.
Collins, Nathaniel, 237.
Collins, Pell, 214.
Collins, Robert, 210.
Collins, Timothy, 3, 91, 93, 95.
Collins, William, 94, 212.
Collon, Abijah, 239.
Collor (Collour), James, 16, 145.
Collor, John, 29.
Collor, see Coller.
Coltson, Moses, 248, 254.
Colwell, Samuel, 138.
Colyer, James, 191.
Colyer, Joseph, 230.
Combs, John, 114, 116.
Comes, Ebenezer, 173, 175.
Cummus (Commos, Commewas).
Cummus, 15.
Commus, Joseph, 16, 108, 184.
Comstock (Cumstock).
Comstock, Daniel, 72, 73, 75, 196, 199.
Comstock, James, 40, 227.
Comstock, Jason, 233.
Comstock, Joseph, 10, 145, 181.
Comstock, Nathan, 40.
Comstock, Phineas, 227.
Comstock, Rainford, 233.
Comstock, Ruford, 233.
Comstock, Samuel, 44, 138, 196, 226, 251.
Comstock, Stephen, 228, 243.
Conant (Connant).
Conant, Shubael, 99, 100, 184, 185, 198, 253.
Cone (Coann, Coen).
Cone, Aaron, 44, 118.
Cone, Cornelius, 72, 73, 75, 80, 114, 116.
Cone, Daniel, 7, 48, 114, 116, 147, 149, 159, 186, 202, 203.
Cone, Ebenezer, 259.

Cone, Ebenezer, Jr., 259.
Cone, Jacob, 212.
Cone, John, 187.
Cone, Jone, 44.
Cone, Joseph, 42.
Cone, Joshua, 227.
Cone, Oliver, 43.
Cone, Ruben, 203.
Cone, Samuel, 118, 160.
Cone, Silvanas, 43, 148, 149.
Cone, Stephen, 173.
Cone, Timothy, 203.
Conlin, John, 63.
Conner, John, 31, 114, 116, 168, 170, 171.
Convers, Joshua, 184.
Conyer, Joseph, 258.
Cook, Amos, 54.
Cook, Amasa, 232.
Cook, Andrew, 229.
Cook, Benjamin, 49, 193, 223, 261.
Cook, Benjamin, Jr., 66.
Cook, Calab, 148.
Cook, Charles, 24, 87.
Cook, Daniel, 100.
Cook, David, 66.
Cook, Demetrius, 225.
Cook, Ebenezer, 203, 234.
Cook, Elam, 49, 235.
Cook, Elijah, 135, 230.
Cook, Ezekiel, 83, 181.
Cook, Henry, 14, 193.
Cook, Hezekiah, 81.
Cook, Isaac, 65, 66, 68, 171.
Cook, James, 203, 256.
Cook, Jesse, 193.
Cook, John, 213, 230.
Cook, Jonathan, 223.
Cook, Josiah, 82, 183.
Cook, Moses, 184.
Cook, Nathaniel, 65, 68, 235.
Cook, Ozial, 144.
Cook, Reuben, 39, 239.
Cook, Richard, 229.
Cook, Thomas, 16.
Cook, Robert, 70.
Cook, Wade, 171.
Cook, Waitstill, 65, 67, 68, 144.
Cook, William, 239.
Cool, Philip, 29, 146.
Cooley (Coley, Coly).
Cooley, Andrew, 72, 73, 75.
Cooley, Benjamin, 155, 221.
Cooley, George, 215.
Cooley, Gershom, 201.
Cooley, James, 266.
Cooley, Jos., 266.
Cooley, Joseph, 155, 196, 261.

Coomes, John, 39.
Cooper, Abraham, 127, 171.
Cooper, Abram, 31.
Cooper, Ammi, 37.
Cooper, Caleb, 252.
Cooper, Jason, 65, 67, 68, 103, 104, 106.
Cooper, John, 12, 252.
Cooper, Joseph, 181.
Cooper, Solomon, 111, 113, 122.
Cooper, Stephen, 127, 252.
Cooper, Stephen, Jr., 31.
Cooper, Timothy, 252.
Cooper, Tors, 133.
Cooper, William, 208.
Cooper, Zepurah, 69.
Copley, Nathaniel, 230.
Copley, Nathaniel, Jr., 39.
Corbin, Daniel, 37, 128, 129, 242.
Corbin, Ezra, 242.
Corbin, Jabez, Jr., 37.
Corbin, James, 38.
Corbin, John, 36.
Corbin, Moses, 238.
Corbit, James, 66.
Corby (Corbe), Samuel, 58, 206.
Cornel, Daniel, 236.
Corning, Ezra, 236.
Corning, Malachy, 239.
Corning, Samuel, 191.
Cornish, James, 214.
Cornish, John, 31, 77, 231.
Cornwall, 24, 140, 141, 185, 247.
Cornwell, Abijah, 234.
Cornwell, Benjamin, 82.
Cornwell, Cornelius, 114, 116, 234.
Cornwell, Daniel, 234.
Cornwell, John, 252.
Cosbee, Michael, 200.
Cosher, Hezekiah, 151.
Cotes, Samuel, 38.
Cotton, Elihu, 114, 116, 229.
Cotton, John, 15, 38, 207.
Cotton, Samuel, 70, 71, 153, 154.
Couch, David, 201.
Couch, Ebenezer, 201.
Couch, John, 114.
Courby, John, 116.
Cousin (Couzens), John, 108, 182.
Covell, Ebenezer, 208.
Covell, Eleazer, 37, 98, 99.
Covell, Philip, 197.
Coventry, 45, 47, 87, 183, 189, 199, 255.
Covert, Denis, 66, 67, 69.
Cowdry, Moses, 43.
Cowdry, Thomas, 42, 203.
Cowell (Couel), John, 116.
Cowell, Joshua, 105.
Cowles, Amos, 239.
Cowles, Eleazer, 239.
Cowles, Phinehas, 239.
Cowles, Samuel, 222.
Cowles, see Coles.
Cox, Jams, 258.
Cox, Ralph, 215.
Cox, Thomas, 257.
Cox, William, 148, 188.
Coy, Benjamin, 71, 190.
Coy, Jonathan, 137.
Coy, Silas, 168.
Coy, Uriah, 215.
Coy, Zedekiah, 16.
Coye, Abia, 232.
Coye, Able, 83.
Coye, Benjamin, 70, 108.
Coye, Ephraim, 108.
Coye, Jonathan, 16, 101, 161, 207.
Coye, Joseph, 83.
Coye, Moses, 183.
Coye, William, 207.
Cozumps, Daniel, 192.
Cozumps, Joseph, 192.
Craft, 18.
Craft, Benjaman, 20, 21, 208.
Craft, Peter, 105.
Cragg, Robert, 83.
Crain, Ezra, 8, 118, 119.
Crain, Jabez, 110.
Crain, see Crane.
Cramton, Jesse, 195.
Cramton, Jonathan, 50.
Crandall, Nathaniel, 236.
Crandall, Samuel, 22, 111, 113, 191.
Crane, Isaac, 248, 254.
Crane, John, 209.
Crane, see Crain.
Cranton, John, 51.
Crary, George, 9, 100, 101, 176, 266.
Crary, Roger, 98.
Cravat, Samuel, 78, 82.
Craw, Jesse, 215.
Creday, John, 219.
Crese, Richard, 34.
Cressy (Cresey, Cresse, Cressey, Cresy, Crissey, Crizzy).
Cressy, Abijah, 32.
Cressy, Daniel, 219.
Cressy, David, 204.
Cressy, Ebenezer, 56, 150, 151, 251, 267.
Crocker, Asa, 10.
Crocker, Champion, 18, 20.
Crocker, Constant, 236.
Crocker, Ebenezer, 69, 71.

Crocker, Elihu, 41.
Crocker, Ezekiel, 70, 203.
Crocker, James, 205.
Crocker, James, Jr., 259.
Crocker, John, 137.
Crocker, Joseph, 198.
Crocker, Peter, 233.
Crocker, Thomas, 236.
Crofoot, Josiah, 56.
Croford, Robert, 99.
Croker, Levi, 247.
Crook, William, 195, 261.
Crosby, Ebenezer, 73, 75, 114, 116.
Crosby, Jonathan, Jr., 248, 255.
Crosman, Pheneas, 198.
Cross, Abel, 6, 99.
Cross, David, 133.
Cross, John, 99.
Cross, Nathaniel, 216.
Crossman, Bartholomew, 52.
Crossman, Thomas, 53.
Crouch, 18.
Crouch, Christopher, 72, 75.
Crouch, David, 19, 72, 197.
Crouch, Thomas Frink, 205.
Crouch, Christopher, 73.
Crow, Christopher, 134.
Crow, John, 229.
Crow, Nathaniel, 239.
Crow, Reuben, 39, 78.
Crow, Roger, 38, 79, 101, 168, 170.
Crow, Zacheus, 39, 79, 135.
Crowfoot, John, 220.
Crowfoot, Joseph, 209.
Crown Point, 7, 9, 21, 32, 87, 91, 99, 100, 106, 116, 119, 121, 140, 149, 160.
Cruttenden (Cretenden).
Cruttenden, Zebulon, 51, 212.
Cudweley, Timothy, 212.
Cuff, Mordica, 66.
Culver (Colver, Culvor).
Culver, Andrew, 193, 261.
Culver, Asher, 199.
Culver, Benjamin, 13, 223, 235.
Culver, Daniel, 28, 49.
Culver, David, 188.
Culver, Ebenezer, 147, 224.
Culver, Edward, 29, 124.
Culver, James, 188.
Culver, Jeremiah, 197.
Culver, Nathaniel, 14.
Culver, Obediah, 205, 257.
Culver, Stephen, 235.
Cummins (Commans).
Cummins, James, 249, 254.
Cummins, Samuel, 72, 73, 198.
Cunningham, John, 44.

Cunningham, Thomas, 197.
Cupper, Thomas, 246.
Curricomb (Corre Comp, Corycomb, Correcum).
Curricomb, Andrew, 72, 74, 75, 102, 103, 104, 193.
Curry, James, 230.
Curtice (Cirtice, Cortis).
Curtice, Benjamin, 252, 258.
Curtice, Bildad, 198.
Curtice, Daniel, 218, 239.
Curtice, Eldad, 224.
Curtice, Eleazer, 206.
Curtice, Henery, 258.
Curtice, Hosea, 148.
Curtice, Isaiah, 206, 207.
Curtice, James, 154.
Curtice, John, 148, 254.
Curtice, Nathaniel, 80, 206.
Curtice, Samuel, 158.
Curtie, Nathaniel, 80.
Curtis (Cortis), 26.
Curtis, Abel, 49, 218.
Curtis, Abner, 152, 200.
Curtis, Abner, Jr., 153.
Curtis, Brewster, 200.
Curtis, Ebenezer, 14, 199.
Curtis, Eldad, 65, 67, 68.
Curtis, Eliphalet, 105.
Curtis, Enoch, 13, 120, 121.
Curtis, Ephraim, 200.
Curtis, Ethan, 65, 66, 68, 120, 121.
Curtis, Ezekiel, 120, 226.
Curtis, Fradrack, 133.
Curtis, Gideon, 28, 204.
Curtis, Giles, 235.
Curtis, Henry, 205.
Curtis, Hoseah, 168.
Curtis, Hoseal, 170.
Curtis, Israel, 62, 200.
Curtis, Jacob, 127.
Curtis, James, 153.
Curtis, John, 248.
Curtis, Nathan, 49, 200.
Curtis, Nathaniel, 69, 138, 161.
Curtis, Phenias, 14, 223.
Curtis, Samuel, 157, 178, 200.
Curtis, Silvanos, 168, 170.
Curtis, Solomon, Jr., 250.
Curtis, Stephen, 35.
Curtis, Thadeus, 204.
Curtis, Thomas, 200.
Curtis, Wath., 71.
Cush, Robin, 105, 106.
Cushman, 161.
Cushman, Isaac, 46, 47, 206.
Cushman, Solomon, 198.
Cushman, William, 198.

Cuttler, Benoni, 99, 207.
Cuttler, John, 208.
Cuttler, William, 252.
Cyman, James, 111, 113.

Dagget, Samuel, 255.
Dairaw, John, 235.
Dale, Justes, 71.
Daley (Daily, Dailey, Daly, Dayley, Dayly).
Daley, Abraham, 153, 154, 242.
Daley, Benjamin, 247.
Daley, Jacob, 99.
Daley, Jeremiah, 168, 170.
Daley, John, 103, 193, 261.
Daley, Justice, 114, 116, 261.
Daley, Justine, 116.
Daley, Justus, 70, 115, 193.
Dan, Abraham, 56, 138, 139.
Dan, David, 180, 261.
Dana (Deana).
Dana, Benjamin, 37, 242.
Dana, Isaac, 79.
Dana, Jedadiah, 249.
Danbury, 28, 55, 156, 158, 163, 237.
Daney, Jonathan, 249, 255.
Daney, William, 248, 254.
Daniels (Danells, Dannills).
Daniels, Asa, 188.
Daniels, David, 86.
Daniels, Henry, 155.
Daniels, James, 233.
Daniels, John, 196.
Daniels, Timothy, 233.
Daniels, Veren, 207.
Daniels, William, 62, 82, 86.
Danilson, Amos, 214.
Dank, Thomas, 219.
Darbee, Jesse, 208.
Darby, Simeon, 82.
Darin, Arune, 144.
Darin, Stephen, 225.
Darling, Jedediah, 122.
Darrow, Isaac, 251.
Darrow, John, 49.
Darrow, Nathaniel, 56.
Darrow, Richard, 26, 126, 128.
Dart, Joseph, 213.
Dart, Nathaniel, 122, 123, 230.
Daruse, James, 208.
Darwin (Derwin), Samuel, 246.
Dascomb, Thomas, 155.
Dascomb, Thomas, Jr., 155.
Daton (Daten), Abraham, 57.
Daton, Israel, 65, 66, 106.
Daton, Jonah, 156.
Daton, Joseph, 8.

Daton, Josiah, 157, 158, 218.
Daton, Laford, 233.
Daton, Stephen, 180, 261.
Daton, William, 233.
Daton, see Dayton.
Dauchy, James, 180.
Davenport (Devenport).
Davenport, Deodate, 55.
Davenport, Haz, 161.
Davenport, Hezekiah, 120.
Davenport, Samuel, 137, 231.
Davenport, Silas, 252.
Davidson, James, 220.
Davis (Davas).
Davis, Benjamin, 6, 102, 122, 124, 178, 179.
Davis, Benjamin, Jr., 133.
Davis, Ebenezer, 70, 71, 101.
Davis, Enoch, 200.
Davis, Experience, 27.
Davis, Ezra, 32.
Davis, Hezekiah, 151, 152, 241.
Davis, Isaac, 53.
Davis, Jacob, Jr., 211.
Davis, John, 32, 206.
Davis, Josep, Jr., 221.
Davis, Joseph, 148, 215.
Davis, Matthew, 79.
Davis, Nathan, 104.
Davis, Nathaniel, 32, 147, 194, 261.
Davis, Noah, 27.
Davis, Peter, 65, 67, 68, 144, 145, 191.
Davis, Richard, 261.
Davis, Samuel, 198, 253.
Davis, Thadeus, 157, 177, 178.
Davis, Thomas, 141.
Davison, Asa, 108.
Davison, Cypprian, 107.
Davison, Dan, 208.
Davison, John, 18, 20.
Davison, Jonathan, 83.
Day, Aaron, 253.
Day, Benjamin, 204, 205, 259, 265.
Day, Benjamin, Jr., 259.
Day, John, 99.
Day, Oliver, 39.
Day, William, 23, 76.
Dean (Deeain, Deen).
Dayton, Israel, 105.
Dayton, Jehiel, 121.
Dayton, Joseph, 117, 118.
Dayton, see Daton.
Deains, James, 112.
Dean (Deeain, Deen).
Dean, Daniel, 201.
Dean, David, 148, 162, 205.
Dean, Eleazer, 91.

INDEX. 291

Dean, Ephraim, 69, 71, 133, 183.
Dean, Foxon, 184.
Dean, James, 10, 111.
Dean, John, 61, 141, 180, 243.
Dean, Jonathan, 56.
Dean, Joseph, 141.
Dean, Josiah, 209, 241.
Dean, Moses, 141, 206.
Dean, Oliver, 259.
Dean, Reuben, 140, 200.
Dean, Samuel, 32, 140.
Dean, Solomon, 82.
Dean, Uriah, 141.
Dean, Zachariah, 133.
DeForest, Elihu, 201.
DeForrest, Isaac, 200, 225.
Defratus, Lewis, 155.
Deful, Peter, 83.
Delano (Dellino), Jethro, 82.
Delano, Timothy, 215.
Delany, Denis, 87, 111, 113.
Delavan (Delevand).
Delavan, John, 150, 152.
Demerat (Demorat, Dimerat).
Demerat, John, 12, 109, 110, 180.
Deming (Damming).
Deming, Benjamin, 37, 242.
Deming, Elias, 224.
Deming, Francis, 210.
Deming, Gemalial, 152.
Deming, Hezekiah, 173.
Deming, John, 237, 250.
Deming, Joseph, 209.
Deming, Lemuel, 173, 175, 210.
Deming, Samuel, 238.
Deming, Seth, 184.
Deming, Solomon, 210.
Deming, Stephen, 168.
Deming, Wait, 247.
Dena, Jacob, 27.
Denend, Humphry, 252.
Denison (Danison, Deneson, Dennison).
Denison, Andrew, 9.
Denison, Chriso, 191.
Denison, Daniel, 70, 248, 254.
Denison, James, 172.
Denison, John, 202, 231.
Denison, Joseph, 214.
Denison, Robert, 5, 9, 11.
Denison, William, 191.
Denmores, Ichabod, 201.
Dennin, William, 32.
Denslow, Charles, 150, 180.
Denslow, Elisha, 39.
Denslow, John, 25, 150, 151.
Denslow, William, 25, 128.
Densly, William, 231.

De Peyster, John, 75.
Derby, 167, 220.
Dermand, Amos, 116.
Derrick (Derick).
Derrick, Joseph, 53, 145.
Derrick, Sampson, 191.
Deruse, John, 214.
Devall, Daniel, 212.
Devey, Lemuel, 250.
Devey, Nathaniel, 131.
Divine (Devine).
Divine, Nathaniel, 72, 73, 124.
Dewey (Dewy, Duey).
Dewey, Aaron, 46, 79, 250.
Dewey, Amos, 81.
Dewey, Charles, 257.
Dewey, Eli, 246.
Dewey, Elijah, 250, 257.
Dewey, Elijah, Jr., 161.
Dewey, Ely, 85.
Dewey, Ephraim, 99.
Dewey, James, 46.
Dewey, John, 250.
Dewey, Jonathan, 161, 188, 211.
Dewey, Nathaniel, 8, 130.
Dewey, Noah, 46.
Dewey, William, 69, 71, 99, 161.
De Wolf (De Woolf, Dwolf).
De Wolf, Bennoni, 186.
De Wolf, Jehiel, 44.
De Wolf, Matthew, 175.
De Wolf, Nathan, 48, 174.
De Wolf, Simon, 41, 234.
De Wolf, Stephen, 35, 56, 130, 131, 186, 193.
De Wolf, see Dulf.
Dexter (Daxter), Elisha, 254.
Dexter, Isaac, 27, 132.
Dibble (Debill, Deibell, Dibel, Dible, Dibol).
Dibble, Abraham, 62, 168, 170.
Dibble, Benjamin, 58, 206.
Dibble, Daniel, 238.
Dibble, David, 202.
Dibble, Eleazor, 56.
Dibble, Eliezer, 238.
Dibble, Ezra, 238.
Dibble, George, 72, 73, 75, 118.
Dibble, Isaiah, 137, 188.
Dibble, Israel, 211, 224.
Dibble, Jabez, 56, 241.
Dibble, Joel, 14.
Dibble, John, 57, 118, 247.
Dibble, John, 2d, 247.
Dibble, Josiah, 14, 43, 141.
Dibble, Moses, 63.
Dibble, Nathan, 157.
Dibble, Thomas, 144, 196.

Dibble, Zachariah, 206.
Dickens, Joseph, 84.
Dickerson, Moses, 267.
Dickinson, 185.
Dickinson, Azanah, 45.
Dickinson, Dan, 195, 261.
Dickinson, David, 82, 258.
Dickinson, Ebenezer, 209, 210.
Dickinson, Elizur, 209.
Dickinson, Gideon, 214.
Dickinson, Ichabod, 10, 107.
Dickinson, John, 197.
Dickinson, Joshua, 217.
Dickinson, Moses, 59, 130, 186.
Dickinson, Nathan, 157, 158, 177, 188.
Dickinson, Nehemiah, 59, 267.
Dickinson, Oliver, 199.
Dickinson, Richard, 162.
Dickinson, Zadock, 179.
Dickson, Nathan, 178, 180.
Diggins, John, 16.
Dike (Dikes), Gideon, 19, 182.
Dike, Jabez, 250.
Dike, Nathaniel, 66, 67, 69, 110.
Dike, Thomas, 32, 127, 128.
Dikeman, Thadeus, 201.
Dill, David, 197.
Dimock (Demick, Dimeck, Dimick, Dimmock).
Dimock, Benjamin, 12, 103, 104.
Dimock, Jeduthan, 249, 254.
Dimock, Lot, 115, 116.
Dimock, Samuel, 71, 72, 73, 74, 75, 118, 119.
Dimock, Shubael, 3d, 249, 254.
Dimock, Thomas, 240.
Dinney, Jeremy, 148.
Disbrow (Desbrow), Jason, 201.
Disbrow, Joshua, 201.
Dix, Benjamin 23.
Dix, Samuel, 229.
Dixen, James, 38.
Dixon, Robart, 101.
Doane (Done), Eleazer, 26, 95, 264.
Doane, Eliazar, 95.
Doane, Elisha, 173, 175.
Doane, James, 144, 196.
Dodge, Abel, 12.
Dodge, Alixander, 122.
Dodge, Amos, 205, 255.
Dodge, David, 161.
Dodge, David, 3d, 255.
Dodge, Ebenezer, 20, 78, 87.
Dodge, Edward, 236.
Dodge, Ezra, 171.
Dodge, Isaac, 97.
Dodge, Israel, 205, 256.

Dodge, James, 97.
Dodge, John, 122.
Dodge, Joseph, 157, 158.
Dodge, Nathan, 87.
Dodge, Nathanael, 47.
Dodge, Nehemiah, 16.
Dodge, Samuel, 34, 203, 242, 258.
Dodge, Thomas, 188.
Dodge, William, 9, 86, 122, 202.
Dodge, William, Jr., 123.
Doe, Ebenezer, 18.
Dollover, William, 196.
Doney, James, 25.
Doolittle (Dolittle, Dowlittle, Dulittle).
Doolittle, Amos, 49.
Doolittle, Barnabas, 223.
Doolittle, Benjamin, 235.
Doolittle, Daniel, 235.
Doolittle, Ebenezer, 81, 103, 104, 115, 116, 234.
Doolittle, Eli, 235.
Doolittle, Eliezer, 49.
Doolittle, Enos, 102, 160.
Doolittle, Giles, 235.
Doolittle, Isaac, 3.
Doolittle, James, 54, 120, 121.
Doolittle, Joseph, 109.
Doolittle, Michael, 67, 68.
Doolittle, Phil., 235.
Doolittle, Ruben, 235.
Doolittle, Samuel, 235.
Doolittle, Tho., 224.
Doolittle, Thomas, 199.
Dorais (Dorars, Dorus).
Dorais, Richard, 74, 75, 145, 196.
Dorman (Dormon).
Dorman, Amos, 115, 198.
Dorman, Dudley, 198.
Dorrance, George, 101.
Doty (Dooty), Isaac, 206.
Doty, Samuel, 218.
Doubleday, Joseph, 181.
Douglass (Dowglis, Doglass, Dowglas, Duglas, Duwglass).
Douglass, Domini, 157.
Douglass, George, 233.
Douglass, James, 266.
Douglass, John, 44, 212, 240, 245.
Douglass, John, Jr., 118.
Douglass, Samuel, 246.
Douglass, William, 247.
Doves, Richard, 72.
Dow, Aron, 83.
Dow, Levy, 198.
Dow, Nathan, 100.
Dowd (Doud), Ebenezer, 234.
Dowd, Giles, 81, 114, 116, 234.

Dowd, Lemuel, 144.
Dowd, Samuel, 50, 84.
Downer, Abraham, 133.
Downer, Cyprian, 191.
Downer, Ezra, 86.
Downer, James, 236.
Downer, Joshua, 52.
Downer, Stephen, 72, 73, 75, 100, 101, 232.
Downer, Stephen, Jr., 101.
Downer, Richard, 122.
Downer, Zaccheus, 19, 97, 160, 250.
Downing, Christophers, 237.
Downing, Stephen, 240, 244.
Downs (Down), David, 220.
Downs, Ebenezer, 203, 204.
Downs, Jeremiah, 10, 112, 113.
Downs, John, 112, 113, 155.
Downs, Joseph, 171.
Downs, Robert, 180.
Drake, 135.
Drake, Ebenezer, 134.
Drake, Frances, 230.
Drake, Gideon, 134.
Drake, Isaac, 12.
Drake, Job, 134.
Drake, Jonathan, 230.
Drake, Nathaniel, Jr., 207.
Drake, Phinehas, 38, 134.
Drinkwater, Thomas, 72, 73.
Drinkwator, John, 29.
Drummer, Samuel, 112, 113.
Dudley, Barzilla, 247.
Dudley, Beriah, 32, 146.
Dudley, Daniel, 32.
Dudley, Daniel, Jr., 224.
Dudley, David, 50.
Dudley, Gilbert, 202.
Dudley, John, 65, 67, 68.
Dudley, Joseph, 12, 118, 212.
Dudley, Josiah, 65, 67.
Dudley, Silvanus, 44, 145.
Dudley, Zebulon, 72, 73, 74, 117, 118, 188.
Dudley, Zipron, 266.
Duffey, John, 191.
Dulf, Stephen, 120, 261.
Dunbar, James, 188.
Dunbar, John, 26.
Duncan (Dunken), Dan, 201.
Duncan, William, 171, 261.
Dunham, Barnabas, 193.
Dunham, David, 122.
Dunham, Ebenezer, 69.
Dunham, George, 16, 97, 98.
Dunham, Gideon, 14, 229.
Dunham, Isaac, 148, 160.
Dunham, Jabez, 205.

Dunham, James, 209.
Dunham, John, 249.
Dunham, John, Jr., 254.
Dunham, Jonathan, 205.
Dunham, Matthew, 210.
Dunham, Obadiah, 188.
Dunham, Samuel, 206, 217.
Dunham, Silan, 213.
Dunham, Solomon, 206, 229.
Dunham, Thomas, 42, 205.
Dunill, Peter, 241.
Duning (Dauning).
Duning, Ezra, 58, 238.
Duning, Henry, 214.
Duning, Josiah, 132.
Duning, Samuel, 56.
Dunlap, Alexander, 6, 94, 96.
Dunlap, Benjamin, 191.
Dunlap, Robert, 83.
Duplex, William, 25, 77, 128, 171.
Duppee, Charles, 209.
Duran, John, 59.
Durand, Andrew, 235.
Durand, Samuel, 220.
Durgey (Dirgey), Robert, 33.
Durgey, Saben, 83.
Durgey, Timothy, 66.
Durgey, see Durkee.
Durham, 3, 48, 70, 72, 91, 222.
Durkee (Dirkee, Dorkey, Drkey, Durkey).
Durkee, 254.
Durkee, Aden, 208.
Durkee, Bartholomew, 97, 208.
Durkee, David, 219.
Durkee, James, 204.
Durkee, Jedediah, 147, 219.
Durkee, Jeremiah, 248, 254.
Durkee, John, 117, 180, 181, 262.
Durkee, Joseph, 34.
Durkee, Nathan, 236.
Durkee, Robert, 70, 71, 132, 133, 183, 219.
Durkee, Timothy, 67, 124.
Durkee, see Durgey.
Durond, Samuel, 220.
Durrum, Ephraim, 246.
Dutcher (Ducher), Cornels, 199.
Dutcher, Gabriel, 209.
Dutcher, Ruluff, 199.
Dutton (Duten), Charles, 66.
Dutton, Matthew, 204.
Dutton, Samuel, 194.
Dye, Peter, 70, 71.
Dyer (Dyar).
Dyer, Ebenezer, 65, 66, 76, 87, 267.
Dyer, Eliphalet, 34, 36.
Dyer, Henery, 198.

Dyer, John, 240.
Dyer, Joseph, 63.
Dyer, Thomas, 211.
Dyke, Gideon, 17.
Dymon, Thomas, 221.

Earl (Earles, Erles).
Earl, Moses, 66, 68, 152, 154, 207.
East Guilford, 202.
East Haddam, 162, 188, 189, 202, 203, 256, 258.
East Hampton, 213.
Eastman (Estman).
Eastman, Benjamin, 219.
Eastman, Jonathan, 133.
Eastman, Neale, 133.
Eastman, Peter, 249, 254.
Easton (Eston), Abel, 229.
Easton, Bildad, 35, 168, 170.
Easton, Elijah, 64.
Easton, Eliphalet, 199.
Easton, Samuel, Jr., 229.
Eaton, Aaron, 69, 97, 98.
Eaton, Calven, 198.
Eaton, Daniel, 173, 175.
Eaton, Daniel, Jr., 39.
Eaton, David, 216.
Eaton, John, 43, 215.
Eaton, Josiah, 248, 254.
Eaton, Nathaniel, 38.
Eaton, William, 122.
Eddy (Edy), Asa, 191.
Eddy, Barnabus, 46, 133.
Eddy, Labeas, 148.
Eddy, Thomas, 35, 79.
Edgecomb (Edgcomb).
Edgecomb, John, 62, 104, 106, 246.
Edgerton, Daniel, 236.
Edgerton, Elisha, 235, 236.
Edgerton, Jonathan, 6, 136.
Edgerton, Joseph, 112, 113.
Edgerton, Joshua, 236.
Edget, Stephen, 261.
Edmonds, George, 32.
Edmonds, Roburt, 204.
Edmonds, Samuel, 240.
Edmun, William, 219.
Edwards, Benajah, 69, 71.
Edwards, Eliphalet, 198.
Edwards, Jera, 235.
Edwards, Joseph, 198.
Edwards, Nathaniel, 223.
Edwards, Rice, 184.
Edwards, Richard, 84.
Eget, Stephen, 180.
Eggington, John, 249.
Eggleston (Egelstone, Egleston, Eglistone).

Eggleston, Ambrose, 186, 223.
Eggleston, Jedidiah, 230.
Eggleston, John, 39, 72, 75, 134, 168, 238.
Eggleston, John, Jr., 136.
Eggleston, Jonathan, 134, 230.
Eldrich, Elisha, 249.
Eldrige, Nathaniel, 144.
Eles, John, 257.
Elgar, Abner, 8.
Eliot (Elliot, Ellot).
Eliot, Aaron, 201, 202.
Eliot, Asa, 143, 145.
Eliot, John, 202.
Eliot, Joseph, 10, 107, 191.
Eliot, Timothy, 51.
Elithorp, Nathaniel, 242.
Ellicott, Willim, 23.
Ellis, Benjamin, 99, 120, 161, 249.
Ellis, Christopher, 197.
Ellis, James, 25.
Ellis, John, 42, 205.
Ellis, Joseph, 46.
Ellis, Peter, 190.
Ellis, Samuel, 215.
Ells, Lent, 247.
Elmer, Daniel, 179.
Elmer, David, 62, 218.
Elmor, Samuel, 124, 185.
Elsworth (Ellsworth).
Elsworth, Charles, 85.
Elsworth, Giles, 34.
Elsworth, Job, 211.
Elsworth, John, 168, 170.
Elsworth, Nicholas, 65, 67.
Elsworth, Thomas, 122.
Elsworth, Thomas, Jr., 230.
Elton, Ebenezer, 234.
Elwell, John, 225.
Elwell, Samuel, 14.
Elwood, Hezekiah, 201.
Ely (Eley), Benjamin, 121.
Ely, Samuel, 3.
Emeas, David, 244.
Emerson (Emason, Emroson).
Emerson, Joseph, 41, 145.
Emerson, Nathaniel, 41.
Emerson, Stephen, 41, 76.
Emmons (Emons), Daniel, 203.
Emmons, Eli, 224.
Emmons, Wodrof, 247.
Enfield, 38, 245, 246, 265.
England, 267.
Enlish, John, 250.
Ennes, Thomas, 191.
Eno, Joel, 168.
Enos, Benjamin, 198.
Enos, Isaac, 63.

INDEX. 295

Ensign, Eleazer, 239.
Ensign, Elifihelet, 246.
Ensign, Elijah, 239.
Ensign, Ezekiel, 230.
Ephraim (Epharim), Ezer, 8.
Ephraim, Jacob, 112, 113, 182.
Ephraim, John, 189.
Ergetstone, John, 73.
Etherige, Nathaniel, 190.
Evans (Eavens, Evens).
Evans, Benoni, 8.
Evans, Daniel, 16.
Evans, Edmund, 94, 96.
Evans, Elijah, 38, 211.
Evans, James, 209.
Evans, Moses, 8.
Evans, Oliver, 94, 95, 96, 216.
Evans, Samuel, 8, 9, 50, 85.
Evans, Samuel, Jr., 8, 229.
Evarts, John, 140, 212.
Evarts, Jonathan, 212.
Evarts, see Everts.
Everett (Everets, Everit).
Everett, Benjamin, 243.
Everett, David, 243.
Everett, Jeremiah, 18, 20, 115, 116.
Everett, John, 228, 243.
Everett, Jonathan, 25, 117.
Everett, Silvanus, 243.
Everett, see Averett, Averid.
Everton, William, 231.
Everts (Evets, Evirts).
Everts, Ambrose, 202.
Everts, Benjamin, 227.
Everts, Caleb, 235.
Everts, Ebenezer, 51.
Everts, John, 247.
Everts, Jonathan, 160.
Everts, Nathaniel, 140, 247.
Everts, Sylvanus, 227.
Everts, see Evarts.
Evis, Benjamin, 155, 156.
Ewen, Michel, 137.
Ewings, Elaxander, 46.

F[ ], Benjamin, 39.
Fabens, Nathaniel, 101.
Fagans, William, 10, 191.
Fails, Samuel, 113.
Fairbank, Barakiah, 81.
Fairchild (Fairchield, Fairchilde, Farechild).
Fairchild, Alexander, 226.
Fairchild, Andrew, 57, 138, 139.
Fairchild, Benjamin, 57.
Fairchild, Caleb, 115.
Fairchild, Elisha, 115, 234.
Fairchild, Enos, 49.

Fairchild, Giershom, 201.
Fairchild, James, 200.
Fairchild, James, Jr., 200.
Fairchild, Jonathan, 237.
Fairchild, Robert, 115, 234.
Fairchild, Thomas, 201.
Fairchild, Timothy, 221.
Fairchild, William, 157, 160.
Fairchild, Zachariah, 60, 171.
Fairfield, 28, 50, 85, 154, 158, 167, 176, 178, 200, 201, 221.
Fairfield County, 57.
Fairman (Fareman, Farman).
Fairman, Eliab, 72.
Fairman, James, 207.
Fairman, John, 45.
Fairman, Nehemiah, 93, 96.
Fairweather, John, 221.
Fales (Falles), Ebenezer, 236.
Fales, Samuel, 25, 112.
Falkner, Caleb, 254.
Falkner, Charles, 212.
Falmon, Peter, 212.
Fancher, James, 146, 194.
Fancher, John, 223.
Fanning, David, 197.
Fanning, John, 102.
Fanning, William, 197.
Fargo (Fergo), Aron, 84.
Fargo, Ichabod, 83, 188.
Fargo, Jason, 236.
Fargo, Jonah, 135.
Fargo, Moses, 233.
Fargo, Ralf, 135.
Fargo, Robart, 40.
Farly (Fairly, Farlie).
Farly, Alexander, 53, 117, 135, 136.
Farmington, 13, 19, 22, 91, 93, 125, 126, 129, 167, 209, 210, 215, 229, 230, 238, 246.
Farnam, Abner, 202.
Farnam, Eliab, 73, 74.
Farnam, Elijah, 20.
Farnam, John, 133.
Farnam, Joseph, 96.
Farnam, Seth, 32.
Farnam, Stephen, 202.
Farnum, Gad, 140, 199.
Farnum, Isaiah, 16.
Farnum, Joseph, 16, 98.
Farnum, Seth, 223.
Farnum, Solomon, 16, 184.
Farnum, Stephen, 144, 145.
Farrand, Samuel, 58.
Farrington, James, 39, 216.
Farris (Farress, Farriss).
Farris, David, 217.

Farris, Josiah, 138.
Farris, Reuben, 260.
Farris, see Ferris.
Fay, Jedidiah, 45.
Fees, John, 183.
Fellows (Fellers, Felows).
Fellows, David, 209.
Fellows, Jacob, 215.
Fellows, John, 28.
Fellows, Jonathan, 209.
Fellows, Nathaniel, 144.
Fellows, Samuel, 214.
Felshaw, John, 208.
Felt (Phelt), Joseph, 94.
Felt, Samuel, 173, 175.
Fenn, Benjamin, 49, 220, 267.
Fenn, Edward, 235.
Fenn, James, 220.
Fenn, John, 120.
Fenn, John, Jr., 121.
Fenn, Samuel, 194.
Fenn, Thomas, 55.
Fenton, Elijah, 198.
Fenton, Francis, 42.
Fenton, Francis, Jr., 42.
Fenton, Gershom, 201.
Fenton, Jacob, 36, 99, 100.
Fenton, Jacob, Jr., 34.
Fenton, John, 43.
Fenton, Joseph, 184.
Fenton, Nathaniel, 27.
Ferguson (Forgoson, Furgeson).
Ferguson, Daniel, 228, 243.
Ferguson, John, 173, 175.
Ferm, Benjamin, 220, 267.
Ferman, Nehemiah, 93.
Ferrill, Josiah, 70.
Ferris (Feriss), Jabez, 217.
Ferris, James, 180, 261.
Ferris, Joseph, 150.
Ferris, Jude, 225.
Ferris, Nathan, 150, 151, 179.
Ferris, Pack, 151, 180.
Ferris, Peter, 61, 217.
Ferris, Reuben, 60, 150, 151, 179, 260, 262.
Ferris, Samuel, 61, 216.
Ferris, Silvanus, 216.
Ferris, see Farris.
Ferry, Charles, 157, 158, 177, 178.
Ferry, John, 199.
Field (Feild), Ambrus, 223.
Field, Benjamin, 78, 82.
Field, Ebenezer, 51, 202.
Field, Josiah, Jr., 215.
Field, Samuel, 212.
Field, Samuel, 2d, 212.
Fielding (Feilding, Felding).
Fielding, Samuel, 42, 148, 149, 257.
Filleow, James, 251.
Filley (Filly, Philley).
Filley, Abraham, 135.
Filley, Daniel, 38, 78, 122, 123, 230.
Filley, Jonathan, Jr., 230.
Filley, Josiah, 78, 168.
Fillmore, Ebenezer, 236.
Fillmore, Henry, 52.
Fillmore, John, 52.
Fillmore, Nathaniel, 236.
Finch, James, 241.
Finch, Jeremiah, 150.
Finch, Nathaniel, 138.
Finney, John, 46, 184.
Finney, Jonathan, 250.
Finney, Richard, 45.
Fish, Ambrose, 190.
Fish, Jehu, 107, 214.
Fish, John, 10, 144.
Fisher, George, 12.
Fisher, Luke, 218.
Fisher, Moses, 72, 73, 75, 124.
Fisher, Nathan, 72, 73, 148, 149.
Fisk, David, 248, 254.
Fisk, John, 207.
Fitch, Abraham, 17, 19, 160, 250.
Fitch, Adonijah, 180, 181.
Fitch, Augustus, 84.
Fitch, Benjamin, 237.
Fitch, Daniel, 158.
Fitch, Eliezer, 65, 98.
Fitch, Elijah, 70.
Fitch, Ezekiel, 24, 96, 98, 160, 187.
Fitch, Ezra, 52.
Fitch, Ichabod, 111, 112.
Fitch, Jabez, 111, 112, 181, 249, 255.
Fitch, Jabez, Jr., 91.
Fitch, John, 254.
Fitch, Joseph, 160, 249.
Fitch, Joseph Trumble, 209.
Fitch, Matthew, 251.
Fitch, Medina, 5, 121, 122, 124.
Fitch, Nathan, 17, 19, 160.
Fitch, Perez, 241.
Fitch, Samuel, 11, 212.
Fitch, Stephen, 237.
Fitch, Theophilus, 107, 214.
Fitch, Thomas, 197.
Fitch, William, 209.
Flagg, Benjamin, 74.
Fleming (Flaming, Flemming).
Fleming, Francis, 14, 130, 131, 168.
Fleming, Gabrel, 241.
Fletcher (Flicher).
Fletcher, Ebenezer, 140, 228, 243.
Fletcher, John, 35, 99.

INDEX.

Fletcher, John, Jr., 99.
Fling, Thomas, 171.
Flint, Ephraim, 173, 176.
Flint, Nathan, 82.
Flint, Silas, 133.
Flora, John, 155.
Floyd, William, 197.
Fluskey, Owen, 77, 81, 162, 174, 175.
Fobes (Fobs), 18.
Fobes, John, 19, 20.
Fobes, Nathan, 232.
Fobes, see Forbes.
Follett, Benjamin, 108, 254.
Follett, George, 138, 241.
Food, Joseph, 31.
Foot, Abraham, 26, 143, 171.
Foot, Adonijah, 259.
Foot, David, 219.
Foot, Ebenezer, 154, 156, 200.
Foot, Ephraim, 225.
Foot, Isaac, 22, 26, 87.
Foot, Jacob, 60.
Foot, John, 245.
Foot, Jonathan, 225.
Foot, Joseph, 121, 137, 160, 225.
Foot, Moses, 54.
Foot, Nathan, 223.
Foot, Peter, 238.
Foot, Phyneas, 60.
Foot, Samuel, 12, 195.
Forbes (Furbs), Abraham, 239.
Forbes, Edward, 85, 173, 175.
Forbes, Elisha, 228, 243.
Forbes, Joseph, 23.
Forbes, Levy, 31.
Forbes, Moses, 230.
Forbes, Samuel, 209.
Forbes, see Fobes.
Force, William, 10.
Ford (Foard, Foord).
Ford, Daniel, 70, 71.
Ford, David, 32, 206.
Ford, Enos, 55.
Ford, Hezekiah, 25, 140, 206.
Ford, Jesse, 171, 218.
Ford, John, 148, 188, 257.
Ford, Joseph, 53, 237.
Ford, Mathew, 231.
Ford, Nathan, 30.
Ford, Nathaniel, 248, 249.
Ford, Nathaniel, Jr., 254.
Ford, Noah, 247.
Foresey, Nathan, 197.
Foroway, Richard, 153.
Forquar, Robert, 180.
Forsdick, John, 212.
Forsyth, James, 203.

Forsyth, James, Jr., 258.
Fort Edward, 3, 62, 76, 77, 79, 87, 104, 105, 106, 112, 113, 114, 138, 139, 154, 155, 156, 157, 159, 167, 170, 185, 210, 211, 245, 253, 256, 259, 260, 262, 267.
Fort William Henry, 76, 95, 98, 104, 106, 108, 114, 115, 123, 131, 139, 147, 149, 151, 155, 157, 166, 197, 198, 199, 200, 201, 202, 204, 205, 206, 207, 208, 209, 212, 213, 214, 215, 216, 217, 218, 220, 221, 222, 223, 224, 225, 226, 227, 228, 229, 231, 232, 234, 236, 237, 240, 241, 243, 247, 248, 249, 251, 252, 253, 259.
Fortnor, Caleb, 248.
Fosset, Amos, 16.
Foster (Foaster, Forster).
Foster, Abel, 215.
Foster, Abrom, 153.
Foster, Ebenezer, 243.
Foster, Edward, 29, 87, 95, 96.
Foster, Jeremiah, 17, 19, 78, 115, 188.
Foster, John, 186.
Foster, Joseph Naggs, 241.
Foster, Phineas, 230.
Foster, Samuel, 70, 234.
Foster, Thomas, 152, 159, 230.
Fountain, Phinehes, 206.
Fountain, Timothy, 110.
Fowler, Benjamin, 212.
Fowler, Daniel, 184.
Fowler, David, 212.
Fowler, Gurden, 132, 198.
Fowler, Job, 245.
Fowler, John, 64, 223, 239.
Fowler, Jonathan, 220.
Fowler, Joseph, 50.
Fowler, Melezer, 195.
Fowler, Morriss, 233.
Fowler, Thomas, 27, 198.
Fowler, Titus, 49.
Fowler, William, 59.
Fox (Foox).
Fox, Abraham, 82, 205, 258.
Fox, Amos, 10.
Fox, Asa, 188.
Fox, Daniel, 127, 171, 261.
Fox, Elisha, 14, 130, 131.
Fox, Gershom, 148, 205, 255.
Fox, Gideon, 8, 86.
Fox, Isaac, 42, 137.
Fox, Jedediah, 8, 9.
Fox, Joel, 188.
Fox, John, 23, 81, 128, 129, 171.
Fox, Jonah, 209.

298   CAMPAIGNS OF 1755, 1756, AND 1757.

Fox, Jonathan, 182.
Fox, Joseph, 52, 186.
Fox, Joshua, 137, 188.
Fox, Lemuel, 148.
Fox, Luke, 121.
Fox, Samuel, 148.
Fox, Samuel, Jr., 148.
Fox, Silas, 205.
Fox, Thomas, Jr., 37, 242.
Fox, William, 42, 148, 149.
Frairey, Daniel, 51.
Frame, John, 27, 98, 248, 254.
Francis (Frainces), Asa, 103, 235.
Francis, Hezekiah, 210.
Francis, Jacob, 49.
Francis, James, 51.
Francis, Samuel, 247.
Francis, Thom., 266.
Francis, Timothy, 210.
Frankland, John, 227.
Franklin, Daniel, 8, 117, 119, 226.
Franklin, David, 72, 73, 75, 195, 261.
Franland, John, 243.
Frasher, William, 236.
Frasur (Freyzor).
Frasur, Anthany, 40, 145.
Freeman (Freman), Danil, 232.
Freeman, Edmund, 3d, 99.
Freeman, Ezra, 236.
Freeman, Israel, 168.
Freeman, James, 84.
Freeman, Samuel, 25, 77, 144, 160.
Freeman, Zacheus, 188.
French, Ichabod, 8, 195, 260.
French, Jesiel, 200.
French, John, 83.
French, Jonathan, 236.
French, Nehemiah Loring, 200.
French, Philemon, 50, 212.
French, Richard, 211.
French, Samuel, 200, 237.
French, Thomas, 212.
Friel, Abel, 70.
Frik, Elijah, 248.
Frink, Elijah, 254.
Frink, Jonas, 107, 232.
Frink, Joseph, 214.
Frink, Zackriah, 240.
Fripe, Pick, 153.
Frisbe, Israel, 66, 67, 68.
Frisbe, Noah, 204.
Frisbee, Elisha, 225.
Frisbee, Jacob, 225.
Frisby, Benjamin, 206, 224.
Frisell (Frizell), Amasa, 242.
Frisell, Ebenezer, 36.
Frisell, Joseph, 243.

Frost, Benjamin, 155, 156, 178, 179.
Frost, Henry, 240.
Frost, Jedediah, 57.
Frost, Joel, 223.
Frost, Moses, 120, 121.
Frost, Samuel, 120, 121.
Fulford, Gershom, 27.
Fulford, John, 105, 106, 224.
Fulford, Luke, 159.
Fuller, Aaron, 39, 184.
Fuller, Abraham, 58, 206.
Fuller, Amos, 209.
Fuller, Benjamin, 202.
Fuller, Daniel, 203.
Fuller, David, 52, 86.
Fuller, Edward, 72, 73.
Fuller, Ephraim, 202.
Fuller, Isaac, 218.
Fuller, Jacob, 43, 184, 237.
Fuller, James, 141, 228, 243.
Fuller, Jeremiah, 218.
Fuller, John, 215.
Fuller, Jonah, 98.
Fuller, Jonathan, 188.
Fuller, Joshua, 215, 249.
Fuller, Josiah, 97, 181, 198.
Fuller, Lott, 122.
Fuller, Nathan, 162.
Fuller, Samuel, 250.
Fuller, Thomas, 15.
Fuller, Timothy, 219.
Fuller, William, 198.
Furnee, Ephraim, 200.

Gager, John, 236.
Gail, Roger, 241.
Gaines (Gayns), Daniel, 6, 153.
Gaines, Jonathan, 130.
Gaines, Moses, 103, 245.
Gaines, Simon, 8, 9, 230.
Gaines, William, 7, 105, 106, 169.
Gale, Daniel, 244.
Gale, Nathanale, 68.
Gale, Nehamiah, 213.
Gale, William, 150, 179.
Gallup (Gallop), Adam, 158.
Gallup, Ben Adam, 190, 192.
Gallup, Thomas, 36, 100, 101, 266.
Galpin, Benjamin, 186, 219.
Galpin, Caleb, 210.
Galpin, Samuel, 204.
Galusha (Gallucia).
Galusha, Jacob, 58, 218.
Galusha, Timothy, 133.
Gambel, John, Jr., 214.
Gard (Gart), Elisha, 73, 75.
Gardner, John, 233.
Gardner, Stephen, 202.

INDEX.

Gardner, Stephen, Jr., 258.
Garlick, Heath, 217.
Garns, Nathan, 262.
Garnsey, Jonathan, 223.
Garnsey, Petor, 147.
Garnsey, Samuel, 241.
Garnsey, Silas, 241.
Garrald, Thomas, 23.
Garrald, see Jerrald.
Garrett (Garrit, Garrot).
Garrett, Joseph, 70, 71, 144, 191.
Garrison, Aaron, 57.
Gart, Elisha, 144.
Gary (Garey), Ebenezer, 27, 161.
Gary, Joshua, 94.
Gary, Peter, 240.
Gates (Gats), Daniel, 244, 256.
Gates, David, 240.
Gates, Ezra, 82, 86, 205, 259.
Gates, James, 42.
Gates, Jesse, 42.
Gates, Jonathan, 61.
Gates, Joseph, 124.
Gates, Josiah, 121, 122, 123.
Gates, Levi, 203.
Gates, Mathew, 86.
Gates, Matthias, 82.
Gates, Nehemiah, 42, 232.
Gates, Samuel, 251.
Gates, Stephen, 213.
Gates, Timothy, 203, 256.
Gay, Abner, 137.
Gay, Eli, 84, 148, 149.
Gay, Gideon, 162, 250, 257.
Gay, Samuel, 46.
Gaylord (Galard, Gailord, Gayler, Gaylard).
Gaylord, 80.
Gaylord, Aaron, 226.
Gaylord, Agur, 14, 246.
Gaylord, Benjamin, 217.
Gaylord, Charles, 135, 136, 173.
Gaylord, Eleazer, 70, 71, 128, 129, 234.
Gaylord, Eleazer, Jr., 70.
Gaylord, Elijah, 246.
Gaylord, Joseph, 246.
Gaylord, Justus, 209.
Gaylord, Samuel, 69, 71, 126, 128, 129, 208.
Gaylord, Timothy, 58, 224.
Gaylord, William, 84.
Geary (Geery, Gery).
Geary, Joshua, 96, 135, 136.
Geary, Peter, 245.
Gee, Sollomon, 41.
Geer (Gear), Aaron, 100.

Geer, Abel, 232.
Geer, Caleb, 84.
Geer, Elias, 232.
Geer, Jacob, 240, 244.
Geer, James, 232.
Geer, Jedidiah, 183.
Geer, John, 84, 107, 232.
Geer, Reason, 112, 113, 237.
Geer, Solomon, 197.
Gennings, see Jennings.
Gennius, John, 71.
George, Thomas, 151, 152, 180.
German, John, 151.
Gibbins, John, 171.
Gibbs (Gebbs, Gibs).
Gibbs, Benjamin, 223.
Gibbs, Caleb, 199.
Gibbs, Job, 147.
Gibbs, John, 120.
Gibbs, John, Jr., 161.
Gibbs, Justus, 33, 140, 141, 219.
Gibbs, Warham, 33.
Gibbs, Zebulun, 199.
Gibbs, Zebulon, Jr., 224.
Gibson (Gipson).
Gibson, Ephraim, 240, 244.
Gibson, Isaiah, 206.
Gibson, John, 82.
Gibson, John, Jr., 129.
Gibson, William, 59.
Giddens (Giddens).
Giddings, Joseph, 226, 237.
Giddings, Wellcum, 202.
Giddings, William, 44, 118.
Gifford, Caleb, 250, 257.
Gifford, Daniel, 206.
Gifford, James, 250.
Gifford, Stephen, 236.
Gifford, Wilston, 77.
Gifford, Woolston, 32.
Gifford, Zibah, 250.
Gilbert (Gelberd, Gilberd, Gilbord, Gilburd, Guilburt).
Gilbert, Benjamin, 84, 135.
Gilbert, Caleb, 30, 127, 171.
Gilbert, Daniel, 116.
Gilbert, David, 115, 234.
Gilbert, Elnathan, 135.
Gilbert, Hezekiah, 13, 242.
Gilbert, Isah, 219.
Gilbert, Joel, 30, 231.
Gilbert, John, 52, 86, 148.
Gilbert, Jonathan, 203, 230, 258.
Gilbert, Joseph, 11, 218.
Gilbert, Josiah, 210.
Gilbert, Mathew, 253.
Gilbert, Michael, 31, 171.

Gilbert, Noah, 249.
Gilbert, Samuel, 30, 70, 71, 135, 136, 231.
Gilbert, Samuel, Jr., 257.
Gilbert, Thoma, 229.
Gilbert, William, 34.
Gilead, 204.
Giles, Thomas, 190.
Gill, John, 200.
Gill, Thomas, 67.
Gillett (Gyllit), Aaron, 205, 256.
Gillett, Abraham, 225.
Gillett, Benjamin, 211.
Gillett, Charles, 95.
Gillett, Daniel, 137.
Gillett, David, 59.
Gillett, Gideon, 169.
Gillett, Israel, 188, 189.
Gillett, Jere, 161.
Gillett, Jeremiah, 120, 130, 188.
Gillett, John, 228, 243.
Gillett, Jonah, 38.
Gillett, Jonathan, 13, 110, 134, 135, 136, 173, 175, 217, 238, 239.
Gillett, Jonathan, Jr., 38.
Gillett, William, 220.
Gitteau (Gitto, Gittow).
Gitteau, Ephraim, 32, 77, 224.
Gitteau, Francis, 147.
Gittum, Benjamin, 223.
Giveit, Lewis, 11.
Gladding (Glading, Gleeding).
Gladding, Ebenezer, 44, 227.
Gladding, Joshua, 118.
Gladding, Silas, 118.
Glastonbury, 3, 91, 162, 185, 188, 189, 210, 228, 229.
Glazier (Glazar, Glazer).
Glazier, John, 208.
Glazier, Samuel, 208.
Gleason (Gleson, Glosson).
Gleason, Ephraim, 39.
Gleason, Isaac, 230.
Gleason, Nehemiah, 46.
Gleason, Noah, 7, 104, 106.
Gleason, Obediah, 169, 170.
Glover, Henry, 238.
Glover, James, 238.
Godfrey, Daniel, 201.
Godfrey, Ebenezer, 201.
Godfrey, John, 201.
Godfrey, Nathan, 102.
Goff, Jacob, 210.
Goff, John, 186.
Goff, Joseph, 81.
Goff, Josiah, 210.
Goff, Philip, 115, 116.
Goff, Samuel, 81.

Goff, William, 40, 233.
Gold, John, 87, 250.
Gold, see Gould.
Goldsberry (Gooldsberry).
Goldsberry, Joseph, 56, 138, 139.
Goldsmith, John Gardner, 233.
Good[ ], Lackins, 213.
Goodale, Abijah, 208.
Goodale, Isaac, 22.
Goodale, Eliphalet, 37, 242.
Goodale, Elisha, 242.
Goodale, Nathaniel, 208.
Goodale, Richard, 213.
Goodale, Thomas, 78, 128.
Goodell, Isaac, 148, 149.
Goodell, Thomas, 18, 20, 129.
Goodrich, Abraham, 210.
Goodrich, Ashbell, 32, 206.
Goodrich, Caleb, 186.
Goodrich, Charles, 159, 213.
Goodrich, Crafts, 215.
Goodrich, Daniel, 61, 225.
Goodrich, David, 59.
Goodrich, Ebenezer, 209.
Goodrich, Elisha, 210, 235.
Goodrich, Elizur, 22, 24, 28, 30, 32, 87.
Goodrich, Ephraim, 35, 70, 71, 130, 131.
Goodrich, Gideon, 130.
Goodrich, Hezekiah, 210.
Goodrich, Jeremiah, 264.
Goodrich, Josiah, 209.
Goodrich, Moses, 59.
Goodrich, Nathaniel, 209.
Goodrich, Peter, 210.
Goodrich, Solomon, 217.
Goodrich, Thomas, 70, 71.
Goodrich, Timothy, 130.
Goodrich, William, 218.
Goodrich, Zenas, 206.
Goodsell, Samuel, 27.
Goodwin (Godwin), Charles, 32.
Goodwin, Jesse, 239.
Goodwin, Jonathan, 246.
Goodwin, Nathaniel, 84, 199.
Goodwin, Sephen, 247.
Goodwin, Thomas, 228, 243.
Goodwin, Uriah, 230.
Goodyear, Asa, 30.
Gordon (Gorden, Gording, Gourden).
Gordon, John, 32, 77, 224, 253.
Gordon, John, Jr., 231.
Gordon, William, 96, 98.
Gorham, Isaac, 201.
Gorham, Samuel, 177, 178.
Gorton (Gorten), Benjamin, 237.

INDEX. 301

Gorton, Lancaster, 51, 52, 117.
Goshen, 57, 58, 142, 162, 223, 224, 243, 247, 249, 256.
Gott (Got), Daniel, 205, 257.
Gott, Isaac, 244.
Gott, John, 82, 137, 257.
Gott, Story, 266.
Gould (Goold), Abraham, 221.
Gould, Ebenezer, 15.
Gould, Job, 225.
Gould, John, 117, 161, 248, 254.
Gould, Joseph, 218.
Gould, Luther, 201.
Gould, Thomas, 37, 208.
Gould, William, 226.
Gould, see Gold.
Goward, William, 188.
Gowdy (Goudy), Samuel, 173, 175.
Goyt, Isaac, 244.
Graham (Grayham), Barnaby, 61.
Graham, Benjamin, 105, 106, 171.
Graham, Elijah, 211.
Graham, Hugh, 23.
Graham, John, 6, 91.
Grandey, Adman, 46.
Grandey, Edmond, 250.
Granger (Grainger), Aaron, 211.
Granger, Abner, 211.
Granger, Bildad, 95.
Granger, Denison, 31.
Granger, Joel, 94, 95.
Granger, John, 246.
Granger, Josiah, 94.
Granger, Robert, 211.
Granger, Samuel, 95.
Grannis, John, 252.
Grannis, Samuel, 31.
Grannis, Stephen, Jr., 31.
Grant, Alexander, 173.
Grant, Benjamin, Jr., 215.
Grant, Elijah, 147, 223.
Grant, Ezra, 211.
Grant, Jehiel, 224.
Grant, John, 86, 230.
Grant, Matthew, 135, 207, 222.
Grant, Noah, 77, 78, 81, 121, 122, 123, 124, 159, 160, 161.
Grant, Ozias, 38, 134, 136.
Grant, Solomon, 81, 132.
Grant, William, 173, 175, 221.
Grasier, Timothy, 160.
Graves (Greaves), Ebenezer, 50.
Graves, Elias, 51, 202.
Graves, Eliud, 44, 118.
Graves, Ely, 202.
Graves, George, 221.
Graves, Hains, 259.
Graves, John, 144.

Graves, Joseph, 229.
Graves, Josiah, 63.
Graves, Mark, 188.
Graves, Nathan, 51.
Graves, Noadiah, 222.
Graves, Silvanus, 226.
Graves, Sterling, 203, 259.
Graves, Thomas, 43, 72, 73, 74, 75, 78, 182.
Graves, William, 15, 192.
Graves, see Greives.
Gray, Abraham, 251.
Gray, Henry, 148.
Gray, Hezekiah, 201.
Gray, James, 201.
Gray, John, 184, 201, 206.
Gray, Joseph, 226.
Gray, Nathan, 180.
Gray, Obediah, 238.
Gray, Simeon, 250.
Great Britain, 3.
Green, Christopher, 27, 232, 233.
Green, David, 157, 226, 232.
Green, Ebenezer, 201.
Green, Ezra, 180.
Green, Isaac, 140.
Green, Jabez, 69, 184.
Green, Jacob, 100.
Green, James, 217.
Green, Jeremiah, 217.
Green, John, 115, 116.
Green, Jonathan, 56, 139.
Green, Joseph, 23, 114, 116, 184.
Green, Norman, 135, 169.
Green, Samuel, 198.
Green, Thomas, 107.
Green, William, 12, 43.
Green, Winter, 27.
Greenbush, N. Y., 22.
Greenlif, James, 83.
Greenslit (Greanslit, Greensleete).
Greenslit, John, 56, 109, 110, 241, 248, 254.
Greenwich, 179, 216, 217.
Gregory (Grigory), Abraham, 251.
Gregory, Dan, 29.
Gregory, David, 157.
Gregory, Ebenezer, 56, 238.
Gregory, Elijah, 56, 251.
Gregory, George, 79.
Gregory, Gilead, 155.
Gregory, Nathan, 55, 237.
Gregory, Nehemiah, 57, 109, 110, 206.
Gregory, Seeley, 109, 180.
Greives, William, 146.
Gridley, Luke, 173, 175.
Gridley, Noah, 130, 209.

Gridley, Rezin, 239.
Gridley, Samuel, 130.
Griffin, Benjamin, 238.
Griffin, John, 59, 177, 178, 220.
Griffin, Joshua, 213.
Griffin, Stephen, 169.
Griffin, Thomas, 5.
Griffing, Daniel, 40.
Griffing, James, 45.
Griffing, John, 201.
Griffing, Samuel, 195.
Griffing, Stephen, 35.
Griffith, Samuel, 238.
Griffith, Seth, 251.
Griffith, Thomas, 58.
Griffus, Thomas, 147.
Griggs, Abijah, 242.
Griggs, Noah, 235.
Grimes, Benjamin, 14, 173, 175.
Grimes, Ichabod, 211.
Grimes, Isaac, 245.
Grimes, Joseph, 196.
Grinnell (Greenell, Grenall).
Grinnell, Pabody, 44.
Grinnell, Samuel, 196.
Grist, George, 237.
Griswold (Grisewould, Griswell, Griswould).
Griswold, Aaron, 259.
Griswold, Azariah, 218.
Griswold, Benjamin, 65, 67, 68, 140.
Griswold, Daniel, 43.
Griswold, David, 206.
Griswold, Ebenezer, 34.
Griswold, Edward, Jr., 246.
Griswold, Elisha, 228.
Griswold, George, 44.
Griswold, Giles, 224.
Griswold, Jedediah, 226.
Griswold, Joel, 230.
Griswold, John, 40, 72, 73, 75, 117, 118.
Griswold, Jonathan, 36, 130.
Griswold, Moses, 34, 108.
Griswold, Ozias, 209.
Griswold, Roger, 173, 175.
Griswold, Samuel, 236.
Griswold, Solomon, 173.
Griswold, Thomas, 212.
Griswold, Timothy, 210.
Griswold, Zacheus, 57.
Grosvenor, Ebenezer, 208.
Grosvenor, John, 41, 207.
Groton, 158, 190, 197.
Groues, John, 147.
Grover, Benjamin, 208.
Grover, Edmund, 94.
Grover, John, 208.

Grover, Simon, 183.
Grover, William, 11.
Growmon, David, 110.
Guard, Elisha, 72.
Guild, Jacob, 120.
Guernsey, John, 234.
Guile, Jacob, 161.
Guile, John, 190.
Guilford, 11, 48, 50, 143, 194, 201, 202, 212.
Gunn, Abel, 54.
Gunn, Abner, 220.
Gunthy, Jos., 219.
Gurley, John, 137, 181.
Gurney, Barzeleel, 239.
Gurney, John, 210.
Gurney, John, Jr., 13.
Gutre[   ], 136.
Guttree, Ephraim, 226.
Guye, Samuel, 23.
Gypson, John, 128.

H[   ], Jared, 26.
Hacket, James, 53.
Haddam, 227.
Haden, Job, 193.
Hadlock (Haddlock, Hatlock).
Hadlock, James, 6, 94, 96.
Hadlock, John, 186.
Hadlock, John, Jr., 162.
Hadlyme, 162, 188.
Hagar, James, 10, 108, 191.
Hail, Gershom, 83.
Hail, Isaac, 70.
Hail, Nathaniel, 35.
Hail, Thomas, 211.
Hail, see Hale.
Hait, Abraham, 217.
Hait, Gedion, 61.
Hait, Jonathan, 216.
Hale, Benjamin, 173, 175.
Hale, Daniel, 94, 229.
Hale, Elisha, 213.
Hale, Ezekiel, 94, 96.
Hale, Gershom, 99, 100, 237.
Hale, Gideon, 51, 229.
Hale, Joseph, 23.
Hale, Moses, 229.
Hale, Natha, 79.
Hale, Samuel, 60, 171.
Hale, Thoder, 229.
Hale, see Hail.
Half Moon, 105, 106, 129, 157, 210.
Halkens, Ozias, 198.
Halkins, James, 255.
Hall, 254.
Hall, Abijah, 213.
Hall, Abner, 31.

INDEX.

Hall, Abraham, 49.
Hall, Amos, 42, 78.
Hall, Asaph, 247.
Hall, Azariah, 100.
Hall, Bale, 66.
Hall, Bate, 66, 68.
Hall, Benjamin, 39, 211, 222, 234.
Hall, David, 66.
Hall, Eliezer, 156.
Hall, Elizer, 154.
Hall, Elnathan, 226.
Hall, Gideon, 213.
Hall, Gilbert, 50.
Hall, Giles, 143, 263.
Hall, Hait, 54.
Hall, Ichabud, 155.
Hall, Isaac, 6, 201, 245.
Hall, Israel, 14.
Hall, Jabez, 62, 138, 139.
Hall, Jacob, 213.
Hall, Jere, 145.
Hall, Jeremiah, 17, 20, 144.
Hall, John, 16.
Hall, Joseph, 83, 221.
Hall, Joshua, 201.
Hall, Jotham, 23, 121, 186.
Hall, Miles, 235.
Hall, Moses, 54.
Hall, Nahum, 207.
Hall, Nat., 197.
Hall, Nathaniel, 72, 73, 75, 143, 145.
Hall, Philemon, 51.
Hall, Solomon, 6, 122, 124, 173, 175.
Hall, Stephen, 195.
Hall, Street, 65, 66, 68, 69, 267.
Hall, Thomas, 215.
Hall, Titus, 49, 103.
Hall, William, 224, 234.
Halladay, James, 63, 94, 96.
Hallet, Samuel, 214.
Halling, Henry, 187.
Hallowell, William, 177, 178.
Haly (Haley), Caleb, 197.
Haly, Jeremiah, 191.
Hambleton, John, 203.
Hambleton, Peter, 52, 86, 122.
Hambleton, Samuel, 206.
Hambleton, see Hamilton.
Hamblin, Charles, 234.
Hamblin, Christopher, 234.
Hamblin, Elijah, 66, 158, 240.
Hamblin, Giles, 202.
Hamblin, Joel, 29.
Hamblin, Nathaniel, 43.
Hamblin, Silas, 206.
Hamblin, Timothy, 86.
Hamblin, William, 225.

Hamblin, see Hamlin.
Hamilton, David, 192, 260.
Hamilton, Dudley, 206.
Hamilton, John, 224, 237, 258.
Hamilton, see Hambleton.
Hamlin, Cornelius, 218.
Hamlin, Edward, 229.
Hamlin, Elijah, 67, 157, 244.
Hamlin, Jabez, 3, 91, 167.
Hamlin, Nathaniel, 209.
Hamlin, see Hamblin.
Hammer (Hamer), Daniel, 214.
Hammer, John, 77, 161.
Hammer, see Hanmer.
Hammond, Abel, 242.
Hammond, Elijah, 233.
Hammond, John, 248, 254.
Hammond, Joseph, 97.
Hammond, Mathew, 37.
Hammond, Tho., 223.
Hampshire Co., Mass., 88.
Hanchett (Henchet), Amos, 247.
Hanchett, John, 211.
Hanchett, Oliver, 169, 254.
Hanchett, Zacheas, Jr., 245.
Hancock, Jonathan, 228, 244.
Hand, Daniel, 202.
Hand, Lemuel, 48, 192.
Hand, Reuben, 50.
Hand, Samuel, 195, 261.
Hand, Timothy, 51, 144, 195.
Handerson, John, 226.
Handy (Handee, Handey, Hande).
Handy, Barzillai, 240, 244.
Handy, David, 140, 185.
Hanford (Handford), 267.
Hanford, Ebenezer, 138, 251.
Hanford, Gershom, 139.
Hanford, Isaac, 32.
Hanford, Samuel, 55, 57, 251.
Hanford, Stephen, 139.
Hanks, Benjamin, 27, 248.
Hanks, Benjamin, Jr., 254.
Hanks, Uriah, 249.
Hanley, Josias, 160.
Hanmer, Francis, 210.
Hanmer, John, 25, 36.
Hanmer, see Hammer.
Hanniball (Hanabal, Hannaball, Hannabel).
Hanniball, Cornelius, 72, 73, 75.
Harding (Harden), Ebenezer, 213.
Harding, Israel, 8, 78, 86, 128, 129, 132, 133.
Harding, Lemuel, 47.
Harding, Thomas, 188.
Hardy, Rufus, 50.
Hare, Samuel, 114, 116.

Hares, John, 149.
Harger, Jabez, 220.
Harmon, Benjaman, 245.
Harmon, John, 103, 211, 251.
Harmon, Nehemiah, 5, 95.
Harmon, Samuel, 245.
Harrington (Harinton, Harrinton).
Harrington, Isaac, 40.
Harrington, Samuel, 208.
Harrington, Timothy, 79.
Harrington, William, 16.
Harris (Harrais), Abijah, 35.
Harris, Daniel, 233, 240, 244.
Harris, David, 157, 225.
Harris, Ebenezer, 237.
Harris, Elisha, 58, 147.
Harris, Giles, 79, 137.
Harris, James, 43, 45, 117, 118, 119, 161.
Harris, James, Jr., 117, 160.
Harris, John, 16, 148.
Harris, Jonathan, 113, 203, 258.
Harris, Joseph, 114, 116, 186.
Harris, Joshua, 247.
Harris, Nathaniel, 127.
Harris, Samuel, 115, 116.
Harris, Stephen, 100, 240, 244.
Harris, Thomas, 206.
Harrison (Harison), Abel, 194.
Harrison, Daniel, 225.
Harrison, Gideon, 199.
Harrison, Jacob, 224.
Harrison, Moses, 60.
Harrison, Nathaniel, Jr., 225.
Harrison, Simeon, 225.
Harrison, Titus, 13, 199.
Harrison, William, 60, 118, 161.
Harry, Benjamin, 72, 75.
Hart, David, 210, 239.
Hart, Elisha, 239.
Hart, Elnathan, 239.
Hart, Gideon, 239.
Hart, Hawkins, 49, 235.
Hart, John, 186.
Hart, Matthew, 210.
Hart, Noadiah, 186.
Hart, Russel, 228.
Hart, Samuel, 212.
Hart, Simeon, 222.
Hart, Timothy, 12.
Hart, Zechariah, 210.
Hart, Zepheniah, 136.
Hartford, James, 65, 67, 68, 79, 101.
Hartford, 3, 5, 7, 11, 34, 36, 38, 76, 77, 87, 93, 96, 98, 108, 126, 128, 134, 135, 136, 167, 173, 228, 229, 230, 265.

Hartman, Christopher, 216.
Hartshorn, John, 237.
Harvey, Nathan, 215.
Harvey, Richard, 113.
Harvey, Robert, 162.
Harwinton, 246.
Hasdell, James, 246.
Haskell, Jonathan, 37.
Haskil, Gideon, 237.
Haskins, Joseph, 224.
Haskins, see Hoskins.
Hasting, John, 121.
Hasting, Jonathan, 191.
Hastins, Joseph, 211.
Haston, James, 249, 255.
Hatch, Abner, 198.
Hatch, David, 122, 215.
Hatch, Ebenezer, 27, 212.
Hatch, Ichabod, 7.
Hatch, Isaac, 51.
Hatch, Jethro, 217.
Hatch, John, 105, 106, 172, 181, 261.
Hatch, Joseph, 232.
Hatch, Lemuel, 216.
Hatch, Moses, 50.
Hatch, Rufus, 83, 191.
Hatch, Samuel, 162, 188.
Hatchet, Tousey John, 105, 106.
Hatchet, see Tousey.
Hathway, John, 64.
Hatter, Daniel, 12.
Havens, Robert, 16, 101.
Haviland, William, 260.
Hawkins, Edward, 233.
Hawkins, Eli, 171.
Hawkins, Eliazer, 59.
Hawkins, Joel, 211.
Hawkins, Josiah, 70.
Hawkins, Robert, 218.
Hawkins, Samuel, 126.
Hawkins, Syrus, 71.
Hawkins, Zadok, 110.
Hawley (Hauley), Benajah, 204.
Hawley, Ebenezer, 241.
Hawley, Enos, 204.
Hawley, Frederick, 221.
Hawley, Jehiel, 218.
Hawley, John, Jr., 241.
Hawley, Jonath, 206.
Hawley, Nathan, 138, 139, 159, 160.
Hawley, Nathan, Jr., 242.
Hawley, Samuel, 200.
Hawley, Wolcott, 221.
Hawse, Edmond, 226.
Hayden (Hadon), David, 173, 175.
Hayden, Job, 261.
Hayden, Nathaniel, Jr., 216.

Hayden, see Haden.
Hayes (Haise, Hays, Hayse).
Hayes, Dudly, 7.
Hayes, Freegift, 56.
Hayes, James, 238.
Hayes, Jonathan, 157, 158.
Hayes, Judah, 7, 211.
Hayes, Silas, 245.
Hayes, Thomas, 180.
Hayes, Zenos, 245.
Haynes, Caleb, Jr., 197.
Hayward, Benjamin, 176, 249, 255.
Hazard (Hazzod), Jason, 222.
Hazard, John, 205, 258.
Heard (Herd), John, 16, 100, 101.
Heard, Thomas, 36.
Heath, Bartholomew, 218.
Heath, Peleg, 27, 99, 198.
Heath, Thomas, 183.
Heaton, Daniel, 252.
Heaton, Joseph, 253.
Hebard (Hebberd, Hebord).
Hebard, Daniel, 248, 254.
Hebard, Ebenezer, 183.
Hebard, Elijah, 183.
Hebard, Josiah, 249, 254.
Hebard, Joshua, 98.
Hebard, Nathan, 248.
Hebard, Nathan, Jr., 254.
Hebard, see Hibbard.
Hebron, 42, 81, 142, 147, 162, 167, 187, 188, 189, 204, 255, 256, 257.
Hecock (Heckock, Hekock).
Hecock, Benjamin, 14, 130, 131.
Hecock, Daniel, 204.
Hecock, David, 204.
Hecock, Gideon, 204.
Hecock, James, 109.
Hecock, John, 109, 110.
Hecock, Joseph, 204.
Hecock, Silas, 251.
Hecock, Tho., 223.
Hecock, see Hicock.
Hegon, see Suckhegon.
Helms, Christopher, 71, 72, 73, 74.
Hendrick (Hendrix).
Hendrick, Benoni, 157, 158.
Hendrick, Beno, 177.
Hendrick, Ebenezer, 251.
Hendrick, Peter, 221.
Hendrick, Samuel, 178, 198, 201.
Henning, Morriss, 49.
Henrick, John, 208.
Henrix, David, 102.
Henry, Thomas, 182.
Henrys, Benony, 179.
Henrys, Samuel, 179.
Henshaw (Hinshaw).

Henshaw, James, 228, 244.
Henson, William, 52.
Herrick (Harrak, Herick).
Herrick, Andrew, 107.
Herrick, Benjamin, 74.
Herrick, Cypron, 236.
Herrick, Elezer, 108, 232.
Herrick, Elijah, 232.
Herrick, Ezekel, 198.
Herrick, Henry, 232.
Herrick, John, 133.
Herrick, Robert, 232.
Herrick, Samuel, 52.
Herrings, Isaac, 11.
Herrington (Herington, Herronton).
Herrington, Daniel, 176, 178.
Herrington, Elijah, 211.
Herrington, Isaac, 108, 191.
Herrington, Timothy, 83.
Herrington, William, 101.
Hervy, Richard, 52.
Heusted (Hewsted).
Heusted, Jonathan, 251.
Heusted, Joseph, Jr., 241.
Hewett, Jeptha, 190.
Hewett, Joseph, 190.
Hewitt, Benjamin, Jr., 214.
Hewitt, Ephraim, 208.
Hewitt, Jonas, 107.
Hewitt, Jones, 214.
Hewitt, Joseph, 10.
Hewitt, Reubin, 214.
Hewitt, Samuel, 214.
Hewitt, Solomon, 40.
Hewitt, Walter, 228, 244.
Hibbard (Hibbert), Eleazer, 16.
Hibbard, John, 208.
Hibbard, Joshua, 35.
Hibbard, Josiah, 20.
Hibbard, see Hebard.
Hicks, Levi, 37.
Hicock, Amos, 219.
Hicock, Samuel, 28.
Hicock, see Hecock.
Hide, 17.
Hide, Abnor, 236.
Hide, Caleb, 129, 136, 138, 160, 161.
Hide, Christopher, 248, 254.
Hide, Dan, 250.
Hide, Daniel, 236.
Hide, Ebenezer, 46, 47.
Hide, Eliab, 236.
Hide, Elihu, 40, 237.
Hide, Elijah, 250.
Hide, Ezekiel, 236.
Hide, Isaac, 101, 240.

Hide, James, 16, 97, 98.
Hide, Jedidiah, Jr., 40.
Hide, John, 101, 153, 236.
Hide, John, Jr., 237.
Hide, Joseph, 35.
Hide, Levi, 40, 182.
Hide, Matthew, 237.
Hide, Samuel, 28.
Hide, Seth, 208.
Hide, Walter, 250.
Hide, William, 19.
Hierlihy (Heirlehy, Herlihy).
Hierlihy, Timothy, 22, 76, 114, 116, 167, 176, 185.
Higbee (Higby, Higbye).
Higbee, Isaac, 53.
Higbee, John, 209.
Higbee, Joseph, 234.
Higbee, Samuel, 54, 234.
Higbee, Zacheus, 115, 116, 234.
Higgins (Higens).
Higgins, Benjamin, 139, 241.
Higgins, Cornelius, 117.
Higgins, Elkana, 60.
Higgins, Ichabod, 145.
Higgens, John, 201.
Higgins, Samuel, 118.
Higgins, Sylvanus, 81.
Higley, Joel, 211.
Higley, Nathan, 211.
Higley, Samuel, 63.
Hill, Aaron, 50.
Hill, Ahirah, 199.
Hill, Asa, 247.
Hill, Meliaz, 12.
Hill, Beriah, 222.
Hill, Bilious, 127, 128, 247.
Hill, Charlott, 181.
Hill, Daniel, 212.
Hill, Daniel, Jr., 186.
Hill, Eben, 247.
Hill, Ebenezer, 107.
Hill, Elijah, 188.
Hill, Isaac, 177, 179.
Hill, James, 231, 250.
Hill, Jared, 252.
Hill, John, 31, 127.
Hill, Levi, 190.
Hill, Luke, Jr., 147.
Hill, Nathan, 202.
Hill, Phinehas, 200.
Hill, Rufus, 10, 214.
Hill, Samuel, 10.
Hill, Silas, 32, 77, 157, 158, 226.
Hill, Thomas, 50, 248, 254.
Hill, Timothy, 212.
Hill, Titus, 224.
Hill, Zacheus, 72.

Hill, see Hills.
Hillard, David, 144.
Hillard, Joseph, 118, 119.
Hillard, see Hillyard.
Hills, Abner, 137.
Hills, Abraham, 130.
Hills, Amos, 257.
Hills, Beriah, 222.
Hills, Benone, 247.
Hills, Charles, 83.
Hills, David, 209.
Hills, Isaac, 215.
Hills, James, 257.
Hills, John, 78, 82.
Hills, Joseph, 46.
Hills, Medad, 247.
Hills, Oliver, 84.
Hills, William, 210.
Hills, see Hill.
Hillyard, Joseph, 45.
Hillyard, see Hillard.
Hilton, Adkison, 180.
Hincher, Oliver, 248.
Hind, Benjamin, 59.
Hind, David, 30.
Hind, Isaac, 252.
Hind, Joel, 59.
Hine (Hyne), Aaron, 171.
Hine, Abel, 225.
Hine, Benjamin, 124, 171.
Hine, Elijah, 220.
Hine, Hezekiah, 220.
Hine, Nathan, 204.
Hinkley, Ebenezer, 248, 255.
Hinkley, Ichabod, 122, 215.
Hinkley, John, 213.
Hinman (Henman).
Hinman, Aaron, 144, 186.
Hinman, Abijah, 28.
Hinman, Adam, 28, 146, 185, 266.
Hinman, Benjamin, 28, 29, 32, 87, 143, 146, 147, 219, 266.
Hinman, David, 219.
Hinman, Ebenezer, 32.
Hinman, Elihu, 155.
Hinman, Elijah, 28, 147.
Hinman, James, 66, 67, 223.
Hinman, Joseph, 224.
Hinman, Noble, 28, 146.
Hinman, Ruben, 146, 204.
Hinman, Samuel, 204, 247.
Hinman, Timothy, 85.
Hinman, Titus, 28.
Hinman, Wait, 85, 218.
Hinsdell (Hensdill).
Hinsdell, Jacob, 103, 239.
Histing, Edward, 199.
Hitchcock (Hichcock).

Hitchcock, Aaron, 5, 102, 103, 104, 159, 160, 167, 168.
Hitchcock, Amasa, 127.
Hitchcock, Amos, 30, 126, 128, 136, 138, 170, 252.
Hitchcock, Benjamin, 49.
Hitchcock, Caleb, 226.
Hitchcock, David, 225.
Hitchcock, Eliaken, 137, 188.
Hitchcock, Enos, 67, 68, 193, 261.
Hitchcock, Isaac, 218.
Hitchcock, John, 50, 226.
Hitchcock, Matthias, 48, 49, 235.
Hitchcock, Nathaniel, 54, 65, 68, 120, 121, 222.
Hitchcock, Reuben, 67, 69, 193.
Hitchcock, Samuel, 48.
Hitchcock, Titus, 235.
Hitchcock, Volentine, 120, 193, 261.
Hixley, John, 94.
Hoade, John, 67.
Hoadley, Samuel, 59.
Hobby, Benjamin, 217.
Hobby, John, 217.
Hobby, Thomas, 60, 62.
Hodgdon (Hogden).
Hodgdon, Timothy, 177, 178.
Hodge, Ezekiel, 138.
Hodge, Joseph, 161.
Hodge, Samuel, 82.
Hodge, Thomas, 105, 106, 171.
Hodge, Timothy, 138.
Hodgkin (Hoghkin).
Hodgkin, Ebenezer, 113, 181.
Hodgkins, William, 69.
Hoisington (Hoesington, Horsington, Hosington, Hossington).
Hoisington, Ebenezer, 54, 55.
Hoisington, Jacob, 121.
Hoisington, Joab, 14, 120, 222.
Holbrook (Halbrook, Holtbrook).
Holbrook, Caleb, 29.
Holbrook, David, 60, 146.
Holbrook, Ebenezer, 207.
Holbrook, Nathaniel, 18, 19, 20.
Holbrook, Nathaniel, Jr., 250.
Holcomb (Holkom), Eldad, 6.
Holcomb, Eli, 135.
Holcomb, Elijah, 63, 134, 136, 169, 170.
Holcomb, Ezary, 7.
Holcomb, Isaac Terry, 35.
Holcomb, Jesse, 245.
Holcomb, Joel, 234, 235.
Holcomb, John, 134.
Holcomb, Joseph, 34.
Holcomb, Juddah, 245.
Holcomb, Michael, 94, 96.

Holcomb, Mickl, 7.
Holcomb, Obed, 245.
Holcomb, Return, 63, 169.
Holcomb, Silas, 169.
Holcomb, Simeon, 245.
Holcomb, Stephen, 6, 94, 105, 134, 136.
Holden (Holding).
Holden, Benjamin, 16, 97, 98.
Holden, John, 22, 229.
Holden, Jonathan, 229.
Holdridge, Amos, 191.
Holdridge, Hezekiah, 137, 188, 257.
Holdridge, John, 148, 257.
Holdridge, William, 190.
Holladay, James, 245.
Holley (Holly), Abraham, 216.
Holley, Gideon, 219.
Holley, John, 150.
Holley, Nathan, 60.
Holley, Nathaniel, 217.
Holley, William, 201, 238.
Hollister (Holester, Holister).
Hollister, Appleton, 39, 169, 170, 210.
Hollister, Elezer, 85.
Hollister, Elisha, 58.
Hollister, Francis, 186.
Hollister, Gideon, 204, 209.
Hollister, Hill, 35, 154, 186.
Hollister, Nathaniel, 157, 226.
Hollister, Stephen, 229.
Hollon, Abishai, 99.
Hollond, Larrance, 29.
Hollowell, William, 155.
Holmes (Holmbs, Holms, Homes, Homos).
Holmes, Alpheus, 228, 243.
Holmes, Christopher, 203.
Holmes, David, 266.
Holmes, Elkanah, 240, 244.
Holmes, George, 258.
Holmes, Jabez, 100.
Holmes, James, 208.
Holmes, John, 86, 130, 131, 186, 187, 198, 217, 253.
Holmes, John, Jr., 82, 241.
Holmes, Joseph, 46.
Holmes, Lemuel, 248, 254.
Holmes, Reuben, 216.
Holmes, Stephen, 13.
Holt, Ezekiel, 35.
Holt, Isaac, 231.
Holt, Joshua, 249.
Holt, Joshua, Jr., 254.
Holt, Justus, 65.
Holt, Nathan, 43.
Holt, Nathaniel, 35.

Holt, Nehemiah, 248, 254.
Holt, Timothy, 198.
Holt, William, 248, 254.
Holt, Zebadiah, 35.
Homan, Peter, 9, 117, 119.
Honde, John, 220.
Honn, Michel, 219.
Hooker, Asahel, 224.
Hooker, Martin, 186.
Hooker, Nodiah, 239.
Hooker, Samuel, 229, 230.
Hooker, William, 224.
Hoosac (Osuck) Fort, 133.
Hopkins, Benjamin, 181.
Hopkins, James, 246.
Hopkins, Jonath, 239.
Hopkins, Joseph, 133, 210.
Hopkins, Prince, 100.
Hopkins, William, 68, 69, 71.
Hopson, Clemen, 103.
Hopson, Clement, 235.
Hopson, Linus, 54, 235.
Hopson, William, 204.
Hordly, William, 222.
Horner, Thomas, 186.
Horseneck, 217.
Horsford (Horseford, Hosford).
Horsford, Amos, 103, 235.
Horsford, Daniel, 247.
Horsford, Ezekiel, 12.
Horsford, Jese, 199.
Horsfoot, Obadiah, 256, 257.
Horsford, Samuel, 247.
Horsford, Serajah, 239.
Horton, Aaron, 215.
Horton, Ebenezer, 227.
Horton, John, 253.
Horton, Samuel, 44, 79.
Horton, William, 120, 193, 261.
Hoscott, Samuel, 182.
Hoskins (Horskins).
Hoskins, Anthony, 13, 192.
Hoskins, Elijah, 127.
Hoskins, Enoch, 236.
Hoskins, Shuball, 105.
Hoskins, Thomas, 39, 230.
Hoskins, see Haskins.
Hosmer (Horsemore, Horsmer, Osmore).
Hosmer, Aaron, 172.
Hosmer, George, 230.
Hosmer, James, 37.
Hosmer, John, 39, 134, 136.
Hosmer, Stephen, 86.
Hotchkiss (Hodgkiss, Hogkis, Hotskiss).
Hotchkiss, 109.

Hotchkis, Amos, 212.
Hotchkiss, Charls, 252.
Hotchkiss, Elijah, 103, 235, 252.
Hotchkiss, Gideon, 222.
Hotchkiss, Henry, 49, 235.
Hotchkiss, Jabez, 126, 252.
Hotchkiss, James, 209.
Hotchkiss, Jesse, 193.
Hotchkiss, John, 49.
Hotchkiss, John, Jr., 49.
Hotchkiss, Jon, 48.
Hotchkiss, Joseph, 231.
Hotchkiss, Mark, 212.
Hotchkiss, Obediah, 31, 252.
Hotchkiss, Samuel, 58.
Hotchkiss, Silas, 223.
Hotchkiss, Stephen, 252.
Hotchkiss, Thomas, 147.
Hotchkiss, Timothy, 63.
Hotchkiss, Wait, 50, 235.
Hough, Barnabas, 193.
Hough, Benjamin, 67.
Hough, Jonathan, 130, 131.
Hough, Simeon, 196, 261.
Hough, William, 44, 45, 118, 119, 121, 212.
Hough, see Huff.
Houghton (Haughton).
Houghton, Elijah, 42.
Houghton, Ezekiel, 250, 255.
House, Benajah, 250, 255.
House, Eliphalet, 46, 250.
House, John, 57, 137, 138, 139, 180.
House, Stephen, 202.
Hovey, Daniel, Jr., 248, 255.
Hovey, Jonathan, 248, 254.
Hovey, Joseph, 249.
Hovey, Joseph, Jr., 254.
How, Jeremiah, 57.
How, Jeremiah, Jr., 224.
How, Joel, 15.
How, John, 223, 231.
How, Josiah, 240, 244.
How, Nathaniel, 228.
How, Samson, 240.
How, Samuel, 55.
Howard (Howerd).
Howard, Edward, 137, 205, 257.
Howard, John, 255.
Howard, Nathan, 240, 244.
Howard, Zebede, 137.
Howd, Edward, 51.
Howd, James, 225.
Howde, John, 66, 69.
Howell, Henry, 253.
Howell, Nick, 31.
Howell, Nicholas, 77, 171.

INDEX.

Howland, Jabez, 72, 73, 74, 80.
Hoyt (Hoit), Benajah, 251.
Hoyt, Comfort, 238.
Hoyt, Daniel, 251.
Hoyt, David, 3d, 241.
Hoyt, Deodaty, 241.
Hoyt, Ebenezer, Jr., 241.
Hoyt, Ezra, 251.
Hoyt, Gould, 251.
Hoyt, Isaac, 241.
Hoyt, Jonathan, 238, 241, 251.
Hoyt, Joseph, 55, 158, 267.
Hoyt, Josia, 241.
Hoyt, Joseph, 3d, 241.
Hoyt, Moses, 56, 109, 110.
Hoyt, Nathan, 238, 241.
Hoyt, Samuel, 238.
Hoyt, Silvenus, 241.
Hoyt, Stephen, 56.
Hoyt, Timothy, 252.
Hoyt, William, 251.
Huath, Soloman, 236.
Hubbard (Hobbard, Hubard, Hubberd).
Hubbard, 253.
Hubbard, Abraham, 50.
Hubbard, Benjamin, 72, 122.
Hubbard, Caleb, 233, 234.
Hubbard, Daniel, 150, 213, 227.
Hubbard, Ebenezer, 222.
Hubbard, Elisha, 122, 216.
Hubbard, George, 234.
Hubbard, Hezekiah, 234.
Hubbard, Jedidiah, 234.
Hubbard, Jeremiah, 234.
Hubbard, John, 3, 91, 157, 212, 231, 252.
Hubbard, Jonathan, 115, 116, 186, 229.
Hubbard, Joseph, 156, 158, 177, 179.
Hubbard, Josiah, 244.
Hubbard, Leveret, 85, 91.
Hubbard, Nathaniel, 222.
Hubbard, Richard, 115, 116.
Hubbard, Roswell, 14, 131, 132, 186.
Hubbard, Salah, 130.
Hubbard, Samuel, 44, 186.
Hubbard, Timothy, 209, 227.
Hubbard, Zachariah, 208.
Hubbell (Huble), Abijah, 251.
Hubbell, Benjamin, 221.
Hubbell, Enoch, 226.
Hubbell, Gershom, 154.
Hubbell, Jedidiah, 206.
Hubbell, Jeptha, 157, 158.
Hubbell, John, 200, 201.
Hubbell, Samuel, 102, 176, 178, 206.
Hubbell, Shadrak, 218.
Hubbell, Silliman, 177, 179.
Hudleston, Richard, 169.
Hudson, Lot, 49.
Hudson, Samuel, 72, 73.
Hudson, see Hutson.
Huff, Benjamin, 65.
Huff, James, 29, 146.
Huff, Jonathan, 218.
Huff, William, 154.
Huff, see Hough.
Hugens, Samuel, 127.
Hugh[ ], Barnabas, 54.
Hughes, John, 236.
Hulbut (Halbart, Hulbert, Hulburd).
Hulbert, Benjamin, 173.
Hulbut, Daniel, 204.
Hulbut, Ebenezer, 204.
Hulbut, Gideon, 223, 224.
Hulbut, Obediah, 246.
Hulbut, Ruben, 204.
Halbut, Samuel, 66.
Hulbut, see Hurlburt.
Hulet, Michel, 99.
Hull, Elijah, 238.
Hull, Ezekiel, 8.
Hull, Giles, 48, 143.
Hull, James, 201.
Hull, Jedediah, 158, 201.
Hull, Jehial, 223.
Hull, John, 201, 225.
Hull, Jonathan, 247.
Hull, Joseph, 202.
Hull, Lemuel, 7, 226.
Hull, Moses, 43.
Hull, Nathan, 227.
Hull, Peter, 118, 201.
Hull, Sam, 227.
Hull, Samuel, 28, 110, 234, 235.
Hull, Seth, 201.
Hull, Seth, Jr., 201.
Hull, Stephen, 220.
Hull, William, 51, 118, 119.
Humerston, Ebenezer, 30, 231.
Humerston, Jay, 31, 252.
Humervile, Eliphalet, 220.
Humphrevile, Benjamin, 265.
Humphrevile, Lemuel, 253.
Humphrey, Asa, 99.
Humphrey, David, 21.
Humphrey, Dosethus, Jr., 230.
Humphrey, Dudely, 245.
Humphrey, Elisha, 173.

Humphrey, Hezekiah, 62.
Humphrey, Isaac, 58.
Humphrey, John, 105.
Humphrey, Jonathan, 102, 104, 105.
Humphrey, Noah, 62, 63, 102, 103, 104, 173.
Humphrey, Roger, 174.
Humphrey, Samuel, 6.
Humphrey, Silvanus, 63, 173, 175.
Hungerford, David, 54, 223.
Hungerford, John, 42, 203, 238, 239.
Hungerford, Lemuel, 203, 259.
Hungerford, Matthew, 239.
Hungerford, Robert, 203.
Hunt, Charets, 132.
Hunt, James, 123.
Hunt, John, 204.
Hunt, Noah, 39.
Hunt, Russel, 244.
Hunt, Samuel, 46, 250.
Hunt, Simeon, 198, 253.
Hunt, Stephen, Jr., 250.
Hunter, Benjamin, 206.
Hunter, Jonath, 206.
Huntington, Benjamin, 237.
Huntington, Christopher, 52, 113, 182.
Huntington, Daniel, 53.
Huntington, Elijah, 237.
Huntington, Elisha, 236.
Huntington, Ezekiel, 97, 160.
Huntington, Hezekiah, 3, 91, 167.
Huntington, John, Jr., 249.
Huntington, Matthew, 26.
Huntington, Samuel, 107, 215, 248, 255.
Huntington, Thomas, 18, 19, 78, 161.
Huntington, William, 236, 249.
Huntley, Elisha, 113.
Huntley, Jabez, 180, 181.
Huntley, John, 41.
Huntley, Jonathan, 41.
Huntley, Moses, 182.
Hurd, Abijah, 29.
Hurd, Adam, 146.
Hurd, Amos, 29.
Hurd, Daniel, 204.
Hurd, Elnathan, 44.
Hurd, Jahiel, 32.
Hurd, Jedediah, 204.
Hurd, John, 118.
Hurd, Nathan, 204.
Hurd, Samuel, 204.
Hurd, Simon, 196, 261.

Hurlburt (Holibord, Harlbut, Hurlbort, Hurlbut, Hurlbutt).
Hurlburt, Aaron, 146.
Hurlburt, Adam, 146.
Hurlburt, Benjamin, 58, 225.
Hurlburt, Caleb, 14, 194.
Hurlburt, Cha, 210.
Hurlburt, Daniel, 32, 33.
Hurlburt, Ebenezer, 219.
Hurlburt, Elias, 209.
Hurlburt, Elijah, 219.
Hurlburt, Elisha, 228, 244.
Hurlburt, Gideon, 142.
Hurlburt, Isaac, 209.
Hurlburt, John, 201, 219.
Hurlburt, Jonathan, 141.
Hurlburt, Joseph, 219.
Hurlburt, Joshua, 146.
Hurlburt, Noah, 29, 146, 219.
Hurlburt, Nathan, 29.
Hurlburt, Reuben, 28, 169.
Hurlburt, Samuel, 57, 67, 69, 146, 218.
Hurlburt, Titus, 263.
Hurlburt, see Hulbut.
Huston, James, 169.
Hutchens, Edward, 8.
Hutching, Benjamin, 240, 244.
Hutchinson (Hutcherson, Hutchingson, Hutchison).
Hutchinson, Asa, 188.
Hutchinson, Benjamin, 198.
Hutchinson, Edward, 132.
Hutchinson, John, 46, 80.
Hutchinson, Joseph, 61.
Hutchinson, Moses, 148, 149, 161, 181.
Hutchinson, Moses H., 5.
Hutchinson, Ruben, 70.
Hutchinson, Solomon, 206.
Hutten, Thomas, 161.
Hutson, Richard, 196.
Hutson, Samuel, 75, 195.
Hutson, see Hudson.
Huxley, Joseph, 80.
Hyat, Daniel, 251.

Indian, Daniel, 249.
Indian, John, 53, 72, 74, 75.
Indian, Maugunet, 84.
Indian, Wonks, 15.
Indian, see Cummus.
Indian, see Pyras.
Indian, see Suckhegon.
Ingalls, Ephraim, 20.
Ingersol, Simon, 216.
Ingham, Alexander, 188.

INDEX.

Ingham, Ebenezer, 202.
Ingham, Jonathan, 196.
Ingraham, Ephraim, 236.
Ingraham, Henry, 194.
Ingraham, Jeremiah, 214.
Ingraham, William, 202.
Isaacs, Isaac, 55, 57, 109, 110.
Isbell (Isbal, Iisbell).
Isbell, Eleazoer, 195, 261.
Isbell, Peruda, 29, 146, 199.
Isbell, Robert, 51.
Isham, Asher, 39.
Isham, Daniel, 79, 87.
Isham, Zebulon, 134.
Ishum, Daniel, 47.
Ives, Abijah, Jr., 87.
Ives, Aner, 193, 261.
Ives, Benjamin, 224.
Ives, David, 224.
Ives, Elnathan, 30, 235.
Ives, John, 235.
Ives, Joseph, 27.
Ives, Joshua, 235.
Ives, Josiah, 246.
Ives, Stephen, 65, 66.
Ives, Zachariah, 235.

Jack, 31.
Jackson (Jacson), Adin, 221.
Jackson, Daniel, 12, 177, 179, 180, 261.
Jackson, Ebenezer, 52, 181.
Jackson, Ephraim, 201.
Jackson, Frances, 221.
Jackson, James, 23.
Jackson, Jeremiah, 37, 79, 101, 107, 191, 242.
Jackson, John, 23, 136, 219.
Jackson, Joseph, 113, 236.
Jackson, Michael, 102, 104, 211.
Jackson, Mril, 6.
Jackson, Nathan, 28, 146.
Jackson, Samuel, 118.
Jackson, Stephen, 180, 206.
Jackson, William, 221.
Jackson, Zebh, 32.
Jackwise, Robert, 144.
Jacobs, Abraham, 171.
Jacobs, Abram, 67.
Jacobs, Bartholomew, 14.
Jacobs, James, 137.
Jacobs, John, 130, 186.
Jacobs, Joseph, 249.
Jacobs, Joseph, 3d, 254.
Jacobs, Samuel, 178.
Jacobs, William, 15, 128, 195, 260.
Jacock, Samuel, 177.
Jager, Reuben, 180.

Jagger, Jeremiah, 150, 151, 179.
Jagger, Nathan, 251.
James, George, 108, 191.
James, Thomas, 106, 172.
James, Tom, 105.
Japhet, John, 38, 77, 131, 132, 169, 170.
Jaquease, George, 214.
Jaquish, Robert, 191.
Jarman (Jerman).
Jarman, John, 61, 152, 180.
Jarvis, Nathan, 251.
Jarvis, Thomas, 157.
Jefferds, John, 207.
Jeffrey (Jeffery, Jeffry).
Jeffrey, John, 24, 140, 141, 159.
Jeffries (Jefferies), John, 24, 185.
Jenkins, Stephen, 213.
Jennings (Genings, Ginings, Gennings, Jenings, Jennens).
Jennings, Aaron, 201.
Jennings, Abel, 221.
Jennings, John, 69, 133.
Jennings, Joseph, 56.
Jennings, Joshua, 248, 254.
Jennings, Nathan, 46.
Jenors, Samuel, 146.
Jerrald (Jarrald, Jarrall, Jarrals, Jarrold, Jerould).
Jerrald, Harding, 174, 175.
Jerrald, Ruben, 16.
Jerrald, Thomas, 134, 136, 174, 175.
Jerrald, see Garrald.
Jessup, Nathan, 152.
Jesup, Nathaniel, 151, 180.
Jesup, Silvanus, 216.
Jethro, Jabez, 192.
Jewel, Ebenezer, 140, 228, 243.
Jewel, Eliphalet, 199.
Jewel, Jedediah, 67.
Jewel, Joshua, 227, 243.
Jewel, Thomas, 99.
Jewett, Caleb, 206.
Jewett, David, 91, 143.
Jewett, Ichabod, 236.
Jewett, Jedediah, 66.
Jewett, Thomas, 83, 100, 236.
Job, David, 144.
Joel, Negro, 188.
Joes, Stephen, 69.
John, Ephraim, 188.
Johnson (Jonson), 18.
Johnson, Amos, 234.
Johnson, Archibald, 72, 73, 75.
Johnson, Caleb, 20, 78.
Johnson, Charles, 220.
Johnson, Cornelius, 127.

Johnson, David, 122, 169, 204.
Johnson, Davis, 186.
Johnson, Diah, 242.
Johnson, Ebenezer, 59, 229, 253.
Johnson, Edward, 194, 261.
Johnson, Elihu, 59, 118, 119, 215.
Johnson, Elisha, 203.
Johnson, Enoch, 184.
Johnson, Hezekiah, 46.
Johnson, Isaac, 12, 127, 199, 228, 236, 244.
Johnson, Jedidiah, 234.
Johnson, Jesse, 126, 127, 171.
Johnson, Joa, 48.
Johnson, John, 191, 205, 207.
Johnson, John, Jr., 61.
Johnson, Jonathan, 186, 225.
Johnson, Joseph, 41, 113, 181, 232.
Johnson, Maverick, 34, 78, 128, 129, 173.
Johnson, Matthew, 55.
Johnson, Moses, 198.
Johnson, Nathaniel, 50, 177, 179, 212.
Johnson, Obadiah, 240.
Johnson, Peter, 32.
Johnson, Phineas, 212, 220.
Johnson, Samuel, 195, 216, 261.
Johnson, Sherborn, 49.
Johnson, Solomon, 141, 206.
Johnson, Stephen, 133, 144, 234, 248, 254.
Johnson, William, 3, 4, 46, 85, 88, 151, 153, 160, 198, 253.
Johnson, Zack, 84.
Jompo, Daniel, 84.
Jonathan, Zachariah, 113.
Jones (Jons), Aaron, 212.
Jones, Amos, 8, 86.
Jones, Asa, 202, 203, 241, 258.
Jones, Azariah, 83.
Jones, Benjamin, 45, 215, 236.
Jones, Benjamin, Jr., 216.
Jones, Caleb, 54.
Jones, Caleb, Jr., 211.
Jones, Eaton, 32, 33.
Jones, Eliakim, 202.
Jones, Elias, 84, 232.
Jones, Elijah, 107.
Jones, Gideon, 162, 205.
Jones, Harriss, 220.
Jones, Henry, 182.
Jones, Israel, 207.
Jones, Jabez, 40, 113, 181.
Jones, James, 7, 61, 86, 155.
Jones, John, 200, 205, 241.
Jones, Jonathan, 125.
Jones, Joseph, 240, 244.
Jones, Lewis, 16, 107.
Jones, Moses, 16, 107.
Jones, Nathan, 107, 229.
Jones, Parker, 205, 255.
Jones, Reuben, 10, 100, 101, 162, 232.
Jones, Rufus, 237.
Jones, Samuel, 42, 188, 189, 190, 257.
Jones, Thomas, 202, 203.
Jones, William, 86, 215, 255.
Jordan (Jorden, Jurden, Jurdin).
Jordan, John, 11, 86, 216.
Joslin (Johslen, Joslen).
Joslin, Benjamin, 242.
Joslin, John, 99.
Judd, Benjamin, 103.
Judd, Ebenezer, 235.
Judd, John, 239.
Judd, Philip, 205, 256.
Judd, Samuel, 70, 71, 223.
Judd, William, 223.
Judson, Abel, 237.
Judson, Daniel, 200, 204.
Judson, Henry, 155, 156.
Judson, Joshuah, 204.
Judson, Lemuel, 200.
Judson, Peter, 55, 239.
Judson, Roswel, 230.
Judson, Samuel, 200, 219.
Judson, Thadus, 219.
Judson, Timothy, 219.
Jum, Joshua, 241.
June, William, 216.

Kay, John, 232.
Kee, Elexander, 101.
Keef, John, 196, 261.
Keeler, Benjamin, 251.
Keeler, Isaiah, 251.
Keeler, James, 251.
Keeler, Jonathan, 238.
Keeny (Keeney), Alexander, 7.
Keeny, Benjamin, 7, 101, 135, 173, 175.
Keeny, John, 7, 115, 116.
Keeny, Joseph, 9, 239.
Keeny, Joseph, Jr., 8.
Keeny, Samuel, 41, 145.
Keeny, Semeon, 239.
Keeny, Thomas, Jr., 9.
Keeny, see Keney, Kinne.
Kegwin, see Cagwin.
Kelcey, Ephraim, 212.
Kelcey, Hiel, 202.
Kelcey, Jeremiah, 212.
Kelcey, Josiah, 202.
Kelcey, Reuben, 9, 118, 119.

INDEX. 313

Kelcey, see Kelsey.
Kelley (Keley, Kelly).
Kelley, Benjamin, 233.
Kelley, Morris, 61, 180.
Kelley, Reuben, 8, 50, 144, 195.
Kellogg (Keleg, Kelogg).
Kellogg, Ashbel, 246.
Kellogg, Charles, 215.
Kellogg, Elijah, 228, 244.
Kellogg, Eliphalet, 251.
Kellogg, Ezra, 238.
Kellogg, George, 239.
Kellogg, Jonathan, 139.
Kellogg, Joseph, 10, 113, 181, 205, 228, 244.
Kellogg, Joseph, Jr., 258.
Kellogg, Lemuel, 235.
Kellogg, Nathaniel, 205.
Kellogg, Nathaniel, Jr., 256.
Kellogg, Samuel, 29, 205, 258.
Kelsey, Amos, 45.
Kelsey, John, 209.
Kelsey, Jonathan, 227.
Kelsey, Nathan, 169.
Kelsey, Oliver, 227.
Kelsey, Samuel, Jr., 44.
Kelsey, see Kelcey.
Kendal (Kindall), 254.
Kendal, Abijah, 248, 254.
Kendal, Jacob, 198.
Kendal, Joshua, 20.
Kendal, Simon, 211.
Keney (Kenney, Kenny, Keny).
Keney, Benjamin, 134.
Keney, Daniel, 66, 68, 204.
Keney, Jacob, Jr., 62.
Keney, James, 188.
Keney, John, 229.
Keney, Joseph, 134.
Keney, Oliver, 94.
Keney, Richard, 144.
Keney, see Keeny, Kinne.
Kennedy (Kenady).
Kennedy, Daniel, 193, 240.
Kennedy, John, 237.
Kennedy, see Canedy.
Kent, 57, 102, 124, 199, 206, 218.
Kent, Aseph, 168.
Kent, Ashel, 168.
Kent, Charles, 64.
Kent, Elihu, 5, 6, 93, 95, 96.
Kent, Joel, 64.
Kent, Joseph, 99.
Kent, Joshua, 43.
Kent, Noah, 103.
Kent, Oliver, 102, 265.
Kent, Paul, 63, 102, 104, 265.
Kent, Seth, 228, 244.

Keson, Thomas, 225.
Ketch, Benjamin, 242.
Ketchum (Katchum).
Ketchum, Benjamin, 139.
Ketchum, Ephraim, 251.
Ketchum, Ezra, 157.
Ketchum, John, 91.
Keyes (Keys), Ephraim, 46, 132.
Kibbe, Charles, 216.
Kibbe, David, 246.
Kibbe, Isaac, 246.
Kibbe, Noadiah, 216.
Kibbe, Paul, 94.
Kibbe, Silas, 211.
Kibbe, Zerah, 94, 95.
Kidder, Nathaniel, 249, 254.
Kilborn (Killborn).
Kilborn, Benjamin, 223.
Kilborn, David, 210.
Kilborn, Elijah, 122, 202.
Kilborn, Giles, 14.
Kilborn, Hezekiah, 122.
Kilborn, John, 147, 149, 224.
Kilborn, Richard, 35, 154.
Kilborn, Roswell, 32, 223.
Kilburn, Elijah, 258.
Kilburn, Jeremiah, 199.
Kilburn, John, 22, 85, 205.
Kilburn, Jonathan, 204, 205.
Killingly, 36, 100, 133, 208.
Killingsworth, 7, 125, 201, 202, 226, 227.
Killo, Eben, 153.
Killorn, Richerd, 153.
Killum (Kellom, Kelom, Killam).
Killum, Daniel, 70, 71, 128, 129, 222.
Killum, Moses, 105, 172.
Kilworth, William, 32, 141.
Kiman, James, 23.
Kimball, Benjamon, 232.
Kimball, Daniel, 236.
Kimball, David, 232.
Kimball, Eliphalet, 111, 112, 240.
Kimball, Jacob, 232.
Kimball, John, 66, 232.
Kimball, Joseph, 232.
Kimball, Pelatiah, 248, 254.
Kimberly, Abraham, 143, 145.
Kimberly, Ephraim, 251.
Kimberly, Fitch, 157.
Kimberly, Isaac Sherman, 27, 195.
Kindress, Thomas, 70.
Kines, Thomas, 71.
King, Asel, 28.
King, Benjah, 204.
King, Benjamin, 28, 71, 72, 74, 207.

King, Ebeneser, 169.
King, Eldad, 204.
King, Gideon, 8.
King, Hezekiah, 134, 184.
King, Joseph, 6, 103, 104, 236.
King, Parmenus, 207.
King, Seth, 62, 94, 96, 168.
King, William, 253.
Kingland, Benjamin, 73.
Kingsbury, Ebenezer, 240.
Kingsbury, Jacob, 209.
Kingsbury, Jonathan, 248, 253, 254.
Kingsbury, Nathenil, 240.
Kingsbury, Thomas, 184.
Kincade (Kencade).
Kincade, John, 60, 171.
Kingsley, Adonijah, 16.
Kingsley, Eliphaz, 248, 254.
Kingsley, Jabez, 236.
Kingsley, Jeremiah, 237.
Kingsley, John, 236.
Kinis, Thomas, 70.
Kinne (Kenne, Kenney).
Kinne, Asa, 232.
Kinne, Benjamin, 10, 101, 135.
Kinne, David, 83.
Kinne, Delevrensce, 219.
Kinne, James, 83.
Kinne, John, 219.
Kinne, see Keeny, Keney.
Kintland, Gideon, 44.
Kintland, Martin, 44.
Kirby (Kurby), Abraham, 29.
Kircum (Curkem, Kurcom).
Kircum, Elijah, 84.
Kircum, Henry, 14, 152, 154.
Kirtland (Kartland, Kertlend).
Kirtland, Elisha, 72, 73, 74.
Kirtland, Jedi, 226.
Kirtland, Joseph, 202.
Kline, Coonrod, 140.
Knap (Knaap), Amos, 180, 261.
Knap, Brasy, 238.
Knap, Caleb, 150, 151.
Knap, Charls, 226.
Knap, David, 217, 238, 241.
Knap, Ebenezer, 150.
Knap, Elnathan, 57.
Knap, Ezra, 208.
Knap, Israel, 241.
Knap, James, 57, 216, 238, 241.
Knap, John, 155, 156, 179, 217.
Knap, Jonas, 150, 160.
Knap, Jonathan, 37, 98, 99, 242.
Knap, Joseph, 216.
Knap, Nehemiah, 151.
Knap, Peter, 228, 244.

Knap, Thomas, 228, 244.
Kneeland (Keenland, Neland).
Kneeland, John, 78, 162, 186.
Kneeland, John, Jr., 82.
Knickerbocker (Kenickerbaker, Kirnickerbr).
Knickerbocker, Herman, 209.
Knickerbocker, Lawrence, 228, 243.
Knight, John, 16, 97, 98.
Knight, Timothy, 99.
Knowles, James, 213.
Knowles, Samuel, 204.
Knowls, Sith, 213.
Knowls, Thomas, 204.
Knowlton (Knolton, Knoulten, Nolton).
Knowlton, Daniel, 133, 184.
Knowlton, Jarad, 148, 215.
Knowlton, Roswell, 148, 203.
Knowlton, Thomas, 183, 203, 256.
Knowlton, William, 6, 154.
Kyes (Kiys), Epham, 132.
Kyes, William, 248, 254.

Lacy (Lacey, Lasy), 33.
Lacy, David, 28, 154, 156, 159.
Lacy, Ebenezer, 226.
Lacy, Isaac, 155.
Lacy, Seth, 139.
Lacy, Thadeus, 32, 204.
Ladd, Daniel, 236.
Ladd, John, 236.
Ladd, Jonathan, Jr., 215.
Ladd, Timothy, 132, 198.
Laget, Philip, 227.
Lahey (La, Layhah).
Lahey, Michael, 18, 19, 97, 98, 184.
Laird, William, 198.
Lake, David, 200.
Lake, Edward, 33, 219.
Lake, George, 45, 76, 87, 246, 266.
Lake, Groshum, 219.
Lake, James, 58, 226.
Lake, John, 218.
Lake, Phinehas, 200.
Lake, Ruben, 221.
Lamb (Lam), 18.
Lamb, Andrew, 197.
Lamb, Daniel, Jr., 197.
Lamb, Ebenezer, 19.
Lamb, Joseph, 218.
Lamb, Lemuel, 214.
Lamb, Thomas, 18, 20, 72, 73, 74.
Lamb, Timothy, 197.
Lamb, William, 137.
Lambert, David, 220.
Lamson (Lambson, Lampson).

Lamson, 118, 119.
Lamson, Elthura, 170.
Landers, Joseph, 206.
Landon (Lendon), Ambroise, 103.
Landon, Asa, 140, 141, 247.
Landon, David, 223.
Landon, Ezekiel, 228, 243.
Lane, Daniel, 227.
Lane, Hezekiah, 227.
Lane, Nathaniel, 70.
Lane, Noah, 202.
Lane, Stephen, 226.
Lane, Zacheus, 12.
Lankester, James, 237.
Lankton (Lancton), John, 229.
Lankton, Timothy, 186.
Lansford, William, 159.
Lappim, David, 236.
Larken, Amos, 137, 188.
Larkin, Benjamin, 69.
Larkins, Benajah, 117.
Larrabee (Laraby), Ebenezer, 70.
Larrabee, Thomas, 11, 107.
Larrabee, Timothy, 249.
Lasell, Joshua, 255.
Latch, Peter, 186.
Latham, John, 191.
Lattimer (Lattemore, Lattimore).
Lattimer, Amos, 233.
Lattimer, John, 23, 153, 154, 186.
Lattimer, Jonathan, 105, 211.
Lattimer, Jonathan, Jr., 232, 233.
Law (Laws), John, 95, 162.
Lawrence (Larrance).
Lawrence, Amos, 152, 239.
Lawrence, Daniel, 209.
Lawrence, Daniel, Jr., 208.
Lawrence, David, 228, 244.
Lawrence, Elihu, 208, 245.
Lawrence, Gideon, 209.
Lawrence, Isaac, 228, 244.
Lawrence, John, 245.
Lawrence, Jonathan, 236.
Lawrence, Nehemiah, 228, 244.
Lawrence, Rufus, 209.
Lawrence, Samuel, 104, 139, 251.
Lawrence, Thomas, 251.
Lawrence, Timothy, 56.
Lawson, Amos, 249, 255.
Lay, Daniel, 212.
Lay, Ichabod, 181.
Lay, John, 83, 143.
Leach (Leech), 161, 255.
Leach, Ebenezer, 45, 47, 85.
Leach, John, 27.
Leach, Richard, 27, 99.
Leach, Thomas, 41.
Leason, Epraim, 211.

Leathercoat, John, 118, 119.
Leathers, Ezekiel, 102, 177, 178, 261.
Leavens (Levens), Isaac, 37.
Leavens, Peter, 36, 79, 242.
Leavenworth (Lavensworth, Levensworth).
Leavenworth, Calvin, 72, 73.
Leavenworth, David, 219.
Leavenworth, John, 219.
Leavenworth, Nathan, 28.
Leavitt, John, 62.
Lebanon, 17, 18, 19, 20, 21, 26, 87, 117, 136, 161, 162, 188, 189, 249, 255, 256, 266, 267.
Leddel, Henry, 95, 98, 104, 106, 108, 114, 115, 123, 131, 139, 147, 149, 151, 155, 157.
Lee, Abijah, 82, 234.
Lee, Benjamin, 36, 108.
Lee, Daniel, 199.
Lee, Elihia, 196.
Lee, Elias, 43.
Lee, Jedidiah, 184.
Lee, John, 40, 112, 126.
Lee, Jonathan, 91, 93, 95.
Lee, Joseph, 224, 227, 243.
Lee, Josiah, 125, 209, 210.
Lee, Nathan, 250, 257.
Lee, Phinehas, 220.
Lee, Selah, 51.
Lee, Semeion, 207.
Lee, Silas, 60.
Lee, Stephen, 129, 143, 145, 159, 161, 206, 267.
Lee, Uriah, 38.
Leeds (Leads), Carey, 241.
Leeds, Gideon, 197.
Leeke, Timothy, 253.
Leeke, William, 180.
Leete (Leat, Leet).
Leete, Allen, 72, 73, 74.
Leete, Ezekiel, 115.
Leete, Jared, 50, 212.
Leete, Levi, 26, 143.
Leete, Reuben, 212.
Leete, Timothy, 51.
Leffingwell, Benajah, 237.
Leffingwell, Heart, 83.
Leffingwell, Jeremiah, 236.
Leffingwell, Thomas, 236.
Leiwes, Cyrus, 196.
Lemons, James, 172.
Lenien, John, 197.
Leonard (Leanord), Abiel, 78, 82.
Leonard, Ebenezer, 29, 156, 158, 217.
Leonard, Jedediah, 44.

Leonard, Nathan, 107, 231, 232.
Lester, Amos, 197.
Lester, Isaac, 233.
Lester, Nemiah, 144.
Lester, Simeon, 236.
Levake, John, 139, 251.
Levinze, John, 98.
Lewak, John, 139.
Lewis (Lewes, Leuis, Lues, Luis).
Lewis, Adonijah, 228.
Lewis, Ambrose, 84, 191
Lewis, Bela, 14, 131, 235.
Lewis, Bille, 130, 131.
Lewis, Caleb, 49.
Lewis, Charles, 15.
Lewis, Daniel, 186.
Lewis, Edward, 33, 232, 233.
Lewis, Eldad, 53, 55, 222.
Lewis, Eli, 79.
Lewis, Ely, 44.
Lewis, Ezekiel, 13, 126, 128, 129, 167, 168, 239.
Lewis, Foster, 55, 180.
Lewis, George, 41, 137, 200.
Lewis, Hezekiah, 49, 103, 104.
Lewis, John, 194.
Lewis, Jonathan, 10.
Lewis, Joseph, 70, 71, 103, 104, 182.
Lewis, Josiah, 32, 194.
Lewis, Justios, 246.
Lewis, Lemuel, 28, 222.
Lewis, Mathew, 86.
Lewis, Medad, 223.
Lewis, Nathan, 44, 45.
Lewis, Nathaniel, 55.
Lewis, Oliver, 14, 103, 104, 246.
Lewis, Richard, 184.
Lewis, Samuel, 63, 103, 104, 247.
Lewis, Solomon, 27.
Lewis, William, 84, 128, 230.
Lewis, William Josiah, 122, 180.
Lide, Ezikel, 116.
Lifeet, John, 13.
Like, Jabez, 255.
Lilley (Liley, Lille, Lillie, Lilly, Lily, Lylle, Lylley).
Lilley, David, 248, 254.
Lilley, Elexander, 100.
Lilley, John, 63, 97.
Lilley, Jonathan, 198.
Lilley, Nathan, 70, 71, 96, 98.
Lilley, Moses, 245.
Lilley, Phillip, 105.
Lilley, Samuel, 42.
Lilley, Silas, 236.
Lindley (Linley), Joseph, 141.
Lindley, Solomon, 224.
Lindley, see Linsey, Linsley.

Lindsey, David, 186.
Lindsey, John, 186.
Lindsey, Robert, 186.
Lines, Ebenezer, 231.
Lines, Joseph, 29, 87, 124, 225.
Linsey (Lensey, Linsea).
Linsey, David, 130.
Linsey, John, 23, 130, 131, 265.
Linsey, Robert, 14.
Linsey, see Lindley, Lindsey.
Linsley, Isaac, 225.
Linsley, Jacob, 225.
Linsley, Joseph, 199.
Linsley, Samuel, Jr., 225.
Liscomb, Thomas, 208.
Lisk, Andrew, 25, 117, 161, 189.
Lisk, William, 162.
Lisk, see Lusk.
Litchfield, 3, 13, 32, 91, 93, 140, 158, 194, 199, 215, 223, 247.
Little, James, 241.
Lloyd (Loyd), Joseph, 84.
Lloyd, William, 69, 71.
Lobdell, 61.
Lobdell, Ebenezer, 61, 180.
Lobdell, Jacob, 157.
Lockwood, Abraham, 151.
Lockwood, Ephraim, 180, 261.
Lockwood, Ezekiel, 216.
Lockwood, Jeremiah, 61, 150, 152.
Lockwood, John, 56, 109, 110, 180, 251.
Lockwood, Jos., 109.
Lockwood, Joseph, 56, 110, 251.
Lockwood, Josiah, 109.
Lockwood, Lot, 265.
Lockwood, Moses, 151, 152, 179.
Lockwood, Nathan, 216.
Lockwood, Nathaniel, 216.
Lockwood, Peter, 252.
Lockwood, Robert, 180.
Lockwood, Samuel, 151.
Lockwood, Timothy, 150, 151.
Loder, John, 179, 261.
Logan, Samuel, 219.
London, Ambrose, 193.
Long, Josiah, 46, 87.
Long, Samuel, 198.
Long, Silas, Jr., 250, 255.
Loomer (Lomer), John, 53, 237.
Loomer, Joseph, 237.
Loomis (Lomays, Lomis), 86.
Loomis, Aaron, 222.
Loomis, Bariah, 215.
Loomis, Benoni, 8, 130, 131, 174, 175.
Loomis, Caleb, 205.
Loomis, Caleb, Jr., 259.

Loomis, Charles, 39.
Loomis, Daniel, 53, 86.
Loomis, David, 161.
Loomis, Ebenezer, 38, 81, 134, 136, 199, 207, 211.
Loomis, Elijah, 39, 230.
Loomis, Eliphalet, 12, 134, 135.
Loomis, Epaphras, 222.
Loomis, Ephraham, 46, 87.
Loomis, Ephraim, Jr., 189.
Loomis, Ezra, 250.
Loomis, Gideon, 39, 230.
Loomis, Hezekiah, 209.
Loomis, Isechar, 222.
Loomis, Israel, 246.
Loomis, Nathaniel, 135, 228, 243.
Loomis, Solomon, 82, 215.
Loomis, Thomas, 249.
Loomis, Timothy, 18, 19, 250, 257.
Loomis, Zachariah, 255.
Loper, Samuel, 212.
Lord, Asa, 237.
Lord, David, 228, 243.
Lord, Elias, 232.
Lord, Elisha, 91, 93, 95, 167.
Lord, John, 70, 71, 130, 131.
Lord, Samuel, 155, 156.
Lord, William, 73, 75, 201.
Loree, John, 12.
Lothrop (Lathrup, Lotrap).
Lothrop, Arunah, 25, 52.
Lothrop, Jonathan, 236.
Lothrup, Labeus, 237.
Lothrop, Nathaniel, 240.
Lothrop, Thatcher, 215.
Loudon, Earl of, 92, 163, 166, 179, 267.
Lounsbury (Lownsbury).
Lounsbury, Samuel, 120, 194.
Lounsbury, Stephen, 252.
Lovelace, James, 139.
Loveland (Lovland).
Loveland, Elizur, 23, 77.
Loveland, John, 72, 73, 75.
Loveland, Lot, 23, 187.
Loveland, Robert, 205.
Loveland, Samuel, 223.
Loveland, Thomas, 70, 71, 128, 129, 210.
Loveland, William, 209.
Loveland, Ziba, 202.
Lovemon, Robord, Jr., 258.
Loveridge, John, 188.
Lovicey, Olivar, 240.
Low (Lowe), John, 66, 67, 145.
Lucas, Richard, 60, 127.
Luce, Benjamin, 35, 198.
Luce, Jonathan, 248, 254.

Luce, Joseph, 122.
Luding[ ], Joseph, 54.
Ludington (Luddinton, Ludenton).
Ludington, Aaron, 193.
Ludington, Amos, 31.
Ludington, Asa, 231.
Ludington, David, 127.
Ludington, Ezra, 27.
Ludington, Henry, 144, 225.
Ludington, James, 27, 127.
Ludington, Jude, 225.
Ludington, Samuel, 212.
Ludington, Timothy, 172.
Lulel, Jos., 258.
Lumb, Jonathan, 220.
Lunsford, Mickel, 99.
Lusk, Andrew, 187.
Lusk, James, 14.
Lusk, Thomas, 130, 210.
Lusk, William, 250.
Lusk, see Lisk.
Lyman, Caleb, 250.
Lyman, E., 160.
Lyman, Ebenezer, 70, 71, 80.
Lyman, Elihu, 3, 91.
Lyman, Ezekiel, 19.
Lyman, Moses, 247.
Lyman, Phineas, 3, 5, 6, 7, 21, 91, 93, 95, 96, 129, 160, 162, 167, 168, 170, 171, 176, 179, 181, 185, 194.
Lyman, Phinehas, Jr., 94.
Lyman, Simeon, 199.
Lyman, Thomas, 214.
Lyman, William, 25, 117, 161, 249,
Lyman, Zekl, 19.
Lyme, 3, 83, 142, 143, 189, 194, 264.
Lyon (Loyon, Lion), Abell, 155.
Lyon, Abiel, 97.
Lyon, Ammariah, 52, 233.
Lyon, Asa, 29, 146.
Lyon, David, 242.
Lyon, Ephraim, 6, 153, 154.
Lyon, George, 242.
Lyon, Henry, 198, 243.
Lyon, Hezekiah, 177, 179.
Lyon, John, 157, 177, 178.
Lyon, Joseph, 201.
Lyon, Joshua, 97, 159.
Lyon, Lemuel, 37, 179, 242.
Lyon, Nathan, 153.
Lyon, Nehemiah, 41.
Lyon, Noah, 45, 122, 124.
Lyon, Samuel, 66, 67, 68, 155, 157, 158, 178.
Lyon, Stephen, 242.
Lyon, Thomas, 7, 79, 101, 198.

Lyon, Timothy, 221.
Lyon, William, 217.

M[   ], Moses, 152.
McCall, John, 202.
McCartey, Richard, 215.
McClannin (Mack Clenen, Mc-Clennen).
McClannin, John, 117, 138, 139.
McClannin, William, 37.
McCleave (McCleve).
McCleave, Robert, 205, 231, 255.
McCleave, Thomas, 187.
McClelen, John, 174.
McClemmon, John, 53.
McColoney, Patrick, 174.
McCullog, Patrick, 175.
McCune, Daniel, 200.
Macdaniel, John, 105.
McDaniel, Michael, 53, 139.
McDonald, Michael, 117, 139.
McEven, John, 218.
Mcfarding, Makum, 117.
McFarlen, Samuel, 232.
McFarthing, Andrew, 197.
McFelling, Peter, 160.
McGunnego, William, 244.
Mack, Abner, 42, 148, 149, 189.
Mack, Daniel, 206.
Mack, Hezekiah, 42.
Mack, Isaac, 175.
Mack, John, 40.
Mack, Joseph, 11, 181.
Mack, Josiah, 42.
Mack, Orlando, 148, 149, 189.
Mack, Orlando, Jr., 189.
Mack, Samuel, 72, 73, 75, 148, 149.
Mack, Solomon, 44, 79.
Macken, William, 41.
McKenny, John, 215.
McKeough, Timothy, 187.
McKey, George, 234.
McKey, Joseph, 230.
McKinsey, Gilbert, 154.
Mackmaners, John, 140.
McKnight, John, 207.
Mackris, Benjamin, 83.
McKy, John, 229.
McLane, David, 84, 182.
McLarin (McLarran).
McLarin, John, 39, 175.
McNeil, Archibald, 192, 194.
McRay, James, 220.
Mager, Samuel, 145.
Main, Stephen, 214.
Mallery (Malery, Mallory).
Mallery, Abner, 204.
Mallery, Daniel, 30.

Mallery, Isaac, 172.
Mallery, John, 201.
Mallery, Moses, 59.
Mallery, Nathan, 252.
Malleson, Joseph, Jr., 197.
Maltbie, Daniel, 224, 225.
Maltby, William, 193.
Man, Abijah, 162.
Man, John, 155, 156.
Man, Mathew, 155, 156.
Man, Samuel, 155, 156.
Mandell, Richard, 152.
Mandor, Richard, 61.
Mangrel, Richard, 150.
Mannering, Addom, 41.
Mannering, Jubez, 233.
Manning, David, 218.
Manning, John, 249.
Manning, Phenias, 35, 97, 98, 248, 254.
Manning, William, 36, 79, 128, 129, 242.
Mansfield, Dan, 25, 127.
Mansfield, James, 105, 106.
Mansfield, Jonathan, 110, 193, 261.
Mansfield, Joseph, 231.
Mansfield, 26, 69, 93, 98, 99, 100, 114, 132, 183.
Mansor, William, 128, 252.
Marbel, John, 226.
March, Pompy, 108.
Marchant, John, 219.
Marcom, Daniel, 198.
Marcy, Benjamin, 242.
Marcy, Edward, 26, 152.
Marcy, Elisha, 242.
Marcy, Stephen, 242.
Marcy, Uriah, 243.
Marcy, Zebulon, 242.
Mark, Daniel, 3d, 197.
Mark, Joseph, 44.
Mark, see Marks.
Markham (Markam, Markim).
Markham, Israel, 94.
Markham, Nathaniel, 211.
Markham, Stephen, 94, 211, 265.
Markham, William, 73, 75, 115, 116, 203.
Markham, see Marcom.
Marks, Miles, 235.
Marks, William, 234.
Marks, see Mark.
Marlborough, 204.
Marsh, Amos, 34, 255.
Marsh, Daniel, 84.
Marsh, Eben, 247.
Marsh, Ebenezer, 199, 217, 218, 225, 227, 243.

INDEX. 319

Marsh, Edmund, 203.
Marsh, Elias, 115, 116.
Marsh, Elijah, 224.
Marsh, George, 33, 199.
Marsh, John, 199.
Marsh, Jonathan, 3, 91.
Marsh, Joseph, 249.
Marsh, Moses, 63, 246.
Marsh, Silas, 189.
Marsh, Timothy, 134.
Marsh, William, 33, 243.
Marsh, Zebadiah, 37.
Marshall (Mashel).
Marshall, Abner, 35, 211.
Marshall, Amasa, 169.
Marshall, Gad, 222.
Marshall, Job, 134, 169.
Marshall, Joel, 12, 229, 239.
Marshall, John, 217.
Marshall, Mead, 217.
Marshall, Peter, 151.
Marshall, Silas, 151.
Martin, 86.
Martin, Brotherton, 45.
Martin, David, 219.
Martin, Elijah, 134, 160.
Martin, Gideon, 248.
Martin, James, 61, 153, 193.
Martin, Joseph, 248, 254.
Martin, Matthew, 191.
Martin, Robert, 153.
Martin, Robert, Jr., 153.
Martin, Thomas, 70.
Marvel, Thomas, 117, 161.
Marvin (Mervin), Jesse, 206.
Marvin, John, 3d, 206.
Marvin, Joseph, 110, 218, 230.
Marvin, Matthew, 264.
Marvin, Samuel, 251.
Marvin, Stephen, 218.
Marvin, Thomas, 25, 249.
Marvin, Zachariah, 266.
Mason, Jonathan, 211, 224.
Mason, Joseph, 198.
Mason, Joshua, 199.
Mason, William, 23, 77.
Massachusetts, 76, 88, 116, 159.
Master, James, 81.
Mather (Marther), Charles, 246.
Mather, Cotton, 14.
Mather, David, 210.
Mather, Eusebeas, 63.
Mather, Timothy, 211.
Mathews, Coll, 53.
Mathews, Edmun, 76.
Mathews, Jese, 169.
Mathews, Joseph, 235.
Mathews, Moses, 194.

Mathews, Stephen, 222.
Mathews, see Matthews.
Matson (Mattson), Amos, 210.
Matson, John, 174, 175.
Matson, Thomas, 210.
Mattason, David, 113.
Matthews, Coll, 101.
Matthews, Cull, 100.
Matthews, Jesse, 170.
Matthews, Moses, 154, 192.
Matthews, see Mathews.
Mattocks, James, 115, 116, 187.
Mattoon, Abel, 82, 189.
Mattoon, Ebenezer, 235.
Maxley, Joseph, 72.
May, Hezekiah, 97.
May, John, 229.
May, Samuel, 228.
Maynard (Mainard), Elijah, 94.
Maynard, Elnathan, 249.
Maynard, Naum, 197.
Meacham, Abner, 6, 94, 95, 96, 173.
Meacham, Barnabus, 245.
Meacham, Daniel, Jr., 20.
Meacham, Ebenezer, 207.
Mead (Meed), Benjamin, 217.
Mead, Caleb, 216.
Mead, Deliverance, 216.
Mead, Elijah, 217.
Mead, Gershom, 61.
Mead, Henry, 217.
Mead, James, 151, 180.
Mead, Jesse, 217.
Mead, Joseph, 61, 217, 241.
Mead, Joshua, 224.
Mead, Mathew, 56, 109, 110, 251.
Mead, Nathaniel, 61, 217.
Mead, Nathaniel, Jr., 217.
Mead, Thaddeus, 11, 91, 126, 241.
Meanwell, John, 156.
Mears, Lewis, 115, 116, 187.
Meech (Meach), Elkanah, 191.
Meach, Joshua, 232.
Meeker (Meaker, Meeker).
Meeker, Benjamin, 221.
Meeker, Daniel, 155, 194.
Meeker, John, 187.
Meeker, Jonathan, 201.
Megonniail, William, 240.
Meigs (Meges, Megg, Miges).
Meigs, Elias, 202.
Meigs, James, 191.
Meigs, Jannah, 195.
Meigs, Stephen, 212.
Mejon, John, 11.
Melony, Matthew, 191.
Menter, Simeon, 8, 86.
Mercy, Edward, 154.

Merion, Joseph, 54.
Merrett, Henry, 242.
Merriams, Joseph, 235.
Merrill (Merels, Meriels, Merralls, Merrels, Merrils, Merlls).
Merrill, Alexander, 233.
Merrill, Allyn, 230.
Merrill, Asher, 42, 205, 257.
Merrill, Benjamin, 202.
Merrill, David, 222.
Merrill, Edward, 118.
Merrill, Joseph, 247.
Merrill, Noah, 63, 127, 128.
Merrill, Samuel, 63, 246.
Merriman (Merimon), Isaac, 223.
Merriman, Silas, 193.
Merritt (Merite), John, 23, 77.
Merritt, Michael, 195.
Merritt, Noah, 37.
Merten, Brotherton, 45.
Merwin (Marwin, Murwin).
Merwin, Barnabas, 65, 103, 193.
Merwin, Henry, 103.
Merwin, Samuel, 193, 221.
Merwin, Stephen, 66, 68.
Merwin, Thomas, 49.
Messenger (Mesanger, Mesener, Messinger).
Messenger, Daniel, 246.
Messenger, Michael, 61, 150, 151.
Messenger, Nathan, 215.
Messenger, Nathaniel, 54, 121, 222.
Metauk, Talker, 156.
Metauk, Taukus, 155.
Metcalf (Medclaf, Medkif, Metcalf).
Metcalf, John, 46, 80.
Metcalf, Reuben, 250.
Metcalf, Samuel, 70, 250.
Metcalf, Simeon, 250, 257.
Mezen, John, 108.
Middlesex, 242.
Middleton, Thomas, 174, 175.
Middletown, 3, 22, 42, 53, 69, 81, 91, 98, 109, 114, 126, 128, 162, 167, 185, 210, 213, 223, 229, 233, 263.
Miles, Daniel, 105.
Miles, David, 220.
Miles, Joseph, 58, 66, 235.
Miles, Justin, 226.
Miles, Justus, 225.
Miles, William, 147, 194.
Milford, 27, 59, 65, 104, 106, 124, 171, 218, 220, 252, 267.
Millard, David, 206.
Millard, John, 58.

Millard, John, Jr., 206.
Miller, Aaron, 224.
Miller, Alexa, 199.
Miller, Anthony, 65, 66, 69.
Miller, Charles B., 187.
Miller, David, 63, 205, 258.
Miller, Ebenezer, 23.
Miller, Elisha, 142.
Miller, George, 14, 127, 128.
Miller, Giles, 234.
Miller, Ichabod, 234.
Miller, John, 63, 136, 213, 246.
Miller, Jonathan, 210.
Miller, Moses, 57.
Miller, Nathaniel, 70, 71, 234.
Miller, Robert, 43.
Miller, Samuel, 58.
Miller, Thomas, 118.
Millington, 162, 202, 259.
Mills, Amasa, 6, 106.
Mills, Amsey, 105.
Mills, Daniel, 242.
Mills, David, 139.
Mills, Ebenezer, 155, 201.
Mills, James, 197.
Mills, John, 63, 110, 169, 170, 201.
Mills, Jonathan, 13.
Mills, Lewis, 218.
Mills, Michael, 7, 211.
Minard (Minord, Mynard).
Minard, David, 52, 113.
Minard, Jeremiah, 233.
Minard, Jesse, 161, 233.
Minard, John, 161.
Minard, Jonathan, 10.
Minard, Thomas, 233.
Minard, William, 233.
Minor (Miner, Mynor).
Minor, Andrew, 52, 113.
Minor, Christopher, 135, 203, 258.
Minor, Clamont, 143.
Minor, Daniel, 41.
Minor, David, 219.
Minor, Elihu, 42.
Minor, Israel, 147.
Minor, Jonathan, 189, 240, 245.
Minor, Joseph, 11.
Minor, Joshua, 196.
Minor, Nathan, 204.
Minor, Richardson, 30.
Minor, Samuel, 204, 233.
Minor, Samuel, 3d, 214.
Minor, Seth, 204.
Minor, Thoms, 10.
Minor, Thomas, 145, 219.
Minor, William Roe, 190, 192.
Minship, Samuel, 116.

INDEX. 321

Mirick, Joseph, 198.
Mitchell (Mechall, Metchel, Michall, Michel, Mitchle).
Mitchell, Ahijah, 218.
Mitchell, David, 229.
Mitchell, Ebenezer, 33.
Mitchell, Elezor, 218.
Mitchell, George, 105, 106, 172.
Mitchell, John, 25, 126, 148, 153.
Mitchell, Joseph, 148.
Mitchell, Matthew, 85, 203, 204.
Mitchell, Zepheniah, 72, 73, 75, 86, 148, 149.
Mix, Amasa, 182.
Mix, Eldad, 26, 222.
Mix, Isaac, 174.
Mix, Seth, 23.
Mix, Stephen, 67, 68.
Mix, Thomas, 40.
Mix, Timothy, Jr., 231.
Mix, Zebediah, 234.
Moe, John, 152.
Moffit (Mooffitt), Lemuel, 103.
Moffit, Parks, 208.
Moger (Mogier, Mojer).
Moger, Enos, 61.
Moger, James, 151, 152.
Moger, Jehiel, 157, 178.
Moger, Naman, 145.
Moger, see Mosier.
Molton, Daniel, 97, 98.
Molton, Nathanael, 46.
Moltrop, Benjamin, 139.
Montowomuck, William, 184.
Moody, Samuel, 230.
Moody, Zimri, 239.
Moore (Moor, More).
Moore, John, 61, 100.
Moore, Jona, 141.
Moore, Jonathan, 227, 243.
Moore, Jonathan, Jr., 209.
Moore, Joseph, 84, 134, 211.
Moore, Joseph, Jr., 38, 136.
Moore, Lewis, 16.
Moore, Micha, 35, 245.
Moore, Roger, 211.
Moore, Sandras, 63.
Moot, Netheniel, 148.
Mordock, John, 232.
Mordock, William, 248.
Moredock, Andrew, 184.
Moredock, Peter, 160.
Moredock, see Murdock.
Morehouse (Morhouse).
Morehouse, Daniel, Jr., 221.
Morehouse, David, 251.
Morehouse, James, 154, 156, 158, 221.

Morehouse, Jedediah, 66, 68.
Morehouse, Jehu, 155, 156, 178.
Morehouse, Jethro, 155.
Morehouse, John, 45, 242.
Morehouse, Samuel, 177.
Morehouse, Samuel, 3d, 178.
Morehouse, Solomon, 201.
Morehouse, Thomas, 143.
Morey (Mory), Jams, 204.
Morey, John, 46.
Morey, Joseph, 240.
Morgan (Morgain, Morgin).
Morgan, Billi, 247.
Morgan, David, 25.
Morgan, Elihu, 237.
Morgan, Elkenah, 197.
Morgan, James, 200, 201, 258.
Morgan, John, Jr., 197.
Morgan, Jonathan, 58, 124, 233.
Morgan, Joseph, 151, 197.
Morgan, Joshua, 82, 197.
Morgan, Rozel, 232.
Morgan, Timothy, 29.
Morgan, William, 197.
Morier, Samuel, 161.
Morley, Timothy, 229.
Morris (Moris), Asa, 124.
Morris, Henry, 96, 98.
Morris, Joseph, 60, 179.
Morris, Samuel, 96, 98.
Morris, Samuel, Jr., 36.
Morris, Sephen, 180.
Morrison (Moreson, Morison).
Morrison, Theophilus, 13, 130, 131, 174, 175.
Morse (Mors, Morss).
Morse, Benjamin, 240.
Morse, Elihu, 54.
Morse, Isaac, 124.
Morse, Nathaniel, 232.
Morse, Noah, 23, 77, 189.
Mortin, Amos, 219.
Mortin, Nathan, 219.
Mosely, Abisha, 219.
Mosely, Joseph, 73.
Moses, Aaron, 63.
Moses, Abel, 63.
Moses, Ashbel, 174.
Moses, Elisha, 245.
Moses, Isaac, 57.
Moses, Jonas, 196, 261.
Moses, Naman, 53.
Moses, Othniel, 7, 169.
Moses, Timo, 246.
Mosier (Mosure), Jehiel, 179.
Mosier, Noah, 233.
Mosier, Samuel, 11.
Mosier, see Moger.

Moss, Amos, 248.
Moss, Ebenezer, 235.
Moss, Elihu, 222.
Moss, Joa, 49.
Moss, Joseph, 200.
Moss, Nathaniel, 48.
Moss, Noah, 187.
Moss, Timothy, 49, 235.
Mossett, Peter, 182.
Mot, Samuel, 257.
Mott, Abel, 225.
Mott, Edward, 10, 11.
Mott, Nathaniel, 82, 86, 149.
Moulton, Daniel, 18, 19, 20, 189.
Mow, John, 151, 180.
Moxly, Joseph, 75.
Moynot, Peter, 155.
Muck, Hezekiah, 214.
Mudge, Abraham, 206.
Mudge, Ebenezer, 3d, 206.
Mulatto (Molatt), Isack, 74.
Mulatto, Jack, 72.
Mulatto, Simon, 61.
Mulhins, John, 16.
Mullen, John, 135.
Mun, David, 28, 146.
Mun, Gideon, 219.
Munge, Jarvis, 218.
Munger (Mongar, Monger).
Munger, Ebenezer, 202.
Munger, Joel, 224.
Munger, Levy, 50, 51, 118, 119.
Munger, Philip, 25, 141, 244.
Munroe (Manro, Monrow, Munrow).
Munroe, Reuben, 218.
Munroe, William, 12, 109, 110, 240, 244.
Munse, Daniel, 110.
Munsell, Elisha, 16.
Munsell, Gurden, 230.
Munsell, Henry, 237.
Munsell, John, 197.
Munsell, Thomas, 196, 261.
Munson, Abner, 222.
Munson, Ebenezer, 238.
Munson, Hermon, 235.
Munson, Joel, 30.
Munson, John, 225.
Munson, Levi, 193, 261.
Munson, Medad, 54.
Munson, Peter, 235.
Munson, Titus, 60.
Munson, William, 120.
Murdock (Mardock), John, 83.
Murdock, Peter, 52, 118.
Murdock, William, 254.
Murdock, see Moredock.

Murphy (Murfee, Murfey).
Murphy, Edward, 182.
Murphy, James, 11, 52, 116, 145, 187.
Murray (Murey, Murry).
Murray, Amos, 153.
Murray, Elisha, 58, 138, 139.
Murray, William, 157, 160.
Muxley, Joseph, 80.
Mygatt (Mygate), Austin, 102.
Mygatt, Roger, 103, 210.
Mygatt, Thomas, 209.

Nanapum, John, 40, 113.
Napping, Thomas, 257.
Nash, Jedediah, 180.
Nash, John, 84.
Nash, Littlefield, 37, 79, 101, 128.
Nash, Moses, 228, 244.
Nash, Phinehas, 85.
Nathan, Michael, 115.
Natlan, Nicholas, 116.
Nearing, Emanuel, 62.
Nearing, Emond, 106.
Nearing, John Henry, 218.
Necko, Pharoh, 60.
Need (Nead), James, 192.
Need, John, 169.
Neff (Neph), Arnold, 214.
Neff, Clement, 16, 69, 71, 132.
Neff, Clement, Jr., 183.
Neff, William, 183.
Negro, Ambo, 131.
Negro, Backos, 152.
Negro, Benjamin Paull, 38.
Negro, Bristol, 131.
Negro, Cato, 37, 100.
Negro, Cæsar, 37, 101.
Negro, Fuller, 141, 224.
Negro, Gooff, 224.
Negro, Jeffery, 172.
Negro, Joseph, 170.
Negro, Jupeter, 53, 122, 123.
Negro, London, 103.
Negro, Mertin, 226.
Negro, Newport, 141.
Negro, Persons, 215.
Negro, Petro, 211.
Negro, Prince, 53, 122, 123.
Negro, Richard, 15.
Negro, Sipio, 160.
Negro, Tobey, 182.
Negro, Walpole, 169.
Negro, William, 169.
Negro, Zekera, 211.
Negus (Negurs), Joseph, 5, 211.
Nelson, Jeremiah, 245.
Nelson, John, 242.

Nelson, William, Jr., 37.
Nettleton (Nuttleton).
Nettleton, Amos, 157, 177, 179.
Nettleton, George, 44, 117, 118.
Nettleton, Jeremiah, 227.
Nettleton, Josiah, 68.
New Cheshire, 234.
New Fairfield, 217, 225, 226.
New Hampshire, 76.
New Hartford, 246.
New Haven, 3, 22, 24, 30, 31, 65, 76, 85, 87, 88, 91, 109, 124, 126, 136, 167, 171, 192, 200, 231, 252, 265.
New London, 3, 5, 9, 91, 143, 145, 180, 232, 233, 263, 267.
New Milford, 28, 57, 62, 87, 124, 185, 217, 218, 225, 226.
New Salem, 86.
New York, 65, 69, 72, 76, 88.
Newcomb, Simon, 19, 209.
Newell (Nuel), 62.
Newell, David, 193.
Newell, Elihu, 239.
Newell, John, Jr., 229.
Newell, Joseph, 242.
Newell, Robert, 45, 79, 195.
Newent, 235.
Newington, 5, 7, 152, 185.
Newman (Numan).
Newman, David, 150, 151.
Newman, Ezra, 216.
Newman, Isaac, 217.
Newman, John, 56, 150.
Newman, John, Jr., 151.
Newman, Joseph, 216.
Newmen, Isaac, 217.
Newson, Thomas, 209.
Newton, 224.
Newton, Ezekiel, 220.
Newton, Roger, 231, 252.
Newton, Samuel, 31.
Newton, Thomas, 235.
Newtown, 237.
Nicholas (Nicklos).
Nicholas, Elnathan, 155.
Nicholas, John, 62.
Nichols (Nickals, Nickols, Nicols).
Nichols, Abel, 201.
Nichols, Abijah, 242.
Nichols, Andrew, 219.
Nichols, Benjamin, 200.
Nichols, Daniel, 177, 178.
Nichols, Eliakim, 56.
Nichols, Howkins, 200.
Nichols, James, 219, 265.
Nichols, John, 8, 32, 141, 218, 228, 243.
Nichols, Joseph, 157.
Nichols, Moses, 221.
Nichols, Nicholas, 22, 76, 129, 132, 185.
Nichols, Silas, 200.
Nichols, Theophilus, 3, 91, 167.
Nichols, Thomas, 102, 180.
Nichols, William, 84.
Nicholson (Nickalson, Nickerson, Nickerson, Nicolson).
Nicholson, Ambros, 23, 77, 138, 139, 210.
Nicholson, Eliphaz, 157.
Nicholson, Henry, 6, 210.
Nicholson, Isacher, 177, 179.
Nicholson, Richard, 70.
Nicholson, William, 238.
Nickes, Nehemiah, 180.
Niles, Caleb, 214.
Niles, David, 259.
Niles, Robert, 190.
Nobicen (Nobigin, Nobikin).
Nobicer, Wonks, 131, 169, 170.
Noble, Aaron, 174.
Noble, Daniel, 217.
Noble, Hezakiah, 219.
Noble, Israel, 58.
Noble, James, 42, 148, 149.
Noble, Morgin, 226.
Noble, Stephen, 226.
Noble, Thaddeus, 109.
Noble, William, 227.
Nodine, Lewis, 155, 179.
Nonsuch, Joshua, 86.
North, Elnathan, 14, 130, 131, 210.
North, Jese, 201.
North, John, 224.
North, Joseph, 63.
North, Martin, 135, 222.
North, Thomas, 228, 244.
Northam (Northum).
Northam, Elijah, 205, 256.
Northam, John, 42, 86, 87, 137.
Northam, Timothy, 142, 187, 203.
Northam, William, 242.
Northford, 224.
Northrop, Abel, 220.
Northrop, Abraham, 157, 196.
Northrop, Andrew, 59.
Northrop, Ephraim, 59.
Northrop, Jonathan, 59.
Northrop, Lazarus, 220.
Northrop, Moses, 220.
Northrop, Nehemiah, 220.
Northrup (Nortrup), Amos, 238.
Northrup, Jabez, 61.
Northrup, William, 61, 238.
Norton, Andrew, 13.

Norton, Ashbel, 50, 51.
Norton, Beriah, 51.
Norton, Bethuel, 169, 170.
Norton, David, 212.
Norton, Ebenezer, 247.
Norton, Felex, 51, 212.
Norton, Ichabod, 230.
Norton, Isi, 202.
Norton, Issacor, 29.
Norton, Job, 210.
Norton, John, 3, 50, 51, 91, 222.
Norton, John, Jr., 211.
Norton, Jonathan, 245.
Norton, Joseph, 130.
Norton, Lot, 25.
Norton, Mathew, 230.
Norton, Matthias, 182.
Norton, Noah, 195, 266.
Norton, Reuben, 212.
Norton, Samuel, 228, 243.
Norton, Shadrach, 94.
Norton, Thomas, 144.
Norton, Zebedee, 96.
Norton, Zebulon, 29, 94, 212.
Norwalk, 11, 55, 66, 91, 126, 158, 241, 242, 251, 252.
Norwich, 3, 22, 40, 48, 51, 83, 91, 109, 111, 142, 167, 180, 188, 235, 236, 262, 265, 267.
Nott, Epaphras, 48, 186.
Nott, Gershom, 230.
Nott, John, 178, 179, 261.
Nott, Josiah, 44.
Nott, Stephen, 227.
Nott, William, 153, 187.
Nova Scotia, 88.
Nowling, Joshua, 240.
Noyce, William, Sr., 45.
Noyes, Joseph, 214.
Noyes, William, 44.
Nye, George, 215.

Occom (Aucon, Oacom).
Occom, Jonathan, 145.
Occom, Joshua, 40.
Occom, Tom, 145.
Ocornally, Partrick, 39.
Odell (Oddle), Edward, 261.
Odell, Ned, 178, 179.
Odell, Nehemiah Smith, 221.
Ogden, Ebenezer, 201.
Ogden, Jese, 201.
Olcott (Olcutt, Ollcott).
Olcott, Benjamin, 148, 203, 256.
Olcott, Ezekiel, 230.
Olcott, James, 211.
Olcott, Thomas, 246.
Olcott, Titus, 230.

Old, Joseph, 64, 245.
Old, Stephen, 245.
Olds, Jonathan, 63.
Oliver (Ollever), Obediah, 118.
Oliver, Peter, 53, 145.
Olmsted (Umstead).
Olmsted, Caleb, 230, 239.
Olmsted, David, 180.
Olmsted, Ebenezer, 226.
Olmsted, Gardiner, 251.
Olmsted, Ichabod, 56, 251.
Olmsted, John, 179, 221.
Olmsted, Justus, 221.
Olmsted, Nathan, 157.
Olmsted, Roger, 246.
Olmsted, Samuel, 230.
Olmsted, Silas, 251.
Olmsted, Stephen, 239.
Olmsted, Timothy, 230.
Olmsted, William, 258.
Orborn, William, 221.
Orcut, David, 199.
Orcut, Moses, 198.
Ormsbury, John, 174.
Ormsby (Ormby, Ormsbee, Ormsbey).
Ormsby, 18.
Ormsby, Ephraim, 20, 183.
Ormsby, Nathaniel, 20, 37, 96, 242.
Orton, Hezekiah, 199.
Orton, Lemuel, 224.
Orvis, 135.
Orvis, Ebenezer, 22, 134.
Orvis, Gershom, 169.
Osborn (Orsborn, Osbon).
Osborn, Ebenezer, 138.
Osborn, Isaac, 94.
Osborn, James, 218.
Osborn, Jeremi, 221.
Osborn, John, 157, 216.
Osborn, Joseph, 261.
Osborn, Moses, 157, 179.
Osborn, Nathan, 65, 67.
Osborn, Nathaniel, 5.
Osborn, Samuel, 13, 31, 146.
Osborn, Timothy, 148, 189.
Osborn, see Orborn.
Osburn (Osbourn, Ossburn).
Osburn, Aaron, 61.
Osburn, Abraham, 172.
Osburn, Ebenezer, 242.
Osburn, Ezekiel, 241.
Osburn, Hezekiah, 241.
Osburn, Israel, 211.
Osburn, James, 65.
Osburn, Jeremiah, 241.
Osburn, John, 199.
Osburn, Joseph, 172.

INDEX. 325

Osburn, Moses, 158, 177.
Osburn, Nathan, 137, 160.
Osburn, Thomas, 38.
Osburn, Zebedee, 211.
Otis, John, 233.
Otis, Stephen, 182.
Ovet, Benjamin, 218.
Oviat, Samuel, 220.
Oviatt, Thomas, 225.
Owen (Owin), Alvin, 246.
Owen, Asael, 245.
Owen, Azoah, 170.
Owen, Benjamin, 250, 257.
Owen, Daniel, 63, 77, 239.
Owen, Elijah, 134, 216, 247.
Owen, Eliphilet, 140.
Owen, Jonathan, 209.
Owen, Joshua, 33.
Owen, Josiah, 122.
Owen, Samuel, 141.
Owen, Simeon, 82.
Owen, Uziah, 169.
Owen, Uzziel, 148.
Owen, Zachariah, 33.
Owen, Zeckeus, 141.
Oxford, Negro, 189.

Paddock, Robert, 99.
Page, Aaron, 172.
Page, Abraham, 225.
Page, Asa, 67, 69, 235.
Page, David, 65, 67, 240.
Pain, Elisha, 52.
Pain, Isaac, 127.
Pain, Thomas, 24, 76, 126.
Paine, Brenton, 215.
Paine, see Payn.
Painter (Panter), Elisha, 253.
Painter, John, 14.
Palmer (Parmer).
Palmer, Abraham, 81, 205.
Palmer, Amasa, 248, 254.
Palmer, Caleb, 172.
Palmer, Christopher, 34, 109, 111.
Palmer, Christopher, Jr., 214.
Palmer, Daniel, 60.
Palmer, Denham, 216.
Palmer, Eleazer, 34.
Palmer, Elihu, 72, 73, 143.
Palmer, Elijah, 226.
Palmer, Eliphalet, 248, 254.
Palmer, Elisha, 75.
Palmer, Ichabod, 214, 218.
Palmer, Jacob, 180, 261.
Palmer, Jeames, 132.
Palmer, James, 151.
Palmer, Jonathan, 51, 126, 159.
Palmer, Jonathan Wiatt, 214.

Palmer, Joseph, 190, 214.
Palmer, Joshua, 249, 254.
Palmer, Judah, 120.
Palmer, King, 70.
Palmer, Nathan, 172.
Palmer, Nathaniel, 40.
Palmer, Nehemiah, 214, 250.
Palmer, Phineas, 144.
Palmer, Samuel, 42, 151, 180, 207, 211.
Palmer, Silas, 180.
Palmer, Stephen, 198, 225.
Palmers, Joel, 135.
Pangman, Joseph, 228, 244.
Pangmon, Stephen, 206.
Pantusick, 86.
Pardee, Daniel, 253.
Pardee, David, 216.
Pardy, Ebenezer, 62, 139, 226.
Pardy, James, 206.
Pardy, John, 206.
Pardy, Nathaniel, 121.
Park, Benjamin, 10, 101.
Park, Brister, 70, 71, 117.
Park, Jeremiah, 232.
Park, Joseph, 237, 240.
Park, Ruben, 240.
Park, Thomas, Jr., 197.
Park, William, 240, 244.
Park, see Parks.
Parker (Perker), Didymus, 48.
Parker, Eanos, 122.
Parker, Eli, 122, 124.
Parker, Eliab, 16, 121.
Parker, Elisha, 8, 78, 153, 154, 198.
Parker, Ely, 39.
Parker, Enos, 169.
Parker, Ephraim, 39, 54.
Parker, Gamaliel, 235.
Parker, George, 83, 97, 98, 189.
Parker, Gideon, 193.
Parker, James, 66, 67, 69, 153, 198.
Parker, Jesse, 54.
Parker, John, 120, 121.
Parker, Joseph, 203, 256.
Parker, Moses, 27.
Parker, Nathaniel, 118.
Parker, Samuel, Jr., 35.
Parker, Zacheriah, 27, 34, 99, 100.
Parkhurst, Tilley, 240.
Parkhurst, Jonathan, 240.
Parklee, Lawrance, 66, 67, 68, 69.
Parks, Daniel, 217.
Parks, John, 28.
Parks, Nathan, 10, 161, 233.
Parks, Ruphas, 101.
Parks, William, 146.
Parks, see Park.

Parmele (Palmerly, Pamerly, Parmilee, Parmlee).
Parmele, Aaron, 212.
Parmele, Amos, 194.
Parmele, Benjamin, 172, 261.
Parmele, Cornelius, 51.
Parmele, Noah, 238.
Parmele, Samuel, 202.
Parnel, Dan, 227.
Parnell, Daniel, 227.
Parrish (Parish).
Parrish, Ebenezer, 240, 244.
Parrish, Ezekil, 257.
Parrish, Gideon, 68, 69.
Parrish, Joel, 59, 176, 178.
Parrish, Oliver, 248, 254.
Parrish, William, 16, 97, 98.
Parrish, William, Jr., 184.
Parry, Thomas, 6.
Parsons, Eldad, 79.
Parsons, David, 6, 93, 95, 96, 173.
Parsons, Eldad, 174.
Parsons, Hezekiah, 122, 123.
Parsons, Isaac, 153.
Parsons, Jonathan, 95, 246.
Parsons, Nathaniel, 246.
Parsons, Noah, 96, 174.
Parsons, Shobal, 211.
Parsons, Warham, 174, 175.
Parsons, William, 222.
Parsons, see Pearsons, Persons.
Partelo, Amos, 216.
Partin, John, 181.
Pasahauk, Simon, 144.
Pasco (Pascho).
Pasco, Jonathan, 169, 170.
Patchen (Pachen), Andrew, 251.
Patchen, David, 221.
Patchen, George, 110, 251.
Patchen, Samuel, 178, 179.
Patten (Patton), Jonathan, 208.
Patten, Nathan, 43.
Patten, Nathaniel, 43.
Patterson (Paterson, Pattersons).
Patterson, Ashbel, 140.
Patterson, John, 13, 15, 126, 129, 131, 132, 160, 161.
Patterson, Thomas, 209.
Patterson, Timothy, 115, 116.
Patterson, William, 141.
Paul, Benjamin, 38, 97, 98.
Paulding, Joshua, 244.
Pawheague (Pawkaigh, Pockhage, Poheage, Powheage).
Pawheague, Charles, 72, 74, 75, 145, 214.
Pawheague, Jonathan, 70, 71, 144.
Pawheague, Peter, 214.

Pawheague, Stephen, 144.
Payn, Stephen, 45.
Payn, Timothy, 252.
Payn, William, 253.
Payn, see Paine.
Payson, 159.
Payson, Ephraim, 51.
Payson, John, 34, 36, 38, 93, 96, 97, 159.
Payson, Jonathan, 98.
Payson, Nathan, 3, 11, 13, 76, 77, 87, 126, 128, 129, 167, 173, 175, 176.
Peabody (Pabodie).
Peabody, Nathaniel, 237.
Peabody, Thomas, 214.
Peagon, Jonathan, 97.
Peake, Ephraim, 242.
Peake, Joseph, 243.
Pearce, Justice, 147.
Pearce, Thomas, 260.
Pearce, see Peirce, Perce, Pierce, Pirce.
Pearsons, Eldad, 39.
Pearsons, John, 11.
Pearsons, Noah, 39, 94.
Pearsons, see Parsons, Pierson.
Pease (Peeas, Pees).
Pease, Abel, 246.
Pease, Abial, 39.
Pease, Abner, 6.
Pease, Benjamin, 105, 172.
Pease, Christopher, 250.
Pease, David, 265.
Pease, James, 4th, 216.
Pease, Joel, 94, 246.
Pease, John, 247.
Pease, Lemuel, 23, 77.
Pease, Moses, 39, 94, 96.
Pease, Nathaniel, 7.
Pease, Noah, 169, 216.
Pease, Peter, 229.
Pease, Samuel, 209.
Pease, Stephen, 39, 79.
Pease, Timothy, 207.
Pease, Warham, 39, 79.
Peck (Peeck, Peek).
Peck, Amiel, 238.
Peck, Aron, 238.
Peck, Benajah, 252.
Peck, Benoni, 247.
Peck, Charles, 157, 158, 235.
Peck, Colier, 235.
Peck, Ebenezer, 206.
Peck, Eliphalet, 61, 113.
Peck, Elisha, 28.
Peck, Ezra, 238.
Peck, Isaac, 227, 243.

INDEX. 327

Peck, Jabez, 14.
Peck, Jahleel, 52, 111, 112, 236.
Peck, James, 30, 31, 217, 231.
Peck, James, Jr., 30.
Peck, Jesse, 238.
Peck, John, 151.
Peck, Joseph, 61, 110, 217, 253.
Peck, Justus, 246.
Peck, Michael, 220.
Peck, Paul, 147, 224.
Peck, Samuel, 40, 105.
Peck, Thomas, 224.
Peck, Timothy, 31, 128, 129, 199, 252.
Peck, Timothy, Jr., 265.
Peck, Zebulon, 55.
Peehe, Eliphalet, 112.
Peet (Peat), Albirom, 224.
Peet, Benjamin, 33.
Peet, Daniel, 155, 178, 179.
Peet, David, 261.
Peet, Elnathan, 200.
Peet, Jehiel, 219.
Peet, John, 225.
Peet, Samuel, 218.
Peirce, Abel, 240, 244.
Peirce, Amos, 209.
Peirce, David, 211.
Peirce, Francis, 157.
Peirce, Jonathan, 157.
Peirce, Joseph, Jr., 211.
Peirce, Lemuel, 16.
Peirce, Nathaniel, 211.
Peirce, Thomas, 44, 118, 195, 209.
Peirce, see Pearce, Perce, Pierce, Pirce.
Pelcit, James, 240.
Pellet, James, 244.
Pelton, Ebenezer, 72, 73, 74.
Pelton, Nathan, 196.
Pember, Jacob, 236.
Pemfield, Samuel, 250.
Pendleton, Edmund, 200.
Penfield (Pendfield), Isaac, 212.
Penfield, John, 213.
Penfield, Samuel, 49, 50, 221.
Penigue (Pinigue), Keup, 136.
Penigue, Keump, 134.
Pennsylvania, 163.
Penoyer, John, 217.
Penoyer, Thomas, 216.
Pepper, John, 226.
Pepperell, William, 88.
Perce (Pers), Ezekiel, 15, 17.
Perce, Francis, 179.
Perce, Joseph, 204.
Perce, Nemiah, 247.
Perce, Samuel, 229.

Perce, see Pearce, Peirce, Pierce, Pirce.
Percival (Pacifull, Parsifell, Parsival, Parsival, Percifull, Persival, Persivel).
Percival, Timothy, 72, 73, 74, 148, 149, 202, 256.
Perday, David, 151.
Perkins (Perken, Pirkins, Purkins).
Perkins, Daniel, 207.
Perkins, Elias, 246.
Perkins, Israel, 6.
Perkins, Jacob, 236.
Perkins, Jesse, 121.
Perkins, John, 235, 236.
Perkins, Joseph, 237.
Perkins, Joshua, 258.
Perkins, Matthew, 237.
Perkins, Ruben, 246.
Perkins, Simon, 236.
Perkins, Stephen, 67, 69.
Perl, James, 248, 254.
Perrigo (Pereggo, Peregoe, Perige, Perigo).
Perrigo, David, 208.
Perrigo, John Kenp, 174.
Perrigo, William, 72, 73, 75, 191.
Perrin (Perine).
Perrin, Thomas, 205, 257.
Perrin, Timothy, 242.
Perrit (Perot), John, 216, 220.
Perrit, Peter, 59.
Perry (Perrey, Pery).
Perry, Asa, 38.
Perry, Ebenezer, 221.
Perry, Elisha, 157.
Perry, James, 220.
Perry, John, 157, 158.
Perry, Jonathan, 242.
Perry, Joseph, 218.
Perry, Joshua, 68, 69.
Perry, Nathaniel, 60, 220.
Person, Stephen, 63, 130, 131.
Persons, Hezekiah, 38, 79.
Persons, see Parsons.
Perterson, Edward, 229.
Perterson, Thomas, 229.
Peter, 86.
Peter, George, 84.
Peters, Benjamin, 180, 261.
Peters, Gala, 160.
Peters, Jabez, 144.
Peters, John, 204, 205.
Peters, Joseph, 61, 130, 131, 139.
Pettery, Alexander, 33.
Pettibone (Pettybone).
Pettibone, Jacob, 105.

328   CAMPAIGNS OF 1755, 1756, AND 1757.

Pettibone, Jonathan, 62, 64, 224, 245, 246.
Pettibone, Samuel, 57, 58.
Pettingal (Petingal).
Pettingal, Lemuel, 236.
Pettingal, Solomon, 17, 236.
Pettis, Benjamin, 117.
Pettit, Ebed, 33.
Pettit, Ebenezer, 206.
Pettit, Eliada, 220.
Pettit, John, 206.
Petty, John, 10.
Pharoah, Samuel, 251.
Phelan, Joseph, 211.
Phelps, Aaron, 63, 245.
Phelps, Abel, 247.
Phelps, Abner, 103.
Phelps, Abraham, 246.
Phelps, Amos, 42.
Phelps, Asa, 134.
Phelps, Azriah, 63.
Phelps, Barret, 205.
Phelps, David, 42, 207, 224.
Phelps, Eldad, 246.
Phelps, Elisha, 246.
Phelps, Hezekiah, 63.
Phelps, Ichabod, 42, 43, 85, 142.
Phelps, Isaac, 230.
Phelps, James, 206.
Phelps, John, 35, 62.
Phelps, Nathaniel, 205, 257.
Phelps, Noah, 43, 245.
Phelps, Roger, 205, 211.
Phelps, Silvenas, 205.
Phelps, Solomon, 204, 205.
Phelps, Timothy, 245.
Phillips (Philips), Abiel, 238.
Phillips, Gillum, 16.
Phillips, John, 44, 80.
Phinney, John, 201.
Phinny, Oliver, 199.
Phinny, Simeon, 199.
Phipeney, Archibald, 200.
Phippene, Joseph, 154.
Picket, David, 57, 237.
Picket, Ebenezer, 238.
Picket, John, 251.
Picket, Joseph, 224.
Picket, Timothy, 177, 179.
Pidge, Jonathan, 184.
Pierce, Elisha, 77.
Pierce, Ezekiel, 15.
Pierce, Francis, 158, 178.
Pierce, Thomas, 117, 194.
Pierce, William, 206.
Pierce, see Pearce, Peirce, Perce, Pirce.
Pierpont (Pairpoint).

Pierpont, Benjamin, 172.
Pierpont, James, 26.
Pierpont, Thomas, 234.
Pierson, Nathan, 220.
Pierson, Samuel, 220.
Pierson, see Pearsons.
Pike, Asa, 208.
Pike, David, 13, 129, 131, 168.
Pike, Ebenezer, 222.
Pike, Lenard, 198.
Pike, N[   ], 208.
Pike, Samuel, 15, 120, 121.
Pike, William, 55.
Pineo, James, 46.
Pinney (Piney, Pinny).
Pinney, Abraham, 11.
Pinney, Jonathan, 38, 103, 134, 135, 239.
Pinney, Joseph, 35, 103, 104, 169, 170.
Pinney, Josiah, 122.
Pinney, Nathaniel, 103, 104.
Pinney, Philander, 11.
Pinnock, James, 224.
Pique, David, 168.
Pirce, Daniel, 122.
Pirce, Nathaniel, 122.
Pirce, see Pearce, Peirce, Perce, Pierce.
Pitkin, James, 230.
Pitkin, John, 5, 7, 9, 118, 119.
Pitkin, Johna, 230.
Pitkin, Joseph, 207, 215, 229.
Pitkin, William, Jr., 229.
Pito (Perto, Pyto).
Pito, Pite, 27, 99, 184.
Plainfield, 15, 36, 101, 108, 194, 241, 266.
Plant, James, 127.
Plant, Timothy, 27, 172.
Plato, John, 191.
Platt, David, 201.
Platt, Epenetus, 59, 225.
Platt, Epinelus, 220.
Platt, John, 56.
Plumb (Plum).
Plumb, Amariah, 13, 130, 131.
Plumb, Charles, 105, 172, 262.
Plumb, Green, 233.
Plumb, Joshua, 234.
Plumb, Seth, 172.
Plumb, Simeon, 169.
Plymouth, Mass., 91.
Pollard, William, 69, 71, 117.
Pollet, William, 206.
Polly (Poley, Polley).
Polly, John, 250, 257.
Polly, Samuel, 131.

INDEX. 329

Pomeroy, Benjamin, 167, 170.
Pomeroy, see Pomroy, Pumroy.
Pomfret, 15, 17, 20, 21, 41, 79, 100, 101, 108, 154, 176, 207, 208, 262, 263.
Pomham, Joseph, 71.
Pompey, Jacob, 74, 75.
Pompey, Japhet, 72, 75.
Pompey, Tafett, 74.
Pompy, Isaac, 144.
Pomroy, Benjamin, 257.
Pomroy, Joshua, 174.
Pomroy, see Pomeroy, Pumroy.
Pond, Bartholomew, 55, 194.
Pond, Peter, 105.
Pond, Phineas, 144, 160.
Pone, Robert, 75.
Pool, Jonathan, 43, 198.
Pool, Thomas, 17.
Poolen, John, 153.
Poon, Simon, 98.
Pooney, Simon, 97.
Pope, Charles, 251.
Pork, Nathan, 114.
Porrage (Porridge).
Porrage, Ananias, 17, 97, 98, 183.
Porter, 87.
Porter, Amos, 210.
Porter, Asel, 229.
Porter, Ashbel, 54.
Porter, Bartholomy, 46.
Porter, David, 219.
Porter, Elijah, 34, 183, 185.
Porter, Elisha, 23, 77, 250.
Porter, Hezekiah, 84.
Porter, John, 230.
Porter, John, Jr., 239.
Porter, Jonathan, 239.
Porter, Nathan, 198.
Porter, Nathaniel, 3, 24, 79, 114, 116, 117, 159, 160, 209, 250, 267.
Porter, Noah, 14, 230.
Porter, Roger, 239.
Porter, Samuel, 15, 84, 174, 176.
Porter, Stephen, 200.
Porter, Thomas, 63, 198, 199.
Possetous, James, 11, 108, 191.
Post, Ambros, 84.
Post, Benjamin, 84.
Post, Gideon, 205.
Post, Gidon, 258.
Post, Jabez, 40.
Post, Mathew, 212.
Post, Reuben, 212.
Post, Thomas, 42.
Post, Zephaniah, 250.
Potter, Amos, 30, 231.

Potter, Daniel, 222.
Potter, Enos, 66, 67, 68.
Potter, Ichabod, 232.
Potter, Isaac, 31.
Potter, Israel, 231.
Potter, Joel, 30, 126, 231.
Potter, Phenes, 204.
Potter, Philemon, 127, 172.
Potter, Roburt, 204.
Potter, Stephen, 231.
Potter, Timothy, 231.
Pougoneet, Samuel, 141.
Pow (Powe), Robert, 72, 74.
Powell, Ephraim, 115, 116.
Powell, Felix, 33, 77, 127.
Powell, Joshua, 99, 208.
Powell, Stephen, 26.
Powell, Thomas, 70.
Powers (Powars), Ichabod, 233.
Powers, James, 23, 30, 77, 117, 127, 128, 181.
Powers, Petter, 222.
Powers, William, 37, 242.
Pratt, Aaron, 7, 230, 239.
Pratt, Azariah, 172, 206.
Pratt, Benjamin, Jr., 44.
Pratt, Daniel, 94, 174.
Pratt, Daniel, Jr., 44.
Pratt, Elisha, 239.
Pratt, Ezra, 230.
Pratt, Hez, 227.
Pratt, Joseph, 58, 218.
Pratt, Samuel, 44.
Pratt, Samuel, Jr., 44.
Pratt, Simeon, 44.
Pratt, Simn, 227.
Pratt, William, 239.
Prentice, Ebenezer, 83.
Prentice, Elezer, 232.
Prentice, Elisha, 107.
Prentice, John, 107, 214, 237.
Prentice, Joshua, 214.
Prentice, Joseph, 233.
Prentice, Samuel, 214.
President, Peter, 66.
Preston (Presten), Amas, 133.
Preston, Asa, 219.
Preston, Ephraim, 49, 124, 192, 194.
Preston, Henry, 17, 97, 98, 248, 254.
Preston, Jacob, Jr., 20.
Preston, John, 133.
Preston, John, Jr., 248, 254.
Preston, Jonathan, 54.
Preston, Joseph, 22, 69, 184.
Preston, Josiah, 71.

Preston, Nathaniel, 112, 113, 183.
Preston (Praston), 9, 83, 107, 142, 190, 231, 232, 266.
Price, Nathan, 179.
Prichard, Abraham, 222.
Prichard, Elnathan, 120.
Prichard, Isaac, 54.
Prichard, Roger, 223.
Pride, Paul, 182.
Pride, Peter, 237.
Priest, Phillip, 105.
Prime, James, 226.
Prime, Reuben, 124.
Prince, 86.
Prince, Benjamin, 204.
Prindle, Abel, 156, 176, 178, 260.
Prindle, Charles, 220.
Prindle, Daniel, 226.
Prindle, Eben., 26.
Prindle, Ebenezer, 153, 154, 193.
Prindle, Epenetus, 12.
Prindle, Ezra, 153, 193.
Prindle, Isaac, 157.
Prindle, Iseph, 29.
Prindle, James, 238.
Prindle, Joel, 12.
Prindle, John, 157, 238.
Prindle, Jonathan, 238.
Prindle, Joseph, 140, 244.
Prindle, Joshua, 228.
Prindle, Mark, 199.
Prindle, Samuel, 226.
Prior (Prier), Abner, 134.
Prior, Clothier, 175.
Prior, Gideon, 134.
Prior, Joel, 211.
Prior, Josiah, 234.
Prior, see Pryor.
Proad, Jeremiah, 250.
Prout, Ebenezer, 115, 116, 234.
Prout, Harris, 115, 116.
Provoce, Samuel, 180, 261.
Prudden, Fletcher, 220.
Prudden, Joseph, 59.
Prulee, Hezekiah, 219.
Prvor, Ezekel, 246.
Pryor (Pryer), Abner, 38, 135.
Pryor, Clother, 174.
Pryor, Gideon, 38, 136.
Pryor, William, 174.
Pryor, see Prior.
Puffer, James, 10.
Puffer, Lasarus, 257.
Pulphard, Edmund, 196.
Pumham, Joseph, 69, 133.
Pumroy, Dan, 169.
Pumroy, Elijah, 189.
Pumroy, Noah, 6, 96.
Pumroy, Noah, Jr., 94.
Pumroy, Phinehas, 64.
Pumroy, see Pomeroy, Pomroy.
Punise, Jack, 192.
Putnam, 188.
Putnam, Asaph, 36.
Putnam, Israel, 21, 41, 79, 80, 100, 101, 160, 161, 162, 176, 262, 263, 266.
Putnam, John, 83.
Pyras, 87, 160.

Quick, John, 103.
Quiomps, John, 191.
Quocheets (Cocghets).
Quocheets, Peter, 10, 108, 191.
Quocheets, Thomas, 191.
Quocheets, see Cheets.
Quon, John, 86.

Race, Abraham, 140.
Radford, James, 28.
Rading, Edman, 133.
Randall, Abraham, 216.
Randall, Greenfield, 99.
Randall, Joseph, 10, 107, 191.
Randall, Ruben, 190.
Randall, Rufus, 203, 258.
Ranney (Raney, Ranny, Rany).
Ranney, John, 12, 187.
Ranney, John, Jr., 12.
Ranney, Nathaniel, 82.
Ranney, Stephen, 50, 187.
Ranney, Timothy, 70, 71, 128, 129.
Ranney, Willit, 229.
Ransom, Amos, 255.
Ransom, James, 203.
Ransom, John, 206.
Ransom, Mathew, 189.
Ransom, Samuel, 29, 146.
Ransom, Steaphen, 41.
Ranson, James, 258.
Rathbone (Rathbun, Rothbone, Rothburn, Wrathbone).
Rathbone, Amos, 203, 214, 258.
Rathbone, Daniel, 228, 244.
Rothbone, Isaiah, 112, 113.
Rathbone, Jacob, 10.
Rathbone, Job, 209.
Ray, Daniel, 108.
Ray, Patrick, 240.
Ray, Timothy, 227.
Raymond (Raiment, Raimond, Ramand, Rament, Ramond, Rayment, Raymont).
Raymond, Amos, 7.
Raymond, Asael, 251.
Raymond, Daniel, 206.

Raymond, James, 208.
Raymond, John, 145, 267.
Raymond, Joshua, 18, 20, 21, 152, 154.
Raymond, Josiah, 218.
Raymond, Nero, 233.
Raymond, Samuel, 72, 74, 75, 205, 226, 258.
Raymond, Sands, 180, 181.
Raymond, Seth, 12.
Raymond, William, 56, 139, 251.
Rayn, John, 69.
Read, Daniel, 135.
Read, Jacob, 63, 83.
Read, James, 136.
Read, John, 95.
Read, John, Jr., 245.
Read, Joshua, 122.
Read, Josiah, 82.
Read, Moses, 247.
Read, Moses, Jr., 206.
Read, Silas, 245.
Read, see Reed.
Reboe, Andrew, 180.
Redding, 200.
Redding, Edmun, 71.
Redding, Edmund, 183.
Redfield, James, 8, 177, 178.
Redfield, John, 91.
Redfield, Josiah, 227.
Redfield, Peleg, 7, 125, 194, 195.
Reding, Edmund, 70.
Redington, Abraham, 27.
Redington, Daniel, 248, 254.
Redington, Jacob, 6.
Reed, Abijah, 241.
Reed, Daniel, 219.
Reed, Ebenezer, 228, 243.
Reed, Eli, 251.
Reed, Elias, 209.
Reed, Hezekiah, 6, 174, 175.
Reed, Jacob, 182.
Reed, James, 241.
Reed, Jeremiah, 184, 228.
Reed, John, 46, 198, 200, 201.
Reed, Jonathan, 243.
Reed, Joshua, 5, 124, 216.
Reed, Josiah, 17, 99, 132, 184.
Reed, Leonard, 16.
Reed, Peter, 241.
Reed, Shubal, 174, 175.
Reed, Thomas, 10, 101, 209, 241.
Reed, see Read.
Reeve (Reaves, Reive, Reve).
Reeve, Benjamin, 224.
Reeve, David, 44.
Reeve, John, 81, 128, 129.

Reeve, Samuel, 72, 73.
Relcey, Aaron, 8.
Remington (Rimmington).
Remington, Jonathan, 169.
Remington, Joseph, 211.
Resco, Thomas, 139.
Restand, Ambrose, 202.
Return, Johnn, 103.
Rew, Daniel, 116.
Rexford (Raxford, Wrexford).
Rexford, Benjamin, 30, 153.
Rexford, Daniel, 235.
Rexford, Samuel, 49.
Reynolds (Ranolds, Raynolds, Raynols, Renails, Renells, Rennals, Rennells, Renolds, Renols, Runels, Rynolds).
Reynolds, Benjamin, 198.
Reynolds, Caleb, 180.
Reynolds, Daniel, 180, 262.
Reynolds, Ebenezer, 151, 180, 262.
Reynolds, Elias, 214.
Reynolds, Elish, 23.
Reynolds, Eliphalet, 146, 194.
Reynolds, Ely, 150.
Reynolds, Horton, 217.
Reynolds, Jedadiah, 86.
Reynolds, John, 28, 146, 204.
Reynolds, Joseph, 23, 96.
Reynolds, Reuben, 216.
Reynolds, Sackett, 61.
Reynolds, Samuel, 20, 72, 74, 75, 232.
Reynolds, Thomas, 161.
Reynolds, Timothy, 150, 151.
Reynolds, Titus, 151.
Reynolds, William, 229.
Rhode Island, 76.
Rice (Rise), Benjamin, 102, 104.
Rice, Charles, 77.
Rice, David, 115, 184.
Rice, Even, 102.
Rice, Isaiah, 63, 105, 106.
Rice, Isaias, 245.
Rice, John, 6, 69, 71, 77, 169, 246.
Rice, Josiah, 141.
Rice, Nathan, 132, 168, 169.
Rice, Peter, 43, 184.
Rice, Phillip, 27, 173.
Rice, Timothy, 154.
Rich, Peter, 81.
Rich, see Ritch.
Richards, Daniel, 241.
Richards, Elisha, 228, 244.
Richards, Isril, 145.
Richards, Jedediah, 29.
Richards, Piras, 25, 97, 98.

Richards, Samuel, 223.
Richards, Samuel, Jr., 241.
Richards, Tho, 222.
Richardson (Richerson).
Richardson, Amos, 199.
Richardson, Asa, 24, 96, 98, 160, 249, 267.
Richardson, Ebenezer, 189.
Richardson, Humphary, 132.
Richardson, Stephen, 82, 198.
Richardson, Thomas, 139.
Richinson, Gershom, 43.
Richman, George, 140.
Rickey, John, 151.
Rider, Benjamin, 98, 99, 198.
Rider, Joseph, 43, 133, 184, 185.
Ridgefield, 242.
Riedson, Henry, 96.
Rierdon (Riordan).
Rierdon, Daniel, 174, 175.
Riggs, [   ]h, 61.
Riggs, Joseph, 109, 111, 220.
Riley (Ryley).
Riley, Charles, 118, 130.
Riley, John, 159, 210.
Riley, Jonathan, 46, 87, 117.
Riley, Richard, 210.
Riley, Roger, 36.
Riley, William, 234.
Rina, James, 233.
Ripley (Riply).
Ripley, Charles, 17, 78, 128, 129, 183.
Ripley, Joshua, 34.
Ripley, Nathaniel, 16, 95, 96, 98, 168, 170.
Ripley, William, 97, 249, 255.
Ripnear (Ripnier, Rippaneor).
Ripnear, John, 35, 91, 174, 175.
Rippenson, John, 36.
Ripton, 200.
Risden, Elisha, 154, 221.
Rising, Abel, 245.
Rising, John, Jr., 211.
Rising, Jonathan, Jr., 211.
Risley, Benjamin, 230.
Risley, George, 239.
Ritch, Solomon, 108.
Ritch, see Rich.
Rix, Thomas, 232.
Roalingson, John, 66.
Robbins, see Robins.
Robbins, Isaac, 23.
Robbins, Isaac, Jr., 149.
Robbins, John, 113, 229.
Robbins, Jonathan, 187.
Robbins, Jonathan, Jr., 35.
Robbins, Roger, 209.
Roberts (Robards, Robarts, Robbards, Robberds, Robbords, Robrts, Roburds).
Roberts, Abiel, 120.
Roberts, Aron, 213.
Roberts, Daniel, 63, 105, 106.
Roberts, David, 84.
Roberts, Ebenezer, 172, 234.
Roberts, Ebenezer, Jr., 234.
Roberts, Eli, 58, 124, 225.
Roberts, Elijah, 175.
Roberts, Elizer, 174.
Roberts, Ezra, 115, 116, 234.
Roberts, Israel, 52.
Roberts, James, 70, 71, 136.
Roberts, James, Jr., 86.
Roberts, Joel, 25, 120, 223, 234.
Robert, John, 12, 52, 86, 107, 109, 110, 205.
Roberts, John, Jr., 256.
Roberts, Jonathan, 173, 175.
Roberts, Lemuel, 208.
Roberts, Luke, 57, 177, 178.
Roberts, Nathaniel, 228, 243.
Roberts, Recompence, 81, 115, 116, 213.
Roberts, Samuel, 209.
Roberts, William, 103, 179.
Robertson (Robardson, Robartson, Robason, Robbertson, Roberson).
Robertson, Elesar, 133.
Robertson, Elezar, 71.
Robertson, Elijah, 198.
Robertson, Obadiah, 146.
Robertson, Samuel, 199.
Robertson, see Robinson.
Robeson, Simeon, 115.
Robins (Roben), Elishia, 196.
Robins, Isaac, 148.
Robins, Isaac, Jr., 148.
Robins, Jehiel, 17, 183.
Robins, John, 35, 112, 181, 207.
Robins, Nicholas, 13.
Robins, Samuel, 105, 169.
Robins, see Robbins.
Robinson (Robenson).
Robinson, Asa, 137, 205.
Robinson, Benjamin, 239.
Robinson, Daniel, 208.
Robinson, Eleazer, 69, 248, 254.
Robinson, Eliakim, 30.
Robinson, Elijah, 43.
Robinson, Isaac, 97.
Robinson, Jared, 31.
Robinson, John, 31.

Robinson, Jonathan, 201.
Robinson, Nathan, 35, 78, 234, 248, 254.
Robinson, Noah, 49.
Robinson, Simeon, 116.
Robinson, Thomas, 11.
Robinson, see Robertson.
Robison, Benjamin, 17.
Robison, Daniel, 130.
Robison, John, 12.
Robison, Joseph, 17.
Robison, Thomas, 11.
Rockwell, Ameriah, 198.
Rockwell, Daniel, 22, 62, 157, 158.
Rockwell, James, 172.
Rockwell, John, 180, 252.
Rockwell, Joseph, 251.
Rockwell, Josiah, 160, 257.
Rockwell, Samuel, 207.
Rockwell, William, 230, 234.
Rockwood, Samuel, Jr., 216.
Rodden, Ezra, 174.
Roe, Elisha, 33.
Roe, John, 194, 262.
Roe, Tho, 64.
Rogers (Rogars, Roggers).
Rogers, Constant, 115, 116.
Rogers, David, 172, 237.
Rogers, Edward, 172.
Rogers, Ezekiel, 41.
Rogers, Gideon, 225.
Rogers, Hezekiah, 252.
Rogers, Ichabod, 247.
Rogers, James, 203, 258.
Rogers, John, 174, 175, 232, 233.
Rogers, Joseph, 41, 54, 78, 84, 94, 96, 122, 123, 169, 170.
Rogers, Joshua, 72, 74, 75, 129.
Rogers, Nathaniel, 174.
Rogers, Nehemiah, 233.
Rogers, Rowland, 182.
Rogers, Stephen, 59.
Rogers, Thomas, 232, 233.
Rogers, Uriah, 233.
Rogers, Zabdial, 136.
Rollins, John, 127.
Rood, Cyprian, 160.
Roolleson, Willson, 153.
Rooney, Simon, 17.
Root (Roots), Asa, 228, 244.
Root, Caleb, 33, 140, 189.
Root, Ebenezer, 198.
Root, Elakim, 82.
Root, Eleazer, 230.
Root, Jesse, 204.
Root, Job, 210.
Root, John, 198.
Root, Jonathan, 205, 257.

Root, Joseph, 33, 239.
Root, Josiah, 132.
Root, Medad, 198.
Root, Nathaniel, 228, 244.
Root, Rufus, 122.
Root, Samuel, 17, 53, 223.
Root, Samuel, Jr., 198.
Root, Thomas, 204.
Root, Thomas, Jr., 133.
Root, William, 205.
Rooty, Thomas, 8.
Rose (Roce), Abel, 211.
Rose, Daniel, 70, 225.
Rose, Henry, 78, 83.
Rose, John, 65, 141, 199.
Rose, Joseph, 232.
Rose, Josiah, 232.
Rose, Roger, 51, 195, 260.
Rose, Solomon, 225.
Roseford, Benjamin, 154.
Ross, Daniel, 249.
Ross, John, 169.
Ross, Joseph, 101.
Ross, Simeon, 194.
Ross, William, 9, 105, 106, 170.
Rosseter, David, 195.
Rosseter, Joshua, 224.
Rosseter, Stephen, 239.
Roulingson, John, 68.
Roundy, 17.
Roundy, Robert, 25.
Roundy, Robert, Jr., 183.
Roundy, Samuel, 19, 248, 254.
Rouse, Elias, 240, 244.
Rouse, Jabez, 18, 19, 236.
Rouse, Simeon, 108, 190.
Rousk, Reuben, 74.
Row, Joseph, 169.
Rowland, Daniel, 206.
Rowland, John, 118.
Rowland, Thomas, 102.
Rowland, William, 44.
Rowlandson (Rowleson, Rowlinson, Rowlison).
Rowlandson, John, 65.
Rowlandson, Joseph, 27.
Rowlandson, Phineas, 130, 210.
Rowlandson, Wilson, 23, 154, 187.
Rowley (Rowly), Aaron, 218.
Rowley, Eley, 218.
Rowley, Ephraim, 161.
Rowley, Gershom, 72, 73, 148, 149.
Rowley, Israel, 8, 72, 73, 86, 124, 145, 206.
Rowley, John, 205.
Rowley, John, Jr., 259.
Rowley, Moses, 115.
Rowley, Thomas, 218.

Rowley, Timothy, 58.
Rows, William, 168.
Royce (Roice, Roys, Royse), 26.
Royce, Allen, 54, 235.
Royce, Asa, 30, 119, 121.
Royce, Benjamin, 102, 104.
Royce, Charles, 25, 30.
Royce, David, 172, 184.
Royce, Evan, 48, 104.
Royce, Isaac, 25, 235.
Royce, Jacob, 239.
Royce, John, 99.
Royce, Jonathan, 219.
Royce, Nathan, 170.
Royce, Nathaniel, 49.
Royce, Peter, 184.
Royce, Philip, 175.
Royce, Timothy, 25, 152, 235.
Rudd, Elisha, 52, 237.
Rudd, Increse, 236.
Rudd, Jonathan, 248, 253, 254.
Rudd, Joseph, 52, 111, 112, 236.
Rude, Ebenezer, 237.
Rude, Zepheniah, 232.
Rugg, Oliver, 238.
Rugg, Solomon, 210.
Ruggles, Ashbel, 238.
Ruggles, Benjamin, 28, 87, 124, 217.
Ruggles, Joseph, 28.
Ruggles, Timothy, 252.
Rumeril, John, 94.
Rumrell, Nehemiah, 246.
Rumsey, Daniel, 177, 179.
Rundell, Jacob, 61.
Rundell, Joseph, 62.
Runnels, Thomas, 46.
Rusheck, John, 31.
Rusk, Ruben, 75.
Rusk, Ruben, Jr., 72.
Rusk, Ruben, 2d, 74, 75.
Russ, John, 35.
Russ, Jonathan, 197.
Russ, Joseph, 69, 97, 184.
Russell (Rusel), Abel, 231.
Russell, Benjamin, 31, 172.
Russell, Daniel, 30.
Russell, David, 23.
Russell, Icabod, 231.
Russell, John, 37.
Russell, Jonathan, 27, 225, 250.
Russell, Joseph, 60.
Russell, Josiah, 232.
Russell, Josiah, Jr., 37.
Russell, Nicholas, 252.
Russell, Samuel, 24.
Russell, Stephen, 25, 99.
Russell, Thomas, 247.

Russell, William, 105, 106.
Russuck, John, 127.
Rust, Abraham, 133.
Rust, Daniel, 69, 122, 123, 183.
Rust, Daniel, Jr., 69, 71.
Rust, Elisha, 222.
Rust, Jonathan, 12.
Rust, Joseph, 69, 71, 183, 236.
Rust, Nathaniel, 184.
Ryant, John, 9.
Ryaut, John, 8.
Ryon, John, 71.

Sabin (Sabens, Sabins).
Sabin, Israel, 17.
Sabins, Josiah, 207.
Sabin, Nathan, 181.
Sabin, Nathaniel, 37.
Sabin, Seth, 232.
Sabin, Zebh, 242.
Sacher, Samuel, 6.
Sacket, Jonathan, 30.
Sacket, Ruben, 199, 252.
Safford (Sefford), 263.
Safford, John, 235, 236, 240.
Safford, Jonathan, 190.
Safford, Joseph, 240.
Sage, Comfort, 228.
Sage, Ebenezer, 91, 109.
Sage, Gideon, 210.
Sage, Jedidiah, 234.
Sage, Samuel Lewis, 234.
Sage, Solomon, 81.
Saintgood, Adam, 66.
St. John, Daniel, 251.
St. John, Isaac, 139, 180.
St. John, James, 61, 157, 158.
St. John, John, 251.
St. John, Matthias, 251.
St. John, Stephen, 251, 252.
St. John, Timothy, 56.
Salar, Ezekiel, 150.
Salisbury, 32, 33, 91, 93, 199, 227, 243, 247.
Salmon Brook, 245.
Saltonstall, Gurdon, 3, 91, 232.
Sanchuse, Peter, 15.
Sanders (Sandars), Daniel, 12.
Sanders, John, 207.
Sanders, Joseph, 17.
Sanders, Noah, 242.
Sanders, see Saunders.
Sandford, 224.
Sandford, Elihu, 59.
Sandford, John, 220.
Sandford, Joseph, 220.
Sandford, Seth, 201.
Sandford, Timothy, 201.

INDEX. 335

Sanferd, 136.
Sanford, Benjamin, 204.
Sanford, Carpenter, 204.
Sanford, Ebenezer, 153, 210.
Sanford, Elihu, 104, 106.
Sanford, Ezra, 223.
Sanford, Nathaniel, 219.
Sanford, Samuel, Jr., 27.
Sanford, Zachary, 223.
Sanger, Aza, 20.
Sanger, Azariah, 18, 20.
Sanger, Jonathan, 133.
Sangola, 103.
Saratoga, 104.
Saterly, Benedick, 15, 101.
Saunders, John, 51.
Saunders, see Sanders.
Savage, Amos, 82.
Savage, Eben, 234.
Savage, Joseph, 81, 82, 234.
Savage, Josiah, 70, 71, 128, 129.
Savage, Nathaniel, 213.
Savage, Stephen, 212.
Sawens, George, 198.
Sawer, Isaac, 70.
Sawyer, Asa, 41, 145.
Sawyer, Isaac, 81.
Saybrook, 15, 17, 48, 71, 119, 125, 188, 227.
Scarrit, James, 54.
Schenectady, N. Y., 3.
Scipio (Sipio), 139.
Scipio, Solomon, 53, 123, 189.
Scipio, Thomas, 53.
Scofield, Abraham, 241.
Scofield, James, 242.
Scofield, Jonathan, 241.
Scofield, Samuel, 227.
Scofield, Silas, 241.
Scofield, Thaddeus, 241.
Scott (Scoit), Abraham, 37.
Scott, Adonijah, 210.
Scott, Benjamin, 6, 54, 94, 96.
Scott, Elijah, 46, 198.
Scott, Eliphalet, 54.
Scott, Elisha, 230.
Scott, Ezekiel, 54, 120, 121, 134, 136.
Scott, James, 217.
Scott, Jedediah, 230.
Scott, John, 54, 141.
Scott, Moses, 187.
Scott, Peter, 241.
Scott, Robert, 222.
Scott, Stephen, 193.
Scott, Timothy, Jr., 215.
Scott, Weith, 223.
Scott, William, 61.

Scovel, Abner, 9, 123.
Scovel, Arter, 203.
Scovel, Elijah, 227, 235.
Scovel, James, 44.
Scovel, Josiah, 234.
Scovel, Micah, 259.
Scovel, Michael, 203.
Scovel, Samuel, 44.
Scovel, Stephen, 81.
Scovet, Denis, 252.
Scranton, Ichabod, 50, 51, 201, 202, 267.
Scranton, Thomas, 13, 144.
Scranton, William, 17, 19.
Scribner, Elias, 251.
Scrivener, Benjamin, 233.
Scudob, Charles, 192.
Seabury (Seebury, Seybury).
Seabury, John, 127, 172.
Seabury, Samuel, 249.
Searles, John, 17.
Sears, Daniel, 44.
Sears, Elisha, 234.
Seate, Richard, 117.
Seaton, John, 240.
Seeal, Samuel, 58.
Seeley (Sealy, Seley).
Seeley, Abel, 221.
Seeley, Abijah, 180.
Seeley, Benjamin, 226.
Seeley, Ebenezer, 218, 225.
Seeley, Ephraim, 155, 225.
Seeley, Ezekiel, 151.
Seeley, Jonas, 251.
Seeley, Justus, 223.
Seeley, Michael, 200.
Seeley, Nehemiah, 139, 177, 179.
Seeley, Samuel, 221, 241.
Seeley, Zadock, 157.
Seeton, John, 245.
Segar (Segers), Joseph, 63, 130.
Segor, Michal, 245.
Sejrus, Daniel, 74.
Selleck (Silleck), Athaniel, 180.
Sellick, Jonathan, 151.
Selleck, Samuel, 55, 109, 110.
Selleck, Seymour, 242.
Selleck, Thadeus, 217.
Sewake, John, 56.
Seward (Seaward, Sewart, Suord).
Seward, Asher, 12.
Seward, Henry, 223.
Seward, John, 49, 56.
Seward, Moses, 48.
Seward, Nathan, 48.
Seward, Samuel, 194, 241.
Seward, Solomon, 225.

Seward, Timothy, 162.
Sexton (Saxtone), Asahel, 39.
Sexton, Daniel, 173, 175.
Sexton, Daniel, Jr., 215.
Sexton, Ebenezer, 55.
Sexton, Semieon, 195.
Seymour (Saymore, Seamore, Seymar).
Seymour, Allyn, 230.
Seymour, Charles, 230.
Seymour, David, 34, 36.
Seymour, Eliakim, 35, 36.
Seymour, John, 239.
Seymour, Jonathan, 108.
Seymour, Matthew, 251.
Seymour, Moses, 265.
Seymour, Richard, 223, 265.
Seymour, Stephen, 56.
Seymour, Theodore, 210.
Seymour, Timothy, 128.
Seymour, Uriah, 246.
Seymour, William, 11, 109, 110, 246.
Shaddock, Joseph, 69.
Shanket, Sampson, 113.
Shapley, Thomas, 243.
Shapley, William, 17.
Sharon, 24, 206, 217, 218, 247.
Sharp, Eli, 33, 177, 178.
Sharp, Elijah, 207.
Sharp, Uriah, 29.
Sharper (Sharpor, Sharpes).
Sharper, Charles, 72, 74, 108.
Shattuct, Timothy, 229.
Shaw, Benjamin, 112, 113.
Shaw, Caleb, 72.
Shaw, Cors, 6.
Shaw, Ebenez, 53.
Shaw, John, 51, 52, 72, 74, 75, 145, 152, 181, 203.
Shaw, Nathaniel, 201.
Shawcott, Sampson, 84, 112, 182.
Shayler, Ephraim, 187.
Shayler, Rubn, 227.
Sheentup, Jeremiah, 101.
Sheffield, 85, 215.
Sheldon (Shelding), Caleb, 229.
Sheldon, Daniel, 95.
Sheldon, James, 241.
Sheldon, Jonathan, 245.
Sheldon, Seth, 211.
Shelley, Shuball, 212.
Shelley, Timothy, 155, 177, 178.
Shelen, Andrew, 39.
Shenteys, Jeremiah, 17.
Shepard (Sheapard, Shepeard, Sheperd, Sheppard).
Shepard, Amos, 174.

Shepard, Daniel, 213.
S[ ]pard, David, 100, 101.
Shepard, Jered, 212.
Shepard, Jonathan, 195.
Shepard, Simeon, 238.
Shepard, Stephen, 231.
Shepard, Thomas, 81, 82, 116.
Shepard, Uriah, 239.
Shephard (Shepord).
Shephard, Benjamon, 240, 244.
Shephard, Jonas, 240, 244.
Shephard, Thomas, 115.
Shepherd, Amos, 175.
Shepherd, James, 49.
Shepherd, John, 157.
Shepherd, Jonathan, 8, 195.
Sheperson, John, 203.
Sherman (Sharman, Sharmon, Shearman, Sheermon, Shirman).
Sherman, Adonijah, 231.
Sherman, Amos, 252.
Sherman, Benjamin, 100, 101.
Sherman, Daniel, 204.
Sherman, James, 18, 20, 183, 253.
Sherman, Jeans, 133.
Sherman, Jotham, 238.
Sherman, Phinehas, 200.
Sherman, Tom, 75, 156, 179.
Sherman, Thomas, 72, 74, 75, 155.
Sherman, William, 208.
Sherrin, Joshua, 137.
Sherwin, John, 250, 255.
Sherwood (Sherod), Abell, 139.
Sherwood, Eleazer, 221.
Sherwood, Gideon, 200.
Sherwood, Isa, 177.
Sherwood, Isaac, 12, 179, 238.
Sherwood, Jabez, 177, 179.
Sherwood, John, 179.
Sherwood, Samuel, 180.
Sherwood, Thomas, 159, 179.
Shew, Richard, 239.
Shield (Schield, Shiels).
Shield, Daniel, 9.
Shield, John, 5, 122, 124.
Shilling (Shiling).
Shilling, Samuel, 23, 134, 136, 187.
Shipman, Benjamin, 47, 80, 87.
Shipman, Daniel, 82, 86, 137, 189.
Shipman, Edward, 202.
Shipman, Edmund, 196.
Shipman, John, 212.
Shirley, William, 88, 91.
Shirtliff (Shertleef), John, 94.
Shore, John, 53.
Shuntup (Shontup).
Shuntup, Henry, 40, 112, 113.

INDEX.

Shuntup, Jeremiah, 100.
Sibely, Ezare, 133.
Sibly, Benjamin, Jr., 43.
Silby, David, 200.
Sickels, Eliakim, 180.
Silkrig (Silkreg, Silhrig, Silkrag).
Silkrig, John, 70, 71, 223.
Silkrig, Nathaniel, 172, 262.
Silkrig, Thomas, 70.
Sill, David, 61.
Sill, Fithen, 226.
Sillsberry, Jonathan, 61.
Silsbe (Silsby).
Silsbe, Jonathan, 138, 139.
Simmons, Francis, 72.
Simons, Aron, 7.
Simons, Asahel, 174.
Simons, Benjam, 246.
Simons, David, 47, 87.
Simons, Eli, 135.
Simons, Elijah, 15, 96, 98, 183.
Simons, James, 118, 122, 187, 211.
Simons, John, 206.
Simons, Jonathan, 190.
Simons, Joseph, 46, 87, 196.
Simons, Nathan, 33.
Simons, Philip, 6, 94, 95, 96.
Simons, Silas, 211.
Simons, Theodore, 18, 20.
Sims (Simes), James, 46, 87, 255.
Sims, John, 240, 244.
Simsbury, 62, 102, 104, 108, 173, 207, 245, 246.
Sina, Joseph, 182.
Sip, Peter, 66.
Sirus, Daniel, 72, 75.
Siscatt (Siscult).
Siscatt, Obediah, 56, 109, 110.
Sizer, Daniel, 116.
Sizer, Lemuel, 234.
Skate (Scate), Richard, 53, 182.
Skesucks, John, 10, 108.
Skiff, Joseph, 249, 254.
Skilijen, 244.
Skinner (Skiner).
Skinner, Daniel, 140, 250.
Skinner, Ebenezer, 82, 189.
Skinner, Elias, 230.
Skinner, Elijah, 25, 247.
Skinner, John, 240.
Skinner, Jonathan, 174.
Skinner, Oliver, 230.
Skinner, Samuel, 141, 228, 243.
Skinner, Thomas, 189, 257.
Slapp, John, 69, 71, 132, 133, 160, 183, 185.
Slason, Peter, 180.

Slason, Silvanus, 180.
Slason, see Slawson, Slosson.
Slate, Joseph, 23, 128, 129.
Slater, Benjamin, 85.
Slater, John, 207.
Slaughter (Slawter).
Slaughter, George, 6, 94, 95, 96.
Slaughter, John, 62, 102, 104, 207.
Slawson (Slauson), David, 251.
Slawson, Elisha, 58.
Slawson, Ebenezer, 150, 151.
Slawson, Isac, 150.
Slawson, Israel, 152.
Slawson, John, 57, 218.
Slawson, Silvanus, 150, 151.
Slawson, see Slason, Slosson.
Sloan, Alexander, 11, 109.
Sloan, David, 251.
Sloan, Ebenezer, 110.
Sloan, Robert, 230.
Sloem, Alexander, 180.
Slooper, Ambrose, 54, 222.
Slosson (Sloson, Slossen).
Slosson, Ebenezer, 56.
Slosson, Elijah, 124.
Slosson, Esrael, 56.
Slosson, John, 56.
Slosson, Salvanis, 262.
Slosson, see Slason, Slawson.
Slossman, Israel, 151.
Sluicer, David, 110.
Smaley, Elijah, 206, 207.
Smalley, James, 161.
Smedley, Ephraim, 199.
Smedley, James, 221.
Smedley, Jedidiah, 194.
Smedley, John, 177, 178.
Smedley, Nehemiah, 14.
Smith (Smioth), 61.
Smith, Aaron, 195.
Smith, Abijah, 236.
Smith, Abraham, 58.
Smith, Amos, 238.
Smith, Asahel, 239.
Smith, Austin, 56.
Smith, Benjamin, 23, 153, 154, 210, 234.
Smith, Besa, 20.
Smith, Cain, 6.
Smith, Cephas, 229.
Smith, Charls, 219.
Smith, Chiliab, 224.
Smith, Daniel, 110, 160, 227, 240, 245.
Smith, David, 49, 162, 205, 216, 220, 221.
Smith, Ebenezer, 17, 135, 139, 203, 245, 251.

Smith, Edward, 204.
Smith, Eebr, 251.
Smith, Eldad, 239.
Smith, Eleazer, 7, 128, 129, 201.
Smith, Elihu, 219.
Smith, Elijah, 25, 42, 77, 109, 205, 255.
Smith, Eli, 49.
Smith, Elnathan, 118.
Smith, George, 45, 122.
Smith, Gershom, 23, 153, 154.
Smith, Gideon, 216.
Smith, Henry, 149, 160.
Smith, Hezekiah, 36, 198, 201.
Smith, Isaac, 23, 57, 94, 148, 149, 229.
Smith, Israel, 66, 67, 150, 151, 172, 230.
Smith, Jacob, 240.
Smith, Jacob, Jr., 224.
Smith, James, 52, 225, 241.
Smith, James, Jr., 211.
Smith, Jedediah, 139.
Smith, Jeduthun, 210.
Smith, Jehiel, 220.
Smith, Jethro, 40, 78.
Smith, Joel, 28, 146, 211.
Smith, John, 49, 60, 70, 83, 107, 171, 194, 208, 227, 236, 239.
Smith, John, Jr., 241.
Smith, Jonah, 248, 254.
Smith, Jonathan, 20, 34, 215.
Smith, Jorden, 60.
Smith, Joseph, 62, 102, 104, 201, 214.
Smith, Joshua, 205, 216, 236, 259.
Smith, Josiah, 6, 46, 180, 183, 224.
Smith, Jurden, 225.
Smith, Justus, 230.
Smith, Lamberton, 220.
Smith, Lieut., 84.
Smith, Matthew, 55, 239.
Smith, Matthias, 25, 87, 127, 128, 266.
Smith, Menas, 210.
Smith, Moses, 150, 153, 180, 229.
Smith, Nathan, 241.
Smith, Nathaniel, 225.
Smith, Nehemiah, 10, 86.
Smith, Noah, 251.
Smith, Oliver, 220, 249, 254.
Smith, Phenias, 237.
Smith, Polycarpus, 81, 86, 147, 149.
Smith, Reuben, 230.
Smith, Richard, 139, 197, 219.
Smith, Samon, 23.

Smith, Samuel, 59, 66, 68, 69, 105, 106, 159, 211, 217, 220, 224, 228, 229.
Smith, Seth, 214, 229.
Smith, Shubel, 162.
Smith, Simeon, 197.
Smith, Stephen, 13, 146, 239, 247.
Smith, Whitman, 216.
Smith, William, 34, 135, 136, 174.
Snow, Arunah, 133, 161, 189.
Snow, Edmond, 227.
Snow, Joseph, 249, 254.
Snow, Moses, 198.
Snow, Robert, 6.
Snow, Salvanis, 133.
Snow, Zephaniah, 39, 174, 175, 176.
Sobuck, William, 41, 78.
Solwell, Elezar, 160.
Somers, 215.
Soper, David, 169, 170.
Soper, Joel, 38, 239.
Soper, John, 135, 239.
Southbury, 203.
Southington, 53, 222, 223.
Southmead, Daniel, 234.
Southwell, 6.
Southwell, Phinehas, 103, 104, 211.
Southworth, William, 19, 117, 160.
Sozer, Daniel, 114.
Spafford, Abraham, 254.
Spafford, Abram, 248.
Spafford, Asa, 249.
Spafford, Moses, 248.
Sparhawk, Simon, 70, 71.
Sparks, Jonathan, 12, 128, 129.
Sparks, Joseph, 123, 216.
Sparks, Moses, 17, 97, 98.
Sparks, Nathan, 130.
Sparrow (Sparrer).
Sparrow, James, 137, 203, 259.
Sparrow, Nathaniel, 203.
Sparrow, Richard, 42.
Spaulding (Spalden, Spalding, Spolding).
Spaulding, Abel, 53.
Spaulding, Andrew, 16, 101, 240.
Spaulding, Asa, 167.
Spaulding, David, 240, 244.
Spaulding, Dier, 52.
Spaulding, Edward, 36.
Spaulding, Jacob, 17, 228, 244.
Spaulding, Lenord, 29.
Spaulding, Moses, 228, 244.
Spaulding, Nathaniel, 37.
Spaulding, Phinas, 247.
Spaulding, Timoth, 206.

Speek, Daniel, 194, 262.
Spees, John, 157, 158, 177, 178.
Spelman, Samuel, 70, 115, 116.
Spencer, Alexander, 206.
Spencer, Daniel, Jr., 245.
Spencer, David, 65, 66, 153, 154.
Spencer, Eliakim, 72, 74, 149, 203.
Spencer, Elisha, 103.
Spencer, Elphalet, 95.
Spencer, Fredrick, 203.
Spencer, Jabez, 74, 75, 80.
Spencer, Jared, 259.
Spencer, Jedediah, 85.
Spencer, Joel, 239.
Spencer, John, 34, 103, 104, 231.
Spencer, Joseph, 174, 175, 205, 215, 255.
Spencer, Judah, 9.
Spencer, Mark, 212.
Spencer, Nathaniel, 97, 183.
Spencer, Obadiah, 216.
Spencer, Peleg, 121.
Spencer, Philep, 247.
Spencer, Ruben, 211.
Spencer, Stephen, 72, 74, 75, 203.
Spencer, Thomas, 44, 197, 211.
Spencer, Timothy, 12, 59, 212.
Spencer, Zaccheus, 43.
Sperry (Spary, Spery).
Sperry, Abraham, 246.
Sperry, Amos, 252.
Sperry, Ebenezer, 174, 175.
Sperry, Eden, 25, 172.
Sperry, Enos, 25, 77, 127, 128.
Sperry, Ezra, 30.
Sperry, Isaac, 252.
Sperry, Israel, 231.
Sperry, Joseph, 24, 126, 171.
Sperry, Joshua, 31.
Sperry, Nathaniel, 252.
Sperry, Reubin, 252.
Sperry, Samuel, 222.
Spiar, Zepheniah, 137.
Spicer, Abel, 197.
Spicer, Benjamin, 237.
Spiler, Samuel, 237.
Spining, Nathaniel, 12.
Spofford, Moses, 254.
Sprague, Elijah, 249.
Sprague, James, 115, 116.
Sprague, John, 208, 228, 244.
Spring, Nethaniel, 245.
Squer, David, 49.
Squibb, Christopher, 189.
Squier (Squair, Squiar, Squior).
Squier, Benjamin, 102.
Squier, Daniel, 18, 133, 184.
Squier, David, 223.
Squier, Gideon, 204.
Squier, Moses, 130.
Squier, Nathaniel, 180.
Squier, Philip, 45.
Squier, Reubin, 147.
Squier, Samuel, 130.
Squier, Solomon, 29, 146, 219.
Squier, Timothy, 18, 20.
Squire, Andrew, 33.
Squire, Charles, 70, 71, 194.
Squire, Daniel, 14, 20, 37, 97, 98, 216.
Squire, David, 204.
Squire, Ezra, 58.
Squire, Ichabod, 206.
Squire, Israel, 120, 121, 193.
Squire, John, 14, 153.
Squire, Joseph, 221.
Squire, Samuel, 25, 210, 219, 227.
Squire, Stephen, 219, 242.
Squire, Thadeus, 201.
Squire, Timothy, 98, 99.
Squuntup, Joseph, 101.
Stadder, Brian, 224.
Stafford, 199.
Stamford, 27, 55, 150, 158, 179, 241, 242, 267.
Stanclift (Standliff, Stantleff).
Stanclift, Josiah, 8, 134, 136, 216.
Standish, Israel, 115, 116, 198.
Stanly (Standley, Stanlay).
Stanly, Abraham, 235.
Stanly, Gad, 230.
Stanly, John, 12.
Stanly, Jonathan, Jr., 230.
Stanly, Josiah, 65, 66, 68, 105, 106.
Stanly, Nathanell, 247.
Stanly, Thomas, 225.
Stanly, Timothy, 223, 224.
Stanly, William, 230.
Stannard (Stanard), John, 5, 63.
Stannard, Joseph, 83.
Stannard, Samuel, 44, 225.
Stanton, Danel, 232.
Stanton, John, 197, 214.
Stanton, Phineas, 91, 143.
Stanton, Rabard, 86.
Stanton, Samuel, 69, 71, 143.
Stanton, Theophilus, 107.
Stanton, William, 7, 91, 117, 118.
Stanwich, 216, 217.
Staples, John, 201.
Stark, Aaron, 197.
Stark, Benjamin, 184.
Stark, Ebenezer, 197.
Stark, Ichabod, 25, 193.
Stark, Zephaniah, 189.
Starkweather, Benajah, 23, 24.

Starkweather, Stephen, 232.
Starkweather, Woodbury, 70, 71.
Starr (Star), Daniel, 238.
Starr, David, 115, 116, 234.
Starr, George, 115.
Starr, Jehosaphat, 22, 109, 114, 115, 116.
Starr, Jonathan, 238.
Starr, Joseph, 238.
Starr, Josiah, 55, 237, 267.
Starr, Josiah, Jr., 55.
Starr, William, 212.
Start, James, 257.
Start, Stephen, 86, 256.
Start, Timothy, 86.
Statter, Abraham, 208.
Stearns (Starns), John, 6.
Stearns, John, Jr., 215.
Stebbins, Jabez, 52.
Stebbins, Joseph, 109, 242.
Stebbins, Josiah, 61, 179.
Stedman, James, 248, 254.
Stedman, John, 192.
Stedman, Thomas, 189.
Stedman, Timothy, 187.
Steel, Ebenezer, 70.
Steel, Elisha, 50, 239.
Steel, Ezekiel, 224.
Steel, George, 84, 170.
Steel, James, 210.
Steel, John, 239.
Steel, Jonathan, 229.
Steel, Solomon, 224.
Stell, Eliphaz, 173.
Stell, Zacheus, 75.
Stepeson, Silas, 211.
Stephens, Aaron, 116.
Stephens, Abraham, 157, 158.
Stephens, Asa, 96.
Stephens, Christopher, 262.
Stephens, Cypern, 208.
Stephens, Eliakim, 12.
Stephens, John, 208.
Stephens, Nathan, 176.
Stephens, Nehemiah, 240.
Stephens, Noah, 29.
Stephens, Osborn, 45.
Stephens, Peter, 240.
Stephens, Timothy, 51.
Stephens, Uriah, 243.
Stephens, William, 99, 208.
Stephens, see Stevens.
Sterling, Isaac, 176, 178.
Sterling, Selvenus, 221.
Stetson, Eli, 253.
Stevens (Steevens), 18, 163.
Stevens, Aaron, 8, 70, 71, 114, 116, 118, 119, 202.
Stevens, Abraham, 8, 118, 119, 158, 238.
Stevens, Andrew, 209.
Stevens, Asa, 17, 98.
Stevens, Benjamin, 13, 208.
Stevens, Christopher, 144, 195.
Stevens, Ebenezer, 209, 247.
Stevens, Eliakim, 227.
Stevens, Elias, 15.
Stevens, Eliphalet, 227.
Stevens, Ezra, 156.
Stevens, George, 189.
Stevens, Hezekiah, 226.
Stevens, James, 118, 195.
Stevens, Jeremiah, 7.
Stevens, Jesse, 32, 209.
Stevens, John, 57, 156, 158, 210, 227, 243.
Stevens, Joseph, 20, 78, 226, 251.
Stevens, Nathan, 178.
Stevens, Nathaniel, 202.
Stevens, Orsbon, 202.
Stevens, Phenius, 202.
Stevens, Reuben, 244.
Stevens, Robert, 70, 71.
Stevens, Roger, 202.
Stevens, Ruben, 227, 228.
Stevens, Silvanus, 33.
Stevens, Thomas, 8, 110, 118, 119.
Stevens, Timothy, 118, 119.
Stevens, Uriah, 227, 243.
Stevens, Uriah, Jr., 228, 244.
Stevens, William, 135, 172, 173, 174, 175.
Stevens, see Stephens.
Stevenson, Robert, 70, 71, 128, 129.
Steward, Alexander, 259.
Steward, Daniel, 180.
Steward, James, 150.
Steward, James, Jr., 162.
Steward, Luke, 218.
Steward, see Stuard.
Stewart, Alexander, 203.
Stewart, Charles, 241.
Stewart, James, 206, 251.
Stewart, Lemuel, 10, 191.
Stewart, Samuel, 191.
Stewart, Timothy, 205.
Stiles (Stils), Benony, 211.
Stiles, David, 219.
Stiles, Isaac, 231.
Stiles, Job, 205, 258.
Stiles, John, 35.
Stiles, Noah, 211.
Still, Ezekiel, 44.
Still, Zach, 227.
Still, Zacheus, 74.
Stillman, Elisha, 229.

INDEX. 341

Stillman, Joseph, 229.
Stillwell, Benjamin, 54.
Stilson, Thomas, 238.
Stinson (Stemson, Stimpson).
Stinson, John, 11, 115, 116, 145, 183.
Stocking, Amos, 213.
Stocking, Elijah, 81, 82.
Stocking, George, 264.
Stocking, Jonathan, 229.
Stocking, Marshel, 213.
Stockwell, Samuel, 214.
Stockwell, Simeon, 141, 226.
Stoddard (Stodard, Stodder, Stoddord, Stoder).
Stoddard, Aaron, 223.
Stoddard, Abijah, 219.
Stoddard, Anthony, 219.
Stoddard, Aviram, 66, 68.
Stoddard, Benjamin, 23, 198.
Stoddard, Cleomant, 137.
Stoddard, David, 24, 99, 100.
Stoddard, Ebenezer, 197.
Stoddard, Elisha, 169, 204, 210.
Stoddard, Gideon, 203, 204.
Stoddard, John, 199, 204.
Stoddard, Jonathan, 210.
Stoddard, Joseph, 25.
Stoddard, Josiah, 247.
Stoddard, Mortimore, 197.
Stoddard, Moses, 158.
Stoddard, Samuel, 78, 83, 84, 191.
Stoddard, see Stadder.
Stone, Abraham, 51.
Stone, Ashnar, 212.
Stone, Beriah, 223.
Stone, Charles, 50.
Stone, Daniel, 144.
Stone, Isaac, 37, 101, 242.
Stone, John, 56, 180.
Stone, John, Jr., 37.
Stone, Joseph, 212.
Stone, Noah, 199.
Stone, Peleg, 204.
Stonington, 9, 69, 91, 107, 109, 143, 189, 214.
Storer, Francis, 117.
Storer, Joseph, 12.
Storrs, 254.
Storrs, Huckens, Jr., 99.
Storrs, Joseph, 93, 98, 99, 159, 160, 267.
Story, Daniel, 237.
Story, Francis, 53, 161.
Story, Joseph, 232.
Story, Solomon, 197.
Story, Thomas, 197.
Stote, Joseph, 213.

Stoten, John, 222.
Stoughton, 93.
Stoughton, John, 95, 167, 168.
Stoughton, Oliver, 207.
Stoughton, Samuel, 215.
Stow, George, 234.
Stow, Giles, 42, 78, 187.
Stow, Jonathan, 229.
Stow, Josiah, 54, 193.
Stow, Nathaniel, 244.
Stow, Samuel, 233, 234.
Stow, Simeon, 15, 120, 121, 187.
Stowell (Stoel), Isaac, 198.
Stowell, Nathaniel, 207.
Strange, James, 40, 117.
Stratfield, 156, 218, 221.
Stratford, 3, 28, 32, 34, 36, 76, 91, 102, 129, 138, 158, 167, 200, 218, 221.
Stratton, Cornelius, 201.
Stratton, David, 155, 178, 179.
Stratton, Enoch, 23, 130, 131.
Stratton, Isaac, 187.
Stratton, Serajah, Jr., 211.
Street, Elnathan, 66.
Streeter, John, 12, 96, 98.
Strickland (Strickling).
Strickland, John, 30, 121, 215.
Strickland, Samuel, 228, 244.
Strong, Aaron, 132.
Strong, Aaron, Jr., 216.
Strong, Amos, 189.
Strong, Asa, 35, 162, 198.
Strong, Asahel, 256.
Strong, Benajah, 160, 250.
Strong, Benjamin, 115.
Strong, Charls, 219.
Strong, David, 250.
Strong, Elijah, 206, 216, 250, 257.
Strong, Ezekiel, 23, 136, 160.
Strong, Jaben, 258.
Strong, Jabue, 148.
Strong, Job, 215.
Strong, Joel, 224.
Strong, John, 38, 134, 135, 228, 243.
Strong, Josiah, 218.
Strong, Josiah, Jr., 218.
Strong, Levi, 174.
Strong, Noah, 209.
Strong, Ozias, 35.
Strong, Return, 204.
Strong, Ruben, 137.
Strong, Selah, 204.
Strong, Simeon, 25, 239, 247.
Strong, Timothy, 230.
Strong, William, 245.
Stuard, Daniel, 226.

Stuard, Timothy, 257.
Stuard, see Steward.
Stuart, James, 58.
Sturdevant, James, 57.
Sturdevant, Peleg, 218.
Sturgis (Stirges), Daniel, 201.
Sturgis, Joseph, 176, 178, 221.
Sturgis, Seth, 221.
Sturgis, Thomas, 102, 178, 179.
Stutson, Eli, 248.
Suckenup, Caleb, 110.
Suckhegun, 8, 153, 154, 172, 261.
Suffield, 3, 5, 62, 77, 91, 93, 102, 167, 245.
Sullivan, Thomas, 105, 106.
Summers, Abel, 172.
Summers, Benjamin, 29, 218.
Summers, Ebenezer, 157.
Summers, Francis, 74, 75, 145, 191.
Summers, Gershom, 238.
Summers, Henry, 59.
Summers, Hezekiah, 81.
Summers, Robert, 29, 124, 176, 178, 260.
Sumner, Beng, 258.
Sumner, Ebenezer, 42, 147, 148, 149.
Sumner, Israel, 146, 219.
Sumner, John, 81, 114, 116, 185, 198, 207.
Sumner, Thomas, 98, 99, 148, 205.
Suncemon, Isaac, 153, 154.
Suncemon, John, 97.
Sundurling, Peleg, 79.
Sunkanay, John, 86.
Surdam, Tunas, 199.
Surthworth, Nathan, 212.
Sutlick, Samuel, 44.
Sutliff, John, 50, 222.
Swaddle, John, 40, 41, 117, 197.
Swain, Isaac, 199.
Swain, Jonathan, 206.
Swan, Joshua, 214.
Swan, Nathaniel, 214.
Swan, William, 214.
Sweat, Stephen, 51.
Sweet, Griffen, 230.
Sweet, Jediah, 139.
Sweet, Joseph, 137.
Sweete, Thomas, 70, 71.
Sweetland (Sweatland, Swetland).
Sweetland, Azariah, 255.
Sweetland, Benjamin, 250.
Sweetland, Caleb, 58.
Sweetland, Ebenezer, 45.
Sweetland, Elijah, 189.
Sweetland, Jonathan, 46, 87.

Sweetland, Luke, 206.
Sweetland, William, 255.
[   ]swell, Dan[   ], 199.
Swelling, Caleb, 124.
Swift, Heman, 58, 206, 213.
Swift, Perez, 250.
Swift, William, 214.
Symes, James, 250.
Symonds, Stephen, 214.

Tacker, John, 72, 74, 75.
Talcott (Talcet, Tallcott).
Talcott, Benjamin, 248.
Talcott, Caleb, 123.
Talcott, Elizur, 228.
Talcott, John, 205, 257.
Talcott, Nathaniel, 228.
Talcott, Samuel, 210.
Talington, James, 160.
Talmage, Joseph, 225.
Talmage, Timothy, 24, 126.
Taney, Thomas, 110.
Tannar, John, 141.
Tanner, Amos, 112, 113, 181.
Tanner, Ebenezer, 84, 112, 113.
Tanner, Nezer, 181.
Tanterpan, William, 27.
Tartar, 263.
Tatman, Stephen, 237.
Tatson, Rubin, 182.
Tatson, Samuel, 106.
Tattington, James, 123.
Tattington, Levis, 149.
Tattington, Lewis, 86.
Tatton, Isaac, 138, 203, 259.
Tauquin, Philip, 109.
Taylor (Tailor, Talor).
Taylor, Abner, 238.
Taylor, Abram, 29.
Taylor, Asahel, 203, 259.
Taylor, Barak, 110, 180.
Taylor, Christian, 170.
Taylor, David, 35, 174, 175.
Taylor, Elijah, 83, 86.
Taylor, Epharam, 257.
Taylor, Forts, 229.
Taylor, Gemaliel, 251.
Taylor, Jacob, 103.
Taylor, John, 179.
Taylor, Joseph, 149, 205.
Taylor, Joseph, Jr., 149, 256.
Taylor, Josiah, 19, 250.
Taylor, Justus, 81, 213.
Taylor, Levi, 56.
Taylor, Moses, 29, 38.
Taylor, Nathaniel, 149, 203, 259.
Taylor, Phinehas, 180, 244.
Taylor, Preserved, 61, 102.

INDEX. 343

Taylor, Reuben, 179.
Taylor, Seth, 251.
Taylor, Stephen, 10, 86, 130, 210.
Taylor, Thadeus, 251.
Taylor, Timothy, 45, 210.
Taylor, Zebulon, 223.
Teall, Samuel, 72, 74, 75.
Tecomwass (Tawdecommewas, Tecommowas, Tocomwas).
Tecomwas, Abraham, 40, 112, 113.
Tecomwas, Isaac, 84, 112, 113, 182.
Tecomwass, Peter, 23, 182.
Teequips, Joseph, 113.
Teese, John, 153.
Tem, Peter, 54.
Tennant, John, 203, 258.
Tenney, Elijah, 236.
Terrill (Terrel), Amos, 237.
Terrell, Israel, 193.
Terrill, Isaac, 120.
Terrill, James, 226.
Terrill, Josiah, 71.
Terrill, Oliver, 121.
Terrill, Timothy, 204.
Terrill, see Turrell.
Terris, Pack, 152.
Terry, Jacob, Jr., 94.
Terry, John, 17, 19, 20, 21, 87.
Terry, Jonathan, 245, 246.
Tew, William, 141.
Thanks, Edward, 152.
Thorp (Tharp), Aaron, 250, 257.
Thorp, Amos, 25.
Thorp, Daniel, 61, 65, 67, 68, 105, 106, 172, 180, 262.
Thorp, David, 30.
Thorp, Edward, 61, 151, 241.
Thorp, Eliphalet, 25.
Thorp, Elnathan, 55, 235.
Thorp, Jonathan, 31.
Thorp, Josiah, 153.
Thorp, Moses, 231.
Thorp, Oliphr, 97.
Thorp, Oliver, 160.
Thorp, Stephen, 177, 178.
Thorp, Timothy, 25, 136, 160.
Thorp, William, 102, 177, 178.
Thatcher, Jared, 189.
Thatcher, Joseph, 116.
Thayer, Seth, 121.
Thayer, William, 215.
Thayer, Zephaniah, 46, 123.
Theley, William, 161.
Thomas (Thoms), Austin, 113.
Thomas, Daniel, 51.
Thomas, David, 45, 118, 119.
Thomas, Elijah, 9, 86, 129, 136, 205.
Thomas, Isaac, 227.
Thomas, James, 127, 172.
Thomas, John, 46, 66, 67, 68, 104, 106, 120.
Thomas, Love, 54.
Thomas, Richard, 70.
Thomas, Robert, 244.
Thomas, Ruben, 219.
Thomas, Samuel, 25.
Thomas, Solomon, 104.
Thomas, Stephen, 30, 77, 127, 128, 172, 262.
Thomirlin, Abijah, 219.
Thompson, Abraham, 231, 253.
Thompson, Ahiel, 51.
Thompson, Alex, 146.
Thompson, David, 127.
Thompson, Eliphalet, 127, 231.
Thompson, Elijah, 218.
Thompson, Elisha, 224.
Thompson, Isaac, Jr., 233.
Thompson, Jabez, 59, 171.
Thompson, James, 231, 253.
Thompson, Jered, 198.
Thompson, Joel, 118.
Thompson, John, 16, 198, 224, 253.
Thompson, Joiel, 195.
Thompson, Robert, 250.
Thompson, Samuel, 231, 233.
Thompson, Stephen, 57.
Thompson, William, 39.
Thomson, Benoni, 230.
Thomson, Eliphalet, 25.
Thomson, Hezkiar, 218.
Thomson, Hugh, 211.
Thomson, John, 30.
Thomson, Joseph, 144.
Thomson, Nathaniel, 40.
Thomson, Thomas, 40.
Thomson, William, 168, 170.
Thomson, see Tompson.
Thonson, Stephen, 247.
Thorington, Samuel, 190.
Thorn, William, 232.
Thorncraft, Jacob, 13.
Thornton, Samuel, 83, 107, 190.
Thrall (Trall), John, 35.
Thrall, Moses, 215.
Thrall, Moses, Jr., 215.
Thrall, Samuel, 6, 211.
Thrall, William, 6, 103, 104.
Throop, Benjamin, 3.
Throop, Dan, 162.
Throop, John, 36.
Throop, Josiah, 19.
Throop, Mercy, 70.
Thurston, Daniel, 206.
Tibbals, Nathan, 206, 207.

Tickner, Isaac, 199.
Tickner, William, Jr., 206.
Tidd, Benjamine, 70.
Tietson, Samuel, 69.
Tiff, John, 29, 146.
Tiff, Joseph, 245.
Tiff, see Tift.
Tiffany (Tefany), Ephraim, 43.
Tiffany, John, 250.
Tiffany, Nathaniel, Jr., 216.
Tiffany, Silas, 137, 138.
Tifft, John, 232.
Tift, Joseph, 214.
Tift, see Tiff.
Tiller, Obidiah, 144.
Tilley, Abraham, 222.
Tilley, Josiah, 35.
Tillotson (Tilison, Tillerson, Tilletson, Tillison, Tillson, Tylletson).
Tillotson, Daniel, 205.
Tillotson, Ebenezer, 39.
Tillotson, Elisha, 12, 131, 169.
Tillotson, Jacob, 41.
Tillotson, Jonathan, 205, 258.
Tillotson, Joseph, 127.
Tillotson, William, 41.
Timus, John, 185.
Tinker, Benjamin, 149.
Tinker, Ellis, 189.
Tinney, Richard, 196.
Tirsby, Edward, 219.
Titerson, Elisha, 130.
Titus, Enos, 33.
Titus, John, 30, 77.
Titus, Onesimas, 194.
Titus, Orrisimus, 124.
Toba, Jesse, 247.
Toby, Elisha, 250.
Toby, Joseph, 72, 75.
Toby, Joshua, 192.
Todd (Tod, Tode, Toodd).
Todd, Abner, 231.
Todd, Abraham, Jr., 217.
Todd, Benjamin, 30.
Todd, Gershom, 231.
Todd, Isaac, 25, 127, 231.
Todd, Ithermer, 231.
Todd, Jonah, 26, 58.
Todd, Oliver, 252.
Todd, Samuel, 72, 74, 75, 108.
Todd, Stephen, 60.
Toles, Henry, 252.
Toles, Jeremiah, 252.
Toles, Nehemiah, 252.
Toley, Joseph, 74.
Tolland, 215.
Tollees, Gershom, 195.

Tolles, Samuell, 105.
Tom, John, 65, 68.
Tom, William, 66, 68, 69.
Tomblin, Elish, 139.
Tombling, Stephen, 226.
Tomes, Robert, 141.
Tomlin, Elisha, 139, 159.
Tomlinson, Abraham, 200.
Tomlinson, Eli, 220.
Tomlinson, Gideon, 154, 156.
Tompson (Tomson), Joel, 119.
Tompson, John, 132, 180, 257.
Tompson, see Thompson, Thomson).
Tomrus, Robert, 228.
Toney, George, 192.
Toney, John, 192.
Toney, Lemuel, 145, 191.
Toney, Reuben, 72, 214.
Tonge, James, 242.
Toocker, John, 118, 262.
Tooley (Toolly, Tooly, Tuley).
Tooley, Christopher, 72, 74, 75, 195.
Tooley, James, 233.
Tooley, John, 210.
Tooley, Joseph, 195.
Tooley, Samuel, 72, 74, 75, 118, 119, 195, 262.
Toroomp, John, 72.
Torrence, Robert, 33, 146.
Torrey (Torey, Torry, Tory).
Torrey, Calvin, 243.
Torrey, James, 184, 185.
Torrey, Micajah, 46, 47, 79.
Torrey, Timothy, 198, 199.
Torrey, William, 250.
Torrill, Josiah, Jr., 70.
Torrington, 222, 246.
Torrowara (Torroway), 18.
Torrowara, Richard, 15, 19, 154.
Tossitt, Thomas, 131.
Totson, Samuel, 66.
Toucy, Chareuel, 74.
Toucy, Robben, 74.
Touey, Lemuel, 72.
Tousey (Touse, Towsey).
Tousey, David, 15, 131, 132, 169.
Tousey, Hatcet, 15.
Tousey, John Hatchet, 172.
Tousey, Thomas, 238.
Tousey, see Hatchet.
Tousley (Towsley).
Tousley, Matthew, 228, 243.
Tousley, Samuel, 247.
Town, Joseph, 242.
Towner, Abra, 226.
Towner, Abraham, 156.

INDEX. 345

Towner, Abram, 60.
Towner, Benjamin, 59, 119.
Towner, Samuel, 65.
Towump, John, 74.
Tozer, John, 255.
Tracy, Eleazer, 52, 142, 180, 181.
Tracy, Ezra, 84, 232.
Tracy, Hezekiah, 236.
Tracy, James, 15, 96, 98.
Tracy, Moses, 237.
Tracy, Prince, 17, 19.
Tracy, Samuel, 70, 107, 236.
Tracy, Simon, 232.
Tracy, Thomas, 206.
Trapue, Daniel, 63.
Treadnay, Amos, 19, 250.
Treadway, Asa, 162.
Treadwell, Ephraim, 155.
Treadwell, see Tredwell.
Treat (Treet), Isaac, 59.
Treat, John, 187.
Treat, Jonathan, 130.
Treat, Stephen, 229.
Treat, Timothy, 218.
Tredwell (Treedwell).
Tredwell, Epram, 221.
Tredwell, Jacob, 155.
Tredwell, John, 154, 156.
Tredwell, Timothy, 221.
Tredwell, see Treadwell.
Trescott (Triscott), John, 184.
Trescott, Savage, 128.
Tribble (Trebble, Treble).
Tribble, John, 41, 78, 122, 123.
Trickey, Thomas, 127, 172.
Trim, Benjamin, 172.
Tromp, John, 75.
Trowbridge (Trobridge).
Trowbridge, John, 55, 138, 139, 237.
Trowbridge, Ralph, 226.
Trowbridge, Seth, 226.
Trowbridge, Stephen, 238.
Truesdell (Trusdell).
Truesdell, Ebenezer, 60.
Truesdell, John, 18, 20, 101, 208, 252.
Truesdell, Joseph, 16, 97, 98.
Truesdell, Samuel, 139, 144, 159, 177, 178.
Truesdell, William, 201.
Trumble (Tromble).
Trumble, Ammi, 207, 211, 265.
Trumble, J., 20.
Trumble, Jonathan, 19, 20, 87, 88, 161, 162, 202, 203, 205, 249, 256, 257, 259.
Trumble, William, 247.

Tryon, Amos, 234.
Tryon, Asahel, 226.
Tryon, Edward, 44, 79, 202.
Tryon, George, 39, 123, 124.
Tryton, 62.
Tubbs (Tubs).
Tubbs, Benajah, 9, 86, 122, 123.
Tubbs, Benjamin, 8.
Tubbs, Ezekiel, 24, 77.
Tubbs, Lebbeus, 8, 9.
Tubbs, John Miller, 196.
Tubbs, Samuel, 237.
Tubbs, Zebulon, 112, 113, 250, 255.
Tucker, Abijah, 208.
Tucker, Benjamin, 149, 169, 208.
Tucker, Daniel, 252.
Tucker, Isaac, 3, 38, 39, 123, 124, 163.
Tucker, John, 127, 196.
Tucker, Joseph, 230.
Tucker, Stephen, 232, 243.
Tucker, Zephaniah, 110, 220.
Tuller, Jacob, 63, 106, 174, 175.
Tuller, James, 169.
Tulley, Ichabod, 33.
Tulley, see Tooley.
Tumbling, Elisha, 61.
Tumbling, Stephen, 61.
Tunell, Daniel, 154.
Tuper, Mahue, 24.
Turner, Abraham, 195.
Turner, Amos, 33.
Turner, David, 244.
Turner, Isaac, 7, 117, 118, 226.
Turner, James, 31, 231.
Turner, John, 46, 249, 254.
Turner, Joseph, 35.
Turner, Reuben, 8, 118, 119.
Turner, Samuel, 144.
Turner, Thomas, 187.
Turner, Timothy, 66, 68, 127.
Turnner, Joseph, 199.
Turrell, Benjamin, 54.
Turrell, Ephraim, 155, 30.
Turrell, Nathan, 155, 156.
Turrell, Oliver, 222.
Turrell, see Terrill.
Tusner, David, 228.
Tuthill, Ebenezer, 235.
Tutsson, Samuell, 106.
Tuttle (Tutel, Tutle, Tuttel, Tuttill).
Tuttle, Aaron, 172.
Tuttle, Ambrose, 27, 172.
Tuttle, Amos, 127.
Tuttle, Andrew, 172.
Tuttle, Caleb, 253.
Tuttle, Daniel, 25, 30, 126.

Tuttle, David, 251.
Tuttle, Ebenezer, 231.
Tuttle, Edward, 49.
Tuttle, Eliphalet, 14.
Tuttle, Enos, 251.
Tuttle, Ezekiel, 31, 172.
Tuttle, Gershom, 239.
Tuttle, Gideon, 29, 204.
Tuttle, Hezekiah, 25, 127, 171, 252.
Tuttle, Ichabod, 219.
Tuttle, Jabez, 55, 128.
Tuttle, James, 127.
Tuttle, John, 25.
Tuttle, Jonathan, 176, 189.
Tuttle, Joseph, 149, 205.
Tuttle, Nash, 219.
Tuttle, Nathan, 242.
Tuttle, Noah, 219.
Tuttle, Samuel, 231.
Tuttle, Stephen, 224, 241.
Tuttle, Thomas, 33, 141, 247.
Tuttle, Uri, 252.
Tutler, Jabez, 129.
Twing, Benjamin, 169.
Twiss, Joseph, 54.
Tyler (Tylor), Abram, 60.
Tyler, Abraham, 235.
Tyler, Amos, 218.
Tyler, Daniel, 49.
Tyler, Enos, 49.
Tyler, John, 9, 24, 142, 231, 232.
Tyler, Jonathan, 174, 175.
Tyler, Nathaniel, 70, 108.
Tyler, Phinias, 127, 240.
Tyler, Samuel, 235.
Tyler, Solomon, 11, 251.
Tyly, Thomas, 227.

Udal, Samuel, 233.
Ufford, John, 213.
Uncas (Uncos, Uncus, Unkus).
Uncas, Benjamin, 112, 113, 182.
Uncas, Pompey, 112, 113, 181.
Uncas, Samuel, 40, 113, 115, 182.
Underwood, Joseph, 240, 244.
Union, 199.
Upam, Luke, 242.
Upson, Daniel, 54.
Upson, Samuel, 54, 193.
Usher, Hezekiah, 162, 203, 259.
Utley, Daniel, 183.
Utley, David, 214.
Utley, James, 254.
Utley, Jeremiah, Jr., 18, 20, 191.
Utter, John, 139.

Vaghan, John, 161.

Vallance, John, 33.
Vanduser (Venduzer).
Vanduser, Hartman, 209.
Vanduser, Hendrik, 199.
Vansant, Christopher, 49.
Vansant, John, 213.
Vargison, John, 191.
Vauhn, John, 249.
Veal, Joseph, 199.
Vedito, John, 157.
Verdin, Peter, 179.
Viel, Benjamin Humphrey, 171.
Vine, Robert, 14.
Vineger, Garret, 206.
Vineing, John, 207.
Voluntown, 100, 176, 214, 241.
Vorce, Lemuel, 237.
Vorse, Henry, 189.

Wabber, Richard, 133, 248.
Wabber, see Webber.
Wackwett, Samuel, 181.
Waddams, John, 82, 147.
Waddams, Jonath, 224.
Wade, Jonathan, 112, 114, 127.
Wade, Stephen, 106.
Wadsworth, Hez, 239.
Wadsworth, John, 48.
Wadsworth, James, 239.
Wadsworth, Joseph, 250.
Wadsworth, Samuel, 189.
Wadsworth, William, 238, 239.
Waggs, Benjamin, 72, 75.
Wagner, Jacob, 146.
Wainright, William, 200.
Wait, Charles, 211.
Wait, Thomas, Jr., 44.
Wakefield, Simeon, 99.
Wakely (Wakelee, Waklee).
Wakely, Abell, 155.
Wakely, Deliverence, 221.
Wakely, Jacob, 200.
Wakely, Jonathan, 223.
Wakeman (Wakman).
Wakeman, Daniel, 178.
Wakeman, Ebenezer, 201, 221.
Wakeman, Squire, 177, 178.
Walbridge, Ebenezer, 112, 113.
Walbridge, Henry, 230.
Walbridge, Joseph, 236.
Walbridge, Thomas, 69, 112, 113, 181.
Walbridge, William, 108, 189.
Walden, Jonathan, 112, 113, 236, 254.
Walder, Ebenezer, 127.
Waldo, Cornelious, 244.
Waldo, John, 249.

Waldo, Jonathan, 20, 248.
Waldo, Zachariah, 245.
Waldor, Corneales, 240.
Waldor, Zecheriah, 240.
Waldow, Jena, 83.
Waldow, John, 255.
Walen, John, 104.
Walen, Samuel, 219.
Wales, Azariah, 132.
Waley, Jonathan, 156.
Walker, Benjamin, 46.
Walker, Eliakim, 200.
Walker, Elnathan, 242.
Walker, Gideon, 219.
Walker, Isaac, 83.
Walker, John, 219.
Walker, Josiah, 176, 178.
Walker, Nathaniel, 37, 98, 99.
Walker, Obediah, 184.
Walker, Phineas, 209.
Walker, Timothy, 33, 204.
Walker, Zachariah, 33.
Walker, Zorakiah, 219.
Walkins, John, 224.
Walkley, Zebn, 199.
Walkley, Zebulon, 49.
Wallace, James, 175.
Wallace, Richard, 23.
Wallaps, Benjamin, 139.
Waller, Cele, 219.
Waller, Elijah, 226.
Waller, Matthew, 184.
Waller, Samuel, 66, 67, 68.
Wallers, Abraham, 222.
Wallice, James, 174.
Walling, John, 14.
Wallingford, 65, 87, 91, 124, 192, 194, 223, 234, 235.
Wallis, Jonathan, 37.
Wallis, Joshua, 226.
Wallis, Nathaniel, 29.
Wallis, Richard, 230.
Walls, David, 61.
Walls, Solomon, 198.
Wallyn, John, 103.
Walner, Ebenezer, 252.
Walston, Thomas, 68.
Walter, Nathan, 61.
Walter, Pierce, 77, 224.
Walters, Joseph, 259.
Walters, Parce, 33.
Walworth, James, 197.
Wampanegg, John, 182.
Wamponey, John, 112.
Wanepoom, John, 163.
Wanzer, Chesher, 226.
Ward, 119, 267.
Ward, Abel, 252.

Ward, Abijah, 16.
Ward, Ambros, 253.
Ward, Amos, 215.
Ward, Andrew, 11, 13, 145, 146, 194, 195, 196, 266.
Ward, Andrew, Jr., 48, 50, 51, 143, 150, 159, 160.
Ward, Belias, 11, 13.
Ward, Fenner, 81, 213.
Ward, Jehiel, 50, 51, 144, 145.
Ward, John, 13, 235.
Ward, Jonathan, 23, 115, 116, 174.
Ward, Joy, 202.
Ward, Luman, 195, 266.
Ward, Moses, 198, 244.
Ward, Phenner, 114, 116.
Ward, Phineas, 116.
Ward, Samuel, 155, 264.
Ward, Semio, 6.
Ward, Stephen, 234.
Ward, Thelus, 212.
Ward, William, 29, 234.
Wardel, James, 150.
Wardel, Uzel, 225.
Warden, Daniel, 106, 220.
Warden, Samuel, 13, 129.
Wardwel, James, 151.
Ware, Joseph, 23, 130, 131, 187.
Waring, James, 216.
Warner (Wonor, Wornor).
Warner, 266.
Warner, Abraham, 226.
Warner, Andrew, 187.
Warner, Benjamin, 204.
Warner, Charles, 120, 222.
Warner, Daniel, 202, 239.
Warner, Eben, 66.
Warner, Ebenezer, 67, 69, 147, 212.
Warner, Ebenezer, Jr., 146.
Warner, Eli, 203.
Warner, Elizur, 217.
Warner, Ely, 6.
Warner, Ephraim, 200.
Warner, Israel, 78, 123, 216.
Warner, James, 72, 74, 75, 131.
Warner, John, 162, 249, 255, 264.
Warner, Joseph, 127, 222, 253.
Warner, Lemuel, 57.
Warner, Mertin, 225.
Warner, Nathaniel, 6, 211, 218.
Warner, Samuel, 55, 169, 217.
Warner, Timothy, 3.
Warner, William, 247.
Warner, Zebulon, 230.
Warre, Sangore, 104.
Warren (Waren).
Warren, Daniel, 228, 243.
Warren, John, 35, 78, 110.

Warren, Robart, 11.
Warren, Stephen, 251.
Warren, William, Jr., 229.
Warrensburgh, N. Y., 3.
Washburn (Warshborn, Washbon).
Washburn, John, 187, 220.
Washburn, Jonathan, 74, 75.
Washburn, Joseph, 58, 204.
Washburn, Nathan, 110, 220.
Washburn, Solomon, 43.
Washburn, Thomas, 161.
Washburn, William, 198.
Waterbury (Warterbury, Waterberry).
Waterbury, David, 150, 151, 179.
Waterbury, David, 3d, 27, 150, 160, 179.
Waterbury, Ebenezer, 180.
Waterbury, Gideon, 157.
Waterbury, Josiah, 241.
Waterbury, Nathaniel, Jr., 242.
Waterbury, Peter, 150.
Waterbury, Samuel, 242.
Waterbury, Thomas, Jr., 241.
Waterbury, 27, 222, 223, 267.
Waterhouse, Nathaniel, 233.
Waterman, Bildad, 205, 255.
Waterman, Daniel, 249, 254.
Waterman, Darius, 19, 96, 98, 160.
Waterman, E., 77, 78.
Waterman, Elisha, 83, 267.
Waterman, Ezekiel, 52, 236.
Waterman, Ezra, 237.
Waterman, Jedediah, 83, 136, 190, 192.
Waterman, John, 236.
Waterman, Silas, 181.
Waterman, Thomas, 236.
Waterman, Zebulon, 123.
Waters (Warters, Worters).
Waters, Abraham, 54.
Waters, Benjamin, 229.
Waters, Deliverence, 203, 259.
Waters, Henry, 82, 86.
Waters, Jacob, 249, 255.
Waters, John, 79, 135, 170.
Waters, Joseph, 162, 230.
Waters, Nichols, 132.
Waters, Samuel, 149, 174, 175.
Waters, Stal Worthy, 205.
Waters, Thomas, 239.
Waters, Timothy, 82, 86, 149.
Waters, William, 82, 149.
Waters, William, Jr., 86.
Waters, see Wouters.
Watkins (Wadkins, Wodkins).
Watkins, Darius, 37, 242.

Watkins, John, 132.
Watkins, Nathan, 46, 198.
Watkins, Thadeah, 46.
Watrous (Waterous), John, 35.
Watrous, Joseph, 202, 205.
Watrous, Josiah, 50.
Watrous, Samuel, 50, 212.
Watrous, Walter, 52.
Watson, Cyprian, 175.
Watson, John, 18, 19, 97, 98, 160.
Watson, Thomas, 6, 65.
Watson, Zipron, 174.
Wattles, Joseph, 96.
Wattles, Mason, 9.
Watts, John, 118, 196.
Waugh, Elex, 199.
Waugh, Joseph, 141, 224.
Way, David, 23, 187.
Way, John, 233.
Way, Joseph, 49.
Way, Phylemon, 219.
Way, Thomas, 55.
Webb (Weeb), 253.
Webb, Abner, 174, 175.
Webb, Benjamin, 216.
Webb, David, 25.
Webb, David, Jr., 241.
Webb, Disborow, 155, 156, 176, 178, 260.
Webb, Gideon, 44, 79, 195, 262.
Webb, James, 8, 86, 123.
Webb, John, 262.
Webb, Jonathan, 150, 152, 153, 180.
Webb, Nathan, 24, 122.
Webb, Samuel, 60, 79, 196, 262.
Webb, Thomas, 72, 74, 75, 137, 203, 259.
Webben (Wobbon).
Webben, Benjamin, 208.
Webben, Hezekiah, 97.
Webber, Christopher, 248, 254.
Webber, Richard, 69, 71, 254.
Webber, see Wabber.
Webster, Abell, 137.
Webster, Abijah, 246.
Webster, Abram, 189.
Webster, Asel, 189.
Webster, Ashbil, 22.
Webster, Benjamin, 223.
Webster, Cyprian, 239.
Webster, Elijah, 250, 257.
Webster, George, 170.
Webster, Israel, 46.
Webster, John, 54.
Webster, Jonathan, 174, 175, 210.
Webster, Levi, 78, 82, 149, 189.
Webster, Matthew, 239.

INDEX. 349

Webster, Moses, 103.
Webster, Oliver, 189.
Webster, Samuel, 118.
Webster, Shadrack, 19.
Webster, Stephen, 199.
Webster, Zepheniah, 128, 174, 175.
Wedge (Weedge).
Wedge, Josiah, 137, 160.
Wedge, William, 100.
Weed, Andrew, 60.
Weed, Charles, 56, 251.
Weed, Daniel, 12.
Weed, Ebenezer, 55, 109, 110.
Weed, Epenets, Jr., 241.
Weed, Jacob, Jr., 242.
Weed, John, 77, 159.
Weed, Jonas, Jr., 241.
Weed, Jonathan, 150, 152.
Weed, Nathaniel, 55, 120, 193, 251, 260.
Weed, Ruben, Jr., 241.
Weed, Youngs, 150, 151, 180.
Weeks, Jethro, 52, 145.
Weeks, Jonathan, 11, 145, 181.
Weisle, Samuel, 84.
Welch, David, 223.
Welch, Ebenezer, 112, 236.
Welch, Fitch, 220.
Welch, James, 61.
Welch, John, 112.
Welch, Jonathan, 12.
Welch, Joseph, 181.
Welch, Joshua, 52, 84, 86.
Welch, Paul, 217.
Welch, Rufus, 237.
Welch, Solomon, 249, 254.
Welch, William, 202, 258.
Welden, John, 243.
Welding, Jefrie, 23.
Welding, Jesse, 77.
Welding, John, 228.
Weldon, Peleg, 209.
Welks, John, 139.
Weller, Amos, 218.
Weller, Benjamin, 58, 124.
Weller, Coolee, 58.
Weller, Zacheas, 29, 219.
Welles, Chester, 210.
Welles, Edmund, 187, 190.
Welles, Eliphalet, 42.
Welles, Ephraim, 189.
Welles, John, 229.
Welles, Josha, 229.
Welles, Samuel, 189.
Welles, see Wells.
Wellman, Benjamin, 195.
Wellman, Elihuia, 195.
Wellock, Elihua, 195.

Wells, Amos, 205, 255.
Wells, Ashbell, 239.
Wells, Azariah, 82.
Wells, Benjamin, 24, 159.
Wells, Edmund, 147, 149, 160, 190.
Wells, Eleazar, 250.
Wells, Eliphalet, 87.
Wells, Ephraim, 52, 86, 123.
Wells, Ephraim, Jr., 123.
Wells, Hezekiah, 215.
Wells, Ichabod, 123, 159.
Wells, John, 181.
Wells, Joseph, 197.
Wells, Levi, 10, 86, 99, 100.
Wells, Nathaniel, 70, 107.
Wells, Oliver, 197.
Wells, Ruben, 86.
Wells, Samuel, 8, 86, 123, 173, 176, 187, 200, 240, 250.
Wells, Samuel, Jr., 173.
Wells, Silas, 38.
Wells, Solomon, 122, 124, 215.
Wells, Thomas, 3, 91, 257.
Wells, see Welles.
Welsh, Ebenezer, 114.
Welsh, James, 187.
Welsh, John, 113.
Welsh, Partrick, 167, 168.
Welton, Eliakim, 222.
Welton, John, 194.
Welton, Oliver, 119.
Welton, Stephen, 222.
Wempy, Elijah, 239.
Wentworth (Wintworth).
Wentworth, Benjamin, 182.
Wentworth, Jered, 40.
Wentworth, William, 83, 112, 114.
West, Aaron, 187.
West, Abner, 215.
West, Benjamin, 149.
West, David, 81, 187.
West, Eleazar, 216.
West, Ezra, 43, 184.
West, Francis, 215.
West, John, 149.
West, Joshua, 256, 257.
West, Rufus, 215.
West Indies, 263.
Westchester, 86.
Westcoat (Wescot, Weskott).
Westcoat, David, 251.
Westcoat, Nathaniel, 12, 56, 109, 110, 180.
Westland, Amos, 135.
Westland, Robart, 136.
Westland, Robart, Jr., 38.
Weston, Darius, 234.
Weston, Noah, 205.

Weston, Samuel, 14, 15.
Westover, John, 159.
Westover, Jonathan, 103.
Wethersfield, 22, 154, 210, 229, 266.
Wetmore, Abner, 223.
Wetmore, Benjamin, 54.
Wetmore, David, 54.
Wetmore, Elias, 54, 110, 115, 116.
Wetmore, John, 72, 74, 75, 162, 189.
Wetmore, Oliver, 234.
Wetmore, see Whitmore.
Whaley, Jonathan, 155.
Whaling, John, 222.
Whaples, Eli, 35, 153, 154, 210.
Whaples, Elisha, 210.
Whaples, Ephraim, 14.
Whaples, Wait, 187.
Wheadal, David, 127.
Wheatley, John, 267.
Whedon (Wheadon, Wheden).
Whedon, David, 59.
Whedon, Jehoida, 27, 172.
Whedon, Reuben, 60, 225.
Whedon, Samuel, 55, 65, 193.
Wheeler (Whealer, Wheler).
Wheeler, Aaron, 178, 179.
Wheeler, David, 77, 154, 156, 177, 178, 219.
Wheeler, Ebenzor, 219.
Wheeler, Elnathan, 221.
Wheeler, Ephraim, 52, 139.
Wheeler, Hesekiah, 200.
Wheeler, Jedediah, 226, 238.
Wheeler, John, 240, 245.
Wheeler, Jonas, 240.
Wheeler, Jonathan, 240, 245.
Wheeler, Joseph, 224.
Wheeler, Joshua, 44, 45, 227.
Wheeler, Obediah, 204.
Wheeler, Pennygreen, 250.
Wheeler, Purgran, 257.
Wheeler, Resolved, 70.
Wheeler, Samuel, 190.
Wheeler, Simeon, 33, 146, 224.
Wheeler, Timothy, 123.
Wheeler, William, 49, 223, 233, 235.
Wheeler, Zeccharius, 145.
Wheeler, Zaccheus, 53.
Whelply (Welply).
Whelply, Daniel, 61, 150, 152, 216.
Whelply, Isaac, 179, 260.
Whelply, Jonathan, Jr., 110.
Whetner, John, 222.
Wheton, Johogada, 144.
Whipple, Daniel, Jr., 197.

Whipple, Jeremiah, 52, 145, 233.
Whipple, John, 107.
Whipple, Nathan, 94.
Whipple, Samuel, 216.
Whipple, Silas, 233.
Whipple, Zebulun, 189.
Whisk (Whesk).
Whisk, Isaac, 174, 175.
Whitaker, Henry, 99.
Whitaker, Samuel, 244.
Whitcker, Samuel, 228.
Whitcomb, John, 205.
Whitcomb, John, Jr., 258.
Whitcomb, Joseph, 215.
White (Whitte), Aaron, 234.
White, David, 61, 180.
White, Ebenezer, 162.
White, Ezekiel, 44, 79.
White, George, 33, 43, 124, 206.
White, Jacob, 123.
White, James, 162.
White, James, Jr., 230.
White, John, 7, 94, 96, 206, 245.
White, John, Jr., 230.
White, Joseph, 198, 234, 236.
White, Moses, 195, 260.
White, Samuel, 37, 79, 135.
White, Stephen, 216.
White, Thomas, 62, 81, 213.
White, William, 46, 94, 120, 121.
White, William, Jr., 161.
Whitehead, John, 221.
Whiting, 159, 160, 265.
Whiting, Charles, 83, 109, 111, 112.
Whiting, David, 53.
Whiting, Ebenezer, 216.
Whiting, Gamaliel, 227, 243.
Whiting, Nathan, 3, 22, 24, 25, 76, 77, 87, 126, 128, 162, 167, 171, 172, 194, 266.
Whiting, Samuel, 28, 52, 102, 159.
Whiting, William, 48, 51, 52, 53, 109, 111, 112, 118.
Whitlock, David, 238.
Whitlock, Nehemiah, 238.
Whitlock, Oliver, 201.
Whitmore, Caleb, 264.
Whitmore, David, 79.
Whitmore, Edward Collins, 234.
Whitmore, Elias, 29.
Whitmore, Fransis, 153.
Whitmore, Ira, 144, 195.
Whitmore, Jacob, 208, 233, 234, 253.
Whitmore, John, 220.
Whitmore, Oliver, 103.
Whitmore, William, 242.

INDEX. 351

Whitmore, see Wetmore.
Whitney, Aron, 69.
Whitney, Aron, 71.
Whitney, David, 53, 208.
Whitney, Elijah, 238.
Whitney, Ezekiel, 70, 71, 101.
Whitney, George, 191.
Whitney, Henry, 106, 220.
Whitney, James, 61, 157, 158.
Whitney, Joshua, 208.
Whitney, Josiah, 70, 71, 172.
Whitney, Moses, 70, 71, 153, 154.
Whitney, Peter, 133, 198.
Whitney, Tarball, 28, 29.
Whitney, William, 228, 244.
Whiton, Wilson, 184.
Whitticore, Henry, 43.
Whitticus, Jo, 106.
Whittle, Isaac, 144, 191.
Whittlesey, Eliphalet, 5, 7, 9, 152, 153, 154, 159, 160, 185, 187.
Whittlesey, Nathan, 187.
Whittlesey, Samuel, 118.
Whittlesey, Stephen, 202.
Wiard, Aaron, 246.
Wickham, Jonathan, 210.
Wickham, Uriah, 210.
Wicks (Wiks), Jethro, 233.
Wicks, Jonathan, 226.
Wicks, Zephaniah, 147.
Wickwire, Christopher, 27.
Wickwire, James, 86.
Wickwire, Josiah, 250.
Wickwire, Nathan, 149, 159.
Wickwire, Samuel, 233.
Wickwire, Solomon, 149.
Widger, John, Jr., 197.
Wilcocks, Hoseah, 168.
Wilcocks, Martain, 247.
Wilcocks, Wait, 128.
Wilcocks, see Willcocks.
Wilcox, Daniel, 209.
Wilcox, Daniel, Jr., 210.
Wilcox, Edward, 218.
Wilcox, Hosea, 170.
Wilcox, John, 33.
Wilcox, Waitstill, 81.
Wilcox, see Willcox.
Wilcoxson, Hoseah, 169.
Wildman, Daniel, 156.
Wildman, John, 139.
Wildman, Richard, 157, 158.
Wileman, Abraham, 238.
Wileman, Samuel, 238.
Wileman, Timothy, 238.
Wilford, Joseph, 50, 267.
Wilke, Thomas, 83, 137, 237.
Wilkinson (Wilkeson, Willkson),

Wilkinson, James, 131.
Wilkinson, Jonathan, 240.
Wilkinson, Willim, 23.
Wilks, John, 57, 139, 238.
Will, Nathaniel, 71.
Will, Thomas, 106.
Will, Tom, 106.
Willard (Williard), Samuel, 212.
Willbour, Uriah, 214.
Willcocks, Ebenezer, 205.
Willcocks, Ephraim, 207.
Willcocks, Ezekiel, 245.
Willcocks, Ezra, 202.
Willcocks, Giles, 8.
Willcocks, Jehiel, 50, 202.
Willcocks, Jeremiah, 245.
Willcocks, Joseph, Jr., 245.
Willcocks, Salvenes, 63.
Willcocks, William, 214.
Willcocks, see Wilcocks.
Willcox, Adam, 51.
Willcox, Benjamin, 45.
Willcox, Ebenezer, 42, 257.
Willcox, Isaac, 214.
Willcox, John, 229.
Willcox, Stephen, 246.
Willcox, Wait, 129.
Willcox, see Wilcox.
Willey, Abel, Jr., 162.
Willey, Allen, 205, 259.
Willey, Barzilla, 117.
Willey, Benjamin, 137.
Willey, David, 203.
Willey, Lemuel, 203.
Willey, Nathan, 42.
Willey, Samuel, 118, 189.
Willey, see Wylley.
Williams (Willems).
Williams, Aaron, 134, 159.
Williams, Albert, 109.
Williams, Amos, 35, 130, 131.
Williams, Asa, 233.
Williams, Azariah, 239.
Williams, B., 72.
Williams, Benajah, 197.
Williams, Benjamin, 121, 238.
Williams, Boaz, 74, 75.
Williams, Charles, 150, 151, 180, 227.
Williams, Daniel, 197, 203, 223, 256.
Williams, David, 229.
Williams, Ebenezer, 101, 197, 201, 240.
Williams, Eleazor, 56.
Williams, Elemuail, 240.
Williams, Elijah, 83.
Williams, Elisha, 39.

Williams, Ezra, 108, 237.
Williams, Isaac, 17, 19, 20, 108.
Williams, Isaiah, 224.
Williams, Jacob, 101.
Williams, Jahiel, 250, 257.
Williams, James, 207.
Williams, Jed, 197.
Williams, Jehiel, 51.
Williams, Jesse, 107.
Williams, John, 24, 38, 99, 131, 182, 265.
Williams, Joseph, 16, 107, 197, 205, 237, 240.
Williams, Lemuel, 37, 244.
Williams, Nathan, 251.
Williams, Nicholas, 24, 131.
Williams, Neckels, 132.
Williams, Robert, 197.
Williams, Samuel, 83, 187, 250.
Williams, Solomon, 230.
Williams, Stephen, 117, 191.
Williams, Stephen Harding, 17, 19, 160, 189.
Williams, Tho., 223.
Williams, Thomas, 209, 214.
Williams, Willida, 55.
Willington, 199.
Willoughby (Willebe, Willobey).
Willoughby, Joseph, 181.
Willoughby, Salvanus, 123.
Willoughby, Waitwl, 141.
Willoughby, Wertil, 224.
Wills, Daniel, 236.
Wills, Eliphalet, 86.
Wills, Hezekiah, 38, 230.
Wills, Joshua, 236.
Wills, Solomon, 6.
Wilmouth (Willmoth).
Wilmouth, Francis, 150.
Wilmouth, Zopher, 61, 180, 262.
Wilson (Willson, Wylson).
Wilson, Archer, 210.
Wilson, David, 7, 174, 175.
Wilson, Elihu, 169.
Wilson, Francis, 85.
Wilson, Jerem, 242.
Wilson, John, 174, 175, 241.
Wilson, Joseph, 18, 20, 132.
Wilson, Michael, 95.
Wilson, Noah, 222.
Wilson, Thomas, 37, 98, 99, 133.
Wilson, William, 12, 198, 217.
Winchell, Benjamin, 152, 210.
Winchell, Jacob, 211.
Winchell, Jehiel, 35.
Winchell, John, 95, 169.
Winchell, Jonas, 151.
Winchell, Joseph, 38, 77, 78.

Winchell, Martin, 35, 103, 104.
Winchell, Robard, 238.
Winchell, Stephen, 15, 94, 96, 102, 168.
Winchell, Thomas, 62, 104.
Winchell, Thomas, Jr., 211.
Windham, 15, 17, 20, 34, 65, 96, 108, 129, 133, 183, 248, 249.
Windsor, 5, 34, 38, 77, 78, 81, 91, 108, 121, 134, 167, 211, 215, 229, 230, 246.
Winkley, Wait, 214.
Winship, Samuel, 114.
Winslow, John, 91, 141.
Winslow, Nathaniel, 228, 243.
Winslow, Zebulon, 38, 134, 136, 169.
Winston, Daniel, 54, 172, 262.
Winston, Stephen, 54.
Winter, John, 141.
Winter, Joseph, 99.
Winters, Obadiah, 225.
Winton, Daniel, 238.
Wise, John, 97, 161, 162, 250, 257.
Wise, John, Jr., 250.
Wise, Samuel, 46, 115, 234.
Wisk, Isaac, 12.
Wix, Zepheniah, 194.
Woes, James, 132.
Wolcott (Walcut, Wilcott, Woolcot, Woolcutt).
Wolcott, Alexander, 174.
Wolcott, Caleb, 14, 153, 154.
Wolcott, Ebenezer, 30.
Wolcott, Elisha, 229.
Wolcott, Gideon, 229.
Wolcott, Giles, 38, 168.
Wolcott, Henry, 134.
Wolcott, Jeremiah, 247.
Wolcott, John, 184.
Wolcott, Joseph, 30, 103, 104.
Wolcott, Moses, 249, 254.
Wolcott, Nathaniel, 208.
Wolcott, Noah, 30, 252.
Wolcott, Peter, 39, 230.
Wolcott, Samuel, 210.
Wolcott, Simon, 6, 207.
Wolleps, Benjamin, 139.
Wolling, Daniel, 169.
Wolling, John, 169.
Wompanage, John, 114.
Wonks, 132.
Wood, Asa, 215.
Wood, Charles, 216.
Wood, Cypio, 183.
Wood, Ebenezer, 94, 112, 113, 242.
Wood, Elijah, 218.
Wood, Elisha, 226.

INDEX. 353

Wood, Halsted, 217.
Wood, Isaiah, 248, 254.
Wood, Job, 84, 237.
Wood, John, 112, 113, 156, 159, 160.
Wood, John, Jr., 197.
Wood, Jonathan, 31, 174, 175.
Wood, Joseph, 262.
Wood, Josiah, Jr., 216.
Wood, Nathan, 39.
Wood, Sipe, 132.
Wood, Stephen, 174.
Wood, see Woods.
Woodbury, 28, 71, 85, 91, 143, 146, 185, 199, 203, 218, 224, 266.
Woodcock, Barnabas, 106, 220.
Woodford, Samuel, 63.
Woodhoues, Daniel, 229.
Woodrough, John, 59.
Woodrough, Joseph, 59.
Woodruff, 267.
Woodruff, Apelton, 63.
Woodruff, Benjamin, 199.
Woodruff, Charles, 32, 140.
Woodruff, David, 220.
Woodruff, Elijah, 22.
Woodruff, Jacob, 199.
Woodruff, Joseph, 220.
Woodruff, Judah, 239.
Woodruff, Samuel, 222.
Woodruff, Seth, 222.
Woodruff, Solomon, 239.
Woodruff, Timothy, 239.
Woods, John, 158.
Woods, Joseph, 178.
Woods, see Wood.
Woodstock, 87, 93, 98, 129, 133, 266.
Woodward, Aaron, 82.
Woodward, Benedick, 58, 124, 206.
Woodward, David, 120, 161.
Woodward, Gaskin, 231.
Woodward, Gideon, 24.
Woodward, Hanar, 132.
Woodward, Henry, 6, 7.
Woodward, Isaac, 115.
Woodward, Israel, 119, 121.
Woodward, James, 240, 244.
Woodward, Jonas, 232.
Woodward, Nathan, 121.
Woodward, Samuel, 31, 45, 120.
Woodward, Samuel, Jr., 161.
Woodwor, Isaac, 19.
Woodworth, Benjamin, 25, 72, 73, 74, 117, 120, 121, 161, 189, 197, 249.
Woodworth, Benjamin, Jr., 25.
Woodworth, David, 25, 97, 98, 189.

Woodworth, Elijah, 97.
Woodworth, Eliphalet, 250.
Woodworth, James, 46, 87, 117, 161.
Woodworth, Jehiel, 47, 117.
Woodworth, Lemuel, 161.
Woodworth, Peleg, 18, 19, 120, 121, 163.
Woodworth, Reuben, 25, 120, 121, 161.
Woodworth, Sylvanus, 228.
Woodworth, Syrenus, 243.
Woodworth, Walter, 250.
Woodworth, William, 141.
Woodwoth, David, 160.
Woolfinch, Bedgood, 233.
Woolworth, Rubin, 211.
Wooster (Woster), Abraham, 54.
Wooster, David, 109, 110, 111, 131, 162.
Wooster, Edward, 66, 68, 110.
Wooster, Elisha, 60, 104, 106.
Wooster, Henman, 121.
Wooster, Henry, 110, 172.
Wooster, Joseph, 36.
Wooster, Moses, 66, 68, 69, 172.
Wooster, Peter, 59, 104, 106.
Wooster, Wait, 193.
Wooster, Weight, 55.
Wooster, see Worster.
Worden, Andrew, 61, 62.
Worden, Daniel, 68, 69, 106.
Worden, Nathaniel, 158.
Worden, Samuel, 262.
Wordin, Samuel, 78, 180.
Works, John, 198, 199.
Worster, Daniel, 220.
Worster, Edward, 220.
Worster, Elisha, 220.
Worster, Henman, 121.
Worster, Henry, 220.
Worster, Joseph, 34.
Worster, Samuel, 220.
Worster, see Wooster.
Worthington, Elijah, 255.
Worthington, Jacob, 205, 255.
Woutors, Staulwortha, Jr., 258.
Wouters, see Waters.
Woves, James, 15.
Wover, James, 131.
Wright (Right, Write).
Wright, Abel, 225.
Wright, Ameziah, 46.
Wright, Amos, 210.
Wright, Asaph, 57, 58, 224.
Wright, Benjamin, 250.
Wright, Beriah, 82, 189, 257.
Wright, Charles, 265.

23

Wright, Daniel, 14, 15, 187.
Wright, Ebenezer, 45.
Wright, Elias, 210.
Wright, Elihu, 210.
Wright, Elisha, 248, 254.
Wright, Ephraim, 82, 257.
Wright, Ephraim, Jr., 189.
Wright, Ezekiel, 130.
Wright, Hezekiah, 84, 112, 114, 191.
Wright, James, 145, 150.
Wright, John, 18, 20, 51, 78, 137, 138, 247.
Wright, Jonathan, 65, 66, 68, 120, 121, 153, 187, 230.
Wright, Joseph, 36.
Wright, Joshua, 144.
Wright, Josiah, 152, 167, 186.
Wright, Miles, 8, 118, 119, 195, 205, 256.
Wright, Moses, 8, 118, 119, 193, 224, 262.
Wright, Nathan, 121, 133, 193, 262.
Wright, Samuel, 23, 39, 131, 132, 137, 205, 247.
Wright, Seth, 214.
Wright, Solomon, 228, 244.
Wright, William, 66.
Wright, Wise, 202.
Wylley, Hugh, 250.

Wyllys, James, 197.

Yale, Aaron, 49.
Yale, Charles, 235.
Yale, Nathaniel, 65, 67.
Yale, Solomon, 49.
Yale, Stephen, 235.
Yale, Street, 235.
Yale, Thomas, 49.
Yarrington (Yerington).
Yarrington, Amaziah, 214.
Yarrington, Ebenezer, 107.
Yarrington, Ezekel, 10.
Yarrington, Rufus, 70, 128, 129.
Yarrington, William, 248, 254.
Yeant (Ycout, Yeout).
Yeant, John, 72, 74, 75.
Yeomans, Colins, 213.
Yeomans, Daniel, 214.
Yeomans, David, 191.
Yeomans, Jonathan, 43.
Yeomans, Joseph, 191.
Yeras, Nathan, 180.
Young, Joseph, 207.
Young, Silvanus, 203, 256.
Young, Simion, 213.
Young, Steadman, 15.
Young, William, 6, 123, 124, 160, 219.

Zone, Lemuel, 75.

www.ingramcontent.com/pod-product-compliance
Lightning Source LLC
Chambersburg PA
CBHW071953220426
43662CB00009B/1107